Eileen Gray

Eileen Gray

Her Work and Her World

Jennifer Goff

IRISH ACADEMIC PRESS

First published in 2015, reprinted 2016, by
Irish Academic Press
10 George's Steet
Newbridge
Co. Kildare
Ireland
www.iap.ie

In association with the National Museum of Ireland
(www.museum.ie)

© 2015 National Museum of Ireland

British Library Cataloguing in Publication Data
An entry can be found on request

978-07165-3276-7 (paper)
978-07165-3277-4 (cloth)

Library of Congress Cataloging in Publication Data
An entry can be found on request

Designed by www.sinedesign.net

Printed and bound by Gráficas Castuera, Spain www.graficascastuera.com

Previous:
1. *Pirogue* chaise longue, 1919-1920, lacquered wood, silver leaf
© Virginia Museum of Fine Arts, Richmond, Gift of Sydney and Frances Lewis

museum
National Museum of Ireland
Ard-Mhúsaem na hÉireann

2. *Guéridon table,* circa 1922-25, wood and natural lacquer ©
Archives Galerie Vallois - Paris, Arnaud Carpentier

3. *Wendigen* rug, 1923, hand woven wool carpet, the rectangular field
knotted in shades midnight-blue and black © Christies images

Contents

Acknowledgements

The National Museum of Ireland Eileen Gray exhibition and collection was made possible through the belief of Dr Patrick F. Wallace and the previous Minister of the Arts Heritage, Gaeltacht and the Islands, Síle de Valera in the importance of bringing home Ireland's greatest female designer. I want to thank Dr Wallace who in 1999 afforded me the incredible opportunity to research and work on this wonderful collection.

Within the National Museum of Ireland, I am very grateful to The Director, Raghnall O Floinn and the previous Keeper, Art and Industrial Division, Michael Kenny, who appointed me curator of this collection and especially for their generous support and guidance over the years. Thanks to all my colleagues in the National Museum of Ireland and the Office of Public Works especially the following departments: Art and Industry, Graphics, Education and Outreach, Marketing, Retail, IT, Administration, Facilities and Services. All of these departments have continually supported, promoted, and maintained the Eileen Gray exhibition and collection over the last decade. I would like to especially acknowledge the work of the Conservation department, and the Registrar's department in relation to the vast amount of work which has been completed on this collection over the last decade. The excellent photography of the Eileen Gray collection has dramatically enhanced this publication. Both Valerie Dowling, Head of Photography, NMI, and Peter Moloney, Photographer, must be sincerely thanked and acknowledged for their contribution to this publication. I am also grateful to Anne Keenan and Richard Weinacht of the Photography Department, NMI. It is impossible to name each person individually in the museum with whom I have worked on this extraordinary collection and permanent exhibition over the past decade, however to each of you I sincerely and warmly 'thank-you'.

Acknowledgement and sincere thanks go to Dr Kathleen James Chakraborty, Professor, School of Art History & Cultural Policy, University College Dublin under whose supervision the author's doctoral thesis on 'the Eileen Gray collection at the National Museum of Ireland' was written, for her editorial work and overwhelming support. Acknowledgement

4. *Le Destin* (The Destiny) four-panelled screen, 1913, wood, red and blue lacquer, engraved, raised colours © Archives Galerie Vallois Paris, Arnaud Carpentier

and thanks also to Dr Christine Casey, History of Art and Architecture Department, Trinity College Dublin, for her guidance and supervision through the early stages of my research.

My warm thanks to my sponsor Mark E. Brockbank who has literally made this book possible – I am indebted by your kindness and generosity. To those in Irish Academic Press especially Conor Graham, senior editor Lisa Hyde and editor Fearghal McClelland for believing not only in me and this book, but especially for standing by me, encouraging me and making it become a reality. To the designer Sinéad McKenna whose wonderful design brings Eileen Gray to life.

My profound thanks to the following institutions who have granted me access to their collections and archives and, afforded me the opportunity to find more magical things in the world of Eileen Gray. This publication would not have been possible without their involvement.

To the following (stated alphabetically); Les Art Décoratifs, Musée des Arts Décoratifs, Paris, Bibliothèque des Art Décoratifs, Paris, Bibliothèque Kandinsky, Paris, Bibliothèque nationale de France, Paris, Bristol Museum and Art Gallery, Fondation Le Corbusier Paris, Bibliothèque, collections Jacques Doucet, Paris, British Architectural Library, London, Centre Nationale d'art et de culture Georges Pompidou, Paris, Irish Architectural Archive, Dublin, Musée national de la Marine, Paris, Musée Rodin, Paris, National Library of Ireland, Dublin, National Portrait Gallery, London, Rare Book and Manuscript Library, Columbia University, New York, Richview Library, University College Dublin, Dublin, Royal Institute of the Architects of Ireland, Dublin, RIBA Library Drawings, London, Slade School Archives, UCL, Tate Library and Archive, Tate Britain, London, The Museum of Modern Art, New York, The National Irish Visual Arts Library, NCAD, Dublin, Victoria and Albert Museum, Trinity College Dublin Archives, Virginia Museum of Fine Arts, Richmond, Vitra Design Museum.

Thank you to the following galleries for their help and assistance; DeLorenzo Gallery, New York, Galerie Ann-Sophie Duval, Galerie Doria, Galerie Dukto, Galerie Jacques De Vos, Galerie Peyroulet and Galerie Vallois, Paris.

It is a great pleasure to acknowledge the contributions of all those who helped with memories, advice, letters, interviews, access to private collections and archives, hospitality and conversation. Peter Adam,

5. The *Siren chair,* circa 1919, sculpted wood, natural lacquer, velvet upholstery © Anthony De Lorenzo

Renaud Barrès, Carolyn Burke, Julie Blum, Dominique Chenivesse and Giles Peyroulet, Mathias Schwartz-Claus, Roger Conover, Caroline Constant, Arnaud Dercelles, Jacques De Vos, Joe and Marie Donnelly, the late Mairead Dunlevy, Adriena Friedman, Philippe Garner, Pierre Antoine Gatier, Sarah Glennie, Roger Griffith, Charles Hind, Marie-Laure Jousset, Barbara Kenny, Sean Kissane, Elizabeth Kujawski, Ronald and Jo Carole Lauder, Anthony Lorenzo, Serge Maudit, Kathryn Meghen, Frédéric Migayrou, Mary Mc Guckian, Colum O'Riordan, Marco Orsini, Shane O'Toole, Evelyne Possémé, Donna Romano, Justin Russo, Daniel James Ryan, Joseph Rykwert, Justine Sambrook, Barry Shifman, Francis Spalding, Ruth Starr, Cheska and Bob Vallois, the late Dorothy Walker, Simon Walker, Eva White, Christopher Wilks, Wendy Williams.

A special acknowledgement goes to Cloé Pitiot for all of her help and assistance which has been greatly appreciated, and who continually shares her rich perspective and encyclopaedic scholarship on Eileen Gray. I am indebted to you my friend.

Grateful acknowledgement is made to the Rare Book and Manuscript Library, Columbia University, New York, for permission to quote from the Stephen Haweis papers; to Trinity College Dublin Archives, Dublin, for permission to quote from the Paul Henry papers, and The National Irish Visual Arts Library, NCAD, Dublin to quote from the Dorothy Walker papers.

Photographs have been reproduced with the kind permission of Anthony DeLorenzo, New York, Archives Galerie Giles Peyroulet, Paris, Bristol Museums, Galleries and Archives, Ceadogan Rugs Ltd, Centre Pompidou, Mnam-CCI, Christies Images, Collection of the Dunedin Public Art Gallery, Courtesy Galerie Vallois, Paris, Commerce Graphics Ltd, Courtesy Galerie Vallois, Fondation Le Corbuiser, Paris, Freer Gallery of Art, Smithsonian Institution, Washington D.C, RIBA Library Drawings and Archives Collections, Simon Walker Architects, Smithsonian American Art Museum, The Alexander Turnbull Library, Wellington, New Zealand, The Irish Museum of Modern Art, Collection of the Dunedin Public Art Gallery, The Library of Congress Prints and Photographs Division Washington, The Marine Biological Laboratory Archives and the History of Marine Biological Laboratory website, The Museum of Modern Art, New York, The National Portrait Gallery, London, The Slade School of Fine Art, London, Topfoto/Roger Viollet,

Victoria and Albert Museum, London, Virginia Museum of Fine Arts, Richmond.

While every effort has been made to trace copyright holders, I would be grateful to hear from those who may have escaped my notice so that I can amend accordingly.

On a personal note I am humbled by certain friends and family, both here and abroad, who have, for the past decade, encouraged me when I was truly despondent with this project. To Patrick Boyle, Yvonne Doherty, and Sarah Nolan – it is lovely to work with friends, especially those who have continually listened. Of special mention is my kindred spirit Sheila Ozechowski, who believed in me during the most difficult of times, I am blessed to have a best friend who is also my family. To those who have nourished my thoughts and shown continued friendship – to my soul sisters Eleanor Butler, Sandra Heise, Majella Lynch, Audrey Whitty and by default my soul brother Ciarán Woods. To Patricia and Wick Walsh – you have stood by me since the very beginning and continue to do so. To the late Teresa Meghen who kept telling me that I could do it. To the tour-de-force that is Joan Butler, who, without agenda, spent countless hours editing my thesis, and who comes to every lecture – I can never repay you. To the amazing Sharon Goff, who spent numerous hours sorting images and helping with all of the machinations of a PhD and, to Jason Goff – for all the countless technical glitches which you fixed. To Finnan and Rowan Goff who kept me laughing throughout. I am especially appreciative of my parents Tom and Eileen Goff – there are no words which can do you justice – except to say thank you for your ceaseless belief in me, your love and strength got me through this long, and at times, never-ending journey. Lastly this book is in memory of my loving husband and best friend Conor Meghen. I miss you every day and hope that you are somewhere quietly proud.

Jennifer Goff, September 2014

Introduction

For much of the twentieth century Eileen Gray remained an elusive figure. Born in Ireland, Gray trained as an artist in both London and Paris and continued to produce artwork throughout her life. She is renowned primarily for her work in France during the 1910s and 1920s as a furniture and interior designer. Gray was also a photographer, capturing artistic images in form, light and shade. Forming a successful partnership with lacquer artist Seizo Sugawara (1884-1937), Gray became the first twentieth-century European artist to adapt traditional Asian lacquer techniques to contemporary Western furnishings. Along with her friend Evelyn Wyld (1882-1973) she designed wall hangings and carpets which were sold at her shop *Jean Désert,* opened in May 1922. The house *E.1027* and its furnishings are undoubtedly her best known work. Despite the house being published in *L'Architecture Vivante* in 1929, the design was attributed to other architects and the success which Gray had early in her career as a furniture designer and interior designer was soon forgotten. As a direct result Gray was omitted from the canon of modern architecture until her work was revived by a series of articles written from 1968 onwards and the record prices her work began to achieve at auction.[1]

6. Eileen Gray, by Berenice Abbott, 1926, black and white photograph © NMI

Beginning in 1923, Gray experimented with architectural form. She was advised by and collaborated with a number of architects from that period. This resulted in the realisation of interior design projects and new buildings. In her archive there are numerous architectural projects which remain unresolved. As a furniture designer Gray constantly varied the media she used; chrome, celluloid, plastics, perforated metal and cork. Her work was multi-functional, user-friendly, ready for mass production yet succinctly unique, and her designs show great technical virtuosity. Initially she had hoped to mass-produce her lacquer work, but the sheer expense of the process proved prohibitive. As an interior designer, especially in the commissions from Mme Mathieu-Lévy (Juliette Lévy) for her *Rue de Lota* and *Boulevard Suchet apartments*, she excelled in the creation of architectonic environments. The planning of walls, decors, lighting and fixtures created a modern interior concept. The *Rue de Lota apartment* was completed in two stages – the first from 1919-22 and the second from 1922-24. The *Boulevard Suchet apartment* was completed from 1931-32 and again Gray used white blocks to cover the wall mouldings.[2] From this simple yet radical interior, Gray continued to show a rare homogeneity of style, exhibiting the *Monte Carlo room* in 1923. This ambitious project, based on a dual-purpose multi-functional living area with a bedroom boudoir, received much negative criticism from French critics. However, members of the De Stijl art group, set up in Amsterdam in 1917, took notice, praising her. Some, such as J.J.P. Oud (1890-1963), wrote to her requesting copies of reviews of her work and in referring to her native Ireland inquired, 'Do you have any modern movement in your country?'[3]

As an architect, she was self-taught, and by 1926 had begun to experiment directly with architectural forms, resulting in *House for an Engineer*, 1926. Her six-year collaboration with Jean Badovici (1893-1956) provided her with the final impetus for an independent career. Gray was introduced to Adrienne Gorska (1899-1969) whom Badovici had met while studying at architectural school. Gorska tutored her in architectural drawing. Gray's architectural archives reveal over 100 sketches, drawings, plans, elevations, descriptions and notes. Some projects were collaborative – such as the work that Gray completed with Jean Badovici at Vézelay. Some projects were realised such as *E.1027,* 1926-29; the bedroom renovations of her apartment in *Rue Bonaparte,* 1930; Jean Badovici's *Rue Chateaubriand* apartment, 1929-31; *Tempe a Pailla*, 1931-34 and *Lou Pérou,* 1954-61. She produced numerous models for the *Ellipse house,* 1936; the *House for Two Sculptors,* 1933-34; *Vacation and Leisure centre*, 1936-37 and a huge model of the *Cultural and Social centre*, 1946-47. Sadly, many projects were left unrealised and unresolved. In response to legislation in 1936 requiring employers to grant workers paid leave, Gray designed the *Vacation and Leisure centre,* including the *Ellipse* housing in the project. She exhibited her *Vacation and Leisure centre*, in Le Corbusier's *Pavillon des Temps Nouveaux* at the Exposition Internationale des Art et des Techniques appliqués à la Vie moderne of 1937.

Gray took copious photographs of her work throughout her career. In the case of her architectural project *E.1027,* the photographs were published

7. Black lacquer block screen, 1922-3, wood, aluminium, lacquer © Anthony De Lorenzo

along with her architectural ideas. These were articulated in a dialogue, in a special issue of *L'Architetcure Vivante,* in 1929. She exhibited frequently at the Salon d'Automne, was a member of the Société Nationale des Artistes Décorateurs and a founding member of the Union des Artistes Moderne.

Despite such achievements, Gray remained aloof from her contemporaries, and throughout her career her architectural work attracted critical attention only infrequently, although she continued to design throughout her life. Then, in 1968 and 1972, the architectural historian Joseph Rykwert (b.1926) published a series of enlightening articles which reappraised Gray's architecture.[4] In November 1972, at the auction of Jacques Doucet's (1853-1929) collection at the Hôtel Drouot, her screen *Le Destin* realised a record price. This revived a global interest in her work which still continues since 24 February 2009 after the *Serpent chair* fetched a world record price at auction. Collectors vie to own her furniture; historians compete to document her life. Many theses, articles, publications, catalogues raisonné and exhibitions examine the artist, designer, architect, her oeuvre, her buildings and her legacy. Some emphatically authenticate her work while others refute it. Collections of Gray's work exist in museums and private collections across the world. Of those who met her towards the end of her life, some got to know her, while others assumed they did. During her later years Gray attempted, and mostly succeeded in destroying her personal papers, as she wanted to be remembered for her designs and her architecture rather than her personal history. From the archives and ephemera that remain, another fact becomes clear: despite having an aristocratic family background and an illustrious career in France (where she remained all of her working life) Eileen Gray was born in Ireland and she remained throughout her life an Irishwoman at heart.

The primary source material for this publication is drawn from the Eileen Gray collection and archives at the National Museum of Ireland (NMI), which were acquired from 2000–2008 and consist of 1,835 objects. Secondary material was consulted in the collections and archives of the following institutions; the Victoria and Albert Museum, the Royal Institute of British Architects (RIBA), the Tate Gallery Archives, Trinity College Dublin (TCD), the Royal Institute of the Architects of Ireland (RIAI), the Irish Architectural Archive (IAA), The National Irish Visual Arts Library (NIVAL), the Centre Pompidou, the Fondation Le Corbusier, the Musée Rodin, Museum of Modern Art (MoMA) and Columbia University. Relevant Eileen Gray material was also researched in the collections of the Metropolitan Museum of Art, New York, the Virginia Museum of Fine

Art, the Getty Centre, Los Angeles, the Portsmouth, Leicester and Bristol City Art Galleries, the Musée des Arts Décoratifs, Paris, the Mairie de Menton, the Musée National de la Marine, Bibliothèque Littéraire Jacques Doucet and the Vitra Design Museum, Germany. Private collections were also consulted through galleries and through the auction houses of Christie's, Sotheby's, Bonham's and the Maison Camard.

Gray's reputation has been consolidated by galleries and museums acquiring collections of her work since the early 1970s and through retrospective exhibitions at the Royal Institute of British architects, London, the Museum of Modern Art, New York, the Victoria and Albert Museum, London, the Design Museum, London, the Centre Pompidou, Paris and the Irish Museum of Modern Art, Dublin.

The Eileen Gray Collection at the National Museum of Ireland represents a veritable anthology of Eileen Gray's varied career as a designer and architect. This collection embraces so many different disciplines which interested Gray throughout her life, including art, photography, graphic art, new media, lacquer work, architecture and furniture and carpet design. It represents the stream of consciousness of Gray's design process through a variety of media. It is an intensely personal collection – coming directly from Gray herself. It is Gray's own assembly of souvenirs, furniture and architecture, which she kept until her death in 1976. The wealth of documentation, correspondence, magazines, books, exhibition catalogues, personal archives, photographs, portfolios and oral history which emerged from this collection provided the information in this book on Gray's work, probing into her design and architectural thinking. This sheer mass of documentation, which testifies to the lengthy, meticulous process that she applied to every aspect of her design, marks her out not as a feminised subject ruled by emotions and materials, but rather a designer and architect guided by logic and order.

It also affords the opportunity to examine her early years as an artist and her recent past in the latter years which up until now was still lacking in the publications on Gray and how these periods contributed to her career and to her philosophy. This collection, viewed as an ensemble, offers a beacon of light into understanding Gray, the woman and the professional. It gives an appreciation of the world that shaped her, however hard she attempted to shape it, or hide it, by destroying a large amount of her work and documents. It gives an understanding into the one area for which Gray wanted to be remembered: her work.

1

From Ireland to Paris 1878-1907

Eileen Gray was Irish. Numerous documents, letters and papers from her personal archive reveal unremittingly that she was incredibly proud of this fact. Notes on her life and work, which she kept as records of dates of various important projects, reveal that despite her family background that Gray constantly referred to herself as 'Irish' and viewed herself as an Irish expatriate. Towards the end of her life, when her work was revived with global enthusiasm, Gray sought to rectify a number of issues surrounding her life and work. As a result she wrote numerous notes or lists regarding projects and dates which were important to her career. She also addressed the issue of her nationality. 'Born in Ireland (South) Co. Wexford', she wrote, and again in another document, but this time in French, she typed 'Né en Irlande à Enniscorthy' (Born in Ireland at Enniscorthy).[1]

1.1 Eileen Gray, 1883, black and white photograph © NMI

Eileen Gray's family history was unconventional. However much she affirmed her Irish patrimony she also could not escape or ignore that her family, on her mother's side, was very distinguished. Her grandmother, Lady Jane Stuart (1802-1880) was the granddaughter of Francis Stuart (1737-1810), the ninth Earl of Moray and his wife Jean Gray (1743-1786). On Francis's father's side of the family the first Earl of Moray, James Stewart, was the illegitimate son of King James V. Jean Gray was a descendant of the first Lord Gray who was the first master of the household of King James II of Scotland.[2]

Lady Jane was fifth in the line of succession after her four brothers to the title of Baron of Lord Gray. However, her four unmarried brothers all died without issue and she then inherited the title becoming Baroness Lady Gray. Lady Jane Stuart married Sir John Archibald Drummond Stewart (b.1794) of Grandtully on 25 January 1832. He died on 20 May 1838. Just three months after his death she married Jeremiah Lonsdale Pounden (d. 3 March 1887), Eileen Gray's grandfather, on 25 August 1838. Pounden was an Irishman and a Doctor of Medicine. The couple renewed their vows at the end of 1840 when Jane was pregnant with their only child, a girl. Eveleen Pounden was born in Dresden on 3 May 1841, but was baptised in Ireland.[3] Eveleen caused quite a scandal when she eloped to Italy in 1863 to marry a 31-year-old middle-class painter, James Maclaren Smith (d.1900) who was from Hazelgrun in Lancashire.[4] Though this union, which did not last, was not welcomed by the family, the couple returned to live at Brownswood House, in Enniscorthy, County Wexford.

Gray's grandfather Jeremiah Lonsdale Pounden, having amassed a large fortune, had bought Brownswood estate at the beginning of the nineteenth century for £5,500.[5] The Georgian manor was an elegantly proportioned early nineteenth-century house with two storeys and five bays. The centre bay broke forward and the house had a pillared porch and an eave roof.[6] Eileen Gray was born on 9 August 1878 at Brownswood, the youngest of five children.[7]

1.2 Eveleen Pounden Gray, 1860, black and white photograph © NMI

1.3 James Maclaren Smith, 1860, black and white photograph © NMI

1.4 Brownswood House, Enniscorthy, Co. Wexford, Pre 1895, black and white photograph © NMI

Her well-documented childhood was spent between the family's London residence at 14 Boltons in South Kensington, a brief spell at school in Dresden, and Brownswood House in Ireland. Photographs and memorabilia reveal trips to Milan, Genoa, Paris, Nice, Egypt, America and skiing trips in the Alps.[8] There are numerous photographs also of the family's life in Ireland which she kept with her throughout her life. These included images of her brother Lonsdale using the horse and trap, Gray horse riding through the Brownswood estate, on a picnic with her sister Thora and the family with friends playing croquet on the lawn in front of the family home.[9] On the back of one photograph Gray purportedly reports that the family had the first Fiat in Ireland.[10]

1.5 The Gray family, from left to right, standing, her sister Ethel, her father, her brother James; seated, her brother Lonsdale, Eileen on her mother's lap, and her sister Thora, 1879, black and white photograph © NMI

1.6 Ethel and Eveleen Gray in Egypt, 1880s, black and white photograph © NMI

1.7 Eileen Gray on skis, 1893-94, black and white photograph © NMI

1.8 Eileen Gray at the front of Brownswood house with a croquet mallet in her hand, 1896, black and white photograph © NMI

1.9 The Gray family on holidays in the Alps, Eileen is wearing the white hat, pre 1900, black and white photograph © NMI

1.10 Eileen Gray on horseback, circa 1917, black and white photograph © NMI

Different descriptions of her childhood have materialised. In some, Gray describes her upbringing as 'lonely and unloved' at the estate. 'Despite considerable wealth and many servants, life was far from comfortable at Brownswood. In the cold wet weather the children had to put on coats to cross the icy halls and staircases'.[11] Gray herself stated that 'even the nursery seemed never to warm up'.[12] However, in an interview in 1976 with Irish journalist and writer Maeve Binchy (1940-2012), Gray recollects

1.11 Thora and Eileen Gray picnicking in Wexford, circa 1895, black and white photograph © NMI

1.12 Watercolour by James Maclaren Smith, circa 1870, black and white photograph © NMI

Brownswood somewhat differently. 'It was a happy childhood that seemed like one long sunny summer when she looks back to it, days and days of being with the horses and down by the river and picking great branches of flowering bushes for the house. They used to go to the Dublin Horseshow and her mother would walk around dreamily looking at the great hunters and show jumpers and saying how nice it would be to have horses like that at home'.[13] Gray also recalled the peacefulness and beauty of the surrounding countryside while taking her boat out onto the river Slaney, which ran through the estate. She had very fond memories of Ireland, describing it as home.

Eileen Gray's father, James Maclaren Smith was an artist, a minor figure in Victorian painting of portraits and landscapes. He was also quite an accomplished watercolourist. Her father was well connected in the art world and corresponded with great artists of the time such as William Holman Hunt (1827-1910), John Brett (1831-1902), William Powell Frith (1819-1909) and John Everett Millais (1829-1896).[14] He sublet his studio to Hunt. Eileen Gray often travelled with her father in Italy and Germany as he painted a lot in these countries, and in Switzerland.[15] When her parents separated he remained in Italy permanently except for a few visits. Gray 'couldn't understand why he (her father) had to spend such a long time in hot landscapes where even the ground and walls looked parched in villages instead of painting cool green things that were shiny and silky in Wexford'.

After her father's departure, many things began to change. On 23 July 1888 Gray's eldest sister Ethel (1866-1946) married Henry Tufnell Campbell (d.31 January 1945), the Earl of Lindsay and the grandson of Sir Henry Bethune, first Baronet of Kilconqhaur, Scotland. The 1891 census reveals that 33-year-old Henry was a stockbroker and married to 25-year-old Ethel. The couple divided their time between England and Brownswood. Throughout the 1890s Henry and Ethel lived in London at 1 Creswell Gardens and then moved to 7 Collingwood Gardens. Eileen's relationship with Ethel and her husband would remain a tentative one throughout their lives.

On the death of her uncle George Philip Stuart, fourteenth Earl of Moray and eighteenth Lord Gray, on 16 March 1895, Gray's mother Eveleen stood to inherit the title Baroness Gray in the peerage of Scotland and her son-in-law Henry persuaded her to claim it. Following this Gray's father received royal licence in 1897 to change his name from Smith to Gray and the children's names were changed accordingly. This news appeared in Irish newspapers at the time. On 27 April 1895 *The Enniscorthy News* and *County of Wexford Advertiser* reported, quoting from an article in the *Dundee Advertiser* on 10 April 1895:

1.13 James Gray, Henry Tufnell Campbell, Rick Campbell and Eileen Gray, at Brownswood, 1890s, black and white photograph © NMI

> Mrs. MacLaren Smith who in consequence of the death of the fourteenth Lord Moray has succeeded to the Barony of Gray is a granddaughter of the tenth Earl and the vicissitudes of families have been remarkably illustrated in her case, in as much as her mother, through whom she inherits, was originally only the seventh in the succession to the title as she had six brothers, all of whom however died without issue. She married first Sir John Archibald Drummond Stewart of Grentully and after his death Mr. Lonsdale Pounden of Brownswood, County Wexford, who had amassed a large fortune, and the present Baroness Gray being the only child of the marriage. Lady Gray married in 1863 Mr. MacLaren Smith of Hazelgrun Lanchashire and has two sons (the second of whom is an officer in the Carabineers) and three daughters.

Another article appeared in the same newspaper on 11 July 1895 under the headline 'Gray Peerage Successful Claim of an Irish Lady'. The article reported that:

> A somewhat curious case came before the committee of privileges of the House of Lords on Tuesday, in which a Mrs. Eveleen Smith, the daughter of Mr. Jeremiah Lonsdale Pounden of Brownswood Co. Wexford, established her claim to the title of Baroness Gray, in the peerage of Scotland. Mr. Lindsay who appeared on her behalf said that the only difficulty in connection with it was that of finding direct formal documentary evidence of the petitioner's birth. Her mother was Lady Jane Stuart daughter of the 10th Earl of Moray, and sister of the 11th, 12th, 13th and 14th Earl of Moray (all of whom died unmarried), was united in matrimony to Sir John Archibald Drummond Stuart (sic) of Grantully who died in May 1838 without leaving issue. Three months after the death of Sir John Stewart, the lady married again by license to Jeremiah Lonsdale Pounden, a physician of Irish birth. In 1840, two years after the original marriage the lady having reason to believe she was about to become a mother, again went through the marriage ceremony with Mr. Pounden. That was in August 1840, and the only issue of that marriage was the present petitioner, who had always been led to believe that she was born in Dresden on or about the 3 May 1841 nine months after the date of the second ceremony, which second marital ceremony had been gone through in consequence of some doubts having been suggested as to the validity of the first. In those days there was no official registration of births and deaths. There was however a registration of baptisms and it would be proved that the petitioner was baptised in Ireland as the daughter of Mr. Pounden and Lady Jane Stuart. She was not however baptised in infancy, and therefore the certificate of baptism was not direct evidence of the date of birth. Except as to the latter point the proofs were conclusive and the Earl of Moray had promised to state the facts, which had always been accepted by the family. Evidence was then adduced and

several letters written by the late Earl of Moray were put
in to show that the deceased peer fully acknowledged the
relationship with the petitioner.

Gray herself would rarely use her own title 'The Honourable Eileen Gray';
she was not close to her sister Ethel or Henry Tufnell Campbell due to
this situation of her mother reclaiming the title. Gray's mother was also
persuaded by Henry to redevelop Brownswood House. This work was
carried out between 1895 and 1896 by the architect Sir Thomas Drew (1838-
1910) making it 'a magnificent specimen of Elizabethan architecture,
with a charming parterre laid out in faultless style; the entrance lodge,
which has recently been completed, is quite a gem'.[16] In Gray's opinion it
was an ostentatious mock–Tudor structure.[17] New additions were added,
firstly a new stable block, 1889, a new cowshed, 1890, and additional
stable buildings, 1892, by Drew's close friend architect William Mansfield
Mitchell (1842-1910). Throughout her life she was unable to forget this
act of vandalism; the destruction of Georgian purity for flamboyant
Elizabethan decoration. 'It was the destruction of her childhood home,
more than anything else that finally drove her from Ireland'.[18] In the final
years of her life Eileen Gray remained upset at the changes that occurred to
her family home. She described the style of the house as 'unimaginative'[19]
and constantly showed visitors two images she kept of the early Irish
Georgian house and the later nineteenth-century conversion.[20]

Many believe that Gray never returned to either Brownswood or
Ireland after the death of her mother on 24 December 1918. Due to the
previous death of Gray's father and both her brothers the Brownswood
estate was inherited by her sister Ethel and Henry. On 17 July 1926 *The Irish
Times* advertised the sale of Brownswood estate by Battersby and Company.
The description is quite impressive:

> Brownswood Co. Wexford on 150 acres freehold for sale with
> possession. Beautiful modern country house overlooking
> the River Slaney which flows through the property, with
> magnificent views of Mount Leinster and Blackstairs.
> Two and one half miles from the station and 24 miles
> from Rosslare harbour. Lands including gardens, pleasure
> grounds, farming land, woods etc in all about 150 acres, if

1.14 Brownswood House, circa 1896, black and white photograph © NMI

desired or less. The pleasure grounds are unusually beautiful, containing terraces, formal Italian garden, walks, pergola, herbaceous borders, kitchen garden etc. Five reception rooms and winter garden, 20 bed and dressing rooms, 3 bathrooms, excellent white tiled offices, electric light, central heating, excellent water; also magnificent stabling for 20 horses, garages, out houses etc. All most up-to-date and fitted with electric light. Three lodges, four cottages. Good hunting with two packs.

The family's connection with Brownswood finally ended on 4 March 1929 when the estate was sold to the Wexford Health Board for £5,000. By 5 September the Health Board had tendered for conversion of outbuildings at Brownswood into a residence and for half a century the house served as the County Medical Hospital's sanatorium.

In the 1976 interview with Maeve Binchy Gray stated, without giving specific dates, that she had returned to Ireland:

> Yes, she had been back to Ireland a few times, but very briefly, and once by chance when she found that a plane was going to stop there. She also returned to her beloved Brownswood. She decided to get off and go look at her old home, and she thought she would have again all these lovely feelings of peace and innocence like she had as a child. But it had changed, and nothing was the same. It wasn't just that everything the lawns, the fields, the river were smaller, she knew that would happen, it was all knocked down and built again, in a most unimaginative style. It made her sad.

Gray admitted to Binchy that on seeing her old home in this condition she never went back again.[21]

Later Binchy recalled that despite her illustrious career in France,

Gray simply refused to tell her about all the great and famous things she had done in her life. She was much more interested in 'what I (Binchy) thought of County Wexford, and who were the bright young designers in Ireland'.[22]

Despite her grandfather being Irish, Gray was a young lady from an aristocratic Protestant-background family. Her family belonged to a faith which had always been a minority one in Ireland, and which symbolised wealth and power. Gray benefited from growing up in a politically secure Ireland and in a period of cultural optimism. As was usual as a member of her class Gray's formal education came from governesses and a period of study at a boarding school abroad, in her case in Dresden. Local newspapers in Wexford reported frequently on the art world in London and Paris, advocating the new improved approaches to art education.[23] The fashionable art schools that proliferated during this period in London were widely accepted as suitable finishing schools for young ladies before they married. During the last quarter of the nineteenth century, for artists to achieve recognition or status, they had to go abroad to gain experience and education. This was partly due to the social, political and economic situations then prevailing in Ireland. They went to London and mainland Europe, most notably Paris, many returning once they had honed their craft and technique.

By the 1890s Gray was a very striking and fashionable young woman.[24] As a young lady from an aristocratic Anglo-Irish Protestant background she was seemingly destined for marriage to an eligible bachelor. During her lifetime there was no shortage of suitors, many of them quite famous.[25] Gray's intentions for art school were delayed after the loss of her father and later her brother Lonsdale in the Boer War in 1900.[26] After a brief diversion with her mother to Paris for the Exposition Universelle, Gray enrolled in the Slade School in London in 1900 and remained registered as a student studying fine art until 1902. English schools were full of young ladies from the upper and middle classes. The choice of school was important, and social propriety was paramount. Gray's choice was quite unconventional as

Eileen Gray, 1897, black and white photograph © NMI

the Slade was considered 'advanced'.[27] From its creation in 1871, the school had admitted women. Initially, women were only permitted to work from the draped model and the antique. By the 1870s rules were relaxed to the extent that students could have access to the partially draped living model. By 1901, the practice of separating the sexes was no longer enforced, except in life drawing classes. Models and students were strictly forbidden to converse, and communication was restricted to short words of command.

1.16 Slade School, Class of 1905 © Slade School of Fine Art

One of Gray's contemporaries Randolph Schwabe (1885-1948) who attended fine art classes at the Slade the same years as Gray did observe that the teaching of female students had progressed from the days when the Slade Professor of Fine Art could not be seen with students in the women's Life Room while a nude female was posing. Women students had to file out when he came in, and he then could enter, write his criticisms, in their absence, around the margins of their drawings.[28] Gray was one of 168 women students in a class of 228.[29] Classes varied from antique drawing to life classes. Attendance at these classes was granted to the more proficient artists. However, while women from the working or artisan classes were accepted into schools for the applied arts, the study of fine art was yet to be recognised as a suitable profession for them. Fine Art was regarded as the preserve of the middle and upper class that were looking for a suitable pastime. Upper middle class women who showed talent in fine art in the state-sponsored system were steered away from pursuing art as a profession, as public education was regarded as charity for the poor. During its early years the Slade School, with over half of the student body being taken up by women, had been at the centre of the debate in relation to the rights of professional female artists and in the rights of education for women.[30]

The 'Sladers' had a somewhat flamboyant, bohemian character with a disregard for reputation. Slade women were described as 'new women'. However, Eileen Gray remained unimpressed with the academic approach of the teachers. Her professors were renowned painters of the period, Wilson Steer (1860-1942), Henry Tonks (1862-1831) and Frederick Brown (1851-1941). Steer had been influenced by the Impressionists, especially Claude Monet (1840-1926) and Edgar Degas (1834-1917), during his Paris sojourn in 1882, and he had attended the Académie Julian, Paris, in 1882. Yet he insisted on structural drawing and emphasis on the old masters. Brown and Tonks were influenced by the Pre-Raphaelites and the writings of Ruskin. Brown avidly advocated the return to the practice and draughtsmanship among the old masters including Jean-Auguste-Dominique Ingres (1780-1867). Brown destroyed many paintings that did not satisfy him – Gray later would continue his practice, destroying almost all of her early student works. Students did charcoal diagrams and sketches continuously on drawing paper. Brown emphasised drawing more so than painting enforcing his motto 'action, construction, proportion'. Gray worked mostly in charcoal or sanguine in his classes. Brown was renowned for recognising talent and promise with female students, having himself become an admirer of and patron of the work of Ethel Walker (1861-1951). Tonks emphasised faithful reproduction to scale in drawing and sketching. He set high standards for his pupils continuing a Slade tradition of pre-eminence in drawing. He was described as 'dour and irascible ... an unfortunate development that cut him off from the more gifted of his pupils'. He also berated students and was noted for his sarcasm. However, it was recorded that in one of Gray's classes 'a certain woman student used, when she considered herself unjustly bullied, to reason gravely and firmly with him, and this from her, he tolerated'.[31] Tonks's paintings were noted for their dryness of technique, known as 'Tonking'. It consisted of soaking up the absorbent material with excess material. This technique Gray used later in many of her collages. Steer's area of expertise was painting – especially watercolour. But Steer was criticised for not taking a lively interest in his teaching, so if a student persisted in questioning him, his acute judgement and great knowledge would be brought to bear.[32]

Gray's frustration with the Slade School may have stemmed from the fact that students seldom spent more than a day on one drawing, where hours were spent in the crowded Antique Room until four o'clock. Then from four until five o'clock students drew short poses in the Life Room.[33] There were also stories of students never moving from the Antique Room to the Life Room, drawing with unabated zeal for three or four years.[34] Her dissatisfaction with the Slade School was apparent from her lack of attendance. She recorded that she first met Dean Charles in 1901, in Dean Street, Soho in London. Charles was a furniture restorer and was the first to introduce Gray to lacquering techniques.[35] Whilst at the Slade Gray solicited lessons from the firm in traditional Asian lacquer techniques, making numerous notes. She remained friends with Charles for years afterwards.[36] Dean Charles used mostly coloured European varnishes to repair screens but also had red Chinese lacquer which Gray began to use.

Her attention turned to the artistic centre of Paris, but the friendships she formed in London would influence her artistic propensities and her thinking for years to come. Gray departed for Paris along with several friends, including Wyndham Lewis (1882-1957), Gerald Festus Kelly (1879-1972),[37] Kathleen Bruce (1878-1947) and Jessie Gavin (1876-1939). She had settled there temporarily by 1902, with Gavin and Bruce, at a pension at 7 rue de Joseph Bara in the artist quarter near Montparnasse. Gray told

Maeve Binchy that she 'arrived as an Irish immigrant to Paris in 1902. She didn't really intend to stay there forever, but somehow things worked out that way. It was very different to home in Wexford'.[38] They continued their drawing studies, enrolling at the École Colarossi in late 1902 to 1903, a popular art school among foreign students.[39] Rivalry among students was apparent but also considered engaging. Gray, Kelly and others soon transferred to the Académie Julian by 1903, a private fee-paying school, where students were trained primarily for admission to the École des Beaux-Arts. The Académie prided itself on segregated studios, yet women were taught by the same professors as their male counterparts.

Gray had many admirers during this period of her life, Kelly being one of them. 'To Eileen he seemed someone quite extraordinary, and she took to this talkative Irishman, he was good company'.[40] Kelly was born in London in 1879; however, his Irish ancestry could be traced back to the tenth century. His father was of direct Irish descent while his mother was half Irish.[41] Kelly said, 'I'm of Irish blood, you know, and apparently in France they imagined that Ireland being damp, was full of people with gout'.[42] He was educated at Eton College and then Trinity College Cambridge. He attended the Slade School at exactly the same dates as Gray. He went to Paris in 1901, where he remained for many years. He exhibited at the Salon in 1904. He travelled extensively during his lifetime, to exotic locations such as Burma and Africa, as well as closer countries such as Italy and Spain for his inspiration. He painted many pictures of young Burmese ladies, sometimes dancing, often posed. Although he had a somewhat varied subject matter he is renowned primarily for his portraits. He executed several State portraits, paintings of society ladies and gentlemen, bishops and lords of the time, among them a portrait of

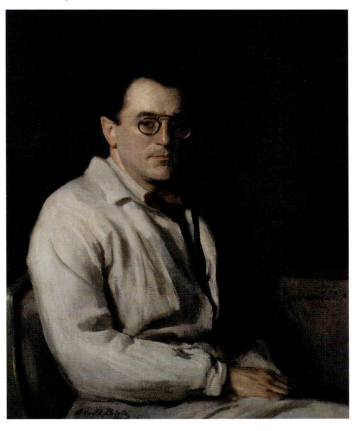

1.17 Sir Gerald Kelly, by Sir Oswald Birley, 1920, oil on canvas © National Portrait Gallery, London

1.18 Auguste Rodin, by George Charles Beresford, 1902, half plate glass negative © National Portrait Gallery, London

Lady Augusta Gregory (1852-1932)[43] and a fine three-quarter length portrait of Sir Hugh Lane (1875-1915).[44] He exhibited over 300 works at the Royal Academy in London between 1909 and 1970 and held the Presidency there from 1949 to 1954.

Though they had a number of close mutual friends, Kelly was responsible for introducing Gray to a much wider Parisian circle. His cousin wrote a letter of introduction that brought about an invitation to the home of the great art dealer Paul Durand-Ruel (1831-1922). Through Durand-Ruel he befriended the artists Edgar Degas, Pierre-Auguste Renoir (1841-1919), Claude Monet, Auguste Rodin (1840-1917), Paul Cézanne (1839-1906) and the French sculptor Aristide Maillol (1861-1944) among others. In 1902 Gray was introduced to Rodin by Kelly and wrote to him looking to purchase one of his bronze statues – the *Danaid*.[45] Kelly also owed many glowing Parisian memories to the Jewish essayist and critic Marcel Schwob (1867-1905) and his wife the actress Marguerite Moreno (1871-1948). Kelly drew her hands. He introduced Eileen Gray to the Schwobs at their house.[46] They were concerned for Kelly's welfare, and Marguerite was worried because Kelly's French was poor. As a result they organised for him to dine twice a week with a young writer, Paul Léautaud (1872-1956). Eileen Gray also met Léautaud at the Schwobs while visiting with Kelly some time during 1904. According to his diaries Léautaud pursued Gray with amorous intent, albeit unsuccessfully.[47]

Gray remembers spending many evenings in Kelly's studio listening to him describe a meeting with Rodin, or the art dealer Paul Durand-Ruel, or the actresses Eleonora Duse (1858-1924), and Maillol or just waiting with Aleister Crowley for something 'magic' to happen.[48] In Cambridge Kelly had befriended the controversial figure Aleister Crowley (1875-1947). Crowley was an influential English occultist, mystic and ceremonial magician responsible for founding the religious philosophy of Thelema. He was a member of the Hermetic Order of the Golden Dawn as well as a co-founder of the spiritual organisation the A A and leader of Ordo Templi Orientis. A controversial poet, playwright and social critic, he revolted against the moral and religious values of the time through a hedonistic lifestyle espousing a form of libertinism based on the rule of 'Do What Thou Wilt'. When he left Cambridge in 1896 Crowley severed all ties with Christianity and began to read up on the subject of occultism and mysticism, reading books by alchemists and mystics and books on magic. In May 1896 Crowley met and befriended Kelly. Their friendship was fostered by shared artistic ambitions and parallels in their background.[49] Occultism was fashionable in intellectual circles at the time and in their first years of friendship Crowley enticed Kelly to dabble in magical ritual.[50]

Not everyone in their circle was considered respectable. Crowley was also a notorious Lothario and womaniser. Kathleen Bruce describes the Englishmen of the quarter as 'an unsavory collection'.[51] Many ladies feared the loss of their reputation if Crowley displayed an interest in them and it was said that 'no young thing could remain alone in the same room with him in safety'.[52]

Crowley had come to Paris in 1902 and Kelly introduced him to Gray.[53] In his autobiography Crowley comments amusingly on Kelly's ability in portraiture. 'He (Kelly) once picked out an old canvas to paint over and had gone some distance before he discovered that it was his favourite portrait of the Hon. Eileen Grey (sic)'.[54] This portrait is now unknown.

Initially Crowley was a figure of amusement in Gray's early years in Paris. At times she found her sessions with him rather boring and full of nonsense. However, Gray owned a series of publications by him which she kept throughout her life. His writings and ideas influenced her early lacquer work and carpet work. They also developed her ideas in philosophical thinking.[55] His ideas regarding the occult were intriguing and she acquired a copy of *The Mother's Tragedy*, one of Crowley's earliest books on poetry and drama.[56] This publication is one of the earliest to incorporate the occult teaching of the Golden Dawn, and was written in the years following Crowley's initiation into the order, largely during his travels in Mexico and Asia. She eventually designed a rug in homage

1.19 Aleister Crowley, 1900s, black and white photograph © Topfoto/ Roger Viollet

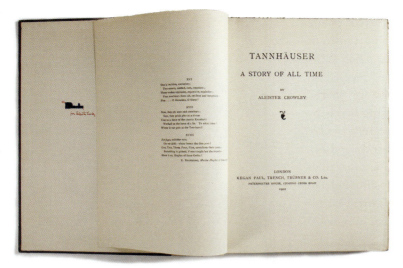

1.20 *Tannhäuser, a Story of All Time,* by Aleister Crowley, 1902, showing Crowley's signature © NMI

to his dark arts called *Magie Noire – Black Magic.* By the end of 1902 Crowley had become somewhat fascinated by Gray, gifting her a diamond brooch.[57] Firstly he gave her a copy of his book *Tannhäuser, a Story of All Time* which tells the tale of a knight and a poet who discovers the home of Venus, where he spends a year worshipping the goddess. Inside Crowley wrote an inscription 'To Eileen Gray from Aleister Crowley'. The book was described by Crowley as a self-portrait, however it was more the philosophical aspects of the play that appealed to Gray. Tannhäuser is ignorant of his identity with the Supreme Being or God. The various characters in the book all form parts of Tannhäuser's consciousness, and are not real persons at all. All of these characters either help or hinder his realisation of his true unity with life. Crowley explained that it was through Tannhäuser's love of Venus refined to pity that he at last attains Supreme Knowledge. Crowley says that play is 'a series of introspective studies; not necessarily a series in time, but in psychology, and that rather the morbid psychology of the Adept than the gross mentality of the ordinary man'.[58] Since childhood, Gray had nurtured a deep and profound interest in philosophy, studying the ideas of other dimensions, the conscious and subconscious mind, and the mind being able to create other personas or even worldly realms. Crowley's controversial approach intrigued her.

Gray may have been interested in his philosophy but not in relation to his ideas regarding men and women. In his poem *The Star and the Garter,* of which Gray also owned a copy,[59] Crowley satirised a number of their friends and clearly defined his opinion of the role of man and woman. 'Sometime later I added an appendix of a very obscure kind. The people of our circle, from Kathleen Bruce (since Lady Scott and Mrs Hilton Young) to Sybil Muggins and Hener Skene (later accompanist to Isadora Duncan) are satirised. Their names are introduced by means of puns or allusions and every line is loaded with cryptic criticism. Gerald (Kelly) and I, as educated men, were frightfully fed up with the presumption and poses of the average ass – male or female – of the quarter'.[60] He continued; 'Another affectation of the woman art students was to claim to be treated exactly as if they were men in every respect. Gerald, always eager to oblige, addressed one of his models as old fellow, to her great satisfaction. Then he excused himself for a momentary absence in the terms which he would have to use for another man. On his return, the lady had recovered her "sex and character," and had bolted. Women can only mix with men on equal terms when she adopts his morality lock, stock, and barrel, and ceases to set an extravagant artificial value on her animal function. The most high principled woman (alleged) insists on the supreme value of an asset which is notoriously of no value whatever in itself. *The Star and the Garter* deals frankly with this problem'.[61]

A surprise turn of events occurred in late summer 1903 when Crowley eloped with Rose Kelly (1874-1932), sister of Gerald Kelly. Kelly was furious. Despite describing this as the happiest day of his life in letters to Auguste Rodin, Crowley gave little consideration to his wife's feelings in his autobiography when describing his brief engagement nine months earlier to an unnamed Englishwoman in January of 1903.[62] Referring to the unnamed fiancée in his autobiography, Crowley informs us that, 'This lady claims the notice principally as the model for several of my poems'. He informs the reader that 'this Englishwoman was "the Star" in *The Star and the Garter* which I wrote at this time'. He claims that this woman served as the model for several poems, notably in the publication *Rosa Mundi and other Love Songs,* written under the pseudonym of H.D. Carr, in 1905. Of the list of poems which he dedicates to this secret fiancée, one was titled *The Kiss* and the other *Eileen*. This poem was dedicated to Eileen Gray. Whether Gray was Crowley's secret fiancée is speculative, however she returned the gift of the brooch, not wanting to cause embarrassment to Rose, Crowley's wife.

Prior to his arrival in Paris, Crowley was in India and on 20 and 21 March in 1902 where he composed *Berashith An Essay in Ontology and Ceremonial Magic*. It is Hebrew, meaning 'in the Beginning; the first word of Genesis'. The book reflects Crowley's interest in nineteenth-century philosophy and in Buddhism. His ideas again had an influence on Gray as the book discusses the theory of the universe according to Crowley. Included is a discussion of ceremonial magic where magic is viewed as a preparatory training for yoga. His theory explores the divergences between the great forms of religion – Buddhism, Hinduism and Christianity – adapting them to ontological science through mathematics. Crowley finishes the publication with 'Om Mani Padme Hum' the six sounds of the sacred Buddhist prayer meaning 'Hail the Jewel in the Lotus' – this being the title of one of Gray's lacquer screens, exhibited in 1913. The book was eventually published privately in Paris in 1903.[63] In the Paris edition the author is given as 'Abhavanda'. This was Crowley's chosen Hindu name during his yogic tutelage under Allan Bennett (1872-1923). By December 1903 Gray and Crowley were amicable to the point that Crowley once again sent her a copy of his book, writing his pseudonym 'Abhavanda to Eileen Gray 9 December'. Crowley's ideas on yoga also influenced Gray later, as she developed her theories on meditation which culminated in the *Meditation Grove project,* in 1941, where she designed a meditation garden on a hypothetical site outside St.Tropez. Gray purchased other publications on the subject, but starting with Crowley such publications form a part of Gray's philosophical thinking in relation to her more socially motivated projects.

Many of the group to which Kelly and Gray belonged frequented both the Café de Versailles and an upper room at the Chat Blanc. Included were Wyndham Lewis; William Somerset Maugham (1874-1965) whom Gray also met; one of Kelly's best friends,[64] Clive Bell (1881-1964) who stated that Kelly was his close friend during the summer of 1904; Enoch Arnold Bennett (1867-1931) whom Kelly had met through Schwob; Aleister Crowley, and Stephen Haweis (1878-1969), a friend of both Gray's, Kelly's and Crowley's. Gray states that sometimes she was brought along to these soirées.[65] The Chat Blanc in the rue d'Odessa was also popular with a circle of Anglo-American painters, sculptors, illustrators, writers and their female friends. Between 1904 and 1906 regulars at the restaurant included novelists Bennett, Maugham, Bell and Crowley. Among the many artists were the Americans Thomas Alexander Harrison (1853-1930), Penrhyn Stanlaws (1877-1957), Robert Root (1864-1937), Paul Bartlett (1865-1925), Canadian James Morrice (1865-1924), Welshman Gabriel Thompson (1861-1935), Englishmen George Barne (1887-1972) and Joseph Milner Kite (1864-1946). The Irish artist Roderic O'Conor (1860-1940) also visited the Chat Blanc. Gray's attendance at the Chat Blanc is only indicated in her biography and in Maugham's book *The Magician*, 1908. Maugham's main protagonist in the novel is Oliver Haddo, who was Crowley, and he describes a young lady, Margaret Dauncey, who had come to Paris from London to study art. Dauncey's character dined frequently at the 'Chien Noir' – Maugham's fictionalised name for the Chat Blanc.[66] The similarities with Gray in this novel are purely coincidental.[67] It is possible that the character of Margaret is an amalgam of Gray and Gerald Kelly's sister Rose.

Even if she had not met O'Conor at the Chat Blanc, Gray would certainly have known about this Irish painter through her circle. O'Conor came from Castleplunket, County Roscommon. He attended Ampleforth College in York and by 1879 had enrolled in the Dublin Metropolitan School of Art and then later at the Royal Hibernian Academy. To further his education he studied first in Antwerp at the Academié Royale des Beaux Arts in 1883 and went to Paris in 1886. He travelled and painted between Grez and Brittany for some years and finally moved back to Paris in 1904. He had participated in the inaugural exhibition of the Salon d'Automne in

1.21 William Somerset Maugham, by Howard Coster, 1930, whole glass plate negative © National Portrait Gallery, London

1903 and continued to exhibit there, with the exception of a few years, until 1935. It was during this period that O'Conor met Bell, Maugham, Bennett, Crowley and Kelly. Maugham did not like O'Conor and O'Conor compared Maugham to 'a bed bug, on which a sensitive man refuses to stamp because of the smell and the squashiness'. [68] Many of the habitués of the Chat Blanc wrote about O'Conor and by all accounts he apparently reigned there as the accepted pontiff.[69] Maugham often used fictional characters as devices with which to comment on or to attack his enemies, as he seems to have done in *The Magician* in the case of Crowley and possibly Gray. Similarly, he used O'Conor as the model for his character the painter O'Brien, also in *The Magician*.[70] O'Conor like Gray became a permanent expatriate and lived the rest of his life in France, chiefly in Paris. And like Gray he suffered the fate of being ignored, until recently, in his native land.[71]

It was also during this period that Gray met the English artist Stephen Haweis. Kelly was a mutual friend from Cambridge as was Crowley. Both Kelly and Gray had a lengthy correspondence with Haweis in the later part of his life. His best friends were the Scottish painter Francis Cadell (1883-1937) and the Irish artist Paul Henry (1876-1958). Belfast born, Henry had arrived in Paris in 1898 and like Haweis and Cadell enrolled immediately in the Académie Julian. It was here at the Academy that the three struck up a close friendship. In both Henry's and Haweis's memoirs a number of people are mentioned as attending the Académie at that time. Constance Gore Booth (1868-1927), the future revolutionary from Dublin and her husband Casimir Markievicz (1874-1932); the Chilean painter Manuel Ortiz de Zárate (1887-1946); Lucien Daudet (1878-1946); Francis Cadell; the Birmingham-born portrait artist Katherine Constance Lloyd (op.1923-1940), who had also attended the Slade School in 1896-1897, and the woodcut artist Mabel Royds (1874-1941).

1.22 Sir John Lavery, by unknown photographer, circa 1909, platinum print © National Portrait Gallery, London

When and where Gray and Henry were first introduced remains unclear and is only hinted at in letters from Haweis to Henry in their renewed correspondence during the 1950s. Haweis lived in Paris until 1914; however Henry, in his memoirs, records Haweis as briefly returning to London sometime in 1901-02.[72] It is during this period that Gray and Henry became acquainted, either in London prior to her leaving for Paris, or in Paris before Henry left for London. Gray is listed in Haweis's memoirs as being part of their social circle in the 1900s, along with Henry, Cadell, Crowley, Maugham, Kelly, Kathleen Bruce, Jessie Gavin, Katherine Constance Lloyd and others. It is suggested in Haweis's letters that it was at Kathleen Bruce's salon that Paul Henry met Gray.[73] It was also at Bruce's salon that Gray was introduced to John Lavery (1856-1941), who also corresponded with Haweis.

Of this circle of friends that Gray developed during these formative art school years it was a Reverend's son from London, Stephen Haweis, who gave much insight into Gray's life during this period and would continue to have an influence on Gray's work for the rest of her life.

ENDNOTES

1 NMIEG 2003.508 and NMIEG 2003.510, notes on Eileen Gray's work.

2 *Debrett's Peerage, Baronetage, Knightage and Companionage*, London, Dean and Son Limited, 1906, p.392.

3 *The Enniscorthy News and County Wexford Advertiser,* Saturday 11 July 1895.

4 *Dundee Advertiser,* 10 April 1895. NMIEG 2000.211, NMIEG 2000.212, Eveleen Pounden Gray. NMIEG 2000.213, NMIEG 2000.214, NMIEG 2000.215, James MacLaren Smith.

5 Adam, Peter, *Eileen Gray: Architect/Designer: A Biography,* London, Thames and Hudson, 2000, p.11.

6 Bence-Jones, Mark, *A Guide to Irish Country Houses,* London, Bass Printers Limited, 1996, p.49. NMIEG 2000.201, Brownswood House pre-1895.

7 NMIEG 2000.205 and NMIEG 2000.206, the Gray family, circa 1879. James McLaren Stuart, Gray's eldest brother, was born in 1864 and Ethel Eveleen, her eldest sister, was born in 1866. Gray's second brother Lonsdale was born in 1870, but died in 1900 from drinking poisoned water during the Boer War. Her sister Thora Zelma Grace was born in 1875 and finally Eileen in 1878.

8 NMIEG 2000.219-226 and NMIEG 2003.566, the Gray family, Pre 1900.

9 NMIEG 2000.201-204, the Gray family, James Gray, Henry Tufnell Campbell, Rick Campbell and Eileen Gray, at Brownswood, circa 1890s. NMIEG 2000.217, Lonsdale Gray, Ireland, NMIEG 2000.218, Thora and Eileen, Ireland. NMIEG 2003.558, Eileen Gray on horseback, circa 1917.

10 NMIEG 2000.242, a *Fiat* car.

11 Ibid, Adam, p.12.

12 Ibid, Adam.

13 Binchy, Maeve, 'A Far from Demure Life', *The Irish Times,* 16 February 1976.

14 Spalding, Francis, *Prunella Clough Regions Unmapped,* London, Lund Humphries, 2012, p.12.

15 NMIEG 2000.209 and NMIEG 2000.210, James MacLaren Smith at his easel.

16 Ibid, Adam, p.17.

17 NMIEG 2000.202, Brownswood house, circa 1896.

18 Ibid, Adam.

19 Ibid, Binchy.

20 Aquarius Interview, Thames Television Production, 11 November 1975. Gray illustrates photographs of the original Georgian house and the Mock Tudor house of 1896.

21 Ibid, Binchy.

22 Binchy, Maeve, *The Irish Times,* 4 November 1976.

23 In the *Enniscorthy News* and *County of Wexford Advertiser*, the *Enniscorthy Correspondent* and the *Enniscorthy Recorder,* from 1890 to 1900 there are regular articles concerning art and architecture, leading artists of the day, contemporary exhibitions, theoretical proposals and a new approach to teaching art being put into practice at London Art Schools.

24 NMIEG 2000.227, Eileen Gray, 1883. NMIEG 2000.231, Eileen Gray, 1897. NMIEG 2000.237, Eileen Gray 1898-1900. NMIEG 2000.228, NMIEG 2003.539, and NMIEG 2003.564, Eileen Gray 1888-1890. NMIEG 2003.545, Eileen Gray, 1894. NMIEG 2003.548, Eileen Gray, 1896. NMIEG 2003.559, Eileen Gray, 1896-1897. NMIEG 2003.553, NMIEG 2003.557, Eileen Gray, 1897-1898. NMIEG 2003.560, Eileen Gray, 1900. NMIEG 2003.550, Eileen Gray 1900-1902.NMIEG 2003.560, Eileen Gray, 1900.

25 NMIEG 2000.238, Eileen Gray with Henry Savage Landor, possibly at the Villa Gherdisca near Florence. Savage Landor was a serious suitor, one that the family approved of, and had studied at the Académie Julian. He was an explorer and when they were introduced he had already travelled quite extensively. The Landors lived in Italy and owned a large villa, the Villa Gherdisca, near Florence. NMIEG 2000.236, Eileen Gray with an unknown gentleman. NMIEG 2000.245 and NMIEG 2003.565, Eileen Gray with three gentlemen.

26 NMIEG 2000.216, James MacLaren Smith taken towards the end of his life. Gray has written lovingly 'papa' on the back. NMIEG 2000.217, Lonsdale Gray. Lonsdale Richard Douglas Gray was born 3 March 1870. He died while on active service, unmarried, on 10 June 1900 at aged 30 whilst in South Africa. He fought in the Boer War and gained the rank of Captain in the Sixth Dragoon Guards. Gray was heartbroken at his death.

27 Burke, Carolyn, *Becoming Modern: the Life of Mina Loy,* New York, Farrar, Straus and Giroux, 1996, p.37.

28 Schwabe, Randolph, 'Three Teachers: Brown, Tonks and Steer', *The Burlington Magazine for Connoisseurs,* Vol. 82, No.483, June 1943, p.141.

29 Adam, Peter, *Eileen Gray: Architect/Designer: A Biography,* London, Thames & Hudson, 1987, pp. 21-2.

30 Postle, Martin, 'The Foundation of the Slade School of Fine Art: Fifty-Nine Letters in the Record Office of University College London', *The Volume of the Walpole Society,* Vol.58, 1995/1996, p.147.

31 Ibid, Schwabe, p.145.

32 Ibid, Schwabe, p.146

33 Ibid, Schwabe, p.141.

34 Ibid, Schwabe, p.142.

35 Aquarius Interview, London Thames Television Production, November 1975. Eileen Gray states that she studied initially with D. Charles on Dean Street in Soho.

36 V&A Archives, AAD9/11-1980, business correspondence, AAD/9/3-1980, notebook.

37 Ibid, Adam. pp.23, 34. Adam states that Kelly was at the Slade and this is where Gray befriended him. However, there is no mention of Kelly attending the Slade in Derek Hudson's biography on Gerald Kelly. In the Slade School records there is an F.M. Kelly registered to study fine art in 1900-1901.

38 Ibid, Binchy, *The Irish Times,* 16 February 1976.

39 Holland, Clive, 'Student Life in Paris', *The Studio and Illuminated Magazine of Fine and Applied Arts*, Vol.27, 1903, p.38.

40 Ibid, Adam, p.35.

41 Hudson, Derek, *For the Love of Painting, The Life of Sir Gerald Kelly,* London, Chaucer Press, 1975, p.1.

42 *The Times,* 18 March 1969. As quoted in Hudson, Derek, *For the Love of Painting, The Life of Sir Gerald Kelly,* London, Chaucer Press, 1975, p.18.

43 O'Connor, Ulick, 'The Abbey Portraits', *Irish Arts Review,* Dublin, Vol.21, No.3, Autumn 2004, pp.104-107.

44 Ibid, Hudson, p.24.

45 Musée Rodin Archives, three letters from Eileen Gray to Auguste Rodin, December 1902, January 1902 and 20 January 1902.

46 Ibid, Adam, p.38.

47 Bilbiothèque Jacques Doucet, fonds Paul Léautaud, MS 24133, deux lettres de Paul Léautaud à Eileen Gray. Paris, 24 February and 30 April 1904.

48 Ibid, Adam, p.37.

49 Sutin, Lawrence, *Do What Thou Wilt, A Life of Aleister Crowley,* New York, St Martin's Press, 2000, pp.49-50.

50 Crowley, Aleister, *The Confessions of Aleister Crowley,* London, Bantam Press, 1971; originally published by Mandrake, 1929, edited by John Symonds and Kenneth Grant, pp.166, 347-350.

51 Bruce, Kathleen, *Self Portrait of an Artist,* London, John Murray, 1949, p.71.

52 Hamnett, Nina, *Laughing Torso, Reminiscences of Nina Hamnett,* New York, Roy Long and Richard Smith, 1932, p.31.

53 Crowley, Aleister, *The Confessions of Aleister Crowley,* London, Bantam Press, 1971. Originally published by Mandrake, 1929, edited by John Symonds and Kenneth Grant, pp.166, 139-140, 347-350.

54 Ibid, Crowley, Aleister, p.370.

55 NMIEG 2003.59, *The Mother's Tragedy,* 1901. NMIEG 2003.56, *Tannhäuser, a Story of All Time,* 1902. NMIEG 2003.57, *An Essay in Ontology with some remarks on Ceremonial Magic.,* 9 December 1903. NMIEG 2003.58, *The Star and the Garter,* 1903.

56 NMIEG 2003.59, Crowley, Aleister, *The Mother's Tragedy,* London, Privately Printed, 1901.

57 The Warburg Institute Archives, the Yorke Collection, OS D6, letter from Aleister Crowley to Gerald Kelly, 12 August 1903. Crowley denies to Kelly in this letter that they were lovers – however the fact that he gave her the brooch was an indication of affection on his part. It is insinuated that Gray and Crowley were engaged.

58 NMIEG 2003.56, Crowley, Aleister, *Tannhäuser, a Story of All Time,* London, Kegan Paul, Trench, Trubner & Co. Ltd, 1902, pp.13-15.

59 NMIEG 2003.58, Crowley, Aleister, *The Star and the Garter,* London, Watts & Co, 1903.

60 Ibid, Crowley, *The Confessions of Aleister Crowley,* p.371.

61 Ibid, Crowley, pp.371-2.

62 Musée Rodin Archives, Aleister Crowley papers.

63 NMIEG 2003.57, Crowley, Aleister, *Berashith: An Essay in Ontology with some remarks on Ceremonial Magic,* Paris, Clarke and Bishop, Printers, 1902.

64 Ibid, Adam, p.40.

65 Ibid, Adam, p.38.

66 Maugham, William Somerset, *The Magician,* London, Vintage Books, 2000, p.19.

67 Ibid, Adam, p.40.

68 Ibid, Crowley, p.364.

69 Tate Gallery Archives, Prunella Clough Collection and Archive, letter from Alden Brooks to Denys Sutton, 12 July 1936.

70 Bennington, Jonathan, *Roderic O'Conor*, Dublin, Irish Academic Press, 1992, p.95.

71 Ibid, Bennington, p.93.

72 TCD Archives, Paul Henry Papers – 7429.2, transcript of Paul Henry's autobiography.

73 TCD Archives, Paul Henry Papers – 7432/71-109, letter from Stephen Haweis to Paul Henry, undated, and letter from Stephen Haweis to Paul Henry, 4 March 1952.

2

A Moveable Feast: Stephen Haweis, Students and Paris

Throughout Eileen Gray's life she kept many publications, letters, articles, magazines and photographs of people whom she knew and who shaped her life, both personally and professionally. Included in this interesting contemporary milieu were Wyndham Lewis, Aleister Crowley, Gerald Festus Kelly, Clive Bell, Kathleen Bruce, Jessie Gavin, Roger Fry (1866-1934), Natalie Clifford Barney (1876-1972), Nancy Cunard (1896-1965), Loïe Fuller (1862-1928), Lucie Delarue Mardrus (1874-1945), Chana Orloff (1888-1968), and Gabrielle Bloch. It is through the diaries, notes, letters and archives of those family, friends, acquaintances and associates who featured in her life during this time that a fuller understanding of Eileen Gray, from art student to artist emerges.

Gray's library also contained a number of publications by the writer and painter Stephen Haweis and letters from his niece René Chipman (1903-1986).[1] Haweis was described, by some, as a suitor and a fellow student who emigrated to Dominica and kept writing to Gray all of his life, sending her 'unasked for' photographs 'looking like a very, very old chimpanzee'. Gray commented, 'No sense of *pudeur* (modesty)'.[2] However, Gray wrote to Haweis until Haweis's death on 17 January 1969. It is

2.1 Eileen Gray, 1898-1900, black and white photograph © NMI

2.2 Loïe Fuller dancing the Tanz de Lilie, 1896, black and white photograph © IMAGNO/Austrian Archives/Topfoto

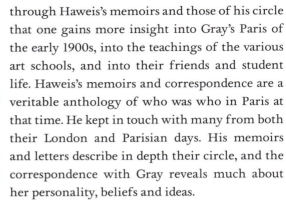

through Haweis's memoirs and those of his circle that one gains more insight into Gray's Paris of the early 1900s, into the teachings of the various art schools, and into their friends and student life. Haweis's memoirs and correspondence are a veritable anthology of who was who in Paris at that time. He kept in touch with many from both their London and Parisian days. His memoirs and letters describe in depth their circle, and the correspondence with Gray reveals much about her personality, beliefs and ideas.

Eileen Gray and Stephen Haweis had much in common. Haweis, like Gray, came from a distinguished family which was also marked with controversy and scandal. His maternal grandfather Thomas Musgrave Joy (1812–1866) was a fashionable portrait painter who gave drawing lessons to Prince Albert and did portraits of the royal children and their pets at Windsor Castle. Mary Eliza Haweis, Stephen's mother, was born in 1848. When she was eighteen, she sold a painting to the Royal Academy and painted two portraits on commission. The following year she married the renowned Reverend Hugh Reginald Haweis of St James's Church, Marylebone. The young couple became very popular in London society and were presented at Court. Mary Eliza became an arbiter of fashion during the 1870s and 80s and was one of the cognoscenti. The couple's first child died in infancy, and thereafter his parents had two sons and a daughter. Like Gray, Haweis was the youngest; he was born Stephen Hugh Willyams on 23 July, 1878.

The Reverend was a little over five feet tall, crippled from childhood in one leg because of a pony riding accident, and of an ivory complexion (his grandmother was a native of the British Indian province of Baluchistan).

2.3 Stephen Haweis, 1923, sepia tint photograph © Photo courtesy of the Marine Biological Laboratory Archives and the History of Marine Biological Laboratory website (history.archives.mbl.edu)

Like Stephen, he became renowned for his small stature. He became a spellbinding preacher, wrote many popular religious books, and was in great demand as a public lecturer. His sermons drew admiring crowds for decades. Gray said to Haweis, 'About your father I remember my mother and eldest sister (Ethel) eleven years older than me used to go on Sunday evenings (was it to Camberwell I can't remember) to listen to your father preaching, immensely impressed and convinced of his importance'.[3] Gray recalled 'hearing people speak of him as a brilliant seductive person!'[4] The Reverend was appointed Lowell Lecturer in Boston, Mass. in 1886 and went on lecture tours in America in 1893-94. When he was a curate, the Archbishop of Canterbury had regarded him as his protégé, but because of indiscreet behaviour he fell out of favour and was offered no preferment; though, prudently, nothing was done to put its outstanding preacher outside the boundaries of the Church.

Stephen's mother strove to repair the effect of her husband's extravagances on their income by writing and illustrating a number of magazine articles and books for women on dress, deportment and decoration in the home, through which she gained an enviable reputation. Her magazine columns on interior decoration and fashion encouraged readers to reject Victorian fussiness in favour of the new 'Art' furniture. She also encouraged her readers to choose the best aspects of the Aesthetic Movement in their dress. Her books *The Art of Beauty,* 1878 and *The Art of Decoration,* 1881 were illustrated with Pre-Raphaelite and Aesthetic designs. She was also renowned for her literary adaptations, notably *Chaucer for Children,* 1877 where she retold Chaucer's tales, making them suitable for Victorian readers. She was a very proud woman in that despite having to earn money she retained the status of a gentlewoman. Her assiduous work enabled her to pay for Stephen's education at Westminster School and to send him to Peterhouse College, Cambridge.

Again like Gray, Haweis had to convince his family, especially his mother, to allow him to take up art lessons. He said, 'Mother was against my taking up art unless I thought I was going to do really well. With support better than starvation I should have done far more and better, but everybody believed that I should have done well but I had only £63 to spend on my first year in Paris. My heart broke down through my father's complete neglect and robbery of about a third of my inheritance'.[5] His mother died in 1898, before he could take a degree, whereupon he decided

2.4 James Maclaren Smith, Firenze, 1880s, black and white photograph © NMI

2.5 Lonsdale Gray, Eileen, Thora and a friend Captain French in the French Alps, year unknown, black and white photograph © NMI

not to continue at Cambridge as he wished to become a painter, and to that end he went to study in Paris in 1899. He never forgot his mother. His studio in Paris was described as being filled with family treasures, notably mementos of his mother. His cape was lined with the dress she wore when presented to Queen Victoria. He kept place cards from his mother's dinner parties, inscribed with the names of important Londoners. He saved her clothing, her amber beads, sewing boxes full of tiny heirlooms, mother of pearl daisies wound with silk thread, miniature patchwork quilts, embroidered baby clothes, a copybook belonging to his great-great grandfather, an hourglass, a leather hood which adorned the family's falcon, the plaster cast of the hand of his brother who had died in infancy and an Etruscan vase which contained the ashes of his mother's dog.[6]

Haweis's father died early in 1901. He had greatly resented his son who, devoted to his mother, appears to have been a quiet, attractive, hard-working young man. He had a streak of stubbornness in his make-up, for his mother had once written, 'Stephen has the Haweis temper'. His father had undoubtedly cheated Stephen of a substantial legacy, but his mother had left sufficient money to make him not entirely dependent on the sale of his work and, indeed, enough to enable him to travel.

Both Haweis and Gray were the children of broken marriages. Despite the Gray family's position in society, Gray recalled her parents eating dinner in silence at either end of a very long table.[7] Just as Haweis lost his mother in 1898 and his father in 1901, Gray lost her father, and she went to Territet in Switzerland to bury him, much grieved in late February 1900.

In June later that year she lost her brother Lonsdale who drank poisoned water while in South Africa. As Gray had doted on her father, Stephen adored his mother. However, unlike Haweis, Gray destroyed many of her family papers. Throughout their correspondence Gray and Haweis discussed such personal matters. On 5 June 1958 Gray wrote, 'I was very interested in the letter talking about your father though you don't say really in what way he was responsible for your

unhappiness'. She continued, 'My own childhood was probably as unhappy
and worse in many ways than yours and the shaky hand is a consequence
of years of sleepless nights and misery of many kinds but as Kipling used
to say that's another story'. Despite Haweis's strained relationship with
his father, Gray dryly comments towards the end of this letter: 'Anyway
you had a mother who loved you'. Gray had a terrible shake in her hand
towards the end of her life. In another letter Gray says that the shake in her
hand is due to her childhood. 'It all comes from having been so frightened
at night (for years) when I was a child and there is no cure for it'.[8]

The Haweis family quarrels continued through Haweis's brother
Lionel, who took the side of his father. The bitterness and feuding caused
by his family remained with him throughout his life. In a poem written
in 1960 Haweis wrote his own epitaph; 'Who shall say what I might have
said, killed by a father's hate and heart, before I failed in love and art,
when I lie dead'.[9] It was through his niece René Chipman that the truth
of what his father and brother did to Stephen was finally acknowledged.
When Lionel died, Haweis wrote to his friend Jean Roosevelt saying of
his family, 'I think nobody has ever needed me and certainly nobody has
ever needed my sister, so this grand and glorious family which began in
about the twelfth century is passing out of the picture regretted by none
and noticed by few'.[10] John Ellis Roosevelt said, 'We learned from Mrs
Chipman and from reading through Hawys' (sic) papers that he, Hawys,
(sic) had come to the conclusion that his father was an S.O.B and a crook,
with psychological and sexual problems to boot and that Hawys' (sic)
brother Lionel (Mrs Chipman's father) was at best a dam (sic) fool'.[11] In the
last year of his life Chipman went through her father's memorabilia and
wrote to Stephen apologising to him for 'my disbelief of you in the past'.
Astonished and horrified at her father and grandfather's behaviour she
confessed to Stephen 'so far I have wronged you'.[12]

Similarly Gray's situation with her family became strained due to
her sister Ethel's marriage to Henry Tufnel Campbell. This man had an
overwhelming influence on her mother. In her letters Gray describes
equally complicated family stories. 'My brother who was left all my
grandfather's money, as I told you he [Gray's grandfather] was angry
with my mother and left her nothing, which provoked feuds (my mother
entirely under the influence of my brother-in-law who grabbed and
ruled) in Ireland'.[13] Gray's grandfather Jeremiah Lonsdale Pounden died

in 1887, leaving his estate to James Mclaren Stuart Gray, twentieth Lord Gray – who had become Lord Gray upon the death of his mother on 24 December 1918. However, on 6 May 1919 *The Irish Times* reported:

> The death occurred at Brighton, after a short illness, of the right Hon. James McLaren Stuart Gray, Baron Gray. He succeeded his mother, Eveleen Baroness Gray, on her death in December 24 1918 and became the twentieth holder of the title. His sister, the Hon Ethel Eveleen, wife of Henry T Campbell Esq of 7 Collingwood Gardens, London SW and Brownswood Co Wexford, succeeds him to the title.[14]

2.6 Thora and Eileen Gray, Palermo, 1895-1897, black and white photograph © NMI

Gray describes quite an uncomfortable situation amongst family members after this. 'The shadow of that horrible atmosphere is still there as it seems to be with you it is undeniable that those are the years that mark one for life. My sister was very popular at school, she was a great flirt and took things easily, and then married and escaped. I escaped too, to Paris'. Gray remained close with her sister Thora (1875-1966) and Thora's husband Eric Clough Taylor (1883-1947). In her later years, like Haweis, contact with her family was with her niece Prunella Clough (1919-1999). This she shares with Haweis, and in one letter affectionately sends Haweis 'poems written by my brother-in-law (Clough Taylor) before he died as I think you might like them'.[15]

For Gray the Slade School had been the initiation into the avant-garde, the world of the déclassé and cosmopolitan artists. However, the school did nothing to encourage individuality, particularly in a woman. In Haweis's memoirs Gray is listed as amongst his circle of friends from the 1900s. Haweis arrived in Paris in 1899 befriending Irish artist Paul Henry and Scottish artist Francis Cadell when they all enrolled in the Académie Julian. In his memoirs he says that he was there between 1899 and 1900. He then returned to England sometime in 1900, but was back in Paris at the École Colarossi in 1902 where he was attending night drawing classes and where he met his future wife Mina Loy (1882-1966).[16] Gray and Haweis attended the École at the same time.

In Paul Henry's autobiography *An Irish Portrait*, 1951, he provides much insight into the city of Paris at that time and what the Académie Julian was like for Gray when she enrolled in 1903.[17] 'Paris in those years was filled with students from all over the globe, all filled with a high resolve to learn as much as they could and to seize every opportunity to perfect themselves in their particular arts'.[18] Henry describes in detail the Académie, which was in stark contrast to the Slade. 'The Académie Julian was not in any sense of the word a teaching institution. It was not a school with regular classes and teachers, it granted no degree, and there were no prizes. As long as you paid up, behaved properly and did not steal the easels, you were free'.

Haweis's circle was described as a blend of dabblers in black magic, spinsters and elderly ladies.[19] Descriptions of Haweis also vary. Loy described him as preferring the female sex to his own and added that his lady friends were not an attractive lot. According to Loy he served as a token of masculinity in their lives. Many found Haweis irritating because he attempted to ingratiate himself with those with a more luxurious standard of living, and he was known for charming women with a monthly allowance.[20] Haweis's memoirs and letters reveal a man who had an equal number of male as well as female friends. He compensated for his lack of stature by an eccentric personality and dress. He is described as having 'flashing black eyes, olive skin, and glossy dark hair, hanging down like a curtain about his head, gave him the appearance of a young Italian who had stepped from a picture by Raphael'.[21] Haweis wanted to stand out. Paul Henry wrote of him, 'we had to find other ways of showing to the world that we were not as other men'. He continued; 'Stephen Haweis was just down from Cambridge and he was one of the most colourful persons in the quarter, his small neat figure was dressed in brown corduroy, he wore a black beret and his long hair was cut straight across his forehead like a Florentine page; collarless he looped around his neck or throat a long string of amber beads. Sometimes in place of the beads he wore a jade green live snake which often caused much commotion in the studio when it wandered among the easels'.[22] Haweis at times flaunted his eccentricities possibly because he had to live up to the reputation of his father. Henry says that 'Haweis, like his father, was something of an oddity, but I liked

2.7 Eileen Gray, 1902, black and white photograph © NMI

2.8 *Self Portrait of an Artist*, by Kathleen Bruce, 1949, detail showing Bruce inside the front cover of the book © NMI

him in spite of his eccentricities which I cannot describe as poses because they were the natural expression of a very vivid personality'.[23]

Gray also was strikingly attractive. In her autobiography Kathleen Bruce gives a description of Gray during this period, as lovable but remote in personality.

> She was fair, with wide set pale blue eyes, tall and of grand proportion, well born and quaintly and beautifully dressed. But for a rather vague look and an absent minded manner, she would have been wonderful. I thought she was wonderful, when, one night she told me that she lived her whole life in terror because there was madness in her family. I thought her not only wonderful to look at, but also the most romantic figure I had ever seen.[24]

Gray's appearance also caught Haweis's attention. He describes many female painters, sculptors and society women in his memoirs. He considered Gray one of the beauties of those Paris days.

> There were several amazingly beautiful girls in our Paris of the early 1900s. Mina (Loy) was half English, half Jewish Hungarian, whose complexion was so perfect that the students betted upon its truth, and would not believe their eyes when a scrub on the studio towel left it ... perfectly white. Her mouth was an incredible wonder and almost plum coloured. It was as beautiful as Eileen's shoulders, which were the most perfect I ever saw ... things beautiful which live forever in memory and for which to be grateful. Of course there are always beauties where many young people of different nationalities are gathered together, yet some remain like planets among the stars, more radiant than others.

These notes in his memoirs are typewritten but at the end of the paragraph describing these women Haweis pencilled in 'The Hon. Eileen Gray'. He continued,

It is not only for their beauty that these girls are to be remembered, nor for their talent, though some of them were talented enough and one was a genius. They marked the end of an era, and created a new one without knowing very much about it. To repeat, ad nauseam, most of the girls were as poor as the men, but they cared for 'beauty' and were not content to be dull echoes of the prevailing fashion.[25]

2.9 Eileen Gray, 1900s, black and white photograph © NMI

The Anglo-Irish aristocracy based their ideas of the French on the popular novels of la vie de bohème and thus saw France as a nation of seducers. The artistic quarter of Montmartre was depicted as a sordid area with dangers lurking in every side street. In George Moore's (1852-1933) *Confessions of a Young Man,* 1886, stories of free love were just the sort of thing which concerned respectable people. Haweis also knew Moore, who came to Paris sporadically with Walter Sickert (1860-1942). Haweis said that Moore and Sickert were old friends and 'frequently dined with us at the Restaurant Garnier in the Boulevard Raspail. They both enjoyed young people, though it appeared to me that Moore's interest in them was highly specialised and referred principally to girls'.[26] Moore was an Irish novelist, short-story writer, poet, art critic and dramatist. He came from Carra, County Mayo. Originally he wanted to be a painter and studied in Paris during the 1870s, where he befriended the many leading French artists of the day. Whether Gray was ever introduced to him is unclear; but through Haweis she must have been aware of this Irishman who had made such an impression in Paris. Haweis's comments about Moore and Sickert are quite revealing. 'We treated George Moore with great respect. He was a celebrity, but some of us rather enjoyed the off-hand, friendly contempt with which Walter Sickert treated him and which Moore never quite seemed able to tackle'.[27] The sordidness, which Moore described in his novel *Confessions of a Young*

Man, 1886, of this district of Paris with its bohemian artists and free love seemed unreal at times to Haweis, 'I went to study in Paris and incidentally I did not find it any wickeder than anywhere else. Whether it be that I am so pure that evil cannot touch me or whether I am so depraved that evil is the natural breath of my nostrils I have never been able to determine but I often think of Nietzsche saying "behold when I looked at wickedness of men it was seldom more than four shoes broad and three months long"'.[28] He differed somewhat from Gray who explained in a letter to Haweis years later that 'At that time, I was always in a dream, and had no grasp on realities so-called: parental sternness, and terror by night left me with a complex, dread of people that I still have. Until I knew them well, they leave me with a feeling of frustration, because the real "Me" retreats to an immense distance, while the creature that is apparent, seizes on any nonsense to pretend that it is really there. Probably to you this doesn't make sense'.[29] Gray's personality always tended towards introversion and in her later life she tells him, 'that I am "en marge de la vie" and have no grasp on material, practical realities. I know that I would like to be quit of them, and yet problems of another kind interest me enormously'.[30]

Montparnasse by all accounts in 1902 was a pastoral outpost on the edge of the city and still retained traces of peaceful country life. The area would soon undergo rapid transformation. Work had just begun on extending the Boulevard Raspail and houses and shops were being replaced by multi-storied modernist buildings and artists' studios. Across the Seine women art students may have been leading disciplined and respectable lives – however as art students they were still viewed with disdain. Bruce summed up public opinion in her autobiography. 'In the first years of the twentieth century to say that a lass, perhaps not out of her teens had gone prancing off to Paris to study art was to say that she had gone irretrievably to hell'.[31] Nonetheless, women artists were already studying there in increasing numbers, and lived without outraging public opinion. Clive Holland, a British journalist, wrote, 'That the life they lead differs from that led by their male companions, both as regards its freedom and its strenuousness, goes without saying; but its (sic) sufficiently Bohemian for the most enterprising feminine searcher after novelty'.[32] Haweis described life as exceedingly difficult for artistic women who, when left to their own devices, had few choices once their financial support ran out, other than prostitution. The American expatriate painter Romaine Brooks

2.10 Paris VI – Montparnasse, circa 1900, black and white photograph, © Roger Viollet /Topfoto

(1874–1970), a friend of both Gray and Haweis, recalled her adventures in the turn-of-the-century Montmartre, where her attempts to earn a living included stints as an artist's model and a brief career as a music-hall performer. Many female art students boarded in family-style pensions; the more emancipated found their own apartments. Most young women rented rooms in the studio complexes around Montparnasse and set up housekeeping on a modest budget. Many students, including Paul Henry, first lodged at the Hôtel de la Haute Loire, at 203, boulevard Raspail. Haweis amusingly comments that 'the memoirs of the concierge in the old Hôtel de la Haute Loire should be interesting reading. There are so many who went there in search of cheap accommodation who were poor, but very often talented. It was from there so many of us went away when we had found even cheaper roofs shared in stern virtue or unquestionable sin'.[33] Within a short time, Henry and Haweis managed to find a 'ramshackle, and out-at-elbows, but adorable studio' in a now-demolished building in the rue de la Grande Chaumière, a street more redolent of art and artists.

2.11 Countess Markievicz in uniform, 1915, photographic negative glass, Keogh Photographic Collection © National Library of Ireland

There was a well in the garden, from whence they drew water, and the toilets, which were in the courtyard, were appalling. Haweis describes in detail the studio off the courtyard where he lived. It was clearly subdivided between those with money and those without. 'At one sad moment I lived in an underground studio in Paris, a cellar which had once been endured by two brothers who became famous illustrators in the *Saturday Evening Post*.[34] Its claim to be a studio at all rested upon its having a top light; it had no other. Above my head, on the ground floor, dwelt Countess Markievicz and her very large Polish husband, but they did not concern themselves with those who frequented the bowels of the earth beneath'. In later notes that he had edited he said:

> Before I married I had a studio which had a top light only for the good and sufficient reason that it was underground. Above was the studio of the beautiful Miss Gore Booth, the Irish patriot, who was married to a Polish Count Markievicz. I knew them slightly, but was not included in the gay parties which often took place over my head. I complained of the light in that wretched studio, which by the way had formerly been occupied with the Leyendecker brothers who made brilliant pictorial covers for the Saturday Evening Post in the USA. Rodin did not seem to think the light of a studio made much difference. 'I can paint anywhere,' he said. 'I spread my watercolours out on the floor and colour them all together. Anywhere any light is good enough, no?' It helped cure me of the superstition that a studio must have a north light.

Paul Henry also recalled Constance Gore Both. 'The only other person I knew was Miss Gore Booth who afterwards married Count Markievicz, who had been one of my fellow students at Julians. The Gore Booth as we called her was very attractive and gay'. Whether Gray ever had the opportunity of making this Irish patriot's acquaintance is mere speculation. Gavin and Bruce later took a studio together at rue Delambre, as did Loy. Bruce also found a studio for Wyndham Lewis on the rue Delambre. By 1902 Haweis had a studio on the rue Campagne Première as did Gerald Kelly. Gray independently rented a flat in the rue des Saints-Pères on her own. Gray's mother thought that her daughter's life was 'modest and terribly proper' because her apartment looked so ordinary.[35] Those who had less money shared studios. Haweis recorded 'we shared what we had with the nearest; girls and boys lived in studios side by side in an intimacy unthinkable in any other place in the world, often as virtuously as though they had two chaperones apiece, of course sometimes they drifting into free unions, that were often not without beauty and dignity'.[36] Haweis talks about those with money and then says 'but those who inhabited Poverty Corner had little to do with them. They ate at restaurants (when they ate) like Garnier's which became Leduc's, Henriette's, or the Hole in the Wall'.[37]

The artistic woman student had to quickly find her feet and work slavishly to achieve her goal. Without guidance and financial support student life in Paris, especially for a woman, was exceedingly difficult. 'There is plenty of human wreckage floating about in the Quarter; and the tragedy of unfulfilled promise, unaccomplished hopes, is closely knit with student life'.[38] Haweis noted in his memoirs that there was almost a competition amongst the students to see who could live for less, as he noted, 'I knew one ever so cheerful girl who beat me to the minimum by ten pounds'.[39] He also noted how 'death took a hand once in a while' when a young shy Russian woman art student was found dead of starvation in her studio, her arm outstretched, holding a letter containing a cheque from home. He recalled many casualties from poverty in the artistic field. 'She was not the only one to die of Paris, and privacy and poverty. It was impossible to pause, we were working. One did not listen to hard luck tales except from one's nearest and dearest; there were too many of them'.[40]

Gray arrived in Paris just a few years after it became possible for men and women to work together in any class, let alone in life drawing – where the question of the nude was on everyone's mind. Frenchwomen already attended the École des Beaux-Arts, but they were still barred from the Prix de Rome, a coveted award that assured official recognition following a year's study in Italy at the Villa de Medici. In 1903 women finally won the right to compete for this fellowship, as did foreign art students, who had been excluded until then and who rejoiced at the news. Not all women welcomed the opportunity as it was considered liberal to study the nude alongside a male student, and some doubted that 'the female art student who was kept at a distance from real art because of the nude model would accept the shared life of the Villa Medici with young men'.[41] Foreign female art students, like Gray, who were Irish, English or American, were long regarded by French men as more masculine than their French sisters, who were thought to represent the quintessentially feminine.[42] As the numbers of foreign female students increased at the turn of the century their presence would have presumably constituted less of an affront to propriety. Foreign students usually enrolled in the popular academies of the Latin Quarter or Montparnasse, where no entrance exams were required and women could choose from a variety of classes. All followed a similar structure. An instructor known as the *maître* chose models, collected fees, and saw to the details of daily life. The École Colarossi was popular among foreign students, and classes had been integrated there for several years when Gray arrived.[43] The more conservative Académie Julian offered separate instruction for women, with three different studios 'arranged to satisfy different sensibilities – one for drawing from the nude model, one for working from a draped model, and a third which had a separate staircase and entrance for amateurs who didn't wish to even glimpse a nude model'.[44] The more experienced women artists felt that access to the male model, draped or nude, was not the most important issue. They maintained that only their full participation in the academic system through membership of the salons' selection committees would put an end to hostilities between the

2.12 Mixed art class, England, 1900, black and white photograph ©Topfoto

sexes. Although women painters had won a more equitable status, their success was thought to depend primarily on their social standing. As in London and Dublin, women were seen as amateurs who would either marry or become teachers.

The choice of art school was paramount, since it put the painter in touch with her future mentor. Gray and her friends choose the École Colarossi. Noted for its informal tone and modest fees, the school was located at 10 rue de la Grande Chaumière,

2.13 Académie Julian mixed class, 1904, black and white photograph, © Roger Viollet/Topfoto

2.14 Académie Julian life drawing class, 1910, black and white photograph, © Roger Viollet/ Topfoto

above a plethora of studios. It was open from 6 a.m. until 10 p.m. There was an abundance of ateliers, and life drawing classes were not segregated. In the morning, models posed for genre painting which depicted everyday life, or ordinary people in work or recreation, while afternoon classes were devoted to the practice of *croquis* or quick sketches. There were the standard drawing, painting, watercolour and sculpture classes. These were supplemented by free instruction in anatomy at the Beaux Arts. In addition there were special classes in costume and in decorative arts. Gray attended the drawing classes. 'Life of the schools is intensely interesting, often amusing, and sometimes even tragic'.[45] In her autobiography Bruce describes how new figure models were chosen every Monday morning. 'At the end of the studio passed one by one a string of nude, male models. Each jumped for a moment onto the model throne, took a pose, and jumped down. The model for the week was being chosen'.[46] Clive Holland describes how female and male students worked alongside one another. 'The stronger natures among the girl art students will probably decide upon attending one of the mixed classes, and there they will work shoulder to shoulder with their brother art students, drawing from the costume or the living model'.[47] However, Bruce was shocked to view Gray attending such classes alongside male students, especially while drawing a male nude model. She describes her as 'standing composedly with her head critically on one side'. Gray is calmly 'appraising'.

In Bruce's autobiography she explains that at first none of the three friends (Gray, Gavin and herself) spoke French. Bruce also gives in-depth details of her daily routine and daily expenditure on food. She rose early at 6 a.m and went bathing. Then she had 'a roll for breakfast with a cup of chocolate when funds were good, and so back to work at the art school at 8 a.m. At twelve, lunch in a little restaurant, and back to work at one. No tea. Dinner at seven. Occasionally back to the night class, occasionally a club dance or the gallery of the opera, but more usually home to bed'. Bruce's daily expenditure on food was 95 centimes. She won a competition shortly after arrival and as a result did not have to pay fees. She was then appointed *Massier* where she became responsible for posing the model on the Monday morning, calling time for classes, stoking the fire and opening windows at lunchtime.

The integration of the students often resulted in men's conversation evolving around whether the various foreign women were *gentiles* (sexually encouraging) or a *nouvelle* (a new female student). One female student at the Colarossi wrote 'what seems simply rowdy in the men immediately appears unattractive in the girls ... we do have it harder'.[48] Haweis also remarks on this in his memoirs, 'Soon clean, neatly dressed American and English girls were seen in the Latin Quarter and they had come to study art but not so assiduously as the art students studied them'.[49] Of the Parisian lack of reserve one student noted, 'There is a childish joy in living, in letting oneself go the way nature seems to like it best, without much concern about whether it is good or bad'.[50] Haweis noted that those ladies who fell for this Parisian lack of reserve sullied their own reputation. 'Due to champagne and association with French girls a few girls encountered trouble and such risks had to be curtailed. An American girls club started which tried its best to provide protection for pure maidens – with considerable success – but the sinful remained outside'.[51] Anatomy classes at the École des Beaux-Arts provided a forum where students watched their professor articulate the movement of the bones with plaster casts, skeletons and at times cadavers. Mina Loy describes in detail one such anatomy class. 'It (the cadaver) was hung from an iron hook fixed in its cranium to a seated posture on a rickety chair', she recalled, 'When the lecturer hurrying across the platform to specify a muscle lifted its arm and, on being dropped, that arm slid off the dead man's thigh'.[52] The corpses for this class were mostly fished out of the river Seine.

Certain teachers were particularly admired in the Colarossi. Raphael Collin (1850-1916) was one such. 'His force and exaltation of temperament impresses one as being the rare gift or the finer inflorescence of character'.[53] Others were the Orientalist Louis Giradot (1858-1933), Gustave Courtois (1852-1923), the Czech Alphonse Mucha (1860-1939) who taught decorative arts, Pascal Dagnan-Bouveret (1852-1929) and the Norwegian Christian Krohg (1852-1925). Night-time drawing classes were also available, where it was said the level of accomplishment was higher. Both Loy and Haweis attended these classes.[54] The Colarossi's reputation grew and it drew large numbers of students. One could learn as much outside of class as in. The most interesting discussions took place in the cafés – as described in Chapter 1. However, to attend the cafés a lady needed to be chaperoned. One solution was to visit other students in their studios or to dine in expensive restaurants. Students would also hire models to their studios and share the cost.

Gray soon transferred to the Académie Julian. Of the private schools the Académie, founded in 1868 by Rodolphe Julian (1839-1907), reproduced most faithfully the discipline of the École des Beaux-Arts and they were seen as rivals. If one wanted access to the most successful painters of the day it was the place to enrol. Its liberal enrolment policies attracted many international students and, though it received no subsidy of any sort, Julian rented ateliers, which he could open and close as demand dictated, keeping costs at a minimum. 'Paris in those years was filled with students from all over the globe, all filled with a high resolve to learn as much as they could and to seize every opportunity to perfect themselves in their particular arts'.[55] The academy prospered and so could award prizes and fees were reduced to a moderate sum. The staff included a number of the professors from the École des Beaux-Arts or some who had previously studied there. But, as Henry noted, it was more than just the professors who contributed to the school's reputation. 'I often thought that in the free companionship there and mixing with a large cosmopolitan crowd I learnt more than could ever be taught by the formal masters in the schools'.[56] Julian felt that women should be given the same opportunities afforded to male artists, and the presence of women in the ateliers is recorded as early as 1873. Due to impropriety and some awkwardness in the shared studios, studios were established exclusively for women in 1876-77. Julian responded more to the needs of bourgeois families, who felt that the study of art was essential for the education of their daughters but they were fearful of mixed classes.[57] The school's brochure actually prided itself on its segregated classes, where in 'an atmosphere of impeccable character and advanced technical values', a woman could 'acquire a professional attitude which, quite unlike the plague of amateurism, had made these women's classes successful'.[58] Women were taught by the same professors as their male counterparts. Marie Bashkirtseff (1858–84), who enrolled in the Académie in 1877, elected to attend the women's atelier primarily because she felt that there was no essential difference between the classes, since the women also drew from the male nude.[59] Henry noted that during his time at the Académie 'There was also an Académie Julian for women somewhere or another... but the number of women students must have been considerable to judge by the number of portfolios which I passed daily'.[60]

An elaborate system of competitions involving both men and women took place. Rivalry among students was apparent but also considered engaging. Once a month all the students competed together. Examining professors did not know either the sex or the name of the students until the results were announced. Women often fared much better in these competitions, especially in portraiture.[61] Standards remained high and competition was keen. Those who showed talent were encouraged, and received valuable advice and criticism. Exhibitions of work and prizes prepared the students for the experience of exhibiting in the Salon where standards were exceedingly high. In fact Julian was confident that his students' work would be shown in the Salon. The Salon was the official art exhibition of the Académie des Beaux-Arts in Paris. From 1881 onward it was organised by the Société des Artistes Français. In 1903 a group of painters and sculptors led by Auguste Rodin and Pierre-Auguste Renoir organised the Salon d'Automne in response to what many believed to be a bureaucratic and conservative organisation.

Professors were chosen for their ability to teach and for the influence that they exerted on their students. Some students favoured one instructor, whereas others worked with several. The programmes of studies for men and women were similar. Henry wrote 'In the studios nude models, male and female stood all day. The students of sculpture worked in one set of studios and painters in another. Twice a week the masters came in to inspect our work. If for any reason you did not feel inclined to have your work criticised you either absented yourself or just turned the drawing around with its face to the wall'.[62] The school was described as an overcrowded hive of activity, 'a congerie of studios crowded with students, the walls thick with palette scrapings, hot airless and extremely noisy'.[63] Henry also describes life at the Académie. 'The studios of the Julian group were crowded and overflowing, and teachers and masters of all kinds were available'.[64] Women were provided with the services of a 'bonne' or assistant who ran errands for them. As in the men's studios the work was almost entirely technical, with long sessions of life classes. By 1885 there was a course of lectures on anatomy and perspective and dissections of dead bodies were performed in the students' presence. Fees were double for women, possibly because of the extra expense of providing segregated studios. The first women's atelier was located on the second floor at 27 Galerie Montmartre in the Passage des Panoramas. It was 'located near one of the principal boulevards and approached by a flight of steps leading up to the first landing. A small door opened into a moderate sized room with a skylight, a stove in the centre, an evident lack of ventilation and a platform on which sat a draped model'.[65] As the number of students increased, a second studio for women was opened in the nearby rue Vivienne, but this

2.15 Jean-Paul Laurens in his studio, 1912, black and white photograph © Roger Viollet /Topfoto

later closed. The main studio for men moved to the rue du Faubourg St Denis. Eventually the Passage des Panoramas became the site of Jean-Paul Laurens's (1838-1921) studio, the site of popular women's classes which continued until the beginning of the First World War. Haweis describes Laurens. 'He was very kind to me, but he could be quite the reverse at times. He was a big man, not unlike a highly civilised gorilla, and it was the custom of the class to follow him around from easel to easel, listening to all the criticisms he made upon the different studies'. In 1888 another women's studio was added at 28 rue du Faubourg Saint-Honoré, and a more permanent atelier soon opened at 5 rue de Berri, just off the Champs Élysées, with 400 square metres of space. In addition to classes for drawing and painting, there were sculpture, watercolour and miniature painting classes. William Bouguereau (1825-1905) taught there. Henri Chapu (1833-1891), followed by Raoul Verlet (1857-1923) and Paul Landowski (1875-1961) taught sculpture. About 1890 two more women's studios opened, one at 28 rue Fontaine and the other adjacent to the men's atelier at 5 rue Fromentin. Jules Lefebvre (1836-

1911) and Tony Robert-Fleury (1837-1912) took charge of these studios. In that year the main studio for men was transferred to 31 rue du Dragon. A further women's atelier opened at 55 rue du Cherche-Midi nearby and occupied the entire building. This is possibly where Gray studied.

Other popular ateliers for women were those run by well-known painters such as Carolus-Duran (1837-1917) and Édouard Krug (1829-1901). Women often studied at several of these academies simultaneously, or progressed from one to another, or entered one to continue later at another. Paul Henry offers an explanation as to why students, such as Gray, moved on from the Académie Julian saying 'a prolonged course of making accurate drawings from the nude model had taught me that however earnest and painstaking I might be, I might go on for years just doing this one thing and I had seen enough of the results of such teaching in the schools to realise it was a blind alley'.[66]

Haweis in his memoirs said that he did not remain long at the Académie as he decided to study at other studios in the Montparnasse quarter. He studied at the Académie Julian in 1899-1900. Henry and Haweis later enrolled in a new art school, the Académie Whistler, better known as the Académie Carmen, where they became inseparable. The two friends, along with Scottish artist Francis Cadell explored Paris, meeting frequently for walks around the city and immersing themselves in its artistic and cultural life. He then went on to study in other studios under the famous Czech artist and illustrator Alphonse Mucha and Eugène Carrière (1849-1906). Haweis is recorded as attending evening classes at the École Colarossi in 1902. After becoming interested in photography, he met Auguste Rodin and subsequently photographed many of the sculptor's pieces.

Attending several studios enabled students to compare what each offered and choose what they wished from each. During her early years in France, Gray apparently took summer classes in Caudebec-en-Caux, Normandy under the guidance of Frances Hodgkins (1869-1947).[67] Hodgkins became the first female teacher employed at the École Colarossi in 1910. Regrettably, Gray destroyed her artwork from this student period. Only a very competent

2.16 Frances Hodgkins, November 1912, black and white photograph © Alexander Turnbull Library, Wellington, New Zealand

2.17 *Old Woman, Caudebec*, by Frances Hodgkins, 1901, watercolour and gouache © Collection of the Dunedin Public Art Gallery

2.18 Gertrude Stein with her brothers, Paris, 1906, black and white photograph © The Granger Collection/ Topfoto

figurative study remains.[68] That Gray became an accomplished artist during these formative years at the Académie Julian is proved by the fact that she had a painting accepted at the Salon. Writing to Haweis on 17 October 1965 she says; 'I was pleased to get a painting received at the Salon, chiefly because it reduced the family opposition to my staying in Paris'.[69]

After completing their art studies both Gray and Haweis's lives went in separate directions. Gray settled permanently in Paris, taking her apartment in the rue Bonaparte by 1906, and she continued the studies in lacquer which she began in London. Haweis, now married, began working for Rodin. Gray's circle expanded, primarily through her flowering profession as a designer of lacquer furniture and with developing friendships and acquaintances with many from the Left Bank cognoscenti. Stephen Haweis maintained contact with many of their circle throughout his life, including Gertrude Stein (1874-1946), Augustus John (1878-1961), Romaine Brooks, Gerald Kelly, John Lavery, Katherine Constance Lloyd (op. 1923-1940) and William Somerset Maugham. But by 1950 he wrote to Eileen Gray that he heard 'very little from anybody of Paris from their early days'.[70] However, through their letters they discuss what happened to the people in their milieu.

Out of their Parisian circle of 1902-3 Gray remained close with Jessie Gavin. Gavin was born in 1876 to Crichton Strachan Gavin and Ann Sophia Lord. In 1915 she married René Raoul Duval, a wealthy restaurateur, and subsequently changed her name to Jacqueline (Jackie). After Haweis married Loy, Gray and the Duvals went on holiday for four weeks to Tunisia. In 1905 Gray also travelled to Algiers with the Duvals, where she caught typhoid and nearly died. She convalesced in the south of France in Hyères. In her letters Gray writes how she was so very fond of Gavin. A distance had occurred for a time between them due to the influence of two other friends, Yolande de Gail and Olive Pixley who was also friends with Gray's sister Thora.[71] Gavin died in 1939. Gray wrote to Haweis saying; 'One by one all those friends have gone and even others who came after, but I still miss Gavin'.[72]

Kathleen Bruce changed her name to Scott on her first marriage, and later became Baroness Kennet, subsequently enjoying a career as a renowned British sculptor. Bruce had befriended Gray and Gavin at the Slade and had lived with Jessie Gavin when they first arrived in Paris. Bruce remained at the Colarossi until 1906. She befriended Rodin, but returned to London by 1907 where she met Captain Robert Falcon Scott (1868-1912) and married him in 1908. In February 1913, while sailing back to New Zealand to greet Scott on his return, she learned of his death in Antarctica the previous March in 1912. In 1922 she married Edward Hilton Young, first Baron Kennet (1879-1960). She exhibited at the Royal Academy between 1913 and 1947, and was very successful as a sculptor, primarily of bronze portrait busts and semi allegorical figures. Her style conformed to conventional academic sculpture and did not reflect new trends. A book of photographs, *Homage, a book of Sculpture* by Kathleen Scott, with a foreword by Stephen Gywnn was published in 1938.

2.19 Kathleen Scott (née Bruce, later Lady Kennet) with her son Sir Peter Markham Scott; (Edith Agnes), by Graphic Photo Union, 1913, bromide print © National Portrait Gallery, London

Bruce in her letters to Haweis informed him that she had fallen into great poverty after Scott's death.[73] Haweis empathised with her. Gray was not as understanding. For reasons known only to Bruce she gave Jessie Gavin and Gray – her two friends – pseudonyms in her autobiography. Eileen was Hermione and Jessie was Joselyn. Bruce thought Gray's behaviour at the École Colarossi unconventional and unbecoming of a lady.[74] The friendship between Gray, Gavin and Bruce became strained when Bruce noticed an affection developing between Gray and Gavin, of which she disapproved. 'I was never at ease with them, but it was many years before I discovered why'.[75] 'One evening a tall, thin, shy, nice looking youth in corduroys and a Norfolk jacket came in. This was Joselyn [Jessie], wearing a wig and a slightly blackened moustache. "We'll go to places and play chess where you can't go without a man"'.[76] After certain hours is was considered highly improper for a lady to be unchaperoned by a gentleman in certain cafés. Gray seemingly recalled 'with much amusement the time when she and Jessie entered a bar and the band struck up the Spanish national anthem because Jessie in her male attire looked so Spanish'.[77] This was unorthodox behaviour in Bruce's eyes.

Bruce's tentative relationship with Gray finally fell sour when Bruce's cousin Henry, a musician for whom she had affection became enamoured with Gray. Henry Bruce was half Greek, half Scottish and often took Gray out all night. Gray described him as good-looking and well read.[78] Gray forgot nothing. Betrayal even in small doses remained with her for many years. Writing to Haweis many years later in 1958, Gray remarked about Kathleen Bruce that she was 'a treacherous creature under an exterior of remarkably good fellowship'.[79] In a later letter she remarked; 'Her (Bruce's) life was a steady and gloriously calculated ascension. She did write her memoirs but I don't remember the name of the book'.[80] Gray lied to Haweis, as she actually owned a copy of Bruce's memoirs, *Self Portrait of an Artist* published in1949.[81]

Gray had lost touch with Gerald Kelly when he returned to London.[82] Kelly stated that the reason the group of friends disbanded and lost contact was due to Haweis's marriage to Loy. He wrote: 'Stephen Haweis had a curious position among the students in Paris. He married a very beautiful woman but I never saw anything of him afterward'.[83] Kelly's Irish connections were exceedingly strong and he exhibited regularly at the Royal Hibernian Academy (RHA) between 1905 and 1969, at the Oireachtas Art Exhibition in 1932 and the Ulster Academy of Arts in 1948. Kelly's first patron was the Irish art collector, dealer and critic Sir Hugh Lane. He was recommended to Lane by another Irish artist, Sarah Purser (1848-1943), resulting in Lane awarding Kelly his first twenty commissions. Kelly was knighted in 1945 and died in London in 1972. Gray followed Kelly's successful and prestigious career, writing to Haweis 'that certainly Kelly had the right temperament to be successful as an artist'.[84] By the 1960s she rarely visited London but wrote in a letter to Haweis dated 27 November 1961, 'I didn't get to see Kelly's show at the RA or hear anything about it, I am rarely in London, but had I been, would certainly have gone'. Despite his success in England Gray felt that, 'No one outside of England has ever heard of Kelly, yet he was of the same generation as Picasso, Léger, Miró, Rouault, Modigliani and their light shines all over the world'.[85]

Haweis lamented the loss of his friendship with Paul Henry. In the late spring-early summer of 1900 Henry met Emily Grace Mitchell (1868-

1953), who would become his wife in 1903. This relationship came between the two men, as Grace saw Haweis as an unfit associate who would lead Henry into sinful ways.[86] In December of 1900, due to lack of finances and the need to earn a living, Henry departed Paris for London. Years later, just as with Gray, Henry and Haweis resumed correspondence.

They also all separated from Crowley. If Gray was secretly engaged to Crowley there is the suggestion that she did it to render Stephen Haweis jealous. Gray and Haweis lost contact with Aleister Crowley after his marriage to Rose Kelly. Gerald Kelly fell out with Crowley due to the scandalous elopement with his sister.[87] Gray appears to have remained amicable with him, whereas Haweis seems quite resentful about Crowley. He describes in his letters how people fell under Crowley's influence and how he had a lifelong regret at losing two particular friends due to a 'quarrel promoted by that rascal Crowley'.[88] In another letter he refers to him as, 'that leper Aleister Crowley'.[89] Despite losing her contact with Crowley, Gray remained interested in the occult, which had been advocated and practised by Crowley and their group during their time in Paris. In her letters to Haweis, Gray reveals that she has purchased two books by the American writer Max Freedom Long (1890-1971). Long had lived a long time in Hawaii as a teacher, and witnessed the native Hawaiians practising magic. He was taught a great deal by Kahunas (natives who have occult knowledge). Absorbed into the culture and thinking, from 1936 Long published a series of books on his teachings called the Huna. He also set up a foundation called the Huna Fellowship in 1945. Fascinated by his ideas Gray firstly purchased The *Secret Science Behind Miracles* in 1948, saying to Haweis how Long 'discovered an unknown religion which strange to say, worked'.[90] Then in 1953 she bought *The Secret Science at Work* telling Haweis that 'the book has been written for people who intend to learn seriously their theory and to practise it'.[91]

Mary Katherine Constance Lloyd is mentioned in several letters between Gray and Haweis.[92] Lloyd was from Birmingham and her career flourished during the 1920s and 30s. She had attended the Slade in 1896-97. She was good friends with Gwen John (1876-1939), who had also attended the Slade in 1895-98. Both Haweis and Gray also knew Augustus John. Gwen John became Rodin's model in 1904 and eventually his lover. By 1903 Lloyd was in Venice painting

2.20 Augustus John, by George Charles Beresford, 1902, sepia platino type print © National Portrait Gallery, London

a series of cityscapes. During the 1950s Haweis learned that 'Lloyd was still painting and had her first successful solo show at 72 years of age at Groupils in London'.[93] Lloyd went to Dominica and stayed with Haweis for two months at the beginning of 1953. He looked forward to her visit writing, 'I think it will be great fun meeting one who belongs to our time in Paris'.[94] Gray asks after Katherine Constance Lloyd in numerous letters.[95] Fearful that many from their milieu have died, Gray complains that 'All the old birds are giving up'.[96] However, Gray indicates that they were merely acquaintances, Gray being told that Lloyd disliked her.[97]

ENDNOTES

1   NMIEG 2003.449, NMIEG 2003.450 and NMIEG 2003.451, letters from Renée Chipman to Eileen Gray, 9 February 1974, 16 January 1975, and undated.

2   Adam, Peter, *Eileen Gray: Architect/Designer: A Biography,* London, Thames and Hudson, 2000, p.11.

3   Rare Book & Manuscript Library, Columbia University in the City of New York, Stephen Haweis Papers, Arranged Miscellaneous Memoirs Box 2, letter from Eileen Gray to Stephen Haweis, Easter Monday, year unknown.

4   Rare Book & Manuscript Library, Columbia University in the City of New York, Stephen Haweis Papers, Arranged Miscellaneous Memoirs, Box 2, letter from Eileen Gray to Stephen Haweis, 5 June 1958.

5   Rare Book & Manuscript Library, Columbia University in the City of New York, Stephen Haweis Papers, Arranged Miscellaneous Memoirs, Box 2, memoirs dated 20 February 1900.

6   Burke, Carolyn, *Becoming Modern: the Life of Mina Loy,* New York, Farrar, Straus and Giroux, 1996, p.82.

7   Spalding, Francis, *Prunella Clough Regions Unmapped,* London, Lund Humphries, 2012, p.12.

8   Rare Book & Manuscript Library, Columbia University in the City of New York, Stephen Haweis Papers, Arranged Miscellaneous Memoirs, Box 2, letter from Eileen Gray to Stephen Haweis, 25 January 1966.

9   Rare Book & Manuscript Library, Columbia University in the City of New York, Stephen Haweis Papers, Arranged Miscellaneous Memoirs, Box 9, Haweis writing his own epitaph, date unknown.

10 Rare Book & Manuscript Library, Columbia University in the City of New York, Stephen Haweis Papers, Arranged Miscellaneous Memoirs, Box 2, letter from Stephen Haweis to Jean Roosevelt, 1942.

11 Rare Book & Manuscript Library, Columbia University in the City of New York, Stephen Haweis Papers, Arranged Miscellaneous Memoirs, Box 2, transcript from John Ellis Roosevelt on Stephen Haweis's life, date unknown.

12 Rare Book & Manuscript Library, Columbia University in the City of New York, Stephen Haweis Papers, Arranged Miscellaneous Memoirs, Box 2, letter from René Chipman to Stephen Haweis, 7 May 1968.

13 Rare Book & Manuscript Library, Columbia University in the City of New York, Stephen Haweis Papers, Arranged Miscellaneous Memoirs, Box 2, letter from Eileen Gray to Stephen Haweis, Easter Monday, year unknown.

14 'Fashionable Intelligence', *The Irish Times,* 6 May 1919, p.6.

15 Rare Book & Manuscript Library, Columbia University in the City of New York, Stephen Haweis Papers, Arranged Miscellaneous Memoirs, Box 2, letter from Eileen Gray to Stephen Haweis, 12 February1968.

16 Ibid, Burke,p.76.

17 Henry, Paul, *An Irish Portrait,* London, Batsford, 1951.

18 TCD Archives, Paul Henry Papers -7429/1, transcript of Paul Henry's autobiography, p.19.

19 Ibid, Burke, p.81.

20 Ibid, Burke.

21 Musée Rodin Archives, *Pall Mall Gazette,* 'Two English Gentlemen in the Latin Quarter', January 1904.

22 TCD Archives, Paul Henry Papers – 7429/1, transcript of Henry's autobiography, p.25.

23 TCD Archives, Paul Henry Papers – 7429/1, transcript of Henry's autobiography, p.26.

24 Ibid, Bruce, p.5.

25 Rare Book & Manuscript Library, Columbia University in the City of New York, Stephen Haweis Papers, Arranged Miscellaneous Memoirs, Box 3.

26 Ibid.

27 Rare Book & Manuscript Library, Columbia University in the City of New York, Stephen Haweis Papers, Arranged Miscellaneous Memoirs, Box 3.

28 Ibid.

29 Rare Book & Manuscript Library, Columbia University in the City of New York, Stephen Haweis Papers, Arranged Miscellaneous Memoirs, Box 2, letter from Eileen Gray to Stephen Haweis, 14 February 1963.

30 Rare Book & Manuscript Library, Columbia University in the City of New York, Stephen Haweis Papers, Arranged Miscellaneous Memoirs, Box 2, letter from Eileen Gray to Stephen Haweis, possibly December 1964.

31 Ibid, Bruce, p.23.

32 Holland, Clive, 'Lady Art Student's life in Paris,' *International Studio,* 1903-4, pp.225-226.

33 Rare Book & Manuscript Library, Columbia University in the City of New York, Stephen Haweis Papers, Arranged Miscellaneous Memoirs, Box 3, undated memoirs.

34 The two brothers were American illustrators Joseph Christian Leyendecker (1874-1951) and his brother Frank Xavier Leyendecker (1876-1924).

35 Adam, Peter, *Eileen Gray: Her Life and Work,* London, Thames and Hudson, 2009, p.20.

36 Rare Book & Manuscript Library, Columbia University in the City of New York, Stephen Haweis Papers, Arranged Miscellaneous Memoirs, Box 3, undated memoirs.

37 Ibid.

38 Ibid, Holland, p.38.

39 Rare Book & Manuscript Library, Columbia University in the City of New York, Stephen Haweis Papers, Arranged Miscellaneous Memoirs, Box 3, undated memoirs.

40 Rare Book & Manuscript Library, Columbia University in the City of New York, Stephen Haweis Papers, Arranged Miscellaneous Memoirs, Box 3, undated memoirs.

41 Goyon, Maximilienne, 'L'Avenir de nos filles,' *L'Académie Julian*, December, 1903, p.3.

42 Clausen, Meredith, 'The École des Beaux-Arts: Towards a Gendered History,' *Journal of the Society of Architectural Historians*, Vol. 69, No. 2, June, 2010, p.155.

43 Holland, Clive, 'Student Life in Paris', *The Studio and Illuminated Magazine of Fine and Applied Arts*, Vol. 27, 1903, p.38.

44 Burke, Mary Alice, *Elizabeth Nourse, 1859-1938: A Salon Career,* Washington, Smithsonian, 1983, p.31.

45 Ibid, Holland, p.38.

46 Scott, Kathleen, *Self Portrait of an Artist,* London, John Murray Editions, 1949, p.26.

47 Holland, Clive, 'Student Life in Paris', *The Studio Magazine,* London, S.N., Vol. 27, 1903, p.38.

48 Woods, Alice, *Edges,* Indianapolis, Bowen-Merrill, 1902, p.232.

49 Rare Book & Manuscript Library, Columbia University in the City of New York, Stephen Haweis Papers, Arranged Miscellaneous Memoirs, Box 3.

50   Modersohn-Becker, Paula, *Paula Modersohn-Becker: The Letters and Journals,* editions Gunter Busch and Liselotte von Reinken, New York, Taplinger, 1983.

51   Rare Book & Manuscript Library, Columbia University in the City of New York, Stephen Haweis Papers, Arranged Miscellaneous Memoirs, Box 3.

52   Ibid, Burke, Carolyn, p.77.

53   Whiting, Lilian, *Paris the Beautiful,* Boston, Little Brown and Co., 1908, p.377.

54   Ibid, Burke, Carolyn, p.76.

55   TCD Archives, Paul Henry Papers – 7429.1, transcript of Paul Henry's autobiography, p.19.

56   TCD Archives, Paul Henry Papers – 7429.1, transcript of Paul Henry's autobiography, p.14.

57   Fehrer, Catherine, 'Women at the Académie Julian in Paris', *The Burlington Magazine,* Vol. 136, No. 1100, Nov. 1994, p.753.

58   Fehrer, Catherine, 'New Light on the Académie Julian,' *Gazette des Beaux Arts,* 1984, p.212.

59   Bashkirtseff, Marie, Journal de Marie Bashkirtseff, Paris, Mazarine, 1980, p.314.

60   TCD Archives, Paul Henry Papers – 7429.1, transcript of Paul Henry's autobiography, p.16.

61   Ibid, Fehrer, p.754.

62   TCD Archives, Paul Henry Papers – 7429.1, transcript of Paul Henry's autobiography, p.16.

63   Ibid, Adam, p.28.

64   TCD Archives, Paul Henry Papers – 7429.1, transcript of Henry's autobiography, p.19.

65   Klumpe, A.E., *Memoirs of an Artist*, L. Whiting, Boston, 1940, p.52.

66   TCD Archives, Paul Henry Papers – 7429.1, transcript of Paul Henry's autobiography, p.35.

67   Constant, Caroline, *Eileen Gray*, London, Phaidon, 2000, p. 9.

68   NMIEG: 2000. 115, drawing of a nude study.

69   Rare Book & Manuscript Library, Columbia University in the City of New York, Stephen Haweis Papers, Arranged Miscellaneous Memoirs, Box 2, letter from Eileen Gray to Stephen Haweis, 17 October 1965.

70   Rare Book & Manuscript Library, Columbia University in the City of New York, Stephen Haweis Papers, Arranged Miscellaneous Memoirs, Box 2, letter from Eileen Gray to Stephen Haweis, 17 October 1965. Ibid?

71   NMIEG 2003.306, letter from Eileen Gray to Gavin, undated.

72   Rare Book & Manuscript Library, Columbia University in the City of New York, Stephen Haweis Papers, Arranged Miscellaneous Memoirs, Box 2, letter from Eileen Gray to Stephen Haweis, 1 November 1966.

73   TCD Archive, Paul Henry Papers – 7432/71-109, letter from Stephen Haweis to Paul Henry, 4 March 1952.

74   Ibid, Scott, p.26.

75   Ibid, Scott, p.25.

76   Ibid, Scott, p.36.

77   Ibid, Adam, p.21.

78   Adam, Peter, *Eileen Gray: Architect/Designer: A Biography,* London, Thames and Hudson, 1987, p.34.

79   Rare Book & Manuscript Library, Columbia University in the City of New York, Stephen Haweis Papers, Arranged Miscellaneous Memoirs, Box 2, letter from Eileen Gray to Stephen Haweis, 5 June 1958.

80   Rare Book & Manuscript Library, Columbia University in the City of New York, Stephen Haweis Papers, Box 1 catalogued correspondence, letter from Eileen Gray to Stephen Haweis, 5 July 1958.

81   NMIEG 2003.52, Scott, Kathleen, *Self Portrait of an Artist,* London, John Murray Editions, 1949.

82   Rare Book & Manuscript Library, Columbia University in the City of New York, Stephen Haweis Papers, Arranged Miscellaneous Memoirs, Box 2, letter from Eileen Gray to Stephen Haweis, 27 November 1961, letter from Eileen Gray to Stephen

Haweis, 14 February 1963, and letter from Eileen Gray to Stephen Haweis, 17 October 1965.

83 Rare Book & Manuscript Library, Columbia University in the City of New York, Stephen Haweis Papers, Arranged Miscellaneous Memoirs, Box 2, letter from Gerald Kelly to Mrs Philip J. Roosevelt, 8 April 1969.

84 Rare Book & Manuscript Library, Columbia University in the City of New York, Stephen Haweis papers, Box 1, catalogued correspondence, letter from Eileen Gray to Stephen Haweis, 27 November 1961.

85 Rare Book & Manuscript Library, Columbia University in the City of New York, Stephen Haweis papers, Box 1 catalogued correspondence, letter from Eileen Gray to Stephen Haweis, 14 February 1963.

86 TCD Archives, Paul Henry Papers – 7432.102a, letter from Stephen Haweis to Paul Henry, 2 March 1953.

87 Adam, Peter, *Eileen Gray: Her Life and Work,* London, Thames and Hudson, 2009, p.25.

88 TCD Archives, Paul Henry Papers – 7432/71-109, letter from Stephen Haweis to Paul Henry, 21 November 1951. Ladbroke Black (1877-1940), a journalist, who was on a brief trip to Paris in autumn 1899. Haweis had introduced him to Henry and Black had been at Cambridge with Crowley, Kelly and Haweis. TCD Archives, Paul Henry Papers – 7432/71-109, letter from Stephen Haweis to Paul Henry, 4 March 1952.

89 TCD Archives, Paul Henry Papers – 7432/71-109, letter from Stephen Haweis to Paul Henry, 15 June 1952.

90 Rare Book & Manuscript Library, Columbia University in the City of New York, Stephen Haweis Papers, Arranged Miscellaneous Memoirs, Box 2, letter from Eileen Gray to Stephen Haweis, 20 November 1967.

91 Rare Book & Manuscript Library, Columbia University in the City of New York, Stephen Haweis Papers, Arranged Miscellaneous Memoirs, Box 2, letter from Eileen Gray to Stephen Haweis, 12 February 1968.

92 TCD Archives, Paul Henry Papers – 7432/71-109, letter from Stephen Haweis to Paul Henry, 19 June 1952.

93 TCD Archives, Paul Henry Papers – 7432/71-109, letter from Stephen Haweis to Paul Henry, 21 November 1951.

94 TCD Archives, Paul Henry Papers – 7432/71-10, letter from Stephen Haweis to Paul Henry, 23 December 1952.

95 Rare Book & Manuscript Library, Columbia University in the City of New York, Stephen Haweis Papers, Arranged Miscellaneous Memoirs, Box 2, letter from Eileen Gray to Stephen Haweis, 30 March 1962, letter from Eileen Gray to Stephen Haweis, Monday 17 December possibly 1962, letter from Eileen Gray to Stephen Haweis, 14 February 1963, letter from Eileen Gray to Stephen Haweis, 17 October 1965, letter from Eileen Gray to Stephen Haweis, 1 November 1966, letter from Eileen Gray to Stephen Haweis, 8 August 1968.

96 Rare Book & Manuscript Library, Columbia University in the City of New York, Stephen Haweis papers, Arranged Miscellaneous Memoirs, Box 1 catalogued correspondence, letter from Eileen Gray to Stephen Haweis, 17 December year unknown, and letter dated 30 March 1962.

97 Rare Book & Manuscript Library, Columbia University in the City of New York, Stephen Haweis papers, Arranged Miscellaneous Memoirs, Box 1 catalogued correspondence, letter from Eileen Gray to Stephen Haweis, Sunday 1 November year unknown.

3

The Artist: Painting, Sculpture, Photography

In the first two decades of the twentieth century, Paris was the artistic centre of the avant-garde. Fauvism, Cubism, Futurism,the Russian avant-garde, De Stijl and Surrealism coupled with a rejection of academic tradition made artists and designers question traditional picture-making and sculpture techniques through other media. Gray's art student years at the Slade, the École Colarossi and then at the Académie Julien were pivotal to so many aspects of her future work – especially her lacquer work and her carpet designs. Both mediums continued to demonstrate her painterly skills. It was during these formative years that Gray met many of her artistic circles; artists, writers, sculptors, photographers, theorists and philosophers, who would have such a profound influence on her developing ideas.

Gray regrettably destroyed most of her artwork during her student period, with the exception of a very competent figurative study which dates approximately to 1903. This sketch shows the muscles, ligaments, a rib cage, body organs and a right-side profile of a woman.[1] Her talent as an artist was apparent after she had a painting, *Derniers Rayons de soleil d'une Belle Journée,* received at the 120 Salon des Artistes Français au Grand

3.1 Drawing of a nude study, 1903, paper, pencil, charcoal © NMI

Palais.[2] Gray took her apartment on the rue Bonaparte in 1907 and by 1908 was already working directly in lacquer.[3] From this moment Gray began to follow, and acquire into her library, the manifestoes from many major art movements. Gray's library had numerous books on art history, painters, sculptors, architecture and their theories. Many were written by fellow artists or acquaintances whom she knew and many were signed by the original authors.

Gray also owned a number of art books which pre-date her formal art training in both London and Paris. Three particular texts were of importance; *The Renaissance,* 1873 by Walter Pater, *The Gentle Art of Making Enemies,* 1890 by James Abbott NcNeill Whistler and *The Early Work of Aubrey Beardsley,* 1899 by John Lane. These three publications along with the writings of Irish writer Oscar Wilde (1854-1900), in whom Gray also had a profound interest, reveal Gray's interest in the Aesthetic and Decadent movements. These movements were also linked with the Symbolist movement in France which had its beginnings with Charles Baudelaire's (1821-1867) poem *Les Fleurs du Mal,* 1857 (Gray later used the title of Baudelaire's poem *Invitation au Voyage* as a coded symbol and decorative feature on the wall of the living in the house *E.1027* in 1929). The Symbolist movement's ideas were anticipated in the work of the idealising neo-classicist Puvis de Chavannes (1824-1898), in whose work Gray also expressed an interest. The influence of the ideas expressed in these publications is revealed in Gray's artistic development; especially in her figurative artwork, her use of symbolism and her ideas on decorative art. They are significant not only in her early artistic career but also in her later career as a designer and architect.

The Aesthetic movement in England was influenced by the writings of the Oxford professor Walter Pater (1839-1894) and his essays, which he published in 1867-68, culminated in the book *Studies in the History of the Renaissance* in 1873 and later renamed in the second and later editions *The Renaissance: Studies in Art and Poetry.*[4] In this controversial book Pater maintained that our thoughts and lives were in constant flux and for this reason he emphasised that people should get the most out of life through sharp and eager observation. It was more as a designer and architect than as a painter that Gray adapted Pater's ideas to suit her own requirements. She acutely observed the way that people interacted with her furniture and her architectural interiors, adapting her designs as such.

James McNeill Whistler (1834-1903) and Aubrey Beardsley (1872-1898) were two of the key artists associated with the Aesthetic movement. They became the main leaders of the movement along with Oscar Wilde. Rejecting John Ruskin's (1819-1900) idea of art as something useful or moral they advocated that art did not have a didactic role – rather they emphasised its aesthetic values. Nature was considered crude, lacking in design when compared to art. The use of symbols, sensuality and the correspondence between words, colours and music were key components. Gray related to these movements' ideals of synaesthesia. Rather than conveying moral or sentimental messages they professed that the arts should engage with the haptic and cognitive senses, providing refined sensuous pleasure. Later Gray refined her ideas on synaesthesia especially in her lacquer work and interior design, creating rooms with furniture and furnishings which directly engaged with all of the occupant's senses.

Whistler's book *The Gentle Art of Making Enemies* emphasised how art was its own end and that nature was rarely right, relying upon the artist to improve it through his own vision.[5] The artist's responsibility was not to society but to himself to interpret through art, and neither to reproduce nor moralise what he saw. This book invited controversy, a self-authorised publication critical of those such as Ruskin, who accused him of throwing a pot of paint in the public's face after Whistler had exhibited *Nocturne in Black and Gold: The Falling Rocket* in The Grosvenor Gallery, London in 1877.[6] Gray maintained this distance in her treatment of her natural subject matter. One particular undated abstract, untitled, monograph completed in pencil and charcoal suggests the figure of a nude woman standing on rocks in front of a waterfall or possibly trees.[7] Gray's lack of colour and use of bleak monochromatic tones develops a muted, yet harmonious composition.

3.2 Drawing of a nude figure in a landscape, unknown date, paper, paint, crayon, pencil, collage © NMI

A separation between the background and foreground occur with Gray's simplistic treatment of the nude figure. The only suggestion of colour is developed through the pale blurred lines of a faint yellow, suggesting the reflection of the moon. As with the majority of Gray's artwork this piece is unsigned.

Gray remained interested in the life, ideas and work of Whistler, purchasing in 1908 *The Life of James McNeill Whistler* written by his friends Joseph (1860-1926) and Elizabeth Pennell (1862-1952)[8] which had an illustration of *The Peacock Room* which he completed in 1876-77.[9] Whistler's palette of brilliant greens and blues influenced the choice of colours used in some of her early lacquer work and in an early gouache completed in the same colours which was probably intended for a carpet.[10]

Gray's interest in the work of Aubrey Beardsley was surprising as his work has become known in the larger context of Art Nouveau – a movement that Gray did not appreciate. She stated: 'I don't care to be absorbed into it as representing willingly a disciple of Art Nouveau'.[11] Gray owned a copy of *The Early Work of Aubrey Beardsley*, 1899 by John Lane.[12] But it was Beardsley's use of a defined line with his caricatures which intrigued her. Her interest in caricatures also led her to purchase *Les Caricatures de Puvis de Chavannes,* by Marcelle Adam in 1906 and a copy of *James Ensor,* by Emile Verhaeren, in 1908.[13] The nineteenth century became the heyday for caricature and by the mid-nineteenth century there was an enormous output of graphic and sculptural caricature, with a great number of artists like Beardsley, de Chavannes and Ensor dedicated to it. Caricatures by Aubrey Beardsley, James Ensor (1860-1949) and Puvis de Chavannes directly inspired the drawings which eventually culminated in Gray's *Ballet des Animaux,* (The Animals' Ballet) 1916-1919 and her fresco drawings from the 1940s. She appreciated these satirical drawings and their use of the grotesque. Whereas the caricatures of Beardsley, Ensor and de Chavannes mocked the salon, or the establishment, or documented relationships with other artists or friends, Gray's characters are noted more for their graphic adventurousness rather than their allegorical nature.

The drawings for *Ballet des Animaux* are a surprising contrast to Gray's better known abstract art work which adheres to the ideas and principles of early twentieth-century art movements. They also reveal Gray's interest in children. Gray's designs have looked to children on several occasions and she had explored furniture for their rooms and playrooms.[14] Throughout her career Gray was considered withdrawn, reserved, a devotee of her work, aloof and somewhat stuffy, however the light-hearted theme for this ballet and its characters reveal her conviviality, her sense of irony and her wit.

Another influence for the creation of this ballet was Sergei Diaghilev's (1872-1929) Ballet Russes production of *Schéhérazade* which opened on 4 June 1910 at the Théâtre National de l'Opéra in Paris. The music was by Nikolai Rimsky Korsakov (1844-1908) and the set and costumes were created by Léon Bakst (1866-1924). Gray purchased two reproductions of Bakst's drawings of the décor and costumes but it is uncertain whether she actually saw the performance.[15] The ballet had a profound effect in French artistic circles, sending a rippling effect through the decorative arts, with the use of fauve and symbolist colours, sumptuous and exotic materials and a strong sense of exoticism. Gray rejected the exoticism yet the use of colour and unusual materials appeared in her work throughout her lifetime.[16]

Gray had a long-time interest in stage design and encouraged by her friend the famous actor Marisa Damia (1892-1978)[17] who was introduced to her by Gaby Bloch (1879-1957), she began the drawings of scenario and character sketches dated 1916-1919 for *Ballet des Animaux*. At that time a number of artists were designing ballets. Rolfe de Mare (1888-1964) along with the

3.3 Damia, by Paul O'Doye, 1909-12, black and white photograph © NMI

3.4 Le Batiscope for *Ballet des Animaux*, 1916-19, paper, pencil, ink © NMI

post-impressionist painter Nils von Dardel (1888-1943) created the Ballet Suédois at the Théâtre de Champs-Élysées and by 1924 Giorgio de Chirico (1888-1978) curated the scenography and the costumes for Pirandello's *La Giara*.[18] Before the First World War Comte Étienne de Beaumont (1883-1956) and his wife, a leading couple in Parisian society known for their extravagant parties and masquerade balls, financed a number of ballets, and with the assistance of Jean Cocteau (1889-1963) presented at the *Soirées de Paris* which combined ballet, poetry and theatre at the Théâtre de la Cigale in Montmartre. Throughout her life Gray had a particular interest in the combined illustrative and poetry work of filmmaker Jean Cocteau, whom she knew through her circles, and she purchased a copy of *Dessins,* in 1923.[19] She also saw his film *Le Testament d'Orphée* (The Testament of Orpheus) in 1960 and stated that she was bitterly disappointed with it.[20] Gray also had a copy of Belgium poet Paul Méral's (1895-1946) *Dit des Jeux du monde,* a poem which was adapted into a play.[21] The costumes and dance were created by Guy. P. Fauconnet (1882-1960) and the music by Arthur Honegger (1892-1955). Honegger was commissioned to write the score in 1918. It was a mimed ballet and was staged at the Théâtre Musical Moderne du Vieux Colombier, directed by J. Bathoiengel. It was recited by actors wearing masks peaking in unison. All of these different sources influenced Gray's design.[22]

The characters for the ballet were given nonsensical names such as *L'Inconnu, Le Cerf Vicieux, La Fau Freluche, Le Mandibus, Le Batiscope, Le Nincompoop* - who walks backwards - and *La Pravasse*.[23] The sketches for costumes and masks illustrate the human figures inside them and highlight how they would move. They are playful and ingenious in their concepts. Gray states in the sketches that it is 'a ballet for animals, pardon, a ballet by animals for animals, or maybe a book'.[24] However, the designs were never realised into an actual production.

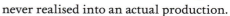

3.5 Characters for *Ballet des Animaux*, 1916-19, paper, pencil, ink © NMI

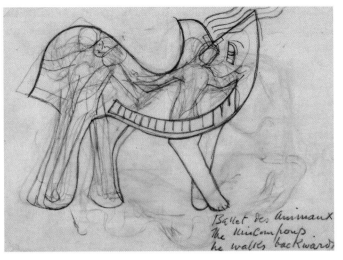

Ballet des animaux
The MisComPoup.
he walks backwards

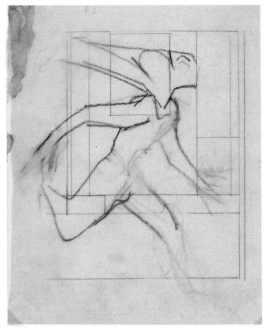

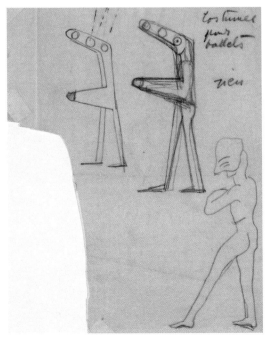

costumes
pour
ballets

rien

Esterer Grey 1916

le chat s'ennuie. je voudrais faire quelque
chose pour le distraire. Un Ballet. fait
par les animaux pardon - par les Bêtes
pour les bêtes.
on peut-être un livre. des images avec inscription
je commencerai par la Faufreluche.

la Faufreluche
Inscription.
Réflexion faite et l'une dans l'autre
je ne suis pas plus retirée qu'une autre.

la Paraverse
Inscription
Quand on me saisi je fiche le Camp
Car seul, je me nourris de l'Air du Temps.

le Batiscope
Inscription
les Batiscopes ça mangent des pierres
ça sine la purée - d'Héliotrope.

l'inconnu
Inscription
Ô femme regardez-moi - me voyez-vous
2 blanches 1 noire ça forme mon tout.
on recherche l'auteur

Le Corps vicieux.
mes goûts sont un peu sadiques
j'adore semer la Panique
les Zopilotes les Axolotls les animaux étranges &
sans oublier la Mante Divine que personne ne dérange.
Auteur Inconnu.

le Mandibus
Inscription retenez bien ceci
Ô ménagères ... là avec du Riz.

During the 1940s Gray revisited the characters which she had created for *Ballet des Animaux* and combined her artistic talents with her architecture when she completed a series of studies for murals. By this time Gray had purchased *Les Ballets Russes de Serge de Diaghilew, Décors et costumes,* 1930 by Michel Georges-Michel and Waldemar George which had illustrations of work by artists such as Pablo Picasso (1881-1973), Natalia Goncharova (1881-1962), Marie Laurencin (1883-1956), Georges Braque (1882-1963), Henri Matisse (1869-1954) and André Derain (1880-1954).[25]

The first drawing was completed for her hypothetical *Children's Day Care Centre*, a two-storey building which had a playroom area.[26] This lyrical drawing was intended for the wall of the nursery and consists of abstract figurative forms and Gray has written in French that it is a mural for children.[27] It was similar to another fresco drawing for a children's bedroom which Gray did in the early 1940s.[28] Gray also revisited these sketches for murals and developed them further when she designed the *Worker's Club project* in 1947.[29] The characters in this fresco appear simplified and more abstract than her previous mural designs. However, her emphasis on line in her rendition of the characters recalls the work of Beardsley, Ensor and de Chavannes.[30] The drawings included dancers, which were cheerful and light-hearted, inspired by the characters created by Matisse and Laurencin, and the costumes of Goncharova illustrated

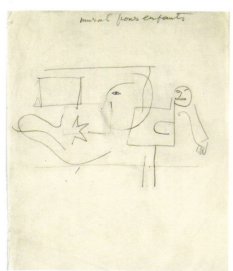

in Michel Georges-Michel and Waldemar George's publication. Gray also included a ferret, the *Nincompoop* again, a donkey and a dinosaur-type reptile with two legs and a long neck with a large head. Each of the characters is treated like a caricature. No sense of naturalism or space is suggested and there is a strong emphasis on line throughout.

Gray arrived in Paris just after the Fauves exhibited at the Salon d'Automne of 1905 causing a sensation through their use of virulent brushstrokes and violent colours. Though short lived, the movement of Fauvism was remarkably international in its range, attracting artists to Paris from different nationalities. Gray appreciated the verve with which they infused their forms with expressiveness but none of her art work displayed Fauvist tendencies. She was also friends with the Fauvist artist George Roualt (1871-1958).[31] Then, with the completion of *Les Demoiselles d'Avignon* in 1907, with its rich diversity of sources in Ancient

Iberian art, African masks and stone carving, Pablo Picasso created a new language which sent ripples through the world of art for years to come.[32] Soon followed by Georges Braque, they took simultaneous viewpoints and produced 'high Analytic' or 'Hermetic' compositions, using a muted palette. Their favourite motifs were still life with musical instruments, bottles, pitchers, glasses, newspapers, playing cards, figures or the human face. Landscapes were rare. Guillaume Apollinaire (1880-1918), the renowned writer and art critic, and an associate of Gray's, became a chief protagonist for the Cubists. Gray purchased his publication *Les Peintres Cubistes*, (*The Cubist Painters)* in 1913.[33] He believed that 'Cubism can in no way be considered a systematic doctrine. It does, however constitute a school, and the painters who make up this school want to transform their art by returning to the original principles with regard to line and inspiration, just as the Fauves – and many of the Cubists were at one time Fauves – returned to original principles with regard to their colour and composition'. This publication explores the work of Cubist painters and their ideas. It was a collection of essays and reviews, written between 1905 and 1912. The text became the essential text in twentieth-century art and presented the poet and critic's aesthetic meditations on nine painters: Pablo Picasso, Georges Braque, Jean Metzinger (1883-1956), Albert Gleizes (1881-1953), Marie Laurencin, Juan Gris (1887-1927), Fernand Léger (1881-1955), Francis Picabia (1879-1953) and Marcel Duchamp (1887-1968). Some of these painters later befriended Gray and with others she later worked on various projects. In the publication Apollinaire advocates a return to pure painting and strives to disentangle four distinct tendencies within Cubism. He speaks of an inner and essential reality whose dictates cubism obeys.

3.11 Abstract drawing, 1916-17, card, pencil, charcoal © NMI

Picasso and Braque's earlier more austere form of Analytical Cubism was short lived, but it still had an effect on Gray's development. Gray looked directly to Georges Braque and Analytical Cubism with an early charcoal drawing dated 1916-17 which became a study for a later lacquer door panel. She was more influenced not by his approach to monochromatic colour but by the patterns of faceted form.[34]

From 1911 the monochromatic colours of Analytical Cubism gave way to the use of bright, vivid colours where pictorial composition became more important than representation. With Synthetic Cubism, as it became known, Picasso and Braque, amongst others, enriched their pictures with references to the physical world, adding words or slogans to paintings. In 1912 Braque began using the technique of papier collé or collage. Newspaper was an early favourite ingredient.[35] Realising the tactile qualities of collage Pablo Picasso added more provocative elements to his papier collé with the inclusion of razor blades and broken glass. These were combined with charcoal or pencil by Braque, while Picasso and Juan Gris combined them with oil. Painting now possessed the tactile qualities of sculpture. Whether Gray actually met Braque is debatable; however, she was introduced to Picasso by the writer Henri Pierre Roché (1879-1959), and an interest in the different types of Cubism and the work of several Cubist painters penetrated every aspect of her work for decades to come.[36]

Synthetic Cubism formed a new pictorial language for Gray and she enriched her pictorial compositions through the use of lettering, sheets of music and newspapers. In one early work on board she also created a collage entirely of newspaper.[37] Gray also explored the use of wallpaper, theatre programmes and posters advertisements. Then from the mid to late 1920s Gray began using geographical motifs from maps in her artwork. Gray was similar to Braque and Picasso in that her use of lettering usually formed a coded visual image for the viewer to decipher.[38] Her fondness for travel and maps appeared on the wall of the living room of the house *E.1027* on which Gray hung a large marine chart with stencilled letters which acted as a code. In her own house *Tempe à Pailla*, in the dining area, she placed a large map of the excavations at Teotihuacán in Mexico. When the *Sunday Times* journalist Bruce Chatwin (1940-1989) interviewed Gray at age 93 in her apartment in Paris he was so impressed by a collage which she had completed of a map of Patagonia that he offered to purchase it.[39] His interest resulted in his journey there and his most renowned publication *Patagonia,* 1977. These geographical locations and motifs from

3.12 Newspaper collage, circa 1920, board, newspaper, paper, paint
© NMI

maps all have meaning and symbolism in Gray's work. As a result she created motifs, representing geographical locations, which she used in her collages. One collage is of the Roquebrune coastline in the south of France and may have been intended as a mural design similar to the marine map with the stencilled words by Baudelaire *Invitation au voyage* in the living room of *E.1027*. The collage consists of a bespeckled ground with black, off white, purple, blue, grey and white. Gray had an enduring interest in remote locales and the overall effect is nautical. A central motif composed of curved line represents the exact location of the house *E.1027* and where it is situated at Roquebrune.[40] Maps appear in other collages which she did during this period using a similar system.[41]

3.13 *Roquebrune* collage, 1926, paper, paint © NMI

Other gouaches contain architectural motifs or represented abstract plans of buildings.[42] One collage completed in 1931-34 is a site plan for her house *Tempe à Pailla*.[43] There are similarities in the shapes, forms and layout of a coloured site plan which is in Gray's archives.[44] This abstract collage is a larger scale version of the plan. Gray had a number of collage pieces which she used as stencils in her collages.[45] These 'design elements'

3.14 Green, white, blue gouache and collage, 1930s, paper, paint © NMI

as she called them were also used in some of her carpet designs and appear in her architectural portfolios.[46] One large square gouache, with a black speckled ground with black linear designs, has in the upper right corner a half circle and plant-like formation similar to the collage elements.[47] Gray used some of these elements to represent trees in a hypothetical architectural project she designed titled *L'Epopée Irlandaise* or the *Irish Epic*. Dating from 1946-47, photographs remain of the model of the stage set, with rocks and trees.[48]

By the 1930s Gray changed her style again, paring down her use of coded letters and words. She began a series of black and white Cubist-inspired paper collages with triangular motifs.[49] She also injected these monochromatic collages with singular motifs completed in bold bright colours.[50] Gray also used circular motifs and circles throughout, with these black and white gouaches which were visually highly effective.[51] Some gouaches she actually signed on the back.[52]

Gray remained interested in the work of both Braque and Picasso. She purchased the surrealist magazine *Documents 3* – published in 1929 which

3.15 Black, grey and white gouache with yellow, 1930s, paper, paint © NMI

had an article written by Carl Einstein entitled *Notes sur le Cubisme* with images by Picasso and Braque.[53] However, in her notes it is the work of Braque in this particular article which caught her attention. The article illustrates four paintings by Braque which he did in 1912-1914; two figurative works dating 1912 and October 1913, *Le Sacré Coeur,* 1913, and a Still Life from 1914.[54] Gray also continued to follow Picasso's career. She attended an exhibition of Pablo Picasso's work and preliminary drawings completed for *Guernica* in 1938, held at the *New Burlington Galleries,* London. Gray also kept the exhibition catalogue in her personal library.[55] She was obviously aware of the social and politically charged art which Picasso produced and by 1938 these were ideas which she herself was exploring at the time. She was very much being directed by an interest in the working-class environment. The idea that modern art was capable of producing an impassioned accusation that was triggered by current political events appealed to Gray greatly. This painting transcended mere social criticism to document the destructive side of human behaviour. Picasso describes in this painting not the German attack on the Basque village but the consequences of that attack. In social terms Eileen Gray's work aspired to address the consequences of a luxurious and elitist lifestyle and she looked to mass-produced pieces and mass-produced housing for the working class. It was different to the social and political statement of Picasso's painting but the underlying social implications were the same. Gray saw the face of destruction first hand during the war and this influenced her approach to creating a modern society which catered to people of all levels. Picasso said that 'Painting was not invented to decorate houses. It is an instrument of war for attack and defence against the enemy'. This statement informed her later attitude against mural painting being used as mere decoration for interiors.

Gray also owned a copy of *Du Cubisme et des moyens de le comprendre* published in 1920 by the painter Albert Gleizes.[56] Gleizes had the most influence over Eileen Gray's early lacquer work and in some of her carpet designs.[57] From about 1910 onward Gleizes had become directly involved with Cubism, both as an artist and as a theorist of the movement. His style had become stripped, linear, consisting of multiple forms and facets where he accentuated colours. He met regularly with Jean Metzinger, Fernand Léger, Robert Delauney (1885-1941) and Henri Le Fauconnier (1881-1946). After exhibiting at the Salon des Indépendants in 1911 and then as a group at the Salon d'Automne where their work caused a sensation, Gleizes was introduced to Picasso by Apollinaire and he joined the Puteaux Group. Influenced by the ideas of Henri Poincaré (1854-1912) and Henri Bergson (1859-1941), both of whom Gray read, Gleizes began to represent an object which was viewed from numerous viewpoints. This technique became known as relative motion. Gleizes believed that to understand the space of Cubist painters one needed to examine the German mathematician Bernhard Riemann's (1826-1866) mathematical series theorems. He also stated that the only way to understand this treatment of space would be to include and integrate the fourth dimension whereby physics, space and time are unified to create a continuum or fourth dimension. Cubism with its multiple viewpoint perspective achieved, in their opinion, a better representation of the world. Gleizes argued that one cannot know the external world; therefore he didn't attempt to analyse or describe an actual visual reality. Instead he said that one can only know sensations. He sought to synthesise the world through sensation, using volumes to create the structure of objects. As a result he simplified his forms and modulated their shape and their colour in relation to one another. Gleizes's theories on the notion of 'Translation and Rotation' are where flat planes are set in motion simultaneously in order to create space and their relationship with the subject matter.

Gray appreciated how the Cubists' aim was to completely eschew time and space in favour of relative motion and how they created a sensory experience and the dynamics of the fourth dimension on a flat canvas. It was to become more relevant in her work as a designer and architect than in her gouaches and drawings which she produced during this period. From 1924-26 Gray did a series of pencil drawings. One abstract drawing completed in charcoal and pencil shows a number of geometrical motifs which she used in her carpet designs from this period. However, her rendition of the geometrical forms reflects the work of Albert Gleizes and Andre Lhote (1885-1962).[58] This drawing also recalls motifs which Gray used on a lacquer door panel dated 1916, completed for the fashion designer Jacques Doucet (1853-1929).[59] Gray's treatment of these motifs and geometrical forms in this drawing look to the ideas of 'Translation and Rotation' as the forms appear in motion, creating space for the subject matter.

Apollinaire helped create the phrase 'Orphic' Cubism. After Gleizes and Lhote it was Robert Delauney who became its foremost practitioner. This philosophical notion about the passage of time, or simultaneity, was a concept which was also espoused by the Italian Futurists. The later phase of Cubism became thus more colourful and decorative and had many foreign adherents.

There was a remarkable link between the avant-garde artists, sculptors and writers of the pre-war period. Apollinaire created the literary and art review *Les Soirées de Paris*. Along with his contributors Apollinaire acted as impresario and publicist for the avant-garde movement by illustrating its principles in each issue. Gray owned a copy of *Les Soirées de Paris,* No.22, 15 March 1914.[60] She was particularly interested in this issue which contained letters by the Symbolist writer Alfred Jarry (1873-1907) and six colour illustrations by Francis Picabia. One illustration of *Danseuse étoile sur un transatlantique,* 1913 with its abstract planar composition inspired a later charcoal drawing by Gray.[61] In this work she depicts an abstracted seascape of a life boat moored at docklands, with a pier receding into the background.[62] Though completed many years later, the subject matter

3.16 Charcoal
drawing, circa
1934, paper,
pencil © NMI

of this piece is possibly inspired by her close friend and architect Jean
Badovici (1893-1956) who had patented the design for his *E-7* lifeboat in
1934. Gray had kept Badovici's notes on submarine and lifeboat design.[63]

Modernity became a central theme in Paris from 1880 through to the
First World War. Avant-garde artists and writers were acutely aware of the
developing modern landscape. They shared an interest in new technology,
particularly in its relationship to speed. The Italian Futurists celebrated
the railways, the motor car and the airplane. The *Manifesto of Futurism*,
written by Filippo Tommaso Marinetti (1876-1944) was published on the
front page of the French newspaper *Le Figaro* on 20 February 1909. The
Futurists had an enormous impact on the work of Eileen Gray, especially
after she visited an exhibition of their work at the *Galerie Bernheim
Jeune* Paris from the 5-24 February, 1912. Gray kept the catalogue which

contained a joint statement in French by the artists: Umberto Boccioni (1882-1916), Carlo Carrà (1881-1966), Luigi Russolo (1881-1947), Giacomo Balla (1871-1958) and Gino Severini (1883-1966).[64] It also contained a copy of the Futurist manifesto. The group advocated modernism. Their ideas were controversial, extolling war as the only hygiene of the world. They revelled in technology, a similarity evident with Gray. Dynamism, motion, movement and speed were all an incantatory formula for the Futurists which led to Marinetti's proverbial saying that a racing car was more beautiful than the Nike of Samothrace.

From the moment that Gray saw the exhibition at the *Galerie Bernheim Jeune* she adopted their ideas. A charcoal and pencil drawing which Gray did shows a Futurist-style landscape with roads and crossroads and abstract forms.[65] In 1912 Gray had also visited America with her sister Thora, and two friends Gaby Bloch and Florence Gardiner (1878-1963). Gray was fascinated by New York, especially the skyscrapers of Lower Manhattan. The Futurists adored the industrial city with its skyscrapers and tunnels,

3.17 Charcoal drawing, circa 1920, paper, pencil © NMI

advocating that new cities be built as the old were torn down. Gray was impressed with their ideas on modernity and machinery.

The success of the new art movements and the successful reign of internationalism in the Paris arts was also in part due to the powerful xenophilism of the upper middle classes and of the enlightened aristocracy. The presence of such large numbers of foreign artists transformed the art scene in Paris by serving to increase the gap between the official art and independent art (represented by the Salon d'Automne and the Salon des Indépendants). These foreign artists were to contribute enormously to the emergence in France of the avant-garde art movement.

With the developments of Fauvism, Cubism and Futurism, abstraction became a prominent issue for many artists and theorists, who were influenced by the writings of Wassily Kandinsky's (1866-1944) essay *On the Spiritual in Art,* 1910. Extracts were published in 1914 in Percy Wyndham Lewis's periodical *Blast* of which Gray owned a copy.[66] His writings and ideas spread rapidly throughout art circles promoting concepts of pure art, total abstraction and the rejection of subject matter. Gray's development into pure abstraction began a move from figurative, seen in her early lacquer screens and panels which she produced for Jacques Doucet, to pure abstract, such as her interiors completed for Mme Mathieu-Lévy and her total abstract carpet designs of the early 1920s. All throughout linear graphics were a constant. Initially Gray began using large swirling lines, which gradually progressed into sweeping thin sharp lines, inspired by Futurism and the work of Giacomo Balla. Her work then displayed thin curling lines inspired by Paul Klee (1879-1940) which finally evolved into the use of more rigid geometric thin lines and forms. One gouache in black, grey and beige is a perfect example of these swirling geometric lines.[67] Another black and white speckled gouache contains a sweeping lightning bolt motif which runs from top to bottom and is similar to the sweeping motifs of the lacquer panels at the salon in Mme Mathieu-Lévy's *Rue de Lota apartment.*[68]

3.18 Black, grey and beige speckled gouache with swirling lines, 1920s, paper, card, crayon and pencil © NMI

Gray revisited this style of work in the early 1930s using a much brighter palette. One gouache has a bright yellow ground with abstract motifs in white in the centre. Thin black lines, coming from the border's edges, intersect the central motifs. It is incomplete but the design resembles quite closely the back of a lacquer door panel design with raised *sabi* which appeared in an article in *Vogue* in August 1917.[69] The motifs used at the centre are also reminiscent of the designs of the Futurists and the work of Marcel Duchamp (1887-1968), notably the *Nude Descending a Staircase no.2,* 1912.[70] Gray seldom used yellow for the entire background of her gouaches and collages. It is possible that was an early study for another collage which she completed during the early 1930s.[71]

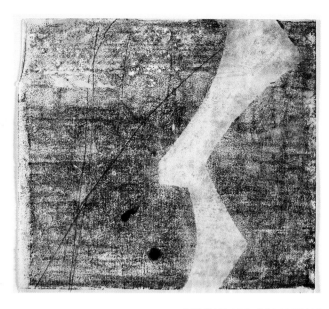

3.19 Black and white speckled gouache with white lightening motif, 1920s, paper, card, crayon and pencil © NMI

From 1918-1921 Gray produced a number of black and white gouaches with thin straight lines. Stylistically these gouaches were a precursor to three lacquer screens, one large one produced for a client called Mme Jean Henri-Labourdette and two small ones, which Gray made in the early twenties – all with a variation on the theme of incised linear decoration in a deep brown lacquer ground. These were shown in *Wendingen*, published in 1924. One black gouache with thin white lines stylistically looks to the simplicity of Paul Klee's artwork from the late 1920s and early 1930s. Like Klee's painting dating from this era Gray's designs are punctuated with symbolic references which are difficult to decipher. They provide an orientation, pointing out directions, set signals, but without entirely answering the pictorial riddle. In one particular gouache a long white line runs horizontally from left to right. Out of this line evolves a series of others completed in chalk.[72]

Russian Suprematism and its successor Constructivism, as well as the Dutch movement De Stijl were deeply rooted in an attempt to change the world and to create a functional, normative art. These movements envisioned a collective, universal art for all, removed from individualism and subjectivity. Russian avant-garde, especially in its Suprematist phase, was rooted in pre-revolutionary anarchism and later condemned by the Russian communist revolutionary and politician Vladimir Lenin (1870-1924). Suprematism was more romantic and mythical, while Constructivism was more futuristic and technological. Gray's artwork and series of carpet gouaches which she designed in 1918-1921 also recalls the work of Kazimir Malevich (1879-1935) and Ivan Kliun (1873-1943). Both Malevich's *Suprematist Composition*, 1915[73] and Kliun's painting *Suprematism*, 1915-16[74] reoccur in several of Gray's compositions. Malevich and Kliun used thin lines in various colours on a white ground. Malevich emphasised reducing objects to their primary forms and colours. Kazimir Malevich's use of the black squares was revisited by Gray several times and she produced a series of squares directly inspired by his ideas, either being a play on the square itself or with the deliberate interjection or placing of a circular or triangular motif; *Navy blue square with a white stripe,*[75] *Black and speckled square,*[76] and *Black with white circle.*[77]

3.20 Black with white circle gouache and collage, 1920s, paper, paint © NMI

Gray owned a copy of *Classique Baroque Moderne,* written by Theo van Doesburg (1883-1931) which was an important publication expressing the ideas of the De Stijl movement.[78] The movement emphasised a return to basic, primary colours, and the use of geometric and rectilinear shapes through abstraction. This often involved balancing one colour and one form against another. Gray also acquired for her library *Neo Plasticisme* by Piet Mondrian (1872-1944) who advocated these ideas and envisaged in his art the formulation of a universal ideal of happiness.[79] He considered himself to be the prophet and his essay *Neo Plasticisme* was dedicated to its ideals. Having read this document Gray established her first contact with the De Stijl architects after she displayed in Amsterdam in 1922. Gray saw their work at the 1923 De Stijl Architecture Exhibition at Léonce Rosenburg's

Galerie l'Effort Moderne. It was to be of seminal importance to her career and ultimately led to friendship with many of the key members of the movement. Mondrian advocated in his publication that 'It is not enough that form be reduced to its quintessence, that the proportion of the whole work be harmonious; on the contrary, the entire work must be only the plastic expression of relationships and must disappear as particularity'. For Gray's De Stijl-inspired artworks she set out to create a pure art composed of pure elements where straight lines, angles and bold graphic designs came into play. Gray produced a body of work with asymmetrical, rectangular grids lines of varying widths. In comparison to her earlier work she produced large-scale gouaches playing with various ideas, using different colour schemes or smudging the edges of her compositions. One brown and beige large gouache clearly demonstrates ideas from the De Stijl, however, Gray's painterly effects are apparent as she uses washes not blocks of colour.[80] Another large gouache painted in bold red and pink dating from 1925 consists of pure geometric shapes, its overall design being highly effective.[81] It is a second variation of another gouache which Gray had worked on, where she had decided to enlarge the central abstract motif and change the palette.[82]

3.21 Brown and beige gouache, 1925, paper, paint
© NMI

During the 1930s and 1940s Gray created a number of gouaches and artworks that were not informed by any one particular art movement. These included a body of work with a speckled ground in a variety of colours which display her more painterly techniques.[83] Many of these have a dark black or green ground with speckled forms that extend inward either horizontally or vertically.[84] By mid-1935 to the early 1940s this speckled painterly aspect of Gray's artwork at times took over the entire picture plane.[85] Sometimes the speckled effect took on specific shapes like jigsaws – which are cut-outs mounted on card and then deliberately placed on the gouache.[86] Initially the colours and motifs used in the collage elements on such backgrounds were vivid in colour.[87] By the mid to late 1940s Gray's palette became increasingly monochromatic and at times these gouaches were indebted to the artwork of the American Abstract Expressionist Jackson Pollock (1912-1956) and others within that movement. The way in which Pollock did not obfuscate technique in his drip paintings and the way he textured the canvas, building up layers of paint through the use of various pigments and methodologies intrigued Gray. But she was later quite critical of this movement in letters to her niece sent during the 1960s. Her choice of palette and this Pollock-type speckled effect occurs in a body of work which Gray produced from 1940-1949.[88]

3.22 Speckled blue gouache with blue abstract motifs, late 1930s, paper, paint © NMI

Certain themes are also apparent in her artwork. During the early 1920s nautical themes become apparent. One gouache has an abstract fish motif, as if it was an imprint, and details include its mouth and upper and lower fins.[89] Fish appeared in Gray's work as early as 1916, and in *Vogue* magazine, August 1917, a sand-grey lacquer table top decorated with white fish which dart about in a black pool was shown.[90] Gray also did a carpet design of the Japanese koi fish and titled it *Poissons* which was completed between 1913 and 1917.[91] With another green, white and blue collage and gouache Gray created an underwater effect.[92] The colour and palette which she uses in this collage resemble another which she produced during the same period.[93]

At times Gray's palette is unconventional, evading the use of bold colour she opted in some of her pastel work soft browns, blues and pale

3.23 *Hantage*, 1930s, paper, crayon, chalk, paint © NMI

oranges. In one artwork entitled *Hantage* Gray has treated the motifs in a sfumato technique, smudging the outline of what appears to be a still life.[94] Another unfinished abstract collage of the early 1930s has a ground in a beige colour with two superimposed stripes which run vertically to the left and right in a deep burnt orange and brown colour.[95]

During the 1950s, 1960s and 1970s Gray worked on monotypes, collages, and bas-reliefs. She constantly challenged herself and felt that artists who had focused on decorative art had not always succeeded because 'Decorative Art which ought not to be decorative but means making new forms from old and sometimes new materials; pottery, cork aggloméré, straw, inventing'.[96] Gray returned to the various styles and movements which had influenced her. In one particular collage she paid homage to Eduardo Chillida (1924-2002), a Spanish sculptor noted for his abstract, monumental pieces. His first exhibition in France was in Paris in 1950. He continued to have solo exhibitions in the *Galerie Maeght* and the *Galerie Bertram* in Paris during the 1950s and 1960s. Using an original poster as the medium on which to begin her design, Gray returned to her sources of Analytical Cubism, painting out the lettering and then stencilling it in the corner.[97] As with many of Gray's experiments it remained incomplete.

André Breton (1896-1966) and Louis Aragon (1897-1982) published the Surrealist Manifesto in 1924 and a second in 1930. Gray had a copy of the first edition and had dealings with both men through an interior design commission which she received from Jacques Doucet in Paris. At that time she socialised in their circles, having many mutual friends in common.[98] The group was led by Breton, Paul Éluard (1895-1952) and Pierre Reverdy (1889-1960). Surrealism was concerned with visualising the inharmonious, dissonant side of human existence. Surrealists proclaimed the significance of the unconscious mind, which Gray was deeply interested in – states of hallucination; dream, intoxication and ecstasy which Breton stated were just as real as situations from everyday life. Gray's interest in dreams also enticed her to purchase *No.63 Visages du Monde,* 15 May 1939 with an edition devoted to *Le Rêve dans L'Art et La Littérature* (The Dream in Art and Literature).[99]

The mission the Surrealists set themselves was to expose previously repressed feelings and images, visualising the whole human existence, which included its absurd contradictions, its terrors and underlying humour. Breton pronounced that it was pure psychic automatism, that is to say that the Surrealist artist would delve below the conscious mind with its controls and inhibitions and reproduce what his or her subconscious inspiration dictated. Besides a copy of the manifesto Gray also had two issues of the periodical *Le Surréalisme au Service de la Révolution,* 1931 and *Le Surréalisme en 1947.*[100] *Le Surréalisme en 1947,* also known as *Prière de toucher* (Please touch) was the limited edition catalogue that accompanied the *Exposition Internationale du Surréalisme* – the first post-war Surrealist art exhibition to be staged in the *Galerie Maeght* in Paris in July–August 1947. Centred upon the theme of myth, the exhibition was organised by Marcel Duchamp and André Breton. The venue was transformed by Gray's friend and architect Frederick Kiesler (1890-1965) into a complex labyrinth of orchestrated rooms intended to spiritually reawaken French society after the horrors of World War II. Inset in the catalogue are 24 original prints by leading Surrealist artists including Max Ernst (1891-1976), Joan Miró (1893-1983), who Gray knew and Yves Tanguy (1900-1955). The catalogue was covered in hand-painted, pre-fabricated foam and rubber breasts that were adhered to a circular piece of black velvet and affixed to the cardboard slip-cover of the catalogue. In the typically mischievous manner of Surrealism, the back of the catalogue playfully read 'please touch'; inviting the readers to fondle the artificial breast adorning the cover before accessing the pages of the manuscript. The Surrealist movement interested Gray, and though her artwork never displayed surrealist tendencies, their influence was felt in her treatment of her subject matter in her artistic photographs. This was seen in artistic photographs by Breton and Éluard which she saw in *Le Surréalisme au Service de la Révolution*.

Throughout her career Gray had composed a visual photographic anthology of her furniture, interiors and her architecture, comprising of 1,070 images. This was not just a portfolio of her work – there were subtle details in the photographs which became Gray's trademark. As a result pieces – for example tables – had objects placed on them, cups and saucers, or books. Her photographs had a humanist element to them as if someone had just left the room. She was an excellent commercial photographer, taking photographs of her furniture displays at her shop *Jean Désert*, and often placing objects on furniture to give them a human touch and make the objects appear as if they were used. Many of these commercial images she treated as though they were still lifes. She also took all the photographs of her house for the magazine *L'Architecture Vivante* and for her portfolios of work which she compiled in 1956.[101]

Beginning in the 1920s Gray began taking artistic photographs which concentrated on light and shade. Inspired by the photographs taken of Rodin's sculptures by her friend Stephen Haweis and Henry Coles (b.1875) Gray embarked on a series of Still Life and Tablescapes in the 1920s. Haweis and Coles were the first of Rodin's photographers to experiment with artificial lighting using acetylene gas lamps for example. This type of lighting provided a strong contrast in their images which was reinforced by the biochromated-gelatin print. Now associated with the Pictorialist movement, the two British artists took about 200 photographs for Rodin in under two years. Pictorialists manipulated the photograph, by 'creating' an image not just recording it. Some of Gray's still life portraits of the 1920s follow this strain, appearing to lack a sharp focus with blurred shadows. She at times treated these photographs like paintings, creating an atmosphere by way of projecting an emotional intent into the viewer's realm of imagination. Other still life photographs are clearly modernist in style and are sharply focused, recording minutiae in a picture. Then in the late 1920s and throughout the 1930s two other movements had a profound effect on her photographs. The first was Surrealism. Gray owned a copy of *Le Surréalisme au Service de la Révolution* – a periodical issued in Paris from 1930 and 1933. Gray owned a copy of the issues no.3 and 4 from 1931.[102] Issue no. 3 had a numbers of Illustrations, including photographs of Surrealist objects by Breton, Gala Éluard (1894-1982), Valentine Hugo (1887-1968), Joan Miró, Alberto Giacometti (1901-1966) and Salvador Dalí (1904-1989). Gray's *Tablescape,* dating from the 1920s and consisting of an African mask hanging on the wall and a still life composed of inanimate objects, directly looks to Breton and Éluard's still life studies in this issue. Her treatment of the composition and the choice of subject matter are directly inspired by their work. The other movement was the Bauhaus, which directly inspired her photographs of the 1930s, especially the work of László Moholy-Nagy (1895-1946). Gray owned a copy of *Malerei, Fotografie, Film* (Painting, Photography, Film).[103] This landmark Bauhaus publication highlighted the debate between the media of painting, photography and film, especially in the recognition of the two latter being considered as art forms. In 1937, 35mm Kodachrome film first became available and Gray embarked – especially during the war years – on a series of images, creating fluid abstract compositions. In this series of images Gray emphasised photography as an extension of human sight, which compensated for the shortcomings of retinal perception, notably in the works *Anneaux de rideaux,* 1930s, and *Torse en marbre du 21 rue Bonaparte,* 1930s. Then by the 1950s Gray began to concentrate on natural and industrial landscapes, which were empty and devoid of human contact, with the series *Église à Saint Tropez* and *Port Grimaud.* By the late 1950s she had returned to outdoor still life compositions consisting of wood in the series *Bois pétrifié.*

3.24 *Still Life,* 1950, black and white photograph © Private Collection

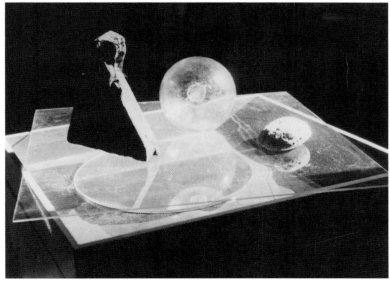

3.25 *Tablescape*, 1920, black and white photograph © Private Collection

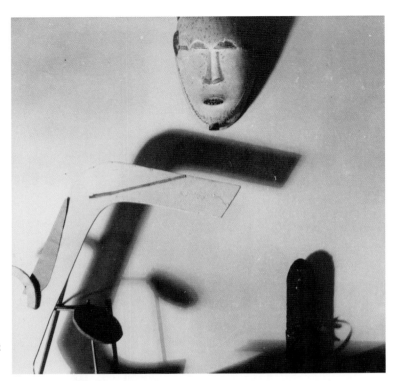

3.26 *Still Life,* 1920s, black and white photograph © Private Collection

3.27 *Torse en marbre du 21 rue Bonaparte,* 1930s, black and white photograph © Private Collection

3.28 *Port Grimaud,* 1950s, black and white photograph © Private Collection

3.29 *Bois pétrifié,* late 1950s, black and white photograph © Private Collection

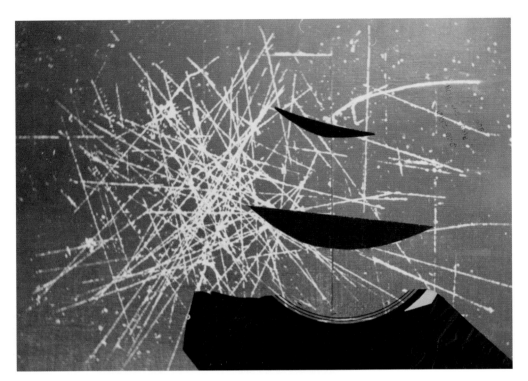

3.30 Photographic
collage, circa 1920,
photographic
paper, paint © NMI

From the 1930s through to the 1960s Gray also produced a series
of photographic collages. The earliest dates from 1935 and consists of a
photograph of white scratched lines haphazardly arranged in accordance
with three adhesive black, plastic curvilinear and straight cuts running
through the centre.[104] It recalled the Paul Klee-like lines on the back of the
1913 red lacquer screen *Le Destin,* and the swirling line motifs on the walls
of the salon of the *Rue de Lota apartment.* With this early photographic
collage she was simply exploring abstraction through the use of
photographic forms. The collage, unfinished, also appears in photographs
on Gray's desk in her home, *Tempe à Pailla.*

In the late 1950s and early 1960s she returned to photographic collage,
producing two large collages, which are nearly identical to one another.[105]
On each black and white photographic collage two separate forms are
assembled in an abstract manner. The first is composed of an off-white
ground with grey or beige triangular shapes and rectangles superimposed
on it. Running horizontally across this are strips, a small thin triangle and
a large triangle in speckled dark black and off white. The second consists

of two different ground colours; a white/cream ground on the left and a speckled black and beige on the right. Superimposed on them is a half circle with five spokes (resembling a hand) joining together and extending outwards. The second form in speckled black and cream is surrounded by a large thick black border and has an acute rectangle in cream in the centre. Stylistically these collages are similar to other gouaches and collages which she produced during this period.[106] They are pure abstraction.

Gray had studied sculpture in both London and Paris and in her archive sketches for sculptural pieces and a number of sculptural heads remain. However, it is difficult to place Gray into the canon of twentieth-century sculpture because so few known examples of her work survive. At the end of 1903 or the beginning of 1904 Gray wrote to Auguste Rodin. From the letters that remain she visited the renowned sculptor at Meudon, greatly appreciative of the time they spent together, and subsequently she purchased a small bronze of *La Danaïde*.[107] Gray's friend Kathleen Bruce went on to study with Rodin and became a successful sculptor in her own right. Rodin sparked the flame of modern sculpture, and students flocked to his studio to meet or study under his tutelage. His work was drenched in pools of light and shadow, and he openly undermined the classical movement by allowing his figures to intrude into the viewer's real space.

The emergence of modern sculpture between 1906 and 1913 took place almost entirely in Paris. From 1913 other movements and forces began to emerge against the hegemony of Paris. Gray's work focuses on three movements which influenced her – Cubism, Futurism and the Russian avant-garde – and the work of a number of sculptors, whom she knew, inspired her developments.

From 1906-1916 in the world of sculpture the human form was liberated and a new vocabulary began to be created. There was a block-like archetype, and every sculpture was a solid mass that was modelled, constructed or created. Space penetrated sculpture, and hollow space was treated with equal validity. New subject matter such as still lifes appeared and new media such as metal, glass, plaster, cardboard and wire were all being used. From the moment Gray had arrived in Paris she was exposed to the debates over French colonial policy in Africa that took place in 1905-6 and the resulting outcry of anticolonial opposition from socialists and anarchists at that time. Two representations of African art appeared in modernist culture of the time. The first came from French West Africa with stories appearing in the press of sacrifice, witchcraft, animism and fetishism which created a mystical, almost romanticised, view of native African culture. The second came from the French and Belgian Congos with the destruction of tribal life through white colonists. Since the end of the nineteenth century pre-historic, African and Oceanic art were being explored as new sources for sculpture. Gray's sculpture developed directly from these sources and a key aspect of Gray's sculpture was the discovery of tribal art. Artists began addressing anew the aesthetic qualities of the ethnographic collections in the museums of London, Paris, Dresden and Berlin. The rhythmic proportions of African wooden sculptures standing firmly on legs, set parallel and slightly bent at the knee, offered an alternative to classical contraposto.

Gray was also primarily inspired by a number of Cubist sculptors, notably Ossip Zadkine (1890-1967), Amedeo Modigliani (1884-1920), Chana Orloff (1888-1968), Joseph Csáky (1888-1971) and Jacques Lipchitz (1891-1973). She also had a number of publications directly relating to their work notably 'Lipchitz' by Maurice Raynal, in *Art d'Aujourd'hui,* 1920 and an exhibition catalogue of *Ossip Zadkine* by André de Ridder from the Palais des Beaux-Arts, Brussels in January 1933.[108]

Originally from Smolensk, Zadkine had come to Paris in 1909 after firstly studying at the London Polytechnic School of Arts and Crafts. Gray was introduced to Zadkine by Chana Orloff, another Russian, who later exhibited in *Jean Désert*. By nature he was not an Analytical Cubist but more a sculptor of elementary forms. He has been described as the 'only genuine wood sculptor' of the Classical Modernist period.[109] From early in his career Zadkine's approach was to animate and dominate his material, be it wood, stone or marble. During his 'African' phase the critic André de Ridder stated that it was as though Zadkine went directly into the forest and sculpted straight from a tree trunk. From this period his work evolved, rejecting popular, African and primitive art, and after a trip to Greece his work entered a long Cubist phase. Zadkine modelled his Cubist figures with short legs, long torsos and large heads according to African proportions. Though his work became monumental in size they maintained a simple and passionate sensibility, whilst demonstrating supple movement and harmony.[110] Gesture was just as important as sentiment and movement.[111] Zadkine emphasised the importance of light by manipulating his forms through the use of concave and convex lines, a regime of high and low reliefs, and through the many hollows and bumps that play with light and shade. Ridder writes that it is 'the simultaneous disassociation of form and light which leads to a piece's emancipation'.[112] By the 1920s he moved from Cubist expressions to a more curvilinear, organic art, yet borrowed the Cubist freedom of combining viewpoints and off-setting convex forms with concave. During the 1930s his work entered an agile, Baroque phase where his sculptures were monumental in size.

Gray liked Zadkine's work; however their rapport was distant and somewhat tentative, as Zadkine never mentions Gray in his autobiography, or the fact that he exhibited extensively at Gray's gallery *Jean Désert*. His work frequently appears in the photographs of the furniture installations which Gray took at *Jean Désert*. She owned a still-life photograph taken by photographer Marc Vaux (1895-1971) in 1922 of one of Zadkine's sculptural heads.[113] In 1926 Gray also purchased a sculptural head with rouge painted lips for her collection. This head was lent to an exhibition in Brussels in 1933, and Zadkine sent Gray a catalogue with the inscription 'To Miss E. Gray in remembrance, Jan 1933', but he never signed it.[114] Gray recommended Ossip Zadkine's work to Albert Boeken (1891-1951), De Stijl writer and critic, when he came to visit her in Paris. During World War II Zadkine departed for America where he taught in New York, but returned to Paris in 1945. They remained in contact and he came and visited her in her house in the South of France. He died in 1967.

Gray also knew Amedeo Modigliani through Orloff. The Italian painter and sculptor, moved to Paris in 1906 where he attended the Académie Julian. After receiving critical acclaim early in his career, his dissolute lifestyle and consumption of alcohol and drugs took their toll on his health. What appealed to Modigliani in relation to African sculpture was its stylisation and sophistication. The *Heads,* made from limestone, which he created in 1909-1914, were directly inspired by African tribal masks with their extreme elongation, smooth roundness, graphic scoring, narrow bridged noses and isolated mouths. The masks are expressionless, reduced to symmetrical axiality, and strengthened by a vertical rhythm.

Chana Orloff and Gray had many friends in common. Orloff, born in the Ukraine, came to Paris via Palestine in 1910, intending to train as a dressmaker, but by 1913 was producing prints and sculpture and was exhibiting at the Salon d'Automne. She designed the letterhead for the notepaper for Gray's gallery *Jean Désert*. In the 1920s, widowed and with a young son, she enjoyed immense critical success. She sculpted portraits of architects Pierre Chareau (1883-1950) and Le Corbusier's (1887-1965) teacher Auguste Perret (1874-1954), who designed Orloff's studio, and painters Amedeo Modigliani and Pablo Picasso. Her work was imbued with a quiet grace and sensuality. Her early works retain their solid core, yet geometric angles and hollows begin to break the surface. Her elongated figures with their length distortion served to consolidate and heighten emotional expression.

Hungarian Joseph Csáky developed and perfected a streamlined Synthetic Cubism in his sculpture. Csáky's figures contained rhythmic movements, combined in harmonic, organic, angular forms. The work of Jacques Lipchitz who came from Lithuania completely identifies with Cubism and his unruly figures have a taut angularity in their structure. Lipchitz interwove rhizomatic forms into the figures which drew the surrounding space into the figures themselves. With developments into a more planar, flatly composed Cubist sculpture developing from 1917, his style inherently changed. By 1925 Lipchitz turned away from Cubism, seeking more organic forms filled with concentrated energy. During and after the war Lipchitz's style was affected by the Jewish persecution. However, unlike the other sculptors who influenced Gray, he revisited Cubism for a second time in his career, where he explored the flow of space into volume.

3.31 Drawing of an abstract sculpture, 1920s, paper, pencil © NMI

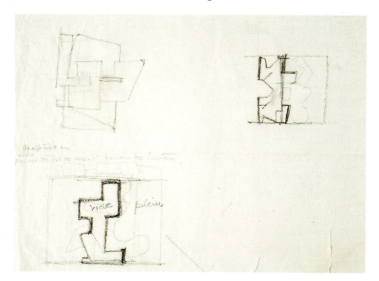

Gray did a series of three sketches for an abstract sculpture. Each drawing consists of these abstract Cubic block forms and each is a play on form and space. She has noted that it was to be made from metal wire and wood blocks.[115] She never realised the sculpture. The sketches recall the work of Alexander Archipenko (1887-1964) who arrived in Paris in 1908. From 1910 he developed his own style of simple, stereometrical, physical volumes in sculpture by creating upwardly spiralling figures. These were created through wedges, acute angles and breaks between form and space. Gray in her drawings addresses the same themes as Archipenko, Lipchitz, Csáky, Orloff and Zadkine, looking at the interaction between volume and space, creating juxtaposition between the two while still producing expressive, lyrical and dynamic forms. It is unknown if Gray ever realised sculptures from these drawings, but they confirm Gray's interest in the rhythmic energies of volumetric masses and in expressive plastic art.

Of the three sculptural heads which remain from Gray's oeuvre, two are made from cork and one from volcanic rock. *Tête,* circa 1929 is a facial sculpture made from a piece of volcanic rock which she found at Roquebrune on the seafront, on which Gray delicately marked the demarcations of facial features. Her choice of material gives the piece a very natural, organic feel.[116] The two sculptural heads or masks are made from cork and directly relate to tribal art. *Tête,* 1920s is primitive, reflecting Gray's interest, along with Modigliani, in African tribal masks from the West African Baule and Guro tribes and Picasso's interest in Iberian sculpture. Eileen Gray created this tribal-like mask when she was in the South of France.[117] It also coincides with the numerous African influences which were appearing in her lacquer work, especially in several furniture commissions completed for Jacques Doucet and Mme Mathieu-Lévy and in her carpet designs. The other sculptural head Gray made during the 1940s was a large sculptural mask of African style, again in the mode of Modigliani, made from cork.[118] She used rubber washers for the eyes and tinted metallic paper to create other facial features. She originally painted it silver and then tinted it grey all over.

Throughout her life Gray never stopped producing artwork. She knew so many artists during her lifetime, but her debilitating shyness thwarted many opportunities to expand on these friendships, attend social occasions or make new acquaintances. In the later years of her life she had regrets, saying that she wished to have known better the artists Picasso, Léger, Miró, Rouault and Modigliani.[119] Her letters reveal associations with some painters which until now were unknown. Gray met prominent Mexican painters Diego Rivera (1886-1957) and his wife Frida Kahlo (1907-1954) in the spring of 1934 when she travelled to Mexico by boat with Jean Badovici. She had visited Acapulco and Oaxaca and while in Mexico City she had lunch with Rivera and Kahlo. Rivera arrived in Europe in 1907, firstly to study in Madrid, and from there went to Paris to live and work in Montparnasse, where he remained until 1920. He became very

3.32 Sculptural head, 1920s, lava rock © NMI

3.33 Sculptural head, 1920s, cork © NMI

3.34 Sculptural head, 1940s, cork, paper, rubber © NMI

good friends with Amedeo Modigliani and Chana Orloff. Despite such introductions Gray was left unimpressed with both his work and the work of José Clemente Orozco (1883-1949).[120]

Gray remained acutely aware of the changes occurring in the contemporary art movements of the 1940s, 1950s and 1960s. However, she had grave concerns.

> No one seems to have any imagination, the current has deviated to science, computers, (ordinateurs) and the new generation are wildly realistic though they have never thought of grappling with the most obvious problems. It is obvious that, as the wheel turns now so quickly, all institutions need profound reforms in their structure and the old birds are always reluctant when it comes to any change.[121]

With the decline in easel painting, with an increase in the use of acrylic instead of oil paint, and the introduction of abstract painting where there was deliberately no meaning to what one painted, Gray felt that contemporary art had lost its identity.[122] To her it was stagnant, in comparison to the socially and politically motivated avant-garde art movements at the turn of the century. Minimalist and Post-painterly Abstract art just simply hypnotised its audience 'like in the story of the Emperor's new clothes'.[123] Critical of the extravagance of new American art – notably Pop and Op Art – Gray wrote, 'Painting seems to be going through a bad patch… Pop Art and now Pop-optics are the latest thing in England, but here the critics who were never capable of understanding abstract art have tried their best to kill it and now painters are totally divided, some going on with more or less the same things and others attempting what they think is a new figuration but without sincerity; the result is frankly mediocre'.[124] She questioned if art could recover from the Pop and Geo-Pop movements.[125] In Gray's opinion Pop Art figurative painting was pretentious as she described it full of 'pompiérisme'.[126]

Gray was interested in the work of a number of contemporary artists; Jean Dubuffet (1901-1985),[127] Barbara Hepworth (1903-1975),[128] Francis Bacon (1909-1992), Bernard Buffet (1928-1999)[129] and Frank Stella (b. 1936). However, she criticised Stella's infamous painting *Hyena Stomp*, 1962 and the Irregular Polygon series.[130] Stella had produced the Irregular Polygon series in 1965-66 where he painted eleven compositions combining varying numbers of shapes to create irregular outlines. He made four versions of each composition, varying the colour combinations of each. *Hyena Stomp* came from a musical tune by the American jazz musician Jelly Roll Morton. Gray didn't understand the work, not realising that Stella was thinking about syncopation while working on the painting. She was both critical and complimentary of fellow Irish artist Francis Bacon when she viewed an exhibition of his work at the *Galerie Maeght* in 1966. Gray wrote, 'Enormous canvases, very thin; light paint, every sort of colour, the kind of realism that one finds in the Bandes Dessinées (cartoons) in Weekly Revues'. However, she then proceeds to describe his style as 'Anecdotal .... No shadows but perspective, and in every painting (if one could call it painting) the faces of the humans were distorted like wicked gnomes or demons... The colours so horrid as if they were imitating comic cuts. This is surely the end of civilization'.[131]

Gray's work as a designer and architect was criticised throughout her life in various publications and by various critics. Though she was freely able to criticise the work of artists in her later years, when it came to someone's review of her own work, who was of her generation, Gray became fearful. Thoughts of ineptitude as an artist persuaded Gray to destroy so many of her early artworks. In the 1960s she wrote to Stephen Haweis, her contemporary from art school, about the incredible body of work she was producing. Her fears returned. She was devoting this time to abstract or semi abstract works and was worried that he, her contemporary, would not like them'.[132]

Gray also criticised art exhibitions or at least the public's reaction to the work of her contemporaries from the turn of the century. At times she is exceedingly protective of her generation's work. It is in moments such as this that she reveals an encyclopaedic knowledge of these artists; their work, their ideologies and the artistic movements from where they came. For example, Gray attended the exhibition *Les sources du XXe siècle: les arts en Europe de 1884 à 1914*, which took place at the Musée Nationale d'Art Moderne from 1960-1961. Works by an impressive array of artists were on display; Paul Cézanne, Fernand Léger, Wassily Kandinsky, Pablo Picasso, Georges Braque, artists from the Expressionist German school, and a selection from the Futurist movement. Gray was critical of the selection, stating that the work of neither Eugène Carrière nor James McNeill Whistler was represented and only a tiny work by Alexander Archipenko was in the exhibition.[133] In another instance, Gray, who knew Alberto Giacometti from his Surrealist years, attended an exhibition of his sculpture in May 1961 at *Galerie Maeght* in Paris. She had gone to view the work which had become his characteristic style – very tall and thin figures. Giacometti had become, by this time, the outstanding sculptor of the era, questioning merging ideas of distance and proximity in frontal, rigid sculpture. Like Gray, he constantly self-questioned his work and the reaction to it. For this reason Gray became highly frustrated. While at the exhibition, a wealthy industrialist approached her and said of Giacometti's work 'you know in my factory, we too, we have a lot of iron or scrap, but it serves an entirely different purpose'.[134]

Despite her criticism of artists or their ideas, Gray always believed in the importance of the artist and especially a respect for the resulting work. At times her view of the status of an artist in society was completely idealistic. To her an artist was precious. She went even so far as to state that artists shouldn't drive, as too much attention to the task at hand prevented artistic thinking or 'wandering' and because driving put constant tension on their eyes.[135] In the years that followed in the role of architect Gray wrote a series of notes on urbanism, and emphasised the necessity of creating a town with special sections for artists, musicians and writers and for all those 'who want to live with pure spiritual matters'.[136] Whether architect, designer or artist the fruition of their efforts was what was important, as for her, they were only the means through which paintings, buildings or furniture were created.

Towards the end of her life she described painting as a whole time job and a constant preoccupation.[137] In 1962 she was actively producing monotypes, collages, bas-reliefs and gouaches. Art played an important role throughout Eileen Gray's life. Her letters reveal that she continued to paint until the year of her death. Painting made her feel alive and she wrote 'It still seems wonderful to be alive, to open one's eyes and be able to work at all, even if it comes to nothing'.[138]

ENDNOTES

1   NMIEG 2000.115, drawing of a nude study.

2   Pitiot, Cloe, 'Eileen Gray, la poésie de l'énigme', *Eileen Gray,* Editions de Centre Pompidou Paris, 2013, p.16.

3   NMIEG 2003.509, NMIEG 2003.510, notes on Eileen Gray's work.

4   Pater, Walter, *The Renaissance: Studies in Art and Poetry,* London and New York, MacMillan and Co., 1888.

5   McNeill Whistler, James, *The Gentle Art of Making Enemies,* New York, Frederick Stokes and Brother, 1890.

6   McNeill Whistler, James, *Nocturne in Black and Gold: The Falling Rocket*, 1875, oil on panel, 60.2 x 46.7 cm, Detroit, Detroit Institute of Arts.

7   NMIEG 2003.126, black, cream and grey gouache with vertical motifs.

8   Pennell, Joseph and Elizabeth, *The Life of James McNeill Whistler,* London, William Heinemann, 1911.

9   McNeill Whistler, James, *Harmony in Blue and gold*: *The Peacock Room*, 1876-1877, oil paint and gold leaf on canvas, leather and wood, Washington, Freer Sackler: The Smithsonian's Museums of Asian Art.

10 NMIEG 2003.94, green Japanese-style carpet gouache.

11 NMIEG 2003.365, letter from Eileen Gray to Prunella Clough, 2 January 1971.

12 Lane, John, *The Early Work of Aubrey Beardsley*, London, The Bodley Head, 1899.

13 Adam, Marcelle, *Les Caricatures de Puvis de Chavannes,* Paris, Librairie Charles Delagrave, 1906. Verhaeren, Emile, *James Ensor,* Brussels, Librairie Nationale d'Art et d'Histoire, G. Van Oest& Cie, 1908.

14 V&A Prints and Drawings Archive, ref nos: E119-1983, E1132-1983.

15 Constant, Caroline, *Eileen Gray*, London, Phaidon, 2000, p.18

16 Ibid, Constant, p.19. Constant puts forward the theory that Gray's architecture was inspired by the Ballet Russes; the way in which Bakst's costumes liberated the movement of the body in motion inspired Gray's interest in liberating the body in its occupation of space. She also states that Baskt's concentration on the expressive potential of the entire group of dancers caused Gray to eliminate the distinction between architecture and furnishings, merging them into an organic whole. Finally she states that Nijinsky's performances, merging masculine and feminine traits, were reflected in the way in which Gray fused furniture and architecture together. Constant suggests that the concept for the Ballet could have been instigated by Jacques Rouche's *Carnaval des Animaux* at the Théâtre des Arts 1911.

17 Born 1892, one of eight children, she changed her name to Marisa Damia after being discovered by Jacques Doherty. By 1912 she was famous and her records sold in thousands.

18 Adam, Peter, *Eileen Gray:Architect/Designer: A Biography,* London, Thames and Hudson, 2000, pp. 108-9. Adam states that Rolf de Mare for the Ballet Suédois commissioned artists such as Francis Picabia, Fernand Léger and Pierre Bonnard to design for him; the Comte de Beaumont rented the Théâtre de Pigalle and commissioned a series of ballets designed by George Braque, Picasso and André Derain.

19 Cocteau, Jean, *Dessins,* Paris, Delamain, Boutelleau et Cie, 1923.

20 NMIEG 2003.337, letter from Eileen Gray to Prunella Clough, 1970s.

21 NMIEG 2003.80, Méral, Paul, *Le Dit des Jeux du Monde*, Paris, Presse de l'Imprimerie Studium, 1918.

22 NMIEG 2000.120 – NMIEG 2000.131, NMIEG 2003.530, drawings for *Ballet des Animaux*

23 Ibid.

24 Ibid, Adam, p.109.

25 Georges-Michel, Michel and George, Waldemar, *Les Ballets Russes de Serge de Diaghilew, Décors et costumes,* Paris, Galerie Billiet, 1930.

26 V&A Archives, AAD/1980/9, un-numbered ground floor plan.

27 NMIEG 2000.132, drawing for a mural for a nursery.

28 V&A Archives, AAD/1980/9, un-numbered drawing for a fresco for a child's bedroom.

29 Adam, Peter, *Eileen Gray: Architect/Designer: A Biography*, London, Thames & Hudson, 1987, p.330, see illustration.

30 NMIEG 2000.133 - 2000.136, drawings for a mural in a daycare centre.

31 Rare Book & Manuscript Library, Columbia University in the City of New York, Stephen Haweis Papers, Arranged Miscellaneous Memoirs, Box 2, letter from Eileen Gray to Stephen Haweis, 14 February 1963.

32 Picasso, Pablo, *Les Demoiselles d'Avignon*, 1907, oil on canvas, 243.7 x 233.7 cm, New York, MoMA.

33 NMIEG 2003.66, Apollinaire, Guillaume, *Les Peintres Cubistes*, Editions Eugène Figuière et Cie, Paris, 1913.

34 NMIEG 2003.150, abstract drawing.

35 NMIEG 2000.173, *Tempe à Pailla* collage.

36 Adam, Peter, *Eileen Gray: Architect/Designer: A Biography,* London, Thames and Hudson, 1987, p.188.

37 NMIEG 2000.176, newspaper collage.

38 Gray's carpet designs were abstract in design but the inclusion of lettering, maps and plans usually referred to a person, place or memory.

39 Clapp, Susannah, *With Chatwin: Portrait of a Writer*, New York, 1997, p.24.

40 NMIEG 2000.172, *Roquebrune coastline* collage.

41 Polo, Roberto, *Eileen Gray-Œuvres sur Papier,* Paris, Galerie Historismus, 2007, p.67.

42 NMIEG 2003.122, black, grey and beige gouache with architectural plan motif. NMIEG 2003.118, black and white speckled gouache and collage.

43 NMIEG 2000.173, *Tempe à Pailla* collage. Dating from 1931-34, this collage shows Gray's experimentation with Synthetic Cubism.

44 NMIEG 2000.90, *Tempe à Pailla* site plan.

45 NMIEG 2000.174, green, white, blue gouache and collage.

46 NMIEG 2000.169, collage elements.

47 NMIEG 2003.118, black and white speckled gouache and collage.

48 NMIEG 2000.169, NMIEG 2003.1569, *Cultural and Social Centre*, Stage design for *Épopée Irlandaise*.

49 Polo, Roberto, *Eileen Gray-Œuvres sur Papier,* Paris, Galerie Historismus, 2007, p.72.

50 NMIEG 2000.177, black and white collage. NMIEG 2003.123, black, grey and white gouache with yellow motif. Polo, Roberto, *Eileen Gray-Œuvres sur Papier,* Paris, Galerie Historismus, 2007, p.77.

51 NMIEG 2003.145, black with green circle gouache and collage.

52 NMIEG 2003.129, black gouache with dark green and speckled motifs. NMIEG 2003.123, black, grey and white gouache with yellow motif.

53 Einstein, Carl, 'Notes sur le cubism', *Documents, No.3,* Paris, 39 rue de la Boétie, June 1929, pp.146-155.

54 Braque, Georges, Le Sacré Coeur, 1913, oil on canvas, 55 x 40.5cm, Lille, Lille Métropole Musée d'art moderne.

55 NMIEG 2003.82, Picasso, Pablo, *Guernica,* London, New Burlington Galleries, October 1938.

56 NMIEG 2003.65, Gleizes, Albert, and Metzinger, Jean, *Du Cubisme,* Paris, Editions la Cible, 1912.

57 NMIEG 2000.74, lacquer panel for a door.

58 NMIEG 2003.150, abstract drawing. The motifs reappear in *Marine d'Abord, Ebony and Ivory, Feston, Black Magic* and *Collage* carpet designs.

59 NMIEG 2000.74,lacquer door panel.

60 Apollinaire, Guillaume, *Les Soirées de Paris,* No.22, Paris, Editions 6 rue Jacob, 15 March 1914.

61 Picabia, Francis, *Danseuse étoile sur un transatlantique,* 1913, watercolour on paper, 75x55 cm, private collection.

62 NMIEG 2003.148, charcoal drawing.

63 V&A Archives, AAD 9/6-1980 and AAD 9/9-1980. These are typed notes by Jean Badovici regarding naval design, life boats and lifesaving.

64 NMIEG 2003.85, *Futurist exhibition catalogue,* London, Sackville Gallery, March 1912.

65 NMIEG 2003.147, charcoal drawing on grid paper.

66 Lewis, Percy Wyndham, *Blast,* issue 1 and 2, London, Bodley Head, 1914.

67 NMIEG 2003.124, black, grey and beige speckled gouache with swirling lines.

68 NMIEG 2003.121, black and white speckled gouache with white lightening motif.

69 NMIEG 2003.125, yellow gouache with white motifs and black lines, early 1930s.

70 Duchamp, Marcel, *Nude Descending a Staircase, No.2,* 1912, oil on canvas, 147.5x89cm, Philadelphia Museum of Art, Louise and Walter Arensberg collection.

71 Polo, Roberto, *Eileen Gray-Œuvres sur Papier,* Paris, Galerie Historismus, 2007, p.73.

72 NMIEG 2003.132, black gouache with thin white lines, 1918-1921.

73 Malevich, Kazimir, *Suprematist Composition,* 1915, oil on canvas, 49x44cm, Lugwigshafen, Wilhelm-Hack Museum.

74 Kliun, Ivan, *Suprematism,* 1915-16, oil on canvas, 89x70.7cm, Moscow, Tretyakov Gallery.

75 NMIEG 2003.93, navy blue square with white stripe gouache, 1918-1921.

76 NMIEG 2003.130, black and speckled square gouache, early 1930s.

77 NMIEG 2003.119, black with white circle gouache and collage, early 1930s. Polo, Roberto, *Eileen Gray-Œuvres sur Papier,* Paris, Galerie Historismus, 2007, p.71.

78 NMIEG 2000.261, Van Doesburg, Theo, *Classique Baroque Moderne,* Paris Edition De Sikkel Anvers et Leonce Rosenberg, December 1918.

79 NMIEG 2003.81, Mondrian, Piet, *Neo Plasticisme,* Paris, Editions de l'Effort Moderne Léonce Rosenberg, 1920.

80 NMIEG 2003.128, brown and beige gouache, 1923-1925.

81 NMIEG 2003.143, red and pink gouache, 1923-25.

82 NMIEG 2003.128, brown and beige gouache.

83 NMIEG 2003.128, brown and beige gouache, 1923-1925. NMIEG 2003.130, black and speckled square gouache, early 1930s. NMIEG 2003.119, black with white circle gouache and collage. NMIEG 2003.120, blackand speckled white gouache. NMIEG 2003.124, black, grey and beige speckled gouache with swirling lines. circa 1930s. NMIEG 2003.129, black gouache with dark green and speckled motifs. NMIEG 2003.122, black, grey and beige gouache with architectural plan motif. NMIEG 2003.123, black, grey, and white gouache with yellow motif. Polo, Roberto, *Eileen Gray- Œuvres sur Papier,* Paris, Galerie Historismus, 2007, pp.55, 71, 85.

84 NMIEG 2003.129, black gouache with dark green and speckled motifs.

85 NMIEG 2003.141, beige and black speckled gouache. NMIEG 2003.118, black and white speckled gouache and collage, circa 1946. NMIEG 2003.149, black, grey and beige speckled gouache, 1939-1949. NMIEG 2003.144, purple, black, grey and white speckled gouache, 1930-1935. Polo, Roberto, *Eileen Gray-Œuvres sur Papier,* Paris, Galerie Historismus, 2007, p.93.

86 NMIEG 2003.144, purple, black, grey and white speckled gouache. 1930-1935.

87 NMIEG 2003.127, speckled blue gouache with blue abstract motifs, late 1930s.

88 Polo, Roberto, *Eileen Gray-Œuvres sur Papier,* Paris, Galerie Historismus, 2007, pp. 93, 95, 97, 99, 103.

89 NMIEG 2003.116, fish-design gouache.

90 NMIEG 2000.251 and NMIEG 2000.252, *Vogue* magazine and article.

91 RIBA Archives, PB546/1, miscellaneous loose designs for carpets and tiles.

92 NMIEG 2000.174, green, white, blue gouache and collage.

93 Polo, Roberto, *Eileen Gray-Œuvres sur Papier,* Paris, Galerie Historismus, 2007, p.68.

94 NMIEG 2003.142, *Hantage* gouache.

95 NMIEG 2000.175, orange and brown collage.

96 Rare Book & Manuscript Library, Columbia University in the City of New York, Stephen Haweis Papers, Arranged Miscellaneous Memoirs, Box 2, letter from Eileen Gray to Stephen Haweis, Thursday 13 February 1964.

97 NMIEG 2000.178, *Chillida* collage, 1950s.

98 Gray's business partner and friend Evelyn Wyld was friendly with Elizabeth de Lanux, who was a journalist and wife of Pierre de Lanux, later becoming professionally and romantically involved with her. They were friends of Jean Cocteau, André Gide, Man Ray and Breton and Aragon. They were also friends of Élisabeth de Grammont, Duchess de Clarement Tonerre, who had written the first French article in *Les Feuillets d'Art* on Eileen Gray.

99 Various authors, *No. 63 Visage du Monde,* Paris, Editions Fernand Sorlot, 15May 1939.

100 Duchamp, Marcel, *Le Surréalisme en 1947,* Paris, Galerie Maeght, 1947.

101 Badovici, Jean, and Gray, Eileen, 'Maison au Bord de Mer', *L'Architecture Vivante,* Paris, Editions Albert Morancé, Winter 1929. NMIEG 2000.250 and NMIEG 2003.1641, portfolios.

102 Various authors, edited by Breton, André, *Le Surréalisme au Service de la Révolution,* issues no.3 and 4, Paris, Librairie José Corti, 1931.

103 Moholy-Nagy, László, 'Malerei, Fotografie, Film', *Bauhausbücher,* Volume 8, 1925.

104 NMIEG 2000.171, photographic collage, circa 1935.

105 NMIEG 2003.133, black and white photographic collage, 1960s. NMIEG 2003.146, black and white photographic collage, 1960s.

106 Polo, Roberto, *Eileen Gray-Œuvres sur Papier,* Paris, Galerie Historismus, 2007, p.107.

107 Musée Rodin Archives, three letters from Eileen Gray to Auguste Rodin, December 1902, January 1902 and 20 January 1902.

108 Raynal, Maurice, 'Lipchitz', *Art d'Aujourd'hui,* No.1, Paris, Action, 1920. NMIEG 2003.63, de Ridder, André, *Zadkine,* Brussels, H. Wellens, W. Godenne rue de Roumanie Editions, 1933.

109 Ruhrberg, Schneckenburger, Fricke, Honnef, *Art of the Twentieth Century,* Taschen 2000, p.142.

110 Ibid, de Ridder, p.6.

111 Ibid, de Ridder, p.7.

112 Ibid, de Ridder, p.8.

113 NMIEG 2003.546.

114 de Ridder, André, *Zadkine,* Brussels, Palais des Beaux Arts, H. Wellens, W. Godenne rue de Roumanie Editions, January 1933. In the catalogue, written in French, Gray's head is No.61 titled 'Head-stone incrusted marble' dated 1926, belonging to Mlle Gray, Paris.

115 NMIEG 2003.528, drawing of an abstract sculpture.

116 NMIEG 2003.535, sculptural head, 1920s.

117 NMIEG 2003.534, sculptural head, 1920s.

118 NMIEG 2000.116, sculptural head, 1940s.

119 Rare Book & Manuscript Library, Columbia University in the City of New York, Stephen Haweis Papers, Arranged Miscellaneous Memoirs, Box 2, letter from Eileen Gray to Stephen Haweis, 14 February 1963.

120 Rare Book & Manuscript Library, Columbia University in the City of New York, Stephen Haweis Papers, Arranged Miscellaneous Memoirs, Box 2, letter from Eileen Gray to Stephen Haweis, 30March 1962.

121 Rare Book & Manuscript Library, Columbia University in the City of New York, Stephen Haweis Papers, Arranged Miscellaneous Memoirs, Box 2, letter from Eileen Gray to Stephen Haweis, 16 May 1968.

122 NMIEG 2003.365, letter from Eileen Gray to Prunella Clough, 2 January 1971. Rare Book & Manuscript Library, Columbia University in the City of New York, Stephen Haweis Papers, Arranged Miscellaneous Memoirs, Box 2, letter from Eileen Gray to Stephen Haweis, February 1968.

123 NMIEG 2003.334, letter from Eileen Gray to Prunella Clough, Wednesday, date and year unknown.

124 Rare Book & Manuscript Library, Columbia University in the City of New York, Stephen Haweis Papers, Arranged Miscellaneous Memoirs, Box 2, letter from Eileen Gray to Stephen Haweis, 8 March (year unknown possibly 1964).

125 Rare Book & Manuscript Library, Columbia University in the City of New York, Stephen Haweis Papers, Arranged Miscellaneous Memoirs, Box 2, letter from Eileen Gray to Stephen Haweis, 16 May 1968.

126 Rare Book & Manuscript Library, Columbia University in the City of New York, Stephen Haweis Papers, Arranged Miscellaneous Memoirs, Box 2, letter from Eileen Gray to Stephen Haweis, Easter Monday, year unknown.

127 NMIEG 2000.189, postcard from Eileen Gray to Prunella Clough.

128 NMIEG: 2003.332, letter from Eileen Gray to Prunella Clough, date and year unknown.

129 NMIEG 2003.337, letter from Eileen Gray to Prunella Clough, 1960. Bernard Buffett (1928-1999) was a French expressionist and member of the Anti-Abstract Group *L'homme Témoin* (the Witness Man). Gray also mentions Annabel Schwob (1928-2005) – Dubuffet's wife, who was an actress, in this letter.

130 Stella, Frank, *Hyena Stomp*, 1962, Alkyd paint on canvas, 77x77cm, London, Tate Gallery.

131 NMIEG 2003.311, letter from Eileen Gray to Prunella Clough, 9 January, year unknown.

132 Rare Book & Manuscript Library, Columbia University in the City of New York, Stephen Haweis Papers, Arranged Miscellaneous Memoirs, Box 2, letter from Eileen Gray to Stephen Haweis, 12 October, year unknown, possibly 1966.

133 Rare Book & Manuscript Library, Columbia University in the City of New York, Stephen Haweis Papers, Arranged Miscellaneous Memoirs, Box 2, letter from Eileen Gray to Stephen Haweis, 27 November 1961.

134 Rare Book & Manuscript Library, Columbia University in the City of New York, Stephen Haweis Papers, Arranged Miscellaneous Memoirs, Box 2, letter from Eileen Gray to Stephen Haweis, 27 November 1961.

135 NMIEG 2003.340, letter from Eileen Gray to Prunella Clough, Monday, late 1960s.

136 Ibid, Adam, p.138.

137 Rare Book & Manuscript Library, Columbia University in the City of New York, Stephen Haweis Papers, Arranged Miscellaneous Memoirs, Box 2, letter from Eileen Gray to Stephen Haweis, 30 March 1962, letter from Eileen Gray to Stephen Haweis, page two part of a letter April 1962 – possibly page two of letter 30 March 1962.

138 Rare Book & Manuscript Library, Columbia University in the City of New York, Stephen Haweis Papers, Arranged Miscellaneous Memoirs, Box 2, letter from Eileen Gray to Stephen Haweis, 27 November 1961.

4

The Realm
of Lacquer

In 1854, after more than 200 years of isolation, Japan reopened its ports to western trade and in so doing provided a fresh source of artistic inspiration to the West. Japanese furniture which came into the European market was praised for its simplicity, purity of form and strong feeling for nature. In a reaction against ornate historical eighteenth-century furniture styles, British designers tried to capture the spirit of the East with its use of lacquered wood finish and an emphasis on structural design. Functional elements such as hinges and key plates became decorative. In England tastes were also being defined by Liberty department store, which became a major outlet for artistic items when it was opened by Arthur Lazenby Liberty (1843-1917) in Regent Street in May 1875. His talent for acquiring tasteful *objet d'art* from Japan and the East was noted by the furniture designer E.W. Godwin (1833-1886) with Godwin describing the excitement of Liberty's customers when a new shipload of goods arrived on the pavement outside the Regent Street shop. This atmosphere was so intense that customers, ecstatic over the silks, fans, rugs, china and enamelware, would demand that the packing cases be opened in the street. This combined with the influence of the Aesthetic Movement compounded

4.1 Eileen Gray, 1896, black and white photograph © NMI

4.2 Eileen Gray, late 1910s, early 1920s, black and white photograph © NMI

the Anglo-Japanese style which developed in the period from 1851–1900. The Museum of Ornamental Art (later the Victoria and Albert Museum) bought Japanese lacquer and porcelain in 1852 and in 1854. In 1875–1897 The National Museum of Ireland had acquired a number of Japanese items, notably lacquer pieces which were displayed in Kildare Street in Dublin. Articles appeared in *The Irish Times* regarding these exhibits from 1885 through to 1890. Gray spent her childhood between London's South Kensington and Enniscorthy in Wexford. Recorded in her archives are day trips spent in Dublin with her mother where it is possible that she saw some of these pieces.

Gray was also exceedingly interested in the Aesthetic, Decadent and Symbolist movements having a number of key publications in her library. These movements emphasised the use of symbols, sensuality and the correspondence between words, colours and music, which defined Gray's ideas of synaesthesia. Lacquer was an ideal medium which encompassed all of these movement's ideas of engaging with the senses, providing the user with a refined sensuous pleasure. It was a craft whereby touch and sight were actively engaged from the beginning of the creative process through to the end result.

By the 1880s the Anglo-Japanese style had become a major influence in these movements culminating in Whistler's *Peacock Room*.[1] Gray owned *The Life of James McNeill Whistler,* 1908.[2] In this publication Gray saw images and read the story behind the commission for *Harmony in Blue and Gold: The Peacock Room* – Whistler's masterpiece of interior decorative mural art. He had painted the panelled room in a rich and unified palette of scintillating blue-greens with an over-glazing of metallic gold leaf. Painted in 1876-77 the interior became an example of the Anglo-Japanese style. The mural decoration of this room dominated the architectural interior and its features. Gray's instinctive reaction against the luxury and

4.3 Room installation, *Harmony in Blue and Gold: The Peacock Room,* James McNeill Whistler, 1876-1877, oil paint and gold leaf on canvas, leather, and wood © Freer Gallery of Art, Smithsonian Institution, Washington, D.C, Gift of Charles Lang Freer

exuberance of the room would culminate in her eventual conviction that 'architecture must be its own decoration'.[3] However Whistler's palette in *The Peacock Room* would later reappear in Gray's lacquer work from 1908 onwards, as she strove to faithfully create and perfect the recipe for blue lacquer.

While attending the Slade School in London in 1900 Gray serendipitously encountered the medium of lacquer.[4] During her lunch hour Gray saw the Asian lacquer displays at the South Kensington Museum, now the Victoria and Albert Museum. She also wandered around Soho looking at shops. By chance she passed a furniture restoration shop on Dean Street belonging to Dean Charles.[5] Offering her services to become a pupil, she was invited to study the materials of lacquer screens that he had been restoring. Charles was an Asian screen and furniture restorer and he used mostly European varnishes to repair the screens but had some varnish from China. When Gray returned from her art studies in Paris for a two-year spell in 1905 she resumed her education in lacquer from Dean Charles, and they remained friends for many years. She continued to ask his advice about colours and she also ordered supplies from him long after she had established herself as a reputable designer in Paris.[6] 'Lacquer always fascinated me', Gray claimed many years later.[7]

It is not clear if Gray purchased the book *A Treatise of Japanning and Varnishing,* 1688 by John Stalker and George Parker, prior to her tutelage with Dean Charles or upon his recommendation, however this publication became important in her instruction. She readily stated that she always had an interest in lacquer. This seventeenth-century book became one of the main manuals on lacquer and japanning not only of that period but for generations afterwards.[8] This publication had been extremely popular in England during the latter part of the seventeenth century, especially amongst women who were encouraged to learn Japanning as a pastime. The book was intended to assist not only amateur decorators, but also professional cabinetmakers. It contains instructions on the use of colours on Japanning and gilding, and the staining or varnishing of wood. The reader not only became a chemist familiarising themselves with proportions, ingredients, quantities and the reaction of chemical precipitates, but also an alchemist, transforming raw materials into textures, which when applied to an object created a work of art. It was similar to magic, appealing to the senses by touch, sight and smell.

Wood stain could also turn vile substances into pure colours, almost like a magical art. For example Brazil wood had to be mixed in stale urine or water impregnated with pearl-ashes to produce a bright red colour. Pale red was obtained by dissolving an ounce of a red gum called dragon's blood in a pint of spirit of wine and brushing over the wood with tincture, until the stain appears to be as strong as desired. The *Treatise* advocated the purchase of a wide selection of colours from druggist's premises, or at that time from colour shops. Gray would eventually import all of her pigments from China. The colours which were popular in the manual included ivory black, lampblack, verdigris, umber, indigo or yellow ochre. The manual advocated the use of only the best varnish which also could be used for varnishing light colours such as white, yellow, green, sky, red, silver or gilded. A black ground was advocated, though grounds could also be, though rarely, white which in the seventeenth century imitated porcelain.

Red lacquer was popular in the seventeenth century and Gray would avidly use it in her screens such as *Le Destin* (The Destiny) and domestic ware, placing it into a contemporary context. The technique as advocated in the *Treatise* consisted of applying coats of heavily pigmented coloured varnish that was initially blended with oil resin formulation, also known as spirit varnish, such as turpentine or essential oil, or with dissolved resin, such as seedlac, sandarac, copal, gum elemi, mastic, Venetian turpentine, gamboge or dragon's blood. Each layer had to be polished and allowed to dry before applying the next coat of varnish. Successive coats had to contain less and less pigment. The last coats required the application of a final white or clear varnish.

4.4 Lacquer samples, 1910s, wood, pigment, lacquer © NMI

The book also provided several sets of prints mainly flora and fauna designs where amateurs could incorporate or copy the patterns or simply cut them out and paste them on the surface of a Japanned object. Advice was given on how to add colour to these cut-out patterns using gold paint. There is one example which serves as the model for painting an exotic bird with a lustrous plumage and the authors instruct the reader on how to make the Japanned pattern shine with various shades of black, silver, gold and brown. To add extra brilliance to compositions, it was recommended to add speckles of gold on the designs, however, the reader was warned to use temperance and measure, to resist the temptation of creating absurd

Chinoiserie compositions. Gray added these gold speckles on the bowls and plates of her domestic lacquer ware, albeit it in an extremely abstract and minimalist manner.

For Gray to expand her fine art skills into the medium of lacquer was not unusual. In England since the seventeenth century it was considered a natural progression in the arts. In the realm of female accomplishments painting was one of the master arts, and Japanning manuals such as the *Treatise* urged for a sound arrangement of designs.[9] Lacquer was a sensuous material, engaging the craftsman's hands, yet it was also an arduous craft. Upon her return to Paris in 1907 she took samples of the work with her and, through Charles's contacts, was introduced to her lacquer mentor Seizo Sugawara (1884-1937), a young Japanese student in his twenties. Gray plunged into a medium that was unconventional and not widely used at all in Paris other than for restoration work. Gray in later years said that the French were suspicious of lacquer because it was too black, too dark and related to the dark arts.[10] Despite lacquer being a difficult medium of expression it captured her imagination, challenging her and intriguing her. It was a very demanding process that required determination, dedication and hard work. She

4.5 Seizo Sugawara, 1910s, black and white photograph © NMI

kept Charles's recipe for lacquer, but Charles used Chinese lacquer which she imported and ordered from him in London but gradually through the influence of Sugawara she changed around to Japanese lacquer which she stated 'The Chinese lacquer has more oil in it and is less resistant than the Japanese one, which is harder'.[11] Gray began ordering directly from a Japanese lacquer merchant Sugimoto Gosuke from Toyko.[12]

Following trips to Ireland and England, Gray finally settled permanently in Paris at the end of 1906 and took an apartment at 21 rue Bonaparte in 1907. During this period the world of the decorative arts in France was in disarray. The rapid development of the German avant-garde design movement, exhibited at the Exposition Universelle, posed a threat to French design. In 1910 the Munich Vereinigte Werkstätten für Kunst im Handwerk held their first Paris exhibition at the Salon d'Automne. Largely employing wood, their simple designs were socially motivated, produced for moderate household budgets and addressed questions of industrial production.[13] The German approach inspired a number of French designers, including Francis Jourdain (1876-1958) and Claude Roger Marx (1888-1977), who believed that, based on the example of Germany and England, one could produce low-cost affordable furniture for the masses. Gray embraced this liberal social philosophy. The Germans posed a threat suggesting a practical, democratic non-historicist approach, whereas the French by not embracing mass production hid behind the veneer of sumptuous interiors and outdated elitism. Indeed on 29 March the French newspaper *Le Matin* proclaimed that the French decorative arts were endangered by an imminent German invasion and as a result French critics assumed a defensive position.[14] Gray felt an immediate affinity with their ideas.

In 1901 the Société Nationale des Artistes Décorateurs, a non-profit organisation, had been formed in France. Its aim was to promote French decorative arts, encouraging artists, craftsmen and designers to break from industrialists and work directly for the public under their own signature. They were insistent on elevating the status of the designer to the same level as that of artist. Gray joined and exhibited with them until 1925. Despite promoting modernity, French decorative arts relied heavily on luxury goods for an elitist clientele and did not consider changing to mass production. In France the emphasis on a nationalist approach to the decorative arts overlooked the developments of the Munich Werkstätten, and in the vacuum left from Art Nouveau there was a revival of eighteenth and nineteenth-century styles with garlands, swags and bouquet motifs and neo-classical references. This, combined with the charms of Orientalism and the exoticism of Les Ballet Russes and Diaghilev's production of *Schéhérazade* in 1909, produced the repertoire of Art Deco which culminated in the 1925 Exposition des Art Décoratifs et Industriels Modernes.

With the initial help of Seizo Sugawara Gray was provided with further instruction, and the two remained as friends and in partnership for many years. They shared the same tools and workboxes, one of the tools even had the initials 'G' and 'S'. Gray also kept Sugawara's cabinet, his professional stamp and she kept a piece of his lacquer for herself.[15] Sugawara was born in Sakata city in Yamagata Prefecture in North West Honshu on 29 January 1884.[16] His early training was with a maker of Butsudan – traditional

4.6 Lacquer tools, 1910-1930, wood, metal, hair, pumice stone, pigment, polishing stones © NMI

Buddhist shrines made in lacquer. He was apprenticed from an early age to a shrine maker in Jahoji.[17] In 1905, at the age of twenty-one he was chosen to accompany Shoka Tsujimura (1867-1929) a professor in lacquer from the École des Beaux-Arts Tokyo to Paris.[18] Tsujimura had been invited by the French government to teach the art of lacquer.[19] Seizo Sugawara was one of Eileen Gray's early lacquer teachers, but the exact date as to when they met still remains unclear.[20] Gray states in her personal notes that by 1908 she was working with a Japanese lacquer craftsman.[21] Gray later stated of their meeting, 'I was very glad when Sougawara (sic) who was lodging with some friends came to see me and we decided to start a workshop'.[22]

The Japanese Pavilion left an indelible impression at the Exposition

Universelle of 1900 where work from the Rimpa School, notably Ogata Korin (1658-1716), was on display.[23] The decision for Sugawara amongst other Japanese lacquer craftsmen to leave Japan for Europe at the time was an indication of how difficult it was to pursue this traditional craft as a career in his native homeland. With the emergence of Art Nouveau at the Paris Exhibition of 1900 the École des Beaux-Arts in Tokyo amongst other schools set up decorative arts departments which permitted artisans like Tsujimura to work in workshops in Paris such as the atelier Gaillard.[24] Some artisans worked in appalling conditions; many returned home, others received government grants for the duration of their stay in Paris. For those who settled in Paris, like Sugawara, they appeared to have lived in the district around rue de Théatre.[25]

Sugawara and Gray formed a very successful partnership. Initially working out of her apartment, they finally opened a workshop in 1910 on the rue Guénégaud where they produced lacquer work.[26] He became Gray's mentor, teaching her this technique, and after she had mastered the art to perfection, he continued to appear on her payroll for lacquer work.

Sugawara was an important lacquer artist in his own right. Jean Dunand (1877-1942), the renowned French lacquer artist who had first met Gray in 1908, came to study under Sugawara after Gray made the initial introduction. Dunand first met Sugawara on 18 February 1912.[27] Sugawara had an interest in the dinanderie work of Dunand and they initiated each other into their respective techniques. The first lesson took place on 16 May 1912 and was followed by twelve more, running to July. Gray remained in contact with Dunand and his son Bernard (1908-1998), who would become one of the most important designers from the Art Deco period.

Lacquer, though it has a remarkable lustrous finish, requires a painstaking method of production. True lacquer is a resin drawn from the Rhus vernicifera, peculiar to China and Japan. In its natural state, once it is filtered from its impurities, it forms a dense liquid which when exposed to oxygen under humid conditions dries slowly to form a hard, impermeable surface. The liquid resin is mixed with powdered stone and then Gray usually applied thin layers onto a wood base. The wood had to be smoothed down with a pumice stone and then the grain was filled in. Then the top is concealed with fine silk or hemp which is pasted on with rice gum. To achieve the required result of a lustrous finish usually twenty to thirty coats had to be applied and each layer took several days to dry. Then they were pumiced over again before the next application. Each of these coats had to be applied in a dust-free environment. The drying process took two to four days and initially the most suitable environment she found was her own bathroom.[28] In her notebook she recorded that 'when lacquer has been left some time before applying a fresh coat or relief always clean well by rubbing over with – for black and solid grounds – charcoal powder and water – for delicate grounds tomoko (a type of Japanese clay) and water'.[29]

Lacquer dries to a rich, dark brown colour when left to dry in its natural form. Yet Gray experimented with natural pigments producing black, brown and brilliant orange and red variations.[30] At one point she experimented with the use of cigarette paper instead of gold or silver leaf.[31] Each of her experiments in colours, materials and techniques she meticulously began to record in a notebook on lacquer which she used for nearly twenty-five years.[32] On how to achieve a rough surface and to give lacquer texture she noted, 'To make a rugged surface in lacquer give a coat of transparent lacquer and on to it drop grains of the powder of colour chosen, wait about three hours and then cover the whole surface with powder brushing it backwards and forwards about three or more times at intervals of a few hours. Leave it dry about two or three days then wash over with sponge and water to wash off sulphurous powder, dry with very fine rag, when perfectly dry give sesame with colour wood'.[33] She learnt the entire process with a lot of patience and when mistakes were made, especially if she applied too much lacquer, it rippled or cracked and she began all over again. The art critic Louis Vauxcelles (1870-1943) observed Gray working and wrote, 'The slightest error forces her to abandon her work and start anew. An assiduous labour. What a paradox in our frenetic times'.[34]

Many of the entries in Gray's lacquer notebook are undated and read like recipes, making them difficult to read but it gives much insight into the laborious and admirable nature of her task and her technique. Gray was the first lacquer artist to successfully achieve the colour blue. Initially her experimentations produced a blue which when dried had a green hue which she disliked. When attempting to achieve this colour she contacted Charles's workshop in London and was given clear directions. Gray later achieved a new and improved recipe. 'For blue ground use common ultramarine, add a little chrome green or crimson lake according to the amount required'.[35] As Gray's technique improved the use of other colours did not elude her and she explored the development of yellow, cinnabar and the colour white.

While Gray's innovativeness is for the large areas of undecorated lacquer, she also recorded in her notebook her achievements in metallic relief, inlaying mother of pearl, eggshell, gilding with both gold and silver and how to incise decoration onto panels. Her research would have been endless if it had not been for the regrettable difficulties in the length of time it took to import lacquer and the fact also that she had hoped to produce for a mass market. In his article in *L'Amour de l'art* Vauxcelles gave much insight into Gray's methodology. 'In the field of the applied arts talent is nothing without professionalism...Eileen Gray knows this. She works with a wise slow method for herself'. He continued, 'She joins oils to the ordinary varnish, iron sulphate, rice vinegar, then the colours, black, yellow, aventurine, red. She then measures out carefully the gum, black animal dye, tea oil, pork bile, cinnabar, cochineal, coromandel, orpiment. This is the reason for her subdued tones, like the night covered in stars, and the lacquer work of our Irishwoman is encrusted with mother of pearl, coral, semi-precious stones, lapis lazuli, all in harmony with the material and the theme'.[36]

4.7 Hamanaka's signature and ideogram signature in coral-red lacquer, detail on sofa, 1935, black lacquer, dyed black rubbed shagreen, wood, coral pigment © Galerie Dutko

Her partnership with Sugawara expanded into a workshop in 1910 at the rue Guénégaud when Gray's apartment became too cluttered with material. Sugawara also produced sculptural heads which Gray exhibited at *Jean Désert*. Their working relationship lasted from 1908-1930, after which Gray closed her shop in rue Faubourg St Honoré. Through Sugawara, Gray was introduced to other craftsmen, Ousouda, Kichizo Inagaki (1876-1951), who worked for Rodin, and Katsu Hamanaka (1895-1982), who was a pupil of Sugawara and became a famous lacquer craftsman in Europe from the beginning of the 1930s. Gray kept a Christmas card from Hamanaka after their initial meeting.[37]

In his own atelier Sugawara employed up to twenty artisans and married one of the polishing assistants.[38] When Gray closed her decorating shop *Jean Désert*, Sugawara took charge of the Rothschild Collection at Cernay-la-Ville. The

4.8 A three-panelled black lacquered and gold leaf screen, black lacquered back, Katsu Hamanaka, 1930s, wood, black lacquer, gold leaf © Galerie Dutko

Rothschilds were clients of Gray's. He also did work for the artist, writer and Art Deco designer Eyre de Lanux (1894-1996) and Evelyn Wyld (1882-1973) when they opened a decorator's shop in Cannes. Wyld and Gray had formed a very successful weaving workshop in the rue de Visconti and had remained friends for many years. Sugawara remained in France until his death on 12 April 1937.[39]

Gray worked with and depended on a number of these Japanese artisans and craftsmen for her commissions. Some were employed for particular tasks and Gray kept records of these.[40] The names which appeared frequently in her ledgers are Inagaki and Ousouda.[41] Between 1912- 1921 Inagaki corresponded and invoiced Gray regarding various items of furniture, handles, Cubist-style lamps and lamp-shades and produced pieces for various commissions, notably some of the work for Mme Mathieu-Lévy's *Rue de Lota apartment*. These notes, invoices and letters give much insight into the materials she used such as parchment, ostrich eggs and ivory and the techniques she employed such as scorching wood and then sanding it down to add to the textures and variety to her pieces. Gray also kept the business cards and details of various craftsmen, suppliers and workshops where she could purchase necessary items suitable to her trade.[42] Any materials which weren't used by these craftsmen Gray kept – often experimenting with them as sculpture – which is what she did in November 1916 with leftover ivory handles for a piece of furniture.[43]

From 1908 onwards Gray began to produce small lacquer pieces but she said that in 1910 she began to produce screens.[44] Indeed her first object she completed in lacquer was a screen.[45] This continued into lacquer panels and furniture ranging from chairs, tables, bureaus, beds and dressing tables. Soon she expanded into domestic pieces, bowls, plates, toiletries. Her first screen which she produced in blue lacquer inlaid with mother of pearl was a large four-panel screen produced for a friend Florence Gardiner in 1912 and was called *La Voie Lactée* (the Milky Way).[46]

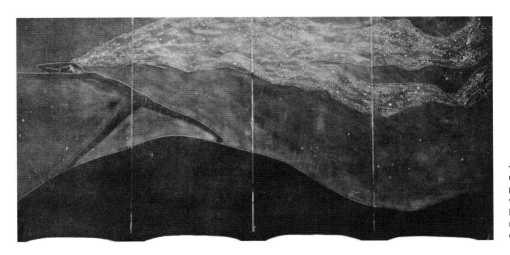

4.9 *La Voie Lactée* (the Milky Way) four-panelled screen, 1912, wood, blue and natural lacquer, engraved, raised colours, mother of pearl inlay © NMI

It was reproduced in *Vogue* magazine in 1917 illustrating an abstract nude figure running over a mountain, a trail of constellations of stars extends across the night's sky, emitting from the figure's head.[47] It was also illustrated in the Dutch magazine *Wendigen* in 1924.[48] The work has now disappeared but it was described in the French magazine *Les Feuillets d'Art* by the Duchess Clermont-Tonnerre saying it depicted 'The dust haze of the Milky Way, made from mother of pearl thrown over the matt of the lacquered leaves of the screen'.[49] At the eighth Salon des Artistes Décorateurs in 1913 Gray exhibited two lacquer panels, a yellow and silver panel for a library, a door panel and a frieze. The first was a blue lacquer panel, *Le Magician de la Nuit* (The Magician of the Night), 1912-13, which attracted considerable attention.[50] The second panel was entitled *Om Mani Padme Hum,* 1912-13.[51] A critic in *Art et Décoration* stated after seeing her display that, 'Miss Gray uses that admirable material lacquer... Seeing her entries one regrets that this beautiful technique is not more favoured by our decorators'.[52]

As with many of her lacquer screens and panels the subject matter is compelling and mysterious. The author from *Vogue* magazine asked 'What is the mystery which impels?'[53] There is a spiritual, enchanting quality to the stories Gray depicts in many of her lacquer panels and screens, evident in the names. Inspired by the contemporary art movements such as Symbolism, Surrealism, Cubism, the subject matter for these pieces is derived from books in her library on mythology (Greek, Persian, Indian and Irish Celtic), poetry, psychology and philosophy.

A number of pieces are possibly inspired by the publications of Aleister Crowley, of which Gray owned various books. Crowley wrote the *Book of Law,* 1904. In this publication Nut, the Egyptian sky goddess who became Nuit or Nut the goddess of Crowley's religion Thelema, asks Crowley to reveal herself to the world in his writings. Gray has looked to Crowley's text and has taken it as an interpretation of a representation of Nuit and of Nut. In many pantheons sky deities are male while earth is female. In Egyptian mythology this symbolism is reversed. For time to begin, sky and earth need to be separated. In the screen Gray carefully divided the entire composition into the sky and the mountainous earth with Nuit traversing through the middle, her arms outstretched to the west where the sun sets and running from the jet stream of stars running across the sky in her wake from the east. Gray's use of the colour blue with the screen is also significant to the story of Nuit, who is often set against a blue night or represented by the use of a deep purple. Gray owned a copy of Crowley's book *An Essay in Ontology with some remarks on Ceremonial Magic.*[54] The book discusses the theory of the universe to the world according to Crowley. His theory explores the divergences between the great forms of religion Buddhism, Hinduism and Christianity, adapting them to the ontological science through mathematics. Crowley finishes the publication with 'Om Mani Padme Hum' the six sounds of the sacred Buddhist prayer meaning 'Hail the Jewel in the Lotus' – which became the title of one of Gray's panels which she exhibited at the eighth Salon des Artistes Décorateurs in 1913.

Another publication which Gray owned is entitled *In the Great God's Hair* by Francis William Bain (1863-1940), published in 1905.[55] Bain was a British writer of fantasy stories which he claimed were translated from Sanskrit. In this publication there is a story entitled 'A Lotus of the World'. Though Gray's edition is dated 1917, *In the Great God's Hair* was initially published in 1905. Gray's blue lacquer panel *Le Magician de la Nuit,* is a rendition of this story of Wishnu and his wife Waterlily. The scene which Gray depicts is just after Wishnu has whispered his wife's name to the sea and the goddess of love emerges from the blue holding a lotus flower which she presents to Waterlily. The critic Maurice Pillard-Verneuil reported in *Art et Décoration* about the Salon commenting 'Miss Gray uses that admirable material lacquer and creates with it interesting and unusual

4.10 *An Essay in Ontology with some remarks on Ceremonial Magic,* by Aleister Crowley, 1903 © NMI

4.11 *Le Magician de la Nuit* (The Magician of the Night) lacquer panel, 1912-13, wood, blue and natural lacquer, engraved, raised colours © NMI

mantelpieces, friezes, and library panels. Seeing her entries, one regrets that this beautiful technique is not more favoured by our decorators.'[56]

Gray's work caught the attention of Vicomte Charles de Noailles (1891-1981) and Élisabeth de Gramont (Antonia Corisande Élisabeth de Gramont, 1875-1954). Though an aristocrat, society hostess and descendant of Henry IV of France (1553-1610) de Gramont was a staunch socialist, opinionated, outspoken and openly bisexual. She married Philibert, Duc de Clermont-Tonnerre and had two daughters. The duchess was a friend of Gertrude Stein and lover of Natalie Clifford Barney, a mutual friend of Gray's. Her left-wing political beliefs earned her the nickname the Red Duchess. Others simply knew her as Lily. Gray knew her as *l'Orage* (The Storm), which was a pun on her name *Tonnerre*, meaning Thunder. Both would become inextricably linked with Gray, as clients and authors and supporters of her work in the years to come.

At the salon the panel *Le Magician de la Nuit* caught the attention of Jacques Doucet, a famous French fashion designer and patron of the arts who had an admirable collection. He visited her in her flat where she was

4.12 *Le Destin* (The
Destiny) four-
panelled screen, 1913,
wood, red and blue
lacquer, silver leaf,
engraved, raised
colours © Archives
Galerie Vallois - Paris,
Arnaud Carpentier

working on another panel called *Le Destin*, (the Destiny) which she began
in 1913 but completed in 1914. He purchased it immediately and insisted
Gray sign it. This four-panelled screen has deep red panels. On one side
it depicts two Greek inspired figures, one his hand outstretched trying
to stop the other from removing a cloak in the form of a human figure.

On the other side it is covered in swirling symbolist lines. At this time Doucet had just sold his impressive eighteenth-century art and furniture collection and had acquired an apartment on avenue du Bois (now avenue Foch).[57] His collection of modern paintings was also astounding, including Pablo Picasso's *les Demoiselles d'Avignon* and *La Charmeuse de Serpents* (The Snake Charmer) by Henri Rousseau (1844-1910).[58] He employed André Breton and Louis Aragon to choose and build up his collection of modern art work, including key works by Constantin Brâncuși (1876-1957), George Braque, Pablo Picasso, Amadeo Modigliani, Francis Picabia, Vincent Van Gogh (1853-1890) and sculpture by Joseph Csáky. In the last years of his life Doucet's project became the redecoration of his studio on the rue Saint-James at Neuilly under the direction of the designer Paul Iribe (1883-1935).[59] Gray was commissioned to design several pieces of furniture for Doucet. Although Paul Iribe employed Eileen Gray, he would later attack the work of progressive and enthusiastic modern designers and architects in his publication *Défense de Luxe,* 1932.

The subject matter for Gray's screen *Le Destin* is possibly taken from three publications which she had in her library telling the same story of *Tannhäuser.* Firstly she owned a copy of *The Early Work of Aubrey Beardsley*, 1899 by John Lane. This publication examined unpublished illustrations, notably the story of *Venus and Tannhäuser* which Beardsley finally published as an erotic novel entitled *Under the Hill* in 1904, which Gray also owned. Beardsley inspired Gray, especially in her treatment of the figures in her screens and panels such as *Le Magician de la Nuit* and *Le Destin.* His black ink drawings with their use of a defined line which were influenced by Japanese woodcuts, his arrangement and handling of his subjects, his treatment of the human figure, and how his use of landscape was subordinate to the decorative effect all influenced her lacquer screens and panels.

The third publication telling the story was again by Aleister Crowley of *Tannhäuser, a Story of All Time* in 1902.[60] The legend of *Tannhäuser* was made famous in modern times through Richard Wagner's (1813-1883) three-act opera completed in 1845. Gray has possibly taken a combination of Crowley's play and Wagner's opera as she depicts a moment from the dramatic last part of the story when Tannhäuser returns to Venusberg. Gray depicts the moment when Tannhäuser is removing his pilgrim cloak – the moment that he is about to learn what true love actually is, only to learn that his true love is actually dead.

Another publication of Gray's – *The Odyssey of Homer,* published in 1903 – is also a possible explanation for the story of *Le Destin.*[61] While the front of the screen *Le Destin* displays a figurative work, the back is artistically modern. Sweeping linear motifs which were the precursor to a typical Gray style from 1918 through to the 1920s appear across the panels. Inspired by Futurism, abstraction and the writings of Wassily Kandinsky's essay *On the Spiritual in Art,* 1910, the back of *Le Destin* embraces total abstraction, where these linear graphics became constant. Gray's use of large swirling lines, was inspired by the work of Giacomo Balla, whereas the thin curling thin lines were inspired by Paul Klee.

From 1913-15 Doucet commissioned Gray to produce several pieces of furniture for his new modern collection and she produced some of her most important early pieces. These include *The Lotus table,* echoing the imagery of the lotus flower which appeared as a central feature in the panel *Le Magicien de la Nuit.* It was the perfect synthesis of form and decoration as Gray uses the legs to spread into flowers to support the top

4.13 *The Lotus table,* 1913-14, black and dark green lacquer, ivory paint, wood
© Archives Galerie Vallois - Paris, Arnaud Carpentier

4.14 *The Charioteer table*, 1913-15, red and black lacquer, wood, with ebony and ivory handle © Archives Galerie Vallois - Paris, Arnaud Carpentier

4.15 *The Charioteer table*, 1913-15, shown in situ in Jacques Doucet's apartment in the hall, in *L'Illustration*, 1930 © *NMI*

of the table. There is a stark contrast between the white of the flower and the deep dark green of the lacquer. It occupied the famed Oriental Cabinet (1926-29) of Doucet's apartment. She also did the *Charioteer table* where Gray used a similar idea, incorporating the charioteer and its wheels into the top of the legs. This occupied the hall in Doucet's apartment. She was also commissioned to do the *Bilboquet table*, which is a low design of two circles supported on block-like legs composed of cubic blocks. It is quite classical and architectonic in form with the legs of the table appearing like columns. It was positioned next to a sofa by Marcel Coard (1889-1975) and with a chest by Paul Iribe and carpets by Jean Lurçat (1892-1966).[62] Bilboquet is a French cup and ball game and Doucet made her add a cup and ball design in red and silver lacquer on the top of the table, a request which she resented. Gray was

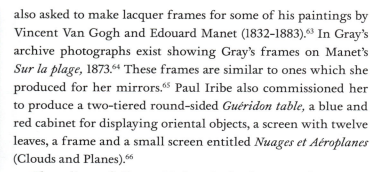

4.16 Lacquer frame, 1913-15, surrounding *Sur la plage*, 1873, by Édouard Manet, black and natural brown Chinese lacquer, wood © NMI

also asked to make lacquer frames for some of his paintings by Vincent Van Gogh and Edouard Manet (1832-1883).[63] In Gray's archive photographs exist showing Gray's frames on Manet's *Sur la plage,* 1873.[64] These frames are similar to ones which she produced for her mirrors.[65] Paul Iribe also commissioned her to produce a two-tiered round-sided *Guéridon table,* a blue and red cabinet for displaying oriental objects, a screen with twelve leaves, a frame and a small screen entitled *Nuages et Aéroplanes* (Clouds and Planes).[66]

The editor of *Vogue*, Madge Garland, reported on Gray in Paris, discussing and illustrating the screen *Le Destin,* a rectangular blue lacquer table, the top decorated with the signs of the zodiac and a planet in the middle, and another table with Koi fish swimming in a pool depicted on the table top which complemented a carpet that Gray had produced at that time.[67]

4.17 *The Children of Lir* lacquer panel, 1916-17, black and natural brown Chinese lacquer, sabi, wood, engraved, raised colours, gold and silver leaf © NMI

It also illustrated part of a lacquer door panel commissioned by Jacques Doucet.[68] The style of the front of the panel suggests Gray's early interest in Cubism, as the form of a woman and a man and two swans have been simplified to basic geometric shapes. The back of the panel is an explosion of Cubic geometric shapes, consisting of lacquer and wood collage. It appears like a form of Synthetic Cubism which has been applied to lacquer panelling. Her use of such motifs was unique for this period and predates the lacquer work of her contemporaries, as it wasn't until 1921 that Jean Dunand first exhibited a lacquer screen with similar type decoration.[69] Gray was influenced by Cubism as advocated by the ideas of the Section d'Or, and adapted it in her work through a variety of media. The back of the Jacques Doucet panel is stripped, linear, consisting of multiple forms and facets echoing the work of Albert Gleizes and the ideas he and Jean Metzinger put forward in the publication *Du Cubisme* in 1912. The forms appear as if depicting a number of viewpoints in rotation, with Gray attempting to create various dimensions. This story on the panel is identifiable as an Irish myth called *The Children of Lir.* Gray was very interested in Irish mythology and the stories of the *Táin Bó Cúalilnge* (The Driving-off of the Cattle of Cooley) and had publications in her library about Irish mythology, notably

L'Épopée Irlandaise (The Irish Epic) by Henri Georges Dottin (1863–1928).[70] This door panel was part of a commission from a series of twelve for Doucet for the doors of the salon; however, it remained incomplete as the couturier cancelled the commission when he saw it published.[71]

Photographs of Doucet's collection were shown in *Fémina* in February 1925, of the interior of Doucet's apartment at avenue du Bois and then, when he moved to Neuilly, of his modern studio at 33 rue de Saint-James, in the magazine *L'Illustration* in May 1930.[72] Gray's name was never mentioned in its credits. In 1929 Doucet passed away shortly after the completion of the studio.[73]

August 1914 saw the outbreak of the First World War. During the war Eileen Gray worked as an ambulance driver for a brief spell and kept her Red Cross armband throughout her life.[74] In 1915 she decided to leave France and return to London. Seizo Sugawara came with her. Taking the majority of her tools and a number of unfinished pieces she rented a property at Cheyne Walk. It had a spare room in the back for Sugawara to sleep. Gray remained at the family house in The Boltons in South Kensington. The family would suffer from many hardships during the war. Gray kept images of her mother and two sisters saying goodbye to her brother James at Tilbury.[75] Her sister Ethel had two sons who fought in World War I; Lindsay, a major with the Royal Field Artillery, was thrice wounded. Mentioned in despatches, he was decorated with the award of the Military Cross. Gray's other nephew, Henry, a Second Lieutenant in the service of the Argyll and Sutherland highlanders, and only 19, was tragically killed in action at Ypres. Gray also kept a photograph of her

4.18 The *Lotus table*, 1913-14, shown in situ in Jacques Doucet's apartment in the Oriental cabinet, in *L'Illustration*, 1930 © NMI

4.19 The *Bilboquet table*, 1913-14, shown in situ in Jacques Doucet's apartment in the studio, in *L'Illustration*, 1930 © NMI brother in law Eric Clough Taylor wearing his uniform, taken by society photographer and Irishman George C. Beresford (1864-1938) in 1917. Beresford had taken numerous portraits of Irish painters, authors and many from her circle, notably Wyndham Lewis and Augustus John. Gray had several portraits taken by him in 1917.

This period in London was stylistically important to the lacquer work which Gray produced after the war. Once again it was primarily through the influence of her circle that Gray's work and ideas evolved. Though she continued doing lacquer she had no commercial success, as she only sold a table while living in London. However, she actively began attending exhibitions and acquiring art literature produce by the Camden Town and Bloomsbury Groups. This period would have a profound stylistic effect on her lacquer work when she would eventually return to Paris.[76]

4.20 Wyndham Lewis, by George Charles Beresford, 1902, half plate glass negative © National Portrait Gallery, London

The Bloomsbury Group rejected the distinction between fine and decorative art and their focus and emphasis on form became notions of inherent value when Gray began producing her lacquer panels and screens. Gray knew many individuals from both groups. Kelly had introduced her to art critic Clive Bell (1881-1964) and his wife Vanesa Stephens (1879-1961) when they were in Paris, and Gray acquired texts by art critic and painter Roger Fry (1866-1934) on their ideas.[77] Gray's friend and fellow artist Wyndham Lewis had been back living in London for a number of years since 1908. In 1909 Lewis was a member of the Camden Town Group along with Augustus John – an artistic group whose work was characterised by Social Realist subject matter, a Post-Impressionist style and experimentation with strong colour. Lewis, like Gray, had a profound interest in caricaturists and his work achieved notoriety for his extreme use of satirical vision and grotesque characters. Both Gray and Lewis were drawn to Filippo Tommaso Marinetti's Futurist movement. Gray was fascinated with the Futurists impressionist attempt to capture moving form with which Giacomo Balla and his colleagues experimented. This was an art of implicit energy and power. In both artists' work from 1912-1916 they rely on Japanese art – Lewis used the canvas as his medium, Gray her lacquer commissions. This oriental aesthetic favoured asymmetry and large areas of empty space on the surface. Just like Gray, Lewis presented key moments in classical tragedy, Gray looked to a key moment to display on her lacquer panels and screens from various sources of mythology.

By 1914 Lewis had become part of a more radical movement, Vorticism, supported by the American poet Ezra Pound (1885-1972), who later became one of Gray's clients. The group produced two issues of the celebrated magazine *Blast*. Gray immediately purchased a copy of *Blast Volume I*.[78] First published in 1914 this literary magazine represented the ideas of the Vorticist movement and its editor was Wyndham Lewis. *Volume I* was written and illustrated by a group of artists which Lewis had assembled and their ideas had a profound influence on Gray's post-war lacquer work.

However, by late 1917 Gray decided to return to France. First she drove to Enniscorthy to say farewell to her mother, and then began making a long and difficult journey back to Paris with Sugawara. In Paris Gray picked up the bare threads of her career. She was still interested in the social thinking of the Munich Vereinigte Werkstätten. Though she had produced commissions prior to the war for a discerning clientele, she had also produced simple bowls, boxes and plates to be used for everyday living in the hope that these low-cost items could be produced in quantity for the needs of the emerging middle class.[79] These simple unadorned pieces are more reflective of Munich Vereinigte Werkstätten's ideologies and of Gray's attitude to her lacquer work. Gray kept very little of her work from her lacquer period except some bowls, plates, a tray and a mirror. However, French manufacturers were still not interested in designers such as Gray who wanted to produce her lacquer work for mass audiences.

4.21 Lacquer tray, 1919, natural brown Chinese lacquer, wood © NMI

In 1919 Gray participated in the Tenth Salon des Artistes Décorateurs displaying a screen entitled *La Nuit*,[80] however it quickly became apparent to Gray that the annual exhibitions at the Salon exhibited the same emphasis on luxurious goods and French elitism as they did prior to the war.[81] Despite the poverty of the working classes the prosperity among the affluent brought a desire to change lifestyles and those with money could afford to change their houses and apartments. The art and activity of redecorating became popular practice among the elite of French society and many people remembered the woman designer who had been involved with Doucet's apartment.[82]

Despite the devastation of the war and the need to address the social changes and problems in the country, the world of the French decorative arts advocated a return to French tradition, the use of French material resources and a move away from all things foreign.[83] A new vocabulary was emerging and the Art Deco style was born. Partly traditional, partly avant-garde, it amalgamated influences from various movements including Dada's machine aesthetic, Surrealism's interest in the subconscious, Cubism and Fauvism's geometry and bold colours, the machine forms of Futurism, Constructivism, Vorticism, the Wiener Werkstätte and the Münchner Werkbund. Art Deco interiors were aimed at the social elite, paraphrasing African art, Egyptian temples, animal fantasy themes, Native American wares, Babylonian ziggurats, Mexican forms and Pre-Columbian architecture. Traditional themes harked back to Baroque furniture and the late eighteenth-century derivatives of Louis XV and Louis Philippe styles.

Lacquer was once again in vogue. The style culminated at the 1925 Paris Exposition Internationale des Arts Décoratifs et Industriels Modernes which included fashion, fabrics, interior decoration, furniture design, as

4.22 The pavilion of the national factory of Sèvres, at the Paris Exposition Internationale des Arts Decoratifs et Industriels Modernes, 1925, black and white photograph © Roger Viollet/ Topfoto

well as architecture from Italy, Russia, Poland, the Netherlands, Austria, Britain, Spain, Belgium, Czechoslovakia, Japan, Denmark, Sweden and France. Though a member of the Société des Artistes Décorateurs, Gray did not participate in the 1925 Exhibition and she clearly stated she did not wish to be associated with this period in design.[84]

An article on Gray appeared in *Harper's Bazaar* which brought her once again to the attention of fashionable society. 'There is in Paris today an artist whose lacquer is exciting much interest among those mondaines who must be among the first to sanction something new, in people, art or drama. When Miss Gray exhibited her first work in this difficult medium the smart world of Paris first stared, then talked, and then of course, accepted it avidly. It was new, distinctly novel and oh so very, very expensive. And so, over night, as it were, lacquer rooms became the rage'.[85] In *Le Journal du Peuple* on 6 April 1919, Gray's lacquer work was described as nothing short of miraculous.[86]

In 1919 Gray was recommended by Madame Tachard, a friend of Doucet's to Juliette Lévy a society hostess and wife of Mathieu Lévy to redecorate her apartment at the rue de Lota. Juliette Lévy was the owner of the fashion house and millinery shop which had been started by Tachard, called J. Suzanne Talbot. Talbot was a celebrated designer known for her hats and stylish clothing amongst elite Parisian circles. Lévy was impassioned about Primitive art and was the owner of an impressive collection of Chinese, Egyptian and African objects and it reflected in the completed commission. This commission offered Eileen Gray the first opportunity to create her first environment and to be an interior designer – an unheard of appointment for a woman during the 1910s. This meant the planning of walls, decors, lighting and fixtures. Gray's friend and client, Élisabeth de Gramont wrote an article on Gray in *Les Feuillets d'Art* in 1922. The article was of seminal importance to Gray's career as it clearly defines Gray as an interior designer. It demonstrates the move from furniture designer and lacquer artist into a new realm where she wanted entire control of the environment which she was creating. The article discusses the mystery of lacquer and how it had long fascinated Eileen Gray. Gramont had noted how Gray aimed to create interiors which were adapted to everyday life. 'Miss Gray wants to create the room as a whole, from the curtains, hangings, the rugs, the fabrics to the lighting, to shape a unity as beautiful as a poem'.[87] Gramont summarises exactly what Gray was attempting to achieve. 'The most difficult thing is the removal of those useless ornaments, traditional ugliness, which embosses walls, cornices and ceilings. Her artistic sense suffers at the thought that the objects she has created will be flung, as it pleases the buyers in any old room so that the owner may say with pride "You see I also like the modern style"'.[88]

The apartment took her four years to complete, from 1918 to 1922, yet the result was luxurious in the extreme and yet of such great simplicity that it stood out radically from the interiors of other decorators. Lévy had specifically wanted the salon to be 'face à une lumière éclantante avoir une ambience reposante' (for the salon to be full of bright light yet having a relaxing atmosphere).[89] Gray firstly had to cover the 'disgraceful mouldings' which covered the hall and the walls of the salon.[90] The salon's walls were decorated with uninterrupted panelled screens, streaked in geometrical designs of linear sweeps with overtones of matt grey, silver and gold which were slightly tarnished in places.[91] Hanging from the salon walls were hand-woven wall carpets. The doors into the salon were decorated with silver inlay. At first glance the lacquer wall panels, the furnishings and the furniture showcased the prevailing French taste for opulence, luxury and exoticism which had been popular prior to the war and which were being readily emphasised in the taste of contemporary interiors. This unique expression of interior decoration shows a rare homogeneity. However, Gray combines French luxury while addressing the ideas of total design of the Munich Werkstätten, where furnishings and the room are integrated. Even her furniture for this commission changed in its language, becoming more sculptural. Lévy wanted something extravagant for the salon, so Gray produced the *Pirogue sofa bed*. It was one of three which she produced during her lifetime. This canoe-shaped daybed with gold cushions was completed in *laque arrachée*. This is where the lacquer is scraped away to simulate an effect of tortoiseshell lacquer. During this period Gray created several domestic objects using this technique – the *Pirogue sofa bed* was the first such large-scale project which she finished this way.[92]

There was a bookcase done in chestnut brown lacquer, where the shelves could be adjusted to suit the height of the books. There was a famous *Serpent chair* or *Dragon armchair* with two serpents completed in natural wood

4.23 Juliette Lévy lying on the *Pirogue sofa bed*, 1918-22, black and white photograph © NMI

4.24 The salon at the *Rue de Lota apartment*, 1918-22, black and white photograph © NMI

and lacquer that were rearing along its sides completed in dotted yellow lacquer. The Cubist fittings and light fixtures were unusual, using lacquer, parchment and ostrich eggs. There was a screen taken from a series which Gray completed in the early 1920s. Each of the screens had a variation on the same theme with incised linear decoration set in deep brown lacquer. The linear decoration displays Vorticist influences and offsets the linear sweeping lines on the salon's wall. It also displays an element which began to appear in a number of Gray's lacquer pieces – the use of three semicircles as a decorative motif. It appears on other lacquer pieces produced such as domestic bowls and on a series of grey console tables which she produced around 1919.

4.25 The *Pirogue sofa bed*, 1918-22, natural brown Chinese lacquer, tortoiseshell lacquer technique, wood © Archives Galerie Vallois - Paris, Arnaud Carpentier

4.26 The *Dragon armchair*, 1917-19, rounded, brown leather, padded arm chair, wood, natural brown lacquer, with orange and silver leaf patina © Christies images

There were also series of carpets, runner rugs and wall hangings, which complemented individual pieces of furniture in the scheme. Many of the pieces linked into Lévy's interest in tribal art – long African-style tables and lamps.[93] She also included in the commission more classical pieces of furniture such as an enfilade, which Gray possibly made and Sugawara assembled in England during the war.[94] Gray saw the enfilade many years later and stated that it had been altered and the handles changed.[95]

The apartment was also clearly an artistic manifestation of Cubism, Futurism and Vorticism which she combined with the prevailing French tastes for Africanism and Primitivism. Gray wholeheartedly had embraced the sweeping lines which she saw in the work of Marcel Duchamp and Giacomo Balla along with the dynamism of line and motifs which she had seen in the work of Wyndham Lewis during her war period in London. This did not go unnoticed by the critics. One writer from *Harper's Bazaar* in September 1920 said of the apartment 'Her style is thoroughly modern… the walls might pose as studies from the latest Cubist exhibition'. At least one panel might be 'The Nude Descending the Staircase'.[96] *Nu descendant un escalier no.2* (Nude Descending a Staircase No.2) was Duchamp's most celebrated work which in 1912 was rejected by the Cubists for being too Futurist.[97] Duchamp had been at the Académie Julian in 1904 – the same time as Gray – and he was one of the Puteaux Group who she had followed with interest.

4.27 Details of Cubist-style parchment lamps from the *Rue de Lota apartment*, 1918-22, black and photograph © NMI

The salon also reveals another developing interest of Gray's at that time. Élisabeth de Gramont summarises Gray's ambition in *Les Feuillets d'Art* saying 'Her difficult ambition is to make suites of perfect cohesion. She wants to create interiors in keeping with our lives, with the dimensions of our rooms, and with the aspirations of our sensitivity'.[98]

The critic and architect Jean Badovici also indicates this in his article on Gray in *Wendigen,* stating that Gray's art expresses a 'sensibility which vibrates with new and rich forms reflecting the new way of life'.[99] Lévy wanted the room to appeal to the senses and sensitivities. This embraced Gray's interest in synaesthesia and her developing knowledge and profound interest in the philosophical ideology of the third and fourth dimension. Gray had numerous books in her library exploring the subject, not only in philosophy but also in art. The concept of creating and embracing another realm was being actively explored by the Cubists, Futurists and the Russian avant-garde at that time. She was particularly

4.28 Details of Cubist-style ceiling lights from the *Rue de Lota, apartment*, 1918-22, black and photograph © NMI

4.29 Details of the lighting in the boudoir from *Rue de Lota apartment*, 1918-22, black and photograph © NMI

interested in the Futurist's approach to Peter D. Ouspensky's (1878-1947) ideas on the *Fourth Dimension,* especially Umberto Boccioni. The walls of the salon of Mme Mathieu-Lévy's *Rue de Lota apartment* are examples of Gray's interest in elemental parallelism and parallel multiplication. Gray later would realise that there was nothing four dimensional about the motion of an object unless it moved off into a new fourth dimension. Gray's choice of colours for the walls of the salon was deliberate; natural brown and black tones covered with flecks of gold and streaks of silver. The use of matt greys, silver and gold contrasted with the reflective qualities of the natural lacquer. Gray conceived a celestial environment, and the sweeping geometric lines and bolts on the panelled walls create an impression of thunder and lighting. Combined with the *Pirogue sofa bed,* a type of boat, and the tactile qualities of the soft furnishings, Gray sought to engage all of Lévy's senses, as if she were to sit in the *Pirogue boat* and embark on a celestial journey into another realm. This celestial theme continued into the other rooms of the commission. In the boudoir Gray lined the upper tier of the wall with lights set on metal strips attached to a shallow vault in the ceiling. They appeared like stars 'tincted with nocturnal blue'.[100]

The hall which led into Lévy's bedroom completed in 1922-24 was a monstrous task and marked a departure in Gray's work. She covered the walls with lacquer blocks, which concealed the original mouldings. They were in matt gold, grey and silver and appeared like bricks or cubic screens. Inagaki worked with Gray creating these blocks. In total there were 450 thin lacquer panels each textured with sabi.[101] Half way along, to subdivide the hall's narrow space into a smaller antechamber before entering Lévy's bedroom, they opened out perpendicular to the wall. This created the idea for her block screens which she later developed as freestanding designs. They were architectural in their concept and some of her most striking inventions because they were like moveable walls, playing with space and light. To add to the continuity of the narrow space and to emphasise the Cubic nature of the blocks, Gray installed lanterns with Cubist designs in parchment, offset by a long runner rug with triangular motifs.[102] They had a semicircular arced top and a rectangular shaped body which finished in a point. Decorated with two semicircular shapes with dots and an upside-down 'L' – their geometric shape and decoration were influenced by the Cubist movement. Her portfolio reveals another suspended ceiling lamp consisting of three tiered elements. The central component was

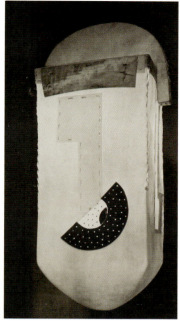

rectangular in shape and it finished in a point facing upward. It was void of decoration, apart from the stitching around the side of the parchment shade. The second and third elements were two rectangular blocks in black parchment, and were again void of decoration apart from the stitching. Towards the end of the hall was a lacquer door in black and gold which led into the bedroom. This architectonic environment was praised by Christian Zervos (1889-1970) in *La Revue de l'art ancient et moderne*.[103] Zervos also featured photographs of her unique furniture in *Les Arts de la Maison* in 1924.[104] Jean Badovici praised her for her ability to create an illusion of space, making a room appear larger than it is. He praises her simple approach to design saying that she has instilled in it a poetical lyricism that she has transcribed into the world of building. The forms she creates, he states, 'are dictated by the function and role which they must fulfil. The smallest details in the overall design are rigorously ordered in relation to the whole object and any useless details, which need to be eliminated, are removed'.[105] Badovici also featured photographs of the apartment to accompany his article on Eileen Gray in *Wendigen* and in *Les Intérieures Français*.[106] Gray wasn't happy with the colour reproductions of the photographs and wrote that the colours were wrong.[107]

4.30 The hall at the *Rue de Lota apartment*, 1922-24, black and photograph © NMI

4.31 Details of Cubist-style parchment lamps in the hall at the *Rue de Lota apartment*, 1922-24, black and photograph © NMI

4.32 Details of the salon walls at the *Rue de Lota apartment*, 1918-22, black and white photograph © NMI

While Gray's commission for Doucet displayed Cubist tendencies, the *Rue de Lota apartment* openly embraced Cubism, Futurism and Vorticism in its design. The word Cubist began to appear frequently in the critics' articles on Eileen Gray's work during this period. Louis Vauxcelles stated of her furniture 'Does one dare pronounce the word cubism? Yes one must'.[108] In *L'Intransigeant* Maurice Reynal wrote how her work was 'a caricature of Cubism and anti-decorative'.[109] The critic L. Watelin states that Gray applied Cubism to 'chandeliers, door handles and drawers'. Her 'ivory is worked in unequal volumes yet maintains a cohesion which is not found in painting'.[110] René Chavance criticised the 'disquieting effects of Cubism'[111] in her work, yet praised her delicate sense of colour which was achieved through suggestions of Cubism.[112]

By the time Gray had completed the *Rue de Lota apartment* she had firmly established herself as reputable designer. On the advice and encouragement of Gabrielle Bloch, Eileen Gray opened a decorating shop as she sought to widen her clientele.[113] On 17 May 1922 she opened her shop *Jean Désert* at 217 rue du Faubourg Saint-Honoré. The exact date as to when Gray first met Jean Badovici is not precisely known but from 1920-21 onward Badovici actively encouraged her to take up architecture. It began firstly with Gray designing the façade for her shop *Jean Désert*, 1922.[114] Wanting the shop to be known for the work, rather than the sex of the designer she aptly named it *Jean Désert*.

However, it is possible that Gray was aware of the book *Les Dimanches de Jean Dézert* by Jean de La Ville de Mirmont (1886-1914) published in 1914. The book was inspired by Jean de La Ville's career as a civil servant. In the book the central character, Jean Dézert lives for his Sundays where he embraces the simple, humdrum of Parisian life, each Sunday being an adventure to be discovered [115] Gray's shop *Jean Désert* was described in *The Chicago Tribune* as an 'adventure: an experience with the unheard of, a sojourn into the never-before-seen'.[116] *The Daily Mail* described the shop as displaying lacquer furniture and furnishings that were both interesting and original.

Gray designed the façade, yet made use of the elements of the original building designed by Charles Letrosne in 1908. She adapted the sculptural elements of the existing façade, placed glass windows in between existing

apertures and completed double entrance doors in black lacquer.[117] In her plans and notes of the layout of the shop she also designed special slabs of blue glass to bring light into the basement, which enabled the passer-by to have a glimpse at what went on there.

4.33 *Jean Désert*, 1922, black and white photograph © NMI

Inside, Gray displayed her own designs (furniture, furnishings and carpets) along with the artwork of Chana Orloff and the sculptures of Seizo Sugawara and Ossip Zadkine.

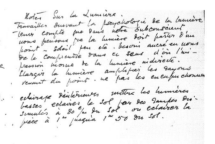

4.34 Notes on light at *Jean Désert*, 1922, paper, ink © NMI

But it was primarily considered a furniture shop according to the official documents.[118] Sugawara produced her lacquer work with the help of Inagaki and about twenty other different artisans at the studio at 11 rue Guénégaud from 1910 to 1930. [119] Evelyn Wyld supervised the rug and carpet weaving at the rue de Visconti workshop from 1910-1924. Everything was sold at the shop. Gray also designed all of the letterheads, cards, invitations and labels for the business, using the Bodoni typeface, an old typeface from the 18th century and showing her interest in typography.[120] *Jean Désert* attracted a distinguished clientele, including well-known politicians, filmmakers, designers, dancers, writers and members of high society from Europe and the United States; film director René Clair, director of the Paris Ópera Jacques Rouché, sculptor Henri Laurens, architects Henri Pacon and Charles Siclis, graphic designer Jean Carlu, politicians Raymond Poincaré and Maurice Thorez, the dancer Loïe Fuller, the fashion designer Elsa Schiaparelli, the opera singer Lucy Vauthrin, the writers James Joyce, Maurice Martin du Gard and Ezra Pound, publisher Sylvia Beach, and the jeweller André Leveillé.[121] Her clients also included Gerald Murphy, the Rothschilds, the Vicomte Charles de Noailles, the Comtesse de Behague, Pierre Meyer, Madame Jeanne Tachard, Madame Jacques Errera, René Raoul Duval who married Gray's friend Jessie Gavin, the car manufacturer Jean Henri Labourdette and the Maharaja of Indore Shri Yeshwant Rao Holkar Bahadur (1908-1961). Since 1906 Gray had been acquainted with and acquired a number of publications by a number of the women who attended Natalie Barney's salon the Temple de l'Amitié on the rue Jacob. Gray's name appears on the frontispiece on the *Poem & Poèmes et autres alliances* published by Barney in 1929 and she also attended the salon on 19 December 1919.[122] Many of these famous women became clients of Jean Désert including Gabrielle Bloch, painter Romaine Brooks, Lucie Delarue-Mardrus, Comtesse Anna de Noailles, the Duchess de Clermont-Tonnerre Élisabeth de Gramont, Élizabeth Éyre de Lanux and Nancy Cunard who opened a shop near Gray on rue Guénégaud.[123]

One famous client was actor and singer Marisa Damia (1892-1978), who was introduced to her by Gaby Bloch. [124] Damia and Gray had a discreet relationship and Damia would come to stay with her at her house in Samois-sur-Seine that she rented from 1921- 1923.[125] In 1919 Gray produced her famous *Siren chair* for Damia. Damia is also listed for a large mirror with a brown and silver frame and Gray lacquered for her a dressing table. The Vicomte de Noailles purchased cushions, a dressing table and rugs for his villa in Hyères.[126] Madame Jacques Errera purchased a large lacquer screen for her bedroom, similar to the one she produced for Lévy.[127] The Rothschilds purchased numerous rugs.[128] The Comtesse de Bahague purchased a large zebra skin throw. Pierre Meyer bought several rugs for his hôtel particulier on the avenue Montaigne. Madame Tachard bought rugs for her villa at La Celle-Saint-Cloud and would later purchase a number of Gray's famous *Bibendum chairs*. Jean Henri Labourdette purchased a black lacquer desk with silver lined drawers and handles in ivory completed by Inagaki, unusual armchairs, three lacquer dining chairs, a lacquer table, another of the lacquer screens similar to the one produced for Lévy, another *Pirogue sofa bed,* this time in natural lacquer, a small stool, a lacquer pouf, a large oak vase and an ostrich egg ceiling lamp.[129] Though Jean Dunand did the lacquer panels which lined Labourdette's salon, Gray later noted in her archives that she arranged the plan of the apartment.[130]

By 1931 Juliette Lévy had moved into a new apartment on the boulevard Suchet, after losing her husband in 1928.[131] Once again Gray was commissioned to do pieces of furniture. Photographs published in *L'Illustration* in 1933 applaud Paul Ruaud as the interior designer, but the photographs reveal that Gray actually did a vast amount of work.[132] The apartment is decorated in light tones in blue and white and silvered glass. Gray, at this time was working with new materials, and this is reflected in the pieces of furniture for the commission; *Bibendum chairs,* a *Transat chair,* and an *Adjustable table*. It was a combination of old versus new (despite the older pieces only being six or eight years old). The *Serpent chair* and the *Pirogue sofa bed* sit very comfortably in the new modern interior. Gray also produced new adaptations of other pieces which she

4.35 The *Boulevard Suchet apartment,* in *L'Illustration,* 1933, black and white photograph © NMI

4.36 The entrance gallery, at the *Boulevard Suchet apartment*, in *L'Illustration*, 1933, black and white photograph © NMI

4.37 The salon, at the *Boulevard Suchet apartment*, in *L'Illustration*, 1933, black and white photograph © NMI

had completed previously – a matt upholstered-covered sofa with lacquer boxes on either end, except this was completed in white. The earlier version was completed in a rusty red colour. This time white blocks cover the linings of the wall of the entrance hall – an evolution from what she had done at the *Rue de Lota apartment*. However, by this stage Gray was now experimenting in architecture; she had moved beyond the realm of interior decoration and beyond the realm of lacquer.

ENDNOTES

1   NcNeill Whistler, James, *Harmony in Blue and gold: The Peacock Room*, 1876-1877, oil paint and gold leaf on canvas, leather and wood, Washington, Freer Sackler: The Smithsonian's Museums of Asian Art.

2   Pennell, Joseph and Elizabeth, *The Life of James McNeill Whistler,* London, William Heinemann, 1911.

3   Badovici and Gray, 'From Eclecticism to Doubt', *L'Architecture Vivante,* Winter 1929.

4   Adam, Peter, *Eileen Gray: Architect/Designer: A Biography,* London, Thames and Hudson, 1987, p.49. Gray returned to England while studying in Paris in 1905 due to her mother's ill health and remained for two years. Adam states that during this period she happened to stumble upon a lacquer repair shop in Dean Street. Constant, Caroline, *Eileen Gray*, London, Phaidon, 2000, p.23. Constant claims that her interest in lacquer was due to the influence of seeing the Asian lacquer work in the South Kensington Museum, now known as the Victoria and Albert Museum.

5   V&A Archives, AAD 9/11-1980, business correspondence, letter from the office of D. Charles, 92 Dean Street and 25 Soho Square Oxford Street, London, letter dated 1913. Dean Charles lacquer repairer appears in the directory of the Soho district in 1902-3. ITV Thames Television. *Aquarius* interview 11 November 1975 stated that in Dean Street she saw that 'they repaired old lacquer screens, the men were very nice, they showed me what they were doing and I was very interested, because I had always wanted to learn lacquer'.

6   V&A Archives, AAD 9/11-1980, letter from the office of D. Charles 92 Dean Street and 25 Soho Square Oxford Street, dated 1914. She also states in the *Aquarius* interview that she remained good friends with them for many years.

7   Ibid, *Aquarius* Interview.

8   Stalker, John and Parker, George, *Treatise of Japanning and Varnishing,* Oxford, 1688.

9   Fesser, Andrea and Daly, Maureen, *The Materiality of Colour,* Farnham, Ashgate, 2012, pp.88-90.

10   Ibid, *Aquarius* interview.

11   V&A Archives, AAD 9/3/1980, notebook.

12   NMIEG 2003.522, notes on an address. This is a note in Eileen Gray's hand giving the address of a Japanese supplier of lacquer and lacquer materials. Gray wrote his name incorrectly but it was Sugimoto Gosuke, Tate Daikucho, Kandaku, Tokio, Japan. Ruth Starr, TCD, in conversation with the author July 2014.

13   Pillard-Verneuil, Maurice, *Le Salon d'Automne*, No. 28, November 1910, p.137.

14   Troy, Nancy, *Modernism and the Decorative Arts in France,* New Haven and London, Yale University Press, 1991, p.63.

15   NMIEG 2000.44, Seizo Sugawara cabinet, NMIEG 2000.45. Seizo Sugawara signature stamp, NMIEG 2000.81, red lacquer table centrepiece.

16   Starr, Ruth, 'Eileen Gray: a child of Japonisme?' *Artefact*, Journal of the Irish Association of Art Historians, Issue No. 1, Autumn 2007, pp.90, 96. Starr cites an obituary on Sugawara which was published in September, 1937 in the Japanese magazine *Atelier,* mentioning his death the previous 12 April 1937. Yanagi, *Atelier,* Obituary page.

17   Ibid, Starr.

18   Ibid, Starr.

19   Ibid, Starr, footnotes Nos. 40 and 41, p.96.

20   Ibid, Starr.

21   NMIEG 2003.510, notes on Eileen Gray's work.

22   Garner, Philippe, *Eileen Gray 1878-1976, Designer and Architect,* Cologne, Benedikt Taschen, 1993, p.11.

23   Jackson, Anna, 'Orient and Occident', in Greenhalgh, Paul (ed.), *Art Nouveau 1890-1914,* London, V&A publications, 2000, p.438.

24   Starr, Ruth, 'Seizo Sugawara, Maître Lacquer', in Pitiot, Cloé, *Eileen Gray,* Éditions du Centre Pompidou, Paris, 2013, p.43.

25   Ibid. see also Tsuda, Seifu *Rougaka no Isshou (Vol 1.), Cyuou Kouron Bijutsu Shuppan,* 1963, pp.225-6, and Garnier, Bénédicte, *Rodin, Le rêve japonais*, Paris, Éditions du Musée Rodin/Flammarion, 2007, p.87.

26 NMIEG 2003.551, Seizo Sugawara, 1900s.

27 Marcilhac, Félix, *Jean Dunand: His Life and Works,* London, Thames and Hudson, 1991, p.170.

28 Ibid, Adam, p.54.

29 V&A Archives, AAD 9/3/1980, notebook.

30 NMIEG 2000.83 - NMIEG 2000.85, lacquer samples, 1920s, NMIEG 2003.280, samples with cigarette paper.

31 NMIEG 2000.82, lacquer sample with cigarette paper.

32 Ibid.

33 Ibid.

34 V&A Archives, AAD 9/13-1980, press cuttings. Vauxcelles, Louis. 'La vie artistique', *L'Amour de l'art,* November 1920, pp.243-245.

35 Ibid, V&A Archives, AAD 9/3-1980, notebook.

36 Ibid, V&A Archives, AAD 9/13-1980, press cuttings, Vauxcelles, Louis.

37 NMIEG 2003.532, Christmas card from Katsu Hamanaka.

38 Ibid, Starr, *Eileen Gray,* Éditions du Centre Pompidou, Paris, 2013, p.43.

39 Ibid, Starr, *Artefact*, Journal of the Irish Association of Art Historians, Issue No. 1, Autumn 2007, p.90.

40 V&A Archives, AAD 9/1-1980, journal cash book.

41 V&A Archives, AAD 9/10 –1980, Inagaki correspondence, AAD9/11-1980, business correspondence.

42 V&A Archives, AAD 9/1-1980, journal from Jean Désert, AAD9/11-1980, business correspondence.

43 NMIEG 2000.30, drawing of handles/sculpture. NMIEG 2000.28, ivory handles.

44 NMIEG 2003.507, notes on Eileen Gray's work.

45 A.S, 'An Artist in Lacquer', *Vogue, late August,* No.29, 1917, p.29.

46 NMIEG 2000.250 and NMIEG 2003.1641, portfolios. Gray has dated this screen in one of the portfolios as 1918, however it was illustrated in *Vogue,* in 1917.

47 Ibid A.S, *Vogue,* 1917, p.29. The article states that 'her first production was a lacquer screen and then fascinated by the difficulties of the work, she made another, afterwards designing tables, chairs, and other objects'.

48 Badovici, Jean, 'L'Art de Eileen Gray', *Eileen Gray. Meubelen en interieurs*, special edition, *Wendigen,* Series 6, Santpoort, Holland, No.6, 1924.

49 NMIEG 2000.253, de Gramont, Elisabeth, 'The Lacquer Work of Miss Eileen Gray', *Les Feuillets d'Art,* no. 3, Paris, 1922, pp.147-148.

50 Ibid, Adam, p.76. Constant, p.33. This panel is also known as *La Fôret Enchantée.* Two other panels of *Le Magician de la Nuit* exist, one in a private collection in California dating the early 1920s, which is exceedingly abstract and almost incomplete. It is a natural brown lacquer. The other, was completed by Seizo Sugawara, signed on the back, in a private collection. See Pitiot, Cloé, 'Eileen Gray La Poésie de L'Enigme', *Eileen Gray,* Éditions du Centre Pompidou, Paris, 2013, p.18.

51 The eighth Salon de la Société des artistes décoratuers took place on 22 February -31 March 1913.

52 Pillard-Verneuil, Maurice, 'Le Salon de la Société des Artistes Décorateurs en 1913', *Art et Décoration,* t.33, janvier-juin 1913.

53 Ibid A.S, *Vogue,* 1917, p.29.

54 Crowley, Aleister, *Berashith: An Essay in Ontology with some remarks on ceremonial Magic,* Paris, Clarke and Bishop Printers, 1902, pp.10-12.

55 NMIEG 2003.70, Bain, F.W, *In the Great God's Hair,* London, Methuen & Co., 1917. Originally published in 1905. Gray dated her copy 4 March 1917.

56 Ibid, Pillard-Verneuil, Maurice, *Art et Décoration,* t.33, janvier-juin 1913, pp.88-100.

57 Possémé, Évelyne, 'Créations Pour Jacques Doucet', in Pitiot, Cloé, *Eileen Gray,* Éditions du Centre Pompidou, Paris, 2013, p.52. See *Collection Jacques Doucet,* en trois parties (Dessins et pastels, sculptures et peintures, Meubles et objets d'art du XVIIIème siècle), Paris, Galerie Georges Petit, 1912.

58 Picasso, Pablo, *Les Demoiselles d'Avignon,* 1907, oil on canvas, 243.7 x 233.7 cm, New York, MoMA. Rousseau, Henri, *La Charmeuse de Serpents,* 1907, oil on canvas, 169 x 189.5 cm, Paris, Musée d'Orsay.

59 Paul Iribe was a French decorative artist who was a spokesperson for the luxurious, opulence of the French tradition reflected in the Art Deco style. He wrote two essays 'Choix' dating 1930 and 'Défense du Luxe' 1932 in which he vehemently attacked the modern style advocated by Le Corbusier and others.

60 Crowley, Aleister, *Tannhäuser, a Story of All Time,* London, Kegan Paul, Trench, Trubner & Co. Ltd, 1902, pp.13-15.

61 NMIEG 2003.71, translation by Butcher, Samuel Henry, and Lang, Andrew, *The Odyssey of Homer,* New York Editions McMillan and Co., 1903.

62 Marcel Coard was a French architect and furniture designer who was active in Paris. Opening up his own shop in 1919 his furniture was inspired by Cubist forms and he was the first designer to cover furniture with parchment. Paul Iribe was a French illustrator and designer in the decorative arts in France. Jean Lurçat was a French painter and tapestry designer who worked for a distinguished clientele. He was devoted to his textile work and was known for the revival of medieval techniques.

63 Ibid, Adam, p.85.

64 NMIEG 2003.869, NMIEG 2003.870, Manet, Edouard, *Sur la plage,* 1873, oil on canvas, 0.6m x 0.735m, Paris, Musée d'Orsay.

65 Vallois, *Eileen Gray, biennale 2000,* Vallois Mobilier 1922-1930 Sculptures XXe Siècle, Paris, 2000.

66 Ibid, Constant, p.34. See also Possémé, Évelyne, 'Créations Pour Jacques Doucet', in Pitiot, Cloé, *Eileen Gray,* Éditions du Centre Pompidou, Paris, 2013, p.52. Possémé quotes from two letters signed Aline Gray on 26 May 1913. See Institut National de l'histoire de l'art (INHA), Jacques Doucet Archives, Int. Ant 641 (22) 77588, 77589, 77590, 77591.

67 RIBA Archives, PB546/1, miscellaneous loose designs for carpets and tiles.

68 Ibid A.S, *Vogue,* 1917, p. 29.

69 Ibid, Adam, p.61.

70 NMIEG 2003.47, Dottin, Georges, *L'Épopée Irlandaise,* Paris, La Renaissance du Livre, 1928.

71 NMIEG 2000.74, lacquer panel.

72 Author unknown, 'Un temple de l'art moderne : l'appartement de M.J. Doucet', *Fémina,* Paris, 1925, pp.29-32. See also Joubin, André, 'Le Studio de Jacques Doucet', *l'illustration,* No. 4548, 3 May 1930.

73 Chapon, François, *Mystères et Splendeurs de Jacques Doucet 1853-1929,* Paris, J.C Lattès, 1984. This publication describes in depth Doucet's apartment in the rue Saint James.

74 Galerie Peyroulet, Paris.

75 NMIEG 2000.243, Eileen and Thora Gray saying farewell to a family friend.

76 NMIEG 2003.485, Fry, Roger, *The New Burlington Magazine,* The Burlington Magazine Ltd, London, no.11.1907.

77 NMIEG 2003.485, Fry, Roger, *The New Burlington Magazine,* The Burlington Magazine Ltd, London, no.11.1907.

78 NMIEG 2003.502, notes on publications.

79 NMIEG 2000.80, lacquer oval box. 1925, NMIEG 2000.75 – NMIEG 2000.77, lacquer plates, circa 1925, NMIEG 2008.2, lacquer tray, 1919-1925, NMIEG 2000.111– NMIEG 2000.113, monogrammed hand mirror with two glass inserts, circa 1920s. Sotheby's, *Collection Eileen Gray: Mobilier, Objets et Projets de sa Création,* Monte Carlo: Parke Bernet Monaco, 1980, p.11, Illustration No.244. Sotheby's, *Important 20th Century Furniture, a Philip Johnson Town House,* New York, 6 May 1989, lot No.96. Galerie Vallois, Paris.

80 Laurent, Jennifer, 'Salon et Expositions: Les Décennies qui Précèdent L'UAM', in Pitiot, Cloé, *Eileen Gray,* Éditions du Centre Pompidou, Paris, 2013, p.73.

81 Ibid, Constant, p.36. Constant states that all except one exhibition under the direction of Tony Selmersheim at the 10th Salon des Artistes Décorateurs featured expensive luxurious furniture. At this Salon Louis Sue and André Mare displayed mass-produced furniture from their Companie des Arts Français, created to challenge from 1919 the German ensembliers and endorse the French decorative arts and furnishings. They were displayed alongside furnishings made by the Atelier Primavera for the Parisian department

store Printemps and Selmersheim's design which he did for the Galeries Lafayette. Gray participated in this exhibition but her furniture was never recorded.

82 Vaudroyer, Jean Louis, 'Le Salon d'Automne II, l'art décoratif', *Art et Décoration,* no.36, December 1919, pp.181-3. The role of the interior designer changed during this period and was heralded as a designer of the 'ensemble' of whole unified interior.

83 Dervaux, Adolphe, 'Le beau, le vrai, l'utile et la réorganisation de la cité', *La Grande Revue,* 90, no.584, April 1916, p.33.

84 NMIEG 2003.365, letter dated 2 January 1971, Paris.

85 Author unknown, 'Lacquer Walls and Furniture Displace Old Gods in Paris and London', *Harper's Bazaar,* September 1920.

86 Ibid, Marcilhac, p.33.

87 Ibid, Gramont, Elisabeth de, *Les Feuillets d'Art,* 1922.

88 Ibid.

89 Ibid.

90 NMIEG 2000.250 and NMIEG 2003.1641, portfolio.

91 Ibid.

92 NMIEG 2000.79, lacquer box, 1918-1919.

93 NMIEG 2003.349, letter from Eileen Gray to Prunella Clough 21 September 1972.

94 Christie's, *Collection Yves Saint Laurent et Pierre Bergé,* Paris, 23-25 February 2009, lot.243.

95 NMIEG 2003.348, letter from Eileen Gray to Prunella Clough.

96 Ibid, *Harper's Bazaar*, September 1920.

97 Duchamp, Marcel, *Nude Descending a Staircase No.2,* 1912, oil on canvas, 57 7/8 x 35 1/8, Philadelphia, Museum of Art.

98 Ibid, Gramont, Elisabeth de, *Les Feuillets d'Art,* 1922.

99 NMIEG 2000. 254, NMIEG 2003. 488, Badovici, Jean, 'L'Art d'Eileen Gray', *Eileen Gray. Meubelen en interieurs,* special edition, *Wendigen,* Series 6, Santpoort, Holland, No.6, 1924, pp.12-15.

100 De Gramont, Élisabeth, 'The Lacquer work of Miss E.Gray', *The Living Arts,* No.3 March 1922, p.148.

101 V&A Archives, AAD/9/10-1980, Letter from K. Inagaki to Eileen Gray, 23 May 1922.

102 NMIEG 2003.257, notes on furniture.

103 Zervos, Christian, 'Les Tendances actuelles de l'art contemporain. Le Mobilier : hier et aujourd'hui', *Le Revue de l'art ancien et moderne,* No.269, January 1925, p.74.

104 Zervos, Christian, 'Choix des œuvres les plus expressives de la décoration contemporaine', *Les Arts de la Maison,* Paris, Winter 1924, pp.18-20.

105 NMIEG.2000.260, Badovici, Jean, 'Eileen Gray', *L'Architecture Vivante,* No.27, Paris, Editions Albert Morancé, Winter 1924, pp.26-31.

106 Ibid, Badovici, Jean, *Wendigen.*

107 NMIEG 2000.263, Badovici, Jean, *Les Intérieurs Fran -çais,* Paris, Editions Albert Morancé, 1925.

108 Ibid V&A Archives, AAD9/13-1980, Vauxcelles, Louis, article undated.

109 Reynal, Maurice, 'Les Arts', *L'Intransigeant,* Paris, 5 June 1922, p.2.

110 Watelin, L., 'The Arts of Decorative and Applied Arts at the Salon d'Automne', *Arts and Artists,* Volume VI, No.32, October 1922, p.111.

111 Chavance, René, *Beaux-Arts,* Brussels, June 1923, p.V.

112 Chavance, René, *Pour Comprendre L'Art Décoratif Moderne en France,* Paris, Librairie Hachette, 1925, p.148.

113 Adam, Peter, *Eileen Gray: Architect/Designer: A Biog- raphy,* London, Thames and Hudson, 1987, p.119.

114 V&A Archives, AAD/1980/9/, four unnumbered drawings and plans for *Jean Désert.* On one Gray has indicated the idea of opening up the floor with glass so that passers-by could view through the display window into the workshop in the basement.

115 Taylor, J, *Paths to Contemporary French Literature,* Vol. 1, New Jersey, Transaction Publishers, 2011, p.35.

116 V&A Archives, AAD/1980/913, 'Odd Designs at Art Studio', *Chicago Tribune,* 7 July 1922. V&A Archives, AAD/1980/913, 'Jean   esert', *The Daily Mail,* 10 June 1922.

117 Two extant drawings exist of the façade. One by the Romanian architect Jean Badovici's which shows a strong horizontal emphasis with steps leading into the entrance. The shop's name was drawn vertically on the right-hand side.

118 NMIEG 2003.265, certificate of de-registration.

119 V&A Archives, AAD9/10-1980, correspondence between Inagaki and Gray between 1919 and 1927.

120 NMIEG 2003.536, stencilling letters and numbers, NMIEG 2003.55, *typography book,* NMIEG 2003.54, *type specimen book,* NMIEG 2000.137-160 and NMIEG 2003.267, 271, 272, paper ephemera from Jean Désert. V&A Archives, AAD9/3-1980, letter concerning the manufacture of rugs from Emile Chaumeron to a Mr Jean Désert. NMIEG 2003.270, exhibition label.

121 V&A Archives, AAD 9/1-1980, this includes Gray's business ledger with lists of clients, workers, etc.

122 NMIEG 2003.78, Barney, Nathalie, *Poem & Poèmes et autres alliances,* Paris, Editions Émile-Paul Frères, 1920. Gray's name appears on the frontispiece on the *Aventures de l'esprit* published by Barney in 1929 and attended the salon on 19 December 1919.

123 NMIEG 2003.77. Delarue Mardrus, Lucie, *Le Pain Blanc,* Paris, J Frenczi et Fils, 1923, Ibid, NMIEG 2003.78, NMIEG 2003.86. Cunard, Nancy, *Nous Gens d'Espagne,* Paris, Labau Press, December 1949.

124 Born 1892, one of eight children, she changed her name to Marisa Damia after being discovered by Jacques Doherty. By 1912 she was famous and her records sold in thousands.

125 NMIEG 2003.533, map of Samois-sur-Seine, NMIEG 2000.191, postcard from Eileen Gray and NMIEG 2003.541-542, NMIEG 2003.561-562, NMIEG 2003.567, photographs of Damia.

126 Deshair, Léon, 'Une villa modern à Hyères', *Art et Décoration,* No.54, July-December, 1928, p.21.

127 Chareau, Pierre, 'Un appartement moderne. Chez Mme Jacques Errera', *Art et Industrie,* No.8, November 1926, p.17.

128 'À la Muette. Chez M. Philippe de Rothschild. Ch. Siclis décorateur', *Art et Industrie,* No.4, 10 April 1928, p.13.

129 'Jean Dunand', *L'Art d'Aujourd'hui,* No.13, Spring, 1927, plate. 17.

130 NMIEG 2003.507, notes on Eileen Gray's work.

131 Koering, Elise, 'Les Intérieurs de Madame Mathieu Lévy', in Pitiot, Cloé, *Eileen Gray,* Éditions du Centre Pompidou, Paris, 2013, p.57.

132 NMIEG 2000.259, 'Appartement de Mme J. Suzanne Talbot', *L'Illustration,* No.4708, 27 May 1933.

5

Knotting and Weaving:
Eileen Gray's Carpet Design

In the first decade of the twentieth century a debate arose between the definition of a work of art and a functional object such as a carpet. Two viewpoints emerged. Some artists believed there was no difference between fine art and the design of a functional object. Others argued that the work of art was imbued with a spiritual essence, normally absent from a utilitarian object. Paris was the artistic centre of the avant-garde where the new artistic movements, coupled with a rejection of academic tradition, artists and designers questioned traditional picture-making techniques through other media.

5.1 Eileen Gray,
1920s, black and
white photograph
© NMI

Eileen Gray's carpet designs displayed her painterly and graphic skills. From the moment she settled permanently in Paris major art movements such as Fauvism, Cubism, Italian Futurism and the Russian avant-garde inspired all aspects of her work. Her library was filled with art books which informed her carpet designs, including the catalogue for a Futurist exhibition in Paris in February 1912 which showed Apollinaire's *Les Peintres Cubistes*, 1913, Theo Van Doesburg's *Classique, Baroque Moderne*, 1918, Piet Mondrian's *Neo Plasticisme*, 1920, and Albert Gleizes's *Cusbism et les Moyens de le Comprendre*, 1920.

Despite her entry into the fields of design and architecture, Gray continued to exhibit her carpets at the salon. She actively produced carpets even after the closure of her shop *Jean Désert* on 24 December 1930. During the 1930s and 1940s she produced gouaches, some of which were carpet designs that never materialised. In her later years she worked on a selection of gouaches commissioned for carpets in her beloved Ireland. Gray felt that artists who had focused on decorative art had not always succeeded because 'Decorative Art which ought not to be decorative but mean making new forms from old and sometimes new materials; pottery, cork agglomére, straw, inventing'.[1] Gray continually experimented with new media throughout her career, constantly challenging the use of materials in her carpet designs and artwork.

During this time many artists and designers opened their own workshops due to a renewed interest in crafts and a revival of a guild system which countered industrialisation. The European schools of *Art Nouveau* were rooted in this philosophy.[2] In relation to the rapid development of the German avant-garde movement French designers struggled to produce a parallel. In 1901 the Société Nationale des Artistes Décorateurs was formed. As a non-profit organisation it promoted the French decorative arts, elevated the status of designer and protected the rights of French designers from industrial exploitation. French copyright law permitted designers to define items of their own artistic origin but not in cases of industrial manufacturing.[3] A revival of eighteenth and early nineteenth styles produced a mixture of different motifs which became the repertoire of Art Deco. Gray joined the organisation, exhibiting with them until 1925. She withdrew her membership due to the society's over-emphasis on craft and that objects were produced for an elitist clientele, not the general public. In 'Ornament and Crime', 1908, Adolf Loos (1870-1933) criticised the *Wiener Werkstätte* and German *Jugendstil* for these reasons. When the Munich Vereinigte Werkstätten für Kunst im Handwerk held their first Paris Exhibition at the Salon d'Automne in 1910, their work contrasted sharply with elaborate French taste. The German furnishings were socially motivated, acknowledged industrial production and were produced for a moderate household budget. Yet they were organised in such a way as if they appeared to be for a cultured wealthy family.[4] Occupying eighteen rooms the group exhibited everything from bedrooms to dining rooms, using industrialisation to their advantage.[5] The carpets on display were criticised for their bulky forms and acidic colours, but the work showed French designers what was possible through a disciplined collaborative effort. Gray had an affinity with their ideas, believing that one could produce low-cost, affordable furnishings for the masses.[6] It was against this backdrop that Gray's repertoire and her approach to carpet design developed from 1909 onwards.

Gray's carpets and wall hangings were produced at an atelier at 17-19 rue de Visconti that she had set up with her American friend Evelyn Wyld in 1910. Wyld initially studied as a cellist at the Royal College of Music in London and finally settled in Paris in 1907. She was a childhood friend of Gray's as their sisters were great friends.[7] It was a productive workshop. Eight women worked in the three rooms on the top floor of the building. The labels on the rugs read 'Designed by Eileen Gray at the workshop of Evelyn Wyld'. Wyld only began designing rugs in the mid-1920s, whereas Gray was the primary designer from 1909. Another young lady, Kate Weatherby (1881-1964) came with Wyld to Paris. Weatherby had encouraged Wyld to embark on a career in rug weaving. In 1908-09 Wyld travelled with Gray to North Africa where they learned weaving techniques and wool dyeing with natural dyes from native Arab women. Upon their return to Paris, Wyld travelled regularly to England in 1909 to further her studies in weaving and knotting, while Gray worked on the rug templates. Wyld returned from England with a teacher from the National School of Weavers to help the overall process.[8]

Handmade tapestry weave and hand-knotted carpets were made in large quantities in Europe during the first half of the twentieth century. By the late 1920s the two most active centres for production were France and Germany. The French made by hand, while the Germans concentrated on industrialisation. In France there were new experiments in rayon and in synthetic dyes, whereas in Germany industrial production of chemical dyestuffs developed. Despite this Gray and

5.2 Handmade tapestry weave and hand-knotted carpets, France, 1930s, black and white photograph
© Roger Viollet/Topfoto

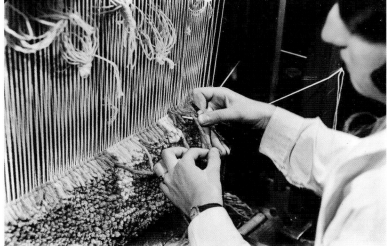

Wyld were probably the first to experiment with natural undyed wools used alongside dyed wools, uneven pile lengths, and juxtaposed plied and unplied yarns in the pile. Their rugs used natural fibres such as wool and cotton. Gray chose wool from various types of sheep, thus providing the end result with unusual tones.[9] The wool came from Auvergne and was dyed in Paris. In *L'Amour de L'Art* a critic stated 'The Art of Eileen Gray retains the flavour of a wild and exotic fruit. Beige and brown, brown and grey, beige and black are her preferred harmonies. But she juxtaposes these lifeless tones with an intentional violence and severity that underscores the weaving methods. Several carpets offer two extremes in wool height; smooth in the customary manner, with a central rectangle composed of a sort of lawn of interwoven wools. The effect is produced by uncut strands that are several centimetres long. The tangled wools recall the mane of some captive beast. It is the complementary effect the artist wanted for the shimmering wood and sharp angles of her furniture. She has also created carpets composed of bands, where a dark band alternates with a light one'.[10] Gray was exceedingly precise in her instructions regarding the wool and the cost of wool to be used.[11] In Gray's notes she discusses the colours of the spun and un-spun wool. The colours included white, black, light and dark grey, beige, yellow cotton and chromed yellow, wild rose, red, havana, rustic red, green and negro black. They had numerous problems dying wool with Veronese green as the colour didn't absorb properly. One of the marks of wool they used was called 'The Good Shepherd'. which was used in several of her carpets. They also kept numerous sample bags from which they could test various weaves.

The atelier also used dyed cotton. At times they used a combination of wool and cotton interwoven together. The majority of their carpets were made from napless fabrics, often with tapestry weave and piled fabric, including knotted pile. Early rugs are entirely tapestry weave where the weaver worked from the back, inserting the weft yarn in blocks of colour which corresponded to the pattern. The weft is then tightly packed down with a comb beater, covering the warps. Some rugs had three or four woven panels which were then stitched together by hand. One such blue rug came from Gray's apartment in the rue Bonaparte. Decorated with geometric motifs, a black line down the middle, a speckled half-moon to the centre and an angled line in the shape of an 'e', these hand-tufted geometric designs were added once the panels were woven.[12]

5.3 Blue carpet, 1920s, wool, cotton © NMI

With pile carpets the original drawing or section of it was transferred onto graph paper, where each square corresponded to a knot – hence the name point paper. Wyld converted the designs to point paper and examples exist for the *Marine d'Abord* and *Kleps* carpets.[13] Many rugs are entirely knotted pile. Executed on a high warp or vertical loom, the knots are tied in a row, cut individually and then the skein is changed in accordance with the pattern. The row of knots is then fixed in place by two or more weft shoots, beaten down with a comb to secure the weave. Other rugs were made in hand-knotted wool and sisal pile in the chenille technique.[14] Gray wrote in French about the process of weaving, the workings of the loom and how to achieve a certain texture which illustrate an in-depth knowledge of technique.[15] In a letter she wanted the rugs to be 'made on a loom, with a shuttle going backwards and forwards through a comb which makes the texture of the rug, the design in wool knotted by hand'.[6]

By 1924 the workshop had become considerable in size, with the account book recording two large looms, seven small looms and one vertical loom.[17] The atelier made samples for clients to view.[18] On numerous carpet template designs, Gray has written specific notes on the thickness of the weave, or has provided samples of wool and colours which she wanted incorporated into the design.[19]

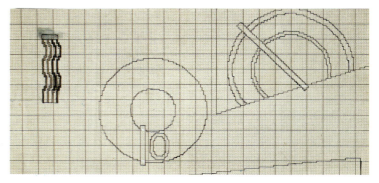

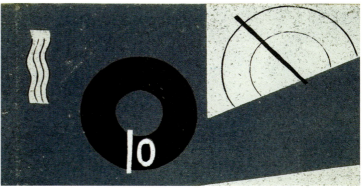

5.4 *Marine d'Abord* carpet drawing, 1926, cream card grid paper, ink © NMI

5.5 *Marine d'Abord* carpet gouache, 1926-29, paper, paint © NMI

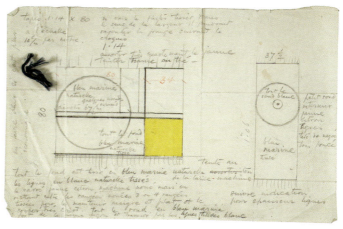

5.6 *Hantelaine* carpet drawing, 1926-29, paper, pencil, ink, yellow card © NMI

Post-war France called for a national style and designs free from German influence. Deprivation during the war years created a surge in the 1920s of consumer goods, creating a prosperous middle class. Immediate post-war designs in carpet making still revealed a German influence. Influenced by the *Wiener Werkstätte* and the publication of numerous pattern books, rectilinear compositions became popular. Fauvism and the *Ballet Russes* influenced the production of very colourful rug designs. French Art Deco rugs were a room's focal point. They displayed bright colours and designs often varied; dense floral designs, medallion compositions, trellis work, chequer patterns, geometrical patterns, reinterpretations of classical motifs, marine themes and figurative carpets. Their format was square, rectangular, oval, round, hexagonal and octagonal and the first irregular formats appeared. An interest in non-Western civilisations, colonised nations and l'art nègre produced a wave of rug designs featuring exotic plants and geometric patterns of Congolese textiles. North African Berber rugs, with their curly pile, un-dyed yarns and use of subdued earth tones had a major influence at the time. In 1917 the *Musée des Arts Décoratifs* held an exhibition of Moroccan art with its simple geometric designs. In Marseille in 1922 the first Colonial exhibition was held fostering interest in tribal art. There was a major demand for designer carpets. Sales reinforced by department stores meant that by the late 1920s designer rugs had become so popular that they were outselling oriental carpets. In the late 1920s modernist abstraction appeared with figurative patterns, muted colour schemes and subdued neo-classical designs. By the 1930s recession and unemployment severely affected the carpet industry. Luxury goods became obsolete. Increased emphasis on hygiene in the home translated into bare walls, simple plain fabrics and carpeting. Designers sought to achieve aesthetic effects through texture and technique rather than composition or colour. The threat of the modern movement in France was noted by Lucien Lainé director of the *Manufacture Française de Tapis et de Couverture.* He spotted the significance of modernism and the threat it posed to the French textile industry by diminishing the role of textiles in the home, noting that the French had failed to respond to this movement.[20] Gray and Wyld carpet designs addressed this social change through the style of carpets which were produced.

Initially Gray's designs were figurative and fluid. Then they became abstract and geometric. Wyld's designs were flowery, becoming more geometric and primitive in style. Many carpet gouaches and rugs are illustrated in Gray portfolios.[21] An early gouache, completed in a sumptuous Jade green, is stylistically unlike any other design produced by the Gray-Wyld workshop.[22] The Asian-inspired design has an off-white border with six decorative circles, some of which are filled with waving stripes in red, pink, maroon and green. Some of the circles are filled with the Buddhist Swastika appearing like the letter 'S' inside. The use of colour recalls the jade in Whistler's *Peacock Room*. While other carpet designers rejected the notions of Chinoserie and Japonaiserie, Gray here explored these ideas with simplified forms, stressing the outlines of shapes, and employing flat areas of colour. The influence for this came from the Hokusai woodcuts which had been known in Paris since the Exhibition of 1867.

Her first series of rugs, produced from 1910-1918 were generally horizontal or vertical bands of colours and line. Gray chose a muted palette, dominated primarily by beige, cream and brown for example with the rugs *Footit I* and *II, Maryland, and Zara*.[23] Sometimes an added motif would also appear such as a triangle or intersecting rectangles in the rugs *Candide* or *Biribi*.[24] Then Gray developed the series further by introducing a richer palette with blue,

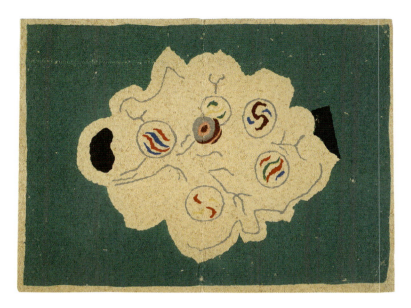

5.7 Japanese style carpet gouache, 1910, textured paper, paint © NMI

5.8 *Biribi* carpet gouache, 1921, card, paper, paint © NMI

5.9 *Poissons* carpet gouache, 1913, paper, paint © RIBA Library Drawing and Archives Collections

5.10 *Vogue* article on Eileen Gray, 1917, illustrating *Le Destin*, the *Zodiac table* in blue lacquer, the *Children of Lir* lacquer panel and a table with koi fish which complemented the rug *Poissons* © NMI

green, purple, brown and orange.[25] Progressing further again, she altered the design slightly by using horizontal curves in the rug *Macédonie* or introducing a square as with the rug *Gustave*.[26]

Other early rugs had identifiable subject matter and were designed to complement Gray's lacquer furniture and her use of natural woods. For example *Poissons,* 1913 complemented a sand-grey lacquer table with white fish that dart about the surface – the lacquer table being illustrated in *Vogue* in 1917.[27] She continued this theme of rugs complementing pieces of furniture throughout her interiors.

Gray was invited to design the interior and furnishings for Mme Juliette Lévy's apartment in the rue de Lota in 1918-24, where the rug *Cluny,* 1922, a geometric blue rug with white lines and abstract motifs hung on the wall, complementing the lines of a lacquer piece called *Cube sofa* which was finished in a rustic red. Lévy's penchant for tribal art also influenced Gray to design an African inspired lacquer table and to complement it she did a dark chocolate brown and beige runner-carpet with three rhino horns and fringing.[28] The design corresponds to an early gouache, where Gray uses a swirling line as used on the *Zodiac* table, which was illustrated in *Vogue,* August 1917.[29] Another photograph of this African inspired table appears with the rug called *Magie Noire,* 1922-23, inspired by the writings of Gray's friend Aleister Crowley.[30] It was illustrated in *Intérieurs Français* in 1925.[31] In the hall of the apartment was a small geometric rug coinciding with a long rectangular rug with triangular forms. The carpets, along with the furnishings, exploited a sensual impact of colour and textures.

A number of gouaches exist that Gray kept which appear to be a combination of ideas from the Vorticist and Russian avant-garde movements that were possibly intended as carpets for the Lévy commission. Gray had explored abstracting further the sweeping-line motif covering the salon walls. In a gouache produced during 1918-21, Gray uses a long white line which runs haphazardly from left to right.[32] Similar to the three lacquer screens which she produced during this period, one for

Lévy, the use of these motifs explore Lewis's Vorticism, yet the style also recalls the work of Kazimir Malevich and Ivan Kliun, where they used thin lines in various colours on a white ground.

Then in 1920 Gray's rug designs began to illustrate identifiable geometric forms in a range of colours and to identify with a variety of types of Cubism. Many designs are formal exercises in abstract art. Use of primary colours and spatial theories reflect the ideas of De Stijl, the Bauhaus and the Russian avant-garde.[33] Numerals, icons and fragmented or abstracted everyday objects were incorporated into her designs and are identifiable.

From 1925 to 1930 Gray refined her method of using a hand-knotting technique by producing rugs with different textures that precluded machine production. Many carpet templates require exact instructions and measurements; some of the designs are signed, and she often produced variants on the same theme. Rugs were frequently named after places she visited, or were inextricably linked to her architectural projects such as *E.1027*. Some rugs were actual architectural plans. Gray's carpet designs were a unique homage to art movements, people she knew, books or publications she read. One rug was in homage to the Union des Artistes Modernes, founded in May of 1929, of which Gray was a member.

Gray had publications in her collection concerning the different types of Cubism.[34] Cubism for Gray was an art of conception and a way of representing a conceptual or creative reality. From 1919 Gray began to introduce abstract and geometric motifs. Initially her palette was muted, beige, deep chocolate

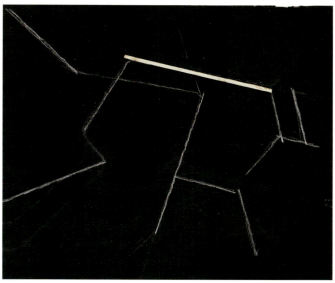

5.11 Black gouache with thin white lines, 1918-21, paper, paint, chalk © NMI

5.12 A six-panelled screen, circa 1921-23, lacquered, incised and painted wood © Christies images

browns and creams.[35] Early carpet gouaches show designs with a beige ground and a central motif in black like a square, triangle or rectangle.[36] Sometimes these motifs busily dominated the all-over design as with *Feston,* 1920, a cream rug with geometric black, grey and pale blue motifs. With others rugs the motifs were enlarged to dominate the all-over pattern. *Côte d'Azur,* 1920-22 was a brilliant blue square rug with a cream border, inset with a small navy square and two vermilion triangles. From 1919 to 1922 Gray introduced circles, arcs and semicircles in her designs. Sometimes the circle dominated the entire composition of the design, sometimes they were interlocking one another, and later she combined them with other primary shapes. Rugs such as *Magie Noire, Bastide Blanche* and *Irish Green* demonstrate this.[37] As is indicated in her notes, such motifs were woven differently to the rest of the carpet to engage the senses. Early studies for these carpets have muted colours of brown and pale yellow.[38] Gray quickly began exploring Anamorphic Cubism. With both her preliminary drawing and final design for the rug *Tarabos* she looks to the work of Robert (1885-1941) and Sonia Delauney (1885-1979), Albert Gleizes and Andre Lhote.[39] With Anamorphic Cubists colour was paramount, yet Gray challenged her contemporaries by developing her own personal

5.13 Preliminary study for *Tarabos*, black and white gouache, 1919-22, paper, paint © NMI

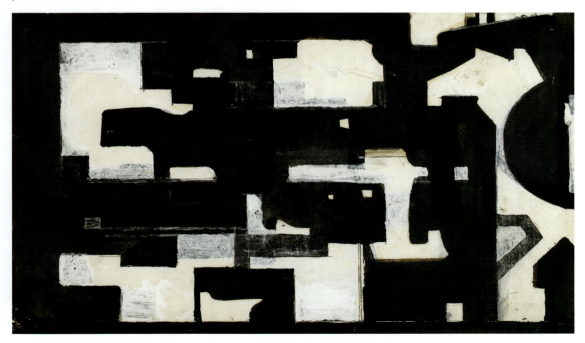

version of this style through the use of black and white. Then, by 1922–23 Gray produced a series of rugs where triangular motifs took precedence and were superimposed on top of one another. These were done in black and white with a burst of colour – often yellow.[40]

By 1925 critics are using the word Cubist to describe her carpets. Waldemar George wrote 'Miss Gray, an Irish woman based in France, is distinguished primarily by the

5.14 Black and yellow carpet gouache, 1922-23, card, paper, paint © NMI

frequent use of massive and simple forms', taking advantage 'of the conquests of Cubism'. He continues, saying that her carpets 'demonstrate the same concern to support a surface, a plane or a volume without involving the element of representation'.[41] Gray was also praised in 1928 for applying 'the bold grammar of Cubism' to her carpet design.[42]

Eileen Gray had an interest in the Bauhaus from the early 1920s through her friendship with Albert Boeken, who was editor of the architectural periodical *Bouwkundig Weekblad*, his articles revealing an admiration for Le Corbusier and Ernst May, particularly the latter's efficient manner of working. He had mentioned the Bauhaus to Gray.[43] The group became of interest to Gray, an interest which continued into the 1930s. Gray purchased the first book published by the Bauhaus *Staatliches Bauhaus in Weimar 1919-1923* in 1923 written by Walter Gropius (1883-1969).[44] It was issued on the occasion of the great Weimar Bauhaus exhibition of 1923, organised at the behest of the Thuringian Legislative Assembly, which wished to have a public display of the accomplishments of the institution's first four years. Gropius chose the theme, 'Art and Techniques: A New Unity'. Gray was interested in the work of László Moholy-Nagy, owning a copy of *Malerei, Fotografie, Film* (Painting, Photography, Film).[45] Gray also subscribed to the journals *Das Neue Frankfurt* and *Moderne Bauformen*. As a result Gray was aware of the developments of Paul Klee who taught for many years at Dessau and Weimar. Klee's art of free fantasy is best described in his own words as 'taking a line for a walk'. Gray designed a rug exploring Klee's work where two lines intersect, the first in a semi arc,

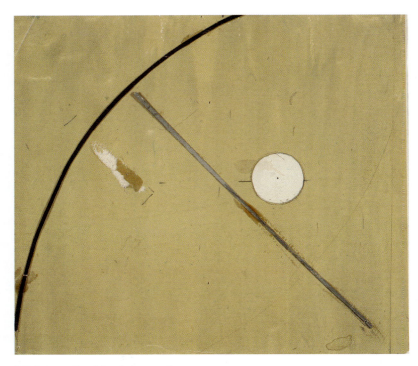

5.15 Beige with white circle carpet gouache with brown arc and silver line, 1923, paper, paint © NMI

running from left to right and coloured a rustic brown.[46] The second nearly pierces this and is straight, running diagonally from right to left. It is a grey silver colour. To the right of this line is a cream circle. The ground is beige.

Kazimir Malevich was in Paris in 1912, and on his return to Russia he claimed to have invented Suprematism – a purer form of Analytical Cubism. His preference for organised lines and the reduction of all of the arts to the primary basics appealed to and had a profound effect on Gray's thinking. The idea of this neologism was to lend supremacy to the basic means of art, colour and form over the mere depiction of phenomena of the visible world. Malevich spoke of this connection, of the supremacy of pure sensation. This romantic tendency appealed to Gray and influenced her in a number of ways through a variety of media – notably her carpet designs. Malevich was fascinated by the beauty of mathematical forms and used them to attempt to achieve absolute painting, cleansed of every objective narrative, reference and allusion. He aimed at 'a new reality of colour, understood as non-objective pictorial creation'.[47] Malevich was one of the first artists to discover the expressive potential of empty space. For Malevich 'the square is not a subconscious form. It is the creation of intuitive reason. It is the first step in the pure creation of art. Before it there were naive deformities and copies of nature'.[48]

Gray produced a series of carpet gouaches exploring the form of the square and the use of primary colours.[49] Her designs centre around the black or white square. Malevich's painting *Black Square on a White Ground* 1913 appealed to Gray.[50] She revisited this painting many times, inspiring her own version of his painting in a carpet design with a white square in a black square, framed by a border of two thin black lines.[51] She also produced a series of black square carpet gouaches – one with a white diagonal running from the top right-hand corner to the bottom left, another with a triangular section taken from the bottom centre and lastly with a speckled square motif superimposed on a black square.[52] The design Gray would later repeat in the garden gate which she produced for *E.1027*.[53] It also inspired a series of large black square-shaped canvases with speckled designs, or motifs in the middle, but these never materialised into carpets.[54]

Gray's interest in the De Stijl's synthesis of colour and elementary forms first began when she acquired copies of Van Doesburg's *Classique, Baroque Moderne,* 1918, and Piet Mondrian's *Neo Plasticisme*, 1920.

5.16 Black and white square carpet gouache, 1920s, paper, paint © NMI

Established in 1917, the De Stijl movement's concern to free contemporary art and design from the limitations of traditionalism, and its approach in synthesising elementary forms and colours appealed to her design ethic. She had seen a De Stijl exhibition at the *Galerie de l'Effort Moderne* in 1923. Her work exhibited in Amsterdam in 1922 caught the De Stijl group's attention, and throughout her career Gray met many from their circle; Gray met Bernard Bijovet (1889-1979), J. J. P. Oud (1890-1963), Jan Wils (1891-1972) and Sybold van Ravesteyn (1889-1983). In 1925 she visited Gerrit Rietveld's (1888-1965) and Truus Schröder-Schräder's *house,* dating to 1924 which is composed of abstract planes, painted in primary colours, white and greys.

Early sketches display Gray playing with motifs and exploring various spatial implications which are similar in design to De Stijl.[55] Gray's early De Stijl and Suprematist style rugs manifest a high degree of abstraction which she adapted to her own personal idiom. Recalling a painting by Vilmos Huszár (1884-1960) entitled *Composition in Grey, White and Black* dated 1918, which was illustrated in her copy of *Classique Baroque Moderne,*

Gray explored the De Stijl use of grey in their paintings, designing a rug completed in grey with a simple, thin 'T' shaped formation coming from the left and running to the centre.[56] In the early 1920s as she began experimenting with architecture, one can also see architectural influences in their spatial control and symmetry. Early De Stijl type designs consist primarily of two or more central motifs featuring rectangles or squares. They also have a beige or brown ground. Many times the carpet designs are outlined by a thin, dark brown border and several measure 1.10 metres x 2.55 metres, suggesting that this was a series.[57]

5.17 Beige, brown and white carpet gouache, 1920-22, paper, paint © NMI

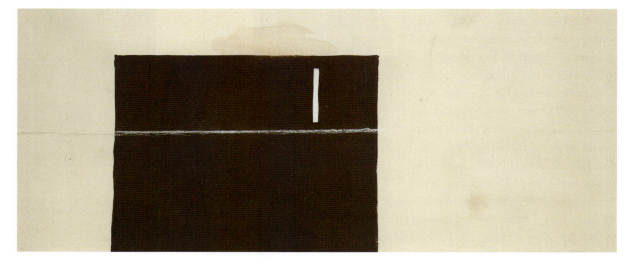

By the early 1920s a change began to occur in Gray's use of colour with her De Stijl and Suprematist rug designs. While still reflecting these movements' ideologies, these designs and subsequent rugs can be viewed as transitional pieces, from her earlier De Stijl inspired carpets where she had used a softer palette, to the primary colours and forms she focused on in her carpet designs from 1923-25. Plain squares and rectangles displayed brown, bright red and tangerine colours. These forms often overlapped the central design, with smaller geometric motifs in white.[58] Others had a beige ground, inset with two squares in primary colours such as blue and white. Above or to the side of the squares Gray would include a line, in a primary and a neutral colour like blue and beige or black and beige.[59] This theme of squares and lines prevailed for a number of designs. From 1921-25 Gray produced a series of rugs in the De Stijl style, with primary forms using a dark purplish brown ground, with black, white, blue and yellow motifs.[60] This series were all rectangular in shape. One was called *Skyline*.[61] Two of them had exactly the same measurements, again indicating that these rugs were part of another series using these colours.[62] This design finally expanded for the last time when Gray used yellow and grey. One carpet gouache consists of a grey ground. Running horizontally on the top

5.18 Brown, blue, yellow and grey carpet gouache, 1921-25, card, paper, paint © NMI

5.19 Brown and grey with black rectangle carpet gouache, 1921-25, card, paper, paint © NMI

left-hand corner are two rectangles – one is larger, the other appearing as a thin line. Both are rustic yellow. In the right-hand corner is a bright yellow square and a thin rectangular line to the right of that. A second gouache has a yellow ground with two grey rectangles in the pattern. One large rectangle runs vertically, the other horizontally, from right to left. Underneath this rectangle is a bright yellow square.[63]

In 1922 Gray designed an untitled rug that pays particular homage to the De Stijl movement.[64] This design consists of rectangles and rectangular form- ations in grey, white, black and red. It is rectangular in shape with one of the short sides bordered in a thin black line. It is more abstract in its colour fields, and it is believed that this abstraction in colour and design heralded the beginning of her studies in architecture. This gouache was made into a rug during 1922-23 and was illustrated in her portfolio.[65] The rug differs slightly in that a long thin black line runs from the top to the bottom on the left hand side and that the black rectangle, which encompasses the red square, does not run to the bottom of the rug. Evelyn Wyld continued using this colour scheme in her later rugs in 1930.[66]

5.20 Grey, white, black and red carpet gouache, 1922, paper, paint © NMI

Sometimes with Gray's De Stijl rugs the primacy of cubic forms took precedence and the entire rug was composed of two forms extending or overlapping one another. In *Hantelaine* a navy blue circle is intersected with white lines and inset with a small yellow square.[67] These block formations are quite severe, but effective. Again as with her other designs muted colours, black, brown and beige dominate.[68] Then they became much bolder with Gray creating dramatic designs using black and red. One design completed in black has a single red square inset.[69] Gray produced a series of large-scale gouaches, with unusual colours such as browns and pinks, where the forms and designs are De Stijl inspired but it was never clear in her records if they were ever intended for carpet designs, and have been interpreted as artworks.[70]

5.21 Black with red square carpet gouache, 1923, paper, paint © NMI

Gray opened her shop *Jean Désert* in May 1922 to sell her lacquer furniture, furnishings, wall coverings and carpets. To complete the effect of the total design of a room, Gray created installations which

5.22 Interior of *Jean Désert* with the rug *Maryland* placed at the top of the stairs, 1922, black and white photograph © NMI

she photographed. Numerous rugs are identifiable. *Côte d'Azur* and *Maryland* sat at the top of the spiral stairs. *Irish Green* with its circles is laid in front of a large red and black lacquer screen with squares in silver leaf.[71] This lacquer screen appears again with a cobalt blue glass lantern, and another screen covered in silver leaf with a large circular rug – a design that Gray would produce in multiple variations. The first version of *Feston* with its semicircles, arcs and geometric motifs complements a large African inspired table. *Tarabos,* 1920-22, purchased by Mme Jean Henri Labourdette, is displayed alongside Labourdette's lacquer abstract screen, *Pirogue sofa bed*, the *Rocket lamp* and a small lacquer table with geometric legs. Gray often placed furniture and rugs together in such a manner that either their forms offset one another or complemented each other. A small irregular form rug, dated 1922, with squares offsets Gray's *Architectural cabinet,* whereas a long runner rug, dated 1922, with chevrons, triangles and diamonds contrasts to Gray's black and white horizontal and vertical *De Stijl table. Hannibal,* 1922, a rectangular rug with two intersecting triangles appears with an image of a sycamore and oak dressing table that Gray later exhibited in the *Monte Carlo room.* A beige rug, dated 1922, with arcs in the shaped of the letter 'C' complements the shape of the legs of Gray's *Adjustable table.* A journalist from the *Daily Mail* newspaper noticed how these installations were successful in showcasing the work and described the specimens of furniture 'displayed on a parquet floor with her handmade rugs of undyed wools, into a depot built for them at 217 Faubourg St Honoré and the effect is as interesting as it is original'.[72] The image of the main shop front also displays this rug in the window with *Wendigen,* dated 1922, a rug designed in homage to the De Stijl publication, that devoted an issue to Gray.[73] From 1922-23 numerous rugs began to appear*; Magie Noire, Cluny, Tarabos, Hannibal,* and a new version of *Feston,* dated 1923, were offered to clients. *Hannibal,* 1922, was produced as a rectangular rug with two intersecting large triangles, one in yellow, the other grey, set on a bright orange ground.[74] The theme of intersecting triangles reoccurred with *Ebony and Ivory.*[75] This beige, rectangular-shaped rug had abstract and geometric motifs which formed the design and were in white and black. A half-arc runs through the central design in red, and there is a small red square at the left hand corner. The design of *Tango,* 1922–23, an orange rectangular rug with sweeping geometric brown motifs and brown fringing, was similar to the salon walls of the *Rue de Lota apartment.* The triangular geometrical theme continued with a yellow rug called *La Bastide Blanche,* dated 1923, which had grey, pink and white motifs. The first of the large circular rugs – of which Gray produced a series, and a circular rug called *La Ronde* appear in photographs from 1922 onwards through to 1930. The rugs from *Jean Désert* received much praise. In *Wendigen,* Badovici describes her wall hangings which he saw on display in *Jean Désert* as reflecting 'lyrical force, an enthusiasm and strength of feeling of this new civilisation and spirit'. Whereas De Stijl architect Jan Wils says that Gray's work was like a well-used rug, 'its noble lines accentuated but its original value retained. In this way, spiritual content, form, and matter fuse together to form a unity of rare delight'.[76] A reporter from the *Daily Mail* praised her for producing her own rugs and wall hangings for their originality and use of neutral tints.[77]

5.23 *Ebony and Ivory* carpet, 1922, cotton, wool, black and white photograph © NMI

Gray began to exhibit her rugs. In 1922, after the opening of *Jean Désert,* Gray exhibited at the Salon d'Automne along with other items of furniture 'un tapis noué en sable, noir et blanc, un petit tapis tissé en blanc, bleu et quetsche, et des tentures à bandes bleues, blanches et noirs' (a sand

5.24 *Monte Carlo room* with *Magie Noire*, 1923, in *Intérieurs Français*, 1925 © NMI

colour hand knotted rug with black and white, a small carpet woven in white, blue and plum, and wall hangings in blue, white and black stripes).[78]

At the Fourteenth Salon des Artistes Décorateurs in 1923 Gray exhibited *Une chambre à coucher boudoir pour Monte Carlo*. From the extant photographs which remain two different rugs appear in the scheme, the first being *Magie Noire,* the second has long fringing which appears to be the top section of either *Côte d'Azur* or *Gustave*. The catalogue also notes that two other rugs were exhibited – *Tarabos* and *Héliopolis*.[79] The rugs contributed greatly to the installation; however, the reaction to the room in the press was exceedingly negative, describing the room as frightening and comparing it to the room of the daughter of Doctor Caligari in all its horrors.[80] *Art et Décoration* discussed the strange bedroom with its disquieting appearance.[81] Another described a display 'constituting an important ensemble...in a melancholic and spiritual tone'.[82] *L'Amour de l'Art* illustrated the room and a knotted pile rug.[83] The newspaper *Le Matin* described a fearsome room but that it caused anguish.[84] Despite this, photographs of the room with the rugs were reproduced in *L'Architecture Vivante*,[85] *Wendigen* and *Intérieurs Français*.[86] However, there was praise. *The Journal* praises Gray's display of furniture, rugs and lacquer which are at least in comparison to the other displays original.[87] George Waldemar comments in *Ère Nouvelle* on the rugs in the room 'decorated purely with geometric patterns'.[88] On 5 January 1924 critic Albert Boeken wrote to Eileen Gray enclosing a reference to an article on her work written by him in *Bouwkundig Weekblad* concerning her work in the XIV Salon des Artistes Décorateurs in 1923.[89] Boeken (1891-1951), a Dutch architect who worked for the office of public works from 1916-26, and then had his own independent practice, came to Paris to report on the Salon des Artistes Décorateurs.[90] He described Gray's display as modest and mystical. He praised the luxurious cushions and her use of exotic fabrics. He praised her for 'choosing muted colours for carpets (some light fabrics, natural colour black design, net and capricious)' which worked together with the lamps to create an atmosphere. The room, however, caught the attention of the De Stijl group. The critic Sybold van Ravestyn linked her work in the *Monte Carlo room* with the De Stijl movement. 'A room by Mlle. Eileen Gray touches us more and expresses balance between "searching" and "finding"'. The relationship with the De Stijl is eye catching, less orthodox, less pure'.[91]

Gray's rug designs caught the attention of other designers and they began to use her rugs in their displays at the Salon. During this period critic Guillaume Janneau (1887-1968) in *Technique du Décor Moderne* described Gray as being 'an agrégé' of Pierre Chareau.[92] At this time there was a topical debate concerning the difference between an 'ensemblier' and a 'tapissier'[93] and later 'architect-decorator' and 'engineer-builder'. When designing an interior Chareau considered the volumetrics of the interior, whereas Gray prioritised her furniture and furnishings to generate a volume from the components of the room; thus she was marked as a decorator. Despite this Gray was commissioned by Chareau for the 1924 Salon des Artistes Décorateurs where he exhibited *La reception et l'intimité d'un appartement modern* (Drawing Room and Inner Portions of

5.25 Dining Room by Émile Jacques Ruhlmann with *Feston* rug by Eileen Gray, in *Intérieurs Français*, 1925 © NMI

5.26 *Tango* rug, 1923, black and white photograph © NMI

a Modern Apartment).[94] Gray's three rugs appeared prominently in the display *Martine, Côte d'Azur* and *Hannibal*. Other designers followed suit. In *Intérieurs Français* Gray's carpet *Feston* appears in a dining room by Émile-Jacques Ruhlmann (1879-1933).[95] During the winter of 1925-26 Gray and Wyld exhibited rugs at the L'Exposition d'art appliqué annuelle, at the Musée Galiera. *Tango* was acquired for Philippe de Rothschild, Mme Jean Henri Labourdette purchased *Tarabos,* and the architect Robert Mallet-Stevens (1886-1945) asked her to contribute rug designs for the Vicomte Charles de Noailles's villa in Hyères.[96] Once again critics returned with praise. George Waldemar wrote that Gray's carpets 'demonstrate the same concern to support a surface, a plane or a volume without involving the element of representation'.[97]

Certain rugs had variations. An early variation of *Tango,* 1920, shows Gray developing the design of the sweeping geometric motifs which cross the rug.[98] Another version takes a section of the geometrical motif and augments it, creating another design.[99] It was finally produced in 1922 with an orange ground with brown fringing and the sweeping geometric motifs were completed in brown.[100] A variant of the completed rug appears in Gray's portfolios from 1923, where the ground is a dark colour and the geometric motifs are in a white.[101] It was a large rectangular rug measuring 2.30 metres x 1.50 metres. The rug *Biribi*, named after a popular French game of chance appears in a portfolio of

work which Gray and Wyld produced from 1910 onward.[102] The design was reflective of Gray's interest in the avant-garde artistic principles which dominated the Cubist, De Stijl, Futurist and Constructivist and Suprematist movements.

The ground of this rug comprises two alternating blocks of colour in light grey and dark brown. The blocks of colour again vary in width. Inset into these, in the middle of the rug design, are block-like motifs in white and dark brown. One of the most popular rugs sold at *Jean Désert* for 400 francs until 1926, when it increased to 500 francs. By 1929 it was 600 francs. A second version appeared in 1921-23.[103] In this version of the carpet the ground comprises two alternating irregular blocks of colour, grey and black. The blocks of colour vary in width. Inset into these, in the middle of the rug design, are rectangular, block-like motifs in white and dark grey-green. Gray wrote that the measurements of the rug were 2.68 metres long and 1.17 metres wide and that the inner rectangle was 0.80 in width. There were two variations of *Feston*; the first appeared in 1920 and had more detail in the central motifs and two lines at one end. The second version which appeared in 1923 was more abstract and the two lines joined together to form a geometric motif.[104] Different abstract forms compose the pattern of the rug *Bobadilla,* later known as *Collage*: seven stripes in green and off white, beige colour rectangular formations to the centre, inset with a brown square and a yellow arrow, and a yellow angular abstract form to the bottom right-hand corner with black wavy lines.[105] Early drawings of this rug were dated 1926-29. There was a series of variations of the design where some of the motifs interchanged and colour altered from blue to yellow.[106] The variation which she decided to use in 1928 included the blue motifs.[107] Gray began to design geometric rugs using primary colours and spatial theories which reflect the ideas of De Stijl.[108] Gray's rug *Wendigen,* meaning

5.27 *Bobadilla* carpet gouache, 1926-29, textured paper, paint © NMI

'turning point', is named after the issue of the De Stijl magazine devoted to Gray's work.[109] *Wendigen* stirred quite a response when it appeared in Holland and the architectural world took notice. De Stijl architect J. J. P. Oud wrote Gray a postcard, mailing it to Ireland, saying how impressed he was with her work and that he would like to see more of it.[110] Gray's links with her De Stijl contemporaries continued throughout her career. *Wendigen's* geometric design reflects their ideas on purity of form and the use of primary colours, especially Piet Mondrian. Measuring 1.75 metres x 1.75 metres, and handwoven, Gray produced two variations, one had a white ground with a rust square and black lines, the other had a blue ground with a dark blue square and black lines.[111]

Multiple variations of the circular rug theme were produced during the 1920s. The most commonly known circular rug design was used in the living room in *E.1027*. The design concentrates on four circles, inset within one another with one half of the carpet in dark colours and the other half in lighter shades. These appear as bands of colour and the difference in each of the design was the choice of colour. Gray marked on many of the designs using the letters 'A' 'C' 'D' and 'E' to denote the various colours and textures as indication to the team of weavers, led by Evelyn Wyld, which shades of grey were to be used. In an earlier design for this rug Gray chose lighter colours – black, beige, grey, beige on one side, grey, beige, grey, white on the other.[112] One version is completed in dark navy blue, dark grey, dark navy blue, light grey on one side and multiple bands of semicircles in various shades of grey on the other.[113] Another variation has one half of the rug in black, beige, grey, beige on one side, while the other is completed in light grey, beige, light grey and cream.[114] A second gouache of this variation appeared in Gray's portfolio alongside a photograph of the completed rug.[115] This rug is shown with photographs of the curved divan which was bought by the Marquise de Brandt and it is possible that she purchased the rug.[116] Another carpet gouache *L'Art Noir* is similar to this, though the colour scheme is slightly darker.[117] Gray changed her palette slightly with another version where one side is dark navy and blue and the other beige and grey.[118] Gray also explored the idea of producing it in a bolder bright yellow and ochre brown except with this design the circles were all inset into a beige square rug design.[119] The circular rug also evolved into the rug *La Ronde* where one side of the circle is black and the other grey with a brown semicircle and at the centre a beige semicircle.[120]

5.28 Circular black, grey, beige and white carpet gouache, 1920s, card, paper, paint © NMI

5.29 Circular black, grey, beige and white carpet gouache, 1920s, card, paper, paint © NMI

5.30 Circular black,
grey and beige
carpet gouache,
1920s, card, paper,
paint © NMI

5.31 Circular dark and
light blue, grey and beige
carpet gouache, 1920s,
card, paper, paint © NMI

Many rugs were named after places she visited like *Côte d'Azur* or *La Bastide Blanche,* others are places where she lived. The *Bonaparte* carpet derives from Gray's apartment purchased in 1910 situated near the quays on the Seine.[121] The motifs on the black ground, with beige and white rectangles and a pink stripe, are an abstract plan of the location of the apartment. It was reproduced during the 1970s by Donegal Carpets. It finally measured 2.10 metres x 1.00 metres and was slightly larger than the original measurement when she designed it in 1921-25. *Roquebrune* was a rug of various shades of blue, grey and white composed of squares and rectangles. It was where she designed and built the house *E.1027,* 1926-29, and it had been the subject matter for a number of gouaches and collages throughout her career.[122] The design of the yellow rug *Castellar* with interlocking brown squares and long thin white line, is derived from a colour site plan of the land of Gray's home *Tempe à Pailla,* which she had already explored in an abstract manner in her artwork.[123] The form on the rug looks to Cubism, De Stijl and the work of Russian artist Kazimir Malevich.[124] Gray produced many variations of the gouache *Castellar* and it featured in M. Matet's *Tapis Modernes* in 1929.[125] The rug was also called *Brentano* – the name of a famous bookshop in Paris. It was finally produced from 1926-29.[126] Gray first travelled to St. Tropez with Evelyn Wyld in 1910 where they stayed at *La Bastide Blanche*. The location had some importance for Gray, Wyld and their friend Kate Weatherby, as all three lived in the region on a permanent basis at some time during their lives. This large, grey circular rug with its white lines is an abstracted site plan of her apartment in St. Tropez on the quai Suffren, where she lived in 1938.[127]

While these rugs linked to her architectural projects, the design of some rugs featured actual architectural plans of buildings or of furniture. An early rug which Gray designed in 1918-21 was the *Tour de Nesle*.[128] The motif is the architectural plan of a twelfth-century Parisian tower, located near her apartment in Paris. The subject matter for the rug could have been derived from an adaptation by film director Albert Capellani (1874-1931) of the novel written by Alexandre Dumas (1802-1870). Capellani's film *La Tour de Nesle* was released in September 1909 in France.[129] The rug was popular with clients in *Jean Désert,* selling for 450 francs in 1924. Two versions of the *Tour de Nesle* rug exist. The early version consists of a pale blue ground and the motif is white

5.32 *Tour de Nesle* carpet gouache, 1918-21, card, paper, paint © NMI

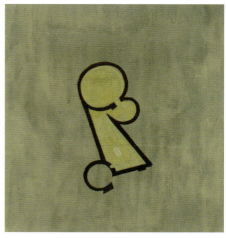

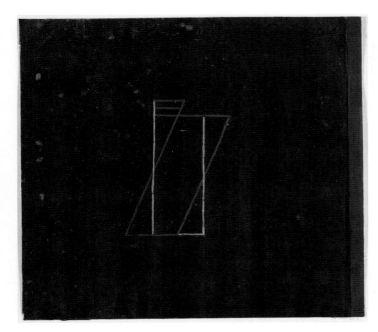

5.33 Blue with white and grey motif carpet gouache, 1926-29, card, paper, paint © NMI

in the middle.[130] The second has a subdued grey ground and a beige coloured motif, outlined with a deep purple border at the centre of the design. Gray's choice of colour reflects the early work of the De Stijl, popular in Paris in 1917-20.[131] Another untitled rug in dark blue and white lines uses architectonic forms which appear like an architectural plan for a house or a piece of furniture.[132] At the top a thick brown line runs the length of the design. A white rectangle to the centre intercrops a grey rectangle which slopes to the left. There are three graded grey lines attached to the bottom which interconnect with the white rectangle and sloping grey rectangle. It first appeared in Gray's carpet designs and templates from the late 1920s, after completing *E.1027*. By the 1930s she was using such forms when designing occasional tables for the housing projects at *Tempe à Pailla* and *Lou Pèrou*.[133] Early drawings show how Gray placed the motif, not to the centre, but towards the bottom of the drawing.[134] Variations of the gouache exist – the first where the carpet ground appears to be much darker, almost black.[135] The second is also similar, the difference being that the centre rectangle is grey and the sloping rectangle is white.[136]

Other rug designs were geographical maps and locations, which appeared in several of Gray's collages and carpet designs. An unnamed gouache is possibly a Mediterranean geographical location, possibly the site of *E.1027*. It is composed of a rich dark navy with striations on it, with a blue half-moon design to the top of the template. To the bottom is blue carbon paper which outlines the sea.[137] During the months of preparation of her studies of *E.1027* Eileen Gray examined closely the terrain on which the house was to be built. Often alone during this period she found solace at the end of the day when she went swimming. This collage explores the theme of the water and the surrounding terrain, not solely concentrating on the house itself, but the elements which surround it. Gray has written measurements on the right-hand corner indicating that her intention was to produce a rug. No evidence exists in her photographs that this design was realised. *Monolith* which measured 2.60 metres x 1.70 metres was a black rug with a pattern of thin, beige lines, 12mm in width, running at angles to each other throughout the design.[138] Gray was interested in ancient sites such as Teotihuacan in Mexico – and this rug is an abstract map of one such ancient site.

In shape, many rugs were square, rectangular or circular – however in the early 1920s Gray began to experiment by producing rugs which were not uniform in shape. Sometime the elements in the design jut out over the edges. She did this with several small rugs during the 1920s, illustrated in her portfolios, which were sold through *Jean Désert*. However, one drawing with measurements suggests that Gray also produced very large designs.[139] One carpet gouache in black and beige has a long thick rectangle extending horizontally from the lower right-hand corner. It is very subtle in the way the form breaks out of the shape of the design.[140]

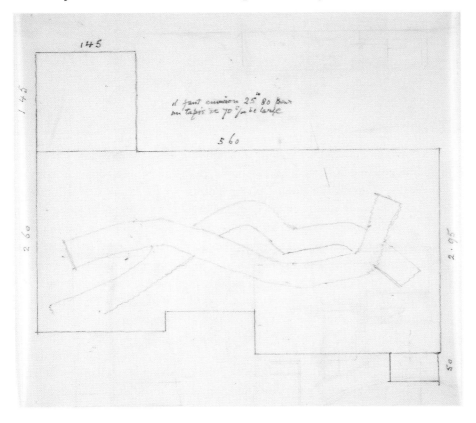

5.34 Geometric carpet drawing, circa 1922, paper, pencil © NMI.

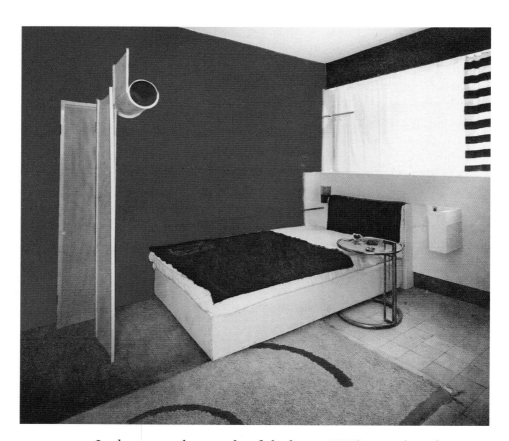

5.35 Guest bedroom at *E.1027* with the beige rug with two dark arcs, 1926-29, in *L'Architecture Vivante*, 1929 © NMI

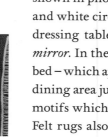

5.36 *Irish Green*, 1926-29, black and white photograph © NMI

In the extant photographs of the house *E.1027* a number of rugs are shown. Some of these are identifiable. In the guest bedroom of the house on the ground floor the beige rug with two dark arcs and a dark border line appears in photographs with the *Adjustable table*. *Irish Green* is also shown in photographs of that room – its colour and motifs of dark squares and white circles complementing the angularity of the multi-directional dressing table. It also features in the bedroom underneath the *Satellite mirror*. In the principal bedroom a long rectangular rug is laid beside the bed – which appears to have triangular motifs as its decoration. In the small dining area just off the living room a square rug, similar to the triangular motifs which Gray used in *Candide*, appears under the cork dining table. Felt rugs also appear in the photographs of the bathroom off the living room and in another image with a circular table. This rug had a perforated design in a square to one corner and the rest of the design was composed of pleated material. It had a thin dark border trim. Felt was good for absorbing

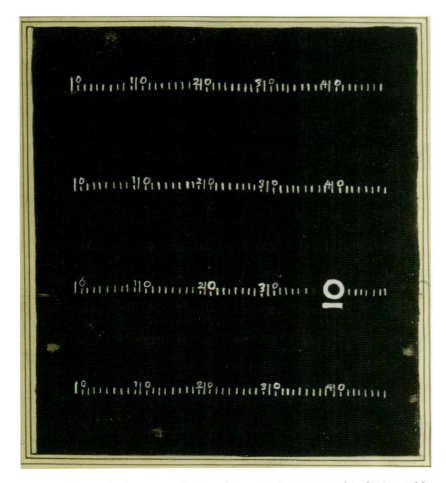

Black Board carpet gouache,
1925-26, paper, paint © NMI

water and Gray had been producing felt rugs since 1922. This dining table features with another long, dark, rectangular rug which has no decorative motifs. In the living room a number of rugs are shown. In photographs of the *Rivoli tea table* two long, rectangular rugs are shown back to back. The first has a dark brown and one single stripe in white-cream divides the rug in two vertically. The second rug, in beige, is of similar size and has a long dark line running diagonally from left to right. The circular rug, of which Gray produced eight variations, takes prominence – one half of the carpet in black with a small semicircle in white to the centre, and the other half in grey and light grey with the corresponding half of the white semicircle in the centre. *Black Board* carpet was a preliminary design for the *Centimètre* carpet, made circa 1926-29 for *E.1027*.[141] Its design had four horizontal scales. The first, second and fourth scales had the numbers running from zero to forty; the third scale had the number ten written vertically. The ground is black, and it had a white border with three thin black lines. From the photographs *Centimètre* appears predominantly in the living room. Its design reinforced and regulated the mechanical aesthetic of *E.1027*.[142] Both *Black Board* and *Centimètre* address the theme of how Gray was drawing architecturally. The metric scale prevails. Both rugs had the number '10' – representing the owner of the house, Jean Badovici and 'J' being the tenth letter of the alphabet. This was the same coding system Gray used for naming the house. Different variations of the *Centimètre* rug exist.[143] As made, *Centimètre* had three horizontal scales. Unlike *Black Board* the numbers were omitted on the scales.[144] On the left-hand edge, running vertically was a series of numbers, and beyond that nearer the edge was a white border line, like a ruler. The number '10' was removed from the scale and was placed directly below the second scale.

The *Marine d'Abord* carpet was one of several designed for *E.1027*.[145] The rug was placed on the living room terrace as Gray stated, 'On this terrace...a heavy brush weave carpet for the terrace garden provides a note of gaiety'.[146] Many of Gray's rugs from the middle to the late 1920s and early 1930s illustrate identifiable geometric forms, numerals, icons, and fragmented or abstracted everyday objects in a range of bold colours were incorporated into her designs and can be identified on close inspection.[147] This ground is predominantly blue throughout. In the centre there is a circular shaped formation with a hole in the middle in black with a superimposed white-coloured open circle and a horizontal white bar in its borders. It is an abstracted life buoy, like those that decorated the railings of the terraces of the house. A cream colour appears in a wave-like motif towards the bottom and to the top is a hemispherical shaped sundial in grey. The theme of the carpet was inextricably linked with its location at *E.1027*. The colour was symbolic and the use of the sundial could possibly be interpreted as the passing of time and stands as a symbol for a new venture, a journey. The sundial also illustrates the importance that light and sunshine play in the construction of the house. The use of blue and the life buoy links with the nautical theme of *E.1027*, found in the many architectural details and furnishings in the house. This carpet was placed on the living room terrace but, like all Gray's designs, it was meant to be moved around. Other examples of this carpet exist.[148] It was illustrated in the Winter edition of *L'Architecture Vivante,* in 1929.[149] It also appears in Eileen Gray's portfolios[150] and appeared in Matet's *Tapis Modernes* in 1929.[151]

Other rugs are mentioned in the literature as also being designed for display or were at some point on display in the house. The first of these was the *Kleps* carpet.[152] There are no photographs showing the rug in situ – however, it was illustrated along with Gray's *Marine d'Abord* rug in the winter edition of *L'Architecture Vivante,* in 1929.[153] The ground for the rug was grey, off white and brown. To the centre, on the left, is a semicircle in grey with black dots. On the top left-hand corner Gray placed a black geometrical motif with the letter 'R' – interpreted as representing Roquebrune, the locality of the house. A vibrant yellow runner rug, originally produced in 1919-24, made in the chenille technique was purportedly made by the Maison Myrbor as part of the furnishings for *E.1027* after the final dissolving of the Gray-Wyld partnership in 1929.[154]

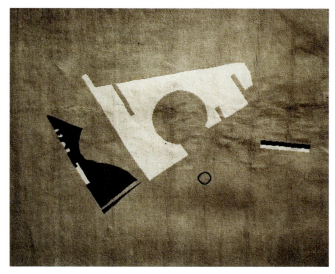

5.38 *La Bastide Blanche* rug, 1923, black and white photograph © NMI

In the studio of Jean Badovici on the rue Chateaubriand (1930-31) one long cream rug appears on the floor next to the daybed. In Gray's apartment in the rue Bonaparte a photograph appears of the rug *La Bastide Blanche* underneath a large lacquer table with a cubic base. Rugs feature rarely in the photographs of *Tempe à Pailla*. There is a plain cream rug seen on the terrace of *Tempe à Pailla* with a dining chair. Another image of the terrace shows a rug thrown across the balcony; it is a thick, hand-woven dark rug with horizontal banding to the edges. Lastly, inside the living room a thick pile rug appears where the design is crossed diagonally with an arc – similar stylistically to the Paul Klee design she had looked at years previously. The yellow rug which supposedly featured in the furnishings of *E.1027* lastly appears on the terrace of her last house *Lou Pérou,* 1954-61. Gray took several coloured photographs of the garden terrace with the rug in situ. This slender rectangular design shows two narrow parallel stripes, one russet-brown, one white, are near the centre of the design along one axis. The ground for this design is a pale brown. A lemon-yellow stripe runs along one long edge and there is a small parabola of the same colour in an opposite corner. A small complete margin to the design left is uncoloured.[155] This unnamed yellow rug appears in Eileen Gray's portfolios, where she placed it with the body of work that she produced

5.39 Yellow carpet gouache, 1919-22, textured paper, paint © NMI

between 1919 and 1922.[156] Her designs for carpets during this period reflected her own personal taste with non-representational composition. Due to her insistence on the hand-knotted technique, her carpets were much more textured than those produced by her contemporaries. This she indicated here through the use of textured paper. The rug has also appeared in Matet's *Tapis Modernes*.[157]

Several rugs had Irish themes – *Kilkenny*,[158] *Wexford*,[159] *Irlande,* dated 1926,[160] and *Irish Green,* dated 1927,[161] reminding her of her homeland. *Wexford* was an early rug design, and the Irish theme for this drawing was probably inspired after the death of her mother on 24 December 1918. Gray's sister Ethel inherited the family home at Brownswood in County Wexford but the family's connection was severed on 4 March 1929 when the house was sold. The rug has a black ground with a beige design. The motif at the centre is a black crown on a beige rectangle with rounded edges to the bottom and pointed edges to the top.[162] *Kilkenny* is one of many carpets which exhibit a high degree of abstraction, derived from De Stijl. In naming this rug *Kilkenny* Gray was remembering her homeland and her Irish roots which remained important to her even though she spent her adult life in France.[163] The choice of the colour green is also symbolic. Some rugs had names such as *Ulysses*,[164] in homage to the Irish writer James Joyce (1882-1941), who was a client.[165]

When their partnership dissolved in 1929 Wyld went to St. Tropez and then to La Roquette-sur-Siagne and opened, albeit only for a year, a décor shop in Cannes with another designer, Eyre de Lanux. Eyre de Lanux and Wyld met in 1927 when Lanux, then a writer and artist was writing an article on Wyld and Gray's designs. After this date to 1932 they became design and business partners. Wyld encouraged Lanux to join the Atelier de Tissage. However, the workshop continued to produce Gray's designs which were sold in *Jean Désert* until it finally closed in 1930. After Wyld's departure to the South of France, they still remained close. After the carpet workshop closed Gray produced during the early 1930s a number of gouaches, some in muted tones, and others highly colourful, with a speckled ground or with geometric motifs that were speckled. It is unclear if they ever were made into rugs.[166]

Gray, Wyld and Weatherby maintained a lifetime friendship. During the Second World War they had to give up their homes and moved to Lourmarin. Wyld would later purchase *La Bastide Caillenco*, at La Roquette-sur-Siagne and Weatherby would return to *La Bastide Blanche*. When Kate Weatherby died, Gray was by her side and wrote to Wyld 'Today our dear Kate died peacefully. I suppose it was for the best, but I am all upset'.[167] Weatherby became key to linking Gray once more to her homeland.

Gray was a crucial figure in influencing the Irish artists Mainie Jellett (1897-1944) and Evie Hone (1894-1955) who studied in Paris during the 1920s.[168] Mainie Jellett and Evie Hone exhibited some of the first abstract painting in Ireland. In 1920 they travelled to Paris where they worked under André Lhote and Albert Gleizes and where in 1921 they explored Cubism and non-representational art. Gray also knew of both Lhote and Gleizes. She later purchased and read Lhote's publication *Traité du Paysage,* 1939.

The two Irish artists befriended Eileen Gray through Kate Weatherby. In June 1922 Eileen Gray is mentioned in letters between Hone and Jellet, both discussing 'the beloved Miss Gray'.[169] Gray and Wyld had the most impact on Mainie Jellett, especially in her rug design. In the summer of 1928 Mainie Jellett had a solo exhibition in Dublin where she displayed her abstract Cubist carpet designs for the first time to critical acclaim by George Russell in *The Irish Statesmen* on 16 June 1928. Though Jellett only exhibited rugs for the first time in 1928, Russell reports that 'Jellett has designed carpets for Maison Mybere (sic) and Miss Evelyn Wyld of Paris which were exhibited at the Salon d'Automne last year'. Not only did Gray have an influence on Jellett's transference into the decorative arts in 1927, but Jellett actually designed and had rugs made in Paris at the Gray-Wyld workshop in 17 rue de Visconti. In 1927 Jellett was curious about how her Cubist rug designs were received at the *Salon d'Automne* of 1927 and she wrote to Gleizes saying 'According to an account of the *Salon d'Automne* I read in one of the principal English papers, the Cubist element though excluded from the pictorial section was very strongly emphasised in the furniture 'Art Decorative section'.[170] Jellett and Gleizes's ideas also inspired the Gray-Wyld portfolio, as the workshop produced a rug entitled *Etude* 1926 which demonstrates Gleizes's ideas of translation and rotation.[171] Though some of Jellett's carpets are formal exercises in Gleizes's theories of abstract cubism, others clearly demonstrate the influence of the Gray-Wyld workshop. A later circular rug designed in 1933 is directly inspired by a rug which Gray created for the living room in 1926-29.[172] However, the influence of Gleizes's abstract Cubism stylistically dominated Jellett's work. In 1924 Eileen Gray had exhibited carpets and draperies in a drawing room created by Pierre Chareau at the Salon des Artistes Décorateurs. In early 1931 through Gray's suggestion Jellett visited Pierre Chareau to show him her designs. But the reaction was not entirely favourable. Jellett wrote 'Chareau was hopeless, they were quite nice but at once said my carpet designs were pictures'.[173] It was also through Gray's contacts with Maison Myrbor that Jellett had rugs produced there, as Gray had a design woven with them also in 1928.[174]

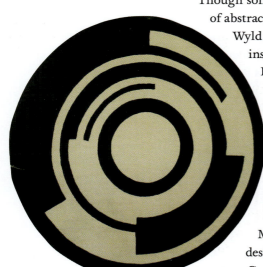

5.40 *No. 12*, by Mainie Jellett, originally produced 1930s, re-edition 2007-8, tufted wool rug © Ceadogan rugs

Gray, Wyld and Weatherby were still in contact with Jellett in 1932.[175] Jellett, back in Ireland, comments that unlike in France 'there is a level of disdain for carpet designs here'. She continued to produce rugs in Ireland until 1938. It seems Gray also had an influence on Jellett with regard to architecture. Though Jellett did not design, she became quite interested, travelling with Evie Hone to Amsterdam in the summer of 1933 where the *Irish Independent* reports she was going to study architecture and Dutch Galleries.[176] She wrote extensively on the architecture there, describing Holland as foremost among European countries in modern movements in painting and architecture. It was an interest which remained with Jellett throughout her life.

In 1973 after Gray's exhibition at the Bank of Ireland headquarters in Dublin in 1973, art critic Dorothy Walker (1929-2002) contacted Gray immediately in the hopes of having her carpets manufactured in Ireland. A lengthy correspondence and subsequent friendship ensued between Walker and Gray. At that time two firms were producing rugs in Ireland – V'Soske Joyce and Donegal Carpets. Gray requested a sample of the weave.[177] The commission was finally realised through Donegal Carpets and began mid-1975. Eight carpets were produced – two of which have Irish themes, *Wexford* and *Kilkenny*. The others illustrate important dates, people or places which affected her career – *Wendigen, Roquebrune, Zara, St. Tropez, Castellar* and *Bonaparte*. One of Gray's last wishes was to have her carpets produced in Ireland. In one letter Gray wrote 'I should so like to have a carpet made in Ireland'.[178] It was through the medium of carpets and rugs that Gray's final wish came true – to have her work made and sold from her home country.

5.41 *St. Tropez* rug, 1975, hand tufted wool rug
© NMI

ENDNOTES

1 Rare Book & Manuscript Library, Columbia University in the City of New York, Stephen Haweis Papers, Arranged Miscellaneous Memoirs, Box 2, letter from Eileen Gray to Stephen Haweis, Thursday 13 February 1964.

2 Campbell, Joan, *The German Werkbund, Politics of Reform and Applied Arts,* Princeton University Press, Princeton, New Jersey, 1978, pp.56, 205.

3 Constant, Caroline, *Eileen Gray*, London, Phaidon Publications, 2000, p.17.

4 Byars, Mel, *The Design Encyclopaedia*, Laurence King Publications, London, 1994 p.396.

5 Pillard-Verneuil, Maurice, 'Le Salon d'Automne', No.28, November 1910, p.137.

6 Ibid, Constant, p.21.

7 Adam, Peter, *Eileen Gray: Architect Designer: A Biography,* London, Thames and Hudson, 1987, p.61.

8 Ibid, Byars, p.598.

9 *The New York Herald,* 20 June 1922.

10 Rosenthal, Gabriel, 'Les Tapis Nouveaux', *L'Amour de l'Art* 7, no.8, August 1926, p.280.

11 NMIEG 2003.87, notes on carpets.

12 NMIEG 2000.181, blue carpet.

13 NMIEG 2003.152, *Hantelaine* carpet drawing, NMIEG 2003.151, *Marine d'Abord* carpet drawing NMIEG 2003.153, carpet drawing on grid paper, NMIEG 2003.155, *Kleps* carpet drawing on grid paper.

14 Day, Susan, *Art Deco and Modernist Carpets,* London, Thames and Hudson, 2002, p.138. NMIEG 2003.105, yellow carpet gouache, NMIEG 2000.250 and NMIEG 2003.1641, portfolios.

15 V&A Archives, AAD/9/4-1980, AAD/9/5-1980, notes on weaving and typed notes on weaving.

16   NMIEG 2003.419, letter from Eileen Gray to Prunella Clough.

17   NMIEG 2003.156, account book for Gray/ Wyld atelier.7, rue de Visconti, Paris, France. 1 July –31 December 1924.

18   NMIEG 2003.278, metal apparatus for displaying carpet samples.

19   NMIEG 2003.96, *Monolith* carpet drawings. This first drawing '*Monolith*' measures 2.60 x 1.70. It had a black ground with thin beige lines running at angles to each other. One line is 12mm in width. The second drawing explains the measurements in detail. The length of the carpet was 2.60 metres with a width of 1.71 metres and a half. The spacing between the edge of the carpet and the main line which cuts through the entire carpet is 1.28 metres, and then 41.5cm to the other edge. The long thick line which runs through the length of the carpet is woven in natural white, cut very short; with a width of 2cm. Other examples of this carpet gouache exist see Sotheby's, *Important 20th century Furniture,* New York, 6 May 1989, Lot.102. Polo, Roberto, *Eileen Gray - Oeuvres sur Papier,* Paris, Galerie Historismus, 2007, p.12. NMIEG 2003.152, *Hantelaine* carpet drawing. There are two rug designs. One is for the *Hantelaine* rug. This design had a single circle which was intersected horizontally by two lines. Gray has included a sample of navy blue wool, measurements, and detailed notes for the weavers. The ground is to be navy blue. The bottom right-hand square is to be yellow. The ground is to be woven in natural navy blue wool. The lines which intersect the circle are to be woven in natural white. The yellow square is to be machine woven placing a knotted row every three to four rows. She wants the rug to be thin, flat and cut very short. The circle itself is to be navy blue, completed in the same way, with two white woven lines intersecting the centre. The rug measures 80cm x 1.14 metres. The diameter of the circle is 67cm. *Hantelaine* also features in Gray's portfolio – see NMIEG 2003.1641. On this second piece of paper to the right is another rug design. It is rectangular in shape. It measures in 1.06 metres x 37.5 cm. The ground for the rug is navy blue with a large circle off centre woven in white. Set into this white circle is a small circle woven in yellow with a black outline. This design was completed during 1926-1929 and was originally in *E.1027* and then at Jean Badovici's house in Vèzelay. See Musée des Arts Décoratifs, No.41971. Woven wool rug in dark indigo, beige with yellow fringing. Offsetting a large beige circle is a small yellow circle in the centre.

20   Lainé, Lucien, 'De la Tente du Nomade au Palais de Ciment', *Renaissance de l'Art Français et des Industries de Luxe,* May 1929, pp.246-262.

21   NMIEG 2000.250, NMIEG 2003.1641, portfolios.

22   NMIEG 2003.94, green Japanese-style carpet gouache.

23   RIBA Archives, Evelyn Wyld collection of drawings ref: SKB378-11 Footit I, SKB378-12 Footit II, SKB378-5 Maryland, SKB378-13 Zara. NMIEG 2003.135, *Zara* carpet drawing, NMIEG 2000.180, *Zara* rug.

24   RIBA Archives, Evelyn Wyld collection of drawings ref: SKB378-9 Candide, ref: SKB378-8 *Biribi*. NMIEG 2000.166, *Biribi* carpet gouache.

25   RIBA Archives, Evelyn Wyld collection of drawings ref : SKB378-1. *Macédonie*, SKB378-15, SKB378-16, SKB378-22, SKB378-23, SKB378-24.

26   RIBA Archives, Evelyn Wyld collection of drawings ref : SKB378-1. *Macédonie*, SKB378-20 Gustave.

27   A.S, 'An Artist in Lacquer', *Vogue, late August,* No.29, 1917, p.29. RIBA Archives, Evelyn Wyld collection of drawings ref: SKB378-1, sketch entitled *Poissons*, ref. in sketchbook 104.176.

28   NMIEG 2003.1641, NMIEG 2000.250, portfolios.

29   NMIEG 2003.124, black, grey and beige speckled gouache with swirling lines.

30   Ibid, NMIEG 2003.1641, NMIEG 2000.250.

31   NMIEG 2000.263, Badovici, Jean, *Intérieurs Français,* Paris, Editions Albert Morancé, 1925.

32   NMIEG 2003.132, black gouache with thin white lines.

33   NMIEG 2000.164, grey, white, black and red carpet gouache.

34   NMIEG 2003.65, Gleizes, Albert, *Du Cubisme et des*

Moyens de le Comprendre, Paris, Editions La Cible, 1912. NMIEG 2003.66, Apollinaire, Guillaume, *Les Peintres Cubistes*, Paris, Eugène Figuière et Cie, Éditeurs, 20 March 1913.

35   RIBA Archives, Evelyn Wyld collection of drawings ref : SKB378-17.

36   NMIEG 2000.177, black and white collage. Ibid, Polo, p.77. RIBA Archives, Evelyn Wyld collection of drawings ref: SKB378-8, an early version of Biribi, SKB378-9, Candide, SKB378-17, Abstract linear rug.

37   NMIEG 2003.119, black with white circle gouache and collage, NMIEG 2003.145, black with green circle gouache and collage, NMIEG 2003.152a and NMIEG 2003.152b, *Hantelaine* carpet drawing, NMIEG 2000.181, blue carpet. Ibid, Polo p.44. Bingham, Neil, *Wright to Gehry, Drawings from the Collection of Barbara Pine,* London, pp.16, 20, 28, 46, 52, 58.

38   NMIEG 2000.168, brown, beige, yellow carpet gouache and collage.

39   NMIEG 2003.131, Black and white gouache. RIBA Archives, Evelyn Wyld collection of drawings ref: SKB 378-7.

40   NMIEG 2003.89, black and yellow carpet gouache.

41   George, Waldemar, 'Le mois artistique – L'Art décoratif moderne', *La Revue Mondiale,* Paris, March 1925, p.84.

42   *Exposition Internationale des Arts Décoratifs et Industriels Modernes,* 1925, general report, Volume VI, Rapport de la Classe 13 – Tissu et Papier, Paris, 1928, p.38. Though Gray is mentioned as being a designer who has demonstrated cubism in her work, she did not take part in the 1925 exhibition.

43   Ibid, Adam, p.145.

44   Gropius, Walter, *Staatliches Bauhaus in Weimar 1919- 1923,* Weimar and München, Bauhaus Verlag, 1923.

45   Moholy-Nagy, László, 'Malerei, Fotografie, Film', *Bauhausbücher,* Volume 8, 1925.

46   NMIEG 2003.97, beige with white circle carpet gouache.

47   Ruhrberg, Schneckenburger, Fricke, Honnef, et al, 'Between Revolt & Acceptance', *Art of the 20th Century,* Spain, 2000, Benedikt Taschen Verlag, p.164.

48   Ibid, Ruhrberg, Schneckenburger, Fricke, Honnef, p.16.

49   NMIEG 2003.93, navy blue square with white stripe gouache, NMIEG 2003.130, black and speckled square gouache, NMIEG 2003.119, black with white circle gouache and collage.

50   Malevich, Kazimir, *Black Square on White Ground*, dated 1913, executed after 1920, oil on canvas, 106.2 x 106.5cm, St Petersburg, Russian State Museum.

51   NMIEG 2003.114, black and white square carpet gouache.

52   NMIEG 2003.91, black and white stripe carpet gouache, NMIEG 2003.93, navy blue square with white stripe gouache, NMEG 2003.114, black and white square carpet gouache, NMIEG 2003.130, black and speckled square gouache.

53   Ibid, Adam, p.169. Adam says that early architectural projects which Gray explored also look to the architectural ideas of Kazimir Malevich and his writings '*Architectons*'.

54   NMIEG 2003.118, black and white speckled gouache and collage, NMIEG 2003.119, black with white circle gouache and collage, NMIEG 2003.120, black and speckled white gouache, NMIEG 2003.129, black gouache with dark green and speckled motifs, NMIEG 2003.145, black with green circle gouache and collage, NMIEG 2003.141, beige and black speckled gouache, NMIEG 2003.149, black, grey and beige speckled gouache.

55   NMIEG 2000.170, carpet drawing.

56   NMIEG 2003.88, grey and white carpet gouache. NMIEG 2000.261, Van Doesburg, Theo, *Classique, Baroque Moderne,* Paris, Editions De Sikkel, Anvers et Léonce Rosenberg, December 1918, Plate.VI.

57   NMIEG 2000.165, beige, brown and white carpet gouache, NMIEG 2003.99, beige with brown square, carpet gouache.

58   NMIEG 2003.95, black, brown, orange and white carpet gouache.

59   NMIEG 2000.167, blue and white square carpet gouache.

60 NMIEG 2003.102, brown, blue, yellow and grey carpet gouache, this rug measured 1.07 metres x 2 metres. NMIEG 2003.104, brown and grey, with black rectangle carpet gouache, this rug measured 1.90 metres in length and 80cm in width and is similar to *Skyline*. NMIEG 2003.107, brown, with white square and black rectangles carpet gouache.

61 Ecart, Paris, *Rééditions*, p.20.

62 NMIEG 2003.104, brown and grey, with black rectangle carpet gouache, NMIEG 2003.107, brown, with white square and black rectangles carpet gouache, both rugs measure 1.90 metres in length and 80cm in width.

63 NMIEG 2003.108, grey, with yellow rectangles and squares, carpet gouache, NMIEG 2003.106, yellow, with grey rectangles carpet gouache. Ibid, Polo, p.25.

64 NMIEG 2000.164, grey, white, black, red carpet gouache.

65 NMIEG 2003.1641, portfolio.

66 RIBA Archives, ref: A489/16, album of views of the interior design work of Evelyn Wyld. Unknown Parisian interior, circa 1930, with black lacquer furniture on a white, grey and red rug.

67 NMIEG 2003.152, *Hantelaine* carpet drawing.

68 NMIEG 2003.109, black and beige carpet gouache.

69 Ibid, NMIEG 2003.92. Sotheby's, *Collection Eileen Gray, Mobilier, Objets et Projets de sa Création*, Monaco, 25 May 1980, lot.285.

70 NMIEG 2003.128, brown and beige gouache, NMIEG 2003.143, red and pink gouache, NMIEG 2003.144, purple, black, grey and white speckled gouache.

71 Victoria and Albert Museum Furniture collection, Ref: W.40:1 to 8-1977.

72 'The Lacquer Work', *Daily Mail*, London, Saturday 10 June 1922.

73 NMIEG 2003.1641, portfolio. See also Badovici, Jean, 'L'Art de Eileen Gray', *Eileen Gray, Meubelen en interieurs,* special edition, *Wendigen,* Series 6, Santpoort, Holland, No.6, 1924.

74 RIBA Archives, Evelyn Wyld collection of drawings

ref : SK378-4 Hannibal see also NMIEG 2003.1641, portfolio, p5.

75 NMIEG 2003.138, *Ebony and Ivory* carpet drawing. NMIEG 2000.250, NMIEG 2003.1641, portfolios.

76 Badovici, Jean, 'L'Art de Eileen Gray', *Wendigen* Series 6, No.6, Santpoort, Holland, C.A. Mees, 1924.

77 'Beautiful Lacquered Furniture', *Daily Mail,* 29 March 1923.

78 *Catalogue des ouvrages de peintures, sculpture, dessin, gravure, architecture et art décoratif exposés au Grand Palais des Champs-Élysées,* 1 November – 17 December 1922, Société du Salon d'automne, Paris, Société français Editions, 1922, No.1077-1081.

79 *Catalogue du 14e Salon du 3 mai au 1er juillet 1923. Paris, Grand Palais des Champs-Élysées. Société des artistes décorateurs,* Paris, Société des artistes décorateurs, 1923, No.308, No.309 and No.310.

80 V&A Archives, AAD/9/13/-1980, unidentified press clipping, 'Le Salon des Décorateurs', 5 May 1923.

81 Chavance, René, 'Le 14e Salon des Artistes Décorateurs', *Art et Décoration 43,* June 1923, p.175.

82 Varene, Gaston, 'Le 14e Salon des Artistes Décorateurs', *Art et Décoration 44,* December 1923, p.178.

83 Mourey, Gabriel, 'Le 14e Salon des Artistes Décorateurs', *L'Amour de L'Art 4,* No.5, May 1923, pp.560-62 and illustrations pp.562-63.

84 V&A Archives, AAD 9/12-1980, 'Le Salon des Décorateurs', *Le Matin,* 5 May 1923, morning editions.

85 Badovici, Jean, 'Eileen Gray', *L'Architecture Vivante*, No.27, Paris, Editions Albert Morancé, Winter 1924.

86 Badovici, Jean, *Intérieurs Français*, Paris Editions Albert Morancé, 1925.

87 Pawlowski, Gaston de, 'Le 14e Salon des artistes décorateurs', *Le Journal,* 10 May 1923.

88 Waldemar, George, 'Le 14e Salon des artistes décorateurs', *Ère Nouvelle,* 8 May 1923.

89 V&A Archives, AAD 9/12-1980, letter from Albert Boeken to Eileen Gray, undated. NMIEG 2000.195, letter from Albert Boeken to Eileen Gray, 16 January 1924. This is a French translation of his article on

the Salon d'Automne, extolling Gray's work and published in *Bouwkundig Weekblad*; the date is unrecorded.

90 Ibid, Constant, p.234.

91 Ravestyn, Sybold van, 'Review of the XIV Salon des Artistes Décorateurs', *Bouwkundig Weekblad*, Amsterdam, 14 July 1923.

92 Janneau, Guillaume, *Technique du Décor Moderne*, Paris, Editions Albert Morancé, 1927, pp.144-146. Agrégé – a person who holds a degree after passing the state examination required for teaching at a French university. It is a rare and prestigious degree. Guillaume Janneau used it to imply that Gray had achieved a professional level of accomplishment with her interiors.

93 Ibid, Constant, pp.61-3.

94 *Catalogue du 15e Salon du 8 mai au 8 juillet 1923. Paris, Grand Palais des Champs-Élysées. Société des artistes décorateurs,* Paris, Société des artistes décorateurs, 1924, p.64 and 76.

95 NMIEG 2000.263, Badovici, Jean, *Intérieurs Français,* Paris, Editions Morancé, 1925.

96 'À la Muette, Chez M.Philippe de Rothschild.Charles Siclis décorateur', *Art et Industrie,* No.4, 10 April 1928, p.13. Deshairs, Léon, 'Une villa modern à Hyères', *Art et Décoration,* No.54, July-December, 1928, p.21.

97 Waldemar, George, 'Le mois artistique – L'Art décoratif moderne', *La Revue Mondiale,* Paris, March 1925, p.84

98 NMIEG 2003.140, abstract carpet drawing.

99 NMIEG 2003.121, black and white speckled gouache with white lightening motif, NMIEG 2003.125, yellow gouache with white motifs and black lines.

100 RIBA Archives, Evelyn Wyld collection of drawings ref : PB546/1, miscellaneous loose designs for carpets and tiles.

101 NMIEG 2000.250, NMEG 2003.1641, portfolios.

102 RIBA Archives, Evelyn Wyld collection of drawings ref : SKB 378-8. *Biribi.*

103 NMIEG 2000.166, *Biribi* carpet gouache.

104 Ibid, NMIEG 2000.250, NMIEG 2003.1641.

105 NMIEG 2003.98, *Bobadilla* carpet gouache.

106 V&A Visual Arts Library, circ.239-1973. This is exactly the same as the National Museum of Ireland gouache. E.535-1980 has a similar layout and design, but some geometric shapes are slightly different. The colours are yellow, blue, grey and green on a brown background. Ibid, Polo, p.75. Sotheby's, *Arts Décoratifs Styles 1900 et 1925.* Monaco, 25 June 1981, lot.251.

107 V&A Prints and Drawings Archive, ref. no. E.535-1980-T.30. It also features in Matet, M, *Tapis Modernes,* Paris, H. Ernst Publications, 1929, plate 12b.

108 NMIEG:2000.164, grey, white, black, red carpet gouache.

109 NMIEG 2003.136, *Wendigen* carpet drawing.

110 V&A Archives, AAD/1980/9, postcard from J. J. P. Oud to Eileen Gray, 31 August 1924.

111 Christie's, *Les Collections du Château de Gourdon,* 29-31 March 2011, lot 802, Camard, *20-21,* 6 April 2009, lot.23.

112 NMIEG 2003.112, circular black, grey, beige and white carpet gouache.

113 NMIEG 2003.110, circular black and grey carpet gouache.

114 NMIEG 2003.111, circular black, grey and beige carpet gouache, this rug is shown in the display photographs which Eileen Gray took in *Jean Désert* in 1922. It is illustrated three times, twice in situ in portfolio NMIEG 2000.250.

115 NMIEG 2003.1641, portfolio.

116 V&A Archives, ADD 9/2-1980, this is the client register for Gray's shop *Jean Désert*, and the Marquise de Brandt is listed for a circular rug.

117 Ibid, Polo, p.47.

118 NMIEG 2003.113, circular dark and light blue, grey and beige carpet gouache.

119 NMIEG 2003.90, circular brown and yellow carpet gouache.

120 Ecart, Paris, *Rééditions,* pp.21-22.

121 NMIEG 2003.137, *Bonaparte* carpet drawing.

122 NMIEG 2000.172, *Roquebrune coast line* collage, NMIEG 2003.155, *Kleps* carpet drawing on grid paper, the letter 'R' respresents Roquebrune in this carpet design.

123 NMIEG 2000.90, *Tempe à Pailla*, site plan, NMIEG 2000.173, *Tempe à Pailla* collage.

124 NMIEG 2003.100, *Castellar* carpet gouache.

125 V&A Visual Arts Library, circ.240-1973. Ibid, Polo, pp.19, 35. Sotheby's, *Arts Décoratifs Styles 1900 et 1925*. Monaco, 25 June 1981, lot.251. Ibid, Matet, M, *Tapis Modernes,* plate 12a.

126 Vallois Gallery, Paris.

127 NMIEG 2008.1, *St. Tropez* rug. Ibid, Polo, p.29. Sotheby's, *Arts Décoratifs du XXe Siècle et Design Contemporain,* Paris, 22 November 2011, lot.136. This rug was sold with an original carpet gouache.

128 NMIEG:2000.163, *Tour de Nesle* carpet gouache.

129 Abel, Richard, *The Ciné Goes to Town: French Cinema, 1896-1914,* Los Angeles: University of California Press, 1994. Bousquet Henri, *Catalogue Pathé des années 1896 à 1914,* Bassac, Henri Bousquet, 1993-1996.

130 RIBA Archives, PB546/1, miscellaneous loose designs for carpets and tiles.

131 Mondrian, Piet, *The Blossoming Tree*, 1912, oil on canvas, Gemeente Museum, The Hague. Theo Van Doesburg, *Heroic Movement*, 1916, oil on canvas, Rijksdienst Beeldende Kunst, The Hague. Van Doesburg, Theo, *Card Players*, 1916-1917, tempera on canvas, Rijksdienst Beeldende Kunst, The Hague. Mondrian, Piet, *Lozenge with Colour Planes*, 1919, oil on canvas, Rijksmuseum Kroller-Muller Otterlo. Mondrian, Piet, *Composition with Colour Planes No. 3*, 1917, oil on canvas, Gemeentemuseum, The Hague. These are some examples of where the use of pastel colours appears in De Stijl paintings.

132 NMIEG 2003.101, blue with white and grey motif carpet gouache.

133 NMIEG 2000.250, there are numerous occasional tables displayed in the portfolios which show this.

134 NMIEG 2003.139, blue with white and grey motif carpet drawing.

135 Ibid, Polo, p.51.

136 Ibid, Polo, p.33.

137 NMIEG 2003.115, blue carpet gouache and collage.

138 NMIEG 2003.96, *Monolith* carpet drawings. Sotheby's, *Important 20th Century Furniture,* New York, 6 May 1989, lot.102. Ibid, Polo, p.12.

139 NMIEG 2003.154, geometric carpet drawing. NMIEG 2000.250, NMIEG 2003.1641, porfolios.

140 NMIEG 2003.109, black and beige carpet gouache. V&A Archives, W.40:1 to 8-1977, lacquer screen. This cubist lacquer screen dated 1928 and features in the photographs which Eileen took of her furniture displays at *Jean Désert*. This screen is wood, red and black lacquer with silver leaf and Cubist composite decoration.

141 NMIEG 2000.162, *Black Board* carpet gouache, NMIEG 2000.250, NMIEG 2003.1641, portfolios, NMIEG 2003.578-581, and NMIEG 2003.1002-1023, photographs of *E.1027*, living room.

142 Ibid, Bingham, p.22.

143 NMIEG 2000.161, NMIEG 2004.124, *Marine d'Abord* carpet gouaches. Ibid, Polo, p.45. This version has omitted the number ten in the middle of its design. NMIEG 2004.124 is the same in design as Polo, p.40, NMIEG 2003.151, *Marine d'Abord* carpet drawing. This drawing, completed on graph paper gives measurements and the rug's name on the back, 1926-29. Ibid, Bingham, Neil, p.22. Sotheby's, *Arts Décoratifs Styles 1900 et 1925,* Monaco, 9 October 1983, lot.144. Sotheby's, *Important 20th century Furniture,* New York, 6 May 1989, lot.103. This lot resold at Christie's, *Les Collections du Château de Gourdon,* 29-31 March 2011, lot. 801.

144 This may have been because of the difficulty of weaving figures in wool at this time.

145 Garner, Philippe, *Eileen Gray 1878-1976, Designer and Architect,* Cologne, Benedikt Taschen, 1993, p.118.

146 Gray, Eileen, and Badovici, Jean, 'Description of E.1027', *L'Architecture Vivante,* Winter, 1929, Paris, Editions Albert Morancé, pp.23-8.

147 Wang, Wilfred and Constant, Caroline, *An Architecture for All Senses*, edited by Marietta Andreas, Rosamund Diamond, Brooke Hodge, Tubingen, Wasmuth, Harvard University Press, 1996, p.20.

148 Ibid, Polo, pp.38, 40, 42. Ibid, Bingham, p.22.

149 Gray, Eileen, and Badovici, Jean, 'Maison au Bord de Mer', *L'Architecture Vivante,* Winter, 1929, Paris, Editions Albert Morancé, p.50.

150 Ibid, NMIEG 2000.250, NMIEG 2003.1641.

151 Ibid, Matet, Plate 12.

152 NMIEG 2003.155, *Kleps* carpet drawing on grid paper.

153 Ibid, Gray, Eileen, and Badovici, Jean, p.50.

154 Ibid, Day, p.138.

155 NMIEG 2003.105, yellow carpet gouache. Ibid Polo, p.37. V&A Visual Arts Library, circ.238-1973.

156 NMIEG 2000.250, portfolio.

157 Ibid, Matet, Plate 36.

158 NMIEG 2000.179, *Kilkenny* rug.

159 NMIEG 2003.103, *Wexford* carpet gouache.

160 RIBA Archives, Evelyn Wyld collection of drawings, album of views ref: A490/13.

161 RIBA Archives, Evelyn Wyld collection of drawings, album of views ref: A491/2.

162 NMIEG 2003.134, *Wexford* carpet drawing.

163 Ibid, NMIEG 2000.179. Sotheby's, *Important 20th century Furniture,* New York, 6 May 1989, lot.100.

164 RIBA Archives, Evelyn Wyld collection of drawings, ref: skb378-1(6).

165 V&A Archives, AAD 9/2/1980, client list book.

166 NMIEG 2003.127, speckled blue gouache with blue abstract motifs, NMIEG 2003.122, black, grey and beige gouache with architectural-plan motif, NMIEG 2003.123, black, grey, and white gouache with yellow motif, NMIEG 2003.133, black and white photographic collage, NMIEG 2003.146, black and white photographic collage. Ibid, NMIEG 2003. 118, NMIEG 2003.120, NMIEG 2003.124, NMIEG 2003.129, NMIEG 2003.141, NMIEG 2003.144, and NMIEG 2003.149. Ibid, Polo. pp. 48, 57, 58, 60.

167 Ibid, Adam, p.365.

168 Arnold, Bruce, *Mainie Jellett and the Modern Movement in Ireland,* Yale University Press, London, 1991, p.67.

169 NIVAL, NCAD library, Bruce Arnold Papers – Mainie Jellett Collection, box 7.

170 NIVAL, NCAD Library, Bruce Arnold Papers – Mainie Jellett Collection, letter from Mainie Jellett to Albert Gleizes, 28 November 1927.

171 RIBA Archives, Evelyn Wyld collection of drawings, album of views ref: A490/12.

172 Ibid, NMIEG 2003.110-114.

173 NIVAL, NCAD Library, Bruce Arnold Papers – Mainie Jellett Collection, letter from Mainie Jellett to Albert Gleizes, 11 February 1931.

174 Day, Susan, *Art Deco and Modernist Carpets,* London, Thames and Hudson, 2002, p.138

175 NIVAL NCAD Library, Bruce Arnold Papers – Mainie Jellett Collection, letter from Mainie Jellett to Albert Gleizes, 9 October 1932. After severe weather Jellett writes to Gleizes that she hopes that 'Weatherby in her little house by the sea was not swept away.'

176 *The Irish Independent*, 'Leaves from a Woman's Diary', 9 June 1933.

177 NIVAL, NCAD library, Dorothy Walker collection, letter from Eileen Gray to Dorothy Walker 22 November 1973.

178 NIVAL, NCAD library, Dorothy Walker collection, letter from Eileen Gray to Dorothy Walker 17 September 1973.

6

Engaging the Senses:
Eileen Gray and Furniture

Gray joined the Société des Artistes Décorateurs in 1913 and started exhibiting her furniture at the eighth Salon d'Automne. It began with her lacquer furniture, notably the panels 'Om Mani Padme Hum' and 'La Magicien de La Nuit'. After the tenth Salon when the Munich Werkstätten exhibited their work, the French economic journals described a German invasion of the French furniture manufacturing district of the Faubourg Saint-Antoine. At the exhibition the German furniture, notably by designers Bruno Paul (1874-1968) and Richard Riemerschmid (1868-1957), displayed fine proportions, undecorated surfaces, was strikingly modern and worked in total harmony with each room. Taking on board the Germans' ideologies Gray had always hoped to mass-produce her lacquer work for a moderate household budget.

In reaction to the German movement the Société des Artistes Décorateurs proposed to the Chamber of Deputies an international exhibition of modern decorative arts to be held in Paris in 1915.[1] The exhibition was to showcase a modern French style through a collaboration of art and industry and to allow for the development of international markets. The exhibition was cancelled after French delegates returning

6.1 Chest of drawers, 1919-22, zebrano, lacquer top and ivory handles © NMI from Dresden felt that France could not compete with Germany. The promotion of French decorative art was hugely important at home and abroad and Gray exhibited a piece of furniture with decorative lacquer panels as part of the French pavilion at the Panama-Pacific International Exhibition in San Francisco in 1915.[2] After the World War Gray returned from London to Paris and in 1919 she displayed a lacquer screen, 'La Nuit, at the Salon'.[3] France resumed its plans for the Exposition Internationale des Arts Décoratifs et Industriels Modernes in July of that year but with the country wracked by war, the planning of such an enormous event had economic, political as well as artistic implications. With various commissions in her new role of interior designer and the opening of her shop in 1922, Gray also participated in two exhibitions. A change was becoming apparent in her work with a move away from the exoticism of lacquer and experimentation in new materials. Like the Germans, Gray began to use plain unadorned wood, and introduced new media such as scorched wood. The first exhibition was at the Salon d'Automne where Gray exhibited a scorched zebrano chest of drawers with a lacquer top and ivory handles, a lacquer screen, and a variety of rugs and wall hangings.[4] She kept some of her experiments in scorched pine and zebrano wood for this chest of drawers.[5] Scorching the wood provided a rough texture, however when sanded it revealed a wonderful effect on the grain. She also scorched a large sycamore vase commissioned by the car manufacturer Jean

6.2 Vase, circa 1920, scorched pine and lacquered oak © Archives Galerie Vallois - Paris, Arnaud Carpentier

Henri Labourette[6] and for a commercial lamp by Bernard Albin which Gray purchased for herself and to which she added a base of scorched wood.[7]

In the winter of 1922 she participated in Amsterdam at an exhibition Exposition Française d'Amsterdam Industries d'Art et de Luxe organised by the Ministry of Foreign Affairs. Gray asked Jan Wils to make adjustments to her display where she exhibited a lacquer screen, a lacquer mirror, and an early version of the *Transat chair*.[8] Wils noted that her work was out of place, due to its contemporary feel, amongst the other French monstrosities.[9] One of the key pieces exhibited at this exhibition was the *Transat chair*. Its design, and the media which Gray used, displays her virtuosity. It shows her changing ethos from lacquer furniture to modern designer.

The *Transat chair* was inspired by the folding deck chairs of steamers and ocean liners.[10] In her portfolio Gray describes the chairs in the following manner, 'Fauteuils démontable en sycamore relié par des traverses en ferchromé; matelas suspend' (Sycamore armchairs which can be easily taken apart, connected by crossbars made from chromed iron with a suspended mattress).[11] It was developed using curved jointing and nickelled steel fittings. Several variations of the *Transat chair* were produced and are in existence. Some are upholstered in leather, others ponyskin. In some of her notes she stated that one was

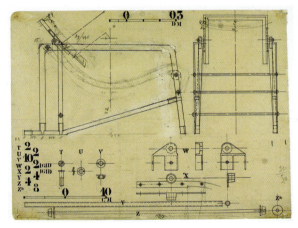

6.3 Drawings of *Transat chair*, 1920-22, paper, ink, pencil © NMI

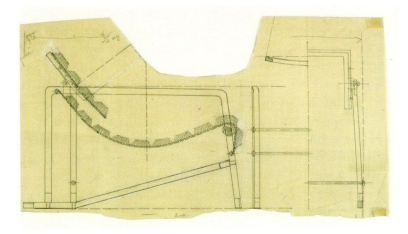

6.4 Drawings of *Transat chair*, 1920-22, paper, ink, pencil © NMI

upholstered in light brown or beige skai.[12] Many of them are displayed in her portfolios and were placed in a body of work which she dated from 1922-1930.[13] They were sold through *Jean Désert*.[14] The chairs either had a black, handcrafted, lacquered frame with brass or chrome fittings or they had a plain, utilitarian sycamore wood frame. Each had the seat set into the frame like a hammock, and the hinged, padded headrest of the chair could tilt for comfort. Both versions of the chair were still being produced in 1930 as Gray's portfolios illustrate dated photographs of both a lacquer version of the chair covered in ponyskin 'model no.1139-1' and a sycamore version upholstered in black leather 'model no.1139-2'. Both chairs are dated 13 January 1930.[15] Depending on the client, the padded head rest either had three padded cushions, or four, and the length and width of the chair also varied. The drawings which Gray made for the *Transat chair* were published in *L'Architecture Vivante*.[16] Some drawings of the *Transat chair* show a side elevation with its suspended mattress and a view of the framework.[17] The chair appears in photographs, elevations and drawings of her various architectural and interior design projects; for the Maharaja of Indore's house *Manik Bagh* for Jean Badovici's at *E.1027*, his apartment at rue Chateaubriand in Paris, and they also feature in drawings for the house on rue de l'Argentine at Vézelay.[18] Gray also ordered two *Transat chairs* for her house *Tempe à Pailla*.[19] The chair was a key piece in the change of Gray's design thinking. The chair which she created for *E.1027* was designed in 1925.[20]

At the fourteenth Salon des Artistes Décorateurs in 1923 the change in Gray's work culminated with 'Une chambre à coucher boudoir pour Monte Carlo' (bedroom boudoir for Monte Carlo). The concept behind the *Monte Carlo room* 'was that of a retreat, to provide a sanctuary for the individual by engaging the senses through the use of space, materials and relaxation'. Within the Modern Movement a conflict had arisen between the individual and their collective needs. In an attempt to explain her ideas Gray says, 'Just as individuals are profoundly different, so there are always common traits and desires among them; human nature always emerges amidst the labyrinth of ideas and contradictory passions'.[21] Her intention was to provide a balance between the individual and collective aspirations saying that 'it is thanks to the intimate fusion of the general and the particular that beautiful works give us the impression of a definitive stability, the impression that nothing can be added to them or taken away, the impression that they are eternal'. [22]

6.5 *Monte Carlo room* lamp, circa 1920, sculpted and polished ivory, mahogany base, material lampshade © Archives Galerie Vallois - Paris, Arnaud Carpentier

Originally called 'Hall 1922' Gray later named it the more significant 'bedroom boudoir for Monte Carlo' – equating the place name Monte Carlo with leisure, and boudoir signifying a woman's private space.[23] Of the room Gray said, 'The walls were white and there were dark red and matt white lacquer panels behind the bed. The door was very dull brown and dull gold lacquer. There were two small white screens; the carpet was dark blue and brown'. The room consisted of a lacquer door which led onto the boudoir, with a large cubist lamp centred at the ceiling which pointed downwards. The room contained a daybed, a small octagonal *guéridon* table, rugs called *Magie Noire, Tarabes* and *Héliopolis*, a small lacquer lamp with a parchment shade, and a zebrano stool.[24] Gray produced an early model for the *guéridon* table which was similar to one which she produced for Damia.[25] It was also a derivative of another occasional round table which had a hexagonal top similar to the *guéridon* table yet had four legs similar to the *Bilboquet table* which she designed for Jacques Doucet.[26] Gray had also produced several variations of the small lacquer and ivory lamp which sat on the *guéridon* table.[27] They usually had parchment shades with abstract, geometric motifs in bright colours.

For the room Gray also produced a black lacquer writing desk identical to the one produced for her client Labourdette with handles by Kichizo Inagaki.[28] For the first model of this desk Gray was not happy with the handles. Kichizo Inagaki was a talented Japanese floral artist of cherry blossoms who came from Murakami, Japan. After obtaining his diploma from the École des Beaux-Arts in Tokyo he came to France with a number of his friends on 8 June 1906, where he would remain for the rest of his life. He is recorded as being at various addresses and quickly found work as an ebonist. He lived with Seizo Sugawara and three others at 16 rue de Théâtre. In Paris he continued giving lessons in Japanese floral art, lacquer work, and also sculpted small figurines in wood which he sold on the street in Saint Michel and Saint Germain. He was introduced to Auguste Rodin and he began working for him in 1912. A lacquer artist and a dyer of wood he also made hinges. He married Laure Peltre, his French teacher, on 11 June 1914. He undertook commissions for Auguste Rodin and Paul Poiret (1879-1944). He eventually represented Japan at the 1925 L'Exposition des Art Décoratifs and was a member of the jury.[29] Inagaki made several ivory handles for Eileen Gray's furniture. In the *Jean Désert* account book dating 1923-25, several payments to Inagaki are recorded

6.6 *Monte Carlo room* lacquer table, circa 1922, black lacquer table, with silver inlaid drawers, with red lacquer console, coloured photograph © NMI and there is correspondence between them about various items, many of which are handles.[30] There is an invoice relating to two ivory handles for work completed on 31 December 1920 for 280 francs. In a letter dated 10 December 1921 he states that there are problems with the wooden models Gray gave him as the wood was too hard and the proportions too big. Ivory was an expensive commodity and not being someone who threw items away Gray made a drawing of the handles depicted as a free-standing sculpture.[31] The drawers of this desk were lined with silver leaf – something which Gray had experimented on when she did her own lacquer powder puff bowl which was plain on the outside and lined on the interior.[32] Though not apparent at first glance these are transitional pieces. With the promotion of French decorative arts and the development of the Exposition Universelle well under way there was an expressed return to the styles of the eighteenth and nineteenth centuries, an emphasis on classicism and rotundity. Surface treatment was the essence of French style. Gray's lacquer furniture shown in the *Monte Carlo room* is an indication of her preference for purity of form and line. The desk was angular with sharp lines completed in black lacquer with an unadorned surface.

6.7 *Monte Carlo room* dressing table, circa 1920, oak and sycamore, © Archives Galerie Vallois - Paris, Arnaud Carpentier

A small antechamber was situated to the left off the main room with a small sycamore and oak dressing table and an unusual armchair which Gray kept in her apartment afterward. Gray also designed a futuristic rocket lamp in brown lacquer with a parchment shade composed of Cubist designs for the room. Many years later the shade had to be replaced.[33]

A blue Japanese lantern hung at the centre of the room, the light reflecting off a silver orb at the centre. Gray gave this description, 'The hanging lamp was made from wood in dull gold lacquer and the ceiling lamp (a Japanese lantern) consisted of circles shielding lights; the centre was illuminated'. The cobalt blue glass planes are cubic in design with superimposed rectangular and triangular forms in gold leaf and were originally designed and made in 1920.[34] The lantern and the blue glass inserts are photographed on display in *Jean Désert* in 1922. Gray liked this lantern so much that she hung one in her own apartment in rue Bonaparte. Noted in Gray's client list for *Jean Désert* is that a square lantern of blue glass was commissioned by Gray's close friend Kate Weatherby in 1930. It is possibly similar to the one which she completed for the *Monte Carlo room*.

The daybed was flanked on either side by two white block screens. White versions of the block screen first appeared in 1923.[35] Painted white, each screen was composed of forty-five large and ten small painted wood panels. They consist of alternating double and single rectangular shapes. Gray did numerous drawings of the screen's pivoting mechanism.[36] The initial idea for the blocks appeared in Mme Mathieu-Lévy's *Rue de Lota apartment*. Gray subdivided the long narrow hall and an antechamber by creating a pair of interlocking screens in black lacquer which projected perpendicularly from the panels of the wall.[37] The first white screens were originally designed for the *Monte Carlo room*.[38] After the exhibition they returned to *Jean Désert* where they feature in photographs alongside other furniture on display.[39] Gray sought to sell them to Duncan Miller for his gallery in London. His wife Madeline Miller wrote to Gray saying 'We do want the two white screens we saw there – do not bother to touch them up at all as by the time they get here they will have to be done again anyway'.[40] However the sale fell through at the time and Madeline Miller wrote to her apologising saying, 'I'm afraid we're so broke at the moment that we cannot afford to buy anything'.[41] It emerges in later correspondence dated 11 May 1936 that Gray granted permission to the Millers to sell the screens on her behalf, and Madeline Miller enclosed a photograph of the screens in the shop window.[42] Gray eventually took the screens back and extant photographs show them incorporated in her apartment on the rue Bonaparte and her last home *Lou Pérou*.[43] She reduced both screens in height by removing one row to suit the domestic proportions of her apartment. Both screens remained in Gray's possession.[44] Gray produced multiple variations of the screen, one in plain wood, some painted, some in black lacquer, some with inset blocks, all of various sizes, heights and widths.[45] In 1971 Gray stated that she made ten block screens – five of which she stated were painted white.[46] There are six recorded black lacquer screens, one off-white and two textured white wood.[47]

6.8 *Monte Carlo room* lantern glass, 1922, blue cobalt glass, gold and silver paper © NMI

6.9 *Monte Carlo room* lantern, in blue cobalt glass, with gold and silver paper geometric designs, 1922, black and white photograph © NMI

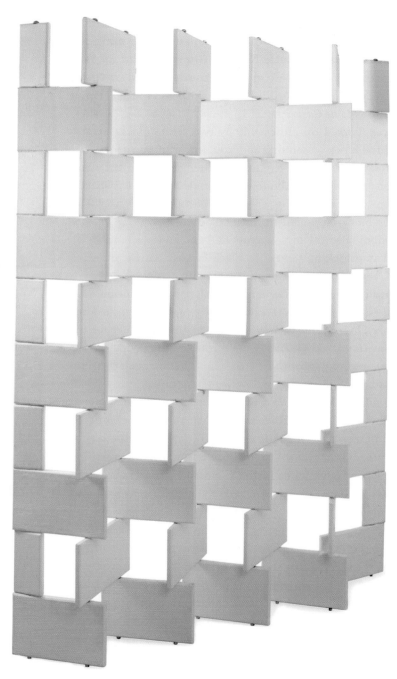

6.10 *Monte Carlo room* white block screen,
1923, wood, white paint © NMI

Gray at one point also explored the possibility of producing a variation of the block screen with triangular divisions.[48] The task of producing triangular blocks and forming them into a cohesive ensemble proved a challenge; hence on the model which she created the chevron motifs were only partially cut out. At one point Gray experimented with producing a block screen covered with silver paper.[49] In 1925 she produced a model for the block screen made from glass.[50] Black lacquer has been painted onto a glass frame, with silver foil applied onto the lacquered panels. This little model reflected Gray's preoccupation with the play of light on and through objects. The function of the block screen was to permit or prevent light from passing through into the room, or onto the sitter. Her experimentation of making a screen from glass, reflects her interest in developing a new alternative to serve a primary function. The block screens did just that. Gray also had numerous notes and drawings on the various block screens which she created – some of which were created in the later years of her life.[51] In the years preceding her death clients returned looking to acquire block screens of various dimensions. Gray employed a lacquer craftsman Pierre Bobot and using both old lacquer blocks from the 1920s, and combining them with new lacquer blocks, Bobot assembled and made new screens under her supervision. She even produced some new block screens – one was completed in red lacquer.[52]

Photographs of the room were reproduced in *L'Architecture Vivante*,[53] *Wendigen*[54] and *Intérieurs Français*.[55] Albert Boeken praised the cobalt blue lantern, the parchment and the ostrich lamps. 'Those wondrous lamps with their mysterious lighting ... are they wondrous works of art? Are they of this time? ... In its geometrical abstraction, like her interiors, with their elementary contrasts is certainly of this time. The lamps are much more than mere demonstrations of constructions and techniques of modern aesthetics ... certain new things, a certain character, purity, a strength bordering on perversity emerges which places the artist in a special category of her own'.[56] The novel room presented a controversial approach to interior design through its use of materials, bold colours and cubic formed furnishings. The parchment lamps, with striking cubist designs in white, red and ivory, were criticised for having an unsettling appearance.[57] René Chavance stated that the room reflected 'some regrettable experiments with disquieting cubism' yet in its eccentricity represented a curious harmony.[58] However, others such as George Waldemar praised the architectural aspects of the design, commenting on

6.11 *Monte Carlo room* rocket lamp, 1923, sculptured and lacquer wood base, with parchment lampshade © Virginia Museum of Fine Arts, Richmond, Gift of Sydney and Frances Lewis, Inv:85.169A

the frank and energetic conception of the room and describing individual pieces of furniture which worked well within the architectural construct.[59] The De Stijl contingent under Sybold van Ravesteyn praised its originality of concept.[60] In 1923 Albert Boeken, a Dutch architect who worked for the office of public works from 1916-26, and then had his own independent practice, came to Paris to report on the Salon des Artistes Décorateurs. Gray had submitted her *Monte Carlo room* and he was overwhelmed by her work. He sent her a copy of the review signed by him dated 5 January 1924 praising the abstract quality of her furniture and commenting on various items which he felt merited his praise. He was very critical of her contemporaries but praised the work of Gray, Robert Mallet-Stevens and Pierre Chareau.[61] Boeken then wrote to her on the 16 January 1924 after calling on her at her apartment in Paris, where their discussion centered mainly on architecture. Boeken mentioned a book to her concerning the applied arts of the Weimar Staatliche entitled *Bauhaus Weimar 1919-1923*.[62] Gray purchased it immediately.

In 1925 the Exposition des Arts Décoratifs et Industriel Modernes opened. It became the most important exhibition which celebrated French style, craft, luxury and elegance in the modern decorative arts. Thousands of designs from around the world were housed in large pavilions and 16 million visitors came to see the displays. Britain, Austria, Hungary, Poland, the Netherlands, Czechoslovakia, Italy, Sweden, Spain, Denmark and Russia were all represented, but notably absent were Germany and the USA. Each pavilion housed designers from different countries, department stores and international manufacturers. It was the height of the Art Deco style, a style which had many novel designs, but a style nonetheless which expressed the reluctance of designers and manufacturers to abandon tradition altogether. As a result the decorative innovation was sometimes short-lived as in the years which followed many European countries either returned to tradition or moved toward a functional Modernism. Three pavilions were noted exceptions: Robert Mallet-Stevens's *Pavillon du Tourisme*, Le Corbusier's *Pavillon de l'Esprit Nouveau* and Konstantin Melnikov 's (1890-1974) *Pavillon de l'U.R.S.S.* In France the Art Deco style dominated during the years following the exhibition. A number of exhibits displayed experiments in moulded steel. Mass production and functionalist furniture only began to be shown at the Salon d'Automne of 1928. Gray had begun her first experiments

6.12 *Satellite lamp*, 1919, cream-painted aluminium, composed of three superimposed flat rings in ascending scale mounted in alternation with three stepped conical shades in descending scale © Christies images

in metal in 1919 with the *Satellite lamp* – composed of three suspended concentric rings of painted aluminum alternated with stepped conical shades. Embracing minimalism and futurism, the *Satellite lamp* was a transition away from lacquer to industrial materials and it foreshadowed Gray's most acclaimed functionalist furniture.[63] Gray was notably absent from the Exposition Universelle of 1925, primarily for the reason that she had already begun numerous experiments and realised projects in architecture. Gray's change in relation to her thinking toward furniture was influenced by the arguments surrounding modernity in the decorative arts led by Le Corbusier and espoused by Jean Badovici. Le Corbusier's support for the French decorative arts tradition belied his fundamental disdain for the decorative arts overall which he elaborated in *L'Esprit Nouveau*. Paris may have been the centre for the arts, but Germany was the centre for production. This was clear in his pavilion where he displayed sculpture and painting alongside standardised mass-produced furnishings. Le Corbusier's statement that a house is a machine for living was demonstrated clearly in the design of his *Maison Citrohan* of 1920 which emulated the German ideology. This, however, was considered unpatriotic, as it challenged the aims of the 1925 exhibition and further contributed to the suspicion of French furniture designers toward mass producing their work, forgoing tradition and forging new initiatives with manufacturers. His ideas were supported by other architects notably Auguste Perrett. With Gray's *Monte Carlo room* she had focused on the furniture and furnishings of the room – and not looked at the space and the volume of the room. Badovici says this in his article on Gray in *Wendigen*. 'If she possessed a more confident and precise knowledge of architecture and relied a bit less on her creative instinct, she might well be the most expressive artist of our time'.[64] Christian Zervos, friend to Badovici and editor of *Les Arts de la Maison* and *Cahiers d'Art* stated similarly, 'The artist (Eileen Gray) is gaining greater insight by working towards more architectonic concepts of furnishings and interiors. Her screens, lacquer work, carpets and lighting fixtures already give evidence of her potential'.[65] Le Corbusier argued that the solution to the quelling of the excess in the field of decorative arts lay in an architectural approach to the modern interior.[66]

It is from this moment on that Gray is notably absent from the decorative arts exhibition circuit and her research into the problems of contemporary architecture also reflected her research into the problems of furniture. However, in applying the developing modern idiom Gray still combined the old with the new. Her work still fully engages with ideas of synaesthesia – by engaging the user's sensory abilities, but this time pieces were created for flexible environments and interiors.

After Gray had exhibited in Amsterdam she created a piece in homage to the De Stijl group whose ideas were challenging her design and architectural thinking. Gray's De Stijl table begins to incorporate all of the ideas which she was developing at the time. Composed of simple planes of oak painted black, to look like ebony, and white, she kept this piece in her apartment after she closed her shop. Gray took the ideas of the publication *Neo-Plasticisme* of 1920 which she had in her library and Theo van Doesburg's 'Sixteen Points Toward a Plastic Architecture'. Van Doesburg advocated that Neo-plastic furniture be asymmetrical, and that there should be a synthesis of elementary forms and colours. Piet Mondrian maintained in his publication that 'It is not enough that form be reduced to its quintessence, that the proportion of the whole work be harmonious; on the contrary, the entire work must be only the plastic expression of relationships and must disappear as particularity'. Gray agreed with Mondrian when he espoused a rejection of decorative arts, stating in this pamphlet 'The decorative arts disappear in Neo-plasticism, just as the applied arts – furniture, pottery etc – arise out of simultaneous action of new architecture, sculpture, and painting, and are automatically governed by the laws of the new plastic'. In this context Gray treats the design of the table as if it were an architectural model for a house. Even in her drawing of the design of the table Gray used a graphic device which the De Stijl architects had revived from eighteenth-century architecture, in which she depicts the table rotated with four elevations around the plan. This she continued to use in her architectural drawings. She also countered Van Doesburg's ideas, adapting them to suit her design. Rather than subdividing each element of the table into individual black and white horizontals and verticals Gray continued the use of the black or white colour through the horizontal and vertical plans articulating them in a single plane. The piece is multidirectional – to be viewed in the round.

6.13 Table, 1922-24, oak and sycamore, paint © Virginia Museum of Fine Arts, Gift of Sydney and Frances Lewis, INV:85.114

6.14 The architectural cabinet, 1924, sycamore, metal and chromed handles © Joe and Marie Donnolly collection

The second piece of furniture which marks a transition in her creative thinking was the architectural cabinet, 1926 – one which she designed for herself, the other for the architect Henri Pacon (1882-1946). Taking the concept of the traditional campaign chest she treats the design of the piece as equipment as well as furniture. The cabinet expands sideways, and has sliding and pivoting drawers created to accommodate large drawings and plans. It directly engages with the user in that she designed the chrome plated handles differently to suit each individual function. Gray had possibly seen displays with moveable furniture at the 1925 Exposition Universelle and critics such as Christian Zervos endorsed this type of furniture, alongside creating furniture which integrated into the architectural interior. Gray concentrated her developing designs on having her furniture emerge from the walls of her domestic projects. She first started doing this in the interiors at Vézelay, but it culminated on a philosophical level with the pieces of furniture which she produced for *E.1027*. The designs and ideas which she subsequently developed and produced for *E.1027* predate the work which was exhibited at the Weissenhofsiedlung Werkbund Exposition, 'Die Wohnung' in Stuttgart in 1927, as well as the steel furnishings which were shown at the Paris salons of 1928.

For her domestic projects notably *E.1027*, she engrossed herself into the processes of living, analysing the functions of the body and mind: relaxing, sleeping, eating, reading etc. Looking directly to what she called the 'camping style' – furniture was lightweight, easily transportable, multidirectional and multifunctional. She challenged the traditional materiality of furniture exploring celluloid, cork, aluminium and tubular steel all the while engaging with the physical, philosophical, psychological and spiritual needs of the person using her pieces. Her integration of furniture and architecture incorporated multiple uses in each space. Her objective was clear 'to create an interior atmosphere that is in harmony with the refinements of modern life while utilising current technical resources and possibilities'. To create furniture and furnishings that take into consideration practical comfort and expressed a universal style Gray created what she called the 'camping style'.

Straight away at the entrance of *E.1027* Gray built into the wall a niche for hats in transparent celluloid with shelves made from netting, to prevent dust from settling. A tube that ran the length of the partition could accommodate umbrellas. This also had a cupboard which could store chairs.

6.15 The living room at *E.1027*, showing the *Bibendum chair*, the daybed, the large divan, and the *Transat chair*, 1926-29, black and white photograph © NMI

Gray furnished the large living room with items suitable for its purpose; a space to be utilised for work, sport and entertaining.[67] She created a large divan where one could sit, or stretch comfortably. Opposite the dressing area was a small alcove with a small bed which had storage cupboards for pillows, mosquito netting, a kettle and books. A flexible table with two pivots extended outwards so one could read when lying down. This alcove could be partitioned off by a large screen for which Gray kept the model.[68] The dimensions and form of this large screen model indicate that the realised screen was used in the living room of *E.1027*.[69] It cornered off the daybed area and was placed next to the partition which concealed the dressing room with shower and cupboards. The colour used on the model is pale blue but the screen produced for *E.1027* appears to be a dark blue or black. Another drawing exists of the folding screen illustrated with a telephone chair and a circular rug.[70] Gray stated that the furniture and furnishings for this room were created to 'contribute to an atmosphere of intimacy'. When looking back at the entry partition which created a pause before entering the room, and subdivided the entrance and the main body of the house, Gray had adapted the partition, on the living room side to hold a gramophone and hold records. It was the music corner and the partition acted as a sound barrier. For the dining room Gray created what is now commercially called the *Rivoli tea table*.[71] Her design for the *E.1027* tea table was made from tubes that could retract. Covered in cork to avoid the impact and noise of cups, the piece included discs for fruit and cakes and a narrow end to rest a cup. However, an earlier version shown in Gray's portfolios was made in lacquer – as Gray noted 'Table à thé laque avec disques en aluminium mat pour gâteaux et fruits' (Tea table with lacquer discs in matte aluminium for cake and fruit).[72]

In numerous photographs of the room Gray records furniture which incorporates her ethos of the camping style: lightweight, portable and flexible pieces of furniture which could accommodate a number of activities and were adaptable. The *Transat chair* in plain wood with brass fittings appears in the living room or on the terrace, acting like a deck chair on an ocean liner. During the period of 1922-1930 Gray made twelve chairs. This example was specifically adapted to Jean Badovici's physique, was longer and wider in its proportions to the early lacquer *Transat chairs* and had four upholstered cushions on the headrest. The *Bibendum chair* was composed of a stacked cylindrical backrest and padded seat with ivory-white fabric upholstery, on chromed tubular steel frame. Its name drew from 'Mr Bibendum' or the 'Michelin Man' whose body was built up from a stack of white tyres. The early *Bibendum chairs* were made of skai, similar to leather, and are shown in extant photographs of *Jean Désert*. The chair is first shown in Gray's portfolios and was first mentioned in the winter edition of *L'Architecture Vivante* in 1929. The *Bibendum chair* of *E.1027* was upholstered in fabric. When *Jean Désert* closed in February 1930 three *Bibendum chairs* are recorded – two were purchased by Madame Pierre Meyer and one by Madame Labourdette.[73] In September 1931 Gray ordered the bases of three *Bibendum chairs* to be manufactured by the Parisian firm of *Aixia*, commissioned for Lévy, Tachard and one for her.[74] Mme Mathieu-Lévy purchased two chairs and they were illustrated in the *Rue de*

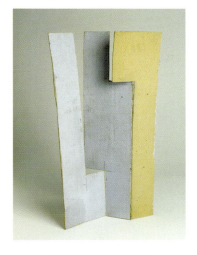

6.16 Model of the living room screen at *E.1027*, 1925, paper, paint © NMI

6.17 *Bibendum chair*, 1930,
stacked cylindrical backrest
and padded seat with ivory-
white fabric upholstery, on
chromed tubular steel frame
© Christies images

Lota apartment.[75] Before 1930 Gray had been experimenting with modern materials and continued to design variations on her furniture. With the *Bibendum chair* she experimented with rubber as described 'Fauteuil recouvert de caoutchouc' (chair covered in rubber).[76] In correspondence between herself and Prunella Clough, Gray noted that Madame Tachard had two *Bibendum chairs* in St.Tropez.[77] However in a later letter of 1971 Gray wrote that an antique dealer had actually acquired four *Bibendum chairs* which belonged to Mme Tachard.[78] Gray had hoped to acquire one or get one on loan so that she could have copies made by *Aram*.

Another chair which is shown in the photographs of the living room and in the bedroom is the *Non Conformist chair*.[79] Just as she did with the drawing of the De Stijl table Gray drew four, detailed elevations of the *Non Conformist chair* which was illustrated in the 1929 winter issue of *L'Architecture Vivante*.[80] The underlying theme of the chair's design is that of comfort. It was a nickelled tubular-framed chair with a stitched upholstered seat and back rest. The curved armrest on the left hand side was upholstered and ran the length of the arm, whereas the right side simply incorporated a slanted chrome steel bar. The drawing itself is an example of Gray's perfectionism in the way that she details every aspect of the chair including the textured upholstery. There are also drawings of a variation of the *Non Conformist chair* that plays on the aspect of asymmetry.[81] In the final drawing and subsequently realised projects Gray obviously examined the practicality of the earlier design. The title *Non Conformist* was reflective of Eileen Gray's non conformist personality and her mocking spirit.[82] The chair was ergonomically designed to provide comfort for the human body, as she understood that the average human has a tendency to sit slightly to the side when seated comfortably. She stated 'in the dining room, observe the very distinctive and comfortable form of the chair: one has removed one of the armrests to give greater liberty to the body, which can lean to one side and look or turn to the other without any discomfort.'

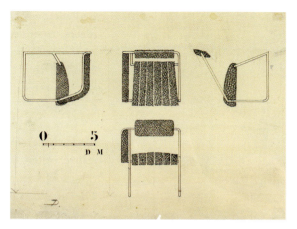

6.18 *Non Conformist chair*, 1925, drawing, paper, ink © NMI

6.19 *Non Conformist chair*, 1926-29, chrome, steel, upholstery, re-chromed and re-upholstered 1970 © NMI

As a result the *Non Conformist chair* for Jean Badovici was upholstered the length of the armrest. Badovici's *Non Conformist chair* was made from nickel and had a navy blue or black seat covering. The upholstery, Gray noted in her portfolios, was hand woven. Whereas the *Non Conformist chair* which Gray took with her from *E.1027* and kept in her apartment in rue Bonaparte she had re-upholstered and re-chromed in the 1970s to suit her needs. It was only partially upholstered on the armrest as Gray tended to lean on her elbow rather than use the full length of her arm, like Jean

Badovici, whilst seated. The *Non Conformist chair* is one of her signature pieces, intended eventually to be mass produced, but at the time of its conception Gray still had only a small workforce under her supervision. The fact that Gray created several versions of the *Non Conformist chair* demonstrates that she did not confine herself to just one prototype for mass production.[83]

Gray also designed a dining chair for *E.1027*. Several variations of the early version of the *dining chair* were produced; some are covered in fabric, others in green plastic, brown leather or suede.[84] In the first series the cross bars at the back are quite angular, and are made from nickel. They are also distinguished by the angular 'A' which is marked on the back of the feet. The back has a soft curvature. Several variations exist of the first series of this dining chair. Early images of the chair illustrated in her portfolios show the chair on display in *Jean Désert,* upholstered in leather, in nickel with no tips on the feet. It was one of only five drawings of furniture which Gray published in *L'Architecture Vivante* of 1929.[85] In extant photographs of *E.1027* the early chairs were upholstered in cream cloth and again did not have tips on the feet.[86] Another early chair which came from *E.1027* created in the first series has the addition of African rosewood tips and is upholstered in the original leather.[87] Gray then designed a series of six for *E.1027* which were later painted white with black seats in 1929.[88] Photographs exist showing the dining chair in Jean Badovici's apartment in rue Chateaubriand, 1929-1931, covered in brown leather. Gray unhappy with the way people sat in the chair revisited the design in 1934-35. The first edition of the second series was produced in chrome, completed in 1935.[89] The earlier productions of the second series show the chairs without rosewood tips on the feet. Slight variations were designed to provide the user with more comfort.[90] With the second series Gray increased the curvature of the back to provide greater comfort for the sitter and to aid digestion.[91] The second editions of the second series were not produced until 1965. These chairs were made from chrome and the feet also feature the addition of the rosewood tips.[92] They were re-upholstered with a brown suede seat in 1970.

Gray refined many of her drawings for the furniture at *E.1027* before deciding on the final piece. Numerous drawings exist of various chairs from the house in tubular steel.[93] Some chairs which appear in *E.1027* also appear in other domestic projects such as *Tempe à Pailla*. The *Aerosol chair*

6.20 Dining chair, 1965-70, chrome steel, suede leather © NMI is a nickelled tubular steel side chair with floor level stretchers which Gray originally designed for *E.1027*.[94] It also appears in photographs at *Tempe à Pailla*. Gray evolved the design removing the floor stretchers, and the resulting chair also appears in photographs at *Tempe à Pailla* where it was used on the terrace. In extant photographs the chrome framework of this chair is painted white.[95] It again appears in photographs on the terrace at *Tempe à Pailla* upholstered in a navy blue stitched canvas. It appears later at Gray's apartment in rue Bonaparte and at *Lou Pérou*. Another version of the chair is wicker upholstered with the metal frame painted blue. A drawing also exists of this chair with the stretchers showing a side elevation, rear elevation and a plan.[96]

Gray also did numerous drawings for tables which incorporated a lamp into its design or the lamp was attached to the side.[97] When designing the dining table for the eating area off the living room of *E.1027* Gray drew an early design of a table with an attached lamp soldered to the side with chrome metal legs which taper outward from the centre of the table.[98] A cross bar interconnects the legs. The lamp had a conical shaped shade and is attached to the table and could be moved by a lever. These drawings eventually culminated in her design for the *E.1027* dining table which was used in the area off the living room.[99] This extendable table which was made from nickelled tubular upright legs with a nickelled tubular extension. The table top frame was made from white-painted wood on which was laid a thick layer of cork.[100] The steel-tubing supports are designed in such a way that one can move and stretch one's legs without discomfort.[101] Gray stated 'the dining table is surfaced in cork to avoid the noise of plates and place settings. The table is supported on legs of tubular steel that can be extended or adjusted effortlessly. At the end of the table, a leaf and two runners covered in leather provide a place to set down a serving tray. During the summer one can either push the table onto the terrace, or, by sliding the terrace doors open, expose the dining room to the exterior'.[102] From the

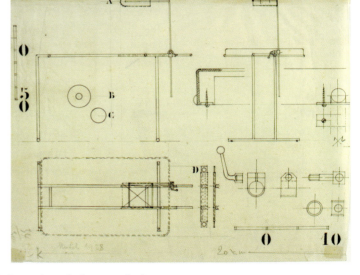

6.21 Drawing of *E.1027* dining table, 1925, paper, ink © NMI

extant photographs it appears that a mobile lamp was fixed to the sides.[103] On the drawing, the area where the lamp is attached to the sides is marked A, and the drawing shows that it can be lowered or raised. Light in weight, the table could be easily transported onto the terrace or moved into the living room. The areas marked B and C on the drawing are for small discs set into the table for plates and bottles. A drawing exists of the metallic frame for the legs of the dining table which is similar to the frame of the final table.[104] Gray did another study for an extendable table which is stylistically very similar to this one. In it she detailed the tubular extension for plates and dishes and also focused on the fixable lamp.[105] This simple table set Gray apart from many of her contemporaries due to it being multifunctional, mobile and specifically designed to its user's requirements. Charlotte Perriand (1903–1999) designed an extendable table for her small apartment in October 1927, which she later modified in 1928 and again in 1930. It was exhibited at the Salon of the *Union des Artistes Modernes* in Paris in 1930. One questions if the two designers, via Le Corbusier, were aware of each other's design. Gray's dining table was reproduced for Jean Badovici's study apartment in rue Chateaubriand, but this design had a lacquer or painted black table top. The drawing for the design was published in the 1929 winter issue of *L'Architecture Vivante*.[106]

6.22 Occasional table, 1925, pine, chrome tubular steel, zebrano veneer 1970 © NMI

In March 1974 Gray came back to re-examine the designs for the table and the lamp in the hopes to have it mass produced. In her drawings she closely examined the part of the dining table which extended with a leaf and two runners which provided a place to set down a serving tray.[107] Gray wrote that each room in the house was fitted with a table unit which served as a writing desk and if entertaining they could be brought into the living room, stretched out, with the supports adjusting one inside the other and made into a very large dining table that was lightweight but perfectly stable.

Gray also designed lightweight portable tables that could be moved from room to room with ease. The occasional table as meant for mass production and sold in *Jean Désert*.[108] Adaptability remains of paramount importance.[109] The original prototype was made from sycamore, which she later re-veneered with zebrano veneer and re-chromed in 1970. These tables formed the basis for numerous occasional table designs.[110] Eileen Gray actually made several versions of this table, with variations on a similar theme; the top was sometimes circular, sometimes rectangular, some were painted wood, others varnished, and some were left plain.[111] Variations are shown in her portfolios.[112] With some of the tables the metal arm was painted, but many were left plain. They were easily transported from one room to another. They consisted of a top and bottom linked by an oblique bar which acted as a handle.[113]

Another occasional table which Gray produced at this time had a painted blue surface and black painted tubular steel legs.[114] The table was possibly a maquette originally for a piece of furniture for *E.1027,* due to the use of the blue colour, but the piece didn't work in situ and no extant photographs survive of it in the house, and was eventually used in her last home *Lou Pérou.* It is an experimental piece. The table top has an anamorphic design. Gray has written underneath the table top indicating that 2cm were to be removed from the length of the table. Two bars run the width of the table underneath which were intended to hold a drawer. Gray has written in pencil that the drawer was to be 25cm in width and 30cm in length. There are three chrome legs which curve and are soldered together at the top. These were to be attached by three bolts to a piece of wood underneath the table. They are very delicate in design. The piece has been well used and suggests that it was used in the interior of one of her other domestic architectural projects.

6.23 Occasional table, 1926-29, sycamore wood, tubular steel, painted blue © NMI

6.24 The *Adjustable table*, 1925, chromium plated tubular steel with metal
tray chrome frame re-chromed 1970, metallic top 1970-71 © NMI

One particular table for which Gray has become associated was the *Adjustable table* which appears in photographs for *E.1027*. It is probably Eileen Gray's most famous piece of furniture.[115] It was a multipurpose table with an adjustable arm. It served as a bedside table or a breakfast table, was light-weight and easily transported.[116] It had an adjustable arm in order to alter the height of the table. Of the surviving tables no two are the same. There are six in existence. They are made either from painted or plain metal, chromed steel, aluminium or nickel. The table top is made from metal, Plexiglas or aluminium.[117] One has a lacquer top.[118] A table similar to this exists with a metallic top.[119] Their dimensions also vary; the original is 61.76cm high with a top of 50.5cm in diameter. A number of the table tops were made for *E.1027* and were made from Plexiglas.[120] There are three which survive.[121] It was also reproduced for Jean Badovici's apartment on the rue Chateaubriand. It appears in numerous photographs on display in *Jean Désert* which Gray took for her portfolios.[122]

The Parisian firm *Aixia* made most of the metal pieces. Letters between Gray and her niece Prunella Clough show that Gray kept the first version of the table, which she re-chromed. She also had the Plexiglas table top replaced with a metallic one which she preferred in the early 1970s so that it could be displayed on exhibition.[123] Though intended for mass production, Gray's small workforce and meticulous supervision of every stage of production meant that only a limited number of tables were originally produced.

In the more intimate areas of *E.1027* Gray attempted to heighten bodily awareness. The bathroom was filled with reflective and shimmering materials, filled with cupboards and shelves. Everything was designed to facilitate the ease of movement. The bedroom included a boudoir studio. The studio had a writing table, a metal chair and a low hanging light diffuser of frosted glass and a metal filing cabinet. Gray did numerous rough sketches for the filing cabinet which she created for *E.1027*. A rough sketch for a shelving system shows that it measured in length 170cm and 52cms in width.[124] The final drawing for the system of shelves illustrates eight drawers whereas the cabinet created for *E.1027* had nine. It was made from perforated and industrial metal.

A dressing cabinet in aluminium and cork conceals a washstand which, when opened, revealed a mirror. Despite being very shallow it contained drawers to hold containers used for grooming. Again using cork to muffle the sounds of toiletries in case someone was sleeping in the adjacent bed, Gray harks back to her lacquer desk which she designed for the *Monte Carlo room* as the cork drawers of the cabinet are lined with silver. This use of shimmering or reflective materials invokes a sense of the erotic marking the house and its furniture as an experience of a sensual being.[125] This aluminium cabinet worked in conjunction with a hinged wall mirror.[126] This square mirror is comprised of chrome and glass. The top left-hand corner is on a pivotal hinge, which enables this section of the mirror to move forward, permitting one to see oneself from all sides. Gray created a version of the mirror for herself in 1925, which she had in the *Rue Bonaparte apartment* and later was brought and installed in *Lou Pérou*. The glass was replaced due to breakage in February 1978; it was noted in Prunella Clough's notebooks at the time that the mirror, the top left-hand corner now broken, had 'survived wars, revolutions and my trundling it back and forth'.[127] The mirror at *E.1027* differed from Gray's mirror as her mirror has small round bolts intermittently placed around the edge. The *E.1027* mirror, made from nickel, was produced for the wash corner of the main bedroom. It complemented the aluminium washstand with its full-

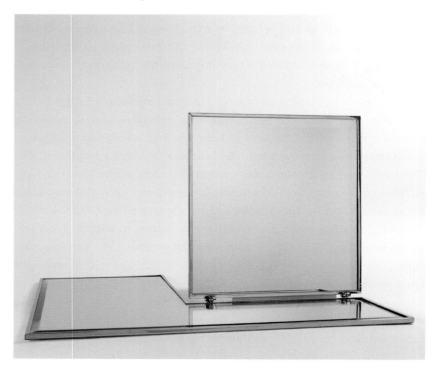

6.25 Hinged wall mirror, 1925, glass, chrome metal frame 1925-1929, re-chromed 1971, piece of new glass added in 1978 © NMI length mirror.[128] Several mirrors were made for *E.1027* – all highly flexible, functional and effective. Each was intended to heighten body awareness and was created with the user's needs in mind. The bed had a plywood head board with built-in lamps – one for night-time reading- a moveable bedside table and electrical outlets. The guest bedroom also comprises a studio – here photographs of Gray's *Non Conformist chair* appear, and a dressing area. This is where she placed the *Satellite mirror* used to magnify the image for shaving. Other mirrors were purely for putting on make-up, or for gentlemen who liked to look at the back of their necks.[129] It was here one *Adjustable table* was placed. Gray described it as an off centre table with a tubular steel base that can be adjusted to hold the breakfast tray at the desired height. It was also in this room that 'a small portable dressing table in leather and tubular steel has pivoting drawers'.[130] It was made of sycamore and nickel and had two pivoting drawers with a top made from leather which was covered by a sheet of glass.[131]

The original prototype of this dressing table which Gray kept for herself is composed of a sycamore carcass with the main frame made from chromed tubular steel.[132] The design of the dressing table displayed the use of hinged swivel drawers and shows similarities to the architectural cabinet that Eileen Gray made originally for the architect Henri Pacon. They also appear in later works on a more grandiose scale such as the swivel door in the sculptor's atelier in the *House for Two Sculptors,* 1933-34. Several studies exist on swivel and other types of hinges. The dressing table is multi directional and spatially adaptable to the owner's desires. In 1970-71 she covered her dressing table in a zebrano veneer imported from England and re-chromed the piece. In her correspondence with Prunella Clough Gray states that hers was the 'original maquette', or original model. Gray's dressing table differs from the one completed for *E.1027* in the addition of smaller drawers. She had the metal frame of the piece re-chromed to make it presentable. Gray's choice of materials produces decorative effects. The chrome handles used on the front of the dressing table are identical to the chrome handles used on the storage cupboards in the spiral stairwell of *E.1027* and also on the wardrobe that she designed for Jean Badovici in the guest bedroom of *E.1027*.

6.26 Dressing table, 1925, pine and rosewood carcass, zebrano veneer, tubular steel, metal frame 1925, pine 1925, zebrano veneer 1970 © NMI

By 1929 the salons in Paris of 1928 had begun to show the metal furniture of René Herbst (1891-1982), Charlotte Perriand, and Djo-Bourgeois (1898-1937). Herbst's display in the Salon consisted of two chaise longues in tubular steel. Perriand had been collaborating with Le Corbusier since 1927 and displayed her *table extensible* and four *sieges tournants* (turning stools or seats) in red leather and chromed tubular steel. These also recall Gray's stools with turning seats which she designed for *E.1027*. Gray's work at *E.1027* predates all of this work shown at the salons during this period. However the Wall Street crash of 1929 overwhelmed the French economy for nearly two years. The French Fine Arts Administration reduced its support of modern design arguing that a new decorative arts policy needed to be implemented as mass production of the decorative arts would undermine French traditional crafts and create unemployment. When the Société des Artistes Décorateurs invited the Deutscher Werkbund to exhibit in 1930 tensions were exceedingly high. The German display was dynamic, with functional lightweight equipment, furniture and light fixtures. The absence of decorative features imparted a solemn almost spiritual quality to the pieces. This abstraction in the German display was to become Gray's new paradigm for modern living when she began the furniture for *Tempe à Pailla*. French critics were scathing in their review of the German section especially as there was the assumption that the Werkbund's work would establish a model which would become the norm for design on an international level. This called into question not just French decorative arts, furniture design and architecture but also France's position both economically and politically.[133] As a result the *Union des Artistes Modernes* (UAM) was founded in November 1929.[134] Its members included René Herbst, Charlotte Perriand, Francis Jourdain, Sonia Delauney, Hélène Henry (1891-1965), Gustave Miklos (1888-1967), Jan and Joel Martel (both born and died 1896-1966), Jean Puiforcat (1897-1945), André Lurçat (1894-1970), Raymond Templier (1891-1968), Robert Mallet Stevens and Eileen Gray.[135] Its initiative was to break with the Société des Artistes Décorateurs as its members wanted to move away from the traditional system of official juries and prizes. They wanted to achieve a unity in the arts and to combine new production methods with the promotion of modern materials such as chromed steel, glass etc. Foreign designers were invited to exhibit in their annual exhibitions. Gray promoted the UAM but never attended the meetings except for one in 1953.[136] She paid the membership fee in

1930-33 and exhibited at the first two exhibitions showing photographs and plans of *E.1027*.[137] However, none of her furniture from the house was shown – only work by Perriand. Gray again showed with Badovici in 1931 recent work from rue Chateaubriand. Gray eventually became angered by the UAM when in 1956 after organising an exhibition of the work of Jean Badovici, photographs of *E.1027* credited the house to him with the furniture completed by Eileen Gray.[138] Gray lodged a complaint with the president René Herbst, but got nowhere.

One especially important commission which Gray received came in 1931. This was for furniture commissioned by the Maharaja of Indore. The twenty-five-year-old Maharaja Shri Yeshwant Rao Holkar Bahadur (1908-1961) employed German architect Eckhart Muthesius (1904-1989) in 1930 to commission various pieces of furniture and to build a modern palace, Manik Bagh, in India for him in the state of Madhya Pradesh. Muthesius's approach to the entire project was one of comfort, elegance and simplicity.

With the Weissenhofsiedlung Werkbund Exposition, 'Die Wohnung' of 1927 in Stuttgart, it became clear that a new direction in design was becoming visible: a combination of De Stijl, Bauhaus, functionalism and constructivism interlinked with Cubism, Purism and Neo-Plasticism. The transparent geometric shapes and 'scarce, severe and clean type of interior design',[139] contrasted radically with the exuberant surface decoration of French art deco. The prince and Muthesius had a strong link with the UAM and with the works which were exhibited in Paris. Carpets were ordered from Ivan Da Silva Bruhns (1881-1980), crystal chandeliers from René Lalique (1860-1945), silver from Jean Puiforcat, and furniture from Émile-Jacques Ruhlmann, Le Corbusier, Charlotte Perriand and Eileen Gray. The furniture ordered for Manik Bagh was to be economical and inexpensive – affordable for everyone. The use of furniture which was produced in series stood in direct contrast to the representative decorative style of the 1920s where designers sought to decorate entire interiors with lavish, individualistic and unique pieces. Some pieces found at Manik Bagh, especially the work of Émile-Jacques Ruhlmann, typified the luxurious art deco style, but stylistically

6.27 Maharaja of Indore, 1920s, black and white photograph © Christies images

they were transitional pieces with functionalist elements as they were series produced. Muthesius's work was produced by the Berlin Werkstätten and could have been produced in series in furniture factories. Many links are seen between the commission of Manik Bagh and the Vicomte de Noailles's house, the *Villa Hyères*, 1923-25, at Toulon in the South of France built by Robert Mallet Stevens. The client, the architect and the artists chosen were all working members of the UAM and links can be seen between the artists participating at the residence of the de Noailles and the architecture and the interior design at Indore.[140] The furniture, other designed objects, plans and models for Manik Bagh were exhibited at the end of 1931 and the beginning of 1932 at the *Porza House* in Berlin.[141] Much acclaimed by the press, the display was visited by over 3,000 people. After the exhibition, three ships from the Hansa line transported the furniture and the pre-fabricated building material from Hamburg to India. Due to the project's distance from Europe the palace and its contents was almost forgotten until it was rediscovered by a French journalist in 1970.[142]

Numerous pieces for the project which were produced in France were proposed by Henri-Pierre Roché.[143] Roché knew Gray from the time she had worked for Jacques Doucet. She described him: 'this very noble, enthusiastic man was a kind of introducer, he knew everybody'.[144] Roché brought the Maharaja to the Parisian artist's studios and acted as an agent on commission among them.

Gray ordered the chroming, polishing, and remounting of a batch of parts for the Maharaja's armchair referred to in an invoice.[145] This was for a *Transat chair* she provided under the commission.[146] The chair, made from lacquered wood, metal and chrome parts, upholstered in leather, was completed in 1931.[147] Gray writes that it was paid for on 15 February 1932. The chair was situated in the bedroom.[148]

6.28 *Aixia* invoice for the Maharaja of Indore, 1931, paper, commercial ink, pen © NMI

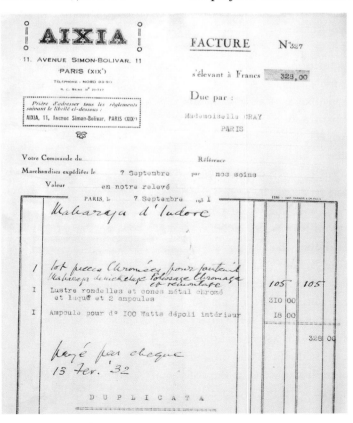

6.29 Maharaja of Indore's *Transat chair*, 1931 black lacquer, chrome fixtures, brown leather upholstery © Private Collection

6.30 Maharaja of Indore's *Transat chair*, 1931 black lacquer, chrome fixtures, brown leather upholstery © Private Collection

The colour scheme for the bedroom was carried out to Muthesius's plans. The walls were in a gold beige tone with a rough surface. The headboard was sprayed red. There were beige coloured mosquito nets. He designed the lighting fixtures which were made by Max Krüger, Berlin, and the dressing table, produced by Johann Eckel, Berlin-Lankwitz. Most of the other furniture in the Maharaja's bedroom was designed by Parisian artists, members of the UAM, and had been exhibited in Paris. The bed made from aluminium and chrome plated metal was designed by Louis Sognot (1892-1970) and Charlotte Alix (1897-1987) and was produced in collaboration with the Société Duralumin. It was exhibited at the 1930 Salon d'Automne and again in 1932 at the third exhibition of the UAM. The chaise longue was designed by Le Corbusier, Pierre Jeanneret and Charlotte Perriand and was exhibited at the Salon d'Automne in Paris in 1929. The couch was produced by Thonet in series in 1930. The invoice also includes a lamp, described as: 'Lustre rondelles et cones métalchromé et laqué', (ceiling light with chromed and lacquered discs and cones). This description is of the *Satellite lamp* except it has two bulbs instead of three.[149] Gray illustrated in her portfolios the earliest version of this cone and disc lamp hanging from the ceiling in her apartment in rue Bonaparte. Dating to 1919, it was composed of three superimposed flat rings which ascended in scale and alternated with three stepped conical shades which descended in scale. It was chromed and then painted in an ivory shade.[150] Gray had produced drawings for other lamps from this early date of 1919. Geometrical in its outline, one sketch has similarities with Gray's *Satellite lamp* of 1919.[151] A drawing exists of the *Satellite lamp* and the similarity in concept, shape and design of the lamp places them in and around the same date.[152] In her portfolio Gray dates the *Satellite lamp* in the same body of work as the pieces which she produced for the *Rue de Lota apartment*. Gray's lamp designs vary, no theme or particular style dominate for long, and her work varied from Cubist pieces emphasising the use of pure geometric forms, which the design of this lamp exemplifies, to multifaceted and multi-coloured De Stijl style forms, to Japanese lanterns, and rocket-like floor lamps. The material that would be used for this lamp is not specified, yet because it is similar in style to the *Satellite lamp* one can assume that it would possibly have been made from painted metal. One of Gray's most unique lamp designs was for a glass hanging lamp which hung in her bedroom in rue Bonaparte. The lamp was inspired by aeroplane flight when she flew with Chéron in 1913 in his bi-plane. The first *Aeroplane lamp* was created in 1922.[153] Its measurements were length 43cm, width 35cm and height 20cm. It was a suspension light of chromed metal fitted with tube lights which were supported by a sheet of blue glass and a sheet of white glass. Four of the aeroplane lamps were sold as part of her estate in 1980.[154] The original had its glass damaged in 1978 and the white glass was replaced with 'flash opal' glass. The other three were re-chromed in 1980. Another lamp was sold to a client Madame Fabre in 1973 for £15.[155] It is noted that this version probably had new glass. Gray's notes are on a piece of paper, written in the later years of her life, stating differences in the various versions of the lamp's size.

The firm who produced these objects was called *Aixia* in Paris. Another key piece which they produced for Gray was the two-tiered curved divan which they made for Gray in 1931.[156] Despite *Jean Désert* closing in 1930 Gray still continued to produce furniture. This was primarily because she was working on several architectural projects and furniture projects simultaneously. In 1931 Eileen Gray was completing work on several architectural projects, many in conjunction with Jean Badovici whilst producing furniture at the same time. These included: the Battachon/Renaudin House, 1926-32, Jean Badovici's House, 1927-31, on the rue de l'Argenterie and the Artists' Housing, 1927-32, on the rue de la Porte in the town of Vézelay. It also included Jean Badovici's apartment, 1929-31, in the rue Chateaubriand in Paris. Gray was still making furniture for *E.1027*, 1926-29. She had also begun work on *Tempe à Pailla*, 1931-34.[157] This two- tiered curved divan composed of four parts, which was nickel plated and then chromed. The structure was made from tubular steel with cupped feet. The firm noted that the divan required a large vat so that it could be successfully chromium plated. The description of the curved divan resembles that of two types which Gray produced. Gray illustrated the first divan in her portfolios. It had a built-in table attached to the curved frame.[158] The second is without the bolster table.[159] Also listed was a 'U' shaped frame for a shelf or a flap manufactured by hand and made from chromed brass, tubular steel feet for armchairs which were nickel-plated and chromed, and a tubular steel bar for a wardrobe or cloakroom which terminated in two fixation points. The firm also supplied Gray with nickel-plated feet for an armchair which were to be chromed in a particular manner, and with feet for two ottoman foot stools, both made from steel and nickel-plated; the first was chromed in a particular manner, the second was to be autogenous, or self-fused without the addition of solder or an application of an adhesive.

The vocabulary of the furniture and the furnishings for *Tempe à Pailla,* her house at Castellar in the south of France, was completely different to *E.1027.* Gray looked to the minimalism that was shown at the German exhibit of the Salon of 1930. The house is more spartan, more compact and specifically tailored to suit her needs. By this time she had also become increasingly interested in the work of Marcel Breuer (1902-1981) and acquired for her library *Moderne Bauformen* in 1931 specifically with photographs of Breuer's interiors for *House for a Sportsman* which he exhibited at the Bauausstellung exhibition in Berlin in that year.[160] Breuer had participated at the Deutscher Werkbund exhibition in Paris 1930 with Walter Gropius, László Moholy-Nagy and Herbert Bayer (1900-1985). One corner of the training room in *House for a Sportsman,* recalled Gray's ideas at *E.1027,* as it also served as a living room with thick cushions serving as a makeshift couch. The kitchen, guest room and second bathroom were separated from the rest of the house and not included in the full-size installation created for the exhibition. Breuer furnished the apartment with Thonet tubular steel furniture and bookshelves and wall units of his own design. Like the *The Hildegard and Erwin Piscator Apartment*, 1926, and the *House for a Gymnastics Teacher*, 1930, this exhibition revealed the contemporary obsession with health and the connection between modernism and hygiene. Taking these ideas, the furniture at *Tempe à Pailla* was created with the idea of minimalism. Abhorring clutter and personal effects being out on display she developed inventive storage compartments and furniture which had dual purposes, many of which were embedded into the walls of the architecture (this was a stark contrast to what she did at *E.1027),* or Gray created moveable furniture which could fold on itself.

There were several pieces which she designed with this concept in mind – the first was the *S bend chair.* She designed this chair in about 1938.[161] The canvas seat is suspended in an S-bend of perforated, laminated wood, and the chair can be folded to half-size for storage. The mattress is divided by bamboo tubing linked together by cord which will form the suspended mattress.[162] There are eleven eyelets which are spaced 4cm apart.[163] It has reinforced rods and rods which traverse at various points along the floor.[164] This chair is a prototype and has never been put into production.[165] Originally it was a derivative of the *Transat chair*, which was inspired by the ocean liner deck chairs which could be easily folded and stored. In her notes Gray says that a second *S bend chair* was produced in 1945 after the war.[166]

She restored an *S bend chair* for the *Heinz Gallery exhibition*, when she had Prunella Clough repaint it in cream and brown, with a brown upholstered mattress.[167] Gray preferred that the later head rest fall over the back of the chair. She also insisted that the stitching on the mattress and cushions be correctly done. Still meticulous to a fault in wanting her work to be presented correctly Gray was never happy with the cushions, advising Prunella Clough that the head cushion for this chair requires more stuffing, and that she wants the bolting system to be rectified. When the exhibition was over Gray learned to her frustration that the cushions of the *S bend chair* were not even put in the display at the *Heinz Gallery exhibition* in the end.[168]

The idea for the terrace chair, a simple deck chair, was a later derivative of firstly, the *Transat chair*, created in the 1920s, and later the *S bend chair*. The idea for all three was inspired by the deck chairs of ocean liners, which could be easily folded up and stored away without taking up too much space. Gray produced a detailed drawing, a model and finally produced two chairs.[169] This simple sycamore terrace chair with the metal parts painted black, was made in Menton by *Dufour & Martin*.[170] Gray writes

6.31 Drawing of the terrace chair, 1938, paper, pencil, ink © NMI

6.32 The terrace chair, 1938, wood, brass © NMI

in her notes that the chair dates to 1938.[171] It is made in two sections from sycamore wood, and folds in the centre and it stands on black-painted metal feet. It originally had an upholstered and padded orange cushion. The second sycamore chair was painted white.[172] These are some of the few pieces which survived the Second World War, when the house was used by the occupying forces. Gray's choice of materials is reflective of the materials used by other designers of the period such as Marcel Breuer and Alvar Aalto (1898-1976). It demonstrates the development from mass-produced tubular metal furniture to organic modernism through the use of woods and other indigenous media. The chair employed a similar hinging mechanism to that used in the *Transat* and the *S bend chairs*. It had brass hinges and thus was similar to the *S bend chair*, it also folded in half to save space when stored. *Tempe à Pailla* was completed in 1934, and items of furniture were still being produced in 1939.[173] The chair also came with Gray to *Lou Pérou*, Gray's last house, and features in a number of photographs, with people actually using the chair on the terrace. In particular drawings Gray indicates that the chair was supposed to be much longer than the final result – in some it measures 165cm, in others the chair measures 136cm, and 143cm. The actual chair when finished measured 98cm in length. One chair remained in *Tempe à Pailla* when the artist Graham Sutherland (1903-1980) purchased the house in 1954, the other remained in *Lou Pérou*.[174]

The *Curly chair* was another folding chair which Gray had produced for *Tempe à Pailla* in 1930-33.[175] It came to her apartment in the rue Bonaparte when the house was sold and is listed as such in her possessions.[176] She altered its design when it left *Tempe à Pailla*, as the little chair had a tendency to rock.[177]

Gray produced a number of tubular chairs for *Tempe à Pailla* for which she produced numerous drawings. In her drawings they appear to be made from metal tubing with a canvas or upholstered covering.[178] The sketches and the final tubular chair produced for *Tempe à Pailla* are similar due to the fact that stylistically both have a straight back with gently sloping seat. The difference between them is that in the sketch the arms of the chair run diagonally from the back upwards, whereas the final design for the terrace chair which Gray produced for *Tempe à Pailla* had no arms.

The furniture at *Tempe à Pailla* was more experimental, much was made locally. With the assistance of local carpenter André-Joseph Roattino she created built-in furniture. The entry hall bench pulls forward to reveal the stairs leading to the cellar, folding steps used for accessing cupboards fold into a seat, and dining tables become small coffee tables. Everything had a dual purpose. Her furniture created for clothing was unique; an extendable wardrobe, a pivoting chest of drawers and a trouser cabinet with chrome bars which acted as hangers which sat neatly into the cabinet.[179] Around 1938 Eileen Gray designed a series of large occasional tables with wood or copper tops with dark tubular or copper legs.[180] Some of the tables were remade after the Second World War when she began a lengthy process of refurnishing *Tempe à Pailla*. One particular chrome metal coffee table echoes back to her use of scorched pine or oak from the 1920s and has a low relief design in the centre.[181] This architectonic motif is actually an abstracted site plan for the house. The framework for the base is in chromed metal. It has four legs which loop in on themselves and interconnect under the table top. It complemented another table from her estate which had a rectangular top.[182] The construction of the metal framework of both tables is identical. Gray had completed detailed

6.33 *Tempe à Pailla* occasional table, 1938, scorched pine with chrome © NMI

designs for the table with the rectangular top giving exact instructions and diagrams for the design of the metal framework of the legs and the underside of the table.[183]

Minimalism is also evident in her work during this period as Gray also produced in 1935 a series of Japanese lanterns during this period which held frosted glass when complete.[184] It was a variation on the theme of the lantern used in the *Monte Carlo room*, with clear frosted glass insets. The glass itself had a central hole to emit the light, which was produced from the four corners of the lantern with tube lighting. Originally a blue glass ball, which reflected the light, was featured in the centre of the lamp; however, later ideas seem to reflect experiments in using plastic silver baubles rather than glass. Eileen Gray had always been extremely witty, inventive and creative in her designs of lamp and light fixtures. Her designs of the *Monte Carlo room* rocket lamp 1923 and the *Satellite lamp* 1919 anticipated innovations in space travel. She used a variety of media such as ostrich eggs, carved ivory and painted vellum. She also painted or chromium plated metal for her lamps and lights, which were pressed into various shapes to produce an assortment of structures, and used metal long before she introduced it to her furniture designs.

Gray was also continually experimenting with screens throughout her life. It is possibly because of the screen's architectonic nature, acting as a moveable wall or partition that Gray revisited screen and their designs continually in her work. Some of her models, like the screen in the living room of *E.1027,* played with cubic forms, strong use of colour and various materials.[185] The way the screen moved was always important to her and Gray did many studies on hinging mechanisms. With other screens it was the choice of material that was of primary importance. Eileen Gray produced three cork screens later in her life, during the early 70s.[186] She went to Montparnasse to choose her materials correctly and had great difficulty selling them upon completion. Stylistically these screens are similar in design to the abstract screens which she produced during the late 1920s. One design was for her last screen which she produced in cork in 1975 and which was shown at the Monika Kinley Gallery, London.[187] Gray's yellow celluloid screen came from the *Rue Bonaparte apartment*.[188] It was originally designed in 1931.[189] This large screen in chromed metal and celluloid consists of five leaves. Each leaf is slightly bowed thus forming a slight arc. It is made from smoked yellow celluloid framed in chromed metal. A horizontal band runs through the centre. Each side is mounted with a handle. It stood in the salon of Gray's apartment.[190] It is noted in an invoice from the *Worbla* factory dated 18 August 1931 that Gray was working with grey, pink and yellow celluloid which she had ordered for projects that she was completing at Jean Badovici's *Rue Chateaubriand apartment*. Drawings exist, though in Prunella Clough's handwriting, of a study of the bowed arc of each of the leaves, how the leaves folded in on themselves and how the hinging mechanism operated.[191] She explored the three sections of a celluloid screen from the top detailing how the screen moves when it is opened this culminated in a detailed study showing exactly how the hinged mechanism worked on the yellow celluloid screen. These were completed later when Clough was studying the measurements of the yellow celluloid screen for a project which Gray was working on in 1975. This project was for a shocking neon pink celluloid screen.[192] By 1975 Gray had already made the model with three leaves. Each of the leaves was bowed and of various widths. It was to have a metal chrome or brass frame and two horizontal bars separating the sections. Initially she looked at creating a two-panelled screen with two leaves. However, the three panel version proved more successful especially in her studies of how the hinging mechanism collapses on itself so that the leaves fit inside one another to form a single panel. Gray got Clough to do the drawings and the measurements for her due to a shake in her hand. The total height which she envisaged for this pink celluloid screen was to be 1 metre

66cm, and the length of the curve was 53cm with the curve width being 9cm.[193] Gray also did numerous drawings of the hinging mechanisms for this celluloid screen.[194] Sadly Gray died before the project ever materialised.

It was assumed that Gray had stopped designing furniture during the 1960s and 1970s. However, the letters to her niece Prunella Clough and the copious notes Gray compiled on her furniture reveal that this assumption has no basis in fact. She continued drawing numerous sketches for tables.

Clough worked with her on some drawings for tubular tables using early prototypes to alternate or update designs.[195] In 1964 Gray compiled a list of furniture which she had to complete.[196] Gray was looking to remount the lacquer blocks into a screen; she wanted to order six more wooden tables from Japan and lacquer panels. Cork and mica are listed to be purchased for use in furniture design. By the 1970s she was looking for new types of foam to stuff chairs which were upholstered with rubber.[197] On one of Gray's lists of 'furniture to finish' written in 1971 she is looking to make a chair using curtain rings, she is in the process of organising the completion of a table with a lampshade, she has to collect three chairs from the upholsterer and finally she wants to create a piece of furniture with leftover bits of ebony.[198] Even in her nineties the weight and construction technique of each piece was important to her, derived from a long process of design.

ENDNOTES

1 Tise, Susanne, 'Contested Modernisms', in Wang, Wilfred (et al), *Eileen Gray: An Architecture for all Senses*, edited by Marietta Andreas, Rosamund Diamond, Brooke Hodge, Tubingen Wasmuth, 1996, p.34.

2 Laurent, Jennifer, 'Salon et Expositions : Les Décennies qui Précèdent L'UAM', in Pitiot, Cloé, *Eileen Gray,* Éditions du Centre Pompidou, Paris, 2013, p.73.

3 Ibid.

4 Ibid.

5 NMIEG 2003.202, piece of wood. 1919-1922.

6 Galerie Vallois, Paris.

7 NMIEG 2003.219, Le Gras lamp. Eileen Gray purchased a Le Gras lamp in 1921 and adapted its design to suit her needs. The lamp is illustrated in photographs showing the architectural cabinet in *Jean Désert* in 1922. The lamp later appears in photographs at *Tempe à Pailla,* where it was mounted on the wall, and hung over her work desk in the living room. The base of this lamp has four holes drilled into it for the purpose of mounting. She also owned a second lamp. See Galerie Peyroulet, Paris.

8 Adam, Peter, *Eileen Gray: Architect/Designer: A Biography,* London, Thames and Hudson, 1987, p.131. According to Peter Adam it is debatable whether the chair was exhibited in Amsterdam in December 1922 as her first sketches appeared in 1924. Gray in conversation with Adam seemed to remember the *Transat chair* being exhibited there – if this is true the model which was sent to Amsterdam was the first version of the chair.

9 V&A Archives, AAD/1980/9, letter from Jan Wils to Eileen Gray, 9 December 1922.

10 NMIEG 2000.31–NMIEG 2000.32, drawings of the *Transat chair,* 1920-1922.

11 NMIEG 2000.250, portfolio.

12 NMIEG 2003.250, notes on the *Transat chair.*

13 NMIEG 2000.250 and NMIEG 2003.1641, portfolios.

14 V&A Archives, AAD 9/11 –1980, business correspondence, AAD/9/2-1980, clients register for *Jean Désert.*

15 NMIEG 2003.1641, portfolio.

16 Gray, Eileen, and Badovici, Jean, 'Maison en Bord de Mer', *L'Architecture Vivante,* winter edition 1929.

17 V&A Prints and Drawings Archive, E1130-1983.

18 V&A Archives, AAD/1980/9, unnumbered drawings, Jean Badovici house, 1926-31, rue de l'Argentine.

19 Adam, Peter, *EileenGray: Architect/Designer: A Bi-ography,* London, Thames and Hudson, 1987, pp.268, 294. Made by *Dufour & Martin* in Menton, Gray stated that they took an eternity to make and that when they arrived they were not of the same 'refined execution'.

20 NMIEG 2003.261, notes on furniture.

21 Badovici, Jean and Gray, Eileen, *Intérieurs Français,* Paris, Editions Albert Morancé, 1925, p.5.

22 Badovici, Jean and Gray, Eileen, *Intérieurs Français,* Paris, Editions Albert Morancé, 1925, p.9.

23 Ibid, Constant, p.52.

24 NMIEG 2000.29, lacquer model for table.

25 Sotheby's, *Important 20th century Furniture,* New York, 6 May 1989, Lot. 90.

26 V&A Archives, E1135-1983, this table had four legs, a circular top with a lower section, both of which were 70cm in width and 46cm in height.

27 NMIEG 2003.252, drawing of an ivory lamp. The base of the lamp was 9cm x 8cm and the shade measured 18.5cm in length. See also Camard, *20-21,* Paris, 31 April 2010, Lot.72. See also Christie's, Paris, 20 May 2003, Lot.38. Resold at Christie's, *An Important Private Collection of mid-20th century Design,* New York, 26 September 2007, Lot.27.

28 NMIEG 2000.28, ivory handles.

29 Musée Rodin Archives, Kichizo Inagaki papers.

30 V&A Archives, AAD 9/10 1980, letters dated 31 December 1920, 16 March 1921 and 10 December 1921.

31 NMIEG 2000.30, sketch for handles/sculpture.

32 NMIEG 2000.78, lacquer powder puff bowl.

33 NMIEG 2003.253, NMIEG 2003.254, drawing of the parchment shade for the *Monte Carlo Room Rocket lamp.*

34 NMIEG 2000.17-23, panels of blue glass, *Monte Carlo Room lantern.* NMIEG 2003.164, portfolio.

35 NMIEG 2000.10, white block screen 1922-23. See also Sotheby's, *Collection Eileen Gray: Mobilier, Objets et Projets de sa Création,* Monte Carlo :Parke Bernet Monaco, 1980, Illustration No.259, pp.30-31.

36 NMIEG 2000.41, drawing of a block screen. NMIEG 2000.42 – NMIEG 2000.43, drawing of two block screens.

37 Author Unknown, 'L'Apartement de Madame J. Suzanne Talbot par Paul Ruaud', *L'Illustration,* 185, No. 4708, 27 May 1933.

38 This was confirmed by research completed by Roger Griffith, MoMA, on taking paint samples from the National Museum of Ireland screen. Griffin, Roger, Delidow, Margo, McGlinchey, Chris, 'Peeling Back the Layers; Eileen Gray's brick screen', Paper given at the Vienna Conservation Congress, September 2012, New York, Manye Publishing, 2012, pp.1-8.

39 NMIEG 2000.250, NMIEG 2003.1641, portfolios.

40 V&A Archives, AAD 9/11 –1980, *Jean Désert* business correspondence.

41 V&A Archives, AAD 9/11 –1980, *Jean Désert* business correspondence.

42 Ibid.

43 NMIEG 2003.1431-1432, interior of *Lou Pérou* with block screen. NMIEG 2000.250, NMIEG 2003.1641, portfolios.

44 The second screen featured in the sale of her estate in Monte Carlo in 1980 see Sotheby's, *Collection Eileen Gray, Mobilier, Objets et Projets de sa Création,* Monaco, 25 May 1980, Lot.259. See also Christie's, *De Lorenzo – 30 years,* 14 December 2010, Lot.21.

45 NMIEG 2003.262, notes on block screens, 23 March 1972. These are notes concerning block screens which Eileen Gray owned. The first was in the entrance of the *Rue Bonaparte apartment* and had 32 large blocks and 8 small blocks. It measured 1 metre 97cm in height. Each of the blocks was 32cm long and 21cm in width. All of the blocks were in relief. The second screen was behind the curtains between the gallery and the salon. It has 18 large blocks and 6 small blocks and measures 1 metre 90cm in height. The bricks are 40cm long and 26cm in width. None of the blocks have relief work. Lastly Gray mentions a white block screen from *Monte Carlo room.* This screen had 45 large blocks and 10 small blocks. It measures 2 metres 13cm in height and the blocks measure 32cm x 21cm

and have no relief patterns. This screen, or the screen in the National Museum of Ireland was photographed later in Gray's *Rue Bonaparte apartment,* opposite a black lacquer block screen, and the two screens are flanking a long rectangular table.

46   NMIEG:2003.361, letter from Eileen Gray to Prunella Clough, undated.

47   The white block screen that is in the National Museum of Ireland Collection is textured white paint on wood.

48   NMIEG 2000.38, model of a triangular block screen.

49   NMIEG 2000.82, lacquer block with silver cigarette paper.

50   NMIEG 2000.37, model of a glass screen.

51   NMIEG 2003.262, notes on block screens, 23 March 1972, NMIEG 2003.237, drawing of a white block screen February 1980, NMIEG 2000.41, drawing of a block screen, NMIEG 2000.42 – NMIEG 2000.43, drawing of two block screens, NMIEG 2003.238, drawing of a block screen, 1971.

52   NMIEG 2000.86 - NMIEG 2000.89, four lacquer blocks. See also Aquarius Interview, London Thames Television Productions, November 1975.

53   Badovici, Jean, 'Eileen Gray', *L'Architecture Vivante*, No.27, Paris, Editions Albert Morancé, Winter 1924.

54   Badovici, Jean, 'L'Art de Eileen Gray', *Eileen Gray. Meubelen en interieurs,* special edition, *Wendigen,* Series 6, Santpoort, Holland, No.6, 1924.

55   Badovici, Jean, *Intérieurs Français*, Paris Editions Albert Morancé, 1925.

56   Boeken, Albert, 'Review of the XIV Salon des Artistes Décorateurs', *Bouwkundig Weekblad*, Amsterdam, 14 July 1923.

57   Chavance, René, *Art et Décoration*, Paris, A. Lévy, June 1923, p.175.

58   Chavance, René, 'Le XIVe Salon des Artistes Décorateurs', *Beaux-Arts*, Paris, June 1923.

59   Waldemar George, *Ère Nouvelle*, Paris, 8 May 1923.

60   van Ravesteyn, Sybold, *Bouwkundig Weekblad,* Holland, 14 July 1923, he states: 'Originality is not one of the great aspects of French furniture designers, the three Louis and their descendants still hybridise architecture … however coming as a surprise, there was also freshness. A room by Mlle Eileen Gray touches us more and expresses balance between searching and finding. The relationship with the De Stijl is eye catching, less orthodox, less pure; French virtues have not been disregarded and feminine frivolity makes itself felt. The work heralds the arrival of a Louis free tendency even in France.'

61   V&A Archives, AAD 9/12-1980, this is a French translation of his article on the Salon d'Automne, extolling Gray's work and published in *Bouwkundig Weekblad*; the date is unrecorded.

62   NMIEG 2000.195, letter from Albert Boeken to Eileen Gray, 16 January 1924.

63   NMIEG 2003.251, drawing of the *Satellite lamp.* This drawing completed by Prunella Clough was measurements and calculations for the *Satellite lamp* which hung in Eileen Gray's apartment. See also Sotheby's, *Collection Eileen Gray: Mobilier, Objets et Projets de sa Création,* Monte Carlo : Parke Bernet Monaco, 1980, p.77, Illustration no.298. See also Collection Marc Blondin. Galerie l'Arc en Seine. See also Christie's, *Collection Yves Saint Laurent et Pierre Bergé,* Paris, 23-25February 2009, Lot.317. See also Galerie Vallois, Paris. Gray also made a *Satellite lamp* for the Maharaja of Indore in 1931 see NMIEG 2003.46. This drawing is similar to the *Satellite lamp* drawing in the Victoria and Albert Museum Collection which dates 1930, see V&A Prints and Drawings Archive, W.105.D.E1136, this is a technical sketch with detailed technical notes and measurements.

64   Badovici, Jean, 'L'Art de Eileen Gray', *Eileen Gray. Meubelen en interieurs,* special edition, *Wendigen,* Series 6, Santpoort, Holland, No.6, 1924, p.12.

65   Zervos, Christian, 'Les Tendances actuelles de l'art décoratif. Le mobilier : hier et aujourd'hui', *La Revue de l'Art,* 47, January 1925, p.74.

66   Le Corbusier, *L'Art Décoratif d'Aujourd'hui,* Paris, Georges Crès et Cie, 1925, p.117.

67   NMIEG 2003.241, drawings of chairs, 1926- 1935.

68 NMIEG 2000.40, model of the *E.1027* living room screen, 1926-29.

69 In conversation with Renaud Barrès. Photographs of the living room at *E.1027* detail this large screen in the corner of the room partitioning off the daybed area.

70 V&A Prints and Drawings Archive, W.105.D.E1141 -1983, folding screen with a telephone chair and a circular rug.

71 NMIEG 2003.257, notes on furniture.

72 NMIEG 2000.199, notes on furniture.

73 V&A Archives, AAD/9/2/1980, clients register from *Jean Désert*.

74 V&A Archives, AAD/9/1/1980, *Jean Désert* cash book.

75 Author unknown, 'Le salon de Mme J. Suzanne Talbot', *L'Illustration,* Paris, 27 May 1933. The magazine shows the additional pieces of furniture Gray designed for Mme Lévy after Paul Ruaud redesigned the apartment incorporating Gray's designs and furniture.

76 NMIEG 2000.199, notes on furniture.

77 NMIEG 2003.300, NMIEG 20003.373, letters from Eileen Gray to Prunella Clough, 1971

78 NMIEG 2003.343, letter from Eileen Gray to Prunella Clough, 1971.

79 NMIEG 2000.250, NMIEG 2003.1641, portfolios, illustrates photographs of this *Non Conformist chair* in the bedroom.

80 NMIEG 2000.34, drawing of the *Non Conformist chair*, NMIEG 2000.1 *Non Conformist chair.*

81 V&A Prints and Drawings Archive, W.105.D.E 1169-1983, there are eight drawings on this piece of paper which is incorrectly dated 1965. This early drawing demonstrates all of the elements realised in the final project; however here the sloping arm is on the left-hand side, and the right armrest is not upholstered. Instead the right side consists of a tubular arm that curves under itself.

82 Adam, Peter, *Eileen Gray: Architect/Designer: A*

Biography, London, Thames and Hudson, 1987, p.200.

83 NMIEG 2003.241, drawings of chairs. See also Galerie Denis Doria, Paris, February 2000, Galerie Giles Peyroulet, Paris, 3 March 2001. Sotheby's, *Arts Décoratifs du XXe Siècle*, Monaco, 13 October 1991, Lot.334.

84 Ibid, Adam, p.229. NMIEG 2000.5, *dining chair*, 1925-1929. Made from nickelled tubular steel which was painted brown, the chair has a brown, upholstered suede seat and came from Gray's apartment in rue Bonaparte. NMIEG 2000.6 - NMIEG 2000.9, *dining chairs*, 1965-1970.

85 Gray, Eileen, and Badovici, Jean, 'Maison en Bord de Mer', *L'Architecture Vivante,* winter edition 1929.

86 NMIEG 2000.250, NMIEG 2003.1641, portfolios.

87 Centre Pompidou Collection, ref. AM.2011-1-35.

88 Sotheby's, *Arts Décoratifs du XXe Siècle*, Monaco, 13 October 1991, Lot.332. See also Galerie Denis Doria, Paris. Christie's, *Important 20th century Decorative Arts,* 8 June 2000, New York, Lots. 80 and 81.

89 Sotheby's, *Collection Eileen Gray: Mobilier, Objets et Projets de sa Création,* Monte Carlo : Parke Bernet Monaco, 1980, pp.54-5.

90 Ibid, Sotheby's, p.54.

91 Ibid, Adam, p.229.

92 Ibid, Sotheby's, see Illustration 279A, dated 1965, p.55. Philips, *20 – 21st century Design Art,* New York, 22 May 2002, Lot.42.

93 NMIEG 2003.241, drawings of chairs, 1926-1935.

94 NMIEG 2003.240, drawing of the *Aerosol chair,* 1931-34. Garner, Philippe, *Eileen Gray, Designer and Architect*, Cologne: Benedikt Taschen, 1993, p.106.

95 Ibid, Sotheby's, Lot 283. Galerie Denis Doria, Paris. Christie's, *Les Collections du Château Gourdon,* Paris, 31 March 2011, Lot 805.

96 V&A Prints and Drawings Archive, W.105.D, E1170-1983, design for a metal framed chair, 1930-1939.

97 NMIEG 2003.232, this drawing is for a table with a prominent table lamp forming part of the table. The base of the table is a cut-off rectangle with two legs

which run through to the height of the lamp shade. The shade measures 35cm, from the table top to the top of the lamp measures 45cm, while the legs of the table measure 60cm. The table top is circular with a circular hole cut in the centre where the stem for the lamp continues. Gray did complete tables and lamps which echo this theme. Another such joint table and lamp design exists with a white circular base, a singular leg which runs through to a white circular table and a long stem which rises up to a white lamp shade. See also Galerie Denis Doria, Paris.

98   NMIEG 2003.233, drawing of a table and lamp, Circa 1920s. The lamp shade measured 30cm, the stem of the lamp measured 80cm, the lever handle 18.5cm and the tapering legs 60cm. Gray didn't indicate the width or the length of the table top.

99   NMIEG 2000.33, *E.1027 dining table.*

100 NMIEG 2003.203, cork lamp base, 1926.

101 Galerie Duval, Paris. Christie's, *Les Collections du Château de Gourdon,* 29 March 2011, Lot. 799.

102 Badovici, Jean and Gray, Eileen*, L'Architecture Vivante*, Paris, Editions Albert Morancé, 1929, p.19.

103 NMIEG 2000.250, portfolio.

104 V&A Archives, AAD/1980/9/188, metallic structure for table in dining room. This is the metallic frame for the legs of the dining table with the cork top.

105 V&A Archives, AAD/1980/9, un-numbered drawings, work drawings and tracings.

106 Badovici, Jean and Gray, Eileen*, L'Architecture Vivante*, Paris, Editions Albert Morancé, 1929, p.20.

107 NMIEG 2003.234, drawing of a table and lamp. March 1974. See also V&A Archives, AAD/1980/9, un-numbered drawings, work drawings and tracings. Gray is exploring the idea of extending the table, which she did to a degree with the dining table at *E.1027*, creating a chrome/aluminium extension for plates and used dishes. Gray also here explores a small section of the table extending vertically.

108 NMIEG 2000.3, occasional table, 1925, zebrano veneer 1970.

109 Ibid, Adam, p.287.

110 NMIEG 2003.209, NMIEG 2003.210, NMIEG 2003.211, models of a decorative design element for furniture, Circa 1920s, NMIEG 2003.205, NMIEG 2003.207, modes of an occasional table base. Circa 1920s, NMIEG 2003.204, NMIEG 2003.206, NMIEG 2003.208, model of an occasional table top, Circa 1920s, NMIEG 2003.214, NMIEG 2003.215, NMIEG 2003.216, NMIEG 2003.217, table tops, Circa 1920s.

111 Ibid, Garner, p.84. See also Vitra Design Museum, ref MST.1033. Musée des Art Décoratifs Collection, ref.41350. Sotheby's, *Arts Décoratifs du XXe Siècle*, Monaco, 13 October 1991, Lots.321 and 322. Sotheby's, *Collection Eileen Gray, Mobilier, Objets et Projets de sa Création,* Monaco, 25 May 1980, Lots no.275 and no.275a. Denis Doria Gallery, Paris.

112 NMIEG 2000.250, NMIEG 2003.1641, portfolios.

113 NMIEG 2003.260, notes on furniture.

114 NMIEG 2003.218, occasional table, Circa 1930s.

115 NMIEG 2000.2, *Adjustable table,* Chrome frame 1925, rechromed 1970, metallic top 1970-71.

116 Badovici, Jean, and Gray, Eileen, 'Maison au Bord de la Mer', *L'Architecture Vivante*, Paris, Editions Albert Morancé, 1929, p.28.

117 Vitra Design Museum, ref. MST.1024. Pompidou Centre Collection, ref. AM.1992-1-3. MoMA Collection, ref. 533.1977. Sotheby's, *Arts Décoratifs styles 1900 et 1925*, Monaco, 25 June 1981, Lot. 250. Re-sold Sotheby's, *Important 20th century Furniture*, New York, 6 May 1989, Lot. 105. Sotheby's, *Arts Décoratifs du XXe Siècle,* Monaco, 13 October 1991, Lots.324, 325, 338. Lot 338 was re-sold at Christie's, *Les Collections du Château de Gourdon,* 29 March 2011, Lot. 29.

118 Peter Adam, private collection, Paris. Adam's table is similar but has a lacquer top.

119 MoMA Collection, ref. 533.1977.

120 Ibid, Badovici and Gray, p.28.

121 Christie's, *Les Collections du Chateau de Gourdon,* 29 March 2011, Lot. 29. Vitra Design Museum, ref MST.1024. Pompidou Centre Collection, ref. AM.1992-1-3.

122 NMIEG 2000.250, NMIEG 2003.1641, portfolios.

123 NMIEG 2004.11, letter from Eileen Gray to Alan Irvine 20 December 1971.

124 NMIEG 2003.243, drawing of a shelving cabinet, Circa 1926-29.

125 Ibid, Constant, p.113.

126 NMIEG 2000.11, hinged wall mirror, 1925-1929, rechromed 1971, a piece of new glass added in 1978.

127 Tate Gallery Collection, Prunella Clough Archives, Box 10, diary entries December 1977 – January 1979.

128 Centre Pompidou Collection, ref. AM.1992-1-6.

129 Ibid, Adam, p.200.

130 This is now in a private collection, France. See Pitiot, Cloé, *Eileen Gray,* Éditions du Centre Pompidou, Paris, 2013, p.174.

131 NMIEG 2000.250, NMIEG 2003.1641, portfolios.

132 NMIEG 2000.4, dressing table, metal frame 1925-1929, pine carcass 1925-1929, zebrano veneer 1971.

133 Berstein, Serge, *La France des années 30,* Paris, 1988, p.81.

134 Ibid, Constant, p.132.

135 Byars, Mel, *The Design Encyclopaedia,* New York, John Wiley and Son, Inc, 1994, p.558.

136 NMIEG 2000.194, letter from Jean Poirier, Union des Artistes Modernes, to Eileen Gray, 20 December 1953.

137 Ibid, Constant, p.133.

138 Ibid, Adam, pp.360-361.

139 Niggl, Reto, *The Maharaja's Palace in Indore: Architecture and Interior,* Arnoldsche, 1996, p.14.

140 Ibid, Niggl, p.22.

141 Werner, Bruno E., 'Ein Maharad schawird Eingerichtet', *Deutsche Allgemeine Zeitung,* January 1932.

142 Descharmes, Robert, 'Manik Bagh', *Connaisance des Arts,* No.223, 1970, pp.51-57.

143 Ibid, Niggl, p.19.

144 Ibid, Adam, p.188.

145 NMIEG 2003.46, *Aixia* invoice to Eileen Gray, 7 September 1931. Invoice in black print on cream paper for furniture completed for the Maharaja of Indore.

146 Ibid, Adam, p.189. Adam states that Gray produced two *Transat chairs* for the Maharaja like those which she had designed for the house at Roquebrune. In 1970 he writes that Gray gave permission for the old *Transat chair* to be produced in a summer version.

147 Sotheby's, *Mobilier Moderniste Provenant du Palais du Maharaja d'Indore,* Monaco, 25 May 1980, Lot 204, p.47. The *Transat chair* is incorrectly dated 1927.

148 Herbst, René, *25 années u.a.m (UAM),* Paris, 1956, p.45 and p.70.

149 Ibid, Adam p.389 and p.333. Adam states that there were two versions of the *Satellite lamp,* dating 1919 and 1925. He says that the *Satellite lamp* produced for the Maharaja came from Jean Badovici and was produced in 1919. This invoice indicates that the light dates 1931. V&A Prints and Drawings Archives, E1136-1983 also indicate this, *Design for a cone shaped light fitting, 1930.* The second light from Eileen Gray's apartment sold in Sotheby's, *Collection Eileen Gray, Mobilier, Objets et Projets de sa Creation,* Monaco, 25 May 1980, Lot 298, p.75, which dates 1919. This lamp appeared at Christie's, Sale 1209 *Yves Saint Laurent et Pierre Bergé,* 23 -25 February 2009, Lot 317, p.276. This catalogue dates the lamp circa 1925.

150 NMIEG 2000.250, NMIEG 2003.1641, portfolios, Gray illustrates one in her portfolios dating the lamp 1919 along with other work for the *Rue de Lota* apartment, *1919-24.*

151 NMIEG 2000.36, drawing of a ceiling lamp, 1919-1924. See also Sotheby's, *Collection Eileen Gray: Mobilier, Objets et Projets de sa Création,* Monte Carlo :Parke Bernet Monaco, 1980, p.77, Illustration No.298. Collection Marc Blondin, Paris. Galerie l'Arc en Seine, Paris. Christie's *Collection Yves Saint Laurent et Pierre Bergé,* Paris, 23-25 February 2009, Lot.317. Galerie Vallois, Paris.

152 V&A Prints and Drawings Archive, W105D-E1136, design for a cone-shaped light fitting, 1930.

153 NMIEG 2003.239, notes on the *Aeroplane lamp.*

154 Sotheby's, *Collection Eileen Gray, Mobilier, Objets et Projets de sa Création,* Monaco, 25 May 1980, Lot no.s. 299, 299a, 299b, 299c.

155 Christie's, *Les Collections du Château Gourdon,* Paris, 29 March 2011, Lot no.28.

156 NMIEG 2003.45, *Aixia* invoice to Eileen Gray, 27 March 1931.

157 The furniture for this house was manufactured by the firm *Dufour & Martin* in Menton, in the south of France.

158 NMIEG 2000.250, NMIEG 2003.1641, portfolios, Gray dates the divan with the built-in bolster table, amongst other furniture, as a body of work produced between 1922 and 1930.

159 Private Collection, Netherlands. This divan is re-upholstered and painted. Pompidou Centre Collection, ref. AM-1992-1-231. See also Sotheby's, *Arts Décoratifs du XXéme Siècle,* Monaco, 13 October 1991, Lot 320, p.114.

160 Author unknown, 'Marcel Breuer, Berlin: Haus für einen Sportsman', *Moderne Bauformen,* August 1931, pp. 377-9.

161 NMIEG 2003.246, drawing of the *S bend chair,* 1931-35.

162 NMIEG 2003.247, notes on the *S bend chair* mattress, 1970s.

163 NMIEG 2003.248, notes on the *S bend chair* mattress.

164 NMIEG 2003.249, notes on the *S bend chair* mattress

165 V&A Furniture collection, ref. Circ.571-1971, *S bend chair.* V&A Prints and Drawings Archive, W.105.D.E.1120-1983, slight sketch of S bend chair, c.1965-70, W.105.D.E.1121, rough sketch of *S bend chair* drawn on back of a sheet of note paper, c.1965-70, W.105.D.E1124, rough sketch of *S bend chair*, c.1965-70. There are several drawings in this collection of the *S bend chair*; it is exactly the same regarding measurements and notes.

166 NMIEG 2003.259, notes on furniture, late 1960s, early 1970s.

167 NMIEG 2003.263, notes on furniture, 1970. See also V&A Furniture collection, ref. Circ.571-1971, *S bend chair.* Gray had her niece Prunella Clough repaint the *S bend chair* and Arthur Wilmore re-upholstered it to go on exhibition at the *Modern Chairs* exhibition at the *Heinz Gallery exhibition* in London in 1970. Gray wanted her work to look pristine. She then donated the chair to the Victoria and Albert Museum.

168 NMIEG 2003.250, notes on the *S bend,* 1970s.

169 NMIEG 2003.242, drawing of the *Tempe à Pailla* terrace chair, 1938, NMIEG 2000.35, model of the *Tempe à Pailla* terrace chair, 1931-34, NMIEG 2003.213, *Tempe à Pailla* terrace chair, 1938.

170 Sotheby's, *Collection Eileen Gray: Mobilier, Objets et Projets de sa Création,* Monte Carlo : Parke Bernet Monaco, 1980, p. 33, Illustration No. 261.

171 NMIEG 2003.259, notes on furniture, late 1960s, early 1970s, NMIEG 2003.261, notes on furniture.

172 Vitra Design Museum, ref. no. MST 1046.

173 Ibid, Adam, p.204.

174 Graham Sutherland bought *Tempe à Pailla* for five hundred and fifty thousand francs (one hundred and fifty seven thousand dollars). Included in the sale were many pieces of furniture, of which only some have been preserved - the cupboards, the work table with a lamp, a dual purpose coffee/dining table, a celluloid screen, a carpet, various mirrors, beds, small occasional tables and a bookcase.

175 Galerie Giles Peyroulet, Paris. Sotheby's, *Collection Eileen Gray: Mobilier, Objets et Projets de sa Création,* Monaco, : Parke Bernet Monaco, 25 May 1980, Lots 270 and 271.

176 NMIEG 2003.264, notes on furniture, 1970s, in reference to the *Curly chair.*

177 Ibid.

178 NMIEG 2003.244, drawing of a tubular chair, 1926-29, NMIEG 2003.245, drawing of tubular chair, late 1920s early 1930s. V&A Prints and Drawings Archive, W.105.D.E.1162-1983, design for a chair with a metal frame, c.1935-39, W.105.D.E.1166-1983, design for a folding metal-framed chair, side elevation, c.1935-39.

179 NMIEG 2003.201, chrome hanger for the trouser cabinet. Galerie Giles Peyroulet, Paris. Sotheby's,

Collection Eileen Gray: Mobilier, Objets et Projets de sa Création, Monte Carlo : Parke Bernet Monaco, 1980, Lot.266. V&A Archives, AAD/1980/9, un-numbered drawings, work drawings and tracings.

180 V&A Prints and Drawings Archive, W.105.D.E1148 -1983, design for an irregularly shaped table, c.1935-39. Sotheby's, *Collection Eileen Gray, Mobilier, Objets et Projets de sa Création* Monte Carlo : Parke Bernet Monaco, 25 May 1980, Lot no.278.

181 NMIEG 2003.212, *Tempe à Pailla* occasional table, 1938.

182 Sotheby's, *Collection Eileen Gray: Mobilier, Objets et Projets de sa Création,* Monaco, 25 May 1980, Lots nos. 272 and 273.

183 V&A Prints and Drawings Archive, W.105. D.E.1142-1983, designs for a table with a formica or veneered word top on an elaborate tubular steel base.

184 NMIEG 2000.12, NMIEG 2000.24, Japanese lanterns, 1930-1935, NMIEG 2000.13 – 2000.16, panels of clear glass for Japanese lantern, Circa 1935. There are four surviving examples of these Japanese lanterns – two were sold at the sale of Gray's estate in 1980 and two are in the National Museum of Ireland collection, see Sotheby's, *Collection Eileen Gray: Mobilier, Objets et Projets de sa Création,* Monte Carlo: Parke Bernet Monaco, 25 May 1980, Lots.296-297.

185 NMIEG 2000.39, model of a screen, Circa 1925.

186 NMIEG 2003.255, drawing of a cork screen, 1973-75.

187 Bristol Art Gallery and Museum Collection, ref no. Na222.

188 NMIEG 2000.39, model of a screen, Circa 1925. Ibid, Adam, p.372.

189 Sotheby's, *Collection Eileen Gray: Mobilier, Objets et Projets de sa Création,* Monte Carlo : Parke Bernet Monaco, 1980, Lot.269. Sotheby's, *Important 20th century Furniture a Philip Johnson Townhouse,* New York, 6 May 1989, Lot.107. Sotheby's, *20th Century Design,* London, 2 March 1999, Lot.35. Sotheby's, *20th century Decorative Arts and Design,* 3 July 2002, Lot.64.

190 NMIEG 2003.776 - NMIEG 2003.781, photographs of the celluloid screen.

191 V&A Archives, AAD/1980/9, un-numbered drawings, work drawings and tracings.

192 Ibid.

193 NMIEG 2003.228, NMIEG 2003.229, NMIEG 2003.230, NMIEG 2003.231, drawings of a celluloid screen, 1970s, NMIEG 2003.221, drawing of a curved partition for a celluloid screen, 1970s.

194 NMIEG 2003.222, NMIEG 2003.223, NMIEG 2003.224, NMIEG 2003.225, NMIEG 2003.226, NMIEG 2003.227, drawing of hinges for a celluloid screen, 1970s.

195 NMIEG 2003.236, drawing of a table, Circa 1960s/1970s

196 NMIEG 2003.524, notes on things to sell, 7 November 1964.

197 NMIEG 2003.258, notes on furniture, Tuesday, 6 January, year unknown.

198 NMIEG 2003.526, notes on furniture to finish, 1971.

7

'A House is not a Machine': Eileen Gray's Domestic Architecture

Eileen Gray realised very few buildings; however material relating to over one hundred architectural projects exist and show that she took the role of architect very seriously. Elements of her domestic architecture which she completed independently or jointly with Jean Badovici still remain at the houses which she worked on in Vézelay. Of Gray's architectural projects, *E.1027,* 1926-29, created for Jean Badovici, and her own home *Tempe à Pailla,* 1931-35, at Castellar, are the only extant architectural works still intact which stand testament to her achievements in the world of European architecture.

7.1 Jean Badovici, circa 1930, black and white photograph © NMI

From an early age Gray expressed an interest in geometry, colour, pattern and architectural theories surrounding the golden ratio. She acquired a copy of *Manuel de Perspective et Trace des ombres à l'usage des architectes et ingénieurs et des élèves des écoles spéciales* (the Manual on Perspective and the movement of shadows for the use of architects and engineers) by P. Planat published in 1899.[1] She also owned a copy of Norwegian historian Frederik Macody Lund's (1863-1943) book *Ad Quadratum* published in 1919, who studied the geometry of several gothic buildings and structures, claiming they were designed according to the golden ratio. Gray's interest in this publication is also linked to her interest in Cubism and the writing of Henri Poincaré, whose book *La Valeur de Science* (The Importance of Science), Gray had acquired in 1903,[2] and also in the Neoplastic artworks of De Stijl all of which study golden ratio proportions. Gray also owned a French copy of the *Grammar of Ornament,* published in 1856 by the English architect and designer Owen Jones (1809-1974). Jones had developed numerous theories on ornament, decoration and polychromy with chapters presenting examples of ornament from diverse, historical and geographical sources. The book stimulated Gray's interest in colour combinations especially in her interiors.

It is not by chance that Gray located and finally settled in her apartment at 21 rue Bonaparte – near the École des Beaux-Arts. Gray must have been aware of the American student of architecture Julia Morgan (1872-1957) the first woman permitted to sit the admission exams to the École des Beaux-Arts in 1898. Morgan had also completed her final exams in 1906. Gray met Jean Badovici, the Romanian architect sometime between 1919-1921. An architect who built little but published widely Badovici was to become one of her early mentors and friends who supported her career as an architect.[3] Only a handful of women had competed for the admissions exams to the school.[4] Many women were not even listed as participating in the admissions examination and it is quite possible that Badovici, a supporter of professional women, and one who recognised women for their work, advised Gray not to pursue studies at the École. Badovici had come to Paris to prepare for the École des Beaux-Arts in January 1915, but enrolled instead in the École Spéciale d'Architecture in 1917 and was awarded his degree in 1919.[5] Badovici was in favour of women architects having an independent career. At some uncertain date between 1919 and 1924 he introduced Gray to the Russian-born Polish architect Adrienne Gorska (1899-1969) who had been living in Paris since 1919. She had studied under Robert Mallet Stevens at the École Spéciale d'Architecture, finally graduating in 1924. One of the few women with an architectural degree, Gorska was one of the architects from whom Gray learned technical drawing. At the same time Gray also began to subscribe to some of the most important architectural publications and journals of the day. She had fifteen volumes of *L'Architecture Vivante*, eight volumes of *L'Esprit Nouveau*, and ten volumes of *L'Architecture d'Aujourd'hui*. Through these key early texts Gray began looking at drawings, plans and elevations of the work of other architects and began devising her own projects.

Gray had been visiting Samois sur Seine since 1912 and she finally purchased a holiday house there in October 1921. She immediately set about making alterations and modifications to the house.[6] The house was at the corner of the rue de Bas Samois and the quays. In October 1923 she purchased the adjoining structure in order to make an atelier for Seizo Sugawara. The exterior of the house was altered by Gray with the help of local craftsmen.[7] She combined the street facades of the two buildings by extending a system of pilasters from the first to the second house. The rear facades were covered in undecorated stucco.[8] On the second floor she extended the balcony to near the corner of the building. To facilitate the parking of the car she built a garage at the back. The interior had a large living room and several bedrooms.[9] Each of the guest rooms was a different colour – echoing her early ideas in the use of colour in interiors. There was also a big studio. She created a skylight by opening up the stairwell.[10] In the service stair she added small metal grid work to windows which is found in other work by Gray.[11]

7.2 Postcard from Eileen Gray to Eveleen Pounden Gray, Samois sur Seine, 19 September 1912, paper, ink © NMI

Gray openly states that by 1923 she was 'absorbed in plans for building'.[12] She may have been referring to her Samois sur Seine project or possibly her study of Adolf Loos's *Villa Moissi*, 1923.[13] Loos had shown his project at the Salon d'Automne in 1923. Owning a copy of *L'Architecture Vivante*

(Winter 1923) where Loos's plan was also illustrated, she adapted his single family house by applying ideas she had studied from Auguste Perret and Le Corbusier.[14] Gray focused immediately on the relationship of the individual to the building. Loos had also used the publication to expand on the ideas in his essay 'L'Architecture et le Style Moderne', advocating the omission of ornament from architecture. Loos stated that a house should look inconspicuous. 'The work of art seeks to draw people out of their state of comfort. The house serves only comfort. The work of art is in its essence revolutionary, the house conservative.'[15] Loos's penchant for engaging the inhabitant's senses appealed to her interest in synaesthesia. Gray's drawing emphasised comfort and privacy shifting the main living quarter from the top floor through to the piano nobile. In looking at the ideas which Le Corbusier had displayed at his *Maison Citrohan,* which Gray had seen at the Salon of 1922, she treated the façade in a Le Corbusian way as a layered

7.3 Postcard of Vézelay, circa 1923, paper, commercial ink © NMI

membrane. She enlarged window openings and added a terrace. In the salon she incorporated strip windows and doubled the height of the salon.

She also added a central staircase which connected the living room floor to the bedroom level – inspired by the *Maison Gaut,* 1924, by Auguste Perret.[16]

In 1923 Jean Badovici received a commission to renovate a private house in Vézelay. Charmed by the town he purchased five derelict properties there with the intention of forming an artist's colony. Between 1927-1932 four houses were built; – *Yves Renaudin house, Jean Badovici house, Artists' housing* and *Christian Zervos house.*[17] Badovici hoped to develop new architectural ideas whilst renovating these houses.[18] Though Gray was a novice at this stage of her career, her work on these projects was quite substantial, yet she received no credit.[19] It is now known that three of the houses at Vézelay during the 1920s are attributable to Gray as they have previously been considered a collaborative project between Badovici and Gray.[20] The houses at Vézelay represent a transitionary period from designer to architect and she kept a postcard of the town as a keepsake.[21] The Vézelay houses fulfilled Badovici's aims as an architect and further facilitated Gray's architectural education, providing her with ample experimental ground to perfect techniques which she later used in *E.1027.*

The *House for an Engineer* was Eileen Gray's first unique architectural project which she made into a model and reflects Gray's interest in the ideas of Loos, Le Corbusier and De Stijl. She dated the project 1926. Several identical versions of the ground floor plan for the house exist, however inconsistencies between photographs in Gray's portfolios and the extant plans suggest that Gray repeatedly modified her drawings before she settled the final plan. [22]

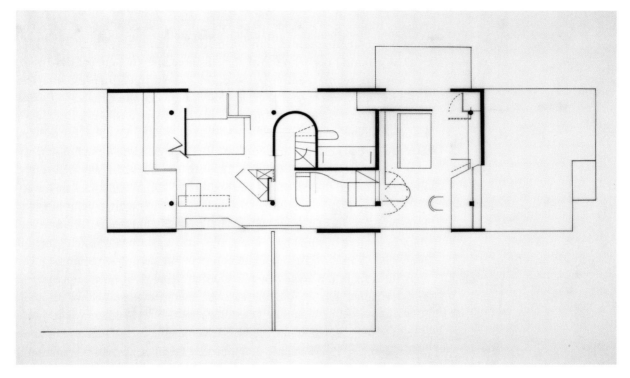

7.4 *House for an Engineer*, first floor plan, 1926, paper, pencil, ink, NMIEG 2003.2 © NMI

The title is significant as it alludes to Le Corbusier's 'Engineer's Aesthetic' in *L'Esprit Nouveau* in 1923. It also recalls Robert Mallet-Stevens's (1886-1945) *Engineer's house* created in 1923 for Marcel L'Herbier's (1888-1979) film *L'Inhumaine*.[23] Mallet-Stevens's *Engineer's house* represents machine ideology where wires, antennas, metal cones and cylinders appear ready to capture electric shadows and the enormous energy of the universe.[24] The house is a rejection of the machine aesthetic in architecture as Gray sought to engage the occupant's haptic sensibilities in both the interior and the exterior. In deliberately seeking to excite the senses Gray shows the influence of Loos's *Raumplan*[25] whereby each room has a volume appropriate to its function making the user engage directly with the space.[26]

She also examined Le Corbusier's 'Five Points of a New Architecture', and countered his ideas in relation to site; Le Corbusier used pilotis and a roof garden to provide conceptual distance at a site, whereas Gray clearly developed the house in direct relation to the site, manifesting the reciprocity between building and garden by using elementary forms and colours linking the interior to the exterior.[27] It was a flat location, but she modulated the surrounding land into discrete terraces.

The ground floor plan shows the entrance, the kitchen, the day room, the washing room, the drying room, the pantry and a sitting room. The sitting room opens onto the terrace. She modulated these spaces to form a series of outdoor spaces each of which is attached to the main house.[28] As a result outdoor and indoor spaces interrelate allowing a spatial continuum, as if the garden and the surrounding site is an extension of the house. Gray also varied the spacing of the columns in the plan, differentiating the spacing between them and the facades.

The first floor plan shows the office/study, the first bedroom, the bathroom, the second bedroom and the terrace.[29] The ideas reflected on this floor plan were inspired by the spatial principles advocated by the De Stijl movement and Neoplastic architecture.[30] In the design of the house Gray took ideas from *Classique Baroque Moderne* through her use of geometric and rectilinear shapes and the balancing of one form against another. She also looked to Theo van Doesburg's 'Sixteen Points Toward a Plastic Architecture', 1924 in which he stated that Neoplastic architecture be anti-cubic, asymmetrical and anti-gravitational. He advocated that there should be a synthesis of elementary forms and colours to break the boundaries distinguishing the interior and the exterior. *House for an Engineer* explored a dynamic balance of elements in the relationship between interior and exterior. Gray also used furniture in the construction of the space and cleverly designed built-in furniture and furnishings. As espoused in Theo van Doesburg's 'Sixteen Points' Gray's plans, on both ground and first floor, are anti-cubic and asymmetrical. From photographs of the model the house appears to be anti-gravitational. Neoplastic architecture combined elementary forms and colours, as displayed in Gerrit Rietveld's *Schröder-Schräder house,* 1924 - which Gray visited in 1925. Through this synthesis of colour and form one overcomes the distinction between interior and exterior. Gray later perfected this idea by combining the elementary forms of the architectural interior/exterior and the furnishings, with coloured floor tiles or natural colours from the garden, as demonstrated in *E.1027, Tempe à Pailla,* and *Lou Pérou.*

House for an Engineer demonstrates how Gray viewed the site as an extension of the house. As with other projects, she extended the elementary forms of the architecture and developed them further into the garden with a square-sunken lap-pool and semi-circular seating area.[31] This dynamic balance of forms and her treatment of the site looked to the *Ideal house,* 1922, which Theo van Doesburg and Cornelis van Eesteren (1897-1988) designed for Léonce Rosenberg (1879-1947).[32]

In the plan of the house Gray applied the ideas of both Adolf Loos's *Raumplan* and Le Corbusier's *Plan Libre.* Loos's dwellings are marked by a maximum of three-dimensional compactness and a connection of length, width and height. Sleeping and living levels are separate. Space on the sleeping level is defined by bedrooms which are individually accessible from the circulation area.[33] In accordance with the *Raumplan* Gray's first floor plan illustrates the bedroom level which has been raised up on pilotis. The principal bedroom/study overlooks the garden area. The space of the rooms is appropriate to their function. The influence of both architects is evident in how Gray isolated the bedrooms on discrete levels and connected them via a short ramp permitting spatial continuity.

The ideas of Loos and Rietveld are also apparent in Gray's plan of the first floor which illustrates furniture as extensions of walls and windows. She differed from Rietveld as the built-in furniture were not just functional pieces, they directly address the occupant's needs for storage, and later she realised storage units which had handles suited to individual function. Gray also draws free-standing tables, chairs and wardrobes. That Gray's furniture forms part of the architectural construct also counters Le Corbusier's mass-produced *casiers* which he advocated as being products of machine technology. Gray's approach to these storage compartments and cabinets was inspired by an article 'Cupboards in the Panelled Wall – An Economical Treatment for a Bedroom where Space is at a Premium' from *House and Garden*, 1920.[34] This article examined the economical treatment of space through panelled walls, promoting a capacious cupboard system which runs the full length of the wall. The space provided a cupboard fitted with deep and shallow drawers, five feet in height fitted with brass rods, not the traditional swivel brackets from where the clothes can be hung. Pigeon holes at the top accommodate hats, boxes of lace and ribbons. There was also a space reserved for boots and shoes. The doors were spring roller blinds which made the cupboards dust proof. These blinds could be easily changed at little expense. By building these storage cupboards into the wall space Gray saw how actual room space could be saved and how the furniture could readily be placed in such a position in the room that it wasn't crowded, and that the furniture itself was properly appreciated.

7.5 Site view of *E.1027*, 1926-29, in *L'Architecture Vivante*, 1929 © NMI

Eileen Gray's first independent, fully-realised, domestic architectural project was *E.1027,* which she created for Jean Badovici. She stated that *E.1027* should not be considered perfect, but rather the house was an attempt at addressing the issues of modern domestic architecture. Gray gave Badovici credit as being a collaborator on the project but significantly all of the extant plans are solely in Gray's hand.[35] Despite inspiration being drawn from various architectural sources, notably Le Corbusier, Gerrit Rietveld and Adolf Loos, it is important to make clear that Gray was the sole designer of *E.1027*. Though she said it was an example – a model on which other architects could improve on her ideas, it was in essence a very personal statement, the sole expression of years of ideas which culminated in what is now considered a masterpiece of twentieth-century architecture. Understanding this allows one to re-examine the Le Corbusier, Jean Badovici and Eileen Gray story and reassess the complex situation which developed afterward. Le Corbusier's pictorial interventions at *E.1027* were his attempt to improve Gray's model – by putting his own authorship on the house. Through her unique plans, design, furnishings, furniture and philosophical approach to the house Gray answered and solved architectural problems which Le Corbusier had unintentionally posed at the house which he had designed for his parents, *Villa Lac Léman,* 1923, at Corseaux in Switzerland. *E.1027* was certainly a case where the student outshone her teachers. Combined with Badovici's role in soliciting the murals and the fact that Le Corbusier felt the need to make his mark on the house demonstrates this further. Their actions underscore the split between their own personal agendas in avant-garde architecture and their lack of understanding of Gray's architectural intentions and aspirations.

Gray created the building for the inhabitant who would occupy it. 'In no part has a line or a form been sought for its own sake; everywhere one has thought of man, of his sensibilities and needs'.[36] Critical of the avant-garde movement Gray felt that architectural theory was insufficient in addressing the requirements of the individual, and that avant-garde architects focused on the exterior and the façade at the expense of the interior and the plan. 'External architecture seems to have absorbed avant-garde architects at the expense of the interior, as if a house should be conceived for the pleasure of the eye more than for the well-being of its inhabitants'.[37]

With regards to her plan for the house Gray felt contrary to Le Corbusier stating, 'The interior plan should not be the incidental result of the façade; it should lead a complete, harmonious, and logical life. Rather than being subordinated to the external volume, it should on the contrary control it'.[38] In responding to Le Corbusier's renowned maxim that a house is a machine for living in, Gray stated 'A house is not a machine to live in. It is the shell of man, his extension, his release, his spiritual emanation. Not only its visual harmony but its entire organization, all the terms of the work, combine to render it human in the most profound sense'.[39]

Gray constructed the house on an isolated, challenging site with rocky slopes along the Mediterranean coastline. After completing several drawings for the site sections,[40] Gray signed the final design on the west site section in pencil with her initials 'E' and '30'.[41] This was published in *L'Architecture Vivante* in 1929.[42] The west site section included: the outdoor kitchen, the main entrance, the balcony that leads off the living room alcove, the main living room terrace, the stairs leading from the garden to the main living room terrace, the sunbathing pit, and the stairs leading to the lower terraces down to the sea. The kitchen is separate to the rest of the house, easily accessible yet sufficiently isolated that no odours could penetrate the living spaces.[43]

7.6 *E.1027*, view from garden, 1926-29, black and white photograph © NMI

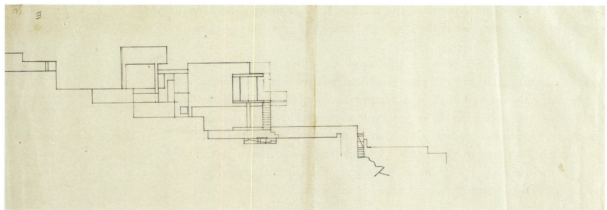

7.7 *E.1027*, west site section, 1926-29, paper, ink, pencil © NMI

Gray also illustrates in the west site section the double door off the living room alcove that gives access to the covered terrace. This metal door was embedded in the thickness of the wall, along with a shuttered door with pivoting slats which allowed practical ventilation.[44] The west side of the house was most exposed to wind, and to provide privacy in the garden Gray closed it off with a narrow storage space made of corrugated metal.[45] On the west site section drawings Gray showed the sunbathing pit with a divan made of sloped paving stones, a tank for sand baths, a mirrored table for cocktails, and benches to either side.[46] Gray did not illustrate on any of the west site sections, the spiral stair leading to the roof top, or the garden gate which was possibly inspired by Kazimir Malevich's *Black Square on White Ground*, 1913.[47]

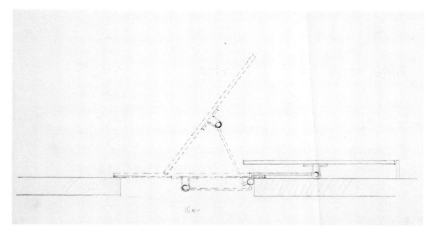

7.8 *E.1027*, drawing for shutters, 1926-29, paper, ink, pencil © NMI

Gray completed a detailed drawing for the shutter and strip window system on the small windows situated on the north façade at *E.1027*.[48] Though Gray designed the system, Badovici held the patents. Gray's system provides a solution to the debate between Le Corbusier and Auguste Perret at that time. For Le Corbusier the strip window was a primary element in his domestic architecture.[49] In his writings, Le Corbusier championed a variety of window types, yet he rejected Perret's use of vertical windows and its fragmented views. Perret had transformed and re-interpreted the traditional vertical window through new construction methods. In rejecting the use of vertical windows, Le Corbusier rejected the figurative or anthropomorphic tradition.[50] Subsequently Perret rejected Le Corbusier's use of strip or horizontal windows, which provided panoramic views. He argued: 'The horizontal window is not a window. A window is a man'.[51] He asserted that the strip window manipulates our spatial vision and perspectival view. They break the spatial continuum; clearly defining the interior and the exterior of a building. In her description of *E.1027,* Gray explains that

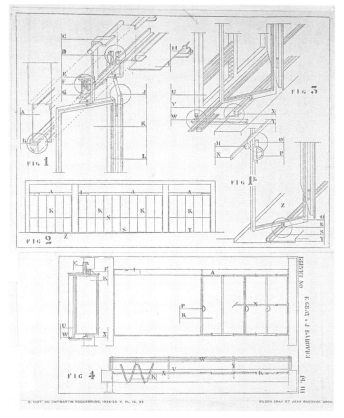

7.9 *E.1027*, plans of windows and shutters, 1926-29, paper, ink © NMI

one of the main issues in the design of the house was:

'1. The problem of windows, for which we have created three types.

2. The problem, often neglected and thus very important, of shutters: a window without shutters is like an eye without eyelids. Otherwise, all the current combinations lead to the same result: insufficient ventilation when the shutters are closed. Our method leaves a large area for the free passage of fresh air while blocking excess light'.[52]

Eileen Gray created horizontal windows, yet she installed panes of glass, which were in proportion to the human body and articulated by shutters. The shutters are a derivative of the traditional Mediterranean form; these sliding shutters pivot vertically and are adapted to a horizontal format. These panes of glass appeared on the northern façade windows and on the doors of the southern façade leading from the living room onto the narrow terrace. These doors pivot and slide sideways like curtains, embracing the modern movement principles and the anthropomorphic tradition.

Gray's system afforded the occupant the choice of completely opening or closing the private recesses of the interior to the outside. They limit the penetration of the sun, and their louvered system provides adequate ventilation during warm months. Various studies for the windows and doors exist.[53]

Gray's treatment of the large living room evoked the plurality of spirit of the *Monte Carlo room,* 1922-23.[54] This multifunctional space is defined by the habits of its occupant: eating, sleeping, entertaining, reading, or moments of reflection.[55] Yet at the same time it is planned so that each of its inhabitants could enjoy total independence, solitude and contemplation if required.[56] Gray achieved this through the camping and the normal method. The camping method responds to an accidental need to an outward expression, whereas the normal method, 'provides an independent and remote centre where the individual can develop his profound powers'.[57] By applying these styles, Gray segregated the space into public and private zones. In the finished room, Gray modified the floor tiles differentiating the various areas of the room.

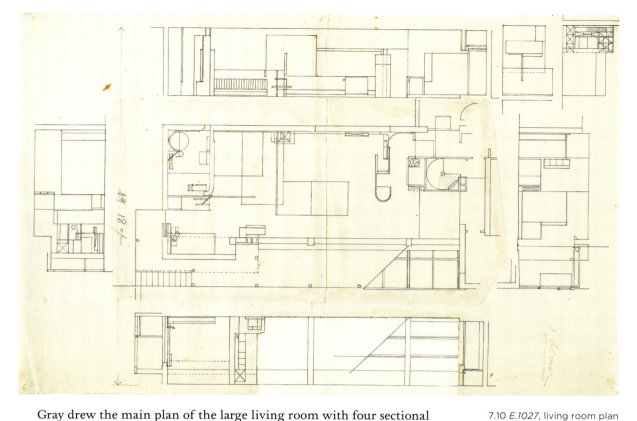

7.10 *E.1027*, living room plan with four elevations, 1926-29, paper, paint, pencil, ink © NMI

Gray drew the main plan of the large living room with four sectional elevations which appear to fold out from the plan.[58] One enters the room from the north, and Gray blocks the view of the room with a partition, heightening the initial experience of the space. With its southern aspect, the room reveals a large, well-lit space. It opens onto a narrow balcony; it overlooks the terrace garden and the sea. To the far left is a dining alcove near the stairs, whereas the far right reveals a small sleeping alcove with a washroom and a screened-off dressing area. Gray states: 'To allow for entertaining numerous guests one has made a convertible room…. Because this room is to be used for other purposes, a low wall at its end that allows the entire ceiling to be visible from any point, conceals a dressing area, complete with shower'.[59] This small alcove has a double door which accesses a private covered terrace, though this is not illustrated on the plan. On the south elevation of the living room plan Gray has drawn the fireplace capitalising on the room's natural light and southerly aspect.

Occupying a central position the fireplace's glowing embers replaced the fading sunlight. This theme she reiterates in *Tempe à Pailla*. Gray states: 'Work often with the psychology of light. Bear in mind that in our subconscious we know that light must derive from one point – sun, fire, etc a need deeply anchored within us'.[60] Placing the fireplace against the window permits one to enjoy firelight and natural light at the same time.[61] Other drawings exist of the fireplace, which display this.[62]

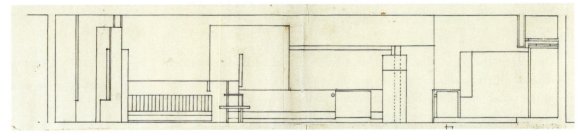

7.11 *E.1027*, living room, the north entrance with partition on the left, and dining alcove near the stairs on the right, 1926-29, black and white photograph © NMI

7.12 *E.1027*, living room, north entrance with partition, 1926-29, black and white photograph © NMI

7.13 *E.1027*, living room, detail of north elevation, 1926, paper, paint, pencil, ink © NMI

On both the plan and elevations (north, east, south and west) of the room Gray clearly outlines pieces of furniture. On the north elevation, Gray illustrates the partition where one enters the room which incorporates shelves for hats or personal items, an umbrella stand, and a coat rack. The large divan, shown on both the plan and the north elevation, recalls eighteenth-century salons with their popular Turkish daybeds. With this large divan and the small divan in the alcove Gray addresses the popular Provencal and Mediterranean culture of siesta.[63] Next to the large divan Gray has affixed to the wall a tubular light and folding shelves.

7.14 *E.1027*, south elevation of living room, showing the fireplace, and sliding doors of the terrace, 1926-29 black and white photograph © NMI

7.15 *E.1027*, living room, detail of south elevation, 1926, paper, paint, pencil, ink © NMI

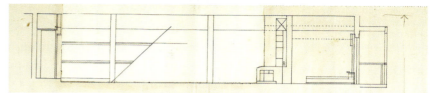

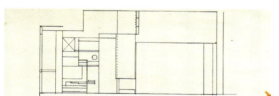

On the west elevation of the sitting room Gray illustrated a large screen attached to the dressing/bathroom area which separated the main part of the living room from the sleeping alcove, for which Gray created a small model.[64] She clearly illustrates the alcove with the small divan with storage and a pivoting table for reading.[65] On both the living room plan and the elevation Gray drew a thin cable, at arm's length, above the small divan which allowed mosquito netting to be extended at night over the bed. On this elevation drawing Gray had not developed the double door system which gives access to the private balcony. In her description of *E.1027* Gray states: 'A double door gives access to a covered terrace sufficiently large to

7.16 *E.1027*, living room, west elevation, with sleeping alcove to the far left, and bathroom behind the wall partition, 1926-29 black and white photograph © NMI

7.17 *E.1027*, sleeping alcove off the living room, west elevation wall, 1926-29, black and white photograph © NMI

7.18 *E.1027*, bathroom adjacent to the sleeping alcove, west elevation of the living room, 1926-29, black and white photograph © NMI

7.19 *E.1027,* living room, detail of west elevation, 1926, paper, paint, pencil, ink © NMI

7.20 *E.1027*, north-east elevation off the living room, with entrance partition, 1926-29, in *L'Architecture Vivante*, 1929 © NMI

7.21 and 7.22 *E.1027*, east elevation off the living room, built into the wall of the stair is a niche for hats and shelves, 1926-29, in *L'Architecture Vivante*, 1929 © NMI

7.23 *E.1027*, dining alcove on east elevation of the living room, 1926-29, black and white photograph © NMI

7.24 *E.1027*, living room, detail of east elevation, 1926, paper, paint, pencil, ink © NMI

hang a hammock. A metal door is embedded in the thickness of the wall, as well as a shuttered door with pivoting slats, to allow practical ventilation and to give the sleeping figure the impression of being outdoors when the first door is left open. A pierced opening high in the fixed part of the glazed frame at the foot of the bed provides for excellent cross ventilation on warm summer nights'.[66]

On the east elevation of the living room plan Gray does not draw the dining alcove with furniture in situ, rather she again illustrates the partition which incorporates shelves, a coat rack and an umbrella stand which blocks the view of the living room from the entrance. In her description of *E.1027* Gray states: 'Built into the wall of the stair to the left is the niche for hats, a half cylinder in transparent celluloid, with its shelves made of loose-knit twine nets, so the dust cannot settle. A tube along the length of the partition accommodates umbrellas'.[67] Though not drawn on the elevation Gray eventually created a drum by the entrance where a system of runners carried hangers for umbrellas. Under the hat niche was a deep cupboard for storage. The east elevation contains the dining alcove and a space used to serve and clear the dining area. The serving table, made from aluminium, also served as a bar, and could fold

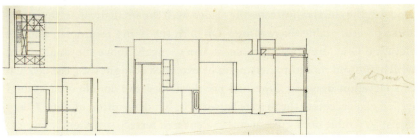

up against the pillar. Other drawings exist of the living room plan with elevations displaying similar details.[68]

The overall idea of *E.1027* was envisaged from a social point of view, through the minimum use of space, yet providing the maximum amount of comfort. Gray stated, 'this very small house thus has, concentrated in a very small space, all that might be useful for comfort and to help indulge in *joie de vivre*'.[69] Gray's minimum use of space in what could be regarded as a relatively luxurious dwelling is unusual for this period as it was normally associated with social housing. Gray also completed a very detailed plan of the ground floor of *E.1027*,[70] similar to the one published in *L'Architecture Vivante* in 1929.[71] The same plan appears in Gray's architectural portfolios.[72] Other drawings of the ground floor plan exist with some variations.[73] Her design reflects a more homogenous idea, created for an individual who would live and entertain there and was conceived from the interior outwards. 'The thing constructed is more important than the way it is constructed, and the process is subordinate to the plan, not the plan to the process. It is not a matter of constructing beautiful arrangements of lines, but above all dwellings for people'.[74] The treatment of the spatial hierarchy of *E.1027* reflects Jean Badovici's penchant for entertaining. The plan reveals an open living room which functioned as a dining room, capable of accommodating guests and had designated zones within the room for sleeping, dressing, washing and working. Gray sought to create an interior atmosphere that would be in harmony with the refinements of modern life while utilising current technical resources and possibilities.[75] In both English and Irish domestic architecture the living and sleeping areas were clearly divided. Gray in her treatment of the living room space adopted the mid-nineteenth century French practice where the salon was an extension of a bedroom, furnished with day-beds, comfortable chairs and tables. During the day and early evening hours it served as a private sitting room, thereby doubling its use when not required for sleeping purposes. At an evening party it served as a main reception room. The English and Irish found the idea of one receiving guests in one's bedroom as peculiar and shocking. Gray adopted the French method in her plan of this room as a way of obtaining two rooms for the price of one.[76]

There were a number of essential issues which Gray sought to address in designing the house: the problem with windows and shutters, the problem with the independence of the rooms and lastly the problem of the kitchen. The kitchen, more than any other room in the house, demonstrates Gray's rejection of the functional dogma of the avant-garde movement. Gray was aware of the time-and-motion studies of Frederick W. Taylor (1856-1915) and the ideas of the Efficiency Movement. Started by Catherine Beecher (1800-1878) in the middle of the nineteenth century and reinforced by Christine Frederick's (1883-1970) publications in the 1910s, the growing trend for viewing household work as a true profession had the logical consequence that the industrial optimisation pioneered by Taylorism spilled over into the domestic area. Frederick's *The New Housekeeping*, which argued for rationalising the work in the kitchen using a Taylorist approach, had been translated into French in 1918 with a re-edition in 1927.[77] Gray's design of *E.1027* explores a choreographic approach which emphasises the qualitative aspects of the body's movement in a space. Being aware of the contemporary trends in kitchen design, Gray had already completed a study of a kitchen for the communal housing projects designed by Russian constructivists Mikhail Barshch (1904-1976), Moisei Ginzburg (1892-1946) and Vyacheslav Vladimirov (b.1898) between 1926 and 1929 prior to her design for the kitchen in *E.1027*.[78] Her sketch included motion efficiency analysis which was directly inspired by Taylor's diagrams. Gray was also familiar with the *Frankfurt kitchen* designed in 1926 by Margarete Schütte-Lihotzky (1897-2000) for the social housing project *Römerstadt* in Frankfurt, Germany, by Ernst May (1886-1970) and then exhibited in Lilly Reich's (1885-1947) exhibition of furniture and fittings at the *Stuttgart Weissenhofsiedlung* in 1927. The low-cost *Frankfurt kitchen* was designed to enable and promote efficient work. Over 10,000 units were manufactured. The kitchens were made for affordable apartments for workers, subject to tight budget constraints and limited space.

Gray designed an independent kitchen which was created adjacent to an outdoor kitchen space located to the left of the main entrance. 'We have separated the kitchen from the rest of the house: one can only go from one to the other by passing through the entry threshold, which is only possible in an exceptionally mild climate'.[79] The ground floor plan illustrates that the kitchen layout has been defined by regional customs where meals are prepared outside during the summer months. Gray states, 'It can be transformed into an open air kitchen by a partition made from glass panels that fold flat. When this partition is opened, the kitchen is nothing more than a paved alcove in the courtyard'.[80] By detaching this space in the plan and by providing access to it from the entry porch Gray broke the interior sequence of the building. She did this so that the kitchen was easily accessible yet sufficiently isolated that no odours could penetrate the living spaces.[81] Gray has also indicated various storage compartments on the plan which actually were a coal store, a niche for wood, a washstand, an electric ice chest, a water softener, a zinc-covered cabinet for bottles, a folding table and an oil-fired oven. There was another oven inside for the winter. She clearly rejected Le Corbusier's and Pierre Jeanneret's (1896–1967) use of standardised cupboards and cabinets which were exhibited in their *Pavillon de L'Esprit Nouveau* in 1925 and looked to compositional notions of De Stijl wall cabinets.[82] Gray perfected her storage designs initially at *House for an Engineer* where she began to use furniture in the construction of the space by incorporating the furniture into the walls. Hence storage spaces and cupboards appear as if they are extensions of the architecture. With *E.1027* Gray developed this further, celebrating the manner in which she brought materials together. Furnishings emphasised an interconnection with one another. Use of joints and hinges appear more frequently. She stated 'Even furnishings should lose their individuality by blending in with architectural ensemble'.[83]

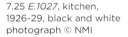

7.25 *E.1027*, kitchen, 1926-29, black and white photograph © NMI

7.26, 7.27 and 7.28 *E.1027*, kitchen, 1926-29, in *L'Architecture Vivante*, 1929 © NMI

The lower level of *E.1027*, containing a guest room, maid's quarters and washing areas, was accessed via the spiral staircase. In Le Corbusier's *Villa Savoye,* 1928-29, the garage and the servants' quarters at ground level are linked by a spiral staircase to the first floor only. The spiral staircase, which Gray has drawn on her plan, leads to the roof, but its primary function is as a source of illumination for the internal descent into the lower level. Though Gray owned a drawing of a view of the roof top garden from the *Villa Savoye,* 1928-29 it is unclear whether she was inspired by Le Corbusier, or whether he was inspired by her design.[84] 'The stair has been built using the smallest possible dimensions, but with deep steps that are grooved to be comfortable underfoot. The stair shaft is much larger than the spiral staircase, so that the volume seems light and airy. Around the spiral stair, which serves like a stepladder, are a series of cupboards that are ventilated, lit, and accessible from both within the stairwell and beyond. The light pours down through the glass shaft above, which provides access to the roof'.[85] The ground floor plan shows how Gray treated each room as being independent of each other. This explains why each of the bedrooms and sleeping areas had private access to the garden.

Gray describes the principal bedroom at *E.1027* as a multi-purpose, studio bedroom enclave. The plan was completed with a study room and adjoining bathroom and the four elevations of the bedroom.[86] As with the guest bedroom, the main bedroom was orientated towards the rising sun. The brightly-lit study overlooked the sea, its southern exposure maximising the daylight. She states: 'The room is sunny from morning to evening, and owing to its shuttered windows, the light and air can be regulated at will'.[87]

In defining the spatial hierarchy of the house into public and private spheres Gray provided the main bedroom with a balcony, and the adjoining bathroom had independent access to the garden.[88] Gray stated 'Everyone, even in a house of restricted dimensions, must be able to remain free and independent. They must have the impression of being alone, and if desired being entirely alone'.[89] The final plan for the bedroom was also illustrated in *L'Architecture Vivante* in 1929. In this publication Gray colours in the various elements, differentiating the areas outlined for sleeping and dressing by modifying the colours of the floor tiles.[90] Gray uses this technique in the actual bedroom, where the tiled floor is grey-black for the studio and grey-white for the room.[91]

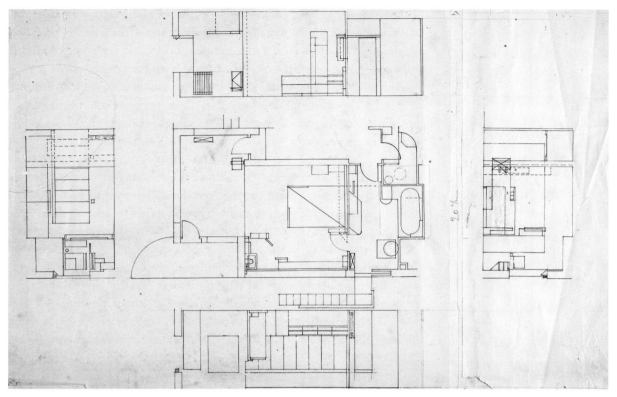

7.29 *E.1027*, bedroom plan and four elevations, 1926-29, paper, pencil, ink © NMI

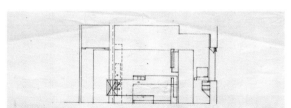

7.30 *E.1027*, bedroom, north elevation, 1926-29, black and white photograph © NMI

7.31 *E.1027*, detail of bedroom, north elevation, 1926-29, paper, pencil, ink © NMI

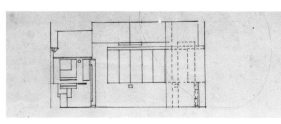

7.32 *E.1027*, bedroom, south elevation, 1926-29, black and white photograph © NMI

7.33 *E.1027*, detail of bedroom, south elevation, 1926-29, paper, pencil, ink © NMI

With her drawing of the main bedroom plan, Gray employed the same technique which she used to illustrate the main living room. This is derived from English nineteenth-century drawings of domestic interiors.[92] This plan shows the bedroom, with four elevations as if they folded out from the plan. Known as the American method, De Stijl architects also used this to illustrate their work, especially in magazines such as *L'Architecture Vivante*. This drawing technique incorporates the total concept of design.[93] It allowed Gray to illustrate every aspect of her design and the multifunctional uses of her furnishings. It emphasised the non-uniformity of her furniture, seen as a series of extrusions, reflective of De Stijl designers' work. In the elevations she illustrated some of the furniture, the storage compartments, reading lights – one in white and one in blue that dims to serve as a night light – and cabinets which project from the wall. It had built-in lamps; a moveable bedside table; electrical outlets for a kettle and bed warmer; mosquito netting in transparent celluloid; and a linen cupboard below the window is placed at the height of the hand, so that the bottom can be reached effortlessly, without bending over. It is hung from the wall, which allows the tiled flooring underneath to be easily cleaned. She noted that the dressing cabinet was made from aluminium

7.34, 7.35, 7.36
E.1027, bedroom, storage compartments, mosquito net, reading lights, 1926-29, in *L'Architecture Vivante*, 1929 © NMI

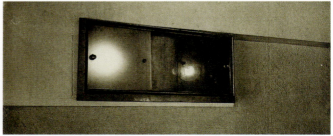

'a beautiful material providing agreeable coolness in hot climates'.[94] Gray also questioned the treatment of the spatial concept of a room, breaking down the boundaries between architecture and furnishings. 'Owing to the layout of this room through shifting alignments, the doors are invisible from the interior'.[95] Drawings exist which Gray did exploring the various spatial concepts for this and the guest bedroom.[96] The plan for the main bedroom also shows the small bathroom. 'The bathtub is an ordinary one covered in aluminium casing, which gives it an agreeable appearance and strikes a glistening note in the tone of the ensemble. The bidet is covered with a seat of rubber foam. The toilet, located near both the living room and the bedroom, is shielded by the entrance canopy, and is ventilated through the roof'.[97] She cleverly chose reflective materials to enhance this private space.

7.37, 7.38, 7.39
E.1027, bathroom off main bedroom, 1926-29, in *L'Architetcure Vivante*, 1929 © NMI

The codified name of house *E.1027* was for the architect and the client – 'E' stood for Eileen, '10' – for the tenth letter of the alphabet which was 'J' (Jean), '2' for the second letter of the alphabet 'B' (Badovici) and '7' for the seventh letter of the alphabet 'G' (Gray). This numerical coding system was again used for a series of lifeboats which Badovici had developed throughout the 1920s. He stated, 'Our task is to educate the public opinion regarding the fundamental possibilities of modern science. Achievement however daring or revolutionary they may seem to us. Public opinion must be aroused from its torpor, and shown the power of scientific appliances which can be introduced everywhere, from the heart of the ship to its natural element the sea'.[98] He compared the design to that of a factory stating 'a ship is reborn modernised fitted up like a factory'.[99] The final lifeboat was designed to inflate on hitting the water. On the bow of the boat was *E-7*, meaning E.G, or Eileen Gray. Le Corbusier was interested in this project and wrote to Badovici requesting him to send a file presenting these lifeboat projects to the Director of Scientific Research who was also involved in the development of wartime inventions.[100] The life boat was produced and eventually exhibited at Le Corbusier's *Pavillon des Temps Nouveaux* at the International Exhibition 1937 in Paris, and Gray kept the exhibition label.[101] He patented this idea later.[102] Certain themes were translated from this project to *E.1027* and vice versa. Badovici's layout for a lifeboat initially developed around a central open planned cabin with a corridor. A stairs leads to all sections of the boat. Similarly *E.1027* revolves around a central open planned living room with a stair which leads to all sections of the house. Badovici emphasised the use of railings, awnings and air conditioning. With Gray nautical themes appear throughout not only in the actual setting, but in the fixtures; ships railings line the terrace, sailcloth is used in the awnings, Gray's version of ocean liner deck chairs called the *Transat chair* appear in photographs, the use of the colour white, the built-in headboards for the beds, and the flagpole on the roof. Many things recall the architecture of boats and their cabins.[103] Even some of the carpets created for the interior notably *Marine d'Abord* decorated with nautical motifs suggest the sea. [104]

By the time Gray began designing *E.1027* she had already begun developing her philosophical ideas in relation to the fourth dimension. Numerous philosophical texts in her library stimulated her interest. During the years 1926 –29 Gray designed a number of important pieces of furniture which addressed notions of the fourth dimension. The Cubists had already adapted the ideas of the Russian esotericist Peter D. Ouspensky (1878-1947) by creating paintings and collages using multiple viewpoints. Henri Poincaré, whose literature Gray also had in her library, advocated in his publication *La Science et Hypothèse*, 1902, that multiple viewpoints are juxtaposed.[105] Gray was also particularly interested in the writing of William Kingdon Clifford (1845-1879), an English mathematician and philosopher.[106] Prior to 1926 Gray's furniture had been described in the context of these themes when Louis Vauxcelles wrote 'Does one dare pronounce the word cubism? Yes one must. Those combination of lines, those geometrical syntheses, this firm and singular precision is the equivalent of our logical painters. The other merit of Miss Gray is that when she designs the architecture of her furniture, she avoids extreme shapes; her forms are simple, straightforward, and functional'.[107] From 1926 onward Gray engrossed herself in the processes of living, analysing mental and bodily functions: relaxing, sleeping, eating, reading and with her furniture and fittings she devised novel solutions which exploited compactness, versatility, respect for function, practicality and user friendliness. By transcribing these ideas into her work, her furniture, especially the pieces designed for *E.1027,* could be viewed from different viewpoints depending on the function that it served. Some pieces were totally integrated into the architecture; others were multidirectional without a fixed position, often serving several functions. In this way she sought to avoid the three-dimensional reading of an object (a piece of furniture in space). In *E.1027* she further developed this notion of her furniture in relation to the fourth dimension. As with her other interiors Gray designed the furniture and furnishings to work with the entire room but with *E.1027* she took this a step further. Not just the furnishings, or the rooms but the house itself was designed to heighten the user's experience – transporting the individual to another dimension or realm. From the time that she was an art student her interest in synaesthesia and how she could heighten a person's sensory experience of her work were central concerns. Combining this with her interest in the third and fourth dimension, *E.1027* was not just another architectural project, it was also a philosophical statement which engaged design and architecture elevating it to what Gray hoped was a new level.

With its nautical theme, its seaside location, and the marine chart on the main living room wall with the stenciled inscription *Invitation au Voyage* (An invitation to a journey), *E.1027* suggests a journey into another dimension. Gray's treatment of the house possibly also looked to the ideas of Charles Howard Hinton (1853-1907), whose writings examined the four-dimensional hypercube. To explain it, he used the analogy of a planar world of two dimensions and the reactions of its inhabitants to the three-dimensional solids passing through the plane. This hyperspace philosophy's two complementary approaches to higher dimensional space are relevant to Gray, whose reference to the fourth dimension occurred in the context of her motion-oriented style. Gray integrated furniture and architecture throughout the house creating multiple illusions of space. This is especially evident in the living room with its open balcony treated like a loggia, screen-like windows, a partition at the entrance incorporating shelves, umbrella stand and coat rack, a sleeping alcove and adjoining showroom in a far-off corner and a dining room all treated to subdivide the three dimensional and elevate it into a fourth dimension. The floor with overlapping rugs and black and white floor tiles compels the inhabitant to pause their movement at various points throughout the room. The space has a plurality of functions.

Space is divided throughout the house into sleeping, dressing and working, modified by the floor tiles, colourings and ceiling heights. Stencils on the walls act as indicators that one is embarking on this journey 'Entrez lentement' (Enter slowly), inviting the inhabitant to pause before embarking. Throughout the house Gray's analysis of the boundaries between **architecture** and furnishings break down the notion of the room being a **singular three**-dimensional entity. She amplifies a space by these means thus **creating wh**at could be described as a fourth-dimensional space.

Hinton's **and Ous**pensky's ideas were also relevant to Gray in the context of **time-and-motion** studies. This has been described as Gray's choreographic **approach** to her architecture. It has been suggested that Gray's inspiration for such an approach was taken from Frederick W. Taylor's time-and-motion studies, Hannes Meyer's (1889-1954) technique for depicting the human circulation in relation to sunlight, Oskar Schlemmer's (1888-1943) affinity with the choreographic approach to the human body and Le Corbusier's concept of the promenade architectural.[108] It is possible that in relation to *E.1027* she looked at how the Futurists, particularly Umberto Boccioni, had used the ideas about the fourth dimension. In a synthesis of Ouspensky's and Henri Bergson's ideas he wrote, 'you must render the invisible which stirs and lives beyond intervening obstacles what we have on the right, on the left, and behind us, and not merely the small square of life artificially compressed, as it were'. He looked to dynamic sensation which was the 'particular rhythm of each object, its inclination, its movement, or, to put it more exactly, its interior force. It is usual to consider the human being in its different aspects of motion or stillness, of joyous excitement or grave melancholy. What is overlooked is that all inanimate objects display, by their lines, calmness, or frenzy, sadness or gaiety. These various tendencies lend to the lines of which they are formed a sense of character of weighty stability or of aerial lightness'.[109] Gray's work had already explored the 'static representation of movement'[110] with the generation of higher dimensional forms. The walls of the salon of the *Rue de Lota apartment* – panelled screens in geometrical designs of linear sweeps - are examples of Gray's interest in elemental parallelism and parallel multiplication. A critic from *Harper's Bazaar* wrote in September 1920 of the apartment 'Her style is thoroughly modern ... the walls might pose as studies from the latest cubist exhibition. At least one panel might be "The Nude Descending the Staircase"'.[111] Just like Marcel Duchamp, however, Gray would realise that there was nothing four dimensional about the motion of an object unless it moved off into a new fourth dimension.

These ideas Gray inferred in the relationship between furniture, movement and the human body in *E.1027*. Though some argue that it drew explicit inspiration from the art of theatre, this aspect of Gray's furniture and architecture has much broader analogies with Ouspensky, Boccioni and the fourth dimension. In this way *E.1027* is Gray's search

7.40 *E.1027*, circulation routes and sun orientation, 1926-29, paper, ink, pencil © RIBA Library Drawing and Archives Collections

for a greater unity between art and life. By emphasising the importance of the movement of the body through the space of the house Gray created an aspect and circulation plan of *E.1027*.[112] This plan depicted both the lower ground floor and the first floor of the house. It showed the circulation routes in relation to the sun's daily path. She delineated the inhabitant's movement around the house using solid lines and those of the maid using dotted lines. While this plan suggests a natural understanding of time throughout the building,

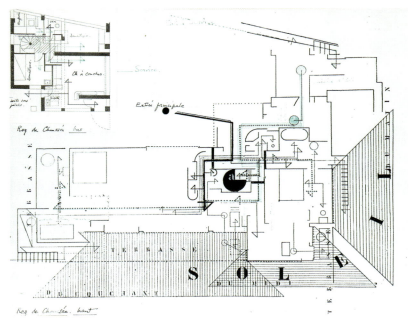

Ouspensky argued that time and motion in three-dimensional space may be considered illusions that result because of our incomplete perception of space. In his book *Tertium Organum* he suggests that beyond the illusions of time and motion four-dimensional reality is static. However, with *E.1027* Gray asserted a positive value of time and motion as an effective indication of a higher dynamic reality or fourth dimension. She did this through the combination of the visual means which controlled the spatial sequence, multidirectional and integrated furniture with a plurality of functions and the use of materials and colours which engaged sound and touch. Gray enhanced the inhabitant's mind as well as their bodily experience.

Gray took numerous photographs of the property and they were published along with an architectural dialogue between her and Jean Badovici in 'Maison en Bord de Mer', *L'Architecture Vivante,* winter edition of 1929. Gray had also looked into having this published in English and had typed up contents pages along with extensive notes in English from the publication.[113] Gray moved out of *E.1027* in 1932, leaving the house to its owner, Badovici. Gray later became upset when Badovici invited Le Corbusier to paint murals on the walls from 1938-39. It was clear that Badovici had not understood what she had tried to achieve at *E.1027*. Even though Gray had described this house as just a model for further exploration, the murals broke the structural integrity of the interior and compromised not just the space but the totality of the house as an ensemble. Gray had just had her first, difficult lesson on the complex relationship between architect and client. In the controversy which ensued in relation to the murals Badovici and Le Corbusier became estranged from one another. Gray and Badovici continued their friendship – Badovici aiding Gray with deliveries when she was doing her own house *Tempe à Pailla*. Badovici died from liver cancer on 17 August 1956. Just prior to this Gray had been in discussions with Badovici about the future of *E.1027*. After his death she had a meeting with Le Corbusier – possibly to discuss the fate of the house. Gray had requested the keys of the property from Badovici's partner Mireille Roupest – however she never gained access to the property. Badovici died intestate and the house was bequeathed to his sister, a nun in Romania, who could not accept such a gift and it was accessioned by the Romanian state. After Badovici's death Le Corbusier's interest in the property only increased. Between 1958 and 1960 Le Corbusier orchestrated long negotiations with the Romanian government and unable to acquire the property himself, he searched for a buyer for *E.1027*. In the summer of 1960 *E.1027* was bought by Marie Louise Schelbert. Le Corbusier took an active hand in preserving not only his murals but the contents of the house and prevented Schelbert from destroying Gray's furnishings when she initiated some modifications work to the house and the furnishings. Schelbert sold the house to her doctor Peter Kaegi in 1974, reserving the right to live there until her death in 1982. Le Corbusier's avid interest in *E.1027* continued to the point that in 1957 he built a hostel directly overlooking the villa, and that in 1950 he had acquired a plot of land, directly above *E.1027,* on which he eventually built his *Cabanon de Vacances* – a modest holiday home. Just as Le Corbusier attempted to have his murals in the house recorded for posterity, Gray had also wanted to reacquire the house that she had designed and built. When this proved impossible she asked her niece Prunella Clough (1919-1999) to compile an inventory of what remained in E.1027 as to perform the task herself would have caused Gray too much pain. Sadly it was only after Gray's death in June 1977 that her wish was fulfilled by Clough.

In August 1965 Le Corbusier died of a heart attack while swimming in front of the house. Before his death Le Corbusier had sought the assistance of André Malraux, Minister of State in charge of Cultural Affairs, in preserving the *E.1027* murals, and in October 1975 the house and its contents were included on France's supplementary inventory of historic monuments.[114] After Schelbert's death in 1982, Peter Kaegi took over *E.1027*, despite Schelbert's children contesting this acquisition which the family lost at trial. Kaegi was murdered in the house in 1996. In January of 2000 Kaegi's two sons sold the house to the *Conservatoire du Littoral et des rivages lacustres,* with a substantial financial support from the community of Roquebrune-Cap Martin. In March 2000 *E.1027* was reclassified as a full *monument historique.*

After the completion of *E.1027* Badovici had asked Gray to design the interior of his small apartment in rue Chateaubriand. She had to design architectural elements which could incorporate several functions. In her plan she subdivided the space into a bedroom-boudoir work area, and at the entrance she designed a compact area which incorporated a kitchenette, a bathroom and storage system. Within the restricted space in the *Rue Chateaubriand apartment* Gray devised a storage system at the entrance area which she exhibited at the UAM in 1931. 'By creating a false

7.41 *Rue Chateaubriand apartment*, plan, 1929-31, black and white photograph © NMI

7.42 View of the false ceiling and the storage system at *Rue Chateaubriand apartment,* 1929-31, black and white photograph, NMIEG 2003.1641 © NMI

7.43, 7.44
Views of the interior of the *Rue Chateaubriand apartment*, 1929-31, black and white photograph © NMI

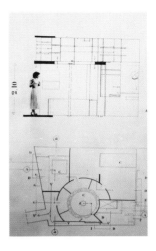

ceiling 2.10 metres from the floor in the zones of circulation and service, one obtains for a habitable dwelling unit of 40 square metres, 13 cubic metres of storage'. This false ceiling had lighting panels and instead of a door to gain entrance to the bathroom Gray used a metallic curtain which would have reflected natural light coming from the living room and the panelled light from the false ceiling. She also had used pivoting mirrors to work with the occupants' small space, and created light in the bathroom by placing a small window with a sliding shutter in the wall from the bathroom to the living room. Gray again drew on the ideas which she had seen in *House and Home* magazine in 1920 on how to integrate cupboard design into an interior with limited space. The ideas discussed in this article found expression in her design for the living room of the apartment on rue Chateaubriand as she masked an irregular angle of the long living room wall with mirrors that expand the space visually whilst also concealing storage compartments. The living room she cleverly divided into designated areas for work, sleep and dining – just as she had done with the living-room of *E.1027*.

Some of the furniture for the apartment was made from beech, which was cut to size by *Société Française du Bois Malléable*, Paris.[115] Gray also ordered thirteen sheets of celulloid: six sheets in smoked grey, two in pink, four yellow and one highly polished transparent sheet to be sent to Badovici's apartment on 18 August 1931.[116] She ordered this material from the *Worbla factory* in Paris. On 11 April 1933 Gray purchased nine leaves of smoked transparent celluloid for the central storage cabinet situated at

7.45 View of the metallic partition at the entrance of the *Rue Chateaubriand apartment*, 1929-31, black and white photograph © NMI

7.46 View of the entrance, the storage system toward the bathroom of the *Rue Chateaubriand apartment*, 1929-31, black and white photograph © NMI

7.47 *Rue Chateaubriand apartment*, plan and elevations of the entrance, kitchen, bathroom, the false ceiling and the storage system, 1929-31, black and white photograph © NMI the entrance of the apartment.[117] Inspiration for these multi-functional storage facilities came from a number of sources. Gray attended The Deutscher Werkbund 1927 exhibition in Stuttgart, and had in her library an article by Le Corbusier on 'The houses of the Weissenhof at Stuttgart' from the summer edition of *L'Architecture Vivante*, 1928 which questioned the function of furniture and storage within standardised block housing. In 1929 Gray also attended the 'Die Wohnung für as Existenzminimum' organised by the Congrès internationaux d'architecture modern, CIAM (International Congresses of Modern Architecture) in Frankfurt. Here Gray viewed the design of a small, standardised home, the furnishing of the home and the prefabrication of the building components. Taking on board all of these ideas Gray began drawing and creating plans, furniture and furnishings for small, standardised spaces. In 1930 the Deutscher Werkbund came to Paris to exhibit at the twentieth Salon des Artistes Décorateurs, just as she finished the apartment on the rue Chateaubriand. It provided an opportunity to renew many of her German contacts, which was reinforced on a trip to Berlin 1931 when she lunched with one of the groups leading architects in Walter Gropius.

7.48 Plan of *Quai Suffren apartment*, St. Tropez, 1934, pencil, paper © NMI

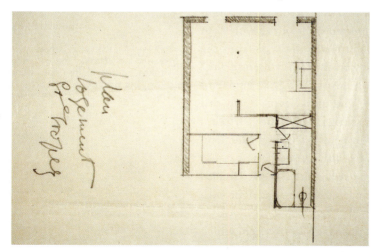

Eileen Gray owned a small apartment on the quai Suffren which overlooked the harbour of St. Tropez. She took refuge here during July and December of each year beginning in 1934.[118] Modifying two rooms to form an open plan area, Gray created a multifunctional room with creative storage facilities by manipulating the depth of the wall. The plan highlights a corridor leading from the entrance.[119] To the left is a closet with a wash area. At the end of the corridor to the right is a bathroom. The corridor terminates in an open plan room with a large fireplace. Gray intended to renovate the apartment in 1938 and in some plans she drew in the measurements especially with regard to the size of the windows, the fireplace and the entrance. [120] As with other architectural projects which Gray had completed at this time a sense of volumetric space and light was key to the apartment at St. Tropez. The

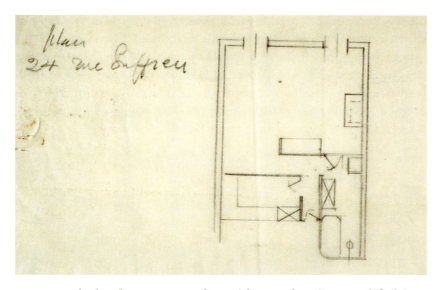

7.49 Plan of *Quai Suffren apartment*, St. Tropez, 1934, pencil, paper © NMI

apartment had only two rooms, but with one plan Gray modified it to create three.[121] She cornered off the entrance to create a small corridor which leads into a bedroom to the left and at the end of the corridor the bathroom to the right. Each has storage facilities. This leads onto a large open space probably the living room. She modified the walls to provide the storage space. The living room was decorated with a circular carpet.[122] She furnished the apartment with a bed made from glass tubes, a *Transat chair,* and several tables.[123] The apartment was destroyed along with her architectural models and drawings on 15 August 1944 when mines were detonated in the harbour.

Starting in 1926 Gray purchased four parcels of land for herself at the village of Castellar, in the district of Menton. Three parcels of land called Belvesassa were acquired on 24 April 1926 and then a larger parcel was acquired in October.[124] Then in 1928 she then purchased another two parcels of land called Lavagnin from Francois Albin, who eventually became Gray's builder.[125] An engineer compiled a report on 12 June 1934 for local planning authorities and on 17 September the mayor's office approved building work to begin on Gray's home *Tempe à Pailla*. Building began at the end of the year of 1934 and was completed at the end of 1935.[126]

A preliminary site plan of *Tempe à Pailla* at Castellar in the South of France shows the parcels of land which Gray originally purchased. It was a constricted site lying below a ridge along a steep winding mountain road, yet it afforded magnificent views of the mountains and sea.[127] Gray was drawn by the views and countryside that surrounded this plot of land. The immediate property included a simple cabanon and three stone cisterns. Gray had already explored plans of a *Maison de Weekend sur Citerne,* 1930s (a week-end house built on a cistern); though undated, the similarity with *Tempe à Pailla* is unmistakeable.[128] In 1932 she bought additional land, demolished the old cabanon and began building her home.[129]

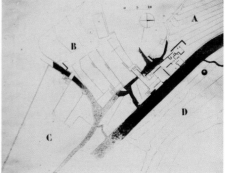

7.50 *Tempe à Pailla*, south façade, 1931-35, black and white photograph © NMI

7.51 *Tempe à Pailla*, view of the terrace and panoramic views, 1931-35, black and white photograph © NMI

7.52 *Tempe à Pailla*, site plan, 1931-35, black and white photograph © NMI

The story of *Tempe à Pailla* cannot be told without reference to a house in Berlin, *Am Rupenhorn,* 1928-30 which made a profound impression on Gray when she and Badovici were guests there, along with Albert Einstein (1879-1955), in 1931.[130] Designed and built by its owner the German architect Eric Mendelsohn (1887-1953) the house was built on a plot that offered breathtaking views of the river Havel and the surrounding lakes.[131] Such an effect did Mendelsohn have on both Badovici and Gray that the following year Badovici wrote a study on Mendelsohn characterising him as one of the prophets of modern architecture.[132] The fact that Gray visited Mendelsohn and this house is of particular importance in relation to *Tempe à Pailla.* *Am Rupenhorn* had a restrained language of classical elegance and moderation. It was decorated with three murals executed by Amédée Ozenfant. *Tempe à Pailla* represented the ideal project, in which Gray herself was the client. Just as Mendelsohn wanted to create *Am Rupenhorn* as a symbol for his wife and their life - so too would *Tempe à Pailla* become a symbol of her independence, a place of retreat and solitude. *Tempe à Pailla* was built on a moderate constricting site but also with breathtaking views of mountains and sea. Mendelsohn's house was on a sloping site leading to a lake. Like *Am Ruperhorn, Tempe à Pailla* opened itself to nature in a dialogue of natural and artistic aesthetics.[133] Gray created her home to appear closed and inaccessible, as was *Am Ruperhorn.* She devised facades that ensured privacy along the roadway and streets. The entrance to the hortus conclusus or enclosed garden in *Am Ruperhorn* was through a controlled and selected route. Gray provided a generous passage from the garden to her house also executed in a deliberate manner. The upper terrace had several points of entry; a staircase rising from the street, an open passage leading to the main entrance, a bridge over the footpath which connects to the garden. Mendelsohn's treatment of his stairs and pathways clearly inspired her.

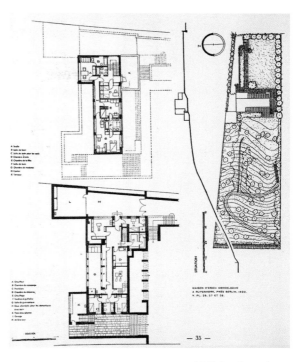

7.53 *Am Rupenhorn,* Eric Mendelsohn, 1930, in *L'Architecture Vivante,* 1932 © NMI

7.54 *Tempe à Pailla,* south façade view from the street, 1931-35, black and white photograph © NMI

However, Mendelsohn's entrance was visible from afar and unpretentious in its design. Gray's entrance continued the theme of seclusion which she created on the external facades. She made the entry façade visually impenetrable by restricting large windows to its upper surfaces, except for a translucent kitchen door. Just as Mendelsohn subdivided his home into public and private zones – so did Gray. Mendelsohn orientated the dining room of his house, used for entertaining, to the northwest, flooding it with light and providing a natural theatre for the setting sun. Gray orientated her living room and the terrace to the southeast to capitalise on the panoramic views down the valley. However, in the built-in furnishings of the living room she inserted a fireplace in the glazed terrace wall so that the embers of the fire in the living room could replace the fading sunlight. She evidently looked to his ideas of incorporating the dramatics of a dying sun into the theatrics of the interior.

Am Rupenhorn boasted a plethora of technical installations such as guillotine windows and a thermostatically controlled oil furnace – however the mechanisms were not on display or shown. Amédée Ozenfant stated that in *Am Rupenhorn* 'Mendelsohn was clever enough to cover the inner organs of this house with a beautiful skin. It is the fashion to admit the existence of every organ. A house is no council of revision, no confessional, no tribunal, no anatomical model, nor museum of mechanics'.[134] *Tempe à Pailla* was more spartan in its material treatment, more compact and more introverted than *E.1027*. At *Tempe à Pailla* Gray minimalised the interior, developing it as over-scaled cabinetry for storage of fittings and fixtures. Gray's technical achievements are in the dual purpose of her treatment of space and fittings. Many pieces are embedded in their architectural milieu. Innovative furniture was designed to decrease in size or could fold in on itself for storage. Gray herself explained 'In small rooms – in small houses, it is important not to encumber the available space. This can sometimes be realised by mechanical means, obtaining several uses for the same object'.[135]

Whilst *Am Rupenhorn* inspired Gray in areas of her design at *Tempe à Pailla,* one questions if perhaps Ozenfant, in writing of Mendelsohn's house, had read her dialogue with Jean Badovici, published in *L'Architecture Vivante*, 1929. Ozenfant, a follower of Le Corbusier's Purism, swore off Le Corbusier's machine aesthetic in *Neues Haus-Neue Welt*, 1932, stating that 'with all our experience no machine is equal to a masterpiece of architecture: the machine has no acropolis'.[136] Gray had criticised Le Corbusier's art of the engineer saying 'The art of the engineer is not sufficient unless it is guided by human needs'. She also responded to Le Corbusier's maxim concluding that 'a house is not a machine to live in. It is the shell of man, his extension, his release, his spiritual emanation'.[137]

With *Tempe à Pailla* Gray departed from Le Corbusier's notion of the *Plan Libre* (free plan), clearly developing each volume as a distinct spatial entity. Rejecting Le Corbusier's emphasis on the horizontal she modulated the floor levels and ceiling heights. She again drew paths of circulation in relation to the transit of the sun. However, she was also preoccupied with ventilation. The living room wall terminates in a shuttered mechanism affording the enjoyment of panoramic views and the morning sun but also permitting the movement of air throughout the house. Gray made a drawing to indicate the paths of circulation in relation to the daily movement of the sun and focused on the principal bedroom at *Tempe à Pailla*.[138] This was divided into two zones, one for sleeping, and one for dressing. She elevated the dressing zone via a step, but also separated them visually by the use of a round aperture in the ceiling which lay exactly

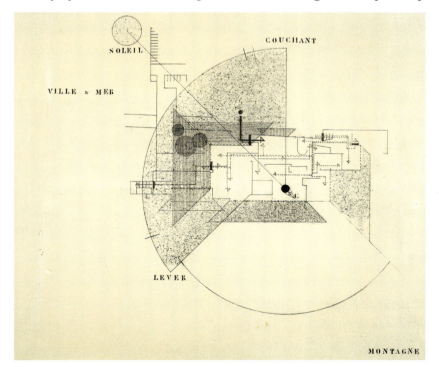

7.55 *Tempe à Pailla*, sun orientation, 1931-35, paper, ink, pencil © NMI

between these two zones. This she has marked on the plan, which she faced towards the southwest. This allowed sunlight to stream into the room during the day. The ceiling disk was operated by a lever. In this diagram she centres the lines indicating the sun's pathway in relation to this ceiling opening. It is suggested this preoccupation with the path of the sun is to gain a greater understanding and awareness of time.[139] Gray might have been influenced by Bauhaus architect Hannes Meyer's preoccupation with ventilation, light, acoustics and smell, and Oskar Schlemmer's declaration that 'the paths of movement, the choreography of every day, form a transition to the conscious'.[140] Schlemmer was more preoccupied with the movement of the body. It is also suggested that she was intrigued by Le Corbusier's concept of the architectural promenade, which he explored in *Maison la Roche,* 1924.[141]

7.56 *Tempe à Pailla*, 1931-35, page from Eileen Gray's portfolio showing the bedroom, plan, the ceiling disc for illumination, the trouser cabinet and the cube, pivoting chest of drawers and the extendable wardrobe, 1956, paper, ink, black and white photograph © NMI

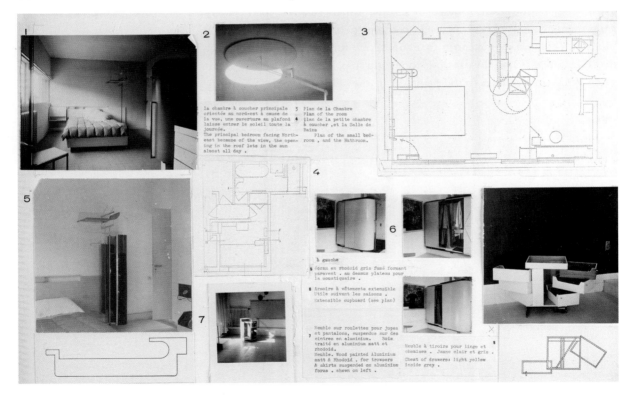

Tempe à Pailla is more fully reflective of Eileen Gray's preference for minimalism. Simplicity in design, concealed storage space and a lack of overtly decorative detail were important to her. The layout of the house is deceptive as everything is not as it seems; rooms and stairwells are hidden and then revealed. The street or east elevation of *Tempe à Pailla* suggests a house which is rather fragmented and compartmentalised.[142] This is due to the fact that Gray used old local stone juxtaposed with white concrete expanses. It indicates how she negotiated the awkward terrain and adapted the house to suit her needs. In 1931 Gray first began drawing the street or east façade.[143] Preferring a quiet setting Gray developed the project on difficult terrain, long and narrow, with a road on one side, cut in two by an access path and a previous building which incorporated three old water cisterns.[144] Gray incorporated these stone cisterns into the design and built the new structure on top of them. The first cistern was converted into a garage with access from the main roadway. The second was made into a cellar, and the third she kept as a reservoir.[145] She clearly distinguished on this façade the cisterns with their rubble surfaces and the new structure created in whitewashed concrete. Gray made the street entrance façade visually impenetrable. She had three similar objectives when she designed this house: solitude, retreat and privacy. She devised the program for this façade to ensure privacy along the roadway and the footpath. The windows were limited to strip windows, set high above the road, which she aligned with an independent shutter system. The open grillwork of the roadside gate gave way to a narrow stair which rose to the intermediate level and then onto the terrace at the main living level. A bridge over the footpath links the terrace to the garden. These were highly visible but the means of access was private. There was also a public entry, beside the footpath and it was a simple, understated passage between the foyer and the elevated terrace.

When Gray initially purchased the land at *Tempe à Pailla* she had painted the existing building white and given it the name *Le Bateau Blanc* or *The White Boat*.[146] Nowhere is the nautical theme more evident than in the early drawing of the east sectional elevation, when she placed a flagpole in front of the living room window. In this east sectional elevation or the street façade Gray outlined the interior of the first floor, the terrace with the sun bed, the living room, the main bedroom and the guest bedroom. Under the terrace a stair leads to a spare room, toilets, the garage and a cellar.[147] There is a longitudinal section from the garden showing the west elevation outlining the dining area, kitchen and service area. The other elevation is of the south façade showing the stairs which lead to another room, lit through an opening in the ceiling.[148]

Gray again drew her plans of the various rooms showing the four elevations. In her plan of the principal bedroom Gray shows how she adapted one of the cisterns into a garage and a bedroom. She also clearly draws details of the storage facilities, washbasin and bed. She ventilated the garage and cellar by maintaining a band of horizontal apertures between the layers, exposing points of contact between the existing bearing walls.[149] The garage door was commercially available, tilted and made by the company *Éclair*. The cellar was accessed via stairs which were hidden behind the bench in the dining room on the ground floor.[150] Her plan with four elevations of the kitchen in *Tempe à Pailla* is evidence that Gray had – as with *E.1027* – taken on board the ideas of Margarete Schütte-Lihotzky's design for the *Frankfurt kitchen*.[151] In comparison to the kitchen at *E.1027*, the kitchen at *Tempe à Pailla* is more conveniently laid out, had its own service entrance and was also adjoined by a pantry.

Though *Tempe à Pailla* was a lot smaller in size than *E.1027*, Eileen Gray made full use of the space provided.[152] In the dining room area a bench opens forwards to reveal a set of stairs to the cellar. A large multi-purpose living room served as a study area. Gray was fascinated by the mechanism of the sliding windows which came from the *Wanner* company.[153] The firm were recommended to her by Le Corbusier who used their windows in his *Clarté apartment* in Geneva in 1928. *Wanner* had won a gold medal at the Paris Exhibition in 1900, and later a silver medal at the 1925 Exposition des Art Décoratifs. They made shutters, lamps and airplane doors and so when creating her strip windows along the street façade and the sliding terrace door she decided to use their products. Their brochure stated that the 'Fenêtres coulissantes V. V (Sliding windows model V. V) permit the maximum of light, have minimal breakage of window panes, excellent closing application and secure sealing to prevent water ingress and they slide easily and would not jam'. Gray purchased the sliding windows on 3 December 1933[154] and they were installed the following month.[155] However, by April 1934 Gray had found a fault with their design, stating they were not as advertised in their brochure.[156]

7.57 *Tempe à Pailla*, 1931-35, page from Eileen Gray's portfolio showing the kitchen, foyer, dining room with the bench, and drawings of the cellar, 1956, paper, ink, black and white photograph © NMI

7.58 *Tempe à Pailla*, 1931-35, page from Eileen Gray's portfolio showing two views of the living room, the elevation facing the footpath, the adjustable coffee/dining table and circular windows, 1956, paper, ink, black and white photograph © NMI

7

Il parait souhaitable, pour les habitations petites ou moyennes, d'employer des moyens mécaniques, augmentant la mobilité des éléments de la vie quotidienne, et réduisant ainsi leur volume .

In small rooms ,in small houses , it is important not to encumber the available space. This can sometimes be realized by mechanical means , obtaining several uses for the same object .

6

1   En haut , une partie de la cuisine

2   La salle à manger ,faisant partie du living room
    Dining room , end of living room

    Table et banquette capitonnée, à charnières;
    Sous la banquette qui se renverse, quelques
    marches conduisent à la cave (ancienne citerne)

    Table with bench on hinges cushions attached;
    under the bench,easily reversable, stairs lead-
    ing to the cellar .

2

4

5

Au dessus du couloir de service , faux plaf
en bois ajouré, quadrillé, servant de placard
(Valises , couvertures de réserves etc)
les marches pour y monter ,mobiles, incorporé
dans la table de service .

Above the passage between the kitchen &
dining room , low ceiling , wood openwork u
ful for storing Valises , etc
Steps for attaining these shewn with the
table used for serving .

Table à deux hauteurs
transferrable instant-
anément .

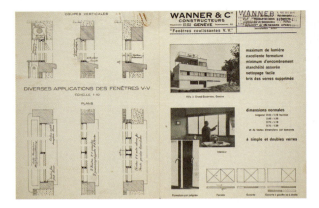

7.59 Promotional leaflets, *Wanner* door company, circa 1930s, commercial ink, paper © NMI

Wanner's promotional brochure also highlighted the *Éclair* garage door which was easy to open, quiet, did not take up too much space, and was economical. The door arrived in five parcels with accessories. From March to May 1934 Gray corresponded with the firm in the design for the door. Badovici was aiding her with deliveries for the project as during this time Gray was staying with him at *E.1027,* while the house was under construction[157] Gray finally ordered a door in April and paid for it in May.[158] It tilted to open which was a unique idea for the time and when installed at *Tempe à Pailla* caused quite a sensation amongst the local community for its novelty.[159]

Gray employed a number of local firms and craftsmen in the construction of her furniture designs for the house and for other projects. Joseph Charles Roattino, a local carpenter, worked on wooden tables, armchairs, lamps, and odd jobs,[160] and she ordered aluminium for furniture from the firm Gaspard Gojon.[161] However, most of the furniture for *Tempe à Pailla* was manufactured by a company in Menton called *Dufour & Martin*.[162] A successful steel and iron manufacturer Gray employed them from March 1936 until its closure in September 1939 when its owner E.Dufour was called up for military service.[163] In the three and a half years of their employ the company carried out the following work. They produced a divan

7.60 Joseph Charles Roattino with an adjustable bench/stool which he made at *Tempe à Pailla*, 1931, black and white photograph © NMI

in 1936,[164] and began the steel framework for the *Tempe à Pailla* deck chairs in 1937 (which were only completed prior to the outbreak of the war).[165] In

7.61 Free-form table, 1938, copper top, wood, chrome legs © Private collection

1938 they produced six tubular steel chairs with perforated upholstery,[166] an extendable wardrobe,[167] Japanese lanterns with frosted glass,[168] a free-form copper table, the chrome framework for free form tables, and an adjustable, folding table, which served as a coffee table and a dining table.[169] Between August and December 1938 they produced folding beds and armchairs, aluminium chairs, adjustable stools and a corner stand for hanging skirts.[170] In 1939 the firm completed the framework of a wooden armchair, and made metal hangers constructed for a trouser cabinet,[171] a cube chest with pivoting drawer, a *Transat chair* with square hinges on the head rest,[172] occasional tables and a small folding chair.[173]

During the Second World War Gray had remained for the first year in Castellar. In April 1942 she was forced to leave, as resident aliens could not live near the sea. Initially she went to St. Tropez where she had an apartment on the quai Suffren. However, she was requested to move inland and settled initially in Lourmarin and in 1943 in Cavaillon in the Vaucluse region. *Tempe à Pailla* was occupied first by Italian, then German and finally American soldiers. A devastating scene awaited her upon her return to the house in October 1946. The retreating troops and vagrants had looted her house, and destroyed most of her possessions, including her architectural drawings and models. Gray drew up lists of items and papers which she needed to have replaced and conducted a room-by-room appraisal of the destruction.[174] She also made lists of local workmen she needed to employ which were required for repairs.[175] The scale of the restoration project was immense: work began in 1946 and would last until 1955.[176] Progress was slow and it was not until 1951 that the restoration project began to accelerate. With work on going in January 1954 she took an apartment at 5 Place des Remparts, St. Tropez.[177]

The repair and reconstruction work was supervised by Badovici.[178] The shutters, doors, the sliding terrace door, railings and windows were replaced.[179] The firm *J.Ciffreo* located in Nice, who did a lot of work at *E.1027,* completed a lot of work, as did Étienne Panizzi, a local mason and her neighbour Francois Albin who was a builder. The house was draught proofed, a heating system installed, external and internal walls were repaired and re-plastered.[180] The entire roof terrace and the garden stairs were completely repaired, as was the famous garage door.[181] Various local workmen did electrical work and plumbing.[182] Much work on the interior was completed by Savoyardo Fortuné, Thomas Casale and Pierre Cannestrier.[183]

Still by 1955 work was incomplete and Gray kept an extensive notebook on *Tempe à Pailla,* with a number of handwritten entries dating from 1955-1957. In it she listed the repair and restoration work which still needed to be completed at *Tempe à Pailla.*[184] It was a monumental task.

Gray had to recreate many pieces of furniture at the house after the war. From 1949 to 1954 Gray employed *J.Bonnet* and the firm *Atelier Moderne* to do furniture restoration and also create new furniture for the house.[185]

Despite all of the repairs being completed on the house, Gray initially looked to sell the property.[186] During 1955 Gray sought a valuation of the property with an estate agent Étienne Carles from the *Agence Charvet Casteu* in Menton.[187] This occurred primarily because her neighbour, Raymond Benoit requested the enlargement of a right-of-way pathway to allow construction materials and machinery to be brought through to his property. Gray's insurance company advised that Raymond's request would not devalue her property or inconvenience her in any way.[188] She still had concerns that this expansion might cause her boundary wall to collapse.[189] As a result she insisted that the expansion of the passage be no more than two metres.[190] During the previous year Carles, and Gray's lawyer Joseph Richard, had been handling requests from interested parties who wanted to purchase the house or the surrounding fertile land. One interested buyer was the artist Graham Sutherland (1903-1980). Sutherland requested to know the exact terrain surrounding the property which Gray owned. She had purchased plots of land around the house over a number of years from three neighbours. The land registry had never updated their records and before any negotiations began with Sutherland Gray had to have the land completely assessed.[191] In addition to Graham Sutherland Gray stated in a letter that three other people had expressed an interest in the property.[192]

Gray's niece Prunella Clough had known Graham Sutherland since 1938 and he expressed an interest in meeting with Gray to view the property. She sent him a telegram inviting him to *Tempe à Pailla* on 22 May 1954.[193] Everything appeared exceedingly promising. Once a large lump-sum was paid up front, Gray agreed that the remaining money could be paid in instalments over two years through Prunella Clough.[194] The price for the house and the lands was initially £3,500 which she then dropped to £3,000 in June 1954. It was a verbal agreement which unfortunately would later cause a series of problems.[195] By August Gray was forced to augment the price to £4,800 as she was not informed about the supplementary monies involved when a non-French resident purchased a home in France.[196] If a foreigner purchased a property in France at this time, upon signing, they were constrained by law to pay the entire amount up front.[197] The Sutherlands naturally were annoyed and Gray offered to fly to London to meet with them in person.[198] To clarify the price of the house Gray wrote to Sutherland explaining that the break-down of this valuation was based on the land surrounding the property, which was valued at one million francs, and the old house which was valued at one million, and that she spent over one million restoring the property. This left the price at 3,250,000 French francs which she felt was a reasonable amount for the house and its fixtures. It was impossible for her to reduce it any further. Sutherland's solicitor came and reviewed the house and offered her £4,900, to include the fridge, which Gray could not accept.[199] Four months went by before Gray heard any news in relation to the sale from the Sutherlands.[200]

In an effort to advance the negotiations Gray offered to include furniture cupboards, a work table with a lamp, a dressing table, a celluloid screen, a carpet, various mirrors, beds, small tables, the chairs/steps and a bookcase in the price of the house.[201] 'A cork faced Chinese type cabinet plus a variety of garden chairs and the cork topped table which is reversible into a high or low position' were added as a further inducement.[202] Letters between Gray and Joseph Richard indicate that negotiations continued throughout 1954 – with the sale nearly falling through by the end of that year.[203] In May 1955 the deal was finalised for the house alone.[204] However, Gray paid for the property tax for that year and further problems ensued when she looked for reimbursement from the Sutherlands for these monies.[205] The Sutherlands didn't move in until May 1956.[206] Despite the misunderstandings Sutherland and Clough remained friends. He permitted students and enthusiasts to visit the house and he remained interested in Gray's career. Pleased to see Gray's work being acknowledged by Joseph Rykwert in *Domus* magazine in 1968 Sutherland wrote to Clough 'this article seems to me to be a very necessary but belated homage to a very good architect indeed, and if you are in contact with her, I would be grateful if you would express to her our really profound appreciation of this house, in which we have now lived since 1956 extremely happily, with daily appreciation of the splendid proportions which she contrived'.[207] In 1969 he wrote to Clough as they were looking to build an extension, in the hopes that Gray would do the project. Gray was suffering from ill health at the time but Clough replied that if it had been six months earlier Gray would have seized the opportunity.[208]

7.62 *Lou Pérou*, extension, 1954-61, coloured photograph © NMI

After selling *Tempe à Pailla* in 1955 Gray's attention turned to another plot of land with a view to building herself another home. *Lou Pérou* was a combination of Eileen Gray's emphasis on human needs combined with the simplicity of her minimal house drawings. The name is derived from Peru, which Gray had visited in 1929 with Jean Badovici.

In 1939 Gray had purchased an abandoned farm house, south of St. Tropez. It was a simple enclosure, with a crumbling stone wall and outhouses. Gray never developed a manifesto in relation to regional architecture; however, she did write numerous thoughts and ideas on pieces of paper which she kept in her archive. In these she wrote that there is something misleading in the return to regional architecture which does not conform to the variety of buildings which are needed. She sees a requirement for a rigorous discipline in the choice of colours in regional architecture from which architects must derive their ideas. For example in arid regions houses should be white-washed, constructed from local stone, with the upper stories painted in ultramarine blue.[209] Nowhere in her domestic architectural projects is this more apparent than with *Lou Pérou*.

Gray wanted to preserve the old farm building from the outset. She had a hydrological survey completed at *Lou Pérou* in 1954.[210] Initially Gray was too frail to draw up the plans for *Lou Pérou* herself so she obtained the assistance, in the same year, of a local engineer Guiccardi Henquez who drew up a series of plans of the existing stone structure and for an extension.[211] Several drawings of the house by Henquez exist.[212] She lodged documents with the mayor's office requesting planning permission for the enlargement of *Lou Pérou* on 3 December 1957. Numerous letters appear between Gray and Henquez. Gray was initially pleased with his designs for the foundations for the building. He hired a builder J. Correria (Gray also spells his name Corréia and Coréa) who he met on several occasions on site in October 1958.[213] At times Gray also drew on his plans, indicating the area for the water and plumbing on the plan.[214] In total Henquez drew two drawings of the renovation and the extension, a study for the septic tank with three drawings, completed in coloured crayon.[215] He also lodged the plans to the administrative department at the Mayor's office. On 3 December 1957 a ministerial order from the mayor's department was issued granting planning permission for *Lou Pérou*. The walls of the old farmhouse were 20cm thick, with a coating, and a height of 2m 50cm. The permit also granted permission for the building of a septic tank and drainage system.[216] However, by now, Gray was reluctant. Despite having planning permission for the renovations she requested the final plan and photographs be sent to her and she didn't hand over the final plan for the extension to the builder.[217] Nevertheless, the renovations on the farm building had begun by 8 October.[218]

Henquez's plan is different to the structure which was eventually built.[219] He treated the original barn as one large room with a humble extension. His plans for the extension show a modest building with a bedroom, bathroom and a tiled kitchen. On the elevation of the extension he drew continuous roller-shutters on Gray's bedroom window and the kitchen window, similar to those conceived by Ben Saul in the early 1950s. In his drawings he also included a curved retaining wall for the terraced garden, a feature which Gray ultimately kept. The material from which the house was constructed was *béton banché* which is a type of rubble concrete. She also used local fieldstone for the walls and the paving in the garden. Gray also asked Henquez to provide a solution to drainage for the property. His plan illustrates a system of shafts which were placed at two corners of the existing structure and the other two corners of the new extension at the bedroom area. These shafts collected water from the roof and the garden terrace.[220]

Despite a tremor in her hands, Gray took control of the project, as she was unhappy with the plans and relieved Henquez of his duties. Gray began making several improvements and modifications. On 11 October 1960 Gray applied for planning permission for the extension – designed by herself.[221] The mayor's office also asked to see copies of any work completed on the site prior to this date. The final certificate was granted for the extension on 29 November 1960.[222]

She focused initially on plans and elevations of the living room and Louise Dany's room, but they remain incomplete, as she erased a lot of the details in her early drawings.[223] However, she began to clearly define the plan, subdividing the interior to create a separate living space for Dany.[224] Dany's room and the living room looked onto the garden terrace. In 1958 Gray added the extension, a wing perpendicular to the original building. In comparison to Henquez, Gray created a corridor with three adjoining rooms. She expanded the kitchen with an open air porch, and she increased the size of the bedroom, with an adjoining room or loggia which led onto the garden. She also increased the amount of light with the addition of a ceiling light in the corridor and another window off the bedroom.

Gray perfected several plans for her version of the project. In early drawings she followed Henquez's

7.63 *Lou Pérou*, early plan of the extension, 1954, paper, pencil, ink, coloured pen © NMI

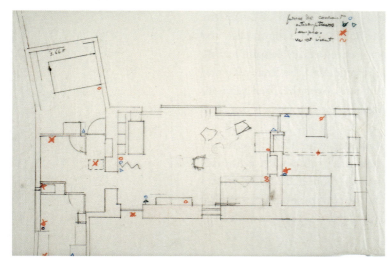

idea and only later did she expand on creating an open air loggia off her bedroom. She also clearly marked out pieces of furniture, beds, tables, chairs and a screen in the living room. Gray marked, in red and blue, the electric nodes and plug sockets.[225] In other early plans she included measurements for existing apertures and for Louise Dany's bedroom in the old farmhouse structure. She was careful in the way she articulated the modern addition in comparison to the original, simple vaulted farmhouse and drew the plans with both the old structure and wing together.

In one plan for the extension, Gray shortens the corridor, extends the kitchen with an outdoor kitchen, and details a small bathroom. She then shifts the axis of the bedroom by ten degrees, making it larger and creating a larger outdoor loggia. This is similar to what she did at *E.1027*, as she shifted the house by ten degrees to gain maximum advantage of the diurnal path of the sun.[226] On another large-scale plan, dated 1958, Gray

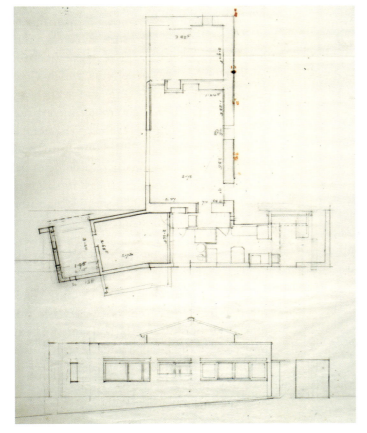

7.64 *Lou Pérou*, plan of the extension with elevation, 1958, paper, pencil © NMI

7.65 *Lou Pérou*, extension, 1958, coloured photograph © NMI

develops this theme showing how the extension was accessed by a small corridor, set off the living room.[227] Initially she had two doors leading off the living room, one directly into a bedroom with an en-suite bathroom, and the other into the kitchen. Both were separated by a large wall.[228]

On the final plan Gray developed drawings of the extension showing three doors leading from this small corridor which was accessed from the living room. It was illuminated by a small window in the north façade, and a square sky light in the flat roof. The first door opens onto a larger kitchen.

Gray situated the kitchen at a distance from the more public domain of the living room and the private quarters of the bedrooms in order to prevent cooking odours from seeping through. In earlier drawings Gray treated this space similarly to the kitchen at *E.1027*. Also similar to the kitchen at *Tempe à Pailla*, this room had its own service entrance at the north façade. It has minimal dimensions yet Gray has included a series of storage compartments and cupboards, along with a cooker and kitchen table. It lacks the practical qualities of the Russian Constructivists which Gray had explored in earlier sketches for kitchens. She rejects Le Corbusier's and Jeanneret's use of standardised uniform cabinets. The storage cupboards are not streamline uniform, and are more compositionally placed, similar to De Stijl ideas. Though modest in size it is more compact in design, illustrating a greater knowledge of function and tailored to Dany's needs.

The second door leads into a small, compact bathroom with a bath, toilet and sink. In another plan Gray gives measurements for the bath, sink and space between the toilet and the wall. As the wall for the bath projects into the kitchen and the sink in the kitchen is adjacent to the bathroom, Gray has carefully integrated the two so that one does not superimpose onto the other.[229]

7.66 *Lou Pérou*, plan of the extension, 1958, paper, pencil, crayon, ink © NMI

7.67 *Lou Pérou*, plan of the extension, 1958, paper, pencil, crayon, ink © NMI

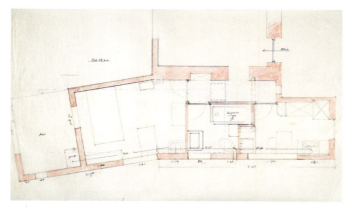

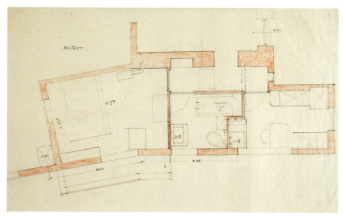

The third door opens into a bedroom with a double bed, a divan, a wash/dressing area, a work desk set against the wall, and a pivoting cupboard which is attached against the wall. This opened onto a modest loggia with boc glass which leads into the garden. Originally she intended to have the bedroom looking directly onto the garden, eliminating the alcove.[230] This would have reduced ventilation on the south façade which was in the direct path of the sun throughout the day. Gray excluded the loggia in one plan and included a south facing window instead.[231]

In 1961 at the age of eighty three Eileen Gray embarked on her second set of adjustments to the design of *Lou Pérou*. She decided to alter and enlarge a number of apertures at the house, in order to allow more natural light into the south façade of the house. Derived from the window and shutter system, which she initially used at *E.1027* and then at *Tempe à Pailla,* Gray's drawings looked at the wooden shutters on the south façade of the house showing the window of Louise Dany's room.[232] This bedroom faced the garden terrace. Gray created these shutters to filter the southern sun and the view. In her drawings she detailed their working mechanism showing how the shutters would slide to the side. Using sliding wooden louvers she could filter the sun, adding or detracting light from within the room, providing shade during the heat of the day whilst simultaneously permitting a constant flow of ventilation. However, due to her age, Gray became frustrated at times with the length of time it took to complete the house, she stated, 'The sliding windows are not even in their place. St. Tropez is not self-supporting. Metal, wood, and all accessories have to come from Toulon or Nice'.[233] Another device she created was a shading device created from bamboo matting which supported a slim metal frame with wheels that could be transported easily around the garden.[234] This could be attached to the garden façade to provide greater protection from the sun. A drawing explains that the metal tubing framing would be assembled in two sections, joined together, each measuring 1.85m x 1. 80m in length and a height from the ground of 2.12m.

Gray drew the elevations of *Lou Pérou* in a modest manner. Her elevation of the entrance façade at *Lou Pérou* indicates a simple vaulted space.[235] Just like she had done at *Tempe à Pailla,* the fenestration and design of the entrance façade is very enclosed and private. It lies in direct contrast to the open, light feel of the south façade, which faces the garden. In her elevations of the extension Gray shows her use of wooden windows and

7.68 *Lou Pérou*, extension, 1954-61, colour photograph © NMI

shutters. She inserted a pattern of blue glass over the doorway at the entrance. She used a barbed metal grill on an adjoining window which recalls work which she had completed on her *House at Samois sur Seine,* 1921-24. In her elevation drawings for the northern and eastern facades to the new extension Gray treated them similarly. With the elevation drawing of the east façade Gray detailed the kitchen, bathroom, bedroom and outdoor alcove which led onto the garden.[236] She drew them in an anonymous vernacular manner using conventional wooden shutters and windows. Just as she did with the plans, the elevations reveal how she relied on the ideas which she developed at *E.1027*. In the early elevations Gray clearly separates living and kitchen quarters as one doorway off the living room led to a small kitchen and an open alcove on the entrance façade.[237] This was concealed from the entrance façade by a large wall, made from local stone which was perpendicular to the kitchen. Visually it would have linked well with the use of the local stone in the garden. Early elevations reveals that Gray originally planned three windows only whereas the finished elevation shows five.[238]

On one drawing of the entrance façade from the entrance from the north facing garden Gray shows a doorway with an open porch.[239] Gray has indicated a rug design in the centre of the room which measures 1.46 metres x 48cm

Problems of damp in the late 1960s and early 1970s forced Gray to deliberate about changing the garage into a small private apartment for Louise Dany. The garage had been added in 1958, and was constructed on the lower terraces of the garden accessed via a stairs. The roof of the garage was covered in grass sods. As with her other houses a choreographic approach was taken in the planning of the house and garden. The garage was viewed as a continuation of the garden, culminating in a projecting terrace from which one could view the sunset. As with her other houses, *E.1027* and *Tempe à Pailla,* the site of *Lou Pérou* matched her stringent sun orientation requirements.

The quotations proved to be quite costly. In her plans Gray doubled the size of the existing structure with a perpendicular addition. The entrance to the apartment would have been where the existing door had been. The garage door was to be converted into a large window. She enlarged an existing window and on the left side of the perpendicular addition she installed two more windows. The end of the new addition would have opened out onto a small garden, where she has indicated vegetation, possibly yucca plants. Neither the drawings nor the elevations for the south and west facades are complete. However she has indicated that the roof would have gradations, which would have enabled the run off of excess water, thus tackling the problem of damp on the roof.

On one drawing, the south elevation of the garage door was to be converted into a large glass panelled loggia, where the roof slightly projects.[240] This would take maximum advantage of the views. Gray treated it similarly to the modest outdoor room which was at the end of the perpendicular wing that she added to the main house at *Lou Pérou* in 1958. The plan reveals that Gray enlarged the width of the structure

7.69 *Lou Pérou*, plan of garage with elevations, 1954-61, paper, pencil, ink © NMI

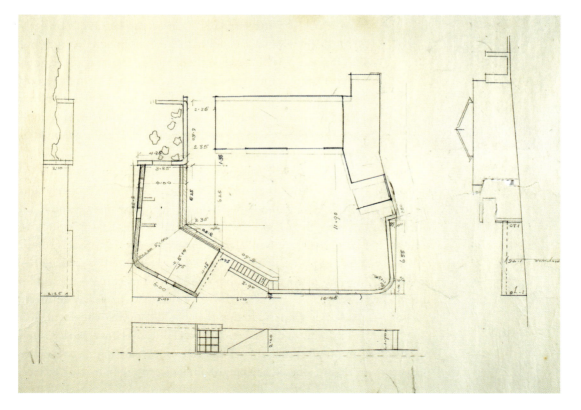

especially at the corners. The building appears to have an open plan, but she has not indicated the subdivision of rooms. This is possibly due to the fact that the light was limited to apertures in the south and west facades. The roof was also covered over. Gray has indicated walls or possibly storage compartments in the plan which subdivides the extension into two spaces on the west side of the house. By opening out the south façade she flooded the interior with light.

In some drawings Gray indicated the width of the walls and had experimented with the creation of a courtyard to the north, drawing a storage area for wood.[241] This conversion would have been cut off from the house providing Dany with privacy. It was never realised. Other drawings of the garage exist indicating that the garage was to house two cars.[242]

7.70 *Lou Pérou*, view of the garden with bamboo awning and curved retaining wall, 1954-61, coloured photograph © NMI

In the garden she created a private enclosure, framing it with a curved retaining wall. Gray also drew a section at the end of the garden terrace at *Lou Pérou* depicting the width of the quarry stone surrounding wall in relation to the garage. Drawings and notes exist which provide measurements and other details of the terrace.[243] During the late 1960s or early 1970s Eileen Gray discussed with her neighbour the building of a fence or a wall between their properties. Gray had a good rapport with her neighbours at *Lou Pérou* and gladly drew up several plans with measurements for a fencing system with a gate.[244] At one point she looked at creating a shed and a small barrier or gate which was to be constructed beside the shed to give access to the garden.[245]

In her later years Gray discovered that measurements made of the property by the land registry were incorrect.[246] The property was surrounded by five neighbouring houses.[247] This would become an important factor as Gray had difficulties with the local authorities and some of her neighbours. *Électricité de France* wanted to run underground cables through her property and her neighbours wanted to enlarge her access pathways to facilitate water pipe laying and to run electric cables into their buildings.[248] Some neighbours wanted Gray to clearly delineate the boundaries of her property so that they could complete these works.[249] Gray tried to find alternative solutions; accessing overhead power lines, or objecting in one instance that if the tree-lined pathway between her property and that of one of her neighbours was enlarged by two metres, it would entail the loss of these trees which provided privacy. She would be left with nothing to protect her property. Once the path was paved she felt the amount of traffic which passed by her land would increase. Without the trees being present between her house and her neighbours or by having to define pathways between the properties Gray felt that it would create the impression of a housing estate – something she wished to avoid at all costs and which went against her architectural thinking.[250] In 1971 she was legally obliged to grant a neighbour right-of-way through her property.[251] By 1976 the year she died Gray had become weary of the problems – she was taken to court by one neighbour and forced to enlarge the access route.[252]

Gray remained respectful of the interior of her own apartment in rue Bonaparte which she had occupied since 1907. The only space which she altered was her bedroom which she modified in 1930 using ideas which she had developed at *E.1027*. She installed a head board with similar lamp, clock and electrical switches that she had used at *E.1027* and a flexible table which was attached to the wall. A De Stijl influenced bookcase hung on the wall. She had painted the bedroom walls white. She again painted the apartment in December 1968, due to a leak from a neighbour's apartment which affected the kitchen and her bedroom.[253] By 1967 Gray's financial situation was becoming an issue. In March Gray approached the agency,

7.71 *Rue Bonaparte apartment*, bedroom, 1930, black and white photograph © NMI

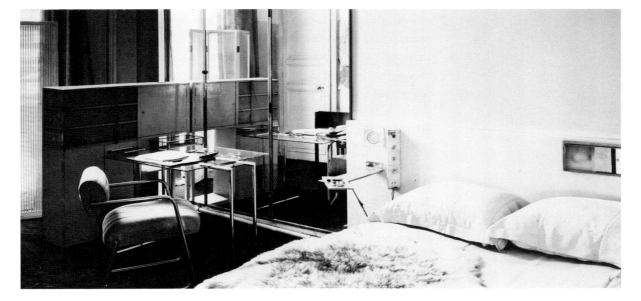

 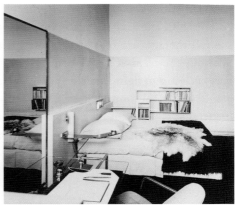

7.72 *Rue Bonaparte apartment*, drawing room, 1930, black and white photograph © NMI

7.73 *Rue Bonaparte apartment*, bedroom, 1930, black and white photograph © NMI

Lloyd Immobilier Français, meeting with R. Larousse to find out the price they proposed for the sale of her apartment.[254] By August of that year they had a client who was interested in the property.[255] She also approached the agent Pierre Joubert, and employed her solicitor Horace Guicciardi to deal directly with them. Gray intended to explore the option of selling her property at a fixed price and being afforded the opportunity to remain living in both her apartment on the rue Bonaparte and *Lou Pérou* until her death.[256] Gray carefully analysed the cost involved in the sale of the apartment, the cleaning of the apartment and the commission for Guicciardi.[257] She took into account – size, situation, stairs, style of the building, and whether it had charm. Though it was an old apartment, the interior had been modernised.[258] By November 1967 a gentleman by the name of J.M Tazi who came from Casablanca, visited Gray and proposed to acquire the apartment for his daughter who was studying medicine.[259] Regrettably, yet with humour, Gray apologised to Tazi as she could not promise him to be dead within the three-year time-frame that he was quoted by Guicciardi. If she agreed the sale with him and was still alive at this time she would be forced to find alternative accommodation for herself and her possessions. Therefore she declined his offer.[260] To raise capital she explored selling *Lou Pérou* and had several valuations completed.[261] *Lou Pérou,* had two large vineyards. A neighbour, Tiburce Fassetti, maintained one of the vineyards until his death in 1959 and his wife continued his efforts. She had the vineyard replanted with a new type of grape in 1972 hoping to become more self-sustaining.[262] In 1970 Gray decided to sell shares from her vineyard to a Wine Cooperative in St. Tropez run by Louis Marie Emil Laudon and his wife Madame Nicole Leveque. They became responsible for the upkeep of the vineyard along with Gray.[263]

Many people question why she became virtually unknown towards the later part of her life. She was constantly plagued with doubt as to whether she was good enough as an architect. In one letter she muses, 'Success or failure – I've begun to realize is absolutely unimportant unless one is a genius'.[264]

ENDNOTES

1   Planat, P, *Manuel de Perspective et Trace des ombres à l'usage des architectes et ingénieurs et des élèves des écoles spéciales*, Paris, Aulanier et cie, 1899.

2   NMIEG 2003.73. Poincaré, Henri, *La Valeur de Science*, Paris, Flammarion Editions, 1903.

3   NMIEG 2003.547, photograph of Jean Badovici.

4   Clausen, Meredith, 'The Ecole des Beaux-Arts, Toward a Gendered History', *Journal of the Society of Architectural Historians*, Vol. 69, No.2, June 2010, p.155. Juliette Billard in 1913, a Mlle Eude in 1917 and, Jeanne Surugue and Juliette Mathé from Versailles in 1918. In 1920 Mlles Mathé, Morel, Bowé, Bernard, Zmaîtch, Lucie Dumbraveanu, and Jeanne Marie Fratacci competed.

5   Archieri, Jean-Francois, 'Jean Badovici: Une historie Confisquée', in Pitiot, Cloé, Eileen Gray, Éditions du Centre Pompidou, Paris, 2013, p.88.

6   NMIEG 2000.191, postcard from Eileen Gray to Eveleen Pounden Gray, 19 September 1912, Samois-sur-Seine, NMIEG 2003.533, map of Samois-sur-Seine, 1921-23.

7   Constant, Caroline, *Eileen Gray*, London, Phaidon, 2000, p.42.

8   Ibid, Constant, p.197, footnote 35, Chapter 2. Badovici could have possibly assisted her with this stucco work as they are unadorned and simplistic like his Le Corbusian-styled work.

9   Adam, Peter, *Eileen Gray: Architect/Designer: A Biography*, London, Thames and Hudson, 2000, p.115.

10 Ibid, Constant, p.42.

11 This type of metal work is also found in a storage room at Vézelay, which according to Constant, Gray designed with Jean Badovici, and in a kitchen window found in *Lou Pérou*.

12 NMIEG 2003.508, notes on Eileen Gray's work, 1970s.

13 V&A Archives, AAD/1980/9/171, AAD/1980/9/172 /1-2, AAD/1980/9/173/1-4, house based on Adolf Loos's *Villa Moissi*, 1923.

14 NMIEG 2003.491, Badovici, Jean, *L'Architecture Vivante*, Paris, Editions Albert Morancé, Winter edition 1923.

15 Loos, Adolphe, 'L'Architecture et le Style Moderne', *L'Architecture Vivante*, Winter 1923, pp.26-34.

16 Constant, Caroline, *Eileen Gray*, London, Phaidon, 2000, p.74.

17 Constant, Caroline, *Eileen Gray*, London, Phaidon, 2000, p.79.

18 Loye, Brigitte, *Eileen Gray, 1879-1976*; architecture, design, preface de Michael Raynaud, Analeph, Paris, 1984, p.86.

19 Ibid, Constant, p.80.

20 Interview with Cloé Pitiot 2014. Pitiot has done extensive research in relation to Gray's work at Vézelay making new discoveries. See also Ibid, Constant, p.80.

21 NMIEG 2000.190, postcard of Vézelay, Circa 1923.

22 NMIEG 2003.1, *House for an Engineer*, ground floor plan. RIBA Archives, PB.496/11-1, this is a ground floor and first floor plan, RIBA Archives, PB 496/11-1-3. V&A Archives, AAD/1980/9, *House for an Engineer* drawings 1-6, AAD/1980/9, small *House for an Engineer* drawings 1-3.

23 Ibid, Constant, p.75.

24 Louis, Michel, 'Mallet Stevens et le cinéma 1919-1929', *Robert Mallet Stevens Architecte*, Brussels, Editions des Archives d'Architecture Moderne, 1980, p.130.

25 V&A Archives, AAD/1980/9/171, AAD/1980/9/172 /1-2, AAD/1980/9/173/1-4, house based on Adolf Loos's *Villa Moisi*, 1923.

26 Ibid, Constant, p.76.

27 V&A Archives, AAD/1980/9/175/9, study for a four storey villa, 1930s, AAD/1980/9/176, axonometric drawing of a Villa.

28 Ibid, Constant, p.75.

29 NMIEG 2003.2, *House for an Engineer*, first floor plan. RIBA Archives, PB.496/11-1, *House for an Engineer*, 1926, this is a ground floor and first floor plan.

30 NMIEG 2000.261, Van Doesburg, Theo, *Classique Baroque Moderne*, Paris Edition De Sikkel Anvers et Leonce Rosenberg, December 1918. NMIEG 2003.81. Mondrian, Piet, *Neo-Plasticisme*, Paris, Editions de l'Effort Moderne Léonce Rosenberg, 1920.

31 V&A Archives, AAD/1980/9/176, four storey villa project, axonometric drawing.

32 Ibid, Constant, p.75.

33 Van de Beek, Johan, 'Adolf Loos – Patterns of Townhouses', Raumplan versus Plan Libre, Delft, Delft University Press, 1991, pp.27-29.

34 NMIEG 2003.489, *House and Garden*, 1920, Condé Nest London, November 1920.

35 NMIEG 2003.508, notes on Eileen Gray's work, Circa 1970s, NMIEG 2000.250, NMIEG 2003.1641, portfolios.

36 Gray, Eileen, and Badovici, Jean, 'Maison en Bord de Mer', *L'Architecture Vivante*, winter edition 1929, p.26.

37 Ibid, Gray and Badovici, p.11.

38 Ibid, Gray and Badovici, pp.113-16.

39 Adam, Peter, *Eileen Gray: Architect/Designer: A Biography*, London, Thames and Hudson, 2000, p.309.

40 V&A Archives, AAD/1980/9/188/5-7, subtle differences exist in these three drawings of the west site section with variations of the external stairs and the private balcony off the living room alcove. AAD/1980/9/188/7 is similar to NMIEG 2003.6 as Gray has formed her ideas, clearly distinguishing the spaces from one another. RIBA Archives, DR166/7-8., this west site section is similar to NMIEG 2003.6.

41 V&A Archives, AAD/1980/9/188/11, just as in NMIEG 2003.6, Gray has signed this site plan drawing 'E.24-30'. When the house was published in *L'Architecture Vivante*, winter edition 1929, Gray and Badovici clearly date the house 1926-29; however some drawings and elevations suggest variations to this date.

42 Gray, Eileen, and Jean Badovici, 'Maison en Bord de Mer', *L'Architecture Vivante*, winter edition 1929, p.10.

43 Ibid, Gray and Badovici, p.16.

44 Ibid, Gray and Badovici, p.18.

45 Ibid, Gray and Badovici, p.26.

46 Ibid, Gray and Badovici.

47 Malevich, Kazimir, *Black Square on White Ground*, dated 1913, executed after 1920, Oil on canvas, 106.2 x 106.5cm, St Petersburg, Russian State Museum.

48 NMIEG 2003.5, *E.1027*, drawing for shutters.

49 Le Corbusier, *Une Petite Maison*, Basel, Birkhäuser Architecture Editions, 1989, pp.30-38.

50 Leatherbarrow, David and Moshen, Mostafavi, *Surface Architecture*, Cambridge, MIT Press, 2005, pp.63-4.

51 Ibid, Constant, pp.107-8.

52 Ibid, Gray and Badovici, p.16.

53 V&A Archives, AAD/1980/9/188, un-numbered drawings for *E.1027*. There are two sketches for strip windows. AAD/1980/9, un-numbered drawings titled *Work Drawings and Tracings*. There are four studies for sliding and pivoting doors and windows, some with detailed measurements. AAD/1980/9, un-numbered drawings titled *Dessins de Jean Badovici*. Though titled Jean Badovici's drawings, the sketches are all in Gray's handwriting. They show drawings for sliding windows, details of shutters, long strip windows and drawings of a double window with louvered shutters on a castor system.

54 NMIEG 2003.8, *E.1027*, living room plan and four elevations.

55 Ibid, Gray, Eileen, and Badovici, Jean, p.16.

56 Ibid, Gray and Badovici.

57 Ibid, Gray and Badovici, p.13.

58 Ibid, NMIEG 2003.8.

59 Ibid, Gray and Badovici, p.18.

60 Adam, Peter, *Eileen Gray: Architect/Designer: A Biography,* London, Thames and Hudson, 2000, p.283.

61 Ibid, Gray and Badovici, p.18.

62 V&A Archives, AAD/1980/9/188/24, this is a plan and elevations of the living room fireplace.

63 Ibid, Constant, p.95.

64 NMIEG 2000.40, this is a model of the *E.1027* living room screen. V&A Prints and Drawings Archive, W.105.D.E. E1140-1983, E1141-1983 – designs, drawings and elevations for a telephone chair, but with a screen similar to the one at *E.1027.*

65 V&A Archives, AAD/1980/9/188/33, this is a plan and elevations for the pivotal mechanism for the swivel-top side table in the sleeping alcove off the living room. Gray has indicated that it measured 18cm in length.

66 Ibid, Gray and Badovici.

67 Ibid, Gray and Badovici, p.16.

68 V&A Archives, AAD/1980/9/188/, un-numbered drawings of elevations.

69 Ibid, Gray and Badovici, p.26.

70 NMIEG 2003.9, *E.1027*, ground floor plan.

71 Ibid, Gray, Eileen, and Badovici, pp.14-15. This published plan also includes detailed plans of the roof top terrace and the entrance.

72 NMIEG 2000.250, NMIEG 2003.1641, portfolios.

73 V&A Archives, AAD/1980/9/188/19, plan and elevations of the main living room and kitchen. AAD/1980/9/188/30, early pencil drawings of the ground floor of *E.1027,* reworked in ink by Jean Badovici. RIBA Archives, DR166/7-4, this is a ground floor plan with the areas clearly labelled into different zones. RIBA Archives, DR166/7-1,this is a display panel of the ground floor plan in Gray's handwriting, differentiating the different areas.

74 Ibid, Gray and Badovici, p.11.

75 Ibid, Gray and Badovici.

76 Olsen, Donald J., *The City as a Work of Art London*: *Paris, Vienna, London,* Yale University Press, 1986, pp.124-5.

77 Heller, Geneviève, *Propre en Ordre,* France, Editions d'en Bas, 1979, p.16, footnote no.469.

78 V&A Archives, AAD/1980/9/, an un-numbered sketch of a kitchen plan.

79 Ibid, Gray and Badovici, p.16.

80 Ibid, Gray and Badovici, p.22.

81 Ibid, Gray and Badovici, p.16.

82 Ibid, Constant, p.119.

83 Ibid, Gray and Badovici, p.20.

84 NMIEG 2004.105, *Villa Savoye à Poissy*, view of the roof top garden.

85 Ibid, Gray and Badovici, p.22.

86 NMIEG 2003.7, *E.1027*, bedroom plan and four elevations.

87 Ibid, Gray and Badovici, pp.19-22.

88 Ibid, Gray and Badovici, p.16 and p.19.

89 Ibid, Gray and Badovici.

90 Ibid, Gray and Badovici, plate.16.

91 Ibid, Gray and Badovici, p.22.

92 Ibid, Constant, p.105.

93 Evans, Robert, 'The Developed Surface: an Enquiry into the Brief Life of 18th Century Drawing Technique', *9H*, No.8, 1989, pp.120-147 as cited in Constant p.105.

94 Ibid, Gray and Badovici, pp.19-22.

95 Ibid, Gray and Badovici, p.22.

96 V&A Archives, AAD/1980/9/188/14, 15, 16, these show the spatial concepts of the guest and principal bedrooms.

97 Ibid, Gray and Badovici.

98 V&A Archives, AAD 9/6-1980 and AAD 9/9-1980, these are typed notes by Jean Badovici regarding naval design, life boats and life-saving.

99 Ibid, V&A Archives.

100 Le Corbusier Foundation Archive, E1-5-116, undated letter from Le Corbusier to Jean Badovici.

101 NMIEG 2003.37, exhibition label for *E-7*, lifeboat.

102 Ibid, Constant, p.234. Badovici finally patented the project in 1934.

103 Badovici was so inspired by these nautical themes that he explored boat architecture see V&A Archives, ADD 9/6-1980 to AAD9/9-1980 in 1929-31.

104 V&A Archives., AAD 9/6-1980, papers marked 'Badovici lifeboats: The Sea Tank'. AAD9/8-1980 and AAD9/9-1980, papers marked 'Life-saving at sea' and 'Le sauvetage maritime.' In Jean Badovici's notes on lifeboats similarities exist in nautical details which appear in the furnishings and in the treatment of the plan of both *E.1027* and *Tempe à Pailla*. See also Rykwert, Joseph, 'Un Omaggio a Eileen Gray, Pioniera del Design', *Domus*, Milan, Casa Editions, December no. 469, 1968, pp.29-31.

105 NMIEG 2003.73, Poincaré, Henri, *La Valeur de Science*, Paris, Flammarion Editions, 1903.

106 NMIEG 2003.74, Kingdon Clifford, William, *Lectures and Essays*, New York, MacMillan Editions, 1886.

107 V&A Archives, AAD 9/13-1980, unknown press clipping from undated article by Louis Vauxcelles.

108 Ibid, Constant, pp.115-116.

109 NMIEG 2003.85, *Futurist exhibition catalogue*, London, Sackville Gallery, March 1912.

110 Duchamp, as quoted in 'Eleven Europeans in America', (Interviews by James Johnson Sweeney), *The Museum of Modern Art Bulletin*, Vol. XIII/4-5, 1946, p.20.

111 Author unknown, 'Lacquer walls and Furniture Displace Old Gods in Paris and London', *Harper's Bazaar*, September 1920.

112 RIBA Archives, DR166/7 (1-8), Roquebrune (France): House, ca. 1927-1929.

113 NMIEG 2003.158, translation notes in English from Maison au Bord de Mer.

114 Ibid, Constant, p.124.

115 NMIEG 2003.189, invoice from Société Française du Bois Malléable on 6 rue Guillaume, Paris, France to Eileen Gray, 7 December 1929.

116 NMIEG 2003.538, invoice from *Worbla Factory* to Eileen Gray, 11 August 1931.

117 NMIEG 2003.537, invoice from *Worbla factory* to Eileen Gray 11 April 1933

118 Ibid, Constant, p.222.

119 NMIEG 2003.12, plan of *Quai Suffren apartment*, St. Tropez.

120 NMIEG 2003.13, plan of *Quai Suffren apartment*, St. Tropez. V&A Archives, AAD/1980/9/, un-numbered plan of Eileen Gray's apartment, quai Suffren, St. Tropez, 1938.

121 NMIEG 2003.14, plan of *Quai Suffren apartment*, St. Tropez.

122 Ibid, Constant.

123 V&A Prints & Drawings Archive, W.105.D/E.1168-1983, this is described as a design for a folding chair in wood, circa 1935-39. This chair was used in the small flat that the artist furnished in St. Tropez in 1939 (sic).

124 NMIEG 2003.1685, act of sale of land at *Tempe à Pailla*, 24 April 1926, NMIEG 2003.1684, act of sale of *Tempe à Pailla*, October 1926.

125 NMIEG 2003.1683, act of sale of *Tempe à Pailla*, 1928, NMIEG 2003.1731, letter from J. Richard to Eileen Gray, 26 June 1954.

126 NMIEG 2003.1686, engineers report for *Tempe à Pailla*, 17 September 1934.

127 NMIEG 2000.90, *Tempe à Pailla*, site plan.

128 V&A Archives, AAD/1980/9/206/1, designed over a single water cistern the *Maison de Weekend* is similar to *Tempe à Pailla*. Built on pilotis this single storey structure is accessed from the main roadway via a stairs.

129 NMIEG 2000.250, NMIEG 2003.1641, portfolios. Gray notes in her architectural portfolio that *Tempe à Pailla* dates 1931-33 and also 1932-34.

130 Rare Book & Manuscript Library, Columbia University in the City of New York, Stephen Haweis Papers, Arranged Miscellaneous Memoirs, Box 2, letter from Eileen Gray to Stephen Haweis, page two part of a letter April 1962 – possibly page two of letter 30 March 1962.

131 Mendelsohn, Eric, *Neues Has, Neue Welt*, Berlin, Gebr Mann Verlag, 1997.

132 NMIEG 2003.499, Badovici, Jean, 'Eric Mendelsohn', *L'Architecture Vivante*, Winter edition, 1932.

133 Heinze-Greenberg, Ita, 'I often fear the envy of the gods', *Erich Mendelsohn: Dynamics and Function*, Germany, Hatje Cantz Publishers, 1999, p.177.

134 Ozenfant, Amédée, 'Für Erich Mendelsohn', *Neues Haus Neue Welt*, Berlin, Gebr Mann Verlag, 1997, p.4.

135 NMIEG 2000.250, NMIEG 2003.1641, portfolios.

136 Ibid, Ozenfant. P. 4.

137 Ibid, Adam, p.309.

138 NMIEG 2003.11, *Tempe à Pailla*, sun orientation.

139 Ibid, Constant, pp.114-115.

140 Schlemmer, Oskar, 'Man' 1928-29, translated by Hans M. Wingler in *Bauhaus: Weimar Dessau Berlin*, Chicago, Cambridge, Mass, MIT Press, 1969, p.523. It was originally published in Bauhaus No.2/3, 1928.

141 Le Corbusier, *Œuvre Complète, 1910-29*, Zurich Editions, 1964, p.144.

142 NMIEG 2004.81, *Tempe à Pailla*, north elevation and longitudinal section of the east elevation.

143 NMIEG 2003.10, *Tempe à Pailla*, longitudinal section of the east elevation. Another drawing exists Centre Pompidou Archives, projets d'architecture, ref. AM 1998-2-202 but without Gray's handwriting of 1931 on the drawing.

144 NMIEG 2000.250, portfolio.

145 Centre Pompidou Collection, projets d'architecture, ref.AM 1998-2-198.

146 Ibid, Constant, p.146.

147 NMIEG 2004.78, *Tempe à Pailla*, longitudinal section of the east elevation.

148 NMIEG 2004.79, *Tempe à Pailla*, south elevation and longitudinal section of the west elevation. Centre Pompidou Collection, projets d'architecture, ref.AM 1998-2-200, AM 1998-2-198, AM 1998-2-200.

149 NMIEG 2004.80, *Tempe à Pailla*, garage and bedroom, floor plan and elevations.

150 Centre Pompidou Archives, projets d'architecture, ref. AM 1998-2-201.

151 NMIEG 2004.83, *Tempe à Pailla*, plan of kitchen.

152 NMIEG 2004.82, *Tempe à Pailla*, living room plan. See also Centre Pompidou Collection, projets d'architecture, ref.AM 1998-2-197.

153 NMIEG 2003.1828, NMIEG 2003.1829, promotional leaflets, *Wanner* door company, Circa 1930s.

154 NMIEG 2003.1833, invoice from *Wanner* door company to Eileen Gray, 3 December 1933.

155 NMIEG 2003.1826, receipt from *Wanner* door company to Eileen Gray. January 1934.

156 NMIEG 2003.1830, letter from *Wanner* door company to Eileen Gray.18 April 1934.

157 NMIEG 2003.1832, letter from *Wanner* door company to Eileen Gray. 24 March 1934. The letter is addressed to Roquebrune, Cap Martin where Gray was previously living with Badovici at E.1027.

158 NMIEG 2003.1827, letter from *Wanner* door company to Eileen Gray. 7 May 1934. NMIEG2003.1831, invoice from Wanner door company to Eileen Gray. 17 April 1934.

159 Adam, Peter, *Eileen Gray: Architect/Designer: A Biography*, London, Thames and Hudson, 1987, p.268.

160 NMIEG 2003.1728, NMIEG 2003.1729, NMIEG 2003.1730, invoices from Charles Roattino to Eileen Gray, 4th March 1930s.

161 NMIEG 2003.1678, invoice from Gaspard Gojon to Eileen Gray. 19 March 1937.

162 NMIEG 2003.1668, invoice from Dufour & Martin to Eileen Gray, 18 March 1936.

163 NMIEG 2003.1661, NMIEG 2003.1662, NMIEG 2003.1664, letters from E. Dufour & Martin to Eileen Gray, 8 September 1939, 22 September 1939 and 31 October 1939.

164 NMIEG 2003.1670, invoice from Dufour & Martin to Eileen Gray, 31 December 1936.

165 NMIEG 2003.1669, invoice from Dufour & Martin to Eileen Gray, 7 June 1937. NMIEG 2000.35, model of the *Tempe à Pailla* deck chair, NMIEG 2003.213, *Tempe à Pailla* deck chair.

166 NMIEG 2003.1654, letter from Dufour & Martin to Eileen Gray, 30 November 1937.

167 NMIEG 2003.1653, letter and a sketch from Dufour & Martin to Eileen Gray, 11 February 1938, NMIEG 2003.1666, receipt from Dufour & Martin to Eileen Gray., 11 February 1938.

168 NMIEG 2003.1656, invoice from Dufour & Martin to Eileen Gray, 17 June 1938, NMIEG 2000.12, NMIEG 2000.24, Japanese lanterns.

169 NMIEG 2003.1667, invoice from Dufour & Martin to Eileen Gray, 1 June 1938.

170 NMIEG 2003.1663, invoice from Dufour & Martin to Eileen Gray, 28 September 1938, NMIEG 2003.1665, invoice from Dufour & Martin to Eileen Gray, 15 December 1938.

171 NMIEG 2003.1657, invoice from Dufour & Martin to Eileen Gray, 6 February 1939, NMIEG 2003.201, chrome hanger for the trouser cabinet.

172 The *Transat chair* had duralumin triangles at the head rest hinges.

173 NMIEG 2003.1658, receipt from Dufour & Martin to Eileen Gray, 6 June 1939.

174 NMIEG 2003.1811, typed notes on inventories, *Tempe à Pailla*, after 1945. It included inventories of the furniture in *Tempe à Pailla* before the war, their valuation in 1939, and an inventory of the pieces now missing, and proof of paid insurance papers signed at the police station for the house before it was looted. NMIEG 2003.1810, NMIEG 2003.1812, NMIEG 2003.1813, NMIEG 2003.1814, NMIEG 2003.1817, notes on damage and repairs, *Tempe à Pailla*, after

1945. NMIEG 2003.1815, notes on objects recovered from *Tempe à Pailla*, after 1945, NMIEG 2003.1816, typed list on damage at *Tempe à Pailla*, after 1945.

175 NMIEG 2003.1767, notes of cost of items, Circa 1946.

176 NMIEG 2003.1671, statement by Eileen Gray, 1946-47.

177 NMIEG 2003.1777, letter from the Mayor's Office to Eileen Gray, 9 August 1954, NMIEG 2003.1771, letter from Eileen Gray to Raymond Benoit, 10 November 1955.

178 NMIEG 2003.1726, invoice from Jean Repaire to Eileen Gray, 21 November 1950, NMIEG 2003.1727, letter from Eileen Gray to Jean Repaire, 3 February 1951. NMIEG 2003.1677, letter from Eileen Gray to Étienne Panizzi, 25 January 1951.

179 NMIEG 2003.1764, invoice from Maurice Lecussan to Eileen Gray, December 1950 – February and March 1951, NMIEG 2003.1763, estimate from Maurice Lecussan to Eileen Gray, 17 July 1951.

180 NMIEG 2003.1710, NMIEG 2003.1711, estimates from J. Ciffreo to Jean Badovici, 17 August 1950. NMIEG 2003.1713, estimate from J. Ciffreo to Jean Badovici, 18 October 1950. NMIEG 2003.1715, NMIEG 2003.1716, estimates from J. Ciffreo to Eileen Gray, 23 October 1950. NMIEG 2003.1714, NMIEG 2003.1717, letters from J. Ciffreo to Jean Badovici, 23 October 1950. NMIEG 2003.1719, letter from Jean Badovici to J. Ciffreo, 30 October 1950. NMIEG 2003.1723, NMIEG 2003.1724, letter and invoice from J.Ciffreo to Jean Badovici, 20 February 1951. NMIEG 2003.1725, receipt from J. Ciffreo to Eileen Gray, 31 March 1951, NMIEG 2003.1720, letter from J. Ciffreo to Eileen Gray, 22 November 1950.

181 NMIEG 2003.1712, letter from J. Ciffreo to Eileen Gray, 18 October 1950. NMIEG 2003.1673, letter from Étienne Panizzi to Eileen Gray, 12 December 1950. NMIEG 2003.1672, NMIEG 2003.1677, letters from Étienne Panizzi to Eileen Gray, 25 January 1951, NMIEG 2003.1676, letter from Étienne Panizzi to Eileen Gray, 2 February 1951, NMIEG 2003.1674, letter from Étienne Panizzi to Eileen Gray, 15 March 1951. NMIEG 2003.1675, estimate from Étienne Panizzi to Eileen Gray, Circa 1951. NMIEG 2003.1721,

letter from J. Ciffreo to Eileen Gray, 18 December 1950, NMIEG 2003.1722, letter from J. Ciffreo to Jean Badovici, 9 January 1951.

182   NMIEG 2003.1648, invoice from André le Bouar to Eileen Gray. 31 Dec 1951 NMIEG 2003.1766, estimate for Zinc work to Eileen Gray, 19 August 1952. NMIEG 2003.1835, invoice from Roger Vilboux to Eileen Gray, 13 April 1955.

183   NMIEG 2003.1765, invoice for works completed by Savoyardo Fortuné, 19 March 1952. NMIEG 2003.1818, invoice from Thomas Casale to Eileen Gray, 15 October 1952, NMIEG 2003.1819, receipt from Thomas Casale to Eileen Gray, 1 April 1953. NMIEG 2003.1770, invoice from Pierre Canestrier to Eileen Gray, 31 January 1954.

184   NMIEG 2003.1682, *Tempe à Pailla*, notebook, January 1955.

185   NMIEG 2003.1706, invoice from J. Bonet to Eileen Gray, 13 January 1949. NMIEG 2003.1707, reminder note for J. Bonet, *Tempe à Pailla*, 13 August 1951. NMIEG 2003.1708, invoice from J. Bonet to Eileen Gray,12 February 1954. NMIEG 2003.1709, receipt from J. Bonet to Eileen Gray,9 March 1954. NMIEG 2003.1649, letter from Atelier Moderne to Eileen Gray, 9 October 1953. NMIEG 2003.1769, estimate for furniture upholstery work for *Tempe à Pailla*, 12 June, 17 June, 2 July, 2 August 1951.

186   NMIEG 2003.1679, valuation notes.

187   NMIEG 2003.1644, business card from Agence Charvet Casteu, 23 rue Partouneaux, Menton, France.

188   NMIEG 2003.1645, letter from Agence Charvet Casteu to Eileen Gray, 22 October 1955, NMIEG 2003.1646, letter from Agence Charvet Casteu to Eileen Gray, 24 October 1955.

189   NMIEG 2003.1771, letter from Eileen Gray to Raymond Benoit, 10 November 1955.

190   NMIEG 2003.1687, notes on *Tempe à Pailla*, 1957. NMIEG 2003.1755, letter from Eileen Gray to J. Richard, 1957.

191   NMIEG 2003.1647, letter from Agence Charvet Casteu to Eileen Gray, 7 November 1955.

192   NMIEG 2003.1690, letter from Eileen Gray to Graham Sutherland, 6 June 1954. NMIEG 2003.1693, letter from Eileen Gray to Graham Sutherland, 19 August 1954.

193   NMIEG 2003.1688, telegram from Eileen Gray to Graham Sutherland, 12 May 1954.

194   NMIEG 2003.1689, letter from Eileen Gray to Mr Evill, 6 June 1954.

195   NMIEG 2003.1696, NMIEG 2003.1697, letters from Eileen Gray to Graham Sutherland, Circa 1954.

196   NMIEG 2003.1693, letter from Eileen Gray to Graham Sutherland, 19 August 1954.

197   MIEG 2003.1697, letter from Eileen Gray to Graham Sutherland, Circa 1954.

198   NMIEG 2003.1691, telegram from Eileen Gray to Graham Sutherland, 18 August 1954.

199   NMIEG 2003.1694, letter from Eileen Gray to Graham Sutherland, 20 August 1954.

200   NMIEG 2003.1695, letter from Eileen Gray to Mr Ward, 8 September 1954.

201   NMIEG 2003.1698, list of furniture at *Tempe à Pailla* included in the sale of the house to Graham Sutherland, Circa 1954. NMIEG 2003.1682, *Tempe à Pailla*, notebook, January 1955. NMIEG 2003.1704, letter from Graham Sutherland to Prunella Clough,2 October 1978.

202   NMIEG 2003.1703, letter from Graham Sutherland to Prunella Clough, 3 April 1977, 15 April 1977, 30 April 1977,12 July 1977.

203   NMIEG 2003.1733, letter from Bachelor Woolrych and Co. to J. Richard, 27 July 1954. NMIEG 2003.1734, letter from J. Richard to Eileen Gray, 4 November 1954. NMIEG 2003.1736, letter from J. Richard to Eileen Gray, 16 November 1954. NMIEG 2003.1737, letter from Eileen Gray, 18 November 1954. NMIEG 2003.1738, letter from Eileen Gray, 19 October 1954. NMIEG 2003.1739, letter from J. Richard to Eileen Gray, 22 November 1954.

204   NMIEG 2003.1745, letter from Eileen Gray to Joseph Richard,18 May 1956.

205 NMIEG 2003.1752, letter from J. Richard to Eileen Gray, 10 July 1957. NMIEG 2003.1753, letter from Eileen Gray to J. Richard's Secretary, 18 July 1957. NMIEG 2003.1754, letter from J. Richard to Eileen Gray, 26 July 1957.

206 NMIEG 2003.1699, letter from the Land Registry Office to Eileen Gray, 21 November 1957. NMIEG 2003.1700, letter from Eileen Gray to the Taxman, 29 January 1959.

207 NMIEG 2003.1702, letter from Graham Sutherland to Prunella Clough, 2 February 1969.

208 Ibid.

209 NMIEG 2003.42, notes on urban architecture.

210 NMIEG 2003.163, water Survey for *Lou Pérou*.

211 NMIEG 2003.25, *Lou Pérou*, 1958, plan of foundations, extension and elevation.

212 V&A Archives, AAD/1980/9/, un-numbered drawing by G. Hanquez. This architectural plan is dated 1959.

213 NMIEG 2003.164, letter from Eileen Gray to G. Henquez, 16 October 1958.

214 Ibid, NMIEG 2003.164. NMIEG 2003.165, NMIEG 2003.1838, letters from Eileen Gray to G. Henquez, 16 October 1958.

215 NMIEG 2003.167, letter from G. Henquez to Eileen Gray, 10 October 1958.

216 NMIEG 2003.171, order from the Mayor's Office to Eileen Gray, 3 December 1957.

217 NMIEG 2003.169, letter from Eileen Gray to G. Henquez, 23 October 1958.

218 NMIEG 2003.166, letter from G. Henquez to Eileen Gray, 8 October 1958. NMIEG 2003.168, letter from G. Henquez to Eileen Gray, 21 October 1958.

219 NMIEG 2003.24, *Lou Pérou*, 1954-58.

220 NMIEG 2003.26, *Lou Pérou*, plan of water drainage and cistern, Circa 1958.

221 NMIEG 2003.172, letter from the Mayor's Office to Eileen Gray, 11 October 1960. NMIEG 2003.173, letter from the Mayor's Office to Eileen Gray, 29 November 1960.

222 NMIEG 2003.170, certificate from the Mayor's Office to Eileen Gray, 29 November 1960.

223 NMIEG 2003.22, *Lou Pérou*, plan of the original building and elevation.

224 NMIEG 2003.15, *Lou Pérou*, plan, 1954-61.

225 Ibid.

226 NMIEG 2003.21, *Lou Pérou*, 1958, plan of extension and elevation.

227 NMIEG 2003.27, *Lou Pérou*, 1958, plan of extension.

228 NMIEG 2003.32, *Lou Pérou*, 1958, plan of extension and elevation.

229 NMIEG 2003.34, *Lou Pérou*, 1958, plan of extension.

230 NMIEG 2003.32, *Lou Pérou*, 1958, plan of extension and elevation.

231 NMIEG 2003.34, *Lou Pérou*, 1958, plan of extension.

232 NMIEG 2003.17, *Lou Pérou*, drawing for windows and wooden shutters. NMIEG 2003.16, *Lou Pérou*, drawings for wooden shutters, south façade. NMIEG 2003.23, *Lou Pérou*, drawing of windows.

233 Ibid, Adam, p.349.

234 NMIEG 2003.35, *Lou Pérou*, drawing for a bamboo awning. V&A Archives, AAD/1980/9/, un-numbered drawings by Jean Badovici. These drawings are all in Eileen Gray's handwriting. Gray measures the patio and adjoining areas, and indicates that the bamboo awning was to be placed at the square part of the terrace.

235 NMIEG 2003.31, *Lou Pérou*, entrance façade elevation.

236 NMIEG 2003.28, *Lou Pérou*, 1958, elevation of extension.

237 NMIEG 2003.32, *Lou Pérou*, 1958, plan of extension and elevation.

238 NMIEG 2003.32, *Lou Pérou*, 1958, plan of extension and elevation.

239 NMIEG 2003.30, *Lou Pérou*, plan of entrance, section of terrace and garage. 1958.

240 NMIEG 2003.20, *Lou Pérou*, plan of the garage with elevations, 1954-61.

241 NMIEG 2003.33, *Lou Pérou*, plan of garage conversion,1958.

242 V&A Archives, AAD/1980/9/, un-numbered drawing. This is a small drawing of a garage with space for two cars. The space measures 35.4m². Gray has marked the beach and the road to St Raphael.

243 NMIEG 2003.29, *Lou Pérou*, section of terrace and garage. V&A Archives, AAD/1980/9/,un-numbered drawing with notes and measurements in French, in Eileen Gray's handwriting. On it she writes 'dallage terrasse 20m2, côté ouest sous arbres 13m2, façade devant 41.25 carré pour volant bambous'. This means 'pavement terrace 20m², west side under trees 13m², front facade 41.25m² moveable bamboo'. This refers to a moveable bamboo awning which Gray created for the garden terrace. It was on wheels so could be moved around the terrace to provide shelter from the sun.

244 NMIEG 2003.18, *Lou Pérou*, sketch for a gate,1954-61.

245 NMIEG 2003.40, notes on architecture.

246 NMIEG 2003.176, letter from Horace Guicciardi to Eileen Gray, 12 July 1967.

247 NMIEG 2003.180, pap of Lands at *Lou Pérou*.

248 NMIEG 2003.179, letter from Horace Guicciardi to Eileen Gray, 6 April 1976. NMIEG 2003.181, letter from Eileen Gray to Pierre Maleville, 5 November 1963. NMIEG 2003.185, letter from Eileen Gray re Madame Henri Fassetti, 6 November 1966.

249 Ibid, NMIEG 2003.181. NMIEG 2003.182, letter from Raymond Marchand to Eileen Gray, 15 November 1968.

250 NMIEG 2003.183, letter from Eileen Gray to Raymond Marchand, 17 November 1968.

251 NMIEG 2003.186, Affidavit for *Lou Pérou*. NMIEG 2003.187, legal report concerning *Lou Pérou*.

252 NMIEG 2003.184, letter from Eileen Gray to Monsieur le Judge, 9 April 1976.

253 NMIEG 2003.191, letter from Eileen Gray to *Miss Petit Syndic,* 30 December 1968.

254 NMIEG 2003.195, letter from R. Larousse to Eileen Gray, 21 March 1967.

255 NMIEG 2003.194, letter from R. Larousse to Eileen Gray, 23 August 1967.

256 NMIEG 2003.192, letter from Pierre Joubert to Eileen Gray, 25 October 1967.

257 NMIEG 2003.193, list of Costs, *Rue Bonaparte apartment*, Circa 1967.

258 NMIEG 2003.196, estimate of value, *Rue Bonaparte apartment,* 1967.

259 NMIEG 2003.198, letter from J. M. Tazi to Eileen Gray, 21 November 1967.

260 NMIEG 2003.197, letter from Eileen Gray to J. M. Tazi, 26 November 1967.

261 NMIEG 2003.177, letter from Horace Guicciardi to Eileen Gray, 12 July 1967.

262 NMIEG 2003.188, letter to the Inspector General concerning the sale of *Lou Pérou* vineyards, 13 July 1972.

263 NMIEG 2003.174, sale of shares, *Lou Pérou*, vineyards, 9 October 1970.

264 Rare Book & Manuscript Library, Columbia University in the City of New York, Stephen Haweis Papers, Arranged Miscellaneous Memoirs, Box 2, letter from Eileen Gray to Stephen Haweis, 5 June 1958.

8

Stories from Dominica and Beyond: Gray, Haweis and the Collage at *E.1027*

Eileen Gray destroyed much of her personal correspondence towards the end of her life. However, Stephen Haweis kept Eileen Gray's letters. Twenty-eight letters from Gray to him remain, revealing a personal relationship which was very important to her. The letters, which survive, date from 1958 through to December 1968, shortly before Haweis's death on 17 January 1969. This personal correspondence reveals much about Gray's personality, her beliefs and her ideas. The letters also throw light on a friendship that would ultimately inspire the large collage, which was composed of a map with stencilled letters, which dominated the wall of the living room of *E.1027,* and the public placement of the map in this central room of the house which she designed for Jean Badovici. Their correspondence was mutually important to both Haweis and Gray. In a letter to his patron Jean Roosevelt, Haweis's niece René Chipman wrote: 'Stephen had many friends to whom he wrote constantly and I really think those further away who were associated with a happier time in his life – were close to his heart'.[1]

Throughout the correspondence the friendship between Gray and Haweis is apparent. In their letters there is an underlying closeness that

8.1 Eileen Gray, by George Beresford, 1916-18, half plate glass negative © NMI

8.2 Watercolour, by Stephen
Haweis, Christmas 1963, paper,
watercolour © NMI

provides evidence that at some point in time Gray did consider their
friendship to be much more. In many letters she sends him blessings,
good wishes or wishes him peace.[2] Others she concludes with 'very
affectionately'[3], 'yours affectionately' [4] or 'affectionate wishes'.[5] Or she
signs off in friendship, sometimes in English, other times in Spanish or
French saying 'Amitié amigo mio' or 'avec mon amitié'.[6] Haweis sent her
books of his poetry – all of which she kept. In one letter Haweis wrote her
a sonnet, which she found 'delightful'.[7] Not all of the poems which he
sent to her were published. In an effort to encourage Haweis to continue
writing Gray informs him, 'I keep <u>all</u> your poems and only wish they
could be published but I know how difficult it is to get poems accepted
by publishers in this materialistic age'.[8] As he continued to send her his
books of poetry she asked him to write her a dedication on one of the front
covers.[9]

They appear to have had a very open friendship, as Gray felt free to ask
if Haweis had a companion.[10] In some letters Gray discussed the notion of
sex and physical love, albeit from a philosophical viewpoint. Gray believed
that 'a good many humans are dual-sexed',[11] or bisexual – as was Gray
herself. In another letter she pondered, 'You speak of sex and evidently
hope to rejoin someone you love. It is very human and natural but I wonder
if two beings can progress along the same lines if united. We shall I think
have left pleasures far behind though there will ultimately perhaps exist
the ecstasy of merging into the infinite'.[12] Without specifying to which
relationship(s) in her life she is referring, Gray did not wish to join someone
in the afterlife as her experience of lovers was one of deception and
disillusion.[13] She obviously had given the matter some thought, writing: 'I
did not think that you associated pleasure with sex, which you say is often
far removed from pleasure at all but as we were concerned mainly with
what happens after death the word pleasure seemed irrelevant since if we
really exist which alas, I doubt we, and those we may have desired on this
earth will be such different beings having no physical inclinations that I
wonder if in those strange conditions one would still aspire to be united'.[14]
Haweis at some point gave Gray a blue turquoise necklace as a gift and she
regretted that 'in a weak moment' she gave it to a younger friend who did
not appreciate it.[15] The letters reveal that both parties in their later years
became a link for each other to the outside world and Gray openly stated
that she was happy he was still there in the unknown.[16] However, she was
also fearful that their renewed friendship was insufficient for him.[17]

As time went on Gray became increasingly concerned for Haweis's physical and mental wellbeing. At that time Haweis was living in abject poverty on the island of Dominica. During World War II he became exceedingly vocal against the authorities there and wrote an article criticising the government's agricultural policy, which resulted in his arrest. The authorities were ill disposed towards him and in many letters to Gray he worries that his post was being tampered with. In reply she says; 'I can't help thinking that you have an exaggerated complex concerning people on your island, to the extent of having to abbreviate names of the people you are writing to (the postman was quite uncertain whether to give me the letter). Have you really reason to think that people would tamper with your correspondence?'[18] Despite her criticisms Gray also began abbreviating the names of people in her letters and correspondence in the later years of her life. Gray expressed sincere concern for his wellbeing, saying that 'Living alone one is apt to imagine all sorts of things'. Ironically Gray herself in her later years did exactly the same thing in her correspondence, identifying people only by their initials. Towards the end of his life Haweis became increasingly embittered and paranoid towards authority, family and friends. In November of 1964 Gray wrote to him with a gentle warning, saying: 'In this material world the slanderers and evil-doers always get the best of it but the real harm they can do is to make us angry and resentful'. Gray says one must rise above it for several reasons. The first is 'because the fault is theirs' and the second 'because in such a short while we shall be free and afford to disregard those sort of things'. Lastly she says; 'We have other preoccupations'.[19] Another time Gray takes into account his difficult life and empathised with him. 'Dear Stephen I wish you often joy and lightness of heart that you always seemed to have, though like so many what you have gone through may have left a bitterness underneath. My past life has, too, but I have put it behind me'.[20]

To relieve his poverty Gray contacted her bank to send a cheque for £100 or the equivalent in dollars so that he would have fewer financial worries. Gray had wanted to help Haweis for a long time but was afraid of offending him.[21] 'Its (sic) surely quite natural that we should help each other and I wanted to do it a long time ago but was so afraid of offending'. Gray also attempted to sell some of his paintings to earn him some money.[22] She constantly wished that his situation would improve and that things would finally go well for him.[23] 'I do wish with all my heart that things should go well for you'. Gray feared at times that he was lonely and said that to him in a number of her letters as she closed.[24] In one quite tender letter Gray wrote; 'I quote two lines to bring you comfort when you are feeling solitary, "So long as we love, we serve. As long as we are loved by others, I would almost say we are indispensable, and no man is useless while he

8.3 Notes on Robert Louis Stevenson, unknown date, paper, ink © NMI

"So lond as we love , we serve . So long as we are loved by others , I would almost say we are indispensable, & no man is useless while he has a friend ."

　　　　　Robert Louis Stevenson .

has a friend"'. She signs the letter 'Robert Louis Stevenson and Eileen to remind you of it'.[25] Writing again later she reminds him, 'Do you remember the quotation of Robert Louis Stevenson. That is what you mean – to me'.[26] Gray kept this quote by Robert Louis Stevenson typed on notepaper in her personal letters.[27]

In the later years of her life Gray withdrew from society, becoming increasingly reclusive. Haweis had always being intrigued as to the reason why the American poet Emily Dickinson (1830–1886) had become a recluse, believing in his naivety that it was due to the misunderstandings of a romantic liaison.

8.4 *Tahiti, the paradise of the Pacific*, by Stephen Haweis, 11 April 1911 © Puck Publishing

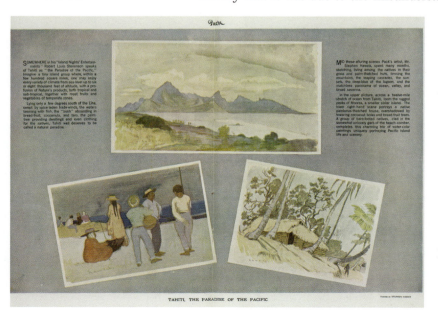

TAHITI, THE PARADISE OF THE PACIFIC

Years later he understand how Gray had become increasingly withdrawn and in one letter to his patron and friend Jean Roosevelt in May 1950 it is possible that Haweis is discussing the relationship between himself and Gray. 'I know of one Irish girl who did something like it, but never married because someone "treated her very badly." He heard about it ten years or so later and was the most astonished of his sex – never having suspected'.[28]

What is apparent is that once Haweis married Mina Loy, his and Gray's relationship changed forever.

Haweis's marriage to the artist and poet Mina Loy was an unhappy one. Loy was four months pregnant with their daughter, Oda, when they got married on the last day of 1903. Born in 1904, the child died on her first birthday. By 1906 Haweis and Loy were already living separate lives. Despite this they moved together to Florence in 1907. Loy was pregnant with her lover's child and Joella was born in 1907. In 1909 Haweis and Loy had a son Giles. Both Loy and Haweis had several illicit affairs throughout the marriage. While in Italy they continued to send paintings to the Paris salons. Haweis had a show in 1911 and again in 1912 at the Ballie Gallery in London. Both in Paris and Florence they were part of the art cognoscenti and became a fashionable couple with friends such as Mabel Dodge Luhan (1879-1962) and Gertrude Stein. They had discussed divorce on several occasions but had remained together so that they would receive Loy's income from her father. In February 1913, however, Haweis left his wife and children to begin his foreign travels, firstly to Australia and the South Seas. The following year he arrived in San Francisco, and proceeded to New York by way of Panama. Financially Loy and Haweis were still tied to one another and to make ends meet Loy rented rooms to foreigners in Florence. All through this time he continued to paint and sketch. Negotiations had begun to have his work exhibited in New York. He published extensively short stories and poems during this time for both American and European periodicals and contributed several articles to *Vanity Fair*. He also published a pamphlet, the *Seven Ages of God*.

Loy arrived in New York in 1916 – leaving the children behind. She sued for divorce and it was granted in America in 1917. Loy had also petitioned for custody of their children and this was granted along with funds for their support from him. Loy became romantically involved with the poet-boxer Arthur Cravan (1887-1918). Cravan disappeared in a boating accident in 1918. Haweis had been refused service in the British army in 1914, and Gray learned that he went to the Bahamas during the war period and painted extensively around Nassau. He published a book, *The Book about the Sea Gardens of Nassau,* in 1917.[29]

In 1921 Haweis returned to Florence and took his son Giles to live with him in the Caribbean. Loy cut off all ties with Haweis, and with her son. Haweis attempted to contact her in 1923, not knowing that she was now

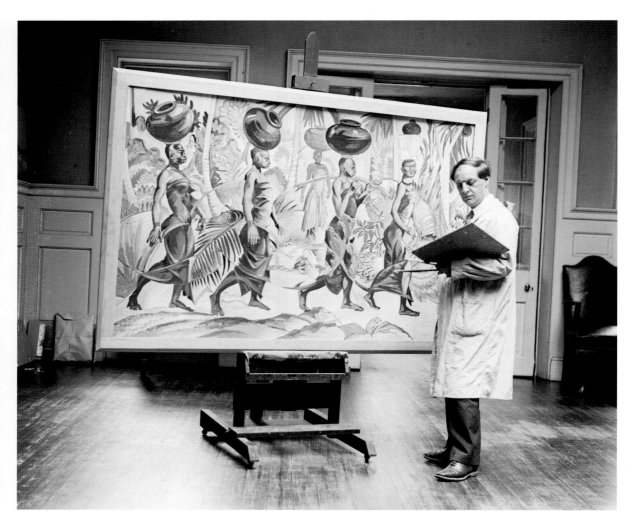

8.5 Stephen Haweis, 18 July 1927, black and white photograph © Library of Congress Prints and Photographs Division Washington

in Paris, after their son Giles tragically died of a rare cancerous growth. Haweis wrote to a mutual friend in Florence: 'Tell Dusie, if you ever find out where she is', that Giles 'lived finely and died bravely, loved and respected by everybody who had anything to do with him'. According to Haweis the child suffered greatly due to having been rejected by his mother.[30] In her letters Gray asked Haweis twice about his wife. Firstly in 1968 she asks, 'A friend here in Paris now remembers your lovely wife Myrna (sic) Loy. Is she still alive and do you correspond and hope to be reconciled? I think that you said she was an ardent Christian Scientist, those that I met a long time ago seemed through their beliefs to have very little heart or sympathy for others'.[31] Through their circle Gray was obviously aware of their divorce, of their affairs, and possibly about the death of his son but she was out of contact with Haweis at the time of the child's death. She returns to the topic asking; 'Sometime ago I heard that you married Mina Loy and that she went off in pursuit of an aviator who was lost in the Pacific. Was that true and is she still alive? Is no reconciliation possible?'[32] Gray was aware that, despite Haweis's numerous affairs, he had been desperately in love with Loy. Gray was also aware that he never fully recovered from the death of his son. Numerous poems and notes are found in his archives that reveal his grief. In one he wrote, 'Your ashes are beside me here, perhaps you were the only person who ever loved me'.[33] It continued to haunt him, especially at the time that he corresponded with Gray. Though Gray and Haweis discuss many personal matters in their correspondence it is suggested that Haweis never discussed the grief and suffering of losing his son. Gray says to Haweis in one letter that he tells her nothing personal about himself:[34] 'You tell me nothing about yourself'. At times Gray feels and fears for his overwhelming depression, as is evident in his poems which he sent her. She wrote: 'My dear Stephen when did that great piece of your soul break loose from its moorings and why? Please explain for that phrase may mean anything'. She continues, 'I feel somehow that you are brooding over something, and hope that you have managed to chase it away! Se laisser envahir par le cafard, (being overwhelmed by depression) so well named c'est une perte de temps, et il nous reste si peu, (it is a waste of time, we only have a little left in this world) let this letter help you, I do so hope it may'.[35]

Gray became one of the few sources of solace and comfort in his later life. Haweis had obviously written to Gray stating how much he wanted a wife and child. Gray in an attempt to divert his grief and offer a sensible reason as to why he was better off in his current situation wrote:

> I understand and sympathize about wanting a wife and children, though what I see around me makes me feel that they are apt to be more of a nuisance than a comfort. The wife by this time might be completely bedridden, and the children, if not actually criminals as so many of the young seem to think natural now would most certainly be allergic to home life in any form and a constant source of worry. I

have cared for certain people too much in my life to feel a real satisfaction in being free, even though it means often (being) completely solitary.[36]

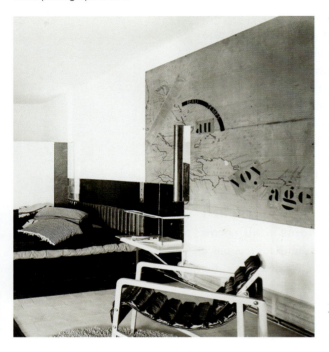

8.6 *E.1027*, living room collage, 1926-29, black and white photograph © NMI

Separately Gray offers an explanation as to why she never married saying, 'one would think that a "man in the house" would take a lot off one's shoulders, but having tried that for some years, I rather doubt it'.[37]

Haweis lost his family's inheritance after the stock market crash of 1929. After this happened he left Bermuda, moving to the West Indian island of Dominica where he would make his home for the remainder of his life. There he wrote extensively about the flora and fauna of the island and for the local newspapers. Gray wanted to know why he went there. 'Perhaps you were in pursuit of some mysterious love, or wished to forget some other fairy, did you come from New York or straight from Italy. As I am being very indiscreet, I remind you that Oscar Wylde (sic) used to say "Questions are never indiscreet, answers sometimes are"'.[38] Haweis's reply is unknown. The letters prove that Gray was acutely aware as to what had happened in Haweis's life. She was also aware of his departure from Europe.

Haweis's foreign travels and the various locations he visited informed the collage, albeit in a coded message, which dominated the living room of *E.1027*. The living room looks out over the Mediterranean Sea. Indeed the house itself appears like a boat embarking on a journey. Nautical themes appear throughout the house not only in the actual setting, but in the fixtures; the railings, the life buoys, the use of sailcloth in the awnings, the *Transat chair*, a type of deck chair, the use of the colour white, the built-in headboards for the beds, the flagpole on the roof. Many things recall the architecture of boats and their cabins.[39] Even some of the carpets and rugs suggest the sea, such as the *Marine d'Abord* carpet rug. The exact date Gray did the nautical chart collage is unclear. However, the large map represents Haweis's travels from 1914 until he finally settled in Dominica

8.7 *Anything about Dominica?* by Stephen Haweis, 1929 © NMI

in 1929. Bermuda, the Bahamas and Dominica all appear on the map. In 1929 Haweis sent her his publication *Anything About Dominica?* Overlaid with the inscriptions 'Invitation au voyage," Beaux Temps', and 'Vas y totor', the collage induces the onlooker to travel further afield. Taken in the context of an artwork, the collage, with its coded message possibly served as a reminder of a person who was dear to her heart on his travels and far away. In this context the reference to Baudelaire's poem, *L'Invitation au Voyage,* had several meanings. The first refers to Peter Ouspensky's ideas of the fourth dimension – in an imaginary land, a dimension only made real through love. It links through a codified message that the house is a representation of this dimension – with its *beaux temps* (sunny weather) and Gray is enticed to go in her car, nicknamed Totor, to get there. In his poem Baudelaire aspired to the spiritual fusion of the lovers, an intimacy that in his universe is irrevocably associated with distance. *L'Invitation au Voyage* is inspired by imaginary love, the hope for a common journey to a land that exists only according to a still unproven legend. It is a land where nature is transformed into art, where harmony, order and peace reign, a land without the threat of contradictions and the sorrows of fragmentation. It represents not only an artistic dream, but also the very image of the beloved – in other words, the chosen land where ideal love would find a haven. By stencilling this inscription onto the nautical chart which represents Haweis's travels it is possible that Gray suggests the illusions of love which once existed between her and Haweis.

By 1929 Gray's relationship with Badovici was tentative and upon completion of the house the couple separated. Gray commonly used enigmas throughout her work. By placing this nautical chart and all that it represents in relation to Haweis, along with the words of Baudelaire's love poem on the wall of the living room of her current lover's house, Gray was making not only a bold statement about her relationship with Jean Badovici, but also her close friendship with Haweis.

What is clear from the collage is that Haweis's travels fascinated her and her interest in that region remained with her throughout her life. She relates, 'Dominic (sic) is unknown here, in fact I saw it written somewhere, but at last I have got hold of an atlas and the island on a French atlas is called La Dominique and is situated in Les Petites Antilles'.[40] As soon as Haweis departed Europe, Gray also began subscribing to *Science et Voyages,* a literary review on scientific and technical information edited by the

Société parisienne d'édition. It was created in September of 1919, ceased in June of 1940, was published again in December of 1945 and continued until 1971. From the 1950s the publication had a much more geographical overtone to it. It was published weekly until issue number 826 and became a monthly during the 1930s. In one issue Gray read that 'a Frenchman goes to Roseau capitale de la Dominique (the capital of Dominique) and a most interesting description of the journey on the island to the fresh water and boiling lakes and the reserve of the caraibe with several photographs. It looks marvellous and I wonder what made you first think of going there'.[41] Once in Dominica, Haweis sent Gray his publications. Gray had a copy of his pamphlet *Anything about Dominica?*, 1929.[42] 'To be frank I feel that it is just written "from the outside" from the point of view of the colonial English or American. I was much more interested by an account in *Science et Voyages* of a French couple who spent two months in the Reserve des Caraibes living with the Natives and sharing their life and occupations'. Later Gray stated that she owned a copy of his publication *Rabbits in the West Indies,* 1948. She wrote of this publication that it was 'extremely well written and amusing, I sometimes think that you have mistaken your vocation. Why not have closer contact with the natives and write about their legends as I once suggested but got no answer. So little is known in Europe about "Les Antilles" as they call them here, more of course about the French islands, but quantities of people would welcome anything that you could write, for one thing because it has the quality of spontaneity'.[43] During the 1960s she obtained a number of publications by him. Haweis sent her copies of two of his poetry books, *Orts and Ends, Dominican Lyrics,* 1963[44] and *Verses of a West Indian Summer,* 1963.[45]

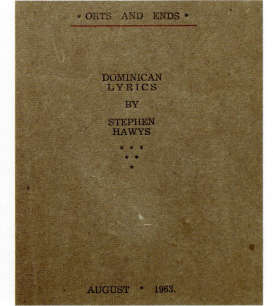

8.8 *Orts and Ends, Dominican Lyrics*, by Stephen Haweis, August 1963 © NMI

Stephen Haweis died on 17 January 1969. Gray corresponded for a number of years with his niece Renée Chipman. Haweis's death was not an easy one. Chipman described it in detail in a letter. She wrote to Gray saying that 'in his case his mind was gone and senility is hard to watch but no (sic) so hard to endure'. Haweis forgot his niece's first name. Their relationship was strained even though she took care of him in his last days. Haweis had become disoriented and when taken to the hospital went into

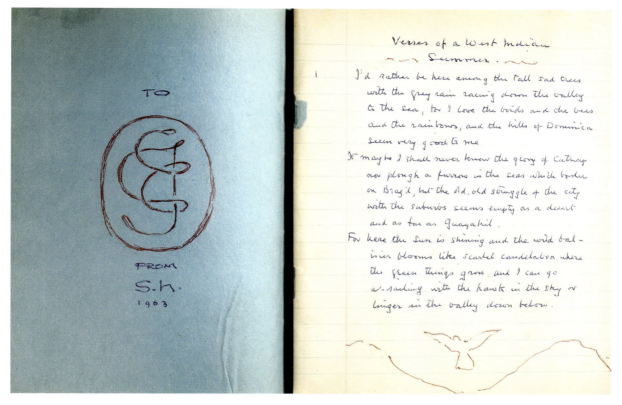

8.9 *Verses of a West Indian Summer,* by Stephen Haweis, 1963 © NMI

shock and died. Chipman organised the funeral and service and had one of his poems read at the service. Chipman describes Gray's one-time suitor; 'Nobody could be more charming and amusing when in the right mood. He was disorganised as a writer, but as a painter, he had great mood merit and technique. He just missed being a genius'.[46] Gray never forgot him.

ENDNOTES

1   Rare Book & Manuscript Library, Columbia University in the City of New York, Stephen Haweis Papers, Arranged Miscellaneous Memoirs, Box 2, letter from René Chipman to Jean Roosevelt, 3 February 1969.

2   Rare Book & Manuscript Library, Columbia University in the City of New York, Stephen Haweis Papers, Arranged Miscellaneous Memoirs, Box 2, letters from Eileen Gray to Stephen Haweis, Easter Monday year unknown, 27 November 1961, April 1962, 13 February 1964, 8 March possibly 1964, 12 October possibly 1966, 17 January 1966, 17 October 1965, 1 November 1966, 8 March 1968.

3   Rare Book & Manuscript Library, Columbia University in the City of New York, Stephen Haweis Papers, Arranged Miscellaneous Memoirs, Box 2, letter from Eileen Gray to Stephen Haweis, 16 May 1968.

4   Rare Book & Manuscript Library, Columbia University in the City of New York, Stephen Haweis Papers, Arranged Miscellaneous Memoirs, Box 2, letter from Eileen Gray to Stephen Haweis, 30 March 1962.

5   Ibid, letter from Eileen Gray to Stephen Haweis, 1 November 1966.

6   Rare Book & Manuscript Library, Columbia University in the City of New York, Stephen Haweis Papers, Arranged Miscellaneous Memoirs, Box 2, letters from Eileen Gray to Stephen Haweis, 14 February 1963, Thursday 13 February 1964, 8 March, possibly 1964.

7   Rare Book & Manuscript Library, Columbia University in the City of New York, Stephen Haweis Papers, Arranged Miscellaneous Memoirs, Box 2, letter from Eileen Gray to Stephen Haweis, 5 June 1958.

8   Rare Book & Manuscript Library, Columbia University in the City of New York, Stephen Haweis Papers, Arranged Miscellaneous Memoirs, Box 2, letter from Eileen Gray to Stephen Haweis, February 1968.

9   Ibid, letter from Eileen Gray to Stephen Haweis, Thursday 13 February 1964.

10   Ibid, letter from Eileen Gray to Stephen Haweis, 30 March 1962.

11   Ibid, letter from Eileen Gray to Stephen Haweis, 8 March possibly 1964.

12   Rare Book & Manuscript Library, Columbia University in the City of New York, Stephen Haweis Papers, Arranged Miscellaneous Memoirs, Box 2, letter from Eileen Gray to Stephen Haweis, 12 May possibly 1964.

13   Ibid, letter from Eileen Gray to Stephen Haweis, 27 November 1961.

14   Ibid, letter from Eileen Gray to Stephen Haweis, Easter Monday, year unknown.

15   Ibid, letter from Eileen Gray to Stephen Haweis, 27 November 1961.

16   Ibid, letter from Eileen Gray to Stephen Haweis, 12 October, possibly 1966.

17   Ibid, letter from Eileen Gray to Stephen Haweis, 16 May 1968.

18   Rare Book & Manuscript Library, Columbia University in the City of New York, Stephen Haweis Papers, Arranged Miscellaneous Memoirs, Box 2, letter from Eileen Gray to Stephen Haweis, 4 August 1965.

19   Rare Book & Manuscript Library, Columbia University in the City of New York, Stephen Haweis Papers, Arranged Miscellaneous Memoirs, Box 2, letter from Eileen Gray to Stephen Haweis, Sunday 1 November 1964.

20   Rare Book & Manuscript Library, Columbia University in the City of New York, Stephen Haweis Papers, Arranged Miscellaneous Memoirs, Box 2, letter from Eileen Gray to Stephen Haweis, 7 July unknown year, possibly 1968.

21   Rare Book & Manuscript Library, Columbia University in the City of New York, Stephen Haweis Papers, Arranged Miscellaneous Memoirs, Box 2, letters from Eileen Gray to Stephen Haweis, 11 July 1965, 12 October year unknown, possibly 1965.

22   Rare Book & Manuscript Library, Columbia University in the City of New York, Stephen Haweis Papers, Arranged Miscellaneous Memoirs, Box 2, letters from Eileen Gray to Stephen Haweis, Monday 17 January 1966, 25 January 1966.

23   Ibid, letter from Eileen Gray to Stephen Haweis, 25 January 1966.

24   Rare Book & Manuscript Library, Columbia University in the City of New York, Stephen Haweis Papers, Arranged Miscellaneous Memoirs, Box 2, letters from Eileen Gray to Stephen Haweis, Monday 17 December, possibly 1962, 12 October, year unknown, possibly 1966, 7 July, year unknown, possibly 1968.

25   Rare Book & Manuscript Library, Columbia University in the City of New York, Stephen Haweis Papers, Arranged Miscellaneous Memoirs, Box 2, letter from Eileen Gray to Stephen Haweis, 27 May, year unknown, possibly 1964.

26 Rare Book & Manuscript Library, Columbia University in the City of New York, Stephen Haweis Papers, Arranged Miscellaneous Memoirs, Box 2, letter from Eileen Gray to Stephen Haweis, Easter Monday, year unknown, possibly 1965.

27 NMIEG 2003.511, notes on Robert Louis Stevenson.

28 Rare Book & Manuscript Library, Columbia University in the City of New York, Stephen Haweis Papers, Arranged Miscellaneous Memoirs, Box 2, letter from Stephen Haweis to Jean Roosevelt, May 1950.

29 Haweis, Stephen, *The Book about the Sea Gardens of Nassau, Bahamas*. New York, PF Collier & Son, 1917.

30 Letter from Stephen Haweis to Ethel Harter, 5 August 1923. Mina Loy Estates. As referred to in Burke, Carolyn, p.327.

31 Ibid, letter from Eileen Gray to Stephen Haweis, 1 November 1966.

32 Ibid, letter from Eileen Gray to Stephen Haweis, 7 July, unknown year, possibly 1968.

33 Rare Book & Manuscript Library, Columbia University in the City of New York, Stephen Haweis Papers, Arranged Miscellaneous Memoirs, Box 10, undated memoirs.

34 Rare Book & Manuscript Library, Columbia University in the City of New York, Stephen Haweis Papers, Arranged Miscellaneous Memoirs, Box 2, letter Eileen Gray to Stephen Haweis, 20 December 1968.

35 Rare Book & Manuscript Library, Columbia University in the City of New York, Stephen Haweis Papers, Arranged Miscellaneous Memoirs, Box 2, letter from Eileen Gray to Stephen Haweis, 8 August 1968.

36 Rare Book & Manuscript Library, Columbia University in the City of New York, Stephen Haweis Papers, Arranged Miscellaneous Memoirs, Box 2, letter from Eileen Gray to Stephen Haweis, 27 November 1961.

37 Ibid, letter from Eileen Gray to Stephen Haweis, 12 October, year unknown, possibly 1966.

38 Ibid, letter from Eileen Gray to Stephen Haweis, 14 February 1963.

39 Badovici was so inspired by these nautical themes that he explored boat architecture; see V&A Archives. ADD9/6-1980 to AAD9/9-1980 in 1929-31.

40 Ibid, letter from Eileen Gray to Stephen Haweis, 14 February 1963.

41 Ibid.

42 NMIEG 2003.60, Haweis, Stephen, *Anything About Dominica?*, Adocate co. Ltd, 1929.

43 Rare Book & Manuscript Library, Columbia University in the City of New York, Stephen Haweis Papers, Arranged Miscellaneous Memoirs, Box 2, letter Eileen Gray to Stephen Haweis, Friday 8 March 1963 or1968.

44 NMIEG 2003.61, Haweis, Stephen, *Orts and Ends, Dominican Lyrics,* Roseau, Bulletin Office Edition, August 1963.

45 NMIEG 2003.62, Haweis, Stephen, *Verses of a West Indian Summer*, handwritten edition, 1963.

46 NMIEG 2003.451, letter from Renée Chipman to Eileen Gray, 1970s.

9

A Tale of Two Houses: Eileen Gray and Le Corbusier

Eileen Gray met Jean Badovici, editor of *L'Architecture Vivante* (1923-1933) and Le Corbusier's close friend, sometime between 1919 and 1921.[1] Badovici was born in Bucharest, Romania, in January 1893. He first came to France in April 1913, but had returned to Romania by October 1914. An accident meant he was exempted from Military service and he returned once again to Paris in January of 1915 where he entered into the atelier of E. Paulin.[2] In 1917 he enrolled in the École des Beaux-Arts in Paris where he studied architecture and in 1919 he received his professional diploma at the École Spéciale d'Architecture. In 1922 he enrolled in the L'Institut d'Urbanisme. However, for reasons unknown, he never received his final diploma. By this stage Badovici was already an influential editor and convinced the publishing house Albert Morancé to develop and publish further on contemporary architecture and design. During Badovici's decade-long tenure as editor, *L'Architecture Vivante* became seminally important in the world of modern architecture not only in France but worldwide with entire issues devoted to De Stijl, Constructivism and Gray's house *E.1027*. Gray's role has been obfuscated from this publication over time but she was involved in the writing of many of the introductory pieces. These appeared

9.1 Eileen Gray, by Berenice Abbott, 1926, black and white photograph © NMI as conversations or dialogues between two people – beginning with an exchange which occurred in the opening pages of the inaugural issue of 1923. This opened with a dialogue drawn from *Eupalinos or The Architect* by the poet Paul Valéry (1871-1945). Other dialogues followed. Badovici published a book on *Intérieurs de Süe et Mare*, 1924 with a dialogue text at the beginning.[3] In 1925 dialogues appeared in issues of *Intérieurs Français* and *La Maison d'Aujourd'hui*.[4] In 1926 and 1929 two final dialogues appeared in *L'Architecture Vivante*.[5] Badovici also produced a number of monographs including *Maisons de Rapports de Charles Plummet*, 1923, *Harmonies: Intérieurs de Ruhlmann*, 1924, *Intérieurs Français*, 1925, *Grands Constructions, béton, armé, acier, verre*, 1927, *Deux études de Paul Nelson: Maison de Santé et Pavillon de Chirurgie*, 1936 and *La Maison Suspendue: recherche de Paul Nelson*, 1939. All of these were published by Albert Morancé in Paris.

Badovici built little during his lifetime, though he was given credit for collaboration between 1926 and 1932 with Eileen Gray on several architectural projects, including the restoration of several houses at Vézelay and the designing and building of *E.1027*, Roquebrune, in the South of France. However, *E.1027* and some of the projects at Vézelay are now known to be solely by Eileen Gray. He wrote considerably and was an influential critic. He patented designs which he completed of a lifeboat[6] and also for a window mechanism which he developed at *E.1027*.[7] Le Corbusier exhibited Badovici's lifeboat design titled *E.7*, 1934, alongside Gray's *Vacation and Leisure centre*, at his *Pavillon des Temps Nouveaux* of 1937.

He joined the *UAM* in 1955, but had exhibited with Gray in 1930 and 1931. After the Second World War, Badovici worked with Maurice Gouvernet under André Lurçat as chief Adjunct Architect for the Reconstruction of Maubeuge and Solesmes. Between 1949 and 1950 Badovici also produced plans for Bavay and Louvroil. In 1956 whilst attending a *CIAM* conference of which he was an active member, he fell ill in Dubrovnik. He died in Monaco on 17 August 1956. Gray grieved deeply and arranged his funeral.[8] The *UAM* organised an exhibition of his work at the *Pavillon de Marsan*, where André Lurçat, Le Corbusier and *UAM* president René Herbst gave talks. Gray's encounter with Jean Badovici and subsequently Le Corbusier was crucially important to her both as a designer and as an architect. At the end of her life Gray owned in her library all the volumes of *L'Esprit Nouveau,* a periodical which was published between 1920-25 under Le Corbusier and Amédée Ozenfant.

Gray was introduced to Le Corbusier sometime in 1922. At this time the Swiss-French architect had already completed his early villas and from 1918-22 had concentrated solely on developing his Purist theory and painting. In the year that they met he had just opened up a studio at 35 rue de Sèvres with Pierre Jeanneret. Gray was immediately interested in his theories and ideas. She discreetly asked Kate Weatherby to ascertain if Evie Hone would lend her two of three copies of *L'Esprit Nouveau*. Evie Hone, in her letter to Mainie Jellett, did not oblige as she feared that Gray or Weatherby would not be able to replace her copies of Le Corbusier's publication. 'The beloved Miss Gray ....had to have them at once on Sunday! But I would not, I am sure I was very disagreeable but it is rather nonsense and I am sure Kate would never get them replaced so I was firm over it'.[9]

9.2 Le Corbusier, Yvonne Gallis and Jean Badovici at *E.1027*, 1930s © Fondation Le Corbusier, Paris

Badovici encouraged Gray to take up architecture and he introduced her to the work of many of the major avant-garde architects and designers of the time. He also involved her in the design on at least four houses at Vézelay between 1926 and 1932. It is not known if Gray was introduced to Le Corbusier by Badovici, or if Gray met Le Corbusier at Natalie Clifford Barney's Temple de l'Amitié where Gray is recorded as being in attendance in 1919. Until this time Gray had only made minor adjustments to her house at Samois-sur-Seine, 1921-24 which she purchased as a holiday home at that time. She also designed the shop front of *Jean Désert* on the rue de Faubourg St Honoré. The letter of 19 June 1922 between Hone and Jellett suggests that Gray had already taken an interest in Le Corbusier's writings and was becoming much more serious about architecture than has previously been thought. In *L'Esprit Nouveau* Le Corbusier was dismissing the contemporary trends of eclecticism and Art Deco, replacing them with architecture that was intended as a stylistic experiment. Gray later saw his *Maison Citrohan* at the Salon d'Automne of 1922 where she exhibited. This was the first time Le Corbusier exhibited a design on pilotis. His spatial organisation of *Maison Citrohan* would later appear in Badovici's house in Vézelay which featured double height living rooms that were overlooked by an entresol, and accessed by a steep, narrow stairs. At this exhibition he also showed a proposal for a standardised house suitable for mass–production. Robert Mallet-Stevens also exhibited his *Pavillon de l'aéro-club de France*, 1922 at this time. Gray's first independent architectural experiment was based on Adolf Loos's project for the *Villa Moissi* and dates to 1923, however, in its design she superimposed Le Corbusier's spatial paradigms on the facade, she enlarged window apertures and added a projecting terrace. Up until this point it has been thought that Gray's initial readings on contemporary architecture dated from the early issues of *L'Architecture Vivante*. It is now apparent from the Hone and Jellett letters that Le Corbusier's writings in *L'Esprit Nouveau* were providing the conceptual and practical bases for her architectural speculations.

Through Badovici's encouragement she took up architecture and also began to make extensive studies of other architects' work, such as *House based on Adolf Loos's Villa Moissi* project circa 1923.[10] She also subscribed to several architectural magazines and periodicals. However Badovici wasn't her only mentor. Between 1923 and 1930 Le Corbusier gave Gray a series of plans and elevations from some of his most significant and personal domestic projects to enable her to improve her architectural-drawing skills. Indeed in examining some of these plans in Le Corbusier's archive, especially *Villa Le Lac,* at Corseaux (Villa, at Lake Léman, Corseaux, Switzerland) reveal Eileen Gray's hand writing on them.[11] Gray reiterated this many years later in 1972 to the architect Alan Irvine whilst working on the *Heinz Gallery exhibition* telling him for the press release that it was Le Corbusier who had encouraged her to branch out into architecture.[12] These drawings and his influence inspired Gray's first hypothetical project *House for an Engineer* of 1926, and became essential to the conception and evolution of her approach to designing *E.1027*. They offer further insight into and explanation of the tentative relationship which evolved between the two architects. They display how Gray's early domestic projects exemplify her interest in adapting Le Corbusier's 'Five Points of a New Architecture' to her experiential aims. Three different projects were given to Gray to study; *Villa Le Lac,* 1923 (Lake Léman, Corseaux, Switzerland), *Petite Maison d'Artistes à Boulogne* also known as *Maison Ternisien,* 1926 (Boulogne, France), and *the Villa Savoye,* 1928 (Poissy, France).[13] All are fundamental in understanding

9.3 *Villa Savoye, Poissy,* view of the roof top garden, Le Corbusier, 1928, paper, ink © NMI

Gray's development as an architect and her approach to design. They are also fundamental in understanding the rapport between the two and how Gray's work, whilst avant-garde, adapted Corbusian themes and how Gray successfully integrated or modified these elements into her own architectural drawings and designs. Finally, they provide an insight into how *E.1027* drew upon Le Corbusier's *Villa Le Lac,* how her resulting work possibly improved unintentionally on the ideas expressed by her mentor and how Le Corbusier developed the garden at his parent's house on the basis of Gray's design at *E.1027*.

Gray and Badovici's rapport and collaboration culminated in Gray designing *E.1027* for him at Roquebrune in the South of France. *E.1027* was a small vacation house that Gray designed and built on an isolated Mediterranean site with panoramic views of the sea. Gray had purchased the land in 1926 and began construction in 1927. Completed in 1929 the house exemplifies Gray's developing architectural thinking at that time. She stated that the house should not be considered perfect, with all of

9.4 *E.1027*, view from the sea, 1926-29, black and white photograph © NMI

the problems of contemporary architecture solved. Instead it should be viewed as an attempt, a moment in a more general pursuit. It was not and should not be considered Gray's final statement and contribution to Modern architecture. That was not what she intended the project to be. It was designed with the client in mind – Jean Badovici, a man who liked to entertain. Badovici and Gray's romantic and professional relationship ended in 1932 when she left the house to work on her own domestic project *Tempe à Pailla* and other projects. They remained friends until his death in 1956.

House for an Engineer was Gray's second hypothetical project.[14] Gray clearly took Le Corbusier's *Vers Une Architecture,* in 1923 and immediately put his ideas into effect in the plans and model. The seven essays in the book had all been published in *L'Esprit Nouveau* between 1921 and 1923. Gray only began to acquire *L'Esprit Nouveau* in 1922, as the letters from Evie Hone and Mainie Jellett suggest. So her adaptation of his ideas to suit her own was quick and reactionary. With this model Gray dismissed the Art Deco trends and instead focused on how the owner would interact with the building. She takes Le Corbusier's ideas about an Engineer's Aesthetic so much into consideration that she titles the project *House for an Engineer*. Almost immediately after Le Corbusier gave her plans for *Villa Le Lac* Gray began exploring his spatial principles at *House for an Engineer*, and combined it with his 'Five Points of a New Architecture'. With the ground floor Gray closely looks at Le Corbusier's 'Five Points of a New Architecture', but still rejected his ideas in relation to the site.[15] Le Corbusier used pilotis and roof top gardens to provide conceptual distance at a site. *House for an Engineer* clearly demonstrates how Gray viewed the garden as an extension of the house. She did this by extending the elementary forms of the house, developing them further into the garden by the use of a square-sunken lap-pool and semi-circular seating area. She later did this with other hypothetical projects such as her *Four Story Villa Project*.[16] The hypothetical location was flat and in the south of France.

With the model for *House for an Engineer* she modulated the surrounding garden and lands into discrete terraces. She created reciprocity between building and garden using elementary forms and colours which linked the interior to the exterior. She also modulated the ground floor spaces to form a series of outdoor areas each of which was attached to the main house.[17] As a result outdoor and indoor spaces interrelate allowing a spatial continuum as if the garden and the surrounding site is an extension of the house. Gray also varies the spacing of the columns in the plan, differentiating the spacing between them and the facades. Gray examined Le Corbusier's *Plan libre* in her treatment of the sleeping level, by raising it up on to pilotis. The principal bedroom overlooks the garden area; however she isolated the bedrooms on half levels connecting them via a short ramp which permitted a spatial continuity. Gray's plan of the first floor also illustrates furniture as extensions of walls and windows, and here she looks at what Le Corbusier's did at *Villa Le Lac*. Later Le Corbusier countered this idea by advocating mass-produced *casiers* which he defended as being products of machine technology.

Gray had begun developing her ideas for *E.1027* whilst she was working on the model for *House for an Engineer*. But extant drawings in Le Corbusier's archive also feature Gray's hand writing on *Villa Le Lac*.[18] Whether these were done at the time that Le Corbusier was working on the project or later as she perfected her spatial theories at *E.1027* is unclear; however the links between the two buildings cannot be ignored, nor the fact that her handwriting appears on the drawings or that Le Corbusier gave her plans and elevations of this house to keep and practice on.

9.5 *House for an Engineer,* model, with ground floor plan, first floor plan and elevations, 1926, black and white photograph © NMI

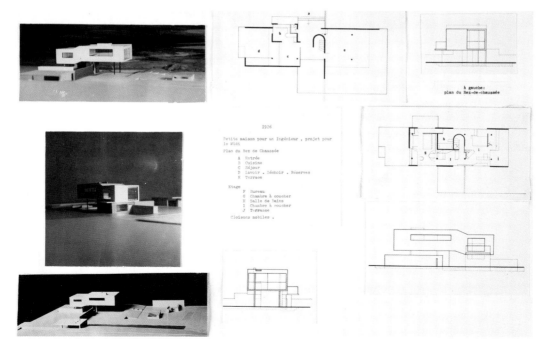

In 1923 Le Corbusier's parents asked him to design for them a small house on Lake Léman, which became known as *Villa Le Lac*, near Corseaux for their retirement. Initially the hunt and selection of the right piece of land had proved exhausting for Le Corbusier and the search is shown, among other things, by a sketchbook filled with drawings of proposed sites and landscapes.[19] The design of the house had to specifically suit Le Corbusier's father's requirements – namely that the design must respond to the landscape. However the house was also innovative through the creation of the 36 foot ribbon window. This was the result of explorations on Le Corbusier's part to theorise on what innovative designs he could produce in relation to the demands of the site. This created what he called a *nouveaux mot* – (a new word) the creation of the window from new construction technologies.[20] It was also the user's testing of the structural, spatial, perceptual and symbolic relationships and benefits.[21] The house needed to be small to satisfy Le Corbusier's parent's need for minimal housing with the maximum efficient distribution of space. The emphasis was on a dual-purpose living room, which emphasised the importance of the view. *E.1027* is a small house, centred on a dual purpose living room that affords panoramic views of the Mediterranean Sea.

The site was a difficult one. Situated on difficult terrain between the lake and the highlands suggested a long narrow plan. Compressed between the road and the lake at Corseaux, the house is concealed from the outside world within a defensive wall, open only to the lake, and even then only in specific ways. Le Corbusier stated in *Précisions* that 'the new elements of modern architecture made it possible to adapt to a site whatever the circumstances'.[22] In a similar fashion Gray chose a very difficult site. *E.1027* is inaccessible from the road, accessed only via a pathway. Le Corbusier had kept a plan of the house in his pocket during his travels between Paris, Switzerland, Italy and Turkey. He had initially

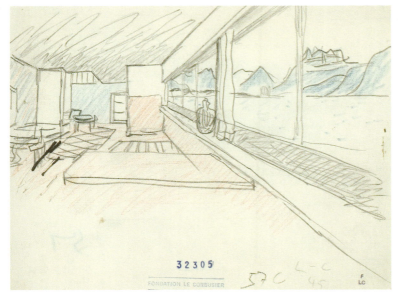

9.6 Drawing of the interior of *Villa Le Lac*, looking onto Lake Léman, Corseaux, Switzerland, Le Corbusier, 1923, paper, pencil, coloured crayon © Fondation le Corbusier, Paris

developed the concept before he had chosen the site, and formulated his initial ideas about *Maison Citrohan* in 1922. Originally the house was placed equidistant between the lake and the road, four metres from each according to Le Corbusier's account in his book on the house entitled *Une Petite Maison,* editions d'Architecture, Zurich, 1954. Gray's choice of the steep slope at *E.1027* was challenging but deliberate. Its placement on the site leads the visitor on a journey from the path to the entrance, through the house, outside to the garden and down to the sea. The similarity of this arrangement in *E.1027* and *Villa Le Lac* confirmed the universal nature of the projects. Both houses

9.7 *E.1027*, entrance path, 1926-29, in *L'Architecture Vivante*, 1929 © NMI

are small – *Villa Le Lac* is barely bigger than a modern urban apartment. Similarities occur between the two houses through an economical treatment plan with no corridor space. Le Corbusier's villa was designed to meet the needs of two people without servants. Both houses were small, using every square metre, and devising economical storage space within the confines of walls and partitions. Gray looked to Le Corbusier's drawings

for shelving and storage space from the laundry room at *Villa Le Lac* when she was drawing the details of the storage facilities and the kitchen at *E.1027*.[23] Gray used stencilling to indicate the function of various storage areas within *E.1027* which looks to Le Corbusier's lettering in his drawings. Moveable partitions and the ability to conceal beds and storage permitted the addition of space when the occupants were entertaining guests at *Villa Le Lac*. Gray also echoed these ideas in the living room of *E.1027* and later again at *Tempe à Pailla* where the kinaesthetic quality of her architecture reached its climax. Benches in

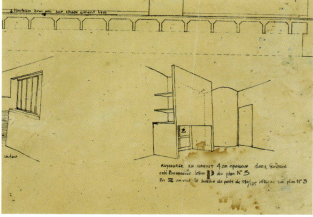

9.8 *Villa Le Lac*, section with drawings, showing storage space in the laundry room, Le Corbusier, 1923, paper, pencil, ink © NMI

the dining room pull forward to reveal stairs to the wine cellar, sliding cupboard spaces reveal fireplaces, and moveable wardrobes expand to form partitions within the main bedroom. Both houses focus all of their energy on the water. It is also interesting to note how another of the

9.9 *Maison Ternisien*, plan, ground floor, Le Corbusier, 1926, paper, pencil, ink © NMI

9.10 *Maison Ternisien*, plan, first floor, Le Corbusier, 1926, paper, pencil, ink © NMI

drawings which Le Corbusier gave Gray, the *Maison Ternisien,* also offered a challenging site for a domestic project. *Maison Ternisien* was created for Paul Ternisien, a musician who wanted a practice studio for himself and a painting studio for his wife, combined with a small residence for the two of them. The house stood at the end of the allée des Pins where it meets rue Denfert-Rochereau on the diagonal. Le Corbusier exploited these peculiarities in a design filled with curves and rectangles.

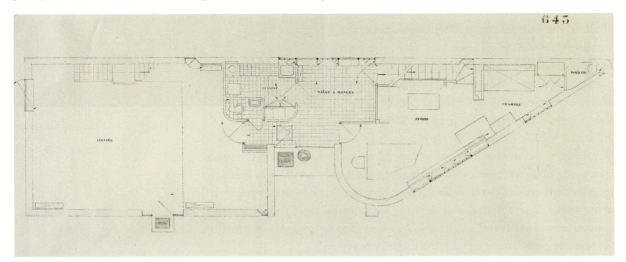

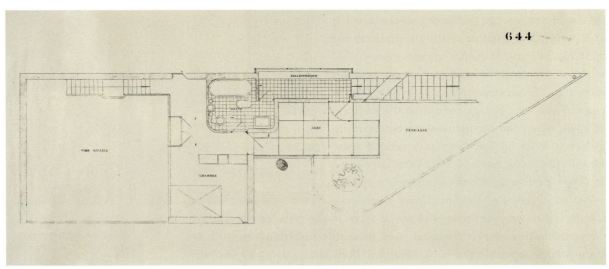

Le Corbusier's treatment of the enclosing garden wall in *Villa Le Lac* acts as a buffer to the external world. He established an 'in between' realm where an internal life might be lived, and retirement might be enjoyed. As Le Corbusier said, 'le paysage omniprésent sur toutes les faces, omnipotent, devient lassant' (Landscape omnipresent on all the faces, omnipotent, deviant wearying).[24] Similarly Gray developed the idea with *E.1027* that one was about to embark on a journey, on a boat out to sea, and that once one entered the house one was transported into another realm.

Both *Villa Le Lac* and *E.1027* are comparable to the houses of the Weissenhof in Stuttgart for the Deutscher Werkbund's exhibition in 1927. During this period the concept of 'Existenz minimum' was both voiced and concretised. Parallel to this, Le Corbusier developed the ribbon window. The north façade of *Villa Le Lac* faced the vineyards, the south façade was opened up by the means of a very wide strip or ribbon window, which ran the length of the sitting room, availing of the most spectacular views of the lake towards the Alps. Le Corbusier also created a small window, a feature which Gray used at *Tempe à Pailla,* on the garden façade, which he punched through the masonry. This window framed the landscape. The idea of the vignette as a window would be repeated at *Villa Savoye*.[25]

The ribbon window was key to this project. On 18 February 1924 Le Corbusier lectured in Lausanne.[26] In his notes for this lecture Le Corbusier explores a history of windows tracing its development in materials and technology up to the point of the development of the ribbon window. The ribbon window combined the interior with the exterior, improving on natural light. He stated that the ribbon window presented 'the immensity of the outdoors, the unfakable [sic] unity of a lakeside with its storms or radiant calms'.[27] Le Corbusier was seeking to create a symbiosis between interior and exterior, whereby the feelings which were created outside amongst nature could be experienced inside. This was exceedingly important to his father who believed that true nature was the place that redeemed and consoled, the goal of authentic experience, and a house overlooking the lake achieved this for him.[28] Le Corbusier's ribbon windows eliminated privacy within the house, whereas at *E.1027* Gray's approach to strip windows was that she created his windows on a human scale, taking maximum advantage of the surroundings views. However, with this Gray sought to provide both spectacular views of the sea at

9.11 *E.1027*, details of windows
and shutters, 1926-29, black and
white photograph © NMI

9.12 *E.1027*, entrance, north
façade, details of windows and
shutters, 1926-29, black and
white photograph © NMI

E.1027, or the mountains at *Tempe à Pailla,* whilst creating a protective membrane. She initially explored Le Corbusier's ribbon window at *House for an Engineer.* She did the same at *E.1027*.[29] On the north façade of *E.1027* she developed, with Badovici, a shutter and strip window system combining Le Corbusier's ideas on the strip window and Auguste Perret's anthropomorphic use of vertical windows and fragmented views. Perret had said that Le Corbusier's use of the strip window broke the spatial continuum, clearly defining the interior and the exterior of a building. At *E.1027,* Gray's horizontal window with a shuttered system left a large area for the free passage of air whilst at the same time blocking excess light.[30] These windows were in proportion to the human body and appeared on the northern façade and on the doors of the southern façade leading from the living room onto the narrow terrace. Interestingly, Le Corbusier had also explored a shuttered system at *Villa Le Lac* on the large strip windows facing on to the garden. These drawings are not dated, but it is possible to see how Gray and Le Corbusier were working in tandem developing similar ideas at exactly the same time.[31]

Le Corbusier also created in the plan an enfilade along the façade through the use of the ribbon window whereby the interior was not separated by walls or doors, instead living room, bedroom and bathroom, become what is described as an architectural enjambment.[32] Gray differed again to Le Corbusier stating also that 'the interior plan should not be the incidental result of the façade; it should lead a complete, harmonious,

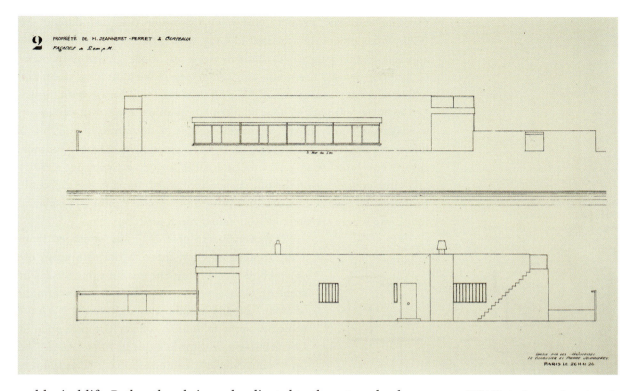

9.13 *Villa Le Lac*, north and south elevation, Le Corbusier, 1923, paper, pencil, ink © NMI

and logical life. Rather than being subordinated to the external volume, it should on the contrary control it'.[33] Gray also still respected the privacy of the user of *E.1027* on the inside, in contrast to the Le Corbusier's open enfilade, Gray created a dual-purpose living room used for entertaining guests, yet within this large space she created alcoves – one with a small divan with its own private terrace, and the other with a dining area which could be transformed into a bar.

By 1929 on completion of *E.1027* Gray was critical of the avant-garde and of architectural theory that failed to address the requirements of the individual. Gray stated that *E.1027* should not be considered perfect, but rather an attempt at addressing the issues of modern domestic architecture. Gray created the building for the inhabitant who would occupy it. She responded to Le Corbusier's renowned maxim that a house is a machine for living in, stating; 'A house is not a machine to live in. It is the shell of man, his extension, his release, his spiritual emanation. Not only its visual harmony but its entire organization - all the terms of the work - combine to render it human in the most profound sense'.[34] However, in comparison to other domestic projects which Le Corbusier designed during the 1920s, what obviously appealed to Gray with *Villa Le Lac* and why she appreciated the design, was that this work was more relaxed than many of his other works. The house uses and dispenses with his ideas when and where necessary to create a singular place of existence for his own family. Le Corbusier even stated 'One concern has been uppermost in my mind: to make the family sacred, to make a temple of the family home'.[35] This house was not a machine to live in. It was a place of meditation, solitude, reverie combined with a new architectural device. Le Corbusier directly takes into consideration the human sensibilities of his parents – especially his father. In essence Le Corbusier viewed this house almost as a personal manifesto where architecture and nature mesh into one.

9.14 *E.1027*, ground floor plan, 1926-29, paper, ink © NMI

9.15 *Villa Le Lac*, ground floor plan, Le Corbusier, 1923, paper, ink, pencil © NMI

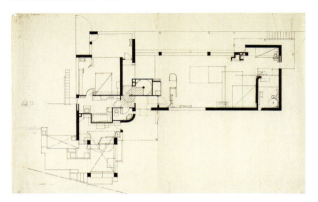

The overall idea of *E.1027* was envisaged from a social point of view, through the minimum use of space, yet providing the maximum amount of comfort. Gray stated, 'everywhere one has thought of man, of his sensibilities and needs'.[36] Gray's minimal space at *E.1027* reflects the influence of Le Corbusier's minimum space in *Villa Le Lac*. 'The thing constructed is more important than the way it is constructed, and the process is subordinate to the plan, not the plan to the process. It is not a matter of constructing beautiful arrangements of

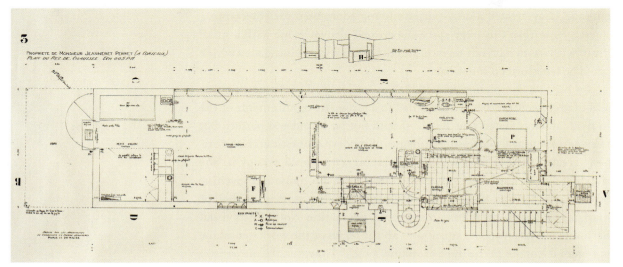

lines, but above all dwellings for people'.[37] Gray adopted the mid-19th century French practice of the bedroom boudoir, where the salon was an extension of a bedroom, in her treatment of the living room space.[38] Le Corbusier created the bedroom as an extension of the living room at *Villa Le Lac*.[39] Here the space was subdivided by a cement partition. Gray once again took Le Corbusier's ideas and developed them by engaging with the visitor's senses and by furnishing the space with day-beds, comfortable chairs and tables. Though a bedroom boudoir implies a more feminine space, Le Corbusier appreciated how she developed the living room at *E.1027,* and it was often used as the work studio when he was there with Badovici. Numerous photographs show Le Corbusier appreciating this bedroom–boudoir environment.[40]

9.16 Le Corbusier, relaxing on the living room divan, *E.1027*, 1930s, black and white photograph © Fondation Le Corbusier, Paris

Le Corbusier also used tiles to define the more domestic areas within the house – the hall, kitchen, toilet and laundry room. Gray would also use tiles in *E.1027;* however she used different coloured floor tiles to indicate changes with the spatial structure or an alternative function of a room. This is seen particularly in the living room and bedrooms of *E.1027.*

Gray created the living room as a space for entertaining. This also resonated with another of the drawings which Le Corbusier gave her. In *Maison Ternisien* Le Corbusier also explored this multifunctional living

9.17 *Maison Ternisien*, view of ground floor, Le Corbusier, 1926, paper, ink © NMI

room theme. An interior view of the living room with a bar on the ground floor again recalls similarities with the multifunctional living room of *E.1027*, with its daybed area and bookshelves set into the wall. Off the sleeping alcove there is a small shower and washroom just as there is at *E.1027,* although at *Maison Ternisien* this area is sectioned off from the rest of the room by a small partition at the end of the stairs. There is a writing desk and storage facilities on the opposite wall.[41]

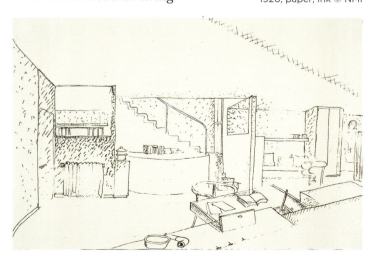

With *Villa Le Lac* Le Corbusier was informed again by the Weissenhof schemes, as his plan was 'a sort of sleeping-dining car combined, with equipment for day and night'.[42] And 'as in a train, many of the desks, tables and storage units are built in as equipment rather than furniture'.[43] Furnishings and furniture at *Villa Le Lac* fascinated Gray as Le Corbusier looked to organise the interior furniture and furnishings so efficiently that they become part of the internal architecture. One drawing fragment which Gray kept of *Villa Le Lac* illustrates a chimney,[44] landing and storage facilities and specifies the materials used for shelving, doors and shutters.[45] The chimney place design which is shown on the elevation is very similar to the design of the chimney in the living room of *E.1027* and the storage facilities are also inspired by these details. Once again at *Maison Ternisien* Le Corbusier uses storage cupboards as room partitions, concealing spaces, yet not cutting them off entirely from the open plan.[46] Gray did this in the living room of *E.1027* and also in the dining area of *Tempe à Pailla*.

9.18 *Maison Ternisien*, view of first floor, Le Corbusier, 1926, paper, ink © NMI

Though completed in 1925, drawings and elevations for this project exist which indicate that in 1930 Le Corbusier was still developing the garden annexes and the garden itself.[47] By this time Gray had completed *E.1027,* and it becomes clear that whilst Gray used *Villa Le Lac* as a model for *E.1027,* Le Corbusier revisited his garden designs after viewing what Gray did with the gardens at *House for an Engineer* and then the realised gardens at *E.1027.*

It is not generally known that Gray had an interest in landscaped gardens and plants. One can see this when one looks at the planed terraces and the total integration between house and garden which she employed at *House for an Engineer, E.1027, Tempe à Pailla,* and her last house *Lou Pérou.* Early in her career her approach to gardens was more structured and architectural – the garden was seen as a projection of the interior of the house. She was disappointed when gardens which were supposed to have structure did not, writing of the maze at the Jardin des Plantes in Paris, 'I found the labyrinth at the Jardin des Plantes was just zero small paths made amongst ordinary trees for children'.[48] Gray also visited Camille Flammarion (1842-1925).[49] He was cultivating plants under coloured glass at his private observatory at Juvisy-sur-Orge to study the effect of the colours on plants.[50] This fascinated Gray.

Later in life Gray took an interest in flowers and plants. Fascinated by the flora and fauna of where Stephen Haweis was living in Dominica, she requested in her letters samples of fruit, vegetables or flowers. On receiving a calabash she wrote, 'It must have been made from some wonderful fruit, surely no coconut could be so big, I was sorry not to see it in its primitive state'.[51] She was also fascinated by anthuriums,[52] the infinite variety of fuchsia,[53] daturas and fig trees.[54] Gray planted yucca and oleander for their wonderful, strange flowers on the terrace of *Lou Pérou.* These grew to one metre sixty in height.[55] Her interest in plants and flowers developed from her time spent in the Midi where she learnt a lot from 'just looking at flowers, the extraordinary variety of their structure; Passion flowers, mimosas de Chine especially but quite ordinary ones, anemones how wonderful'.[56] Gray wrote 'Notes sur des Jardins' (Notes on Gardens), where she maintains that at a garden entrance there should be many black stones, composed into a conical wall, two feet in height. The stones should flow in a curve encircling parts of the garden. Opposite the wall should be a smooth lawn and flowers.[57] But these notes were written later in life at *Lou Pérou* when she had moved away from the more architectural and structural compositions which defined the garden at *E.1027*. Gray's gardens appear, at times, as extensions of her interiors, especially at *E.1027* and less formally at her last house *Lou Pérou*. However the idea of the garden as an outdoor room can be traced back to the Renaissance and to Roman times. Gray modulated the ground floor spaces of the *House for an Engineer* to form a series of outdoor spaces each of which is attached to the main house.[58] She also varies the spacing of the columns in the plan, differentiating the spacing between them and the facades. As a result outdoor and indoor spaces interrelate, allowing a spatial continuum as if the garden and the surrounding site is an extension of the house. This she perfected at *E.1027* to the point that both Badovici and Le Corbusier noticed this extension of architectural design into landscape and her ability to design this outdoor space as an ensemble. Badovici described decorated interiors or ensembles as compositions where furniture were 'entities extending one another', and whose 'geometric shapes merge with the lines of the walls'.[59] Gray took Badovici's analysis of her furniture and incorporated it into to her garden design. Badovici was impressed, along with English architect Ernö Goldfinger (1902-1987), a friend of both Badovici himself and Le Corbusier. They studied the garden space of *E.1027*, marking points on the plan where Gray had plants and shrubs which were strategically planted for maximum effect.[60]

Gray also looked to the ideas of André Vera (1882-1956) who advocated a return to formal mannered gardens, designed now by architects. Vera maintained that garden forms should be treated as direct translations of contemporary

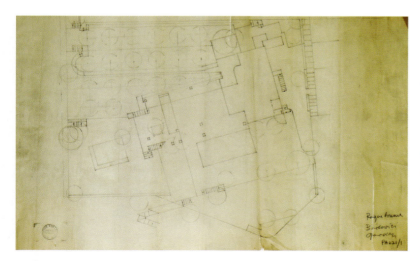

9.20 Drawing of garden at *E.1027*, 1930s, paper, ink, pencil © RIBA Library Drawing and Archives collections

decorative trends in art, the decorative arts and architecture. Architects would compose gardens as they would interiors, concrete and cast masonry reinforcing structure, whilst glass, ceramics, mosaic and the effects of mirrors defined features and effaced boundaries. He also intended a decorative unity to be achieved between the interior and the exterior. He turned away from ideas of transitional spaces moving through the garden, emphasising instead outdoor rooms which balanced and opposed one another. In this way gardens would appear as extensions of the building or as a mirror of the facade. Trees were viewed as punctuation marks in the garden and vegetation played only a minor role.

Gray's design for the garden at *E.1027* echoes some ideas which were first exhibited at the Exposition Internationale des Arts Décoratifs et Industriels Modernes, held in Paris in 1925. Modern garden designs of the 1920s seldom invoked nature as their prime source of inspiration. They were closer to architecture, and many architects at the exposition treated their landscaped spaces as extensions of their architecture.[61] With the repudiation of the romantic garden, designers cited speed, economy of maintenance and modern materials as the factors generating the morphology of their designs.[62] The products of the so-called modern landscape sought a link between the past and present through a renewal of tradition. It simply illustrated a resurgence of the formal garden with France's patrimony.[63] Garden designs of the time countered previous traditions while revealing the need for aesthetic cohesion among the arts.

Gray's use of concrete in her gardens looks to Robert Mallet-Stevens. Stevens along with Jan and Joël Martel had created a garden on the eastern section of the *Esplanade des Invalides* at the 1925 exhibition, called the *Jardin de l'Habitation*. It was more an experiment in contemporary construction than an analysis of contemporary garden design. Their bold use of concrete exploited the material of the machine age. Gray continued to use concrete in her garden designs in innovative patterns and forms. The garden at *E.1027* is architectonic, viewed as a graphic arrangement of planar and volumetric elements through concrete. Just as Le Corbusier had attempted to unify nature and architecture, inside with outside through the use of the ribbon window, Gray had the same aim but intended in using the entire house conjoined with the garden and view to echo one another –

9.21 View of the terrace onto the garden, *E.1027*, 1926-29, black and white photograph © NMI

hence marine colours are used on the interior, architectonic elements are used in the garden, and tiles extend from the interior to the exterior into the garden realm. She attempted to achieve a symbiosis between interior and exterior. Similar to her treatment of the public spaces inside *E.1027* Gray also sought to create privacy in the garden. She wrote 'To give the garden greater intimacy, the side exposed to the wind has been closed off by a narrow space in corrugated sheet metal, where the gardener can store his tools'. The garden too is intended as a continuation of the journey that one experiences in the interior. She wrote 'paving crosses the entire garden up to the space under the house raised on pilotis'.[64] She intended this journey to culminate at the sea, writing 'a small stair enables one to descend directly to the sea to bathe, fish, or sail'.[65] Gray achieved this by grading the landscape and with the addition of seated areas, bathing pool, and pergolas. This also addressed the human being who was interacting with the garden – the seated areas served as a pause as one meandered down the steps into the terraces, the pergola provided shelter and the sun pool provided cool. She wrote 'A reflecting pool, which would attract mosquitoes, has been avoided; instead there is a sunbathing pit with a sort of divan made of sloped paving stones, a tank for sand baths, a mirrored table for cocktails, and benches to either side for chatting'. She strengthened the impact of the overall design and diluted the impression of excessive space. These architectural elements appeared in the gardens of the exposition notably in the work of Jacques Lambert (1891-1948) and Robert Mallet Stevens. Gray could also have been looking at the ideas of Robert Wheelwright (1884-1965) who paired landscape architecture with sculpture, and architecture with painting. Wheelwright maintained that architects draw plans on sheets of paper whereas landscape architects view the land as a sculptural block.[66] This explains the vogue for the architectonic layers of 1920s gardens.

When Le Corbusier designed *Villa Le Lac* he looked at Gray's careful placing of trees and shrubs at *E.1027*. Gray sought to extend the journey

9.22 Sun pool at *E.1027*, 1926-29, black and white photograph © NMI

from inside the house to outside by the strategic planting of trees and shrubs and also to provide privacy from the panoramic exposed sea vistas. Here she looked to the ideas, though not the realised gardens, of Henri (1841-1902) and Achille Duchêne (1866-1947) who strongly favoured a return to the regular garden, where the formal garden became an extension of interior decoration and architecture. Composition and axes incised into the land reflected those of the facade, and the parterre, water pools and canals were treated as graphic motifs. The immediate surroundings of the house became extensions of the sumptuousness of the reception rooms. They created the *Jardin d'Architecture.* Due to the decrease in expenditure and the influence of mechanisation the new garden emphasised simplicity and functionalism, yet remained a creation for an elite.

The garden at *Villa Le Lac* was planted and developed at the time of its completion in 1925, yet Le Corbusier revisited it in September 1930.[67] His design in 1925 for the garden was aimed at shielding the house from the sun and providing privacy by strategic planting of trees and building a large exterior wall. The garden is contained by a rectilinear lakefront wall that is raised on the left side looking toward the lake. It forms a type of white lime-washed screen which opens at the centre. Combined with the hedge on the street side and the enclosing wall in brilliant red on the short side facing east, Le Corbusier's garden becomes an extension of the living space – an outdoor room. At the centre is a concrete table. Just as Gray had done with all of the photographs of her interiors or objects, Le Corbusier had photographs published where the concrete table is set and household objects sit on the windowsill.[68] This added a human element to his work – refuting his ideas that a house was a machine to live in. Looking at this part garden, completed in 1925, by Le Corbusier one begins to see echoes of ideas which Gray expressed in her bedroom boudoir *Monte Carlo room.* Le Corbusier used a mélange of material to entice the senses and engage the person who was sitting in this garden space. The use of white lime wash and brilliant red engages the user's visual senses, and the choice of different materials; the natural stone of the wall, the use of smooth concrete on the table invite touch. Gray had long been exploring ideas of synesthesia and Le Corbusier effectively does this here, albeit in a garden space.

Whereas Gray relied on the natural growth of flora and fauna to obscure views, Le Corbusier relied on varying the height of the wall at strategic points to reveal the views. Both Le Corbusier and Gray were creating membranes to regulate the views in the surrounding garden. Elevations and drawings exist on the garden elevations and annexes of the project with Gray's handwriting in Le Corbusier's archive showing he was still adapting the garden annexes on 19 June, July 1930, 15 August 1930, 8 June 1931.[69] After viewing *E.1027* and upon its completion it is possible that Le Corbusier invited Gray to develop the garden annexes during these dates, taking into account her ideas expressed in *E.1027.* During these dates Le Corbusier strategically planted poplars, willows, acacia, cherry trees, conifers and a paulownia.[70] For whatever reason, thirty years later when he revisited *Villa Le Lac,* Le Corbusier cut down and removed everything. Any vegetation not on a roof-top terrace was now to be kept at a distance.[71]

For the garden at her last house *Lou Pérou,* Gray explored the ideas of Jean Claude Nicolas Forestier (1861-1930) whose garden designs considered the local climate and its corresponding plant palette. For him the garden was a work of art and he exploited architectural composition. His choice of vegetation reflected the changing seasons to ensure an ever-changing choice of fragrances. He was critical of the exactness of landscape designs stating that the modern garden 'returns to a clear, geometric composition without subjecting itself to the symmetrical severity and ample forms of the seventeenth century'.[72] At *Lou Pérou* Gray strategically planted lavender and other scented plants throughout the garden enticing the senses and leading one through the garden to the garage where one could sit on a grass-covered roof and watch the sun go down.

Le Corbusier *Villa Le Lac* was a house which carried deep personal connotations for him, a house where he introduced a new architectural vocabulary, a house which was removed from his 'Five Points', but a house which due to the weight of his personal involvement became a very personal manifesto. However the story of *E.1027* is central to *Villa Le Lac,* the house which Le Corbusier designed for his parents at Lac Léman which he finished in 1923. Gray completed *E.1027* in 1929, publishing her ideas and a monograph in *L'Architecture Vivante* in that year. In many ways Gray took a project which was so personal to Le Corbusier, adapted it, combined it with ideas from other contemporary architects and elevated it, not just in the plan and the interior but also in the exterior and garden. Le Corbusier praised this house at the time and even a decade after its creation. In letters between Jean Badovici and himself, Le Corbusier describes his gratitude for her friendship. He wrote to Badovici in an undated letter, 'I have received the first draft of the book on the Pavilion. It is not bad. There are two pages for you and two pages for E. Gray, which look very good. I hope that you both are satisfied. Please again tell Eileen Gray my gratitude for her friendship. Very happy to have spent these moments with her'.[73] His obvious admiration for *E.1027* is well documented in a letter written in April 1938 to Gray where he expressed praise for 'l'esprit rare' which was evident in the house and its furnishings. 'I would be delighted to relate to you how much those few days spent in your house have made me appreciate that rare spirit that dictates all of its organisation, both inside and outside, and has given modern furniture and equipment a form that is so dignified, so charming and so full of wit'.[74] Le Corbusier became an avid admirer of Gray's architecture. Her work, notably *Vacation and Leisure centre,* was displayed at Le Corbusier's *Pavillon de Temps Nouveaux* along with Badovici's lifeboat model. Despite such praise Eileen Gray's relationship with Le Corbusier was at the best of times ambiguous and though they were on good terms, it was a formal relationship, based on respect.[75]

9.23 Letter from Le Corbusier to Eileen Gray, April 1938, paper, ink © NMI

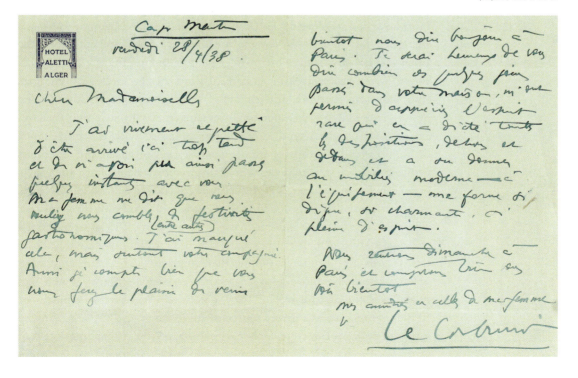

There are many different myths and many viewpoints surrounding Le Corbusier's murals which were sanctioned by Badovici at *E.1027* between 1938 and 1939. Le Corbusier, Jean Badovici and Léger had already developed a theory on mural painting in Vézelay, where both Léger and Le Corbusier had painted in 1934 and 1935. At Vézelay, Léger had painted a mural in 1934 on the courtyard wall. In 1935 Le Corbusier painted his first mural on the upper surface of the living room wall. Badovici was excited by these murals which Le Corbusier and Léger had painted for him at Vézelay and claimed that the three of them had rediscovered spatial painting.[76] His ideas contrasted with those which he shared with Gray in *La Maison d'Aujourd'hui* in 1925 where he stated that painting should not oppose a construction but that it should complement it, emphasising its overall character and stressing its movement. At this house the murals impart a modern spirit to the interior, exploring the sculptural elements of the two-dimensional form of painting in an interior space. Le Corbusier had explored mural painting at *Maison la Roche,* 1923-25 and at the *Ozenfant Studio* in 1923. Badovici invited Le Corbusier to paint at *E.1027* hoping to have the same result produced at Roquebrune as at Vézelay.

Gray had always been interested in Le Corbusier's painting. Influenced by the earlier sketches of Le Corbusier and Amédée Ozenfant she was intrigued by their developments within Purism. As an adolescent Le Corbusier had dreamed of becoming a painter and in the early stages of his career, when he was lacking in commissions, he channelled his energies into painting, drawing and theory. Ozenfant introduced him to the avant-garde and to cubist personalities such as Apollinaire and Fernand Léger. Both Ozenfant and Le Corbusier grappled with the inheritance of Cubism and its allusive plastic syntax. Le Corbusier and Ozenfant evolved their ideas, which were more inspired by the Futurists, with their emphasis on movement, speed, technology, their quest for abstraction, and their interest in proportional systems and symbolic mathematics. They exhibited at the *Galerie Thomas* in autumn 1918 and developed the purist style, which culminated with their catalogue and manifesto entitled *Après le Cubisme*. It emphasised simplicity, logic, calm and order, and represented a move away from the decorative schemes which had taken over the artistic world. They advocated classicism as a means of higher values, not as a direct source of subject matter. Gray's drawing of a mural explores these concepts. Her subject matter is machine-like and static with a mathematical precision and geometric form. Purist subject

9.24 Drawing of a mural, 1920s, paper, pencil © NMI

matter evolved around banal, everyday objects which were reduced down to their most generalised forms of rectangles, curves and flat planes.[77] Le Corbusier's ideas about mural painting were at times ambiguous. Initially his approach was in favour of polychromatic painting and the way in which it had the potential for modifying space in an interior. He thought mural painting antithetical to architecture.[78] But under the influence of Fernand Léger his ideas developed and his exploration with mural painting radically changed. In his lecture in 1938 entitled 'Peinture, sculpture et architecture rationaliste' he claimed that mural painting could surpass the confines of wall space through the illusive creation of space through paint.[79] Believing that rectangles, curves, spaces, proportions and colours could infuse an architectural interior with space and overcome the limits of the wall plane, he eventually applied these ideas to *E.1027*. Gray owned

9.25 *Man with a Cigarette*, Le Corbusier, 1925, black and white photograph © NMI two photographs of Le Corbusier's paintings and was prompted by them to produce a sketch of her own.[80] *Man with a Cigarette* of 1925 is wearing a suit, and sitting at a table in a restaurant.[81] The second photograph shows a painting depicting a woman holding a book and posed on a rug, dating from 1935. Gray was grappling with his evolving ideologies and produced a Corbusian-style sketch as an attempt to understand his approach to mural painting and his ideas, and to try to reconcile these conflicts. However, she soon defined her ideas opposing painting of any kind in an interior.

Le Corbusier was encouraged by Léger to develop his mural painting. In 1938 he discussed the importance of mural painting overcoming the problems and confines of wall space.[82] Jean Badovici had not only encouraged but also commissioned the murals at *E.1027* between 1938 and 1939. The first mural was painted in the living room on a wall which separated the small bathroom and the alcove with the small divan to the rest of the room. Based on one of his paintings *Figure devant une porte blanche* the garish colours clash with the intimate scale of the interior and offset the internal harmony and delicacy of the space. Le Corbusier's mural broke this illusion. Le Corbusier argued that this dark shower corner needed brightening up.[83] The second

9.26 Le Corbusier painting murals at *E.1027*, 1938-39, black and white photograph © Fondation Le Corbusier, Paris

mural painted in 1938 was a controversial mural called the *Sgraffitto*, added to the underneath of the house. This was the fruit of a long gestation composed of three nude figures – the interpretation of these figures has become central in several arguments surrounding Le Corbusier and Gray. Originally the figures were to be three women, then they have been interpreted as a man, woman and child. Some believe that they are derivatives of Eugène Delacroix's painting *Les Femmes d'Algers*, 1834.[84] Others state that the mural is representative of Gray and Badovici. In that same summer Gray ironically attended an exhibition in London at the New Burlington Galleries which exhibited a series of preliminary drawings for Picasso's *Guernica* where Picasso said that 'Painting was not invented to decorate houses'.[85]

Then in a letter from 19 August 1939 Le Corbusier requested to Badovici that he come to Roquebrune as he had 'a furious desire to dirty the walls. Ten compositions are ready, enough to daub everything'.[86] In 1939 Le Corbusier returned to *E.1027* where he added more murals including another one at the end of living room wall. Jean Badovici was pleased with the murals at first.[87] However Léger felt that the colours were too loud.[88] Whilst Gray undoubtedly contributed to the design of Badovici's house in Vézelay, *E.1027* was her work alone. The primary problem with the murals was that they negate and break the spatial choreography which Gray had created inside the house. Her interior was simple, understated, designed for the human environment - a small house in which Gray cleverly created the illusion of space.

Gray at the time was unaware of Le Corbusier's pictorial intervention at *E.1027* which she later deemed an act of vandalism.[89] Gray had stated that 'architecture must be its own decoration. The play of lines and colours should respond so precisely to the needs of the interior atmosphere that all detached painting or pictures would seem not only useless, but detrimental to the overall harmony'.[90] What provoked Gray's annoyance and her reaction through Badovici was that she viewed Le Corbusier's pictorial interventions at *E.1027* as a rebuttal on these ideas, which were published in a dialogue between herself and Badovici in *L'Architecture Vivante,* Winter 1929. Le Corbusier added fuel to this fire by publishing photographs of the murals along with some insulting comments about the house in *L'Architecture d'Aujourd'hui,* 'Unité' no.19, 1948, a special issue devoted to Le Corbusier and again in *Œuvre Complète* 1938-46. He stated, 'This villa which I animated with my paintings was very beautiful and it could have managed without my talents'.[91] In his *Œuvre Complète* 1938-46 he wrote, 'They burst out from dull sad walls where nothing is happening'.[92] Gray retaliated through Badovici, writing to Le Corbusier threatening to eliminate the murals altogether. He wrote, 'What a narrow prison you have built for me over a number of years, particularly this year through your vanity. On the contrary, my attitude toward you has been nothing but joyful and full of happy trust – seven volumes of the heroic era of *L'Architecture Vivante*. My baraque (house) served as a testing ground by sacrificing the profound direction of an attitude that formally banished painting. As purely functional architecture, that was its strength for such a long time: 1925 and you have denied its absolute character with such harshness in your writings, disseminating them through your worldwide authority. You lack any generosity toward me. A correction from you seems necessary; if not, I will be forced to do it myself, thus to re-establish the original spirit of the house by the sea'.[93] Le Corbusier retorted with his own attack. He formally demanded that Badovici photograph his murals. He vehemently replied through Badovici though clearly to Gray saying, 'you want a statement from me based on my worldwide authority to demonstrate "the quality of pure and functional architecture" which is manifested by you in the house at Cap Martin, and has been destroyed by my pictorial interventions. Fine – send me some photographic documents of this manipulation of pure functionalism ... also send me some documents on Castellar, this U boat of functionalism; then I will spread this debate in front of the whole world'.[94] The two parted on bitter terms – never to reconcile.

The actions taken by Le Corbusier in *E.1027* of drawing, painting and photographing the murals have been viewed by some as instruments of colonisation, and as tools to exercise his authority.[95] Thus by drawing he re-territorialises the domestic space.[96] Some view Le Corbusier's murals at *E.1027* as an effacement of Gray's sexuality on the basis that she was openly gay.[97] However, Gray was actually bisexual and it seems less important what Gray's sexual activities were than to try and explain the role that sexuality played in her life.[98] In Gray's opinion Le Corbusier had covered the walls with inappropriate subject matter.[99] If one is to interpret *Graffite à Cap Martin* or *Sgraffitto* as depicting Jean Badovici on the right, Gray on the left and an outline of a head and hairpiece of a seated figure in the middle, then Gray's annoyance is veritably justified. Le Corbusier claimed to friends that this figure was the 'desired child which was never born'.[100] Gray's sexuality played a role in the critical alternative which she offered at *E.1027,* by challenging the dynamics and erotic of vision, which Le Corbusier had been exploring since the 1920s, and which contributes to the reason why Le Corbusier reacted in such a way to the house.[101] *E.1027* is a house filled with secrets, pockets, walls, sliding passages – it hides and reveals simultaneously. It reveals but still remains closeted.

What did result after Le Corbusier published his comments is the misattribution of her work, this house in particular and subsequently her omission from the canon of modern architecture.[102] This occurred not just by Le Corbusier – but by Jean Badovici also. When Le Corbusier published

9.27 Mural at *E.1027*, Le Corbuiser, 1938-39, in *L'Architecture d'Aujourd'hui*, April 1948 © NMI

Œuvre Complète in 1946 and *L'Architecture d'Aujourd'hui* in 1948, *E.1027* was referred to as 'a house in Cap Martin'. Gray's name was omitted. It was almost as if Le Corbusier wanted the world to believe that the house was not built by her.[103] As a result *E.1027* was mistakenly attributed to Jean Badovici.[104] Whilst she graciously gave him credit in the name of the house – it was solely Gray's project. Badovici's role was firstly client and secondly consultant architect.[105] However in the special edition of *L'Architecture Vivante* of 1929 he describes himself as joint architect.[106] At the time of Badovici's death his obituary in *Techniques et Architecture* of November 1956 featured five illustrations of the house, and it was claimed as the basis of Badovici's reputation.[107] In fact all of the architectural projects which Gray had been involved in or actually designed were omitted; these included Badovici's apartment in the rue Chateaubriand which Gray completed after *E.1027* and his house at Vézelay to which she actively contributed.[108] Even Ernö Goldfinger who stayed at *E.1027* and studied the plan of her garden was also party to the assumption that Badovici had completed not only *E.1027* but also *Tempe à Pailla*, writing, 'I don't think she had any architectural pretensions, certainly not that I know of'. [109] Even after *E.1027* and *Tempe à Pailla* were rediscovered, examined and published by architectural historian Joseph Rykwert in 1971, another historian Reyner Banham argued that though competent Gray was not a major talent.[110] Banham believed that Eileen Gray never made a reputation for herself due to her mature fashionable 1920s style and that her work did not reflect the style of the hard core of the International Style. Instead Banham says that Gray's oeuvre was given a brief moment of transcendence by Badovici in *L'Architecture Vivante* and by Le Corbusier by his deigning to paint graffiti on her walls.[111] Banham believed that writers exaggerated Gray's output in design and architecture.[112]

From the late 1930s through the 1940s Gray's relationship with Le Corbusier was tentative, especially after his published comments in relation to the murals which he completed in 1938-39 at *E.1027*. When Jean Badovici died in 1956 the fate of the villa was uncertain. His death only increased Le Corbusier's interest in purchasing it. In 1957 he was involved in the construction of a hostel which directly overlooked *E.1027*. It was situated on an adjoining property, owned by Thomas Rebutato, who conceded the land in 1950 to Le Corbusier enabling him to build his cabanon and the hostel, thus destroying the villa's vistas and privacy. Towards the end of the 1950s, Le Corbusier withdrew more and more from social life and spent increasing periods of time at his cabin at Cap Martin. His plans were halted by the death of his wife Yvonne Gallis in 1957. Gray

9.28 Drawing of hands,
Le Corbusier, 1957,
paper, ink © NMI

sent him her condolences and Le Corbusier replied with a sketch of a man and a woman's hand intertwined.[113] It is dated the evening of 5 October 1957. It is written in French, 'In memory of Yvonne Le Corbusier, thank you L-C'.[114] From this point on Gray empathised with him. Her tone in letters to Clough when referring to him became more understanding. She wrote 'Corbu had such bad luck with all he did; one can't help thinking that it was perhaps done purposely, so many were jealous'.[115] The Gray–Clough correspondence shows that Gray still admired Le Corbusier's work and in her comments was both objective and critical of it from an aesthetic and theoretical viewpoint. In December 1961 while Gray was completing work on *Lou Pérou*, she received a copy of *the Architectural Review* from Clough with an article by Colin Rowe.[116] It featured photographs of Iannis Xenakis and Le Corbusier's *Sainte Marie de la Tourette,* Lyon. Gray wrote that she 'Was fascinated by the photos and account of Le Corbu's Monastery. The first photos I have seen. No one has seen it as of yet in Paris. What a vitality in that man and how much he has learnt from working in India. I like the monastery better than Ronchamp, where certain things like that mass of sloping wall and the roof seemed to me too arbitrary'.[117] In another letter Gray wrote about the *Church at Ronchamp*, 'I have always felt rather yes and no about Ronchamps but would so much have liked to see it'.[118] Her interest in Le Corbusier continued – and she even inspired her niece to attend a lecture at the Open University on his *Maison la Roche*.[119] After forty years Gray obviously felt that she was entitled to critique his work.

In being invited by Badovici to paint, and develop their spatial theories with mural painting at *E.1027,* it is quite possible that Le Corbusier hoped to elevate Gray's ideas represented at *E.1027* further. Undoubtedly he had wanted to make his mark on this house. But the student, so to speak, taking an intimately personal project from her mentor and elevating it to a new status must have quietly hurt his pride. His painting of the murals, his persistent request to Badovici to have the murals photographically documented and his anger towards Badovici for asking him to retract his published comments about his murals at the house, further explain without justifying his reaction. This fear that the ideas he sought to elaborate at *E.1027* with the murals would not be preserved at *E.1027* augmented his interest in the house, especially after Badovici's death in 1956. Le Corbusier was impressed by Gray's building and took a number of photographs of the house, of the interior and from outside. These are the only photographs of modern architecture that he took with his movie camera apart from his mother's house and some images of his own apartment.[120] Whether this is a quiet homage to Gray and this house is unknown however these images record his close attention to the house and to its site, the windows and their ingenious shutters, the canvas on the long balcony and details in the garden notably the sun pit. Despite the later unhappy events Gray took pride in the April 1938 letter which he had written probably because it was the only praise or positive acknowledgement that she would receive from him.[121] Robin Walker (1924-1991) a prominent Irish architect who had studied under Le Corbusier in 1947, noted that Le Corbusier was so impressed with *E.1027* that he kept a model of the house in his work cell at his atelier in Paris.[122]

Le Corbusier wrote in his last book *Creation is a Patient Search,* that 'By working with our hands, by drawing we enter the house of a stranger, we are enriched by the experience and we learn'.[123] In his own way he was paying a compliment to *E.1027* and to Gray. Gray may have learned from the mentor, but the mentor had also learnt from the student.

ENDNOTES

1   NMIEG 2003.547, photograph Jean Badovici. Gray and Badovici possibly met in 1919.

2   Archieri, Jean-Francois, 'Jean Badovici: Une historie Confisquée', in Pitiot, Cloé, *Eileen Gray,* Éditions du Centre Pompidou, Paris, 2013, p.88.

3   Badovici, Jean, *Intérieurs de Süe et Mare présentés par Jean Badovici,* Paris, Editions Albert Morancé, 1924.

4   Badovici, Jean, and Gray, Eileen, *Les Intérieurs Français,* Paris, Editions Albert Morancé, 1925. See also Badovici, Jean and Gray, Eileen, *La Maison d'Aujourd'hui,* Paris, Editions Albert Morancé, 1925, p.16.

5   Badovici, Jean, and Gray, Eileen, 'L'Architecture Utilitaraire', *L'Architecture Vivante,* no. 14, winter 1926, pp.17-24.

6   V&A Archives, AAD 9/8-1980, AAD 9/9-1980, typed notes by Jean Badovici.

7   Constant, Caroline, *Eileen Gray,* New York, Phaidon, 2000, p.234.

8   Adam, Peter, *Eileen Gray: Architect/Designer*: A Biography, London, Thames and Hudson, 1987, p.356.

9   NIVAL, NCAD Library, Bruce Arnold Papers – Mainie Jellett Collection, box 7.

10   V&A Archives, AAD/1980/9/171, house based on Adolf Loos's *Villa Moisi*, 1923.

11   Fondation Le Corbusier, see plans and elevations no.s FLC 09382, 09402, 09403, 09419, 09433, 09434, 09439, 09440, 09446.

12   NMIEG 2004.75, *Heinz Gallery exhibition* press release.

13   NMIEG 2004.131, NMIEG 2004.98, *Villa Le lac Léman*, ground floor plans, NMIEG 2004.130, NMIEG 2004.97, *Villa Le lac Léman*, north and south elevations, NMIEG 2000.182, *Villa Le lac Léman*, section. NMIEG 2004.132, NMIEG 2004.99, *Petite Maison d'Artistes à Boulogne*, cross sections of the ground floor, NMIEG 2004.135, NMIEG 2004.102, *Petite Maison d'Artistes à Boulogne*, east façade, drawings, NMIEG 2004.134, NMIEG 2004.101, *Petite Maison d'Artistes à Boulogne*, first floor plans, NMIEG 2004.133,NMIEG 2004.100, *Petite Maison d'Artistes à Boulogne*, ground floor plans, NMIEG 2004.136, NMIEG 2004.103, *Petite Maison d'Artistes à Boulogne*, views of the first floor, NMIEG 2004.137, NMIEG 2004.104, *Petite Maison d'Artistes à Boulogne,* views of the ground floor, NMIEG 2004.138, NMIEG 2004.105, *Villa Savoye à Poissy*, views of the roof top garden.

14   NMIEG 2003.2, *House for an Engineer*, first floor plan, 1926. See also RIBA Archives, ref. PB.496/11-1 *House for an Engineer,* 1926. This is a ground floor and first floor plan.

15   NMIEG 2003.1, *House for an Engineer*, ground floor plan.

16   V&A Archives, AAD/1980/9/176, *Four Storey Villa Project*, axonometric drawing.

17   Ibid, Constant, p.75.

18   Fondation Le Corbusier see plans and elevation no.s, FLC 09369, elevations of interior and views of furniture and furnishings. FLC 09382, plans and elevations of the garden annexes dated 5 September 1930. FLC 09402 and FLC 09403, series of studies and sketches of the plan in detail with loose sketch of the garden with Gray's writing. FLC 09434, series of sketches and elevation. FCL 09439, study of the plan of the annexes with modifications. FLC 09440, study of the plan of the annexes. FLC 09446, study of a partial plan.

19   Fondation Le Corbusier. FLC Sketchbook 9, drawing FLC 5055.

20   Reichlin, Bruno, 'Corseaux: My Father Lived One Year in This House. The Scenery Fascinated Him', in Louis- Cohen, Jean, *Le Corbusier and Atlas of Modern Landscapes,* New York, The Museum of Modern Art, 2013, pp.65-6.

21   Ibid.

22   Le Corbusier, *Précisions sur un état présent de l'architecture et de l'urbanisme,* Paris, G. Crès & Cie, 1930, p.127.

23   NMIEG 2000.182, *Villa Le Lac*, section with drawings.

24   Le Corbusier, *Une Petite Maison,* éditions d'Architecture, Zurich, 1954, p.22.

25   Curtis, William, *Le Corbusier: Ideas and Forms,* Phaidon. London, 2006, p.575.

26   Ibid, Reichlin, p.66. See also Fondation Le Corbusier. FLC C3-6-30.

27   Ibid, Le Corbusier, *Précisions,* p.130.

28   Ibid, Reichlin, p.68.

29   NMIEG 2003.5, *E.1027,* drawing for shutters.

30   Badovici and Gray, 'From Eclecticism to Doubt', *L'Architecture Vivante*, Winter 1929, p.16.

31   Fondation Le Corbusier, ref. FLC 09361 – Shuttered system on large strip window, garden facade.

32   Ibid, Reichlin, p.68.

33   Ibid, Badovici and Gray, p.13.

34   Ibid, Adam, p.309.

35   Jenger, Jean and Beamis, Caroline, *Le Corbusier: Architect of New Age,* London, Thames and Hudson, 1996, p.151.

36   Ibid, Gray and Badovici, p.26.

37   Ibid, Gray and Badovici, p.11.

38   Ibid, Constant, p.95.

39   Fondation Le Corbusier. FLC 09365 and FLC 09366.

40   Fondation Le Corbusier, FLC.L4-10-22, L4-10-24 and L4-10.30.

41   NMIEG 2004.137, *Petite Maison d'Artistes à Boulogne,* view of the ground floor.

42   Gans, Deborah, *The Le Corbusier Guide,* Princeton Architectural Press, 1987, p.128.

43   Ibid, Gans, p.128.

44   This chimney resembles the chimney place in the centre of the living room of *E.1027.*

45   NMIEG 2000.182, *Villa Le Lac Léman*, section

46   NMIEG 2004.136. Petite Maison d'Artistes à Boulogne, view of the first floor.

47   Fondation Le Corbusier, FLC 09381 and FLC 09382. These drawings are dated 15 and 19 September 1930.

48   Rare Book & Manuscript Library, Columbia University in the City of New York, Stephen Haweis Papers, Arranged Miscellaneous Memoirs, Box 2, letter from Eileen Gray to Stephen Haweis, 27 November 1961.

49   Rare Book & Manuscript Library, Columbia University in the City of New York, Stephen Haweis Papers, Box 2, letter from Eileen Gray to Stephen Haweis, 30 March 1962.

50   Rare Book & Manuscript Library, Columbia University in the City of New York, Stephen Haweis Papers, Box 2, letter from Eileen Gray to Stephen Haweis, page two of a letter April 1962 (or possibly page 2 of the letter dated 30 March 1962).

51   Rare Book & Manuscript Library, Columbia University in the City of New York, Stephen Haweis Papers, Box 2, letter from Eileen Gray to Stephen Haweis, 14 February 1963.

52   Rare Book & Manuscript Library, Columbia University in the City of New York, Stephen Haweis Papers, Box 2, letter from Eileen Gray to Stephen Haweis, 17 October 1965.

53   NMIEG 2003.364, letter from Eileen Gray to Prunella Clough, 1970s.

54   NMIEG 2003.408, letter from Eileen Gray to Prunella Clough, Tuesday, date unknown, 1970s.

55   Rare Book & Manuscript Library, Columbia University in the City of New York, Stephen Haweis Papers, Box 2, letter from Eileen Gray to Stephen Haweis, 17 October 1965.

56   Rare Book & Manuscript Library, Columbia University in the City of New York, Stephen Haweis Papers, Box 2, letter from Eileen Gray to Stephen Haweis, 8 August 1968.

57   Ibid, Adam, p.355.

58   Ibid, Constant, p.75.

59   Badovici, Jean, 'L'Art de Eileen Gray par Jean Badovici, architecte,' *Wendigen,* No.6, 1924, pp.12-15.

60   RIBA Archives, Erno Goldfinger collection, PA621/1, drawing of *E.1027* garden.

61   Imbert, Dorothée, *The Modernist Garden in France,* Yale University Press, New Haven and London, 1993, p.27.

62   Ibid, Imbert, p. 52.

63   Ibid, Imbert, p.53.

64   Ibid, Gray and Badovici, p.26.

65   Ibid.

66   Wheelwright, Robert, 'Thoughts on Problem and Form', *Landscape Architecture Quarterly 21,* No. 1, October 1930, pp.1-10.

67   Fondation Le Corbusier. FLC 09382.

68   Ibid, Reichlin, p.69. See also Boesiger, Willy and Stonorov, Oscar, *LE Corbusier und Pierre Jeanneret: ihr Gesamtes Werk von 1910-1929,* Zurich: Girsberger, 1920, p.74.

69   Fondation le Corbusier. FLC 09381, 09382, 09384.

70   Ibid, Le Corbusier, *Une Petite Maison,* pp.52-6.

71   Ibid, Imbert, p.176.

72   Forestier, J. C. N., *Gardens: A Notebook of Plans and Sketches,* translated by Helen Morgenthau Fox, New York, Scribner's, 1924, p.13. Originally published as *Jardins: carnet de plans et de dessins.* Paris, Émile-Paul Frères, 1920.

73   Le Corbusier Foundation, E1-5-111, undated letter from Le Corbusier to Jean Badovici.

74 NMIEG 2000.183, letter from Le Corbusier to Eileen Gray.

75 Pearson, C., *'Integrations of Art and Architecture in the work of Le Corbusier. Theory and Practice from Ornamentation to the Synthesis of the Major Arts'*, unpublished PhD thesis, Stanford University, 1995, p.301. Cited in Samuel, Flora, *Le Corbuiser Architect and Feminist,* Wiley Academy, 2004, p.36.

76 Badovici, Jean, 'Peintre, Murale ou Peintre Spatiale', *L'Architecture d'Aujourd'hui no 3,* Paris, March 1937.

77 Ibid, Curtis, p.49.

78 Ibid, Constant, pp.121-2.

79 De Franclieu, Pierre, *Le Corbusier, Savina: Dessins et Sculptures,* Paris, Fondation Le Corbusier, 1984, p.18.

80 Ibid, Constant, p.125. NMIEG 2000.184 – NMIEG 2000.185, photographs of Le Corbusier murals. NMIEG 2000.186, drawing of mural.

81 Le Corbusier, *L'Architecture d'Aujourd'hui*, Paris, Editions Albert Morancé, April 1948, p.87.

82 Ibid, De Franclieu, p.18.

83 Benton, Tim, *LC FOTO Le Corbusier Secret Photographer,* Switzerland, Lar Müller Publishers, 2013, p.387.

84 Delacroix, Eugène, *Les Femmes d'Algers*, 1834, Oil on canvas, 180 x 229cm, Paris, Louvre.

85 NMIEG 2003.82, Picasso's *Guernica*, New Burlington Galleries, London, New Burlington Galleries, October 1938.

86 Fondation Le Corbusier, FLC El (5) 34.

87 Fondation Le Corbusier Archives, ref. El-5-53, letter from Jean Badovici to Le Corbusier, 2 July 1941. After the war Badovici claimed that the murals were 'more beautiful and luminous than before'.

88 *Le Corbusier sketchbooks, 1957-164,* Vol. 4, Cambridge, Mass, MIT Press and New York, Architectural History Foundation, 1982, No.778.

89 Adam, Peter, 'Eileen Gray and Le Corbusier', *9H,* no. 8, 1989, pp.150-153.

90 Gray, Eileen, and Badovici, Jean, 'Maison en Bord de Mer', *L'Architecture Vivante,* winter edition 1929, p.19.

91 Corbusier, Le, 'Unité', *LArchitecture d'Aujourd'hui,* No 19, Paris, 1948.

92 Corbusier, Le, *Œuvre Complète 1938-45*, Zurich Editions of Architecture, 1964, p.158.

93 Fondation Le Corbusier Archives, ref, FLC.EI-596-7, letter from Jean Badovici to Le Corbusier, 30 December 1949.

94 Fondation Le Corbusier Archives, ref, FLC.EI-599, letter from Le Corbusier to Jean Badovici, 1 January 1950.

95 Colomina, Beatriz, 'Battle lines-E.1027', *The Sex of Architecture,* New York, Harry Abrams, 1996, pp.167-182. Also Colomina, Beatriz, *Privacy and Publicity – Modern Architecture as Mass Media,* MIT Press, 1996, pp.84-8.

96 Ibid, Colomina, *Privacy and Publicity,* p.178.

97 Ibid, Colomina, 'Battle lines-E.1027', *The Sex of Architecture,* p.171.

98 Walker, Lynne, 'Architecture and Reputation', *Women's Places: Architecture and Design 1860-1960,* London, Routledge, 2003, p.104. Rault, Jasmine, *Eileen Gray and the Design of Sapphic Modernity – Staying In,* Ashgate, 2011, p.95.

99 Barrès, Renaud, 'Eileen Gray, Le modernisme en bord de mer', *L'ŒIL,* Paris, May 2003, pp.36-43. One on the ground floor on the outside was done in black and white. In subsequent years the murals were retouched and the subject matter had been somewhat altered. Barrès claims that the murals completely undermined the spatial integrity of the house, and the aesthetic ideas which Gray sought to achieve on its completion in 1929

100 Colomina, Beatriz, 'War on Architecture', *Assemblage,* No. 20, Violence, Space, MIT Press, April 1993, p.28. This is taken from a letter from Marie Louise Schelbert to Stanislaus von Moos, 14 February 1969.

101 Ibid, Rault, pp.94-118. See also Bonnevier, Katarina, 'A Queer analysis of Eileen Gray's E.1027', *Negotiating Domesticity – spatial productions of gender in modern*

architecture, Routledge, London, 2005, pp.162-180.

102   Ibid, Colomina, 'Battle lines-E.1027', p.173.

103   Ibid, Adam, p.235.

104   Ibid, Adam, p.335.

105   Ibid, Constant, p.5 and p.94.

106   Gray, Eileen, and Badovici, Jean, 'Maison en Bord de Mer', *L'Architecture Vivante,* Paris, Editions Albert Morancé, winter edition 1929.

107   Ibid, Walker, p.101.

108   Blumenthal,   M.,'Jean   Badovici   1893-1956', *Architecture et Technique,* November 1956, p.24.

109   RIBA   Archives,   ref,   GolEr/267/2:   general correspondence files of Erno Goldfinger 1960-1985 includes information on Jean Badovici.

110   Rykwert, Joseph, 'Eileen Gray: Two Houses and an Interior, 1926-1933', *Perspecta: The Yale Architectural Journal,* New Haven, No.13/14, 1971, pp.66-73.

111   Ibid, Rault, p.93.

112   NMIEG 2003.484, Banham, Reyner, *New Society Magazine,* London, Harrison Raison, 1 February 1973.

113   NMIEG 2003.268, NMIEG 2003.284, drawing of hands,

114   Ibid, NMIEG 2003.284.

115   NMIEG 2003.353, letter from Eileen Gray to Prunella Clough, 20 September 1972.

116   Rowe, Colin, 'The Dominican Monastery of La Tourette, aveux sur l'Arbresle', *The Architectural Review,* London, London Architectural Press, 129, No.772, June 1961, pp.400-410.

117   NMIEG 2000.189, postcard from Eileen Gray to Prunella Clough, 1961.

118   NMIEG 2003.354, letter from Eileen Gray to Prunella Clough, Wednesday, unknown date or year.

119   NMIEG 2003.389, letter from Eileen Gray to Prunella Clough, 1 June 1970s.

120   Ibid, Benton, p.386.

121   Ibid, Constant, p.125.

122   Dorothy Walker has reported this several times in various articles, as her husband Robin Walker studied under Le Corbusier. It was also stated by Joseph Rykwert in *Domus* magazine, Milan, Casa Editions, 1968.

123   Le Corbusier, *Creation is a Patient Search,* New York, Frederick Praeger, 1960, p.203. As quoted in *Colomina, Beatriz,* 'Battle lines-E.1027', *The Sex of Architecture,* New York, Harry Abrams, 1996, p. 177.

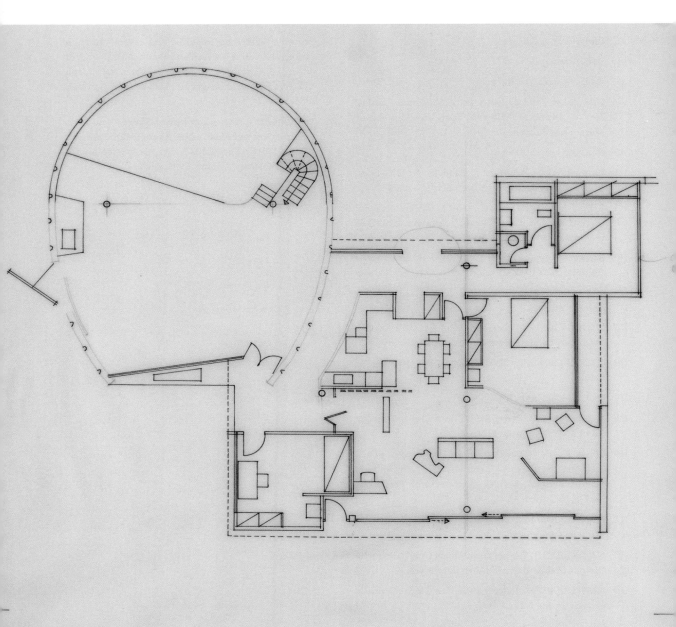

10

For the People: Social and Cultural Architecture

During November 1923 the De Stijl group held their debut exhibition in Paris at Léonce Rosenberg's *Galerie l'Effort Moderne*. The combination of art, architectural drawings and models that were exhibited had a profound effect on Gray. The architectural component in the Rosenberg gallery show was reconstituted in 1924 for an exhibition at the École Spéciale d'Architecture, Paris, where Theo Van Doesburg and Cornelis Van Eesteren distributed a manifesto to visitors entitled 'Towards Collective Construction'. In the summer edition of *L'Architecture Vivante* in 1924 Badovici reviewed the De Stijl exhibition at the École Spéciale d'Architecture. This time it wasn't so much what was on display but how it was displayed which caught Gray's attention. The exhibition space was stunning in its simplicity because it lacked any ornamentation.[1] From the late 1920s Gray began exploring designs for an exhibition and art pavilion but her first private commission for the study of an exhibition, work studio and domestic space was realised with the *House for Two Sculptors*, 1933-34.

The *House for Two Sculptors*, was originally supposed to have been commissioned by the brothers Jan and Joel Martel.[2] The Martel twins were French sculptors and among the founding members of Union des Artistes

10.1 *House for Two Sculptors*, plan, 1933-34, paper, pencil, ink © NMI

Modernes. The project was for a combined art studio with an exhibition area for their sculptures and a domestic space. With this house she explored the use of tree trunks as pillars at the main entrance and used as a corner support, thus adding to the organic nature of the design and providing the inclusion of natural pillars. Gray stated: 'Today's materials are smooth, the result of the monotony of the machine. Try to find rugged materials – like in country houses – some surfaces in rough wood built into smooth walls. Sometimes put (in) pieces of protruding rough wood. Pillars; instead of concrete put stones, rock, granite, tree trunks – trunks of palm trees'.[3]

Gray developed two proposals for this project. The 'U' shaped atelier with an adjoining house was the first proposal put forward for the plan of *House for Two Sculptors*.[4] Gray dated the project 1933.[5] She initially integrated the house with the atelier modifying the design of the studio from an open 'U'. The plan indicates a studio area of two stories with a single-storey residential area. The entrance front had a small pergola with a pierced roof. Extant drawings show that Gray did several variations of the entrance front.[6] This first version had a sloping roof. The common denominator between all of the drawings is a large glass vertical hinged door.

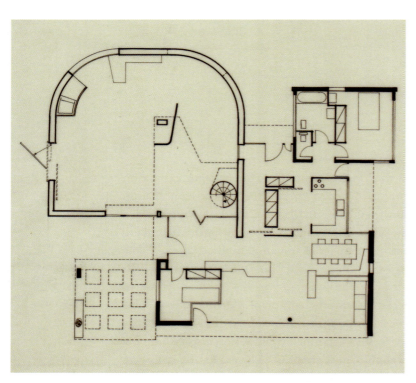

10.2 *House for Two Sculptors*, plan, 1933-34, paper, pencil, ink © NMI

The second plan for the *House for Two Sculptors* shows a simplification of the first design, stripping down the elements to the bare essentials.[7] The front window was enlarged making the overall appearance of the house much more dramatic.[8] Gray inter-linked the two spaces, the atelier and the residential area, through overlapping of the forms and volumes in the plan,[9] though their integration was more successful with the changing of the atelier drawing from the 'U' type form to a truncated oval.[10] In the first plan she relied on the formal differences

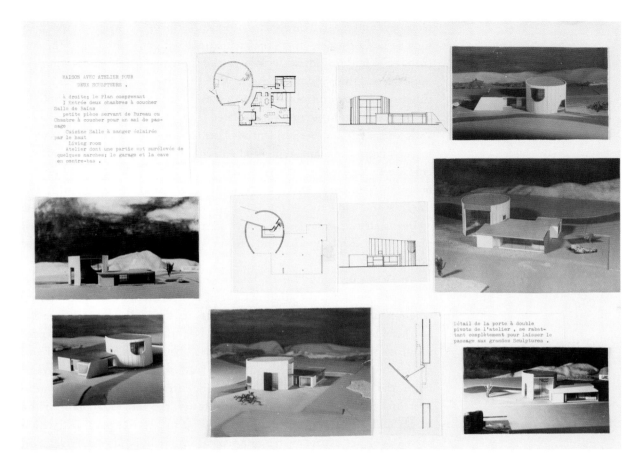

between the house and the studio to isolate their functions but by the time she had developed this plan she was attempting to provide continuity through the integration of their forms. Other changes included a central ceiling light, which illuminated the entire living area and the roof of the atelier was no longer sloping.[11] These alterations were better suited to the function of the house and were more harmonious in composition. Several variations exist of the second plan.[12] Gray developed the second scheme realising drawings with four elevations.[13] This final scheme illustrates the enlarged front window and shows how Gray inter-linked the two spaces, combining the single-storey residential area with the truncated oval plan of the sculptor's atelier.[14] Gray orientated the studio and the living room to the south.[15] In *E.1027* and *Tempe à Pailla* Gray also orientated the architect's

10.3 *House for Two Sculptors*, model, plans, elevations 1933-34, paper, pencil, ink, black and white photograph © NMI work area and the living room to the south, differing from contemporaries such as Le Corbusier. Gray's preoccupations with the rotation of the sun through a building directly inform the floor plan, the ventilation of a building and the window locations. With this project the atelier was also to function as an exhibition area and an area for entertaining. The bedrooms, orientated toward the sun, were isolated from the main kitchen and salon area; and as in her other residential plans, sleeping and washing areas were isolated from the main living and entertaining quarters. There were two entrances – one leading to the atelier, the other to the kitchen and master bedroom. The porch and the main entrance admitted sunlight through the roof and had a tree trunk, which acted as a corner pillar support. The atelier itself was organised into two separate levels. It contained a raised platform for exhibition use and a lower workshop area. The schemes were not realised.[16]

In Gray's drawings for the elevations for the second proposal, each elevation illustrates the combination of a high atelier and a residential single-storey area.[17] The artist's studio was set facing the sun, as were the southern bedrooms and the living room. Gray explores here multipurpose solutions in the design – the bedroom and bathrooms are isolated from the kitchen and living room and sliding walls separate the guest bedroom from the atelier and salon. The main entrance porch had circular apertures, which permitted sunlight through the roof. The plan for the atelier indicate two separate levels, providing a stage-like platform, which served as either a display area or a separate workshop. This arrangement, subdividing the clear division of private domain and public workshop, recalls Robert Mallet-Stevens's *Studio,* 1926-27 for the Martel brothers in the rue Mallet-Stevens, Paris.[18] Whereas Mallet-Stevens created a house on three levels subdividing the public and private spaces, Gray creates a single-storey space, also clearly defining the public and private spheres. Variations of elevations from the second proposal exist.[19] Some are identical.[20] Some are similar yet display further development in the design.[21] Sometimes Gray pencilled in indications of what she would like to do. In one example Gray has indicated a ramp descending into a garage, written in French 'descent vers le garage' – or descend to the garage.[22]

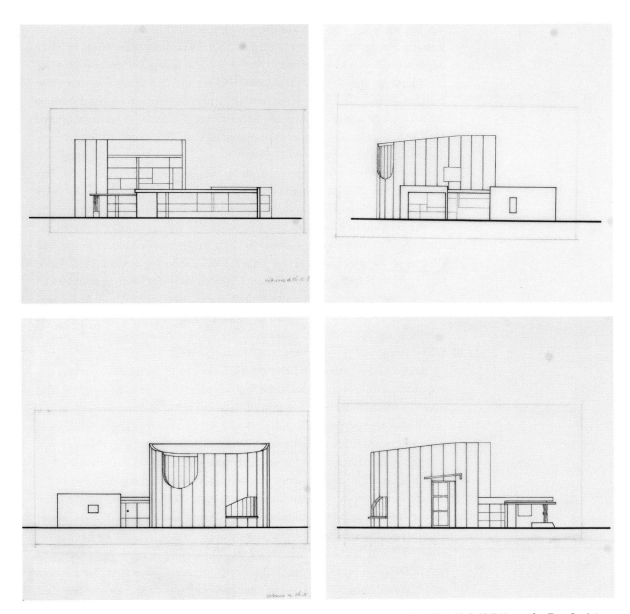

10.4, 10.5, 10.6, 10.7 *House for Two Sculptors*, elevations, 1933-34, paper, pencil, ink © NMI

The highlight of the building is the vertical glass door, which was hung on specially designed hinges that permitted the door to slide or swing open. This door was created for the reception and removal of studio sculptures. The hinging mechanism on this door was one Gray had developed previously with her furniture.[23] There are extant drawings which closely detail the pivot mechanism for this door.[24] The highlight of Mallet-Stevens's project was the large glass door composed of four panels designed by Jean Prouvé (1901-1984).

Gray produced various versions of models for the *House for Two Sculptors*. She also concentrated on producing a model solely of the large workshop, and was particularly interested in using an aluminium alloy on the outside of the walls. [25] Inspiration for the material of the house was possibly inspired from Henri Sauvage's standardised *House in Asbestos Cement* or the *Kiefhook Housing Estate,* 1925-29, by J. J. P. Oud (1890-1963) which appeared in the first issue of *L'Architecture d'Aujourd'hui* in 1930.[26] Oud's housing project demonstrated the use of plymax panels and plywood covered in ribbed metallic alloy. This was similar to what Gray suggested for the outside of the sculptor's atelier and for other projects such as the *Ellipse house.*

Eileen Gray anticipated the creation of a new social order when the importance of recreational time for all classes became a controversial issue in France in the 1920s and 1930s. Some architects such as Le Corbusier viewed this as a political and social threat.[27] Those concerned with liberal politics joined members of various labour organisations in taking an institutionalised approach to the creation of leisure facilities and individual homes for mass production. Gray's earlier designs initially targeted an elite but she now responded with socially motivated designs for leisure centres, vacation centres, social housing and holiday homes. These housing projects were symbolic of working-class solidarity. Her concerns differed from her contemporaries in that Gray's designs began almost immediately to focus on the individual, yet in the hope that her projects could be mass produced. The schemes and elevations for the *Camping tent*, 1930-31 can be seen as a preoccupation with both the public as a whole and the private individual.[28] She stated that it was done in collaboration with Jean Badovici and was exhibited at the *Union des Artistes Modernes* in 1931. Earlier drawings indicate that the original shape of the tent was triangular.[29] All the extant drawings illustrate a simple, folding arched, metal framework that was covered in canvas. It was to be erected by one person, light enough to be carried on a motorcycle or in a car. It had plastic discs wide enough to let the night air in, but small enough to form a barrier against any stray dogs.[30] The tent was quite large, with measurements varying in proportion. The height of the tent extended to 2.20 metres in some drawings, reduced to 2 metres in others.[31] In one specific drawing an unfolded bed appears along with a dining table and an extension opens outwards to form a sheltered sitting area.[32] The *Camping tent* can also be viewed as a cross between furniture and architecture, and how Gray's designs became intertwined. Gray also did this with her ideas for the block screen. At one point Gray was designing a wooden porch consisting of triangular and square-like forms superimposed over each other.[33] Gray had experimented with a triangular block screen; however the project was never realised.[34]

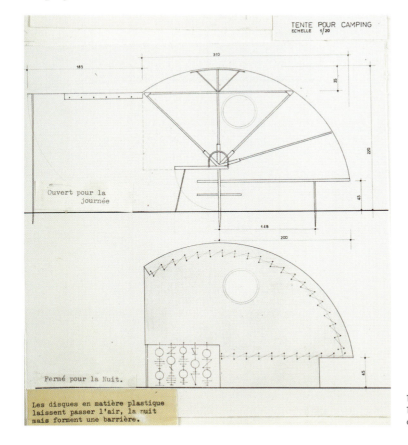

10.8 *Camping tent*, elevations, 1930-31, paper, ink, pencil, colour crayon © NMI

The *Ellipse house,* 1936 was intended as a temporary structure suitable for workers, the homeless or as a temporary leisure home. By this date housing and leisure time for the worker population had become a major political issue in France.[35] After the war the French government brought into law a number of initiatives encouraging the construction of workers' housing. On the 22 December 1922 and 13 July 1928 laws were changed in France to permit workers to borrow money, long-term, so that they could own and build their own homes. This enabled the construction, of *minimal housing* for workers in designated areas of towns and villages. This consisted of small houses, which addressed social and economic issues, and everything that is needed for a modern lifestyle without compromising quality. Workers could actually build their own homes, thus also providing local employment. This initiative encouraged the return of workers to and

10.9 *Ellipse house,* model, plan, elevations, 1936, paper, ink, pencil © NMI

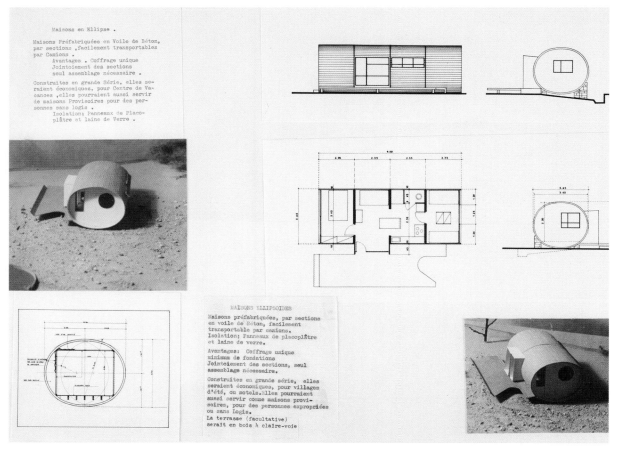

the making of artisanal products in villages which were depopulated after the war. The Popular Front restricted working hours for the working class, which required employers in certain industries to permit their workers paid annual leave.[36] Gray had also been influenced by the writings of the architectural critic Dr. Sigfried Giedon (1888-1968) who had published an essay 'Lesson of the Werkbund Exhibition at Stuttgart in 1927' in the summer edition of *L'Architecture Vivante* in 1928.[37] He is critical that architects in France had not addressed the housing shortage, the creation of housing for lower classes and inexpensive housing. Gray would later realise such ideas with her *Ellipse house*. Giedon's thought developed further after the Second World War – saying that architecture had to begin again, with the single cell, the smallest unit, low cost dwellings, on to the creation of neighbourhoods, cities and regions.

There are several possibilities as to the source of Gray's inspiration for this project. The *Ellipse house* is possibly inspired by Charlotte Perriand's (1903-1999) *Weekend house,* 1934-35, which could accommodate six people and was composed of duraluminium, a corrosion-resistant aluminium alloy that was used for airplanes.[38] Pierre Jeanneret's had also designed a holiday home in 1936 which folded up and was easily transportable. The basis for this housing was the idea of a demountable camping structure, a concept that Eileen Gray had already explored in 1930 with her *Camping tent* as a foldable holiday home made from corrugated metal. The *Ellipse house* could be a freestanding form in its own right or incorporated for holiday centres.[39] It consisted of transportable sections of shell concrete with standard shuttering, minimal foundations and made use of simple jointing so that it could be assembled and taken apart.

In November 1930 Gray and Badovici published an article on 'La Maison Minimum', which was a single family house in the inaugural issue of *L'Architecture d'Aujourd'Hui* in 1930. Also featured was an article on 'La Maison de L'Artisan' (Worker's Housing).[40] The article explained how the government's initiatives were being implemented with finance from state investment, combined with aid from construction companies and building societies for affordable housing. The project ensured the renewal of craft production, a fight against the depopulation of the countryside, the extension of a driving force in small businesses, the promotion of a working family, the training of apprentices, hygienic housing, access to small properties and the best defence against a declining birth rate.[41] It is after this date that Gray became preoccupied with architecture for the working class and that the problem of temporary housing and leisure facilities commanded her attention. The *Ellipse house,* and later projects such as the *Cultural and Social centre* 1946-47 addressed the issues raised in this article. The *Ellipse house* was to be mass produced like her furniture. It was a prefabricated unit developed from interlocking planes of concrete, which could be constructed and dismantled quickly, and could also sleep from three to five people. This particular scheme sleeps five.[42] Gray noted in her portfolio: 'Ellipse houses. Prefabricated houses of concrete panels in sections easily transported on trucks. Advantages. Unique concrete framework. Pointing of sections is sole requirement for assembly. Employing techniques of mass production, they would be economical for the Vacation Centre; they could also serve as provisional housing for homeless persons. Insulation: panels of placo–plaster and fibreglass'.[43]

10.10 *Ellipse house*, plan and elevation, 1936, paper, ink, pencil © NMI

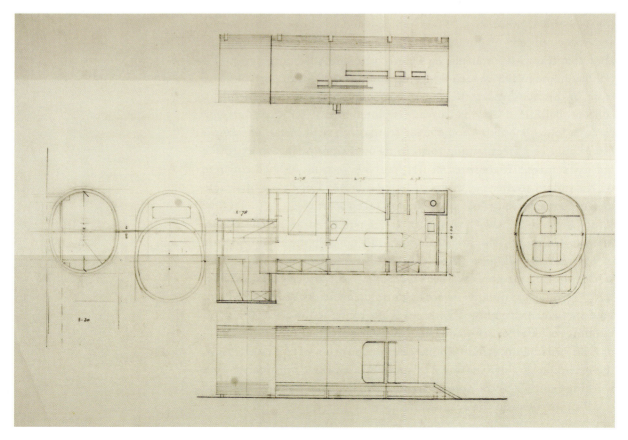

Gray's choice of construction material for the house was possibly inspired by Henri Sauvage's (1873–1932) standardised *House in Asbestos Cement* which appeared in the first issue of *L'Architecture d'Aujourd'hui* in 1930 and by the mass-produced component possibly from the ideas of Le Corbusier.[44] The components for this house could be assembled into various combinations. They ranged in size from 2.05 x 3.0 metres to 2.35 x 3.65 metres. Several schemes sleep three people. These schemes indicate a porch, an entry area, storage facilities, a kitchen area and plumbing.[45] Other schemes focus and develop more the kitchen and dining area.[46] One particular scheme sleeps several people.[47] Gray also indicated the use of aluminium, which she drew in the side section of one of the schemes for this house, which could also be a transcription of ideas from the use of chrome-plated aluminium in her furniture design.[48] She had also explored the use of corrugated metal in an early design for a demountable

10.11 *Ellipse house*, plan and elevation, 1936, paper, ink, pencil © NMI

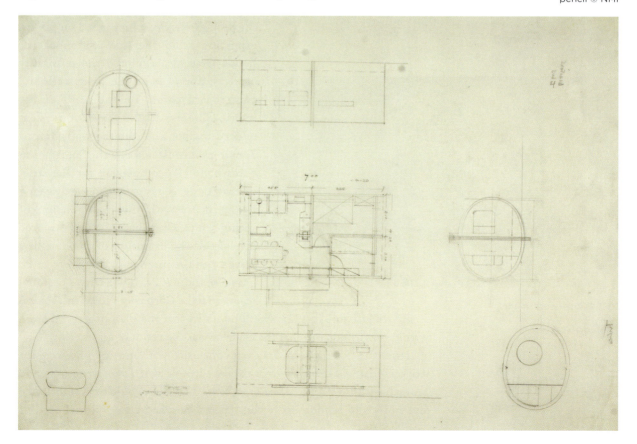

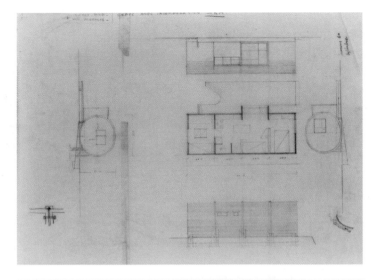

camping structure and anticipated using a water proofing sealant. On one particular scheme and section for the *Ellipse house* Gray wrote; '*Chape avec incorporation SIKA Sifreo Nice*', In French, *une chape* refers to a thick layer of concrete used in construction or industry. Sika is an international company which specialised in the use of chemicals for the construction industry. They focused on products which were used for sealing, bonding, reinforcing and protecting concrete layers used in construction. During the 1920s Sika introduced into Europe an innovative waterproofing product. With the *Ellipse house* Gray anticipated using the Sika product as a water-proofing sealant on the deck extension, which stood on pilotis, extending from the side section of the house. Gray also explored the possibility of using fibreglass on the outer walls and plasterboard panels on the walls of the interior. She also draws a ventilation system under the floor and into the walls. In one drawing she indicated that the flooring was hardwood.[49] To compensate for the strict interior design Gray extended the dwelling out of doors with the manipulation of sitting units. Gray had already explored the idea of the extension of the dwelling place from the interior in the *House for an Engineer* and *E.1027*. It was Gray's personal response to Le Corbusier's ideas in *Towards a New Architecture* in 1923 where he stated that the plan proceeded from within to without and that the exterior was the result of an interior.[50]

From the 1930s Eileen Gray was concerned with minimal housing for workers that would have two or three bedrooms, with steel structures, and moveable walls.[51] As with the *Ellipse house,* 1936, they could be prefabricated and easily and economically constructed. She had also explored projects for workers' colonies in single family prefabricated housing done in 1936-1940. Gray read Paul Nelson's *La Maison Suspendue*, Editions Albert Morancé, Paris, 1939.[52] The publication was produced under the direction of Jean Badovici and was to have a profound influence on several of her social and domestic projects.

Nelson's hypothetical structure was a square block built from uniform foundations that was exhibited at the *Galerie Pierre Loeb* in Paris in 1937 and in New York and Princeton in 1939.[53] Isolation, regeneration and the spiritual and cultural needs of the client were paramount in Nelson's project. The structure was geometrical in form on the exterior and the interior stimulated the client's senses through a play of contrasts in form and volume. It was constructed from a continuous metal lattice which defined the main volume of the house, above which sits the roof, supported by a large metal steel frame. This rigid metal frame, filled with transparent or opaque glass lozenges, each two metres in height, reflected the light, appearing like a mosaic, creating a mezzanine and roof terrace. This open structural cage was a daring architectural experiment which employed the free plan. The reinforced exterior permitted the rooms to be suspended internally from the roof and connected by ramps. All remaining open space was given to the display of art. Each room was constructed from a curved, soldered steel frame which prevented reverberations of sound. The concept of these suspended rooms is that they could be demounted and replaced by another, different in size and form. The house was divided into three levels. The ground floor or staff quarters was composed of reinforced concrete and glass blocks. The living quarters were suspended from the roof. Emphasising the ideology of 'the machine for living', it economically utilised space for living, eating, washing and rest. The third and final section of the house – the space for entertainment, was situated between the ground floor and the living area. It was accessed via a curved ramp which led from the ground floor to this large open entertainment area, used for music, radio, television, etc. By continuing along the ramp one arrived at the first suspended room – the library/office, and then onto two suspended rooms where the client could retire from the rest of the family. Each level was accessed by this ramp and also by a staircase which is enclosed in a column accessed from the service entrance. The house had air conditioning and heating. Nelson stated that the structure was earthquake proof, required little foundations, and that as a concept it was entirely unique.

From this moment on Gray began exploring Nelson's ideas.[54] Gray first used both the title of his book and the expressive architectural forms of the house itself that emphasised spatial fluidity through the use of curvilinear forms for her *Maison de Rapport Suspendues* project.[55] The drawings appear to indicate a tower with curved forms protruding in segments from small alternating bays. It consisted of three-bedroomed apartments, and employed a rectangular arrangement for the dining/living room, kitchen, and bath, with quite inspirational and experimental bedrooms that are subdivided through the use of curvilinear walls with built-in storage facilities and furniture.

In June 1936 the Popular Front government, directed by Léon Blum (1872-1950), introduced legislation whereby France's four million workers were given the right to paid holidays and limiting the working week to forty hours. Paid holidays had been the concern of the Confédération Générale du Travail since 1919 but only became an issue from 1925 onwards. Léo Lagrange was appointed to the post of Under Secretary of State of Leisure by Blum and he sought to reorganise both work and leisure aims in his policies to appeal to French youth. Gray had also visited a number of exhibitions which addressed housing concerns notably the Weissenhofsiedlung exhibition in Stuttgart of 1927, Die Wohnung fur das Existenzminimum (The Dwelling for Subsistence Minimum) exhibition in Frankfurt of 1929, and the Berlin Building Exhibition of 1931. She had subscribed to architectural journals and collected eleven copies of *L'Architecture d'Aujourd'hui* dating from February 1934 to June 1948 which explored a number of standardised housing and urbanisation projects.[56] The magazine had sponsored a competition which examined low cost family housing in 1933. Gray had also been actively exploring her thoughts on Leon Trotsky's (1879-1940) ideas on architecture. She wrote 'Every regime expresses itself through its architecture. The present Soviet epoch is characterised by palaces and official houses, which are the real temples of bureaucracy, houses for the Red Army, Military Clubs ... whilst the construction of houses for the workers is miserable and terribly behind'. She summarised these thoughts quoting Vladimir Ilyich Lenin (1870-1924) saying 'the more the functions of power belong to the entire people, the less they become necessary'.[57] Opposed to Bolshevik extremism Gray looked to create an individualised housing prototype and programme which could be achieved by modular construction. Gray's interest in Russian politics and the idea of power functioning for the benefit of the people inspired her acquisition of *Le Yogi et le Commissaire* (The Yogi and the Commissar) written by Hungarian-British journalist Arthur Koestler (1905-1983). [58] It appeared in France in the mid-1940s where it was publicly heralded for denouncing the Stalinist reign of terror.

As with all of her previous projects Gray sought to engage the direct needs of the people who would use such buildings. In the January 1938 edition of *L'Architecture d'Aujourd'hui* Gray had seen an article by Le Corbusier on modular housing in America and the development of modular urban areas in New York. This issue also depicted the demountable housing by Erik Friberger (1889-1968) which he had created between 1932 and 1937, a modular house *Petite Maison de Weekend* by Charlotte Perriand and a mobile house by W. B. Stout (1880-1956). Whilst similarities can be found with these projects Gray was more concerned about creating a house which addressed the needs of the individual rather than creating a unit using modern materials. Gray was one of the first architects to explore in her architecture the possible results of this new legislation. For a number of years Gray experimented with designs for individual holiday homes, minimal and modular housing which eventually culminated in *Ellipse house* and *Camping tent*. Gray's interest in this type of modular housing became especially useful, but also poignant after the war.

Gray was one of the first who also addressed the broader context of the new legislation and began immediately developing a series of proposals for collective living with a variety of recreational facilities. These eventually culminated in the *Vacation and Leisure centre*, 1936-37. Gray had been studying communal living spaces, cultural centres and large-scale architecture for quite some time, at one point she was interested in designing a communal home based upon the ideas of Paul Nelson's hospital architecture with his unrealised project for a *Hospital in Ismailia, Egypt* 1936.[59] She wrote 'Now that paid holidays are universally recognised, one thinks more and more of leisure time to facilitate the holidays so necessary to families and individuals of limited resources. The aim is to assemble the campers because it has become difficult to obtain authorisation to camp on private land, water facilities are necessary and even in designated camping sites hygiene is often rudimentary. This large-scale architectural project

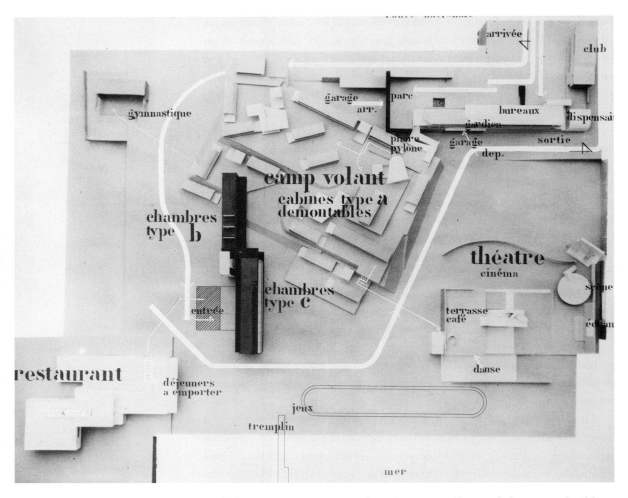

10.14 *Vacation and Leisure centre*, model, 1936-37, black and white photograph © NMI

includes; a restaurant, several washrooms, toilets and showers, a building for backpackers, single people, demountable cabins for families, easily transportable tents. Cafe-cinema-open air theatre'.[60] The hypothetical project was located next to the sea, accessed by a national motorway and was a type of holiday centre. Once again as with her individual and domestic projects Gray organised the buildings in direct relation to the sun and to the light. To the entrance was a service building, a porter's residence and a sheltered parking area. Communal areas were created around an open-air theatre and a restaurant which provided different type of eateries – a coffee shop, a cafeteria and a fine dining restaurant. The restaurant is similar in design to her *House for an Engineer*. Individual types of housing were also created, where she used her *Ellipse houses* – some slept three people, others five. To facilitate shower and toiletry facilities Gray designed a communal bathroom for camp or tent users.[61] She completed the proposal in 1937 and illustrated it in her architectural portfolio.[62] There was also a large apartment/hotel complex – one side created for families, the other for single people.[63] This complex invoked Corbusian ideas as it was raised on pilotis and had a roof top terrace for communal areas. She also varied her treatment of the windows.

10.15 Apartment/hotel complex, *Vacation and Leisure centre*, model, with plans and elevations, 1936-37, paper, pencil, ink, black and white photograph © NMI

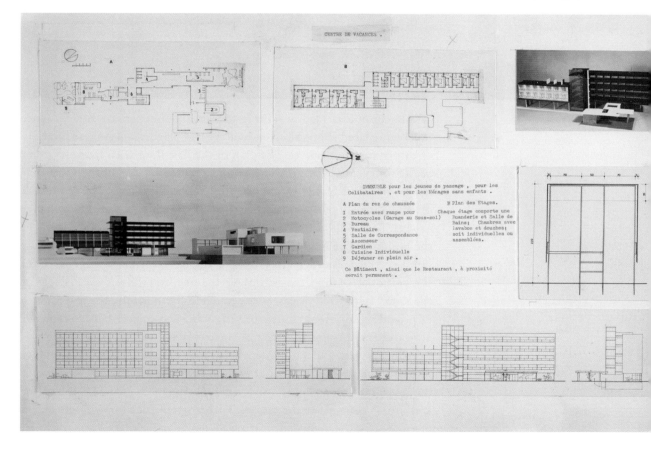

10.16 Restaurant, *Vacation and Leisure centre*, model, 1936-37, black and white photograph © NMI

The communal facility of the restaurant and the open-air theatre/dance hall were placed at opposing ends of the site. The restaurant had a variety of eating areas and spaces. The plan of the first floor with four elevations of the restaurant shows the terrace and a coffee area.[64] The clear, unfussy design and varied fenestration provided panoramic views. The restaurant offered a variety of dining experiences for individuals, families or larger groups. The levels of formality were increased toward the upper levels of the building. The first floor had a fixed price restaurant, and an outdoor dining terrace. The first floor plan of the terrace area of the restaurant shows the coffee shop, the central terrace area, and the self-service area or the eatery with fixed prices.[65] Gray noted in her portfolio the importance of providing different choices of restaurant and coffee shops to cater for all travellers.[66] As with the rest of the complex Gray's primary focus was to attract a variety of holiday makers from diverse social environments. She also completed a number of ground floor plans with two elevations of the restaurant. One plan shows the garage, the main entrance, the coffee area which leads on to the terrace, a large open space for self-service, an office area for the manager, which leads down to the kitchen and the toilet facilities.[67] Her handwriting is visible on this original plan, showing also where she has made modifications to the plan in French stating that she wants to eliminate the doorways and stonework around the stairwells and instead replace them with pilotis near the kitchen area. Another ground floor plan with two elevations of the restaurant shows the garage, the main entrance, the coffee area, which leads onto the terrace, a large open space for self-service for food, an office area for the manager, which leads down to the kitchen and the toilet facilities.[68] Detailed lower floor plans of the restaurant show the wine cellar, fridge area, a preparation room, the delivery area, a fridge freezer and the garage for the manager.[69] An earlier drawing from 1935-36 of the top floor shows Gray pondering the allocation of space for facilities.[70] All floors were linked by a central stairwell.[71] Gray finally completed a detailed floor plan of the top floor of the restaurant complex with glass surrounds and panoramic views of the area. It shows the dancing facilities, the dinner area and the restaurant with à la carte menus.[72] Just as she did with her treatment of the windows on the hotel/apartment complex Gray used different fenestration on the restaurant. In her design for the east façade of the coffee shop, the glass windows open outwards like screens, leaving the passageway free.[73] Whereas on the south elevation of the restaurant the windows pivoted and slid across.[74] In her design for the dance hall, terrace, café and outdoor theatre complex Gray combined building and landscape into one. A precursor to her theatre

10.17 Plan of Restaurant, first floor, *Vacation and Leisure centre*, 1936-37, paper, ink © NMI

10.18 Plan of Restaurant, ground floor, *Vacation and Leisure centre*, 1936-37, paper, ink © NMI

10.19 Model of the open air theatre, *Vacation and Leisure centre*, 1936-37, black and white photograph © NMI

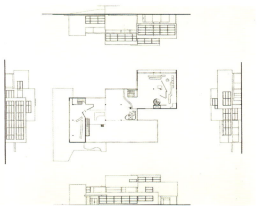
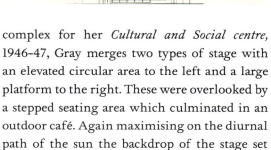
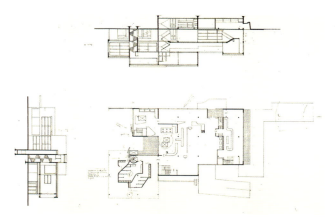

complex for her *Cultural and Social centre,* 1946-47, Gray merges two types of stage with an elevated circular area to the left and a large platform to the right. These were overlooked by a stepped seating area which culminated in an outdoor café. Again maximising on the diurnal path of the sun the backdrop of the stage set would have been illuminated with the rays of the dying sun, adding to the theatrics and drama of any performance.

Le Corbusier's *Pavillon de Temps Nouveaux* was devoted to the theme of modern urbanism where Eileen Gray exhibited her *Vacation and Leisure centre* in 1937.[75] Gray used a small celluloid disc as an exhibition label which read, 'Vacation and Leisure Centre Club Regional Equipment du Logis par Eileen Gray' (Vacation and Leisure Centre with Fitted Dwellings by Eileen Gray). At the *Pavillon* Gray created her own stand, reworking a display originally designed in the 1920s. For this exhibition Gray revised and signed an old exhibition pavilion project, writing on the back that it was 'un vieux croquis' or 'an old sketch'.[76] Gray's pavilion was intended to display her photographs, furniture, models and drawings. It was subdivided to accommodate different types of display and circulation routes from left to right. Models had tall vertical surfaces to display plans, furniture stood on the floor and the walls were lined with drawings and photographs. She also completed a series of drawings of lighting for the space designing a vertical ramp and using mirrors on the adjoining wall to amplify its effects. She engaged the visitor's senses, making the experience tangible and tactile, through a clever amplification of light, by lining the walls with mirrors and by covering eight panels with cork and matte silver.[77]

Her earlier model, made from paper and cardboard had been reworked by André Joseph Roattino, a mason and carpenter from Castellar, who carried out extensive work on Gray's house and executed much of the furniture at *Tempe à Pailla*. Due to feelings of self-doubt Gray did not attend when the pavilion opened. Le Corbusier wrote a letter to Jean Badovici referring to the book *Des Canons, des munitions? Merci! Des logis... s.v.p.*, 1937. He stated how pleased he was with the first draft, which included two pages for Eileen Gray. At the pavilion Le Corbusier created an interior structure in which the walls were literally words and images. It was photographically documented in the publication.[78]

Gray's archive suggests that there were several projects, not just the *Vacation and Leisure centre* which she prepared to be exhibited at the Pavilion. She had also looked to exhibit the shutter and window system drawings from *E.1027,* and her drawings of the false ceiling which she completed for *Tempe à Pailla*. Gray was exceedingly proud of the shutter and window system at *E.1027* and created her own exhibition label for her designs, made from yellow celluloid, and using her stencilling methods. It read 'fenêtres s'ouvrant' or 'opening windows'.[79] At *Tempe à Pailla*, Gray converted three cisterns into rooms. The first was a garage with a false ceiling and a guest room, the second was a wine cellar and the third acted as a reservoir for rain water collected from the roof terrace.[80] Again, Gray designed her own exhibition label for this project. It reads 'Faux plafond dans le garage', or 'False ceiling in the garage'.

Though Gray never wrote an architectural manifesto she did write extensively on architecture, often directly challenging the ideas of some of her contemporaries. In her personal archives Gray wrote a series of notes and short essays on different topics. One essay which she developed on exhibition architecture Gray challenged ideas put forward by Le Corbusier.[81] Eileen Gray claims that poor architecture is due to a lack of sensuality or feeling for the user of the building. Everything is built without reason, without trying to approach the truth and without doing any research. The art of the engineer is insufficient if it is not guided by the primitive needs of man. Reason without instinct makes suspicious the pictorial element of art which is not assimilated by instinct. Gray then draws a building on pilotis, writing in French 'an example of penetration of architecture descending slowly under pilotis'. She continues this train of thought, saying that man is directed by his primitive sensations such as the

10.20 Notes on exhibition architecture, undated, paper, pencil © NMI

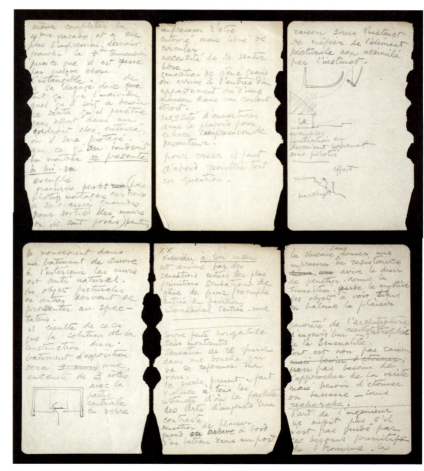

feelings of fear and discomfort. Gray gives the example of entering into an international pavilion, comparing it to an individual entering the mouth of a form which is going to swallow him or her. The twentieth century, she claims, attacked all of man's instincts. The arts of the twentieth century did not. There is a sensation of pleasure one gets when one arrives on board a boat in a port. It gives the impression of being free, of still being able to circulate. This feeling of freedom of movement is vital when one arrives at the entrance of an apartment or a house if accessed by a narrow corridor. As a result there is a necessity to punctuate the ceiling with openings to alleviate the weightiness of the space. Gray says one has to question everything. For instance on page three of this essay she says one has to question the fourth façade, giving it a fourth dimension, making it tangible and tactile. One must give the individual the idea of penetrating into an enclosed space where he/she feels protected. Gray gives the example of using large photographic montages which when placed on the walls would appear as if they are coming out of the walls like paintings. Gray did this with her exhibition pavilion completed initially in the 1920s for Le Corbusier's *Pavillon des Temps Nouveaux,* 1937. In the earlier scheme, a tall, cubic volume is bounded by an L shaped single story space. She later transformed the earlier model, and it is unclear if the latter version was realised.

Gray also states that the movement of the building must follow the interior walls which are anti-natural. Objects and other art forms must present themselves to the spectator. It results in the construction of an exhibition space which will be of three walls and a central section in glass. This Gray clearly developed with a number of projects. In one drawing she explored how to raise objects so that they could be viewed better by the public. She also explored the objects themselves and how they could engage the visitor, by designing a mechanised sculpture. It was operated by a handle which drew up, on a disc, a series of balls into the structure. The balls were released by a spring, landing to the left of the piece on a small platform with a ramp which returns the balls back to the disc, where the process begins again.[82] Gray's *Picture Gallery project,* 1930s, which she actually called *A study in indirect lighting*, is a highly-developed drawing of an exhibition space which encompasses all of her ideas in these notes.[83] It has a meandering circulation route through the gallery space. Vertical panels project from the raised central spine, lit by a clerestory and the space had subsidiary display spaces which were created by alternating at angles wall and window panels which filtered natural light.

Gray also did numerous drawings for the exhibition gallery in the *Cultural and Social centre*.[84] Her *Batiment pour une exposition à étudier* or 'building for the study of exhibitions' again displays her ideas.[85] It consists of a rectangular frame with four storeys, with six areas designated for exhibition space. These were arranged at half levels and connected via a sequence of stairs and continuous ramps. Gray stated in French that the primary function of the building was the movement sequence and the role of light in the display of the objects. Gray was preoccupied with both natural and artificial lighting of the exhibits.[86] The ground floor was located two metres below the first floor, which had a ramp leading to stairs and up to the second floor. The stairs ascend continuously up to the fourth floor, inviting the exhibition-goer to continue through the entire exhibit. Gray arranged a sequence of free form galleries.[87] Using a red line she emphasised the movement through the exhibition. She included trees toward one end of the building, leading to an outdoor stairs at the other end which leads to a restaurant to be located on the lower level of the second floor. Paul Nelson's *La Maison Suspendue* was an inspiration for the project in the way she arranged the free form galleries; however, Gray's design contrasted sharply to the work of Nelson in that his spaces are closed cells and Gray's are open plan.[88]

By 1941 Gray was forced to leave the Mediterranean coast of France as an expatriate and move inland where she remained at Lourmarin in the Vaucluse region. She worked on designs for a house in Casablanca for Badovici which was never realised and on a hypothetical project for a meditation garden for *La Bastide Blanche* in St. Tropez. In her notes she also stated that she was working on a project in Dakar, Senegal – but doesn't elaborate further.[89] In 1943 she moved to Cavaillon and by the end of the war she had returned to St. Tropez taking an apartment at 5 place des Remparts. In 1945 Badovici was appointed Chief Adjunct Architect for Reconstruction in France, and in 1946 Gray was invited to contribute a design for a worker's flat for the International Exhibition of Reconstruction in Paris. In December 1945 Gray had visited London to see family after the war and was horrified by the destruction. Britain had been badly affected during the war. A total of 3,745,000 houses in Britain were either damaged or destroyed. In London only one house in ten escaped some kind of damage. Gray took a keen interest in the British housing crisis and purchased John Madge's *The Rehousing of Britain*.[90] This book illustrated and analysed tenant housing and looks to post-war production of suitable housing in England. Gray had been experimenting with workers' and social housing since the 1930s and had completed detailed plans for the *Ellipse house*. Some of the houses illustrated in this book are light steel frame houses, easily erected and cheap to build. They were exceedingly economical.

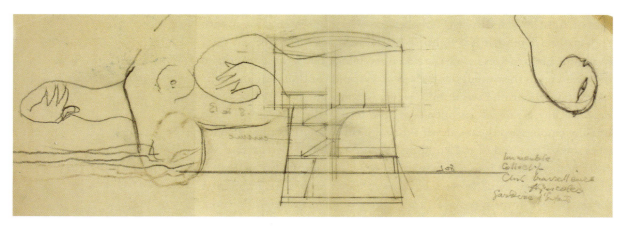

10.21 *Agricultural worker's house*, 1946, paper, pencil © NMI

The ideas expressed in Nelson's *La Maison Suspendue* and John Madge's publication influenced Gray's design for the *Agricultural worker's house*, which she planned in 1946. Gray addressed the issues and conditions of social housing through the provisions in her design of space, light and ventilation.[91] It had a curved roof and double height living room with kitchen, bathroom and bedrooms on an upper level.[92] The project is a derivative of Nelson's house type yet also reflects Gray's social concerns for housing for agricultural workers. Similarities between the two projects are evident; they are both prefabricated workers' housing. Leading from the suspended staircase the rooms appear on the drawings as though they are cell-like structures suspended throughout the main level of the house. Both have a curved roof.[93] Gray's drawing consists of a *maison suspendue* with specifications for ventilation, as areas are marked for the movement of air through the roof. Though the materials are not listed, the curvature of the roof suggests the use of aluminium. The house has three levels, a substructure or basement, a main floor and a first floor. Rooms appear suspended, raised on pilotis within the interior framework of the building. A suspended staircase rises up through the first floor through to the second floor. To the left on the first floor appears a large living area with a curved ceiling. To the right, on the main floor, the stairs cuts through a kitchen which is raised on pilotis. Directly above the kitchen, accessed via the stairs is a bathroom located on the main floor. On the other side of the elevation Gray has writen: 'Immeuble collectif civic travailleurs agricoles garderie d'enfants' which translates as a 'collective building for civic agricultural workers with a day nursery'. Gray's building develops from thick sloping walls which distribute the pressure created by the height of the building evenly throughout the structure.

Even prior to the war, Gray had been developing her ideas in relation to urbanism. Two particular issues of *L'Architecture Vivante* which Gray had in her library looked at urban projects, the first contained an article by Badovici looking at J.J.P. Oud's plans and elevations of inexpensive workers' housing projects in Rotterdam, Tusschendyken 1920-21 and Spangen 1919-20.[94] The second was an issue devoted to Le Corbusier which includes an essay and plans of his *Urbanisation project* for a town in Algiers, 1931-32.[95] For a number of years French officials had been unsuccessful in dealing with the squalor of the growing Parisian slums. In Gray's notes she sought efficient ways to house large numbers of people in response to the urban housing crisis. She points to the need to create spacious areas in built-up zones for recreational services, for children and for those of a freer spirit.[96] The reasons she gives are sanitation and safety, especially for children, and to begin confronting the problems of urbanism and sprawling cities. She emphasised the need to create a collective community for families, single people, and young couples in an urban environment which has a plethora of activities freely available to all.

Gray's notes on urbanism are a direct response to Le Corbusier. During the 1920s he advanced hypothetical large-scale housing projects in response to the growing urban populations and housing shortages of post-war France. The *Ville Contemporaine*, 1922, created for three million people, illustrates rows of skyscrapers placed on stilts to allow for pedestrian passage. They were connected by vast highways and set in parks. The *Plan Voisin,* 1925, envisaged an enormous urban-renewal project replacing historic buildings with a complex of high-rise buildings. These two projects were designed to house the industrial and intellectual elite.

Both Gray and Le Corbusier believed in the concept, common among the modern pioneers, that armed with the right city planning and faith in technology, architecture could revolutionise living patterns, improving the lives of modern city dwellers on a physical, economic and even spiritual level. Le Corbusier's *Ville Radieuse, 1935,* addresses the concept of capitalist authority and a pseudo-appreciation of workers' individual freedoms. Pre-fabricated apartment houses would be available to everyone, not just the elite, based upon the size and needs of each particular family. Standing fifty metres high, and accommodating 2,700 inhabitants they stood on pilotis. Each apartment block was equipped with a laundry and catering section which provided services, if required, for every family. This enabled the individual to think, write or utilise the play and sports grounds which covered much of the city's land. The apartments had roof top gardens and beaches. Children had a day care centre, run by trained professionals. The business centre consisted of Le Corbusier's Cartesian skyscrapers placed every 400 metres. The skyscrapers provided office space for 3,200 workers per building.

Gray's ideas never developed into a concrete proposal. Her notes on urbanism consider the individual's freedoms and there is no emphasis on authority. Sanitation and safety are the central focus of her concept. Le

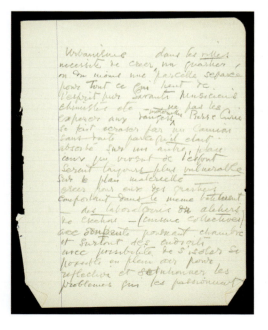

10.22 Notes on urban architecture, 1930s, paper, pencil © NMI

Corbusier does not look to the individual's freedoms; rather he promoted leisure time activities that he enjoyed. Le Corbusier's individuals had no voice in the governance of their lives. They are able to behave, but not to act. There is no room for individuals to act non-rationally. Leisure time is filled with healthy pursuits. There is no extravagance or chaotic excess. Gray's urban ideology focuses on those with a freer spirit. Le Corbusier's vision suffers from a naive conception of human nature and his notion of authority is both patriarchal and bureaucratic. He also assumes that a collective social identity would result from the communal ownership of land whereas Gray discusses urban spaces which are dedicated to social contact. In her notes Gray also briefly looked at how regional architecture could be improved. She has written that there is something misleading in the return to regional architecture which does not conform to the variety of buildings which are needed.[97]

During the 1940s the migration of youth from the country to the major cities in France was becoming an increasing problem, and the French provinces were becoming depopulated. Inspired by the *Maison du Peuple* at the turn of the century and the Popular Front government cultural initiatives with the *Maisons de la Culture* after the war, Eileen Gray created the *Cultural and Social centre*, 1946-47 with the intention of encouraging French youth to remain in their native localities. She aspired to provide employment and a forum that stimulated cultural, intellectual and social, rather than physical activities. Since the 1920s Gray had already clearly defined her ideas in relation to the arts, looking to the ideas and thoughts of Paul Valéry.[98] In 1921 Valéry wrote *Eupalinos or the Architect* and Jean Badovici cited it in the inaugural issue of *L'Architecture Vivante*.[99] Valery's dialogue elucidates architecture's potential impact on human sensibility. In notes in her archive on the subject Gray discusses expanding Valéry's ideas on affecting the senses to all levels of society. She states how the Dramatic Arts and Plastic Arts are reaching a wider audience. With regard to the *Cultural and Social centre* she says that this access to the arts means that designers and architects can broaden the horizon of possibilities for those who can't afford to move up to Paris. She stresses the importance of grouping together cultural and social facilities to open the door to all levels of society. She stresses in her argument in French that 'we are living in a time of immeasurable change where everything that man touches must be put into question'. Man has eyes in front of his head for walking but quoting Valéry she says that currently man is entering the world walking backwards.[100]

Gray's *Cultural and Social centre* project was influenced by a book published by the Arts Council of Great Britain in 1945 called *Plans for an Arts Centre*.[101] According to the book during the destructive wartime years the general population in England as well as in France showed a new appetite for the 'arts of life'. The following paragraph in particular met with Gray's approval 'Art is a concrete expression of human activity, requiring not only instruments of music, scenery and costumes, or painting, canvas and brushes but buildings, where men can congregate both to enjoy it and to make it their own'.[102] During World

10.23 Notes on urban architecture, 1930s, paper, pencil © NMI

War II, especially in the regional parts of France there was a deplorable lack of suitable buildings for the arts. Due to the wartime bombings improvisations had to be made, using every type of building except one properly designed and adequately equipped for the purpose. One of the lessons learned from the wartime experience was that the economic nature of different art forms makes it necessary to accommodate them at different levels.[103] The emphasis was that the Arts should be honourably housed; but their accommodation must be properly related to the side of the community they serve. With the return of men and women from war service the problem of accommodating leisure and communal facilities needed to be addressed. The purpose of the Arts Council of Great Britain's publication was to show how the Arts can be accommodated in a medium-sized town with a population of between 15,000 and 30,000 – a town where it is not economically possible to run a separate art gallery and hall for concerts, but where visiting companies, touring exhibitions, orchestras and concert artists have to be housed in a single multipurpose hall. In the English hypotheses there are three main components, each planned to function independently. The first is a hall to seat 600 with stage, property store, paint shop, studio, dressing rooms and store rooms. The second is an exhibition or lecture room, with adjoining reading or committee room with stores. The third is a restaurant to seat 200, with bar, service counter, kitchen, storerooms, wash up and staff rooms. Gray adapted the British guidelines to the Popular Front's ideologies of post-war France, writing:

> Now that the provinces participate more and more in the diffusion of the dramatic and visual arts, and everyone can experience art, is this not the time to enlarge the horizons of those who are unable to travel to Paris? Shouldn't one group together cultural and leisure activities in one complex, as done in other countries, so that everyone can make use of such facilities? Certainly this is not the best moment to think about such superfluous things, when so many people need basic shelter, but we do live – and will continue to live – in times of enormous change. Times in which everything that touches human beings has to be re-thought. Human beings have eyes in the direction that they walk: forwards, despite the fact that Valéry has said that they enter the world

backwards. Therefore, should we never look ahead? Those that always turn backwards will never see the light. They will always live in the shadow of the past. Those who have enough strength ought to rise and make themselves heard. When one has faith one can transform the world.[104]

Gray also looked to *Town Centre, Avesta,* in Sweden by Alvar Aalto (1898-1976) where in the summer of 1944 Aalto and his Swedish colleague Albin Stark drew up plans for a civic centre in the Svanen (Swan) district around Markustorget (St Mark's Square) in Avesta. Aalto opposed the splitting up of public buildings into small, scattered units and instead believed in assembling several institutions within a single multipurpose building. Aalto hoped to create a gathering place and a mirror for urban identity. His plan, designed to be built in stages, combined the assembly hall and offices of the town hall with a courthouse, city hotel, workers' club, theatre and library to produce an irregular but coherent complex. It encompasses a 'Citizens' Yard' with access to the square from one corner only. The fan-shaped theatre/concert hall (with seating for 700 people) had a stage which could open up towards the Citizens' Yard for major open-air events. Under the theatre is a dance hall and exhibition gallery. Aalto's project had been heavily supported in the Arts Council publication stating that it 'deserves attention if only for the breath-taking generosity of its scale and plan'.[105] Gray had already embarked on a number of hypothetical amphitheatre projects,[106] and stage sets,[107] writing that she 'had begun work on an art centre'.[108] Early drawings concentrate on studies of theatre complexes, which were symmetrical in their design.[109] The final project dates 1946-47, yet Gray signed and dated an early drawing in 1939.[110] There are many extant drawings for this project.[111]

Gray's overall program was highly developed. It included indoor and outdoor theatres, a cinema, an exhibition hall, dining facilities and a library. Gray carefully divided the library and the theatre so that visual and acoustic influences would not cause distraction.[112] Similarities abound between ancient Greek and Roman classical theatre design and Gray's project. The proposed site was flat. As with other projects completed prior to 1946-47, such as *E.1027, Tempe à Pailla* and the *Vacation and Leisure centre* the solar orientation of the site was important.[113] Gray illustrated these solar orientation drawings in her portfolios and she indicated these drawings on several plans.[114] The early drawings concentrate on studies of theatre complexes which were symmetrical in their design.[115] The final project develops Gray's approach to the integration of interior and exterior, resulting in a symmetrical theatre, and asymmetrical visitor centre. Gray repeatedly explores the symbiotic rapport between interior and exterior, architecture and nature, sun, air and light. The main entrance is under the projecting wing of the library, but at the secondary entrance, which leads to the performance hall, a tree column supports a curvilinear roof, recalling the column used in *House for Two Sculptors,* 1933-34.[116] As demonstrated in these orientation drawings the axes of the complex acknowledge the movement of the sun during the day, maximising natural light in the areas most frequented by visitors; the restaurant, the art and sculpture gallery, the library and reading room, the conference room, the theatre, concert hall, and the open-air theatre. Gray explained: 'Work often with the psychology of light bear in mind that in our subconscious we know that

10.24 *Cultural and Social centre,* model, elevations, 1946, paper, ink, black and white photograph © NMI

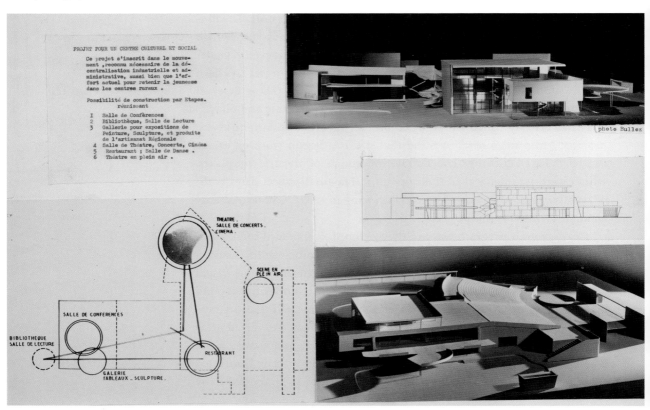

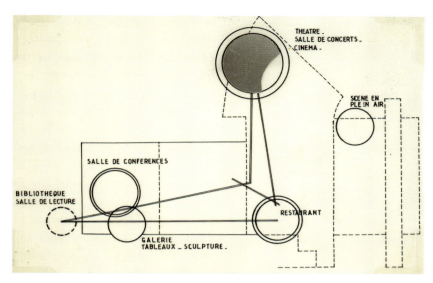

THEATRE .
SALLE DE CONCERTS .
CINEMA .

SCENE EN
PLE IN AIR

SALLE DE CONFERENCES

BIBLIOTHEQUE
SALLE DE LECTURE

RESTAURANT

GALERIE
TABLEAUX _ SCULPTURE .

10.25 Orientation drawing,
Cultural and Social centre, 1946,
paper, ink, pencil © NMI

light must derive from one point – sun, fire, etc a need deeply anchored within us. To understand this explains the morose impression indirect light creates. Enlarge the light, amplify the rays which come from one point, don't encapsulate it'.[117] The combination of the sunlight and ventilation defines the system of routes for people within and around the building, culminating in the open-air roof top theatre.[118] The elimination of the proscenium, the combination of a circular platform and a rectangular stage, and a removable screen towards the back of the stage permit the audience to interact with the surrounding landscape, which acts as a visual backdrop. There were two reflecting pools – a large irregular shaped pool at the side entrance, and a small pool in front of the theatre. In sunlight, these pools would attract groups, fostering a sense of community and continuity from the interior to exterior and from architecture to nature. Gray made a huge model which in photographs took up a large portion of the living room floor space when she was living at *Tempe à Pailla*. The original model still existed in 1970 when she returned to the project as she was invited to exhibit the model at the *Heinz Gallery exhibition*, London.[119] She worked on the project for quite some time, giving detailed notes on the ground, first and second floor plans, and it was to be exhibited alongside other models for the exhibition in 1973.

Gray also looked to Irish subject matter in her architectural projects. Interestingly, one of her proposed projects, a stage set for which she

10.26 *L'Epopée Irlandaise* (The Irish Epic), model, 1946, black and white photograph © NMI

produced a model, was a strong reflection of her Irish heritage. Entitled *L'Epopée Irlandaise* or the *Irish Epic* 1946, this design was directly inspired by a publication by George Dottin in the 1920s, a copy of which she kept in her library.[120] Gray had explored several theatre and amphitheatre projects, leading eventually to the design for the *Cultural and Social centre*. Photographs of the stage-set model dated 1946-47 remain showing rocks and trees.[121] It was Gray's first venture into theatre design since her early set designs done for *Ballet des Animaux*, 1913-16. She gives detailed notes on the design and scene for the stage set.[122] The *Irish Epic* describes at length the various Irish myths and legends of Cúchulainn, amongst others. If realised it would have been an interesting project.

Gray's final architectural project was her last home *Lou Pérou*. After the death of Badovici in 1956 and the misattribution of her work to other architects Gray began to compile three portfolios of her work.[123] Throughout her life Gray constantly questioned her own sense of achievement. Indeed in her personal records she kept newspaper cuttings throughout her life which both praised and sharply criticised her work.[124] In her notes she transcribed four handwritten pages which she copied from the publication *Wake Up and Live* by Dorothea Brande published in 1936.[125] The book concerns the conduct of life and success. The sections which Gray copied offer profound insight into her own personal character and into the psychology of what enabled her to continue in the face of adversity and criticism. She wrote:

> After failure we try again sometimes, many times. But meanwhile we have to experience defeat, failure. The final success does not wipe out from our unconscious a memory of the failures and pain. The unconscious dreads pain, humiliation and fatigue. It bends its efforts ceaselessly to

avoid them. The fact accounts for much of the inactivity, the mess to which we succumb at moments when positive action should be to our advantage.

The hypothetical project for the *Cultural and Social centre* received little publicity and was never actually realised. However, it was published in *L'Architecture d'Aujourd'hui* in 1959.[126] It wasn't until Joseph Rykwert rediscovered Gray with his article in *Domus* in 1968 that the design and architectural world once again took notice, and a revival of interest in Gray's career began until her death in 1976.

ENDNOTES

1   NMIEG 2003.492. Badovici, Jean, *L'Architecture Vivante,* Paris, Editions Albert Morancé, summer edition, 1924.

2   Constant, Caroline, *Eileen Gray*, London, Phaidon, 2000, p.216.

3   Adam, Peter, *Eileen Gray: Architect/Designer, A Biography,* London, Thames and Hudson, 2000, p.291.

4   NMIEG 2000.101, *House for Two Sculptors*, plan. V&A Archives, AAD/1980/186/6, *House for Two Sculptors*, plan.

5   V&A Archives, AAD/1980/9/186/4, *House for Two Sculptors*, plan. Gray has written the date on the plan with the four facades as 1933.

6   RIBA Archives, ref. PB 501/2, six drawings of the *House for Two Sculptors*. V&A Archives, AAD/1980/9/185/1-6, AAD/1980/9/186/1-9, AAD/1980/9/187, drawings of the *House for Two Sculptors*.

7   NMIEG 2000.102, *House for Two Sculptors*, plan.

8   Adam, Peter, *Eileen Gray: Architect/Designer, A Biography,* London, Thames and Hudson, 1987, p.293.

9   Ibid, Constant, p.216. V&A Archives, AAD/1980/9/185/1, study of second plan linking the sculptor's atelier to the main housing complex.

10   Wang, Wilfred and Constant, Caroline, *An Architecture for All Senses*, edited by Marietta Andreas, Rosamund Diamond, Brooke Hodge, Tubingen, Wasmuth, Harvard University Press, 1996, p.172.

11   NMIEG 2000.103, *House for Two Sculptors,* plan with elevations.

12   RIBA Archives, ref. PB.501/1-1, PB.501/1-2, *House for Two Sculptors,* plan with elevations. V&A Archives. AAD/1980/9/185/1, AAD/1980/9/185/2, and AAD/1980/9/186/1, *House for Two Sculptors,* plan with elevations.

13   NMIEG 2000.103, *House for Two Sculptors*, plan with four elevations. This is the same as NMIEG 2000.102 but this plan also shows the four elevations.

14   Ibid, Wang, and Constant, p.172.

15   Ibid.

16   V&A Archives, AAD/1980/9/186/4, *House for Two Sculptors*. This is a finished version of the first plan with north, south, east and west facades. It shows the entrance, bedrooms, bathroom, kitchen, dining room, living room, office, sculptor's studio and a detail of the pivoting double doors from the atelier to the garden via a ramp.

17   NMIEG 2000.97, 2000.98, 2000.99, 2000.100, *House for Two Sculptors*, four elevations.

18   Ibid, Constant, p.216.

19   V&A Archives, AAD/1980/9/185/3-5, AAD/1980/9/186/7-9, six elevations of second version of *House for Two Sculptors*. AAD/1980/9/185/5 is an earlier drawing. RIBA Archives, ref. PR.501/2-3, PR.501/2-5, PR.501/2-6 - three elevations of second version of *House for Two Sculptors*. RIBA Archives, ref. PR.501/2-4, in this elevation the tree has not been included.

20 NMIEG 2000.99 and RIBA Archives, ref. PB.501/2-5, *House for Two Sculptors,* elevation.

21 RIBA Archives, ref. PB.501/2-3, *House for Two Sculptors,* elevation. The elevation NMIEG 2000.100 is similar but later in date to one in RIBA archives as Gray has completely developed both the design of the atelier workshop and the house, whereas in the earlier elevation there is just a workshop adjoining a glass entrance connected to a sloping wall.

22 RIBA Archives, ref. PB.501/2-6, *House for Two Sculptors,* elevation. This elevation shows the ramp, but the elevation is the same as NMIEG 2000.98.

23 NMIEG 2000.4, dressing table 1925-30, the *E.1027* dressing table 1926-29 and the architectural cabinet 1924.

24 V&A Archives, AAD/1980/9/, two un-numbered drawings of the pivoting hinge mechanism. V&A Archives, AAD/1980/9/186/3, detail of the large door and ramp which leads to the garden. NMIEG 2000.250 and NMIEG 2003.1641, portfolios. V&A Prints and Drawings Archive.,W.105D-E1137, 1138-1983, design for a door, plan and position of door and hinges, perspective sketch door and hinge arrangement with the door closed.

25 NMIEG 2000.104, *House for Two Sculptors*, pieces of model.

26 Chalamel, Félix, 'Les Contreplaqués et Leurs Emplois', *L'Architecture d'Aujourd'hui,* Paris, 1930, pp.73-5.

27 Le Corbusier, *The Radiant City*, translation Pamela Knight, Eleanor Levieux and Derek Coltman, New York, Orion Press, 1967. Originally published as *La Villa Radieuse,* Paris, Vincent Fréal et Cie, 1933, p.7. He stated, 'Leisure could turn out to be the menace of modern times ... a social danger, an imminent threat.'

28 NMIEG 2000.91 - NMIEG 2000.93, *Camping tent,* elevations.

29 V&A Archives, AAD/1980/9/189/23, *Camping tent,* elevations

30 NMIEG 2000.250, portfolio. V&A Archives, AAD/1980/9/189/12, Gray has typed in French that these discs provided ventilation and also acted as a protective barrier.

31 V&A Archives, AAD/1980/9/189/9, this is the finished elevation. AAD/1980/9/189/15, this plan and elevation illustrate a fold-out bed.

32 V&A Archives, AAD/1980/9/189/1-23, these twenty-three drawings of the tent give various measurements, details of ventilation, the furniture and the appearance of the tent both open and closed. AAD/1980/9/189/15 displays the inside of the tent which reveals a fold-out bed, which when tucked away acts as either an eating or a seating area, similar to drawings. Ibid, NMIEG 2000.91 - NMIEG 2000.93.

33 NMIEG 2003.256, notes on a triangular wooden block porch.

34 NMIEG 2000.28, model for a triangular block screen.

35 Ibid, Constant, p.171.

36 Ibid, Constant, p.175.

37 NMIEG 2003.495, Giedion, Sigfried, 'Lesson of the Werkbund Exhibition at Stuttgart in 1927', *L'Architecture Vivante,* Paris, Editions Albert Morancé, summer edition 1928.

38 Ibid, Constant, p.173.

39 Rykwert, Joseph, 'Eileen Gray: Pioneer of Design', *The Architectural Review*, London, The Architectural Press, December 1968, p.361.

40 Author unknown, 'La Maison de L'Artisan', *L'Architecture d'Aujourd'hui,* Paris, 1930, pp.61-63.

41 Ibid, *L'Architecture d'Aujourd'hui,* Paris, 1930, p.61.

42 NMIEG 2000.94, *Ellipse house,* plan and elevation. V&A Archives, AAD/1980/9/190/1, *Ellipse house* drawing. It is similar to NMIEG 2000.94 as it sleeps five people. The only difference is in one of the single bedrooms; next to the principal bedroom Gray has drawn a storage cabinet attached to the wall, whereas in the drawing in the National Museum of Ireland Collection this is a swivel cabinet which also serves as a desktop. The other difference is that in the drawing NMIEG 2000.94 Gray has used natural stone on the plinths and there is a double lintel above the windows, whereas in the drawing AAD/1980/9/190/1 there is only one. RIBA Archives, ref. PB.501/3-1. *Ellipse house* plan with two elevations and two sections – there is a difference in the measurements.

43   NMIEG 2000.250 and NMIEG 2003.1641, portfolios. Gray also dates the *Ellipse house* in her portfolios as 1958.

44   Ibid, Constant, p.172. Ibid, Chalamel, Félix, pp.86-7.

45   NMIEG 2000.95, NMIEG 2000.96, *Ellipse house,* plans and elevations. V&A Archives, AAD/1980/9/190/9, this is an early, incomplete drawing and a large plan of the *Ellipse house* where Gray has only begun experimenting with the idea of facilitating three people. The shape of the house is not as delineated as in NMIEG 2000.95. RIBA Archives, ref. PB.501/3-2, this plan in RIBA of the *Ellipse house* sleeps three people and illustrates the entrance, living room and two bedrooms. It measures 3.20m across x two sections of 2.90m. Gray shows the right lateral façade, the left lateral façade, the entrance façade, and the rear façade or posterior façade.

46   Ibid, NMIEG 2000.96.

47   V&A Archives, AAD/1980/9/190/1, *Ellipse house* drawing. It is similar to NMIEG 2000.94 as it sleeps five people. The only difference is in one of the single bedrooms; next to the principal bedroom Gray has drawn a storage cabinet attached to the wall, whereas in the drawing in the National Museum of Ireland Collection this is a swivel cabinet which also serves as a desktop. The other difference is that in the drawing NMIEG 2000.94 Gray has used natural stone on the plinths and there is a double lintel above the windows, whereas in the drawing AAD/1980/9/190/1 there is only one. *RIBA* Archives, ref. PB.501/3-1, *Ellipse house* plan with two elevations and two sections – there is a difference in the measurements.

48   Ibid, NMIEG 2000.95.

49   RIBA Archives, ref. PB.501/3-3, *Ellipse house* section.

50   Le Corbusier, *Towards a New Architecture*, translated from the French by Frederick Etchells, London, The Architectural Press, 1927, p.11.

51   Constant, Caroline, 'Eileen Gray: architecture and the politics of leisure', in *Form: Modernism and History, Festschrift in honour of Eduard F. Sekler*, edited by Alexander Von Hoffman, Cambridge: Graduate School of Design, 1996, pp. 81-94. See also V&A Archives, AAD/1980/9, AAD/1980/9/199/1, AAD/1980/9/201/1-2, AAD/1980/9/202/ 1-2,AAD /1980/9/203/1-2, AAD/1980/9/204/1-6, and AAD/ 1980/9/205/1, these are all designs for minimal housing with steel structure.

52   NMIEG 2000.265, portfolio.

53   Ibid, Constant, p.223.

54   V&A Archives AAD/1980/9, un-numbered drawings. There are four studies for types of *maison suspendue* and an early study for an agricultural worker's plant with writing 'Route de Bailly'.

55   V&A Archives, AAD/1980/9, un-numbered drawings. There are four drawings in total.

56   NMIEG 2003.501, notes on publications.

57   NMIEG 2003.500, notes on yoga [sic] yogi.

58   NMIEG 2003.75, Koestler, Arthur, *Le Yogi et le Commissaire*, Paris, Editions Charlot Press, 1944.

59   NMIEG 2000.264, Nelson, Paul, *Architecture Hospitalière*, Paris, Editions Albert Morancé,1936.

60   NMIEG 2000.250, portfolio.

61   NMIEG 2004.96, *Vacation and Leisure centre,* bathroom for tent and campers.

62   Ibid, NMIEG 2000.250.

63   NMIEG 2003.157, photographs from René Lévy to Eileen Gray. This is an envelope from René Lévy for photographs of Eileen Gray's work which was exhibited with Le Corbusier's *Pavillon des Temps Nouveaux* in 1937. Included and typed in French on the outside of the envelope is the following: 'Vacation Centre including restaurant, Housing and Buildings for Single People.'

64   NMIEG 2004.84, *Vacation and Leisure centre,* plan of restaurant, first floor.

65   NMIEG 2004.88,*Vacation and Leisure centre,* plan of restaurant, first floor.

66   NMIEG 2000.250, portfolio.

67   NMIEG 2004.85, *Vacation and Leisure centre,* plan of restaurant, ground floor.

68   NMIEG 2004.87, *Vacation and Leisure centre,* plan of restaurant, ground floor.

69   NMIEG 2004.86, *Vacation and Leisure centre,* plan of restaurant, lower floor.

70   NMIEG 2004.90, *Vacation and Leisure centre,* plan of restaurant, second floor.

71   NMIEG 2004.93, *Vacation and Leisure centre,* restaurant, cross section of north elevation. NMIEG 2004.95, *Vacation and Leisure centre,* restaurant, cross section of north elevation. NMIEG 2004.94,*Vacation and Leisure Centre,* restaurant, cross section of west elevation.

72   NMIEG 2004.89, *Vacation and Leisure centre,* plan of restaurant, second floor.

73   NMIEG 2004.92, *Vacation and Leisure centre,* restaurant, east elevation.

74   NMIEG 2004.91, *Vacation and Leisure centre,* restaurant, south elevation.

75   NMIEG 2003.38, exhibition label for the *Vacation and Leisure centre.*

76   V&A Archives, AAD/1980/9/,signed axonometric drawing, two plans and four elevations of exhibition pavilion. Adam, Peter, *Eileen Gray: Architect Designer: A Biography,* London, Thames and Hudson, 2000, p.305. Adam states that Gray was dissatisfied with her pavilion and covered eight panes with matte silver and cork.

77   V&A Archives, AAD/1980/9/, four un-numbered drawings and plans with descriptions of the exhibition pavilion.

78   Le Corbusier Foundation, El-5-111, undated letter from Le Corbusier to Jean Badovici.

79   NMIEG 2003.39, exhibition label for *E.1027* windows.

80   NMIEG 2003.36, exhibition label for *Tempe à Pailla.*

81   NMIEG 2003.44, notes on exhibition architecture.

82   V&A Archives, AAD/1980/9/, two un-numbered drawings with descriptions in French of a mechanised sculpture which was to be exhibited and how it functions

83   V&A Archives, AAD/1980/9/18, art gallery.

84   V&A Archives, AAD/1980/9/208, thirty five drawings, plans and elevations, for the Cultural and Social Centre.

85   V&A Archives, AAD/1980/9/184, exhibition pavilion.

86   V&A Archives, AAD/1980/9, un-numbered drawings for *Batiment pour une exposition à étudier.*

87   V&A Archives, AAD/1980/9/184/1, exhibition Pavilion.

88   Ibid.

89   NMIEG 2003.507, notes on Eileen Gray's work.

90   NMIEG 2003.79. Madge, John, *The Rehousing of Britain*, London, Editions Pivotal Press,1946.

91   NMIEG 2000.105, *Agricultural worker's house*, elevation and drawing

92   NMIEG 2000.105 – NMIDF 2000.108, *Agricultural worker's house*, elevation and drawing

93   V&A Archives, AAD/1980/9, un-numbered drawings. This is a drawing for a building with a curved roof with notes on durisol. Gray used durisol, a pioneering noise absorbing material that incorporates a unique proprietary composite concrete material. It provided thermal insulation, energy absorption, non-combustibility, non-toxicity, outstanding exterior durability and a high strength to weight ratio.

94   NMIEG 2003.493, Badovici, Jean, *L'Architecture Vivante,* Paris, Editions Albert Morancé, Spring edition1925.

95   NMIEG 2003.498, Badovici, Jean, *L'Architecture Vivante,* Paris, Editions Albert Morancé, Autumn edition, 1932.

96   NMIEG 2003.41, notes on urban architecture, circa 1930s.

97   NMIEG 2003.42, notes on urban architecture.

98   NMIEG 2003.516, notes on philosophy and proverbs. Circa 1920s.

99   Valéry, Paul, *Eupalinos or the Architect,* translation by William McCausland Stewart, London, Oxford University Press, 1932. It was originally published in France in André Mare and Louis Sue editions,

Architecture, Paris, Editions de la Nouvelle Revue Française, 1921.

100 NMIEG 2003.515, notes on philosophy and proverbs, Circa 1920s.

101 NMIEG 2003.64, *Plans for an Arts centre,* Arts Council of Great Britain, Lund Humphries, 1945.

102 Ibid, The Arts Council of Great Britain p.3.

103 Ibid, The Arts Council of Great Britain, p.4.

104 Ibid, Adam, p.326.

105 Ibid, The Arts Council of Great Britain, p.21.

106 V&A Archives, AAD/1980/9/, un-numbered drawings of six plans and two elevations for an amphitheatre.

107 V&A Archives, AAD/1980/9/, un-numbered drawings, study for a stage set, an open-air theatre, with plan, elevation, stairs section and written descriptions.

108 Ibid, Adam, p.326.

109 Ibid, Constant, p.184. Constant believes that these theatre complex drawings were begun during the war when Gray was in exile in Vaucluse.

110 V&A Archives, AAD/1980/9/208/1-35, amongst the thirty-four un-numbered drawings there is an early, yet complete, drawing for the *Cultural and Social centre* showing the ground floor, first floor and second floor. Gray numbered the various rooms. She dated and signed this drawing '*Gray, 26th February 1939.*' Pompidou Centre Archives, box no.2/3918.117 – 118. This is a photograph of an early model of the theatre complex.

111 V&A Archives, AAD/1980/9/208, *Cultural and Social centre* plan. RIBA Archives, ref. PA408/2(1-10), DR144/4(1-3), *Cultural and Social Centre* plans.

112 Gray, Eileen, 'Projet pour un Centre Culturel', *L'Architecture Vivante*, Paris, Editions Albert Morancé, No.82, 1959, p.XLI.

113 NMIEG 2003.3, NMIEG 2003.4, *Cultural and Social centre,* orientation drawings.

114 NMIEG 2000.250, NMIEG 2003.1641, portfolios. V&A Archives. AAD/1980/9/208, *Cultural and Social centre* plan. There are thirty-four drawings of the *Cultural and Social centre*, un-numbered, of which two are solar orientation drawings.

115 Ibid, Constant, p.184.

116 NMIEG 2000.97 – 98, *House for Two Sculptors*, elevations. V&A Archives, AAD/1980/9/185/5, *House for Two Sculptors*, elevation. *RIBA* Archives. PB501/2(5), *House for Two Sculptors*, elevations.

117 Ibid, Adam, p.283.

118 This is described as Gray's choreographic approach to her architecture.

119 NMIEG 2004.126, notes on the *Cultural and Social centre.*

120 NMIEG 2003.47, Dottin, Georges, *l'Épopée Irlandaise,* Paris, Editions La Reniassance du Livre, 1922.

121 NMIEG 2003.1569, *Cultural Social centre*, stage design for *L'Épopée Irlandaise.*

122 V&A Archives, AAD/9/1980, un-numbered drawings and notes.

123 NMIEG 2000.250, NMIEG 2003.1641, NMIEG 2003.1642, and NMIEG 2003.1643, portfolios.

124 V&A Archives, AAD 9/12-1980 and AAD 9/13-1980, press cuttings.

125 NMIEG 2000.196, Brande, Dorothea, *Wake Up and Live,* New York, Simon and Schusler, 1936. NMIEG 2003.514, notes on philosophy, Circa 1939.

126 Gray, Eileen, 'Projet pur un Centre Culturel', *L'Architecture d'Aujourd'hui,* No.82, 1959, p.XLI.

11

A Kindred Spirit: The Prunella Clough Letters

Prunella Clough (1919-1999) was one of the most interesting British painters of the post-war period and a niece of Eileen Gray. While her work found critical acclaim and attracted a devoted following she was, like Eileen Gray, towards the end of her life not widely known to the general public. Like her famous aunt, Clough was an intensely private person and was devoted to her work, which in nature was similar to Gray's in that it was subtle, considered and complex. By the late 1960s and early 1970s Gray had become increasingly reliant on Clough because of her deteriorating eyesight. With her niece, Gray felt she had found a kindred spirit.[1] Increasingly becoming a recluse towards the end of her life, Gray's friendship with Clough and their exchange of letters became Gray's lifeline until she died.[2] Gray told her, 'Your letters, telling me about yourself keep me alive, and just to see your envelope gives me a thrill'.[3]

Eileen Gray and Prunella Clough's letters give an insight into Eileen Gray's family. They also throw light on Gray's personality, tell us who she knew and had known, and show her interests, her opinions, her design ethic and above all her approach to her work, especially in the later years of her life. Despite her age Gray was exceedingly active, constantly working,

11.1 Prunella Clough in her studio, 1964, black and white photograph © Jorge Lewinski/ Topfoto

11.2 Eileen and Thora Gray,
1884, sepia tint photograph
© NMI

11.3 Eric Clough Taylor, by
George Beresford, 1914-18,
half-plate glass negative
© NMI

questioning, and experimenting with new materials to the end of her life. The letters illustrate the close friendship and bond that developed between aunt and niece during the post-war period. Gray told Clough in one letter that she was the only person to whom she really enjoyed writing.[4] The letters show how these two remarkable women were incredibly similar in their lives and their approach to their work. They reveal how Clough and Gray influenced one another, especially during Gray's later years. A symbiotic relationship developed gradually between these two women on both a personal and professional level. The letters also reveal Gray's wonderful sense of humour. Once when Gray was down in St. Tropez in 1964, she opened her missive to Clough on the festival of the Assumption of the Virgin with 'Not many Virgins here, anyway Dear Prunella ...'[5]

Prunella Clough was born on 11 November 1919 in Chelsea, London, and was brought up in an upper middle-class family. Her mother was Gray's sister Thora, and her father was Eric Clough Taylor. She enrolled in the Chelsea School of Art in 1937. She painted full-time until her death in 1999, interrupted only once during her wartime service. She also lectured at both Chelsea and Wimbledon Schools of Art. She is primarily renowned for her landscape scenes and industrial landscapes of post–World War II Britain.

Like her aunt, Clough talked little about her family background or mentioned that they were descended from Anglo-Irish aristocracy. Similarities abound between aunt and niece in their dysfunctional parental situation. Gray's parents' marriage was short lived, and the changes which occurred in her family when they separated would affect her for the remainder of her life. Clough's mother Thora Zelma Grace (1875-1966), was eight years older than Eric Clough Taylor (1883-1947). It is suggested that Clough's father had been indiscreet with a woman by the name of Ruth Anderson, who befriended both Thora and Prunella later in her life, which caused undue complications and strain.[6] Again like Gray, Clough was exceedingly close to her father and was devastated by his early death in 1947. She had a somewhat distant relationship with her mother, as did Gray with her mother. These coincidences meant that aunt and niece had a common thread between them. They both managed their privacy with skill; both were reticent, both circumvented questions regarding their personal lives. Gray destroyed many of her personal papers towards the end of her life, and in fact instructed Clough to destroy them for her. She wrote, 'I am very glad you tore up the letters. It's disquieting to think that they should still be lying about after all these years'.[7] Similarly when Ruth Anderson entrusted Clough with Eric Clough Taylor's letters to her, Clough closely guarded them. At the time of her final illness, she was particularly concerned for their safety.[8]

From their early letters it becomes clear that Clough kept Gray abreast of news of the Gray family in England. Gray's relationship with her family, especially her older sister Ethel and her husband Henry Tufnell Campbell, had been a tentative one. This was not the case with Thora, who was just a year older than Eileen, and her husband Eric. Thora and Prunella Clough regularly visited Gray in Paris, and Prunella continued to visit on her own on a very regular basis.[9] Thora and Eileen Gray were strikingly similar in looks, and at times it is difficult to distinguish between them in family photographs. They were often pictured together in childhood, later with groups of gentlemen admirers, on outings or holidaying together. From photographs of Prunella Clough, she at times also bears a striking resemblance to her aunt. Gray and her sister Thora were so close that even after Thora's marriage in 1911, she accompanied Gray and two other female friends to New York in 1912. They travelled all over the United States by train, visited the Rocky Mountains and the Grand Canyon, ending up in California.

11.4 Eileen and Thora Gray, 1890s, black and white photograph © NMI

Gray eagerly anticipated news of Thora in Clough's letters. Writing on 10 February 1945, Clough informs her that Thora was inundated with work for the war effort and continued to do everything for the family. Gray was also exceedingly fond of Eric. She proudly sent his poetry to friends, notably to Stephen Haweis, and kept portrait photographs of him taken by the Irish photographer George Beresford who also took a series of Gray's portrait.[10] After the war it became apparent from Prunella's letters that

Thora and Eric would welcome the possibility of Gray's return to England and that the family 'could fix things up for her'.[11] The family would have preferred a permanent return in order that Gray resume 'a relatively normal life'.[12] Celebrations were noted in Clough's diary when Gray did visit London after the war. Despite their warm welcome Gray chose to remain in France.

Gray's difficult relationship with her older sister Ethel became further strained after Ethel married Henry Tufnell Campbell. 'Henry was a snob, and Eileen, who never got on with Ethel, disliked him intensely'.[13] To Campbell manifestations of wealth were important, and he convinced Gray's mother to reclaim the title of Baroness Gray in the peerage of Scotland and to subsequently change the children's family name. He also prevailed on her to have the Georgian family home at Brownswood remodelled.[14] The Gray–Clough correspondence offers more insight into this relationship. Despite marrying well, Ethel's later circumstances were exceedingly tragic. She would outlive both her husband and two of her children. Henry and Ethel had four children, Violet (1891-1942), Lindsay (1894-1945), Henry (1896-1915) and Ian (1901-1946). Henry was killed at Ypres, Belgium, during World War I. Lindsay, despite being thrice wounded in World War I went on to fight in World War II. Clough noted in her diary that in early January 1946 Ian fell ill in Brussels with leukaemia. On his return to London his health declined further, and he died on 21 March 1946. Clough wrote in her diary 'Ethel's tragedy is complete'.[15] Ethel had already been widowed at the time Ian died, as Prunella had informed Gray in February 1945 that Henry Tufnell Campbell had died on 31 January 1945 and that Ethel was now living in a hotel.[16] The following year Ethel herself died, on 2 October 1946. Clough had organised nursing assistance for her until the end of September of that year when, despite Ethel's protests, she was moved into a nursing home.[17] Despite their differences throughout their years, especially concerning the estate and Brownswood, Gray paid her sister's hospital fees.

Clough was horrified to learn that Gray had done this as she hadn't realised that the Campbell's financial situation was problematic. Following Ethel's death Prunella and her mother organised Ethel's and Henry's affairs. In January 1947 they began to clear out 73 Pont Street, the Campbell's former home. They discovered that Henry Tufnell Campbell had kept detailed papers relating to family, business and personal matters in numerous trunks and boxes. Thora and Prunella had to make eleven journeys to Pont Street to remove all the private papers and possessions so that they could sort through them. Many of the trunks were locked and the keys were missing. They discovered one key labelled 'Fowl Bin, Brownswood'. Many of the objects and letters were intended for specific people and were identified accordingly. It was noted that nothing was labelled 'Eileen Gray'.[18] This aside, Gray had still come to London to tend to her sister during Ethel's final illness.

After Ethel's death Gray continued to send cards and gifts to Ethel's remaining two children and her grandchildren. One Christmas she wrote to Clough stating 'I suppose I shall have to find presents and cards for the Campbell Grays who never forget and so many who send them out of duty'.[19] In other letters she discussed presents which she was sending to four of Ethel's grandchildren, all children of Lindsay Stuart Campbell Gray (1894-1945), Angus (1931-2003), Fiona (1933-1991), Calain (1934-1987) and his wife Wendy Helen Katharine Dunlop and Christine (1938-1987). Gray mentions in several letters that Calain was coming to visit her in Paris and that she looked forward to the visit. She also mentions Christmas cards and tells anecdotal stories of the family. Gray asks Clough 'Pruny dear Pruny, do you remember whether you took along a present to send to Cailain (sic), there was a round brooch for Angus, the gold serpent for Fiona (thank you ever so much for sending them) and they wrote that they had got them but what about Cailain (sic) and Christine. Yesterday I found a small diamond serpent which I had thought would please Wendy, perhaps I forgot to give it to you to take, also there was a necklace with some sort of agates that I thought would do for Christine, can't remember if I gave it to you to take or not'.[20] Gray also mentions a family member to whom she had sent cuff links.[21] Gray was greatly saddened by memories of her family's past, telling her niece, 'Other letters that make me sad and that I must get rid of ... other people, all gone now ... into the unknown and again I feel like a ghost, something left behind'.[22]

11.5 Letter from Eileen Gray to Prunella Clough, 19 August 1970s, paper, typed ink, pen © NMI

Paris

Aug 19

CW

Love • Please Pruny you never seem to have a let-off
I think of you so much & worry .
Do hope you are going to have some rest
lately its been my fault

It seems so strange to be back here , almost as if Brittany was a different country; rather tiring arriving at midnight in that new enormous Gâre Montparnasse with its vast spaces where I lost Louise but found a policeman who was such a help .

Yesterday couldn't find anything to pack up the blue mattress to shew F.Stella in case He prefers the stitching but today we have got a carton & though it is too late to get it off today ,it shall go tomorrow without fail for it may take some days to arrive .

Looking for a paper that the Impôt people are wanting I came across some letters from you ,some quite old but so alive that I just can't tear them up & began to read them over again .

I feel Pruny , more than ever that if you are dis-satisfied sometimes with your career as a painter you would be just as gifted (a word I hate) as a writer & have lots to say :Do you ever think of it ?

Other letters that make me sad & that I must get rid of , Gabriel Soudkowski from Canada ,little Haweis & his lamentations from Dominica , Kate . . other people ,all gone now . . into the unknown & again I feel like a ghost ,something left behind. . .

I'm afraid you must be cold now in the hall with this queer August weather , I'm glad to turn on th chauffage here.

Would it be an awful bother to send over some Complan ,Two packets , not to me But to Louise's sister whose husband is very ill. (too complicated to explain now . This is her address
Madame Pierre Le Corguillé
II Rue St Jullien
56 Malestroit

Morbihan   Bretagne .
Two packets will be quite enough to see if it does any good ,am sending you a cheque for 5 pounds as I am su I ____owing you for the others .
Louis_ has just come back from the tapissier (the one who threw up the job) but who kept the padded rod that goes under the mattress for the knees ,but it was not

Gray asserted her Irish background not only in letters to Clough but also to others. And she never forgot Brownswood, the family home and estate in Ireland. Gray talked about Brownswood to Clough, describing once how a friend's sister was detained there for a short time, as her old family home had become 'now a sort of sanatorium'.[23] Clough never mentioned Brownswood or her Irish heritage in correspondence but Clough's mother Thora felt the same way about Ireland as did her sister.

Sunday Dec 26

Pruny dear , it was wonderful to have that long letter
but I've been sort of swamped,getting off these cards &
letters (Fiona had taken the trouble to order a pot of
Hyercinthes sent from some place here I can't think how)
        Yesterday I took round a card for Hamlet & Bun-
ny, today Bunny came round to say that the sister died
last Friday & they are leaving tomorrow . Mackay's sister though I didn't know her then,lived quite near us at
Gorey Co Wexford . She had completely lost her memory &
was interned for a short time at Brownswood ,now a sort
of Sanatorium.!
        You must have enjoyed that day with K-P & the
BBC people I often think of the afternoon we spent at the
Studios   I have had to give up trying to do the maquette of the Coiffeuse . (My Hand has got much worse ,&
yet I don't feel that a plan will be sufficient as I want
to see the proportions with the whole structure ; If I
could have a student .. .. ..
        You have just telephoned & I was in despair not bein
able to hear . The truth is that these little Batteries
when they are rechargeable wear out very quickly ,& when
one is nervous knowing that some one is waiting , it
takes a little time to find the other kind & put it in pl
place . I am so sorry,Was longing to talk to you!
        As you know I went to Bob Walkers new flat & was
very impressed ,the big room was most attractive pale
beige walls & floor ,beige marble ! the floor & walls the
same colour made it look bigger & they had arranged it wi
with only my things 3 Transats, the boat shaped thing &
the long mirrors , Two or three big paintings ,pretty aw
ful sort of Pre-Burne-Jones;the figaro announces a big
exhibition of the preRaphaelites; He said he was hoping
that you would come ,so I didn't say that you had been
here , no questions about more stuff of mine so probably
he thinks he has enough . He found the transats comfortable & they are still in fairly good condition so I hope
Sheila is pleased with his too .
        Yes at night thoughts do accrocher themselves
in one's mind ,magnified , & offer no solution .
Amongst other things I have to decide what to do with the
piece of ground at the back of Lou Perou . The vines are
dead & must be replaced by some thing ,for if the ground
is left bare people will come & park their cars on it

2

If I try & replace the vines I shall have to have a trac
tor to défoncer all the ground , the new vines will have
to be gréffé & will take 4 years before they give raisin
        If I plant fruit trees ,they will have to be wa-
tered which means prolonging the pipes for water & getting a man to look after them ,as it is quite uncertain
whether Jacques will stay with the Fassettis .
        It is important to decide now, later the groun
will be too hard to défoncé; but this morning I have
a very nice letter from the President of the RIBA who
hopes to see me when he comes to Paris & seems pleased
with the maquettes also I have the little table ready
for Irvine but how to get it to him ?
        I didn't mean to bother you with all this ,&
now its late & this will have to wait till tomorrow
to be posted .
I quite agree about the coiffeuse there is a wood calle
Zebrano that I think would be good but the places where
they might have it are Miles away & hard to find .
        Am so glad to know that you are working
the success of that exhibition ought to give you a bi
    boost so just tear up this letter & don't
think of it again . How did you like the Saky
    Strange a japonese shop in Wimbledon

    My love & hoping you have peace in the New Year

11.6 Letter from Eileen Gray to Prunella Clough, Sunday, 26 December year unknown, paper, typed ink, pen © NMI

Clough informed Gray on one occasion that Thora wanted to visit Ireland, whereas Clough preferred going to her aunt in Paris.[24] Thora had gone by ferry to Ireland with Eric and some friends in 1934, 1935 and again in 1937. They travelled by car visiting Achill Island, the Giant's Causeway, Horn Head and Rosapenna in County Donegal. Numerous photographs in the Clough archive show two friends of Gray's, Olive Pixley and Jessie Gavin with Thora and Eric on these journeys.[25] Clough's letters to Gray reveal that Thora continued to travel to Ireland during the 1940s. It is possible that Gray came with them as it is now known that she was visiting Ireland until the 1950s.

It was during her teenage years that Clough first became aware of her famous aunt, whom she saw little of as a child, as Gray was at that time living in Paris.[26] Their early letters give an insight into Gray's life during the war.[27] Letters from 1945 through to 1948 inform us about their lives after the war. After the blitz began in London Clough acted as a fire watcher. Early in 1941 she was conscripted by the Ministry of Labour. In May of 1943 she was with the Military Railways section of the European Theatre of Operations, United States Army, where she was engaged as a mapping and engineering draughtsman.

During the Second World War Gray had remained for the first year in Castellar in the South of France. In April 1942 she was forced to leave, as resident aliens could not live near the sea. Initially she went to St. Tropez where she had an apartment on the quai Suffren. However, she was requested to move inland and settled initially in Lourmarin and in 1943 in Cavaillon in the Vaucluse region. Times were exceedingly tough. The family sent money and packages from London and Gray had thought of going to England but said 'I can't bear the thought of leaving France and feel I should be homesick if I did go'.[28] In an early letter to her niece Gray tells how Clough's letter 'was a joy. It seemed like having a companion somehow. Life at Lourmarin is very solitary'.[29] Gray described in this letter how Kate Weatherby was looking into the possibility of obtaining for herself and Gray visas to travel to England via Lisbon but how Gray is undecided as 'It will be terrible leaving France. I don't yet know what to decide but we are all gradually getting weaker –& more and more enervé at this forced inaction & it reacts on my brain'. She continued: 'Anger is perhaps the greatest inspiration on those days when the individual is separated into so many personalities. Suddenly one is all in one piece'. In 1944 the bombing by retreating forces destroyed Gray's apartment in St. Tropez. Her house *Tempe à Pailla* was also pillaged by retreating forces, and when she returned there in 1946 she had to begin anew to recreate the interior, the furniture and the furnishings. Gray wrote to the family in London during the war years, though her letters sometimes took months to reach their destination.[30] She continued to work producing furniture, gouaches and sculptures, and worked on hypothetical architectural projects. She had financial problems at the time and attempted to obtain money from her bank in Paris. The Germans had put a hold on her bank accounts and assets.[31] Clough in London looked to get art supplies from Paris during this period. She managed to receive parcels from a friend in Paris containing four boxes of crayons and handmade paper so that she could continue to work. Clough in return sent this young friend coffee via Army mail in December 1944 which her friend never received.[32]

11.7 Letter from Eileen Gray to Prunella Clough, 19 September 1942, paper, ink © NMI

By the outbreak of World War II Gray was already renowned as a designer and architect, with a distinguished reputation intact whereas Clough was then only embarking on her career. She produced her first signed and dated significant painting *Sea Composition* in 1940. The Gray-Clough, aunt-niece, relationship blossomed during this period, especially when Clough began to paint. Prunella struggled to work during the war, but towards the end of 1944 her interest was renewed and she kept a diary from November 1944 to February 1947 detailing wartime events. After the liberation she noted in her diary on 3 December 1944 that she was eager for news from Paris. Despite the fact that Gray refused to return to England during the war, she did finally visit her family in December 1945. Clough anticipated this visit writing 'I dare not hope too much, but it is possible'.[33] Gray by this time was sixty-seven years of age, yet her knowledge of art, design and architecture dominated the conversations between aunt and niece. Clough clearly records these in her diary and how the two became close. Clough coded people's names in her diary, often just using their initials – Gray often did likewise in her correspondence, as if aunt and niece shared their own specific language.

During her December 1945 visit to London Gray was introduced to a young architectural student, Richard Pollock. Gray was now completely engrossed in post-war architecture, especially in new housing programmes in distressed and underdeveloped areas, and she was keen to see examples in and around the London area. Pollock phoned Clough and arranged an outing to visit a housing centre in Northolt. They examined prefabricated buildings, modular and industrialised units which Gray had been exploring in designs for collective communities or environments. Clough 'felt out of place and after an abortive visit to the Finsbury Health Centre, built in the 1930s by Tecton, reckoned that her appreciation of architecture would always remain theoretical. She wondered, with some amazement, how her aunt had ever got her mind around the constructional complexities attendant on building'.[34] The threesome also visited the Office of Public Works to view the site of the Tate Gallery which had been badly damaged during the war and, later again, the library at the Royal Institute of British Architects. Here they discussed Jean Badovici, building, painting and methods of training.[35]

After this encounter with Pollock and Clough and on her return to Paris, Gray re-examined in detail her pre-fabricated housing proposal. Gray purchased the booklet *The Rehousing of Britain,* 1946, by John Madge. Gray had been experimenting with worker and social housing since the 1930s and had completed detailed plans for the *Ellipse house*, 1936. Some of the houses illustrated in Madge's book are light steel frame type, easily erected and low cost. Both the ideas in John Madge's publication and the architectural visits contributed to Gray's design for the *Agricultural worker's house*, 1945-46. She

11.8 *The Rehousing of Britain,* by John Madge, 1946 © NMI

addressed the issues and conditions of social housing which she had witnessed first-hand in London through the provision in her design of space, light and ventilation.[36]

Pollock became an avid admirer of Gray and she continued to inquire after him, especially after he became gravely ill with pneumonia. Despite his illness he learnt that Gray had visited London again, 'He's heard somehow that you'd been here – asked about you at once and suggested rushing off to Paris tomorrow to look at buildings'.[37] Clough informed Gray on 1 March 1947 that Pollock has recovered: she had met him at a party where they had a lengthy discussion regarding house property.[38] The encounter with Pollock inspired both Gray and Clough. Gray perfected her prefabricated Post-War housing designs and Clough's appreciation of architectural theory improved. She kept up with developments in the field and subscribed to the *Architectural Review,* which she sent to her aunt in Paris. In a 1961 postcard Gray thanks Clough for the delightful card and 'how very good of you to send the *Architectural Review'*.[39]

From this point onwards Clough noted each of Gray's visits in her appointments diaries. The times spent were recorded as a single word 'talk' or 'Eileen studio'.[40] Clough's development as an artist is carefully recorded in her notebooks. Her stylistic development with her drawings, prints, collages and paintings were acutely watched as well by her aunt. Gray was delighted when Clough moved out of the damp studio in 53 Cadogan Place to a new one in Beaufort Street. Gray was often encouraging, offering her niece advice, coaxing her to push herself further. In one letter she recommended that she take a break from painting, suggesting that Clough should work with other materials. At other times Gray offered advice on how to hang a painting or how to have it mounted or framed. On 1 March 1947 she recommends that Clough use black frames for paintings which were due to go on exhibition.[41] Gray praises Clough when she deemed it merited – sometimes in quite a maternal tone. Gray proudly compliments Clough, saying how she must be pleased that the celebrated abstract artist Bridget Riley (b.1931) had purchased one of her paintings.[42] Gray eventually became a great admirer of Clough's work, and in a letter dated 20 September 1972 she thanked her for the drawing which Clough had given her. 'I love the little drawing you gave me, we can get it framed too, the same way, a colour you could choose.'[43] Gray ended this letter by saying 'good luck to the new painting'.

At other times Gray was critical. Gray did this, not to insult or hurt Clough in any way but to develop the young artist's potential. Clough mentioned in her diaries her irritation with her aunt being critical of her approach to her work during a visit in December 1946 through into 1947. Gray's comments pushed Clough to enrol in the Camberwell School of Art two days a week, but she was still 'Irritated with E who wondered, I think, why I didn't intend to work there every day (a thing I would never do, even in '37): ignoring the work of the war years'.[44]

Gray also saw the potential in Clough's other artistic abilities. She believed that if painting proved difficult that her niece could just as easily succeed as a writer. 'I came across some letters from you, some quite old but so alive that I just can't tear them up and began to read them over again. I feel Pruny, more than ever, that if you are dis-satisfied sometimes with your career as a painter you would be just as gifted (a word I hate) as a writer and have lots to say. Do you ever think of it?'[45] Gray enjoyed her niece's painterly descriptions of things 'I like your description of the daily walk up to the shops on a wet windy morning. I could see it all'. In the same letter Gray says 'Your letters are a joy and I am interested in everything you tell me'.[46] Whilst attempting to destroy personal records she stated 'so many things I ought to have done here in the flat, (& haven't) tearing up old papers, marking what I want to leave people. I hate to tear up your letters, they are so full of life, and you always find just the word that "fits" to describe situations'.[47]

Clough provided the impetus for Gray to continue to produce gouaches, monotypes and collages during her later years. It is not widely realised that Gray was still working in her nineties. However, her tendency to doubt her ability as an artist continued to plague her in later life just as it had done during her student years. She questioned whether it was worthwhile finishing up a few of her monotypes and gouaches as Clough would have to throw them out or tear them up.[48] Clough at times experienced similar self-doubt, questioning her own work and her ability, and she shared with Gray in one letter how she was 'getting out old canvases, and looking at them in a rather bleak way'.[49]

Both women's work was, at times, stylistically similar, one inspiring the other through their interest in surface textures, non-figuration, mark making and experimental techniques. They shared a profound interest in art movements, various artists' work, contemporary exhibitions, photography, maps and philosophy. Both responded to the changes in the artistic and intellectual climate. Gray and Clough 'shared a desire to extract essentials and both frequently resorted to geometry as if it was a personal alphabet'.[50] During the 1950s Clough's work carefully placed objects directly into the composition. This style recalled Gray's carpet gouaches and collages of the early to mid-1920s in their decorative, compositional approach. Clough's *Still Life in Workshop,* 1951 is stylistically and compositionally similar to Gray's *Bobadilla,* 1919-1922.

By the late 1930s Gray's carpet and collage work had become more abstract, reflective of her appreciation for the De Stijl and Russian constructivist movements. She was especially intrigued by Kazimir Malevich's painting *Black Square*, which had a white border surrounding a black square. She also was inspired by his new treatment of spatial references. This black square motif appeared several times in various formats in her gouache work such as in *Black and speckled square* gouache, early 1930s,[51] *Navy blue square with white stripe* gouache, 1918-21,[52] and the two versions of *Black and white square carpet* gouaches, 1918-21.[53]

11.9 Navy blue square with white stripe gouache, 1920s, paper, paint © NMI

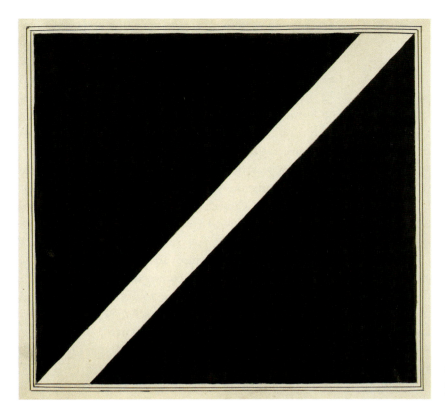

11.10 Black and white stripe carpet gouache, 1920s, paper, paint © NMI

Clough explored similar principles, where her compositions are based on an absolute, pure geometrical abstract art. In these paintings Clough gives primacy to the square form. This language was a suitable expression for her postmodernist industrial painting. Paintings such as *Black Edge/ Yellow,* 1975 (Private Collection), *Brown Wall,* 1974 (Pallant House Gallery, Chichester), *Double Diamond,* 1973 (Private Collection) and especially *Black Gate,* 1979 (Private Collection), directly link to Gray's treatment of Malevich's ideas. Clough differed from Gray in the perception of the 'edge'. This reflected Clough's habit of outlining a shape with a modulated or slightly toned colour, providing an awareness of the edge especially where the other colours of the composition meet.

In 1977 when Clough painted *Black Gate,* Gray had been dead a year. Themes of death surround this painting, executed just after Clough had also lost her close friend the artist Keith Vaughan (1912-1977). The theme of the black and white square appears again where Clough takes Gray's version, blowing it up to monumental proportions – the painting is five feet high.

11.11 *E.1027* showing the black gate, 1926-29, black and white photograph © NMI

11.12 Letter from Eileen Gray to Prunella Clough, 1960, paper, typed ink © NMI

Shall have a try before I go.
          Otherwise there is not very much , or perhaps
I haven't had time to hear about things ; Cocteau
very much to the fore as his film le testament d'Orphée
is being given now . Iwas looking forward to something
really mysterious knowing that the mise en scène
was turned at les Baux , but was disappointed , I think
because of Cocteau's insistence of putting himself
au premier plan throughout . Isuppose you have it in
London
          It must be maddening to feel Mrs T lying in wait f
for you , all the same , when you once get inside
the little court , the Studio has a remote feeling
that would be hard to find elsewhere . Tell me more
about your work . I think its inevitable you should
feel irritable after having had to revise all your
dates . This is also "just to communicate" will
write again

Monday . no post yesterday & it appears that the
Lorry is still waiting for Bernard Buffet's pictures
to go to Cannes ; have you heard about his show now
on , the Birds 99 times as large or rather larger
than Life plus the Lady , Annabel I suppose ,I thought
they were awful ,

          love to both

The title of the painting *Black Gate* has another meaning with themes of life and death. 'Gate' also implies 'threshold', as if one is passing through the nebulous white square and black rectangle to a transformative experience.[54] But the painting also directly links to Gray's architectural work *E.1027*. Gray was inspired by Malevich's painting while designing the garden gate at this house. It is not known if Clough had ever visited *E.1027* prior to her visiting with Peter Adam in 1977 after Gray's death, the same year in which she painted *Black Gate*. The gate formed an important part of the journey through the house from the interior to the exterior. It leads from the living room terrace, the central point in the house, to the garden and marks the boundary between interior and exterior. *E.1027* is also about a journey from the interior to the exterior and explored themes surrounding the third and fourth dimension. It is very possible that Clough's *Black Gate* also marked these journeys.

Clough and Gray in their letters discussed the lives and work of various artists or exhibitions which interested them. Gray felt that contemporary art was losing its identity.[55] In many letters Gray was highly critical of artists and various art movements. In other letters she recommends exhibitions for Prunella and her friend David Carr to visit. Gray believed in the importance of the artist and the resulting work. At times her view of the status of an artist in society was idealistic. [56]

Gray was critical of all aspects of the arts – not just painting. She tells Clough of her disappointment after seeing Jean Cocteau's film *Le Testament d'Orphée* (the Testament of Orpheus). The film directed by and starring Cocteau was the final part of the Orphic Trilogy, following *The Blood of a Poet,* 1930, and *Orphée,* 1950. The film, in black and white, had just a few seconds of colour spliced into it. Gray declared she was truly disappointed because of 'Cocteau's insistence of putting himself au premier plan throughout'.[57]

Gray frequently mentioned people whom she knew or who were important to her in her letters. In many cases she talks about friends who have died and about her early years in Paris. Reminiscing on her student years she wrote to Clough that she was saddened to see a section of the Académie Julian closing down.[58] When discussing the past she became somewhat philosophical. 'Personally I am brainless when in contact with people. Its (sic) only when one feels one can count on being alone, when one can let one's brain free wheel, that one has moments of lucidity getting underneath things'.[59] She quotes another furniture designer, Isamu Noguchi (1904-1988), who said that 'things which are so far back are not like a part of myself, more like the life of somebody else'.[60]

'Other letters that make me sad and that I must get rid of, ... little Haweis and his lamentations from Dominica, Kate (Weatherby) ... other people, all gone now ... into the unknown and again I feel like a ghost, something left behind'.[61] Names are often coded in her letters – in that Gray only wrote their initials. Stephen Haweis gets several mentions. 'The old bird in Domenica, (sic) you remember has been trying to sell his house in Italy (Florence) for years, and thought he'd arranged everything with the tenant, who declared she was ready to buy it, and called the sale off at the last minute. He is, I fear on the rocks, so I want to help. But the silly creature hardly gives me any information, so I've had to send him a list of questions'.[62] Gray frequently sent Haweis things to read – books and articles – and often asked Clough to find publications for her to send to him. In one letter she tells Clough that she has sent him a new work by Peter Scott.[63] Towards the end of his life Haweis was suffering from paranoia and became increasingly ill. In the final letter in which she mentioned him she shared that she was concerned that 'Stephen Hawys (sic) is ill, haven't heard from him'.[64]

Her niece hears about the visit of actress Ginger Moro to her aunt's apartment. Moro, née Hall, worked for Paramount Studio where she had secondary parts in several films. She ended up in Paris where she made her home for sixteen years and appeared in French films and on British television. She was also a founding member of the Studio Theatre of Paris. She studied at the École du Louvre and eventually opened an antique shop in Montparnasse specialising in jewellery and decorative art objects. She married the Italian-American actor and director Russ Moro and eventually moved back to California in the 1970s. In her letter Gray relates that Moro remained with her for three hours and wanted to come back with a photographer to takes images for an article which she was preparing on Gray.[65] Moro lived on rue Bonaparte and describes Gray as extraordinary. She sent Gray a long letter with a photograph after their meeting,[66] which initiated an extensive correspondence between Gray and Moro in 1975.[67] Moro advised her about the work which she was completing at the time, notably block screens, as she found that the price of construction was exorbitant. Moro later commented that they had 'bonded immediately … we respected and admired many of the same designers'.[68]

Gray had travelled to America in 1912. New York had a profound effect on her, especially its recent architecture. After Clough had visited New York, Gray wrote to her saying 'the buildings do look so marvellous especially at night … Europe seems very small when one first gets back.'[69] Gray was in New York again in 1934 and visited the Austrian architect Frederick Kiesler (1890–1965).[70] He had moved there in 1926 but the exact date as to when she had been introduced to him by Jean Badovici is not known – though it happened some time in or around 1925.[71]

Kiesler influenced and inspired Gray in different ways. He exhibited the installation *City in Space* at the Austrian Theatre and Architectural Pavilion at the Exposition Nationale des Arts Décoratifs 1925. The installation, composed of thin wooden beams and supports displaying a theatre set, stage and costume designs, looked to De Stijl spatial principles.[72] Gray had kept a flyer called 'La Contre architecture', written by Maurice Reynal.

Gray had an affinity with Kiesler's spiritual approach to architecture, the layout of the modern interior and the attention paid to the inhabitant who occupied the space. Such ideas informed her dialogue with Badovici in *L'Architecture Vivante,* published in 1929.[73]

Gray sometimes mentions her old circle in Paris, notably Kate Weatherby and Evelyn Wyld. One letter informs Clough that Kate Weatherby is unwell.[74] Weatherby arrived in Paris with Evelyn Wyld in 1907. She came from a wealthy brewer's family, and was a very sporty young lady who loved horse riding.[75] Like Gray, she was independent of character and had a strong personality, coming to Paris to escape the constraints of her family life. Gray was only a year older. Weatherby encouraged and initiated many projects, influencing Wyld to produce rugs, and Gray furniture. During the war she began working with French farmers and moved down south.

When Eileen Gray's relations with Damia soured, Weatherby came to visit her at Samois-sur-Seine. She encouraged Gray to exhibit her work, and open her shop *Jean Désert*. After World War I, Weatherby bought a house at St. Tropez, which was called *La Bastide Blanche*. Gray named one of her carpets after it. It was an attractive location, which she continued to visit for fifty years. When Wyld became involved with Eyre de Lanux, Weatherby remained at St. Tropez. There she was joined by a new friend, Gert Goldsmith, another carpet designer. During World War II Gray, Weatherby and Wyld all had to move to Lourmarin, a small town north of Aix in the Vaucluse region. Weatherby and Wyld rented a little house called Lointes Bastides, while Gray rented an apartment in the town. Gray remained friends with Weatherby, and into her seventies she continued to go to *La Bastide Blanche*. On 14 March 1964 Weatherby died.[76] Gray was upset by her death.

In one particular letter Gray told Clough what had become of Wyld. Sometime in 1927 Wyld met Eyre de Lanux and they began a professional collaboration.[77] Lanux was born Elizabeth Eyre in 1894 and studied at the Art Students League New York. Adopting her grandfather's name, she changed it to Eyre de Lanux in the 1920s. Initially a painter, she designed a few pieces of cubist-style furniture. Her professional collaboration with Wyld lasted from 1927 to 1935. However she became romantically involved with Wyld and left her husband. She moved in 1929 with Wyld to *La Bastide Blanche* and then to *La Bastide Caillenco*. Lanux was a contributor to *Town and Country* magazine in the 1920s with her articles 'Letters of Elizabeth'. When Gray and Wyld's professional collaboration ended, Wyld left with Lanux in 1929 and moved to St. Tropez and then to La Roquette sur Siagne to open a décor shop in Cannes. It lasted only briefly. They designed lacquer work and interiors, with the assistance of Seizo Sugawara. Lanux and Wyld exhibited at the 1927, 1929 and 1932 Salon des Artistes Décorateurs and at the Union des Artistes (*UAM*) in 1930. Wyld's rugs were also shown in 1930 at the Curtis Moffat Gallery, London. In one particular letter Gray gives the impression that Wyld was never responsible for the designs, stating 'Wyld didn't design anything herself but combined with a friend Elizabeth de Lanux and they had for a little time a shop in Cannes but soon gave it up'.[78] This is known to be incorrect. Despite their professional partnership coming to an end Gray and Wyld remained friends. In one letter Clough asked Gray about the location of some of her rugs for display in the *Heinz Gallery exhibition* in London. Gray replied that 'the Germans looted all my rugs in 1940', but that she could write to Wyld who perhaps 'kept some of mine'.[79] Gray also wondered in another letter if after the Gray-Wyld partnership had dissolved and the Lanux-Wyld partnership had formed, whether Wyld 'produced any of the carpets I designed though Elizabeth de Lanux did some rather like mine'.[80] In the early 1970s RIBA curator John Harris was organising an exhibition on Wyld and Lanux. Gray noted in a letter that she was quite pleased that RIBA planned to exhibit Wyld's carpets, some designed by de Lanux, and some by me, at the same time.[81]

The letters reveal as much about Clough as they do about Gray.[82] From one dated 1 March 1947 we learn that Clough has been approached by Hugh Willoughby who was with the Léger Galleries in Old Bond Street, London and was also a friend of Fernand Léger. He had approached her requesting twelve canvases for an exhibition. Clough also corresponded with Léger who told her that Willoughby would deal directly with her regarding the exhibition. Léger had also been a friend and associate of Gray's. However, Willoughby fell ill, and Léger asked Clough to bring fifteen to eighteen paintings for him to select from for the exhibition, which she would share with two other artists. But her session with Léger was disappointing. Clough brought seventeen paintings, and he complained about the varying sizes of her canvases.

Clough hoped that Gray might be able to attend the opening because Clough had already shown her a number of the paintings. She displayed two still lives, *The White Root*, which she painted in 1946, and the large painting of *The Fisherman with Skate*, which she describes with fishing nets and the anchor with ropes. This is now identified as the painting *Nets and Anchor,* 1946. Clough also mentioned a painting titled *Encounter on Scaffolding*. The inspiration for this painting possibly came from Clough's conversations with Gray regarding architecture and painting. It was also inspired by spending an afternoon with her father in Flimwell where she made notes about bricklayers and tilers working on houses.

Clough also stated in a letter that the other paintings included in the exhibition were of a trawler scene with fishermen, a small marsh landscape, a brightly coloured still life, a large boat with a small man who

Sunday Later

have just thought P- took away lasttime some addresses of old clients . Here is the model of a letter which I was to transilate into French , I realized afterwards that these addresses were only of "chance "Clients , those who bought the big things the vendeuse hasn't mentioned I don't want you to have the bother of sending the letters ,especially if it prevents in any way your going off for a rest so please don't bother
       E Wyld didn't design anything herself but com-bined with a friend Elizabeth de Lannux ,& they had for a little time a shop in Cannes but soon gave it up
              Here is K-P

The Model you made for me

11.13 Letter from Eileen Gray to Prunella Clough, Sunday, January 1960, paper, typed ink © NMI is mussel fishing, and two paintings of the quarry. Gray had recommended that Clough use black frames for the exhibition – advice which she took. Clough's exhibition finally opened on 25 March 1947 – delayed due to severe weather which had affected the whole country. Her work was displayed alongside pictures by Walter H. Nessler. Fourteen of her works were displayed.[83]

The Gray-Clough correspondence informs us of Gray's approach to her work and demonstrates her undiminished energy, despite her age, for completing work and various commissions. They also highlight Gray's perfectionism, which was at times obsessive and often debilitating. Gray liked to control not only her environment but also the people around her. After Thora's death on 13 April 1966, Gray flew to London for the funeral. Aunt and niece dined together and next day, following the cremation, Gray returned to Paris. From this point on it appears that Clough became increasingly involved in Gray's personal and business affairs. In some of her letters Gray adopts a very maternal tone towards Clough. Gray never had children, and Clough became the closest thing to a daughter she would have. Gray enjoyed her trips to London to spend time with her niece and missed her terribly upon her return. After one journey she wrote 'I miss you dreadfully, more than the other times, perhaps because I understand a little more. You are a person very hard to know, for outwardly expansive you very rarely let one see what goes on inside'.[84]

At other times Gray's recurring professional or domestic crises exhausted Clough to the point that it affected her health, even after Gray's death.[85] By 1978 Clough's continued efforts to sort her aunt's effects was having an affect on her work. 'So distracted. EG desk, work most of the day – another day – it is so much worse than even last year'.[86]

In 1968 architectural historian Joseph Rykwert approached Clough about writing an article on Gray's life and work. This article was published in *Domus* in December of that year and entitled 'Un Omaggio a Eileen Gray'.[87] It was the first serious appreciation of her work as an architect, re-introducing Gray to new architects and designers.[88] Gray had read about and knew of Rykwert's work, stating that she thought an article he wrote on the Bauhaus was excellent, insightful and extraordinary.[89] Clough had known Rykwert

11.14 Letter from Eileen Gray to Prunella Clough, 26 October circa 1968, paper, typed ink © NMI

Lou Pérou

October 26

Dear Prune , The weather has all changed ,heavy rain last night B& very uncertain today , but I must scrape d down the shutters & give a coat of paint ,if not they will rot .
    Reading over last night the article by J-R on the Bauhaus , I thought it excellent . such insight & total amalgum of a foreign language , I thought extraordinary .
    As for the one for Domus , I am very sorry not to be in Paris ;shall be there on the 5th but that will probably be too late . You did tell him that I was born in Ireland , didn't you , for the few old figures that remain I was known as Irish which I much preferred .

No News here , almost all the people have gone the St Tropezians too as they take their holidays now , painters & maçonr ,one has to do what one can oneself am going now to paint the front door & the courette

    shall hope for a line before I go but I daresay you are too busy

    love

since the 1940s, and he was astonished to learn from her that Gray was her aunt. Gray stressed to Clough that the one piece of information she wanted Rykwert to note in his article was that she was Irish. She wrote 'You did tell him that I was born in Ireland, didn't you, for the old few figures that remain, I was known as Irish, which I much preferred'.[90] Gray described Rykwert as 'Really an extraordinary person'.[91] Following his interview Gray was concerned that she had given him incorrect dates for her studies. She was also fearful of divulging too much information and complained that he brought that infernal machine that records and that 'it may have registered things which I ought not to have spoken about'. The *Domus* article instigated a major revival of Gray's career. She was so proud of the article that she kept two copies in her personal diary.[92] It resulted in the 1972 exhibition at the Heinz Gallery in London, curated by Alan Irvine, showing her buildings, interiors, designs and projects. This was followed by an exhibition with Clough's agent in London, Monika Kinley, who held an exhibition in her gallery in London in 1975. Other exhibitions occurred in Dublin, Paris, Los Angeles and Vienna. To some exhibitions she sent a large amount of photographs – some didn't return.[93]

All of these exhibitions were carefully recorded at length in the correspondence. There are many accounts of Gray working on architectural models or on her architectural portfolios in order to prepare them to go on display in these exhibitions. Of the models which were displayed at the Heinz Gallery exhibition Gray discussed the *House for Two Sculptors*, *the Ellipse house*, *the Vacation and Leisure centre*, and *the Cultural and Social centre*. The original models for the *House for Two Sculptors* are currently in RIBA archives; however, the whereabouts of the *Vacation and Leisure centre* and the *Cultural and Social centre* models are now unknown. One letter reveals that Gray was having difficulty locating the base of the model of the *House for Two Sculptors*, and the *Vacation and Leisure centre* model was missing pillars which due to the shake in her hand she was having trouble replacing. 'The House for the Two sculptors is nowhere to be found and I spend sleepless nights and wary days ransacking every cupboard to find it; for the *Centre de Vacances* takes up too much room and would have to be entirely re-painted, several pillars are missing and with my bad hand, I don't think it is possible'.[94] She became preoccupied about the model for the *Vacation and Leisure centre* writing 'The *Centre de Vacances* looks terribly dull, I wonder whether it would look better if the ground was painted a pale beige ... These caravan places are generally sandy & it might give it more life'.[95] Despite her achievements as an architect the fact that such work was being put on display constantly filled her with doubts as to whether her work was good enough or presentable. She wrote in one letter to the architect of the exhibition Alan Irvine 'I am not sure that any of the models are worthy for an exhibition'.[96]

11.15 *House for Two Sculptors*, original model, 1933-34, wood, paper, card © RIBA Library Drawings and Archive Collections

11.16 *Ellipse house*, original model, 1936, wood, paper, card © RIBA Library Drawings and Archive Collections

When Badovici died in 1956 the *UAM* (Union des Artistes Modernes) organised a memorial exhibition in November of that year. Gray's offer to assist was declined, and as a result *E.1027* was attributed to 'Jean Badovici with the collaboration of Eileen Gray for the furniture'.[97] This prompted her to compile architectural portfolios, of which it was believed there were only two. The Gray-Clough correspondence reveals otherwise. In one letter she stated that the larger architectural portfolios were created from 'four small notebooks'.[98] Writing to Clough, Gray notes 'I am uniting all the small cahiers into the large one. There are a good many explanations in French which I try to translate into English'.[99] In another letter she wrote, 'I am going on with the photos in the big cahier, as it seemed better to try and group things together; I mean Roquebrune, Castellar & the small cahiers of the "culture et loisirs"'.[100] A third small portfolio existed which went on exhibition to Vienna and never returned, but two pages which Gray removed from this smaller portfolio illustrate photographs and plans of the *Vacation and Leisure centre* and still remain.

The existence of another Eileen Gray architectural portfolio is important. The extant portfolios contain the work in which she took the greatest pride. Critics have questioned why some of her early architectural work, such as her study of Adolf Loos's *Villa Moissi,* the houses at Vézelay, numerous private and public housing studies, apartment proposals, exhibition spaces, and her worker's colony were absent from the larger portfolios. The exclusion of this work has been interpreted to mean that she viewed it as too derivative, the private commissions indicative of a lifestyle that she was unable to embrace, and the later work too schematic. Such gaps prove the idealism that governed her work.[101] Nonetheless, the discovery that another smaller portfolio existed clearly calls into question this viewpoint.

Gray spent days typing up the captions for the portfolios; Clough helped her at times. She noted that she regretted giving 'all the importance to carpets and early decorations' as she feels they will be of little interest to anyone. Whereas her architectural work such as *Tempe à Pailla*, the *Vacation and Leisure centre*, *E.1027* and the *Cultural and Social centre* 'are much more important to me but are collected in such a small space that students would never trouble to look at them, the cahiers (portfolios) are so small'. The portfolios were also important because as Gray noted, they include 'a few photos of the Maison en Bord de Mer (*E.1027*) which

were not published in the book', referring to the 1929 Winter Edition of
L'Architecture Vivante.[102]

Throughout her correspondence Gray discusses the domestic
architectural projects which she completed – but much of the
discussion centres around work at her last house *Lou Pérou*. *E.1027* is
Gray's most renowned domestic architectural project. The Gray-Clough
correspondence reveals a surprising opinion expressed by Gray after seeing
photographs of the house in 1970. She wrote to Clough 'I didn't like them
(the photographs), the house itself, without
any shelter to the terrace and plastic on the
roof instead of glass, looked smaller and
lacked atmosphere'.[103] Again in another
letter she wrote 'Had to go to the house at
Roquebrune ten days ago, too complicated
to tell you now, but it was most ghastly
and upsetting'.[104] At this point in her life
E.1027 brought back too many unpleasant
professional and personal memories for
Gray. Peter Adam, Gray's biographer and
Clough's best friend noted in his memoirs
that the first time he asked Gray to go to see
E.1027 she adamantly refused as 'd'anciens
griefs referent surface' (old grievances
resurfaced).[105] When she finally decided
to go, one day in June 1967, they parked at
the pathway which led to the house. Gray
brusquely stopped and said, 'Je ne peux pas y
aller, c'est trop tard de toute façon. Regarde
ce qu'ils on fait de cet endroit' (I cannot go
there. It is too late anyway. Look what they
did to this place).[106]

Despite this, Gray was still interested in
the original furniture which had been in
E.1027. In September 1971 she learned from
an Italian antiques dealer and collector
Madame Capuano, who was based in Monaco
that several original pieces of furniture

11.17 Letter from Eileen
Gray to Prunella Clough,
Saturday, year unknown,
paper, typed ink © NMI

11.18 The *Bibendum chair* in situ in *E.1027*, 1926-29, black and white photograph © NMI

were still in situ in the house and that Madame Schelbert, who bought *E.1027*, wanted to organise a meeting with Gray.[107] However, of more interest to Gray was that Capuano had told her that she was in possession of four *Bibendum chairs*, their form originally inspired by the Michelin man.[108]

These chairs originally belonged to a client of Gray's, Madame Jeanne Tachard, who was a close friend of both Jacques Doucet and Pierre Legrain. She was a woman of refined taste and had been a client of Gray's since 1923. She had purchased a number of rugs and had recommended Gray to Madame (Juliette) Mathieu-Lévy. Gray remembers in her letters that Tachard 'had two (*Bibendum chairs*) at St. Tropez'.[109] Gray began to explore the possibility of getting one of the *Bibendum chairs* returned or at least of being able to copy it for reproduction. She wanted to have at least one on show in the exhibition at the Heinz Gallery in London.[110] She felt that the chairs, though designed in 1926, 'even now would not be too old fashioned'.[111] However, Gray never managed to obtain one of the chairs. Capuano had several pieces by Gray, most notably a small chair which Gray designed for Lévy, and the 'gondola bed' or *Pirogue sofa bed*.[112] Gray was upset to learn that Capuano died shortly afterwards and that her collection had been sold at auction. She signed a contract with *Aram* in 1973 to reproduce this chair.[113]

Gray discusses *Tempe à Pailla* in several letters. It is unknown if Clough visited her aunt at *E.1027*, but she did join Gray at her second home in the summer of 1951. During the war Gray had had to leave *Tempe à Pailla* and on her return found it pillaged and badly vandalised. Gray was in her seventies at the time but she embarked on repairs and making new furniture, listing all the objects, furniture and furnishings which had been stolen or damaged. In a letter dated 6 January 1947 Gray wrote to Clough from the house saying that she has been a week in Menton doing repairs in the freezing cold.[114] The terrace roof was badly damaged and she had to repair it. Due to the sheer scale of the work that needed to be done the project took nearly seven years to complete. Shortly after she had restored the house she sold it to the artist Graham Sutherland. In a letter she states, 'I was sorry to leave that country around Castellar. Up above the village there were lovely walks'.[115] 'Sutherland', she wrote in a letter to Clough, 'seems to have taken roots at *Tempe à Pailla*. I had a letter from Mr Tom

Wilson saying that he was enlargening [sic] the little house in the garden adding "a sitting room, bedroom & bathroom" & wanted "the same light fittings" that I had put in the house & where could they get them'.[116]

Just as with *E.1027,* Gray was interested in reproducing the furniture she had designed for *Tempe à Pailla.* Writing to Clough she stated that she wanted to remake the adjustable dining table which she had sold to Graham Sutherland. However, this time she hoped to make it from rhodoid (which is similar to Perspex), with the supports and the table top being entirely transparent.[117] The table was later reproduced, with *Aram,* though not as Gray had described above.

Her last house, *Lou Pérou,* Gray described as a little 'cabanon', a 'little abris done in a hurry'. Prior to living in *Lou Pérou* she told Clough that she was living in a lodgement which was requisitioned after the war. This was due to the fact that her apartment on the quai Suffren, St. Tropez, which had been properly furnished, 'was blown up by Germans'. Gray explained the provenance of the name of her last house. *Lou Pérou* is 'slang for what one can say – Eldorado but less pretentious. I didn't know what to call the place and had been just reading a sort of Coué Manual called "Affirmez et vous obtiendrez" so I thought I'd affirmez...'[118] Gray previously had given a slightly different explanation to Stephen Haweis in her letters. Until now it has been assumed that building work had been finished at *Lou Pérou* in 1961. However, in many

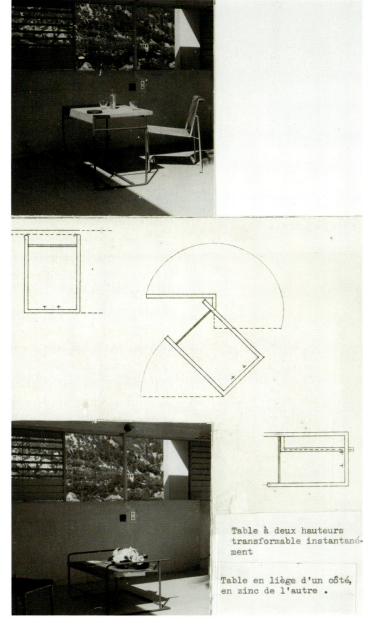

Table à deux hauteurs transformable instantané‐ ment

Table en liège d'un côté, en zinc de l'autre .

11.19 The *Adjustable Dining/ Coffee table* in situ at *Tempe à Pailla*, 1931-34, black and white photograph © NMI of her letters she talks about re-designing and ongoing building and repair work at *Lou Pérou* into the late 1960s: new kitchen shutters, new courtyard windows, a new water cistern, and the rebuilding of boundary walls which caused some controversy. She frequently mentions that the builder and carpenter are also working on various other projects.[119] In December 1961 she wrote, 'The sliding windows are not even in their place for it has hardly stopped raining for weeks. The other windows and doors are not even finished – St. Tropez is not self-supporting, metal, wood, all accessories have to come from Toulouse or Nice and lately the roads have been cut by floods'.[120] Gray discussed her colour scheme for the interior of *Lou Pérou*, saying that she felt 'the living room is not bad'. She added that the room's appearance would improve when she lowered 'the divan and cut its aluminium legs and get the dallage (tiles) polished'.[121] Gray painted the façade a pale green. She wrote 'the pale green seemed to me that which goes best with the big trees round the house and with the landscape'. She is also going to make the sliding shutters on *Lou Pérou* greyer as they are only varnished and she doesn't like the yellow colour.[122] This demonstrates that despite her age Gray continued to supervise every stage of her projects.

From the 1950s on Gray had plans to convert the garage into living quarters for her housekeeper, Louise Dany. Dany was desperately fond of the house, and primarily for this reason Gray thought about having alterations done to the garage with the advice of a local architect. The garage was to have a sod-covered roof which would create a platform from where one could view the sunset.[123] It was to be converted into a room, a bathroom and a kitchen for Dany if she chose to remain there for the purpose of looking 'after the house when it is not let'.[124] But it appears that she feared that such a conversion would be too damp.[125] The modifications to the garage were never completely realised and the letters reveal that it was still an ongoing project in 1968. In one letter Gray says that she has just got more work done on the garage doors and windows, including the addition of protection tiles.[126]

Throughout this time Gray was preoccupied, naturally enough, with the upkeep of *Lou Pérou* and of the surrounding land and vineyards. 'I must scrape down the shutters and give them a coat of paint'. In the same letter, she adds, 'one has to do what one can for oneself and I am going now to paint the front door and the courette (a small outer courtyard)'.[127] Other

11.20 *Lou Pérou*, 1954-61, colour photograph © NMI

letters reveal that she was concerned about the need to replace dead vines, about whether the land was properly ploughed and the vines grafted and whether if she planted fruit trees they would be watered.[128]

Gray was very proud of this her final architectural project and the alterations and additions which she made to the property. When she began to organise her affairs she looked to sell the house. Two prospective buyers were interested in *Lou Pérou*. The first, Gray states, wants to pull the structure down but would have to wait five years, so she would prefer the second buyer who wanted to keep the house as it was.[129] Unfortunately the person who finally bought the house demolished Gray's addition and built new extensions to the original structure. By 1993 only the garden terrace and the garage remained, although there were plans in place to modify the garage.[130] It was primarily due to increasing financial difficulties that Gray considered renting out the house and discussed with Clough selling

11.21 *Lou Pérou*, 1954-61, colour photograph © NMI

the vineyards.[131] Sadly a similar situation arose in relation to her apartment in rue Bonaparte, which she had hoped to leave to Clough in her will, or at least of having the option of selling the apartment while retaining the right to live there until her death.[132] She wrote, 'I would prefer to sell the flat with me in it'.[133]

Gray remained exceedingly active in her carpet production during the later years of her life, and Clough supervised much of the correspondence with various rug manufacturing firms. One of Gray's last wishes was to have her carpets produced in Ireland. The entire project is recorded in the Gray-Clough correspondence. During 1973 - 1974 there was also a possibility of a series of Gray's rugs being produced by Cogolin carpets in France.[134] One of the reasons why she was deterred from the project was that production costs in France in 1970 were exceedingly high, and Gray thought at first that it was pointless as the rugs would make little profit. This was initially the problem with the Cogolin factory.[135] As a result she looked at having rugs manufactured in Asia.[136] Gray visited the Cogolin factory in July of 1973 and commissioned a rug. She signed a contract with both Cogolin and with Donegal Carpets in November 1973.[137] In France, she was impressed with the Cogolin factory, stating in a letter to Clough that the looms were enormous and she described the carpets they produced as 'modern, marvellously finished'. Gray was also impressed that their looms were very wide and as a result they could possibly do two or three at any one time.[138]

11.22 *Monolith* carpet drawing, original drawing, 1918-21, reproduced by the Cogolin factory, 1973-4, paper, pencil © NMI

The rug chosen for this commission was 'a dark charcoal one ... with straight beige lines', and it measured 1.80 metre and cost her 3,450 in new French francs. Despite twenty per cent being removed off the production price Gray still thought it a costly venture.[139] This rug was to be completed for November or December 1973. In several letters it becomes clear that Gray is impatient and wanted the commission completed sooner rather than later. When the firm explained that during the summer months, especially in August, that their work was 'au ralenti (at a slowed down pace) & they would take a year to make rug', Gray was disappointed.[140] The first sample of the rug sent to Gray on 25 June 1974 pleased her. 'It is point noué like we used to make; too close the stitches but that can be arranged'.[141] But in a second letter in July 1974 Gray wrote that 'the Cogolin echantillon (sample) is too dense. I shan't be able to give the real price until I go myself to Cogolin & see what I can arrange. They don't use the laine filée à la main (hand knotted wool), which gave the handmade look, but just the ordinary wool bought anywhere, but I shall know better when I have seen another sample'.[142] The commission was fully realised and the 'new rug from Cogolin' was delivered to Gray around 5-7 October 1974.[143]

Other letters reveal that the fashion couturier Yves Saint Laurent (1936-2008) was interested in commissioning Gray to do a rug for his collection. In one letter she wrote, 'I would willingly do a carpet for Yves St Laurent, but how can I? I don't know what colours, what shapes, what emplacement he would want. It seems to me impossible'.[144] Yves Saint Laurent became an avid admirer of Gray, especially the furniture and rugs she designed for Mme Mathieu-Lévy.[145] She wrote in a letter to Clough, 'Yves Saint Laurent has 2 or 3 meubles (furniture) that belonged to Mme Mathieu-Lévy & is coming on Saturday to take me to see them'.[146] These pieces subsequently appeared at auction making record prices in 2009.[147] One of the pieces was the *Serpent armchair* completed in lacquer with rearing serpents in yellow dotted lacquer. It was originally covered in pale salmon-coloured upholstery with thin stripes.[148] In another letter Gray discussed the sideboard or enfilade that she designed for Mme Mathieu-Lévy for the *Rue de Lota apartment* which Yves Saint Laurent subsequently owned. Her description of the piece is unusual: 'the lacquer had been covered with some stuff, and the handles on the façade changed'.[149]

11.23 *Block screen,* 1922-23, wood, aluminium rods © NMI

Many writers place Gray's furniture from 1900-1925 into the Art Nouveau and Art Deco period; however Gray repeated in her letters that her work never belonged to these movements. She emphasised to Clough, 'As you know I loathe what was produced in 1900'.[150] Again on 2 January 1971 she says in relation to the Art Nouveau movement 'I don't care to be absorbed into it as representing willingly a disciple of Art Nouveau'.[151] The series of block screens made by Eileen Gray were in her opinion foremost among the creations that have come to differentiate her from the Art Deco movement. She states 'the 1920s is a period I loathed and the things I tried to make were really an escape from that, so I don't care to be absorbed into it'. She continued, 'The screens are a revolt as I meant them to be' from Art Deco furniture.[152] Even in the 1970s the block screens were set apart from other Art Deco furniture. Even in 1972-73 when she made a red block screen it was considered too modern in certain circles.[153] Variations exist of the block screens. The original was plain wood painted black.[154] There exists another which is plain wood.[155] This plain wood screen was photographed in *Jean Désert*.[156] The white screens were followed by black screens. Two of these are listed in the stock of the *Jean Désert* gallery.[157] One was bought by Jean Badovici. Two screens appeared in a series of photographs from the 1970s in Gray's *Rue Bonaparte apartment*. She clearly stated in one letter that she had two black lacquer screens 'one in the salon, one in the Entrée' of her apartment.[158] Some of the block screens were composed of plain large lacquer blocks. The width, length and size of the blocks also vary.

Some have inset squares on the blocks themselves. Gray stated that in total she made ten block screens.[159] From the Gray-Clough correspondence and from current scientific research it becomes apparent that the production of Gray's block screens falls into three different categories – screens made prior to 1930, screens assembled during the 1970s using existing blocks which she had left over from the 1920s and screens which were fabricated during the 1970s.[160]

From the correspondence that from 1970 onward Gray was approached by a number of clients who were all interested in her block screens; these included the American collector Robert Walker, Sydney and Frances Lewis who donated their collection to the Virginia Museum of Fine Arts,[161] and the British collectors Charles and Lavinia Handley-Read who later donated their screen to the Victoria and Albert Museum. Madame Capuano's friend Madame Corradini wanted a black lacquer block screen, but Gray had promised 'the last one to a museum' – now the Virginia Museum of Fine Arts.[162] Clough was also good friends with the architect Jim Carbury Brown and Gray stated in several letters that she should like him to have the block screen which eventually went to Handley-Read on loan.[163] It is also clear from the correspondence with Clough that these commissions posed problems for Gray. She had left over blocks from the 1920s, some were 'half lacquered', but she had 'enough plaques to make another screen but they are only half done & will probably be very expensive'.[164] When Gray made inquiries about having them re-lacquered there were only a few selected lacquer craftspeople in Paris at that time. 'No one now uses real Japanese or Chinese lacquer, too expensive to buy & too expensive to employ the necessary main d'oeuvre the polissage & all that. It is very disappointing for it seems stupid to throw them away but impossible to do anything with them as they are'.[165] The only lacquer worker Gray knew at this time was Bernard Dunand (1908-1998) – the son of Jean Dunand (1877-1942).[166] He learned the technique of lacquering from his father, who was credited with inventing the use of egg shell in lacquering, originally called coquille d'œuf.[167]

Gray's letters to Clough document that Gray kept four original screens – two white from the *Monte Carlo room* and two black. Walker wanted one of the surviving screens from the 1920s. Gray thought of making up a screen from the surviving blocks saying to Clough 'it all depends on what you think of doing with them as it would make a third screen and if it was

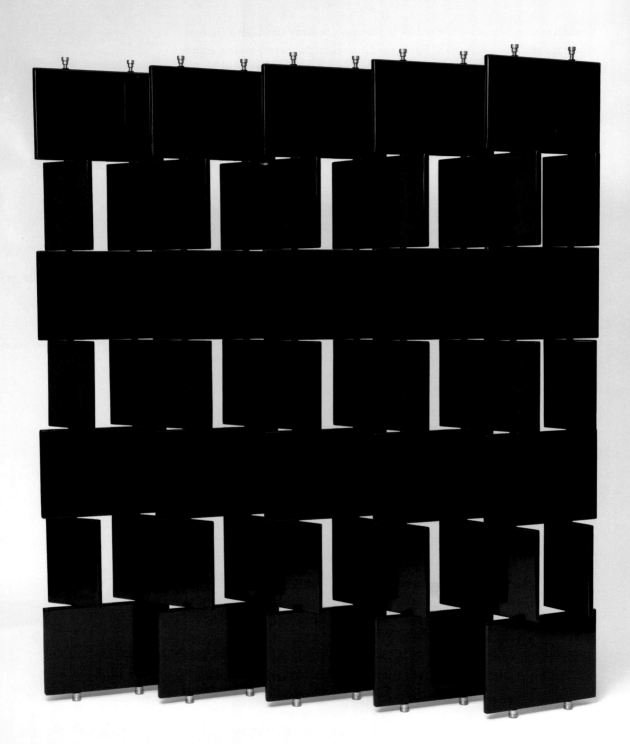

sold to Walker I suppose he would have to be told'.[168] In another letter she questioned, 'Do you think Walker would accept the present-day lacquer if it looked the same? There would then be three screens available'.[169] He had asked for two screens – and Gray felt that one was sufficient. It has been assumed up until this point that the screen which Walker purchased was an original screen from the 1920s and that he then acquired another, the larger screen that had belonged to Jean Badovici'.[70] The Gray-Clough correspondence appears to suggest otherwise. Gray employed Pierre Bobot to do the lacquer work on the blocks and in some cases assemble the screens. From evidence in both the Gray-Clough correspondence and from Bobot's invoices from 1971 to 1974 Gray had a number of screens composed from surviving blocks from the 1920s and requested new lacquered blocks which were then assembled into new screens during these years. In one letter she stated, 'Had a long talk with Bobot who brought the new screen or rather the old one redone in lacquer. He is going to send me the price doing it in wood first. He wanted to know whether I wanted the squares in relief or just plain ... He said he thought the bricks looked better with the relief. But who is going to have the screen?' Gray wondered whether the news screens should 'go to the V&A or Walker'.[171] In another letter Gray contemplated having one of the white screens re-done in black lacquer but it was too costly and she 'thinks it better to leave the white screen as it is'.[172] In this letter she again mentions that the screens which Bobot produced 'for Walker & Reade were 32 big and eight small'. In another letter Gray wrote that Bobot, when he made the screen for Robert Walker, did produce extra blocks.[173]

This suggests that the screens acquired by Walker and Handley-Read were not originally assembled and manufactured in the 1920s, but rather that old bricks were re-lacquered or new lacquer was used on new bricks, applied and assembled by Bobot in 1972. These new screens posed many problems due to the rising costs of their manufacture. Gray complained in one letter that the lacquer was not old lacquer, that Clough was left to negotiate prices with the clients, and that the cost of the materials, notably the wood, was ridiculous. The creating of the blocks also caused problems, in that the piercing of each brick with the rods meant that they had to be especially made. This work alone cost 22,000 francs.[174]

Lastly when the commission from Robert Walker for the new black lacquer block screen was finished and sent to England, Gray wrote to

11.24 Black lacquer block screen, wood, paint, aluminium, lacquer by Pierre Bobot, designed 1922-1923, executed 1973 © Virginia Museum of Fine Arts, Gift of Sydney and Frances Lewis

Clough inquiring whether Walker was pleased and what did he say and what Clough thought of the bricks that Bobot arranged.[175] Despite her age Gray still wanted the client to be content with the end result. 'It would be a relief to know that the rods are all right for that screen as the serrurier (locksmith) didn't keep to what I said and they are a millimetre thicker'. Gray did confirm that the second screen which Robert Walker later purchased 'was done in 1923 and a model in white which exhibited that summer. I will write the line for Walker. But you can tell him I have the photo taken with the date on it'. The white screen she referred to was one of those exhibited at the *Monte Carlo room* at the Salon des Artistes Décorateurs in 1924.[176]

Some of the block screens which Gray describes to Clough at that time are now unknown and are not adverted to in Bobot's invoices. Whether the commissions were ever completed also remains unknown. Gray expresses concern about a screen which Bobot was mounting at one point as he used only small bricks, and Gray felt that it might be better to divide them, making two small screens.[177] It appears from the invoices that Bobot delivered finished blocks for an un-assembled screen, and Gray described to Clough how he was going to 'make a model ... with the rectangle in dulled silver'.[178] The production of a red block screen, for which she is seeking 1,800,000 francs, is teased out in several letters. It is referred to again in Bobot's correspondence with and invoices to Gray. The first reference is on 20 September 1973 when the cost of 'paravent rouge' (red screen) is dealt with and it states that the screen should be finished by 24 September. A communication of 14 January 1974 requested settlement of an invoice sent three days later which confirmed the specific cost of 'laquage paravent panneaux rouge' (lacquering for red block screen). Bobot acknowledged receipt of payment, made by Gray on 18 January 1974.

Clough was also involved in this screen – one letter shows Gray requesting a missing block from Clough so that Bobot could finish assembling it; Clough replies that she had sent it.[179] It is possible that Clough was showing English clients a sample of the block in red. However, the screen wasn't without its problems, and ensuing correspondence with Clough shows just how much of a perfectionist Gray was in dealing with the workmen who worked with her. She was bitterly disappointed with Bobot's assembling of the red lacquer screen, as an error occurred in the placement of the small bricks and the roundels between the bricks were

11.25 Red Lacquer block screen, wood, aluminium, the lacquer by Pierre Bobot, designed 1922-23, executed in 1973 © Private Collection

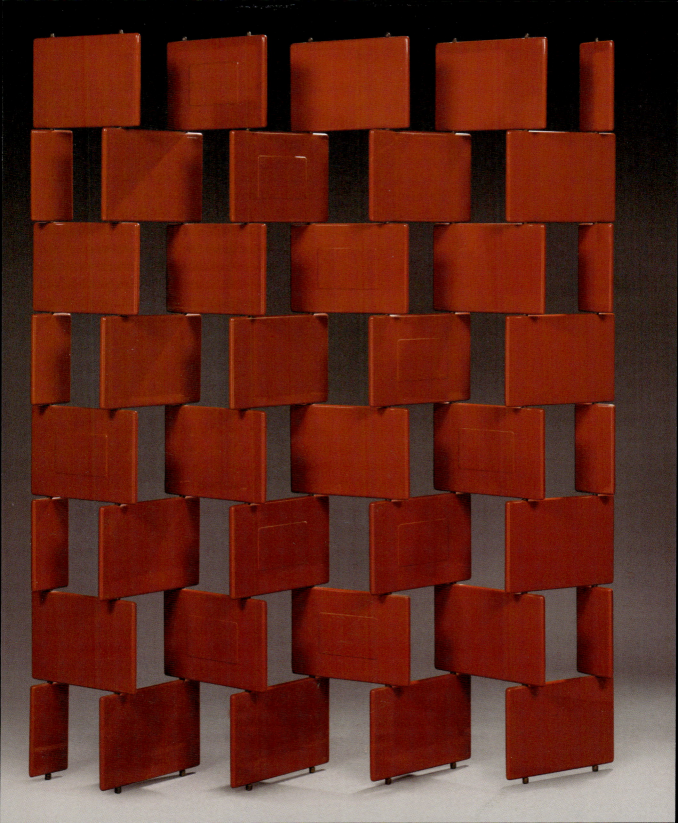

incorrectly positioned. Bobot did this so that the screen would fold more easily, but Gray felt that the piece appeared disjointed.[180] Another problem arose when the original unknown client changed his mind and requested a black screen.[181] The screen was finally purchased by the designer Andrée Putman – but whether she was the original client and whether Gray or Clough prevailed on her to change her mind is unclear.[182]

Gray also went to view the block screen which Bobot had been working on for Sydney and Frances Lewis. After the above mentioned problems arose Bobot did a lot of work on the screen and she was pleased.[183] Gray and Bobot had enjoyed a good relationship, and she was very upset when she learned of Bobot's death shortly afterwards, as he not only had worked on the screens but on other furniture as well. She had not known he was ill.[184]

Manufacturing of custom-made furniture in Paris during the late 1960s and early 1970s was an expensive process. Gray noted in one letter that pieces cost 35,000 or 40,000 francs. As a result she started to restore her old furniture and to produce new pieces which she then put up for sale. Writing about this to Clough Gray complained about the lack of available materials and was disgusted by the thought that she would probably have to use Formica for 'some of those imitations'.[185]

When Gray was not working she became easily frustrated, 'it is boring not to be working at something and it is probably that which gives me such a hump. I am so fed up trying to deal with the accumulated junk, often twenty years old, thrust away into cupboards, everything I try to throw away is put out of sight by L (Louise), and hoarded only to turn up again in some other place'.[186] Several letters show Gray working on brand new pieces; their whereabouts or whether the commissions were completed are unknown. One letter details a screen which measured 1.57 metres and had a curved band of metal and was made from acetate which she wanted in pink. Gray did work with pink Perspex, possibly for a screen that she was working on in 1974.[187] Other letters indicate that it was for Handley-Read.[188] This screen also had a problem – the acetate had splodges on it.[189] Clough sent her new perspex from London.[190]

Numerous letters reveal that Gray worked on furniture for the Victoria and Albert Museum chair exhibition in Whitechapel, London in 1970. Her *S bend* and *Transat chairs* were exhibited there alongside Marcel Breuer's *Steel Tube chair*, Alvar Aalto's *Plywood chair* and Gerrit Rietveld's chair made from packing case wood. In preparation for the exhibition Gray had

11.26 *S bend chair*, 1938, laminated wood, painted, with canvas, repainted and upholstered 1972, inv:circ.579-1971 © Victoria and Albert Museum, London

work completed on both chairs so that they were presentable; the *Transat chair* made from plain sycamore had the wood re-varnished and the metal parts re-chromed and the *S bend* chair was re-upholstered and re-painted in two colours.[191] Gray later offered the *S bend chair* to Victoria and Albert Museum's permanent collection. Writing to the curator, Carol Hogben, Gray revealed that the original *Transat chairs* all dated from 1926. She had twelve chairs 'or more' made to reduce the price, and that all of the *Transat chairs* were sold. She initially wanted the arm rests slightly curved, and the uprights which held the head rest to go straight down, screwed to the base.[192]

Another series of letters to her niece shows us Gray discussing a commission for work on early prototypes of a gift for Peter Adam. She fondly referred to the man who became her biographer as 'Klaus Peter' or 'KP' in her letters. They first met in 1960 when she was eighty-two. His biography is a personal account of her life. The commission began with Gray and Clough approaching Gonzales da Costa to work on a model of a dressing table and an occasional table made initially from plywood and sycamore. Gray had kept them from the 1920s and she used the dressing table as the model for the dressing table made for Jean Badovici in *E.1027* while the occasional table appeared over the years in different adaptations with either square or oval tops. The dressing table had a complicated design with a metal base for drawers, and alongside were two smaller drawers.[193] To spruce them up Gray wanted them re-veneered using zebrano.[194] The zebrano was imported from London via Clough and the work was completed by da Costa.[195] Adam was so thrilled with the gift that he then approached Gray with a commission for a series of six dining chairs which are mentioned in several letters.[196] The dining chairs, dating from approximately 1965-72, belonged to the second series of chairs begun in 1933 where Gray adjusted the back. In one letter she spoke of the difference in design explaining that 'the chairs are more slanted as well as the bars'.[197] The legs of the chairs were also filled with rubber tips so as not to scratch the parquet floor.[198] Discussing the metal ends of the dining chairs she said the craftsman 'left the tube open on purpose to make the rubber fit inside and stay in place'.[199]

In yet other letters Gray mentioned some pieces from the 1910 to 1920 period, including a blue screen called *La Voie Lactée* (location now unknown) that Florence Gardiner bought. Gardiner had gone to America with Gray and other friends in 1912. She says that when Gardiner died her daughter offered her the screen back but Gray told her to keep it.[200] She mentioned in another letter that Robert Walker bought a panel of lacquer depicting people, which dated from 1916. Gray explained that she did this piece 'to try and see the difficulties of doing people in raised lacquer'. She adds 'I hoped never to see it again. It was just done to try and see the difficulties of trying to do people in raised lacquer and is certainly very bad. I should scrape it off if I had it now but what can I do: dates from 1916'.[201] When she visited Walker's apartment, where he had arranged a selection of her furniture in Paris, Gray was impressed, noting that he had, at that time, three *Transat chairs* and that he found 'the *Transat* comfortable and they are still in fairly good condition'. Walker also owned 'the boat shaped thing', which is the *Pirogue sofa bed*, and the long mirrors.[202] This he had purchased from Madame Capuano.

Clough was very involved in Gray's work at times and sent her drawings to help with certain pieces and their fabrication.[203] Clough also painted the white block screen, now in the National Museum of Ireland in her kitchen using an acrylic paint.[204] Clough had pieces re-upholstered, including the *S bend chair,* after Gray had sent samples of fabric and colours to her.[205] A *Transat chair* which the artist Frank Stella commissioned for himself is discussed in several letters to her.[206] Clough helped Gray to order a new blue mattress for the chair. Clough was also involved when *Aram* began producing her designs in London, but Gray was still concerned that prices were too high and that customers would soon lose interest in her work.[207] Another letter between Gray and Clough revealed that *Knoll* were also interested in re-producing furniture from her designs.[208]

In February 1976 Clough learned that Gray had lung cancer. At that time Clough was attempting to arrange the sale of *Lou Pérou*. Gray just got to see an exhibition which was retrospective of the work on display in the 1925 Exhibition at the Musée des Arts Décoratifs. In October of 1976 she fell in her apartment while heading towards her workroom and died eleven days later on 31 October. Clough and Peter Adam arranged a simple funeral at Père Lachaise cemetery where her ashes were interred.

Clough continued to uphold Gray's reputation, organising and helping with exhibitions at MoMA and the Victoria and Albert Museum. Clough also kept a sharp eye on the reproduction of her rugs and her furniture by *Aram*. Her financial situation improved after she inherited Gray's copyright and estate – however she had earned it as Clough estimated that it took her from 1976 to 1978 to sort out Gray's estate and affairs.

ENDNOTES

1   Adam, Peter, *Eileen Gray: Architect/Designer: A Biography,* London, Thames and Hudson, 1987, p.312.

2   One hundred and seventy-four letters, mostly from Gray to Clough during the 1960s and 1970s exist in the National Museum of Ireland. The remainder of these letters are in Peter Adam's collection.

3   NMIEG 2003.410, letter from Eileen Gray to Prunella Clough, Thursday 7 March, year unknown.

4   NMIEG 2003.363, letter from Eileen Gray to Prunella Clough, 1970s.

5   NMIEG 2003.402, letter from Eileen Gray to Prunella Clough, year unknown.

6   Spalding, Francis, *Prunella Clough Regions Unmapped,* London, Lund Humphries, 2012, p.15.

7   NMIEG 2003.315, letter from Eileen Gray to Prunella Clough, Saturday, unknown date and year.

8   Ibid, Spalding, p.15.

9   NMIEG 2003.29, letter from Prunella Clough to Eileen Gray, 1 March 1947.

10 NMIEG 2000.233-234 and NMIEG 2003.554-556, portraits of Eileen Gray by G.C. Beresford. NMIEG 2000.246-247, portrait of Eric Clough Taylor by G.C. Beresford.

11 NMIEG 2003.295, letter from Prunella Clough to Eileen Gray, 1 March 1947.

12 Ibid.

13 Adam, Peter, *Eileen Gray: Her Life and Work,* London, Thames and Hudson, 2009, p.15.

14 Adam, Peter, *Eileen Gray: Architect/Designer: A Biography,* London, Thames and Hudson, 2000, p.15.

15 Ibid, Spalding, p.61.

16 NMIEG 2003.293, letter from Prunella Clough to Eileen Gray, 10 February 1945.

17 Ibid, Spalding, pp.66-7.

18 NMIEG 2003.328, letter from Prunella Clough to Eileen Gray, 21 January 1947.

19 NMIEG 2003.311, letter from Eileen Gray to Prunella Clough, Thursday 9 January, year unknown.

20 NMIEG 2003.360, letter from Eileen Gray to Prunella Clough, Circa 1970s.

21 NMIEG 2003.382, letter from Eileen Gray to Prunella Clough, 15 September 1974.

22 NMIEG 2003.322, letter from Eileen Gray to Prunella Clough, Sunday 9 August, circa 1970s.

23 NMIEG 2003.351, letter from Eileen Gray to Prunella Clough, Sunday 26 December, year unknown.

24 NMIDF 2003.295, letter from Prunella Clough to Eileen Gray, 1 March 1947.

25 Tate Gallery Archives, TGA200511, Prunella Clough archives, Box 16, family photographs.

26 Bumpus, Judith, 'Prunella Clough', *Contemporary Art,* winter 1993-1994, p.13.

27 The earliest letter in the National Museum of Ireland collection dates from 19 September 1942.

28 Adam, Peter, *Eileen Gray: Her Life and Work*, London, Thames and Hudson, 2009, p.136.

29 NMIEG 2003.1758, letter from Eileen Gray to Prunella Clough, 19 September 1942. This is the earliest letter in the archive. However, there remains a collection of letters with Peter Adam.

30 Ibid, Adam, p.136.

31 NMIEG 2003.1773, envelope, 5 June 1943, Lourmarin, Vauxcluse, South of France. NMIEG 2000.193, letter to the taxman.

32 NMIEG 2003.293, letter from Prunella Clough to Eileen Gray, 22 February 1945.

33 Tate Gallery Archives, TGA200511, Prunella Clough archives, Box 1, diary 5 November 1945.

34 Ibid, Spalding, p.60.

35 Ibid, Spalding, p.60.

36 NMIEG 2000.105, *Agricultural worker's house*, elevation and drawing.

37 NMIEG 2003.328, letter from Prunella Clough to Eileen Gray, 21 January 1947.

38 NMIEG 2003.294 and NMIEG 2003.295, letters from Prunella Clough to Eileen Gray, 1 March 1947.

39 NMIEG 2000.189, postcard from Eileen Gray to Prunella Clough, June 1961.

40 Ibid, Spalding, p.169. Tate Gallery Archives, TGA200511, Prunella Clough archives, Boxes 4, 5 and 6.

41 Ibid, NMIEG 2003.294 and NMIEG 2003.295.

42 NMIEG 2003.241, letter from Eileen Gray to Prunella Clough, Sunday 26 December 1971.

43 NMIEG 2003.353, letter from Eileen Gray to Prunella Clough, 20 September 1972.

44 Tate Gallery Archives, TGA200511, Prunella Clough archives, Box 1, diary 18 January 1946.

45 NMIEG 2003.322, letter from Eileen Gray to Prunella Clough, Sunday 9August, Circa 1970s.

46 NMIEG 2003.332, letter from Eileen Gray to Prunella Clough, date and year unknown.

47 NMIEG 2003.413, letter from Eileen Gray to Prunella Clough, Tuesday, date and year unknown.

48 NMIEG 2003.419, letter from Eileen Gray to Prunella Clough, April – May 1974.

49 NMIEG 2003.459, letter from Prunella Clough to Eileen Gray, year and date unknown.

50 Ibid, Spalding, p.169.

51 NMIEG 2003.130, black and speckled square gouache.

52 NMIEG 2003.93, navy blue square with white stripe gouache.

53 NMIEG 2003.91, Black and white stripe carpet gouache, NMIEG 2003.114, Black and white square carpet gouache.

54 Ibid, Spalding, p.188.

55 NMIEG 2003.365, letter from Eileen Gray to Prunella Clough, 2 January 1971.

56 NMIEG 2003.340, letter from Eileen Gray to Prunella Clough, Monday, late 1960s.

57 NMIEG 2003.337, letter from Eileen Gray to Prunella Clough, 1960.

58 NMIEG 2003.424, letter from Eileen Gray to Prunella Clough, Tuesday, 24 month unknown, 1969.

59 NMIEG 2003.390, letter from Eileen Gray to Prunella Clough, 1970s.

60 NMIEG 2003.392, letter from Eileen Gray to Prunella Clough, 1970-1971.

61 NMIEG 2003.322, letter from Eileen Gray to Prunella Clough, Sunday 9 August, Circa 1970s.

62 NMIEG 2003.340, letter from Eileen Gray to Prunella Clough, Monday, late 1960s.

63 NMIEG 2003.390, letter from Eileen Gray to Prunella Clough, 1970s.

64 NMIEG 2003.438, letter from Eileen Gray to Prunella Clough, Saturday, year and date unknown.

65 NMIEG 2003.362, letter from Eileen Gray to Prunella Clough, Saturday 6 July 1970s.

66 NMIEG 2003.382, letter from Eileen Gray to Prunella Clough, 15 September 1974.

67 Interview with Ginger Moro conducted 24 October 2012.

68 Ibid.

69 NMIEG 2003.320, letter from Eileen Gray to Prunella Clough, Sunday, 1970s.

70 Constant, Caroline, *Eileen Gray*, London, Phaidon, 2000, p.236.

71 Ibid, Constant, p.59.

72 Ibid.

73 Gray, Eileen, and Badovici, Jean, 'Maison en Bord de Mer', *L'Architecture Vivante,* Paris, Editions Albert Morancé, winter edition 1929.

74 NMIEG 2003.316, letter from Eileen Gray to Prunella Clough, Tuesday, possibly 12 March, year unknown.

75 Ibid, Adam, p.61.

76 Ibid, Adam, p.365.

77 Byars, Mel, *The Design Encyclopedia*, London, Laurence King Publications, London, 1994, p.598.

78 NMIEG 2003.302, letter from Eileen Gray to Prunella Clough, Sunday January 1960.

79   NMIEG 2003.307, letter from Eileen Gray to Prunella Clough, Christmas, year unknown.

80   NMIEG 2003.344, letter from Eileen Gray to Prunella Clough, Tuesday 2 May 1970s.

81   NMIEG 2003.352, letter from Eileen Gray to Prunella Clough, Monday 25 September, year unknown.

82   There are eight letters from Prunella Clough to Eileen Gray in the National Museum of Ireland. The remainder of Clough's letters are with Peter Adam.

83   Ibid, NMIEG 2003.294 and NMIEG 2003.295.

84   NMIEG 2003.437, letter from Eileen Gray to Prunella Clough, Monday, year and date unknown.

85   Tate Gallery Archives, TGA200511, Prunella Clough archives, Box 10, diary entry for 22 February 1978.

86   Tate Gallery Archives, TGA200511, Prunella Clough archives, Box 10, diary entry for 23 February 1978.

87   Rykwert, Jospeh, 'Un Omaggio a Eileen Gray', *Domus,* Milan, No. 469, December 1968, pp.23-5.

88   Ibid, Adam, p.369.

89   NMIEG 2003.298, letter from Eileen Gray to Prunella Clough, 26 October, year unknown, possibly 1968.

90   Ibid.

91   NMIEG 2003.311, letter from Eileen Gray to Prunella Clough, 9 January, unknown year.

92   NMIEG 2003.486 - NMIEG 2003.487, *Domus,* No.468, 1968, Joseph Rykwert, Milan, December 1968.

93   NMIEG 2003.521, notes on a list of photographs for exhibition in Vienna.

94   NMIEG 2003.342, letter from Eileen Gray to Prunella Clough, 17 October Sunday, Circa 1970s.

95   NMIEG 2003.466, letter from Eileen Gray to Prunella Clough, Tuesday, 24 October, year unknown.

96   NMIEG 2003.453, letter from Eileen Gray to Alan Irvine, 21 October 1971.

97   Ibid, Adam, pp.360-361.

98   NMIEG 2003.317, letter from Eileen Gray to Prunella Clough, Sunday 17 July, year unknown.

99   NMIEG 2003.303, letter from Eileen Gray to Prunella Clough, Saturday, date and year unknown.

100 Ibid.

101 Ibid, Constant, p.12.

102 NMIEG 2003.316, letter from Eileen Gray to Prunella Clough, Tuesday, possibly 12 March, year unknown.

103 NMIEG 2003.296, letter from Eileen Gray to Prunella Clough, 25 November, possibly 1970.

104 NMIEG 2003.315, letter from Eileen Gray to Prunella Clough, Saturday, year unknown.

105 Adam, Peter, *Mémoires à contres-vent,* Paris, Editions de La Différence, 2010, p.328.

106 Ibid, Adam, p.330.

107 NMIEG 2003.297, letter from Eileen Gray to Prunella Clough, 16 September, year unknown.

108 NMIEG 2003.341, letter from Eileen Gray to Prunella Clough, Sunday 26September, year unknown.

109 NMIEG 2003.300, letter from Eileen Gray to Prunella Clough, Tuesday, date and year unknown.

110 NMIEG 2003.4355, letter from Eileen Gray to Madame Corradini, date and year unknown.

111 NMIEG 2003.373, letter from Eileen Gray to Prunella Clough, Tuesday 20 April, year unknown.

112 NMIEG 2003.343, letter from Eileen Gray to Prunella Clough, Tuesday, date and year unknown. NMIEG 2003.350, letter from Eileen Gray to Prunella Clough, 11 September 1971.

113 NMIEG 2004.48, letter from Eileen Gray to Alan Irvine, 26 September 1973.

114 NMIEG 2003.1757, letter from Eileen Gray to Prunella Clough, 6 January 1947.

115 NMIEG 2003.306, letter from Eileen Gray to Gavin, year and date unknown.

116 NMIEG 2003.1762, letter from Eileen Gray to Prunella Clough, Monday, year and date unknown.

117 NMIEG 2003.467, letter from Eileen Gray to Prunella Clough, Thursday 19 October, year unknown.

118 NMIEG 2003.332, letter from Eileen Gray to Prunella Clough, date and year unknown.

119 NMIEG 2003.353, letter from Eileen Gray to Prunella Clough, 20 September, 1972.

120 NMIEG 2000.189, letter from Eileen Gray to Prunella Clough, 1961.

121 NMIEG 2003.315, letter from Eileen Gray to Prunella Clough, Saturday, year unknown.

122 NMIEG 2003.402, letter from Eileen Gray to Prunella Clough, year unknown.

123 Ibid, Adam, p.251.

124 NMIEG 2003.299, letter from Eileen Gray to Prunella Clough, Friday, September, year unknown.

125 NMIEG 2003.305, letter from Eileen Gray to Prunella Clough, Monday, 4 September, year unknown.

126 NMIEG 2003.352, letter from Eileen Gray to Prunella Clough, Monday 25 September, year unknown.

127 NMIEG 2003.298, letter from Eileen Gray to Prunella Clough, 26 October, year unknown, possibly 1968.

128 NMIEG 2003.351, letter from Eileen Gray to Prunella Clough, Sunday 26 December, year unknown.

129 NMIEG 2003.312, letter from Eileen Gray to Prunella Clough, Monday and Tuesday, year unknown, possibly 1975.

130 Ibid, Constant, p.228.

131 NMIEG 2003.296, letter from Eileen Gray to Prunella Clough, 25 November possibly 1970. NMIEG 2003.311, letter from Eileen Gray to Prunella Clough, Paris, Wednesday, year unknown. NMIEG 2003.311, letter from Eileen Gray to Prunella Clough, Thursday 9 January year unknown.

132 NMIEG 2003.30, letter from Eileen Gray to Prunella Clough, Monday 30 October, year unknown.

133 NMIEG 2003.440,letter from Eileen Gray to Prunella Clough, Thursday, year and date unknown.

134 NMIEG 2003.338, letter from Eileen Gray to Prunella Clough, Tuesday 7 October, circa 1970s.

135 NMIEG 2003.362, letter from Eileen Gray to Prunella Clough, Saturday 6 July, 1970s.

136 NMIEG 2004.48, letter from Eileen Gray to Alan Irvine, 26 September 1973

137 NMIEG 2004.48, letter from Eileen Gray to Alan Irvine, 26 September 1973.

138 NMIEG 2003.394, letter from Eileen Gray to Prunella Clough, 1972.

139 NMIEG 2003.370, letter from Eileen Gray to Prunella Clough, 25 July 1973.

140 NMIEG 2003.394, letter from Eileen Gray to Prunella Clough, Paris, Sunday, date unknown, 1974.

141 NMIEG 2003.387, letter from Eileen Gray to Prunella Clough, Tuesday 25 June 1974.

142 NMIEG 2003.386, letter from Eileen Gray to Prunella Clough, 1 July 1974.

143 NMIEG 2003.433, letter from Eileen Gray to Prunella Clough, Saturday, 5 October 1974.

144 NMIEG 2003.400, letter from Eileen Gray to Prunella Clough, Thursday 15 August, unknown year.

145 NMIEG 2003.400, letter from Eileen Gray to Prunella Clough, undated.

146 NMIEG 2003.361, letter from Eileen Gray to Prunella Clough, undated.

147 Christie's, *Collection Yves Saint Laurent and Pierre Bergé,* Paris, 23–25 February 2009, lots 276, 277, 243, and 317.

148 NMIEG 2003.361, letter from Eileen Gray to Prunella Clough, circa 1970s.

149 NMIEG 2003.348, letter from Eileen Gray to Prunella Clough, Tuesday 7 September and Wednesday 8 September 1971.

150 NMIEG 2003.364, letter from Eileen Gray to Prunella Clough, date and year unknown.

151 NMIEG 2003.365, letter from Eileen Gray to Prunella Clough, Saturday 2 January 1971.

152 NMIEG 2003.365, letter from Eileen Gray to Prunella Clough, dated 2 January 1971.

153 NMIEG 2003.420, letter from Eileen Gray to Prunella Clough, Tuesday 9 April, unknown year.

154 GalerieVallois, Paris.

155 NMIEG 2003.775, plain wooden block screen.

156 NMIEG 2000.250 and NMIEG 2003.1641, portfolios.

157 V&A Archives, AAD 9/11-1980, *Jean Désert* business correspondence.

158 NMIEG 2003.398, letter from Eileen Gray to Prunella Clough, Thursday 10 December 1970.

159 NMIEG 2003.361, letter from Eileen Gray to Prunella Clough,undated.

160 Griffin, Roger, Delidow, Margo, McGlinchey, Chris, 'Peeling Back the Layers; Eileen Gray's brick screen', paper given at the Vienna Conservation Congress, September 2012, New York, Manye Publishing, 2012, pp1-8.

161 NMIEG 2003.361, letter from Eileen Gray to Prunella Clough circa 1973.

162 NMIEG 2003.343, letter from Eileen Gray to Prunella Clough, date and year unknown.

163 NMIEG 2003.364, letter from Eileen Gray to Prunella Clough, Paris, Wednesday, date and year unknown.

164 NMIEG 2003.398, letter from Eileen Gray to Prunella Clough, Thursday 10 December 1970.

165 NMIEG 2003.308, letter from Eileen Gray to Prunella Clough, Tuesday, 15 December, year unknown.

166 NMIEG 2003.307, letter from Eileen Gray to Prunella Clough, 1970s.

167 Jean Dunand sculptor, cabinet maker, metal worker and artisan. Born at Lancy near Geneva in Switzerland, he settled in Paris in 1896 and began to work with sculptor Jean Dampt. In 1903 he turned to metalwork after studying coppersmithing. In 1905 he set up a studio in Paris exhibiting Art Nouveau style pieces. In 1909 he turned to lacquer and from 1912 he learnt from Seizo Sugawara who worked and taught Eileen Gray. He became one of the most renowned lacquer artists of the Art Deco period.

168 NMIEG 2003.308, letter from Eileen Gray to Prunella Clough, Tuesday 15 December 1970.

169 NMIEG 2003.309, letter from Eileen Gray to Prunella Clough, Christmas day, year unknown.

170 Christie's, *The Steven A. Greenberg Collection, Master-pieces of French Art Deco,* sale 2651, lot 49, New York, 12-13 December 2012. V&A Archives, AAD 9/11-1980, *Jean Désert* business correspondence.

171 NMIEG 2003.366, letter from Eileen Gray to Prunella Clough, Sunday 10 January, year unknown.

172 NMIEG 2003.376, letter from Eileen Gray to Prunella Clough, 18 January 1970s.

173 NMIEG 2003.476, letter from Eileen Gray to Prunella Clough, 1973.

174 NMIEG 2003.336, letter from Eileen Gray to Prunella Clough, Tuesday 30 March, circa 1970s.

175 NMIEG 2003.331, letter from Eileen Gray to Prunella Clough, Wednesday 10 March, year possibly 1970.

176 NMIEG 2003.336, letter from Eileen Gray to Prunella Clough, Tuesday 30 March Circa 1970s.

177 NMIEG 2003.469, letter from Eileen Gray to Prunella Clough, Sunday 30 September 1973.

178 NMIEG 2003.466, letter from Eileen Gray to Prunella Clough, Tuesday, 24 October, year unknown.

179 NMIEG 2003.476, letter from Eileen Gray to Prunella Clough, 1973 and NMIEG 2003.297, letter from Eileen Gray to Prunella Clough, 16 September, year unknown.

180 NMIEG 2003.335, letter from Eileen Gray to Prunella Clough, circa 1970s.

181 NMIEG 2003.297, letter from Eileen Gray to Prunella Clough, 16September, year unknown.

182 Christie's, *The Steven A Greenberg Collection, Masterpieces of French Art Deco*, sale 2651, New York, 12-13 December 2012, lot 49.

183 NMIEG 2003.368, letter from Eileen Gray to Prunella Clough, 19 December 1973.

184 NMIEG 2003.382, letter from Eileen Gray to Prunella Clough, 8 September 1974.

185 NMIEG 2003.334, letter from Eileen Gray to Prunella Clough, Wednesday, date and year unknown.

186 NMIEG 2003.301, letter from Eileen Gray to Prunella Clough, Tuesday, January 1960.

187 NMIEG 2003.417, letter from Eileen Gray to Prunella Clough, Sunday 10 March, circa 1974.

188 NMIEG 2003.381, letter from Eileen Gray to Prunella Clough, 27 September 1974.

189 NMIEG 2003.355, letter from Eileen Gray to Prunella Clough, 9 September, unknown year.

190 NMIEG 2003.466, letter from Eileen Gray to Prunella Clough, Tuesday, 24 October, year unknown.

191 NMIEG 2003.472, letter from Eileen Gray to Prunella Clough, Thursday, circa 1972.

192 NMIEG 2003.461, letter from Eileen Gray to Carol Hogben, 9 August 1970.

193 NMIEG 2003.375, letter from Eileen Gray to Prunella Clough, 4 June 1971.

194 NMIEG 2003.466, letter from Eileen Gray to Prunella Clough, Tuesday, 24 October, year unknown. NMIEG 2003.465, letter from Eileen Gray to Prunella Clough, 31 October, circa 1971

195 NMIEG 2003.344, letter from Eileen Gray to Prunella Clough, Tuesday 2 May 1970s.

196 NMIEG 2003.422, letter from Eileen Gray to Prunella Clough, 27 November 1974.

197 NMIEG 2000.6 – 2000.9, dining chairs.

198 NMIEG 2003.345, letter from Eileen Gray to Prunella Clough, Monday 5 November, year unknown.

199 NMIEG 2000.6 – 2000.9, dining chairs.

200 NMIEG 2003.350, letter from Eileen Gray to Prunella Clough, 11 September 1971.

201 NMIEG 2003.326, letter from Eileen Gray to Prunella Clough, date and year unknown possibly Sunday or Monday, mid-December, circa 1970s.

202 NMIEG 2003.351, letter from Eileen Gray to Prunella Clough, Sunday 26 December, year unknown.

203 NMIEG 2003.465, letter from Eileen Gray to Prunella Clough, Tuesday October circa 1971.

204 Ibid, Griffin, p.8.

205 NMIEG 2003.329, letter from Eileen Gray to Prunella Clough, Monday 15 June, year unknown.

206 NMIEG 2003.462, letter from Eileen Gray to Prunella Clough, 23 August 1970. NMIEG 2003.461, letter from Eileen Gray to Carol Hogben, 9 August 1970.

207 NMIEG 2003.310, letter from Eileen Gray to Prunella Clough, Thursday, 9 January, year unknown.

208 NMIEG 2003.314, letter from Eileen Gray to Prunella Clough, 1 April, year unknown.

12

Longing for Home: Ireland and Her Later Years

After Jospeh Rykwert's 1968 article in *Domus* magazine, a series of exhibitions of Gray's work were held during the 1970s in London, Graz, Vienna, New York, Los Angeles, New Jersey and Boston. Gray's screen *Le Destin* sold from the collection of Jacques Doucet at the Hotel Drouot in Paris for a record price and reawakened interest in her lacquer work. She was honoured as a Royal Designer for Industry by the British Royal Society of Arts.[1]

In Ireland the Irish art critic Dorothy Walker and her husband, architect Robin Walker (1924-1991) became important figures in the rediscovery of Gray's work that occurred towards the end of her life. Dorothy Walker was a promoter of Irish Modernism, and was a board member of the Irish Museum of Modern Art. She was a co-founder of the Rosc exhibitions of the 1960s, 1970s and 1980s which showed classic modern and contemporary work by artists from Europe and America. Her husband Robin Walker worked and studied under Le Corbusier in France on a French Government Scholarship, and had spent time in the United States, where he worked with Mies van der Rohe. Robin had told Dorothy that he recalled the model for *E.1027* being in Le Corbusier's studio in

12.1 Eileen Gray, by Alan Irvine, 1971, black and white photograph © NMI

12.2 Dorothy and Robin
Walker, 1961, black and
white photograph ©
Simon Walker

12.3 Honorary
Fellowship, RIAI, 24 May
1973, paper, commercial
ink, seal © NMI

12.4 Letter from Eileen
Gray to Prunella Clough
describing her meeting
with Robin Walker, 12
February 1973, paper,
typed ink © NMI

1947-48, which had piqued his interest, upon learning that Le Corbusier
was not the architect. He had initially joined the architect Michael Scott's
(1905-1989) firm in 1948, became an associate in 1956 and, by 1958 returned
to Ireland to work with Scott full time. He became a full partner in 1961
along with Ronnie Tallon (b.1927), forming the firm Michael Scott and
Partners which later became Scott Tallon Walker.

Gray's friendship with the Walkers began when, following an
exhibition of her work in Dublin, the Royal Institute of the Architects
of Ireland (RIAI) decided to acknowledge her life and career with an
Honorary Fellowship. On 11 May 1973 it was proposed that Eileen Gray
gain recognition from her homeland for her work as a pioneer of
Modernism. She was duly elected an Honorary Fellow, and the report stated
'arrangements are being made to have the certificate presented to Miss Gray
by the Irish ambassador in Paris'.[2] In July 1973 Robin Walker was asked to

prepare the citation.[3] Gray was too frail to travel to Ireland to attend the ceremony or even to accept the diploma at the Irish embassy in France. The President of the RIAI Kevin Fox then contacted the Department of Foreign Affairs to see if they could arrange the presentation for some time in September 1973. The Irish Ambassador to France, Edward Kennedy (1971-1974), was to present the award.[4] In letters to her niece Prunella Clough at the time Gray reveals she was too unwell to attend so plans were postponed until 1974. The presentation finally took place in her apartment in April of that year.

In the citation Walker described Gray as 'probably the sole representative from Ireland wholly immersed as an outstanding exponent in the pioneering work of the modern movement'.[5] Her architecture is said to be 'more inventive, more modern' than that of her contemporaries. The unique quality of her work in the field of furniture design is admired for her 'intuitive ability to fuse modern technology with the new aesthetic spirit of the times'. This praise of her work Walker later continued in Gray's obituary[6] and a lengthy tribute was also written by James McQuillan.[7]

Writing to her niece afterwards Gray's delight is evident. 'Dearest, I am now an honorary Fellow of the Royal Institute of the Architects of Ireland. They all came on Friday to bring my diploma the Ambassador and four architects, Members of the Council. It seems so strange, Louise wanted to tell you about it and on Sunday we tried ever so many times to ring you but could not get through'.[8] Gray was so pleased to receive the accolade that she wrote to the President of the RIAI saying 'Please accept my sincere thanks for the great honour of my election to membership as an Honorary Fellow of your Institute. I shall endeavour by my efforts to justify this promotion and this diploma will be a great incentive, and an inspiration to many people to continue their work'.[9]

The impetus for the award to Gray originated in the exhibition of her work with the Royal Institute of British

THIS IS TO CERTIFY THAT

Eileen Gray

Was Elected on the 24th day of May 1973

Honorary Fellow

of the

ROYAL INSTITUTE OF THE
ARCHITECTS OF IRELAND

Founded in the year of Our Lord One Thousand Eight Hundred and Thirty-nine, incorporated One Thousand Nine Hundred and Nine, a Body Politic for the general advancement of Architecture and for the maintenance of the Interests, Status and Uniformity of Practice of the Profession.

In Witness whereof the President, Honorary Secretary and Two Members of the Council have affixed their Names at the Meeting of Council held at 8 Merrion Square, Dublin, this 8th day of June 1973

PRESIDENT

MEMBER OF COUNCIL

HONORARY SECRETARY

MEMBER OF COUNCIL

Frb 12

Pruny dearest at last I can do something I want to do I E write to you .
I had people all last week ,or letters to answer, just as boring . the
walkers came . He is an architect , "sympathique"& today I've written to
thank him for a cahier of recent Architecture ,his & other Irish Architects ,rather inspired by Mies Van der Rohe but interesting though very
monotonous . Your letter is beside me , You say (about the slide , 3
students quite out of place. You mean too good to be students ?
thank you ever so much for rectifying the drawings . The spots on the
one you have drawn are not meant to be there, just accidents ;Could you
remove them . For the frames ,I quite agree Wood would be best only plea
se write down everything you pay , so that I can send you a cheque .
This afternoon they announced "from tomorrow all prices I5% more .
Wood whitened sounds nice but will they do it ?
            Couldn 't finish last night . This morning, its so dark I can
        hardly see the type.or read the letter of Miss Elizabeth Wrightson
Concerning Rugs designed by Evy Wyld ,of which she has some specimens
(probably my designs) but I suppose I better not say so .
As Maecilhac seemed in a hurry I told him I was not going to sell the
Persian paintings for I think you are quite right. No Hurry. though
taxes & contributions to be paid immediately have gone up enormously
But I have enough to meet them I think .
Pruny dearest did you pay into my Bank a cheque . Please tell me. If
so you must have it back for there is really no reason why I should
live on Charity .
Your show opens on the 9th of March . I wish I could go over to see it
When is Easter . Will you be quieter then
My Love & blessings
                                        Eileen

Architects (RIBA) London in March 1973. The RIAI requested that the exhibition travel to Dublin for May - July of that year.[10] Alan Irvine, who designed the *Heinz Gallery exhibition*, contacted Eileen Gray with the request. She replied 'I should be very glad if the things could be shown in Dublin'.[11] The thought of an exhibition in Dublin brought back memories for Gray of her home and writing to Irvine she enclosed 'a photo of my grandfather's house in Ireland, near Enniscorthy, Co. Wexford, overlooking the river Slaney and the Wicklow hills. It is the only print I have and I should be sorry to lose it. Would it be possible to have a copy made?'

The exhibition of Gray's work was to take place at the then new Bank of Ireland Headquarters in Baggot Street, Dublin, in association with the RIAI in May/June of 1973. The location was of importance to Gray as the building was designed by Ronnie Tallon and Irvine reassured her that 'it is an excellent building and the exhibition will look good their (sic)'.[12] The exhibition was titled *Eileen Gray: Pioneer of Design* and ran from 18 May - 15 June 1973. It was organised jointly by the Architectural Association of Ireland and the Royal Institute of the Architects of Ireland. The exhibits included a *Transat chair*, an *S bend chair*, an *Adjustable table*, carpets and numerous images of her architectural and interior design projects. Gray sent from Paris a black lacquer block screen which was insured for £1,000. She had requested that the rods for the screen be adjusted and have a centimetre removed. At 95 Gray was still meticulous about her work being displayed correctly. After the exhibition Gray told the journalist Maeve Binchy that she had received 'a few letters from Irish architects and artists which pleased her very much, she still had them in a little file called "Irlande" and she hoped that she had remembered to reply to them all'.[13] It was at this exhibition that Dorothy Walker saw Gray's carpets and contacted her in the hopes of having her carpets manufactured in Ireland. From then until her death in 2002 Walker was a tireless champion of Gray's work.

In the 1990s, she and Patrick Mellett, an Irish architect based in France, were the driving force behind a campaign for the purchase of *E.1027* by the Irish state. Walker wrote to and met with various Irish political figures, notably Minister for Arts, Culture and the Gaeltacht Michael D. Higgins, Minister for Housing and Urban Renewal Liz McManus,[14] Minister for Finance Ruairi Quinn,[15] President Mary Robinson[16] and her husband

Nicholas Robinson, the Irish Council, the RIAI,[17] the Commissioner of the *Imaginare Irlandais* program and the director of *La Maison d'Architecture* in Paris.[18] Their initial idea, developed by Mellett, was to create an Irish Association and European exchange centre for Irish artists, based in *E.1027*.[19] A written proposal was drawn up acknowledging the importance of *E.1027* in the history of twentieth-century design and its importance to Ireland was stressed to ensure that the building would be restored and preserved for posterity.[20] Though Gray had long been known amongst the Irish architectural cognoscenti going back to the 1930s when students did their internships with Le Corbusier, her work as a woman, as a pioneer, and as an architect had also been deliberately ignored, primarily because it had been assumed that she was an Irish expatriate who had never returned – which was not the case. Just as Gray had been effaced from the canons of Modernism – so too was her name eliminated by her homeland in the writing of Ireland's architectural history. Walker and Mellett had hoped to change this fact. When Mellett made preliminary inquiries in 1995 about how *E.1027* could be purchased he discovered that its ownership was in dispute. *E.1027* was purchased by Madame Schelbert following Badovici's death and she sold it to her doctor. The hopes were that the house could be purchased in conjunction with the inauguration of the *L'Imaginaire Irlandais* programme.[21] The then owner of the house, Dr Peter H. Kaegi was in agreement with the proposal to turn the house into an Irish cultural centre.[22] Kaegi was willing to give the Irish nation priority on the sale of the house and land.[23] Mellett also contacted the Irish *Fund de France*.[24] Sadly all of their efforts failed. In 1991 a campaign was mobilised by DoCoMoMo (The International Committee for documentation and conservation of buildings, sites and neighbourhoods of the modern movement) in an attempt to prevent the dispersal of the contents of the house with a request for the compilation of a complete register of the location of the pieces after the sale. The reason for this campaign was that 'the set of furniture is likely to have been the most complete entity of house and furniture relating to Eileen Gray in existence' and that the 'campaign centred not only on the outstanding quality of the individual pieces, but mainly on the importance of keeping the collection together or, if that would not be possible, to have the new owners registered so that future documentation and scientific research would have remained possible'.[25] DoCoMoMo contacted several museums and collectors in an effort to find someone interested in buying the complete set. The Victoria and Albert Museum, the Design Museum in London and the National Museum of Ireland were unsuccessful in preparing serious bids. In 1999 Dorothy Walker was later heavily involved in persuading the National Museum of Ireland and the Department of Arts, Heritage, Gaeltacht and the Islands to purchase the Eileen Gray collection for the National collections. In this she succeeded.

However, Walker's initial efforts in the 1970s concerned Gray's carpets. One of Gray's last wishes was to have her work produced in Ireland and in one letter to Walker she wrote 'I should so like to have a carpet made in Ireland'.[26] After the exhibition at the Bank of Ireland headquarters, Dorothy Walker contacted Gray immediately in the hopes of having her carpets manufactured in Ireland. Walker, enthusiastically assumed the role of expeditor and wrote to Terence Conran (b.1931) the founder of the Habitat stores since 1964, who had been involved in the Kilkenny Design Workshops and had championed Irish design and designers:

> I am sure you know of the pioneer Irish designer Eileen Gray who produced brilliant carpets and furniture designs in Paris in the nineteen twenties. An exhibition of her work was held in London last May and I was so taken with the designs that I have been discussing the possibilities of remaking her carpets – which were all lost in the last war – with the hand-made carpet makers V'Soske Joyce here in Oughterard in the West of Ireland.

She continued, 'At the time I was also taken with two of the chair designs in the exhibition which were still fresh and original... [it is a] great pity that they are not being manufactured and put on the market now and it occurred to me that you might be the right person who would be able to appreciate the quality of the design and be able to manufacture it'.[27] However, Walker's hopes that Conran would manufacture Gray's designs were ultimately dashed, as in 1973 Eileen Gray granted the worldwide rights to manufacture and distribute her designs to *Aram Designs Ltd*, London.[28]

A lengthy correspondence and friendship developed between the two women. Gray was particularly interested in the Walkers as Robin was an architect and Dorothy a critic. They visited Gray in Paris during this period[29] and she encouraged these visits.[30] Of her friendship with the Walkers she wrote 'I shall keep a very friendly souvenir of the short time that we passed together'.[31] Gray had written to Prunella Clough, when first contacted by Dorothy about producing rugs in Ireland, saying 'Here is Mrs Dorothy Walker's letter ... she is married; Husband an Architect'.[32] Robin kept Gray apprised of recent architectural developments in Ireland including some of his own. Gray in turn wrote 'I am so glad to see that the plans are included and that I shall be able to study them carefully in the evening'. She compliments his architecture stating that the 'general effect of the buildings gives the impression of strength without the heaviness one sees so often in other countries'.[33]

In the Walker-Gray letters Gray frequently discusses Ireland. She states that she wishes that she could have gone to Dublin to have seen the exhibition and wanted to return to her roots as 'Anything to do with Ireland always moves me'. In several letters Gray mentions her old family home of Brownswood in Enniscorthy.[34] In another letter she complains, 'I can't stand the heat here, I long for Ireland, but the old house near Enniscorthy has gone, there is only the hospital'.[35] Later Gray expresses an interest in Irish politics, 'I shall be so glad to have some Irish news and hope there was Peace for Christmas'.[36]

In numerous letters Walker makes clear that she has no commercial interest in the project herself but would simply like to see the carpet designs brought to life again in Ireland.[37] The entire project was supervised by Gray's niece Prunella Clough. Gray made it clear early on that she, like Walker, did not wish to gain financially from the venture. 'As it would be for Ireland I should not want any Bénéfice for the carpet designs or for the copies of the chairs'.[38] Though this was a generous offer on Gray's behalf, Walker felt that the firm who received the commission should still put monies into a fund or an Eileen Gray award to encourage future designers.[39]

12.5 Letter from Eileen Gray to Prunella Clough, March 1973, paper, typed ink, pen © NMI

At that time two firms were producing rugs in Ireland, V'Soske Joyce and Donegal Carpets. It seems Gray researched the commission further. In one letter to Clough she noted that there were actually three firms producing rugs and carpets in Ireland, but that she feared they all used the same system of machine woven carpets.[40] Gray never mentioned the name of the third firm, but she wrote in one letter that she sent three rug drawings to a carpet manufacturer in Kilkenny.[41]

April 19 Friday

Dearest , Did I tell you that when I received the Sample & saw that it wouldn't do I wrote again to Mrs V Soske to explain & sent off the sample back to the Agent as I didn't want you to h have to bother to go there ,your self ,its such a long way.I se there are 3 Firms who make rugs & carpets in Ireland but I expe they all use the same system . We will talk about it when I se you.   I do hope I shall be able to find a small hotel some where ,I feel ashamed to have to ask you to put me up ,which means extra cooking & bothers . Louise will know on the 22cd whether she must go at once.

Must write to Alan now to answer his letter & two others will let you know on the 22 cd ,so sorry about the telephone the other day

Love & blessings & apologies that I am still alive

12.6 Letter from Eileen Gray to Prunella Clough, 19 April 1974, paper, typed ink, pen © NMI

21, RUE BONAPARTE.VI

Friday

Pruny dearest, I received late   this morning the sample. It is not at all what we want, It is made on canvas by what they call a wool gun whereas the rugs I would like to have ,are made on a loom , with a shu shuttle going backwards & forwards through a comb which makes the tec ture of the rug . the design in wool knotted by hand . If possible I will return the sample tomorrow but if the post is shut will send it on Tuesday. better give back the sample , no good to ask for others as all their rugs seem to be done that way. Everything here seems to be in confusion so as louise is going out she will just post this line . very disappointing , but I am sure you agree that the tecture is much too thick & would anyway not do for small rugs that one would catch one's feat in , if they were on the floor.   I went to see the tapissier with Natacha the other day & they promised to send 3 échantillons of stuff for the small chair here ,but have not received anything yet. is it worth while finishing a few of the Monotypes & gouaches , what do you think . It would save you having to tear them up.   There are 3 firms who advertise Hand-made carpets . I wonder i if they all use the same system .

Forgive this hurried line all my love Pruny

12.7 Letter from Eileen Gray to Prunella Clough, April/May 1974, paper, typed ink © NMI

Samedi 28 Sept

Pruny dearest ,I've been a long time without writing ,& there
are so many things to andwer in your lettzrs ; but I wanted to
make another Maquette for the Divan 3Xourbax   (curved) . I rea
lized the first one was too big , 2 metres 40 ,but the wire is
too thin & makes it difficult .
Ist I did get a letter from you enclosing a bad drawing of the
S Chair ,but I had bx not marked enough dimensions for the
cushions as they were not done. I will look for it again .
I did get your letter about the boy from Leeds, it
was"too good to be true " but it cheered me up a lot & help
me to forget my present decrepit state , (hand worde than
ever ,so shaky I can't even make a plan, & deafer)
(The girl who has the room upstairs is doing the menage & making a terrific noise , I suppose ,to emphasize the fact
that she is working. The slumps & glooms as you say seem to
permeate all inhabitants ,& especially here there are cons
tant allusions to England on the downhill grade.
I'll send two or three rug drawings tomorrow & would be so gla
if you would choose one & send it to the Kilkenny people (don'
know their address.
Your letters are like sunshine to me ,I do so thank youtho I
know its a sacrifice ,& I'm horrified when I see you have har
ly any spare time to think about your work which is more ip-
portant than anything. It would be lovely if you could manage
to come here for a few days (please don't think of sending a
cheque) but I expect you are expecting Peter any time now &
want to be in London .
The girl is going & I want her to post this .Will write properly as soon as possible . Louise has avery bad sore throat
& is feeling rotten

My love ,always

12.8 Letter from Eileen Gray
to Prunella Clough,
28 September 1970s, paper,
typed ink © NMI

Walker proposed V'Soske Joyce, feeling that they were slightly more adventurous when it came to designs[42] and also because she thought Donegal Carpets might be too thick for Gray's designs.[43] Gray wrote to Clough that she is sure to like V'Soske Joyce's tapestries because they make handmade tufted carpets.[44] However, writing to Prunella Clough she speaks favourably of both firms. Referring to Dorothy Walker's first letter Gray says 'Both Donegal Carpets and V'Soske Joyce of Oughterard make hand-made carpets of the finest quality - perhaps the Donegal firm might be cheaper'.[45] Ever the consummate professional who supervised all stages of her work Gray was anxious that the commission be done correctly. Gray remained adamant about using the traditional hand-knotted technique – the way that she had woven the carpets during the 1920s. She also insisted to Clough that her designs were only to be copied, not reinterpreted.[46] Gray later also requested a sample of the weave from V'Soske Joyce 'of the tufted sort with rather long strands'.[47] Clough informed Walker that the questions of the size and wool quality depend on Gray's memory but that despite her age, 'she has an amazing recollection of these sort of details'.[48] Gray also suggested that V'Soske Joyce contact Carol Hogben, Curator of the Victoria and Albert Museum in London for permission to copy one of the designs and offers to provide any rugs which they could use to put the design to scale. In addition she offered twenty to thirty designs which she still had in Paris.[49] Gray also wondered if she could have a small carpet made by V'Soske Joyce for herself for Paris, 'which I should be glad to buy, for as you know all my things were taken by the Germans during the last war'.[50]

Walker contacted V'Soske Joyce providing them with a detailed biography and sent them a copy of the catalogue from the RIAI exhibition on Gray's work. The designs of the carpets, which were to be made by V'Soske Joyce, had been donated to the Victoria and Albert Museum and the stipulation was that the firm remake the carpets to Eileen Gray's original 1920s designs.[51] She also informed them that the negotiations would be handled by Gray's niece.[52] The firm were aware of Gray's work and designs but proposed that Stanislav V' Soske would be the artist who should interpret these designs.[53] Stanislav V'Soske also wanted to create a permanent Eileen Gray carpet collection.[54] There was a delay in the decision to pursue the commission. Walker apologised to Gray for the slow progress writing 'I do hope that you have not completely given up hope of having your carpets made in Ireland'.[55] Clough met V'Soske Joyce's agent in London and agreed that if Gray is content with the small samples two designs would be produced on a trial basis.[56] Gray subsequently did give the agent two designs.[57] On 4 April 1974 the firm contacted Gray in a letter which pointed out that the Bauhaus architect Hannes Meyer had been a former client of V'Soske Joyce and that V'Soske Joyce were eager to preserve the important collection that was Gray's work. They aimed to convince Gray to allow them to do the commission stating 'the period in which you produced your designs coincides with that in which the V'Soske brothers were developing the techniques that established them firmly in their craft of hand tufting carpets and rugs in wool - and in which craft they are engaged now in Ireland as well as in the States'.[58]

In another letter of the same date the company informed Dorothy Walker that Gray's wish was to supervise the process, have samples of the weave sent to Paris and the commission of two designs for her own use.[59]

However, Gray – who wanted to supervise and be in charge of every stage of the process, just as she did in her early years as a designer – could not relinquish control and differences in interpretation of the project and manufacturing methods made the project impractical.[60] On the 14 July 1974 Joyce wrote to Walker saying that Clough had made the firm aware of Gray's preference for the knot and weaving methods of rug construction, but hoped Gray might be interested in the firm's technique which in their opinion varied in textures and was faster in production.[61] In a letter to her niece it becomes increasingly apparent that Gray remained adamant about using the traditional hand-knotted technique – the way that she and Wyld had the carpets woven during the 1920s. She stated, 'I received late this morning the sample. It is not at all what we want. It is made on canvas by what they call a wool gun whereas the rugs I would like to have are made on a loom, with a shuttle going backwards and forwards through a comb which makes the texture of the rug, the design in wool knotted by hand'.[62] Sadly and to the regret of the company the commission never materialised.[63]

Despite these setbacks Gray remained undeterred, and it was through Donegal Carpets that her dream was finally realised. The Donegal archives which remain do not mention Gray. However, from Gray's correspondence we learn that the commission began in mid 1975. Prunella Clough wrote to Gray stating that 'I have also made a date with the Donegal man this Friday to discuss the yellow one with rectangles. He sounded keen too!'[64] This rug is called both *Castellar* and *Brentano*. A booklet was produced and the rugs were sold by Monika Kinley, an agent in London. Eight carpets were produced – two of which had Irish themes – *Wexford* and *Kilkenny*. The others also illustrated important dates, people or places which affected her career – *Wendigen, Roquebrune, Zara, St. Tropez, Castellar* and *Bonaparte*.

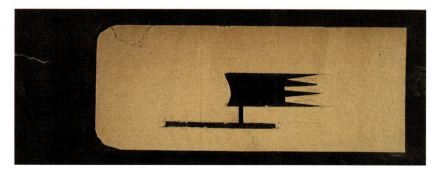

12.9 Wexford carpet gouache, 1919, paper, paint © NMI

EILEEN GRAY
CARPETS

1

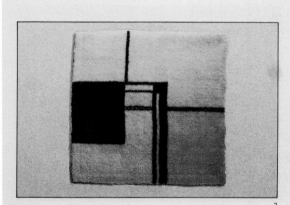

2

3

4

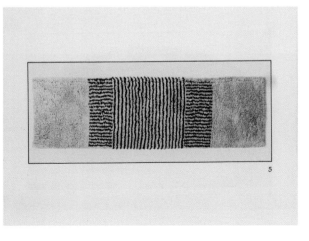

5

6

7

8

12.10 Eileen Gray, Donegal Carpets
booklet, 1975, featuring the carpets;
Wexford (1), *Wendigen* (2), *Kilkenny* (3),
Roquebrune (4), *Zara* (5), *St. Tropez*
(6), *Castellar* (7) and *Bonaparte* (8)
paper, commercial ink, black and white
photographs © NM

12.11 Eileen Gray, 1973,
coloured photograph
© NMI

Walker was also a key figure in realising the arrangement with Monika Kinley. Kinley was a significant figure in the English art world. She supported and helped the careers of many artists. She grew up in Berlin and Vienna and after school and college in England she began work at the Tate Galley during the 1950s. This laid the foundations for her long career in the arts. In the 1960s she worked for short periods with commercial galleries which led her to seek out the work of artists she admired. As a result she exhibited from her apartment in Hammersmith, London. Gray's niece Clough was one of the many artists she exhibited and it was through Clough that Gray's own work was shown. The Walkers knew Kinley and she invited them to an 'open house' exhibition in November 1975 at her then home Digby Mansions, Lower Mall, London to view work by Prunella Clough, Eileen Gray and an abstract Irish artist and collector Cecil King (1921–1986). When Walker had first written to Gray, Clough had replied on 26 September 1973 mailing her letter to *Hibernia* magazine. King had seen the letter and realising its importance forwarded it to Walker.[65] The booklet produced by Donegal Carpets in relation to the commission entitled 'Eileen Gray Carpets' states on the inside cover that 'these carpets are original designs by Eileen Gray, made to order in Donegal Ireland. Each carpet is hand knotted 100% pure wool and can be obtained from Monika Kinley, 213 South Lambeth Road, London'.

Throughout their correspondence Gray, Clough and Walker discussed Gray's furniture projects. Many have assumed that due to her age and relative obscurity in the later part of her life Eileen Gray was no longer working. However, Gray's correspondence with Dorothy Walker, Robin Walker's citation at the RIAI presentation and an interview given by Gray to *Irish Times* journalist Maeve Binchy offer emphatic confirmation that Gray was still creative, designing, having copies commissioned and having furniture made. Binchy wrote 'Eileen Gray is ninety-seven, and, so she says, finds that she doesn't work as she used to. She had some chairs to finish, and she wasn't at all happy about the lines of the backs'.[66] Walker wrote 'Eileen Gray is still alive, aged ninety-four. Living in Paris, and designed a set of new screens last year'.[67] This is further confirmed in a letter from her niece to Walker who says that she is struggling with 'people who are making two new screens to her (new) designs: it is a slow business, but it will be nice to have something from 1973'.[68] Robin Walker's citation highlights that 'still at ninety-four she continues to experiment and to develop ideas, designing

metal and plastic screens and working on furniture using plastic tube frames'. A number of her earlier furniture designs were copied by various people and the firm Aram were in negotiations about a table and a chair.[69] Gray gave American painter Frank Stella permission to have the *Transat chair* copied because he liked the one which was exhibited at the *Modern Chairs exhibition* in Whitechapel in 1973. However, the commission to copy took a long time to manufacture and was expensive.[70] Simultaneously Walker had expressed her interest in having Gray's designs copied in Ireland. In one letter Gray states that she will inquire with Clough to find out who copied them 'for perhaps they made several and I should like you to have one or two'. In the same letter Gray says that she hopes to have 'some new screens and would like you (Dorothy) to see them'.[71] Gray's work on new screens is confirmed in a later letter.[72] Clough again writes to Walker that a friend of hers has one of Gray's early dining chairs from the 1930s which she plans to have copied but depending on the metal work only two of three will be made. In this letter Clough sums up the problems with Gray's early original modern furniture stating that, 'the difficulties lie in so few originals being available, though I could think of one or two perhaps less famous examples of which she has spares'.[73] On 22 July 1975 Eileen Gray wrote to the National Museum of Ireland saying, 'I should have liked so much to have something permanent in Ireland but I suppose it is too late now'.

Gray is widely recognised as one of the most unique designers of the twentieth century. By nature Gray was discreet and self-effacing. She never sought acclaim. By the 1960s her achievements had been largely forgotten. The work of a few committed collectors and historians since the early 1970s has served to effectively reposition her at the forefront of the story of architecture and design in the first third of the twentieth century. Gray died in 1976 while still working on models for new screens. In the year of her death, despite spending her life in Paris, she still thought of herself as Irish, describing herself as another expatriate, 'in the absurd way us expatriates will always do'.[74] When she died the majority of the furniture in her apartment was sold at auction and her archive passed into the care of her niece, Clough, and her friend Peter Adam. In May 2000 the National Museum of Ireland purchased the contents of Gray's apartment and personal ephemera. The Eileen Gray exhibition at the National Museum of Ireland was made possible by the vision of then Director

Dr Patrick F. Wallace and then Minister of the Arts, Heritage, Gaeltacht and the Islands, Síle de Valera. It is now on permanent exhibition. When Joseph Rykwert wrote his initial article in 1968 enlightening the world once again about her architecture Eileen Gray wrote to her niece 'You did tell him that I was born in Ireland, didn't you, for the old few figures that remain, I was known as Irish, which I much preferred'.[75]

ENDNOTES

1   NMIEG 2000.119, Royal Designer for Industry Award.

2   RIAI Report 1974, under the section The RIAI Annual Report of the Council 1973.

3   RIAI Archives, letter from Eileen Blackford to Robin Walker, 23 July 1973.

4   RIAI Archives, letter from Kevin Fox, RIAI President, to Robin Walker B.Arch, FRIAI, 16 July 1973.

5   The citation was written by Robin Walker who had met with Eileen Gray in Paris; Gray had correspondence with Dorothy Walker, his wife, concerning her carpets.

6   RIAI Archives, McQuillan, James, *Eileen Gray – A Tribute*, RIAI Yearbook 1977, pp.108-111.

7   RIAI 1975-76 Yearbook, Eileen Gray obituary written by Robin Walker.

8   NMIEG 2003.339, letter from Eileen Gray to Prunella Clough, 10 April 1974.

9   NMIEG 2003.414. Letter from Eileen Gray to the RIAI, 1973.

10   NMIEG 2004.39, letter from Alan Irvine to Eileen Gray, 6 March 1973.

11   NMIEG 2003.40, letter from Eileen Gray to Alan Irvine, 11 March 1973.

12   NMIEG 2004.41, letter from Alan Irvine to Eileen Gray, 9 April 1973.

13   Binchy, Maeve, *The Irish Times,* 4 November 1976.

14   NIVAL, NCAD Library, Dorothy Walker collection, letter from Michael Murphy, Private Secretary to TD Liz McManus, to Patrick Mellett, 29 February 1996.

15   NIVAL, NCAD Library, Dorothy Walker collection, letter from Hannah O'Riordan, Private Secretary to TD Ruairi Quinn, to Patrick Mellett, 7 March 1996.

16   NIVAL, NCAD Library, Dorothy Walker collection, letter from Patrick Mellett to President Mary Robinson, 29 January 1996. In this letter Mellett explains the proposed renovation project in hope of the President's support. In reply, Colm Butler, Deputy Secretary to the President, writes on 29 February 1996 that the President is interested to learn of the project but as she did not have an executive role is not in a position to offer assistance; however she will meet with Mellett.

17   NIVAL, NCAD Library, Dorothy Walker collection, letter from Dorothy Walker to Patrick Mellett, 9 July 1995. Walker has spoken to the President of the RIAI regarding the project.

18   NIVAL, NCAD Library, Dorothy Walker collection, letter from Office of the Minister, Michael D. Higgins, to Patrick Mellett, 26 October 1995.

19   NIVAL, NCAD Library, Dorothy Walker collection, fax from Dorothy Walker to Patrick Mellett, 16 January 1996.

20   NIVAL, NCAD Library, Dorothy Walker collection, Mellett, Patrick, 'The Growth of an Idea - Villa E.1027', *Eze sur Mer*, 20 April 1995.

21   *L'Imaginaire Irlandais* was a major festival of contemporary Irish art and culture which was inaugurated in Paris on 15 March 1996 by the Minister for Arts, Culture and the Gaeltacht, Michael D. Higgins. The project was unique and had its genesis in a meeting between President Mary Robinson and President Mitterand on her state visit to France in May 1992.

22 NIVAL, NCAD library, Dorothy Walker collection, fax form Peter Kaegi to Patrick Mellett, 30 June 1996.

23 NIVAL, NCAD library, Dorothy Walker collection, letter from Patrick Mellett to Nicholas Robinson, 1 July 1996 and Fax from Peter Kaegi to Patrick Mellett, 6 July 1996.

24 NIVAL, NCAD library, Dorothy Walker collection, letter from Patrick Mellett to Pierre Joannon, 14 March 1996.

25 De Jonge, Wessel, DoCoMoMo Newsletter, No. 6, Eindhoven, the Netherlands, International Secretariat, November 1991, pp.9-10.

26 NIVAL, NCAD Library, Dorothy Walker collection, letter from Eileen Gray to Dorothy Walker 17 September 1973.

27 NIVAL, NCAD Library, Dorothy Walker collection, letter from Dorothy Walker to Terence Conran, undated.

28 NIVAL, NCAD Library, Dorothy Walker collection, letters from Prunella Clough to Dorothy Walker, 23 October 1973 and 16 October 1973.

29 NIVAL, NCAD Library, Dorothy Walker collection, letter from Eileen Gray to Dorothy Walker 13 January 1975.

30 NIVAL, NCAD Library, Dorothy Walker collection, letter from Eileen Gray to Robin Walker 12 February 1975.

31 NIVAL, NCAD Library, Dorothy Walker collection, letter from Eileen Gray to Dorothy Walker, 3 February 1975.

32 NMIEG 2003.417, letter from Eileen Gray to Prunella Clough, Sunday 10 March, year unknown.

33 NIVAL, NCAD Library, Dorothy Walker collection, letter from Eileen Gray to Robin Walker, 12 February 1975.

34 NIVAL, NCAD Library, Dorothy Walker collection, letter from Eileen Gray to Dorothy Walker, 15 June 1973.

35 NIVAL, NCAD Library, Dorothy Walker collection, letter from Eileen Gray to Dorothy Walker written from *Lou Pérou*, 12 August 1973.

36 NIVAL, NCAD Library, Dorothy Walker collection, letter from Eileen Gray to Dorothy Walker, 13 January 1975.

37 NIVAL, NCAD Library, Dorothy Walker collection, letter from Dorothy Walker to Alma Joyce, 16 October 1973.

38 NIVAL, NCAD Library, Dorothy Walker collection, letter from Eileen Gray to Dorothy Walker, 15 June 1973.

39 NIVAL, NCAD Library, Dorothy Walker collection, letter from Dorothy Walker to Prunella Clough, 15 November 1973.

40 NMIEG 2003.423, letter from Eileen Gray to Prunella Clough, 19 April 1974. See also NMIEG 2003.419, letter from Eileen Gray to Prunella Clough, April/May 1974.

41 NMIEG 2003.395, letter from Eileen Gray to Prunella Clough, 28 September 1970s.

42 NIVAL, NCAD Library, Dorothy Walker collection, letter from Prunella Clough to Dorothy Walker, 26 September 1973.

43 NIVAL, NCAD Library, Dorothy Walker collection, letters from Prunella Clough to Dorothy Walker, 23 October 1973 and 16 October 1973.

44 NMIEG 2003.417, letter from Eileen Gray to Prunella Clough, Sunday 10 March, year unknown.

45 Ibid.

46 NMIEG 2003.422, letter from Eileen Gray to Prunella Clough, Tuesday 27 November, year unknown.

47 NIVAL, NCAD Library, Dorothy Walker collection, letter from Eileen Gray to Dorothy Walker, 22 November 1973 and letter from Eileen Gray to Dorothy Walker, 17 September 1973.

48 NIVAL, NCAD Library, Dorothy Walker collection, letter from Prunella Clough to Dorothy Walker, 26 September 1973.

49 NIVAL, NCAD Library, Dorothy Walker collection, letter from Eileen Gray to Dorothy Walker, 22 November 1973.

50 NIVAL, NCAD Library, Dorothy Walker collection, letter from Eileen Gray to Dorothy Walker, 12 August 1973.

51 NIVAL, NCAD Library, Dorothy Walker collection, letter from Dorothy Walker to Alma Joyce, 16 October 1973.

52 NIVAL, NCAD Library, Dorothy Walker collection, letter from Dorothy Walker to V'Soske Joyce, 15 November 1973.

53 NIVAL, NCAD Library, Dorothy Walker collection, letter from V'Soske Joyce to Dorothy Walker, 27 October 1973.

54 NIVAL, NCAD Library, Dorothy Walker collection, letter from V'Soske Joyce to Dorothy Walker, 22 February 1974.

55 NIVAL, NCAD Library, Dorothy Walker collection, letter from Dorothy Walker to Eileen Gray, 1 March 1974.

56 NIVAL, NCAD Library, Dorothy Walker collection, letter from Dorothy Walker to Eileen Gray, 4 March 1974.

57 NIVAL, NCAD Library, Dorothy Walker collection, letter from Eileen Gray to Dorothy Walker, 10 March 1974, letter from Prunella Clough to Dorothy Walker, 3 April 1974.

58 NIVAL, NCAD Library, Dorothy Walker collection, letter from V'Soske Joyce to Eileen Gray, 4 April 1974.

59 NIVAL, NCAD Library, Dorothy Walker collection, letter from V'Soske Joyce to Dorothy Walker, 4 April 1974.

60 NMIEG 2003.422, letter from Eileen Gray to Prunella Clough, 27 November, year unknown.

61 NIVAL, NCAD Library, Dorothy Walker collection, letter from V'Soske Joyce to Dorothy Walker, 14 July 1974.

62 NMIEG 2003.419, letter from Eileen Gray to Prunella Clough, April/May 1974.

63 NIVAL, NCAD Library, Dorothy Walker collection, letter from V'Soske Joyce to Dorothy Walker, 14 July 1974.

64 NMIEG 2003.118, letter from Prunella Clough to Eileen Gray, undated.

65 NIVAL, NCAD Library, Dorothy Walker collection, letter from Dorothy Walker to Prunella Clough, 16 October 1973.

66 Binchy, Maeve, 'A Far from Demure Life', *The Irish Times,* 16 February 1976.

67 NIVAL, NCAD Library, Dorothy Walker collection, letter from Dorothy Walker to Terence Conran, undated.

68 NIVAL, NCAD Library, Dorothy Walker collection, letter from Prunella Clough to Dorothy Walker, 26 September 1973.

69 NIVAL, NCAD Library, Dorothy Walker collection, letters from Prunella Clough to Dorothy Walker, 23 October 1973 and 16 October 1973.

70 NIVAL, NCAD library, Dorothy Walker collection, letters from Prunella Clough to Dorothy Walker 23 October 1973 and 16 October 1973

71 NIVAL, NCAD library, Dorothy Walker collection, letter from Eileen Gray to Dorothy Walker from *Lou Pérou*, 12 August 1973.

72 NIVAL, NCAD library, Dorothy Walker collection, letter from Dorothy Walker to Eileen Gray, 15 November 1973.

73 NIVAL, NCAD library, Dorothy Walker collection, letters from Prunella Clough to Dorothy Walker 23 October 1973 and 16 October 1973.

74 Binchy, Maeve, *The Irish Times,* 4 November 1976.

75 NMIEG 2003.298.

List of Illustrations

3.12 Newspaper collage, circa 1920, board, newspaper, paper, paint, NMIEG 2000.176 © NMI

3.13 *Roquebrune* collage, 1926, paper, paint, NMIEG 2000.172 © NMI

3.14 Green, white, blue gouache and collage, 1930s, paper, paint, NMIEG 2000.174 © NMI

3.15 Black, grey and white gouache with yellow, 1930s, paper, paint, NMIEG 2003.123 © NMI

3.16 Charcoal drawing, circa 1934, paper, pencil, NMIEG 2003.148 © NMI

3.17 Charcoal drawing, circa 1920, paper, pencil, NMIEG 2003.147 © NMI

3.18 Black, grey and beige speckled gouache with swirling lines, 1920s, paper, card, crayon and pencil, NMIEG 2003.124 © NMI

3.19 Black and white speckled gouache with white lightening motif, 1920s, paper, card, crayon and pencil, NMIEG 2003.121 © NMI

3.20 Black with white circle gouache and collage, early 1920s, paper, paint, NMIEG 2003.119 © NMI

3.21 Brown and beige gouache, 1925, paper, paint, NMIEG 2003.128 © NMI

3.22 Speckled blue gouache with blue abstract motifs, late 1930s, paper, paint, NMIEG 2003.127 © NMI

3.23 *Hantage*, 1930s, paper, crayon, chalk, paint, NMIEG 2003.142 © NMI

3.24 *Still Life,* 1950, black and white photograph © Private Collection

3.25 *Tablescape,* 1920s, black and white photograph © Private Collection

3.26 *Still Life,* 1920s, black and white photograph © Private Collection

3.27 *Torse en marbre du 21 rue Bonaparte,* 1930s, black and white photograph © Private Collection

3.28 *Port Grimaud,* 1950s, black and white photograph © Private Collection

3.29 *Bois pétrifié,* late 1950s, black and white photograph © Private Collection

3.30 Photographic collage, circa 1920, photographic paper, paint, NMIEG 2000.171 © NMI

3.31 Drawing of an abstract sculpture, 1920s, paper, pencil, NMIEG 2003.528 © NMI

3.32 Sculptural head, 1920s, lava rock, NMIEG 2003.535 © NMI

3.33 Sculptural head, 1920s, cork, NMIEG 2003.534 © NMI

3.34 Sculptural head, 1940s, cork, paper, rubber, NMIEG 2000.116 © NMI

4.1 Eileen Gray, 1896, black and white photograph, NMIEG 2003.548 © NMI

4.2 Eileen Gray, late 1910s, early 1920s, black and white photograph, NMIEG 2003.567 © NMI

4.3 Room installation, *Harmony in Blue and Gold: The Peacock Room,* James McNeill Whistler, 1876-1877 oil paint and gold leaf on canvas, leather, and wood, Gift of Charles Lang Freer, F1904.61, © Freer Gallery of Art, Smithsonian Institution, Washington, D.C.

4.4 Lacquer samples, 1910s, wood, pigment, lacquer, NMIEG 2000.83 - NMIEG 2000.85 © NMI

4.5 Seizo Sugawara, 1910s, black and white photograph, NMIEG 2003.551 © NMI

4.6 Lacquer tools, 1910-1930, wood, metal, hair, pumice stone, pigment, polishing stones, NMIEG 2000.46 - NMIEG 2000.67 © NMI

4.7 Hamanaka's signature and ideogram signature in coral-red lacquer, detail on sofa, 1935, black lacquer, dyed black rubbed shagreen, wood, coral pigment © Galerie Dutko

4.8 A three-panelled black lacquered and gold leaf screen, leaf pattern on the same tone in slight relief, black lacquered back, Katsu Hamanaka, 1930s, wood, black lacquer, gold leaf © Galerie Dutko

4.9 *La Voie Lactée* (the Milky Way) four-panelled screen, 1912, wood, blue and natural lacquer, engraved, raised colours, mother of pearl in lay, NMIEG:2000.250 © NMI

4.10 *An Essay in Ontology with some remarks on Ceremonial Magic,* by Aleister Crowley, published privately, Paris, 1903, NMIEG 2003.57 © NMI

4.11 *Le Magician de la Nuit* (The Magician of the Night) lacquer panel, 1912-13, wood, blue and natural lacquer, engraved, raised colours, NMIEG 2003.866 © NMI

4.12 *Le Destin* (The Destiny) four-panelled screen, 1913, wood, red and blue lacquer, engraved, raised colours © Archives Galerie Vallois - Paris, Arnaud Carpentier

4.13 *The Lotus table,* 1913-14, black and dark green lacquer, ivory paint, wood © Archives Galerie Vallois - Paris, Arnaud Carpentier

5.9 *Poissons* carpet gouache, 1913, paper, paint © RIBA Library Drawing and Archives Collections

5.10 *Vogue* article on Eileen Gray, 1917, illustrating *Le Destin*, the *Zodiac table* in blue lacquer, the *Children of Lir* lacquer panel and a table with koi fish which complemented the rug *Poissons,* NMIEG 2000.251 © *NMI*

5.11 Black gouache with thin white lines, 1918-21, paper, paint, chalk, NMIEG 2003.132 © NMI

5.12 A six-panelled screen, circa 1921-23, lacquered, incised and painted wood © Christies images

5.13 Preliminary study for *Tarabos,* black and white gouache, 1919-22, paper, paint, NMIEG 2003.131 © *NMI*

5.14 Black and yellow carpet gouache, 1922-23, card, paper, paint, NMIEG 2003.89 © NMI

5.15 Beige with white circle carpet gouache with brown arc and silver line, 1923, paper, paint, NMIEG 2003.97 © NMI

5.16 Black and white square carpet gouache, 1920s, paper, paint, NMIEG 2003.114 © NMI

5.17 Beige, brown and white carpet gouache, 1920-22, paper, paint, NMIEG 2000.165 © NMI

5.18 Brown, blue, yellow and grey carpet gouache, 1921-25, card, paper, paint, NMIEG 2003.102 © NMI

5.19 Brown and grey with black rectangle carpet gouache, 1921-25, card, paper, paint, NMIEG 2003.104 © NMI

5.20 Grey, white, black and red carpet gouache, 1922, paper, paint, NMIEG 2000.164 © NMI

5.21 Black with red square carpet gouache, 1923, paper, paint, NMIEG 2003.92 © NMI

5.22 Interior of *Jean Désert* with the rug *Maryland* placed at the top of the stairs, 1922, black and white photograph, NMIEG 2003.1641 © NMI

5.23 *Ebony and Ivory* carpet, 1922, cotton, wool, black and white photograph, NMIEG 2003.1641 © NMI

5.24 *Monte Carlo room* with *Magie Noire*, 1923, in *Intérieurs Français*, 1925, NMIEG 2000.263 © NMI

5.25 Dining Room by Émile Jacques Ruhlmann with *Feston* rug by Eileen Gray, in *Intérieurs Français*, 1925 NMIEG 2000.263 © NMI

5.26 *Tango* rug, 1923, black and white photograph, NMIEG 2000.250 © NMI

5.27 *Bobadilla* carpet gouache, 1926-29, textured paper, paint, NMIEG 2003.98 © NMI

5.28 Circular black, grey, beige and white carpet gouache, 1920s, card, paper, paint, NMIEG 2003.112 © NMI

5.29 Circular black and grey carpet gouache, 1920s, card, paper, paint, NMIEG 2003.110 © NMI

5.30 Circular black, grey and beige carpet gouache, 1920s, card, paper, paint, NMIEG 2003.111 © NMI

5.31 Circular dark and light blue, grey and beige carpet gouache, 1920s, card, paper, paint, NMIEG 2003.113 © NMI

5.32 *Tour de Nesle* carpet gouache, 1918-21, card, paper, paint, NMIEG 2000.163 © NMI

5.33 Blue with white and grey motif carpet gouache, 1926-29, card, paper, paint, NMIEG 2003.101 © NMI

5.34 Geometric carpet drawing, circa 1922, paper, pencil, NMIEG 2003.154 © NMI

5.35 Guest bedroom at *E.1027* with the beige rug with two dark arcs, 1926-29, in *L'Architecture Vivante*, 1929 NMIEG 2000.256 © NMI

5.36 *Irish Green,* 1926-29, black and white photograph, NMIEG 2003.1641 © NMI

5.37 *Black board* carpet gouache, 1925-26, paper, paint, NMIEG 2000.162 © NMI

5.38 *La Bastide Blanche* rug, 1923, black and white photograph, NMIEG 2004.122 © NMI

5.39 Yellow carpet gouache, 1919-22, textured paper, paint, NMIEG 2003.105 © NMI

5.40 *No. 12,* by Mainie Jellett, originally produced 1930s, re-edition 2007-8, tufted wool rug © Ceadogan rugs

5.41 *St. Tropez* rug, 1975, hand tufted wool rug, NMIEG 2008.1 © NMI

6.1 Chest of drawers, 1919-22, zebrano, lacquer top and ivory handles, NMIEG 2000.250 © NMI

6.2 Vase, circa 1920, scorched pine and lacquered oak © Archives Galerie Vallois - Paris, Arnaud Carpentier

6.3 Drawings of *Transat chair*, 1920-22, paper, ink, pencil, NMIEG 2000.32 © NMI

6.4 Drawings of *Transat chair*, 1920-22, paper, ink, pencil, NMIEG 2000.31 © NMI

6.5 *Monte Carlo room* lamp, circa 1920, sculpted and polished ivory, mahogany base, material lampshade © Archives Galerie Vallois - Paris, Arnaud Carpentier

6.6 *Monte Carlo room* lacquer table, circa 1922, black lacquer table, with silver inlaid drawers, with red lacquer console, NMIEG 2003.862 © NMI

7.8 *E.1027*, drawing for shutters, 1926-29, paper, ink, pencil, NMIEG 2003.5 © NMI

7.9 *E.1027*, plans of windows and shutters, 1926-29, paper, ink, NMIEG 2000.250 © NMI

7.10 *E.1027*, living room plan with four elevations, 1926-29, paper, paint, pencil, ink, NMIEG 2003.8 © NMI

7.11 *E.1027*, living room, the north entrance with partition on the left, and dining alcove near the stairs on the right, 1926-29, black and white photograph NMIEG 2003.1641 © NMI

7.12 *E.1027,* living room, north entrance with partition, 1926-29, black and white photograph, NMIEG 2003.1641 © NMI

7.13 *E.1027*, living room, detail of north elevation, 1926, paper, paint, pencil, ink, NMIEG 2003.8 © NMI

7.14 *E.1027*, south elevation of living room, showing the fireplace, and sliding doors of the terrace, 1926-29 black and white photograph, NMIEG 2003.1641 © NMI

7.15 *E.1027*, living room, detail of south elevation, 1926, paper, paint, pencil, ink, NMIEG 2003.8 © NMI

7.16 *E.1027*, living room, west elevation, with sleeping alcove to the far left, and bathroom behind the wall partition, 1926-29 black and white photograph, NMIEG 2003.1641 © NMI

7.17 *E.1027*, sleeping area off the living room, west elevation wall, 1926-29, black and white photograph, NMIEG 2000.250 © NMI

7.18 *E.1027*, bathroom adjacent to the sleeping alcove, west elevation of the living room, 1926-29, black and white photograph, NMIEG 2000.250 © NMI

7.19 *E.1027*, living room, detail of west elevation, 1926, paper, paint, pencil, ink, NMIEG 2003.8 © NMI

7.20 *E.1027*, north-east elevation off the living room, with entrance partition, 1926-29, in *L'Architecture Vivante*, 1929, NMIEG 2003.496 © NMI

7.21 *E.1027*, east elevation off the living room, built into the wall of the stair is a niche for hats and shelves, 1926-29, in *L'Architecture Vivante*, 1929, NMIEG 2003.496 © NMI

7.22 *E.1027*, east elevation off the living room, built into the wall of the stair is a niche for hats and shelves, 1926-29, in *L'Architecture Vivante*, 1929, NMIEG 2003.496 © NMI

7.23 *E.1027*, dining alcove on east elevation of the living room, 1926-29, black and white photograph, NMIEG 2003.1641 © NMI

7.24 *E.1027*, living room, detail of east elevation, 1926, paper, paint, pencil, ink, NMIEG 2003.8 © NMI

7.25 *E.1027*, kitchen, 1926-29, black and white photograph, NMIEG 2000.250 © NMI

7.26 *E.1027*, kitchen, 1926-29, in *L'Architecture Vivante*, 1929, NMIEG 2003.496 © NMI

7.27 *E.1027*, kitchen, 1926-29, in *L'Architecture Vivante*, 1929, NMIEG 2003.496 © NMI

7.28 *E.1027*, kitchen, 1926-29, in *L'Architecture Vivante*, 1929, NMIEG 2003.496 © NMI

7.29 *E.1027*, bedroom plan and four elevations, 1926-29, paper, pencil, ink, NMIEG 2003.7 © NMI

7.30 *E.1027*, bedroom, north elevation, 1926-29, black and white photograph, NMIEG 2000.250 © NMI

7.31 *E.1027*, detail of bedroom, north elevation, 1926-29, paper, pencil, ink, NMIEG 2003.7 © NMI

7.32 *E.1027*, bedroom, south elevation, 1926-29, black and white photograph, NMIEG 2000.250 © NMI

7.33 *E.1027*, detail of bedroom, south elevation, 1926-29, paper, pencil, ink, NMIEG 2003.7 © NMI

7.34 *E.1027*, bedroom, storage compartments, mosquito net, reading lights, 1926-29, in *L'Architecture Vivante*, 1929 NMIEG 2003.496 © NMI

7.35 *E.1027*, bedroom, storage compartments, mosquito net, reading lights, 1926-29, in *L'Architecture Vivante*, 1929, NMIEG 2003.496 © NMI

7.36 *E.1027*, bedroom, storage compartments, mosquito net, reading lights, 1926-29, in *L'Architecture Vivante*, 1929, NMIEG 2003.496 © NMI

7.37 *E.1027,* bathroom off main bedroom, 1926-29, in *L'Architecture Vivante,* 1929, NMIEG 2003.496 © NMI

7.38 *E.1027,* bathroom off main bedroom, 1926-29, in *L'Architecture Vivante,* 1929, NMIEG 2003.496 © NMI

7.39 *E.1027,* bathroom off main bedroom, 1926-29, in *L'Architecture Vivante,* 1929, NMIEG 2003.496 © NMI

7.40 *E.1027*, circulation routes and sun orientation, 1926-29, paper, ink, pencil © RIBA Library Drawing and Archives Collections

7.72 *Rue Bonaparte apartment*, drawing room, 1930, black and white photograph, NMIEG 2003.1641 © NMI

7.73 *Rue Bonaparte apartment*, bedroom, 1930, black and white photograph, NMIEG 2003.1641 © NMI

8.1 Eileen Gray, by George Beresford, 1916-18, half plate glass negative, NMIEG 2003.554 © NMI

8.2 Watercolour, by Stephen Haweis, Christmas 1963, paper, ink, typed, inside book, NMIEG 2003.61 © NMI

8.3 Notes on Robert Louis Stevenson, unknown date, paper, ink, NMIEG 2003.511 © NMI

8.4 *Tahiti, the paradise of the Pacific*, by Stephen Haweis, Puck Publishing, New York, commercial ink, 11 April 1911 © Puck Publishing

8.5 Stephen Haweis, 18 July 1927, black and white photograph © Library of Congress Prints and Photographs Division Washington

8.6 *E.1027*, living room collage, 1926-29, black and white photograph, NMIEG 2003.1641 © NMI

8.7 *Anything about Dominica?* by Stephen Haweis, Advocate Ltd, Mountjoy, commercial ink, 1929-34 NMIEG 2003.60 © NMI

8.8 *Orts and Ends, Dominican Lyrics,* by Stephen Haweis, Bulletin Office, Roseau, commercial ink, August 1963, NMIEG 2003.61 © NMI

8.9 *Verses of a West Indian Summer*, by Stephen Haweis, 1963 paper, ink, handwritten, NMIEG 2003.62 © NMI

9.1 Eileen Gray, by Berenice Abbott, 1926, black and white photograph, NMIEG 2003.570 © NMI

9.2 Le Corbusier, Yvonne Gallis and Jean Badovici at E.1027, 1930s © Fondation Le Corbusier, Paris

9.3 *Villa Savoye* à Poissy, view of the roof top garden, Le Corbusier, 1928, paper, ink, NMIEG 2004.105 © NMI

9.4 *E.1027*, view from the sea, 1926-29, black and white photograph, NMIEG 2004.106 © NMI

9.5 *House for an Engineer*, model, with ground floor plan, first floor plan and elevations, 1926, black and white photograph, NMIEG 2003.1641 © NMI

9.6 Drawing of the interior of *Villa Le Lac*, looking onto Lake Léman, Corseaux, Switzerland, Le Corbusier, 1923, paper, pencil, coloured crayon © Fondation le Corbusier, Paris

9.7 *E.1027*, entrance path, 1926-29, in *L'Architecture Vivante*, 1929, NMIEG 2003.496 © NMI

9.8 *Villa Le Lac*, section with drawings, showing storage space in the laundry room, Le Corbusier, 1923, paper, pencil, ink, NMIEG 2000.182 © NMI

9.9 *Maison Ternisien*, plan, ground floor, Le Corbusier, 1926, paper, pencil, ink, NMIEG 2004.100 © NMI

9.10 *Maison Ternisien*, plan, first floor, Le Corbusier, 1926, paper, pencil, ink, NMIEG 2003.101 © NMI

9.11 *E.1027*, details of windows and shutters, 1926-29, black and white photograph, NMIEG 2000.250 © NMI

9.12 *E.1027,* entrance, north façade, details of windows and shutters, 1926-29, black and white photograph, NMIEG 2003.1641 © NMI

9.13 *Villa Le Lac*, north and south elevation, Le Corbusier, 1923, paper, pencil, ink, NMIEG 2004.97 © NMI

9.14 *E.1027*, ground floor plan, 1926-29, paper, ink, NMIEG 2003.9 © NMI

9.15 *Villa Le Lac*, ground floor plan, Le Corbusier, 1923, paper, ink, pencil, NMIEG 2004.98 © NMI

9.16 Le Corbusier, relaxing on the living room divan, *E.1027*, 1930s, black and white photograph © Fondation Le Corbusier, Paris

9.17 *Maison Ternisien*, view of ground floor, Le Corbusier, 1926, paper, ink, NMIEG 2004.104 © NMI

9.18 *Maison Ternisien*, view of first floor, Le Corbusier, 1926, paper, ink, NMIEG 2004.103 © NMI

9.19 *Lou Pérou,* view of garden with yucca and oleander plants, 1954-61, coloured photograph, NMIEG 2003.1426 © NMI

9.20 Drawing of garden at *E.1027*, 1930s, paper, ink, pencil ©RIBA Library Drawing and Archives collections

9.21 View of the terrace onto the garden, *E.1027*, 1926-29, black and white photograph, NMIEG 2003.1641 © NMI

9.22 Sun pool at *E.1027*, 1926-29, black and white photograph, NMIEG 2000.250 © NMI

9.23 Letter from Le Corbusier to Eileen Gray, April 1938, paper, ink, NMIEG 2000.183 © NMI

9.24 Drawing of a mural, 1920s, paper, pencil, NMIEG 2000.186 © NMI

11.7 Letter from Eileen Gray to Prunella Clough, 19 September 1942, paper, ink, NMIEG 2003.1758 © NMI

11.8 *The Rehousing of Britain*, by John Madge, Pivotal Press Ltd, London, 1946, NMIEG 2003.79 © NMI

11.9 Navy blue square with white stripe gouache, 1920s, paper, paint, NMIEG 2003.93 © NMI

11.10 Black and white strip carpet gouache, 1920s, paper, paint, NMIEG 2003.91 © NMI

11.11 *E.1027* showing the black gate, 1926-29, black and white photograph, NMIEG 2003.1641 © NMI

11.12 Letter from Eileen Gray to Prunella Clough, 1960, paper, typed ink, NMIEG 2003.337 © NMI

11.13 Letter from Eileen Gray to Prunella Clough, Sunday, January 1960, paper, typed ink, NMIEG 2003.302 © NMI

11.14 Letter from Eileen Gray to Prunella Clough, 26 October circa 1968, paper, typed ink, NMIEG 2003.298 © NMI

11.15 *House for Two Sculptors*, original model, 1933-34, wood, paper, card © RIBA Library Drawings and Archive Collections

11.16 *Ellipse house,* original model, 1936, wood, paper, card © RIBA Library Drawings and Archive Collections

11.17 Letter from Eileen Gray to Prunella Clough, Saturday, year unknown, paper, typed ink, NMIEG 2003.315 © NMI

11.18 The *Bibendum chair* in situ in E.1027, 1926-29, black and white photograph, NMIEG 2000.250 © NMI

11.19 The *Adjustable Dining/Coffee table* in situ at *Tempe à Pailla*, 1931-34, black and white photograph, NMIEG 2000.250 © NMI

11.20 *Lou Pérou*, 1954-61, colour photograph, NMIEG 2003.1443 © NMI

11.21 *Lou Pérou*, 1954-61, colour photograph, NMIEG 2003.1473 © NMI

11.22 *Monolith* carpet drawing, original drawing, 1918-21, paper, pencil, NMIEG 2003.96 © NMI

11.23 Block screen, 1922-23, wood, aluminium rods, NMIEG 2003.775 © NMI

11.24 Black lacquer block screen, wood, paint, aluminium, lacquer by Pierre Bobot, designed 1922-1923, executed 1973 © Virginia Museum of Fine Arts, Gift of Sydney and Frances Lewis

11.25 Red Lacquer block screen, wood, aluminium, the lacquer by Pierre Bobot, designed 1922-23, executed in 1973 © Private collection

11.26 *S bend chair*, 1938, laminated wood, painted, with canvas, repainted and upholstered 1972, inv:circ.579-1971 © Victoria and Albert Museum, London

12.1 Eileen Gray, by Alan Irvine, 1971, black and white photograph, NMIEG 2004.116 © NMI

12.2 Dorothy and Robin Walker, 1961, black and white photograph © Simon Walker

12.3 Honorary Fellowship, RIAI, 24 May 1973, paper, commercial ink, seal, NMIEG 2000.119 © NMI

12.4 Letter from Eileen Gray to Prunella Clough describing her meeting with Robin Walker, 12 February 1973, paper, typed ink, NMIEG 2003-397 © NMI

12.5 Letter from Eileen Gray to Prunella Clough, March 1973, paper, typed ink, pen, NMIEG 2003.417 © NMI

12.6 Letter from Eileen Gray to Prunella Clough, 19 April 1974, paper, typed ink, pen, NMIEG 2003.423 © NMI

12.7 Letter from Eileen Gray to Prunella Clough, April/May 1974, paper, typed ink, NMIEG 2003.419 © NMI

12.8 Letter from Eileen Gray to Prunella Clough, 28 September 1970s, paper, typed ink, NMIEG 2003.395 © NMI

12.9 *Wexford* carpet gouache, 1919, paper, paint, NMIEG 2003.103 © NMI

12.10 Eileen Gray, Donegal Carpets booklet, 1975, paper, commercial ink, black and white photographs, NMIEG 2000.266 © NMI

12.11 Eileen Gray, 1973, coloured photograph, NMIEG 2003.544 © NMI

8. Trouser cabinet, 1930-33, paint, transparent celluloid, aluminium hangers © Private Collection

9. Folding terrace chair, 1930-33, metal frame with upholstery © Private Collection

8. Trouser cabinet, 1930-33, paint, transparent celluloid,
aluminium hangers © Private Collection

Bibliography

Archives and Collections
Centre Pompidou Archives and Collections
Rare Book & Manuscript Library, Columbia University in the City of New York, Stephen Haweis Papers
Fondation Le Corbusier, Paris - Le Corbusier Foundation Archives, Paris
Institut National de l'histoire de l'art – collections Jacques Doucet, Paris
Irish Architectural Archive – McCurdy and Mitchell Collection
Museum of Modern Art, New York – MoMA
Musée des Art Décoratifs, Paris
National Museum of Ireland Eileen Gray Collection – NMIEG
The National Irish Visual Arts Library, National College of Art and Design, NCAD – NIVAL – Library Dorothy Walker Collection
Royal Institute of British Architects – RIBA Archives
Royal Institute of the Architects of Ireland
Tate Gallery Prunella Clough Collection and Archives
Trinity College Dublin Archive – TCD Archive
The Virginia Museum of Fine Art Collection
Victoria and Albert Museum Archives – V&A Archives
Victoria and Albert Museum – Prints and Drawings Archive
Vitra Design Museum

Articles, Newspapers, Journals
Unknown author
'Gray Peerage', *The Enniscorthy News and County Wexford Advertiser,* Enniscorthy, Saturday 11 July 1895
'Gray Peerage', *Dundee Advertiser,* Dundee, 10 April 1895
Pall Mall Gazette, 'Two English Gentlemen in the Latin Quarter', London, January 1904
'Fashionable Intelligence', *The Irish Times,* Dublin, 6 May 1919
'Lacquer Walls and Furniture Displace Old Gods in Paris and London', *Harper's Bazaar,* London, September 1920
'The Lacquer Cult', *The New York Herald Tribune,* New York, 20 June 1922
'Bargain Time', *The Daily Mail,* London, 10 June 1922
'Paris Notes and News: The Lacquer Cult', *The Daily Mail,* London, 10 June 1922
'Odd Designs at Art Studio of "Jean Desert". Furniture in Bizarre forms and Styles', *Chicago Tribune*, Chicago, 7 July 1922
'*Wendigen* se met encore une fois en devoir de nous monter des bizarreries: meubles et intérieurs Eileen Gray', *Telegraaf,* Paris, 27 September 1924
'Un Temple de l'Art Moderne, l'appartement de M. Jacques Doucet', *Femina,* Paris, January 1925
'Jean Dunand', *L'Art d'Aujourd'hui*, No.13, Paris, Spring, 1927
'À la Muette. Chez M. Philippe de Rothschild. Ch. Siclis décorateur', *Art et Industrie,* No.4, Paris, 10 April 1928
'La Maison de L'Artisan', *L'Architecture d'Aujourd'hui,* Vol.1, No.1, Boulogne, November, 1930
'Marcel Breuer, Berlin: Haus für einen Sportsman', *Moderne Bauformen,* August 1931
'L'Appartement de Madame J. Suzanne Talbot par Paul Ruaud', *L'Illustration,* 185, No. 4708, Paris, 27 May 1933
Abel, Richard, 'In the Belly of the Beast: The Early Years of the Pathé Frères', *Film History,* Vol. 5, No. 4, Indiana University Press, 1993

Abram, Joseph and Epron, J.P., 'Les Premiers élèves de Perret: la génération de l'Atelier du Palais du Bois', *Bulletin d'Informations Architecturales,* supplement to No.91, Paris, Institute Français d'Architecture, January 1985

Adam, Peter, 'Eileen Gray and Le Corbusier', *9H. On Rigor,* Cambridge (Mass), The MIT Press, 1989

Anscombe, Isabelle, 'Expatriates in Paris, Eileen Gray, Evelyn Wyld and Eyre de Lanux', *Apollo,* Vol. 115, No. 240, London, February 1982

Apollinaire, Guillaume, 'La Peinture Nouvelle: Notes d'Art', *Les Soirées de Paris,* No.3, Paris, Editions 6 rue Jacob, April 1912

Apollinaire, Guillaume, *Les Soirées de Paris,* No.22, Paris, Editions 6 rue Jacob, 15 March 1914

A. S., 'An Artist in Lacquer', *Vogue,* No.3, London, 1 August 1917

Badovici, Jean, 'Projet décoratif et fresques par F. Léger', *L'Architecture Vivante,* Paris, Autumn 1924

Badovici, Jean, 'Eileen Gray', *L'Architecture Vivante,* No.6, Paris, Editions Albert Morancé, Winter 1924

Badovici, Jean, 'L'Art de Eileen Gray', *Eileen Gray. Meubelen en interieurs,* special edition, *Wendigen,* Series 6, No.6, Amsterdam, 1924

Badovici, Jean, 'Eileen Gray', *Intérieurs Français,* Paris, Éditions Albert Morancé, 1925

Badovici, Jean, 'L'Architecture Utilitaire', *L'Architecture Vivante,* Paris, Winter 1926

Badovici, Jean, 'La Maison d'Aujourd'hui', *Cahiers d'Art,* Vol. 1, No. 1, Paris, January 1926

Badovici, Jean, 'Peintre, Murale ou Peintre Spatiale', *L'Architecture d'Aujourd'hui,* No. 3, Boulogne, March 1937

Badovici, Jean, *Architecture de Fêtes: Arts et Techniques, Paris 1937,* Paris, Éditions Albert Morancé, 1937

Barrès, Renaud, 'Eileen Gray, Le modernisme en bord de mer', *L'ŒIL,* Paris, May 2003

Banham, Reynor, 'Nostalgia for Style', *New Society,* Vol. 23, No. 539, London, 1 February 1973

Banham, Reynor, 'Four Rooms', *Four Rooms,* London, Arts Council of Great Britain, 1984

Benton, Charlotte, 'Le Corbusier, Furniture and the Interior', *Journal of Design History*, Vol. 3, Nos. 2-3, Oxford, 1990

Binchy, Maeve, 'A Far from Demure Life', *The Irish Times,* Dublin, 16 February 1976

Binchy, Maeve, 'Obituary', *The Irish Times,* Dublin, 4 November 1976

Blumenthal, Max, 'Jean Badovici 1893-1956', *Techniques et Architecture,* Vol.16, No.4, Paris, November 1956

Boeken, Albert, 'Moderne Fransche Kunstnijverheld', (Review of the XIV Salon des Artistes Décorateurs), *Bouwkundig Weekblad,* Amsterdam, 14 July 1923

Breton, André, editor, *Le Surréalisme au Service de la Révolution,* No.3 and 4, Paris, Librairie José Corti, 1931.

Brett, Guy, 'Do Sit Down', *The Times,* London, 8 August 1970

Brockmann, Heinz, 'A Remarkable Pioneer', *Financial Times,* London, February 1973

Bumpus, Judith, 'Prunella Clough', *Contemporary Art,* winter 1993-1994

Burch George Bosworth, 'The Philosophy of P.D. Ouspensky', *The Review of Metaphysics,* No.2, December 1951

Chalamel, Félix, 'Les Contreplaqués et Leurs Emplois', *L'Architecture d'Aujourd'hui,* Boulogne, November 1930

Chareau, Pierre, 'Un appartement moderne. Chez Mme Jacques Errera', *Art et Industrie,* No.8, Paris, November 1926

Chareau, Pierre, 'La création artistique et l'imitation commerciale', *L'Architecture d'Aujourd'hui,* Vol. 6, No. 9, Boulogne, September 1935

Chavance, René, 'Le 14e Salon des Artistes Décorateurs', *Art et Décoration,* t. 43, Paris, January - June 1923

Chavance, René, 'Le Salons de 1923', *Beaux-Arts,* Paris, June 1923

Chavance, René, and Vernes, Henri, 'Le mobilier, les artistes meubiliers', *Pour Comprendre L'Art Décoratif Moderne en France,* Paris, Librairie Hachette, 1925

Clausen, Meredith, 'The École des Beaux-Arts: Towards a Gendered History,' *Journal of the Society of Architectural Historians,* Vol.69, No.2, Philadelphia, June, 2010

Clermont Tonnerre, Élisabeth, (Élisabeth de Gramont), 'Les Laques d'Eileen Gray', *Les Feuillets d'Art,* No.3, Paris, February – March 1922

Clermont Tonnerre, Élisabeth, (Élisabeth de Gramont), 'The Lacquer work of Miss E.Gray', *The Living Arts,* No.3, London, New York, February- March 1922

Colomina, Beatriz, 'War on Architecture', *Assemblage, Violence, Space,* No.20, Cambridge (Mass.), MIT Press, April 1993

Compton, Susan P., 'Malevich and the Fourth Dimension', *The Studio International,* Vol.187, No.965, London, April 1974,

Compton, Susan P., 'Malevich's Suprematism – The Higher Intuition', *The Burlington Magazine*, Vol. 118, No. 881, London, August 1976

Constant, Caroline, 'E.1027: The Nonheroic Modernism of Eileen Gray', *Journal of the Society of Architectural Historians,* Vol.53, No.3, Philadelphia, September 1994

De Felice, Roger, 'Le Salon des Artistes Décorateurs', *Les Art Français,* Paris, 1919

De Jonge, Wessel, *DOCOMOMO Newsletter*, No.6, International Secretariat, Eindhoven, the Netherlands, November 1991

Delaunay, Sonia, 'Tapis et Tissus', *L'Art International d'Aujourd'hui,* No. 15, Paris, Éditions Charles Moreau, 1929

Deshairs, Léon, 'Tapis Modernes', *Art et Décoration*, Vol. 38, No. 4,Paris, September 1920.

Deshairs, Léon, 'Le XVᵉ Salon des Artistes Décorateurs', *Art et Décoration*, Vol. 45, No. 6, Paris, June 1924

Deshairs, Léon, 'Une villa modern à Hyères', *Art et Décoration,* t.54, Paris, July–December, 1928

Deshairs, Léon, 'Le Mobilier et les Arts Décoratifs au Salon d'Automne', *Art et Décoration*, Vol. 56, No. 6, Paris, December 1929

Descharmes, Robert, 'Manik Bagh', *Connaisance des Arts,* No.223, Paris, 1970

Dervaux, Adolphe, 'Le beau, le vrai, l'utile et la réorganisation de la cité', *La Grande Revue,* 90, No.584, Paris, April 1916

Diamond, Rosamund, 'Eileen Gray: an introduction', *9H,* No. 8, Cambridge, (Mass), 1989

Dormey, Marie, 'Intervue d'Auguste Perret sur Exposition Internationale des Art Décoratifs', *L'Amour de l'Art,* No. 6, Paris, May 1925

Dormey, Marie, 'Les Intérieurs à l'Exposition internationale des Art Décoratifs', *L'Amour de l'Art,* No. 8, Paris, May 1925

Einstein, Carl, 'Notes sur le cubisme', *Documents, No.3,* Paris, 39 rue de la Boétie, June 1929

Evans, Robert, 'The Developed Surface: an Enquiry into the Brief Life of Eighteenth Century Drawing Technique', *9H,* No.8, Cambridge (Mass), The MIT Press, 1989

Faré, Michel, 'Jean Badovici obituary', *Architecture d'Aujourd'hui,* Vol. 27, Nos. 67–68, Boulogne, October 1956

Fehrer, Catherine, 'Women at the Académie Julian in Paris', *The Burlington Magazine,* Vol.136, No.1100, London, November 1994

Fehrer, Catherine, 'New Light on the Académie Julian', *Gazette des Beaux Arts,* Paris, 1984

Fry, Roger, *The New Burlington Magazine,* The Burlington Magazine Ltd, No.1, London, 1907

Gardiner, Stephen, 'The Magic of Eileen Gray', *Observer,* London, 4 March 1973

Garner, Philippe, 'The Robert Walker Collection Part I', *Connoisseur,* London, September 1971

Garner, Philippe, 'The Lacquer Work of Eileen Gray and Jean Dunand', *Connoisseur,* Vol. 183, No.735, London, May 1973

Giedion, Sigfried, 'L'Architecture contemporaine dans les pays méridionaux: I. Midi de la France, Tunisie, Amérique du Sud', *Cahiers d'Arts,* Vol. 6, No. 2, Paris, 1931

Goyon, Maximilienne, 'L'Avenir de nos Filles', *L'Académie Julian,* Paris, December 1903

Gray, Eileen, 'Intérieur à Paris, 1924', *L'Architecture Vivante,* Paris, Editions Albert Morancé, Winter 1926

Gray, Eileen, and Badovici, Jean, 'E.1027. Maison en Bord de Mer', *L'Architecture Vivante,* Paris, Editions Albert Morancé, winter edition 1929

Gray, Eileen and Jean Badovici, 'La maison minimum', *L'Architecture d'Aujourd'hui,* Vol. 1, No. 1 Boulogne, November 1930

Gray, Eileen and Jean Badovici, 'Wohnhaus am Meeresufer bei Cap Martin', *Der Baumeister,* Vol. 28, No. 10, Munich, October 1930

Gray, Eileen, 'Projet pour un Centre Culturel', *L'Architecture d'Aujourd'hui*, Thirtieth year, No. 82 Boulogne, February–March 1959

Hecker, Stefan, and Müller, Christian, editors, 'Eileen Gray: une approche ludique de la modernité', *Archithese,* Vol. 21, No. 4, Niederteufen, Switzerland, July–August 1991

Holland, Clive, 'Student Life in Paris', *The Studio and Illuminated Magazine of Fine and Applied Arts*, Vol. 27, London, 1903

Holland, Clive, 'Student Life in Paris', *The Studio Magazine,* Vol. 27, London, 1903

Irvine, Alan, 'Pioneer Lady', *Architectural Review,* No.152, London, August 1972

Johnson, J. Stewart, 'Pioneer Lady', *Architectural Review,* No. 152, London, August 1972

Joubin, André, 'Le Studio de Jacques Doucet', *L'Illustration,* No. 4548, Paris 3 May 1930

Kiesler, Frederick, 'Notes d'Amérique', *Cahiers d'Art*, Vol. 6, No. 3, Paris, 1931

Koechlin, Raymond, 'L'art français moderne n'est pas "munichois"', *L'Art français moderne,* Paris, January, 1916

Lainé, Lucien, 'De la Tente du Nomade au Palais de Ciment', *Renaissance de l'Art Français et des Industries de Luxe,* Paris, May 1929

Le Corbusier, 'The murals of Le Corbusier', Œuvre Complète 1938-46, Zurich, Les Editions d'Architecture, 1946

Le Corbusier, 'L'Unité', *L'Architecture d'Aujourd'hui,* No.19, Boulogne, 1948

Le Corbusier, 'Hommage à Jean Badovici', *Techniques et Architecture,* Vol.16, No.4, Paris, November 1956

Lowenstam, Steven, 'The Shroud of Laertes and Penelope's Guile', *The Classical Journal,* Vol. 95, No.4, The Classical Association of the Middle West and South, 2000

Moholy-Nagy, László, 'Malerei, Fotografie, Film', *Bauhausbücher,* Vol. 8, 1925

Mourey, Gabriel, 'Le 14ᵉ Salon des Artistes Décorateurs', *L'Amour de L'Art,* Vol.4, No.5, Paris, May 1923

Norman, Geraldine, 'Sofa in Art Deco Auction', *The Times,* London, 9 November 1972

O'Connor, Ulick, 'The Abbey Portraits', *Irish Arts Review,* Vol. 21, No.3, Dublin, Autumn 2004

Pawlowski, Gaston de, 'Le 14ᵉ Salon des artistes décorateurs', *Le Journal,* Paris, 10 May 1923

Pillard-Verneuil, Maurice, *Le Salon d'Automne,* No. 28, Paris, November 1910

Pillard-Verneuil, Maurice, 'Le Salon de la Société des Artistes Décorateurs en 1913', *Art et Décoration,* t.33, Paris, January-June 1913

Postle, Martin, 'The Foundation of the Slade School of Fine Art: Fifty-Nine Letters in the Record Office of University College London', *The Volume of the Walpole Society,* Vol.58, London, 1995/1996

Raynal, Maurice, 'Les Arts', *L'Intransigeant,* Paris, 5 June 1922

Raynal, Maurice, 'Lipchitz', *Art d'Aujourd 'hui,* No.1, Paris, Action, 1920

Rayon, Jean Paul, 'Eileen Gray : Un manifeste, 1926-29', *Architecture Mouvement Continuité,* No.37, Paris, November 1975

Rayon, Jean-Paul and Brigitte Loye, 'Eileen Gray architetto 1879-1976', *Casabella,* Vol. 46, No. 480 Milan,1982

Rayon, Jean-Paul, 'Eileen Gray: The North Star and the South Star', *9H,* No. 8, Cambridge, (Mass), 1989

Roger-Marx, Claude, 'Le Salon des Artistes Décorateurs', *Le Crapouillot,* No.2, Paris, 15 April 1919

Rosenthal, Gabrielle, 'Les Tapis Nouveaux', *L'Amour de l'Art,* No.8, Paris, August 1926

Rowe, Colin, 'The Dominican Monastery of La Tourette, aveux sur l'Arbresle', *The Architectural Review,* Vol.129, No.772, London, The Architectural Press, June 1961

Rykwert, Joseph, 'Un Omaggio a Eileen Gray; pioniera del design', *Domus,* No. 468, Milan, Casa, December 1968

Rykwert, Joseph, 'Eileen Gray: Two Houses and an Interior, 1926-1933', *Perspecta: The Yale Architectural Journal,* No.13/14, New Haven, 1971

Rykwert, Joseph, 'Eileen Gray: Pioneer of Design', *The Architectural Review*, Vol. 152, No.910, London, The Architectural Press, December 1972

Schlumberger Evelyne, '1913, Irlandaise à Paris: Premier Succès en Laque, 1973, Toujours Parisienne et une Quête d'Innovations', *Connaissance des Arts,* No.258, Paris, August 1973

Schwabe, Randolph, 'Three Teachers: Brown, Tonks and Steer', *The Burlington Magazine for Connoisseurs,* Vol. 82, No.483, London, June 1943

Starr, Ruth, 'Eileen Gray: a child of Japonisme?' *Artefact,* Journal of the Irish Association of Art Historians, Issue one, Dublin, Autumn 2007

Teitelbaum, Mo, 'Lady of the Rue Bonaparte', *The Sunday Times Magazine,* London, 22 June 1975

Vaizey, Marina, 'The Collection of Mr. and Mrs. Robert Walker, Part II', *Connoisseur*, London, April 1973

van Ravesteyn, Sybold, 'Review of the XIV Salon des Artistes Décorateurs', *Bouwkundig Weekblad*, Amsterdam, 14 July 1923

Varenne, Gaston, 'L'Art Urbain et le Mobilier au Salon d'Automne', *Art et Décoration*, t.44, Paris, July-December 1923

Vaudroyer, Jean Louis, 'Le Salon d'Automne II, l'art décoratif', *Art et Décoration*, No.36, Paris, December 1919

Vauxcelles, Louis. 'La vie artistique', *L'Amour de l'art*, Paris, November 1920

Waldemar, George, 'Le 14ᵉ Salon des artistes décorateurs', *Ère Nouvelle*, Paris, 8 May 1923

Waldemar, George, 'Le mois artistique – L'Art décoratif et urbain au Salon d'automne', *La Revue Mondiale*, No.23, Paris, 1 December 1924

Waldemar, George, 'Le mois artistique. L'Art décoratif moderne', *La Revue Mondiale*, No.5, Paris, 1 March 1925

Watelin, L., 'The Arts of Decorative and Applied Arts at the Salon d'Automne', *Arts and Artists*, Volume VI, No.32, Paris, October 1922

Walker, Dorothy, 'Alphabetic Extravaganzas', *Hibernia Magazine*, Dublin, 8 June 1973

Werner, Bruno E., 'Ein Maharadscha wird Eingerichtet', *Deutsche Allgemeine Zeitung*, January 1932

Wheelwright, Robert, 'Thoughts on Problem and Form', *Landscape Architecture Quarterly*, Vol. 21, No.1, October 1930

Zervos, Christian, 'Les Tendances actuelles de l'art contemporain. Le Mobilier : hier et aujourd'hui', *Le Revue de l'art ancien et moderne*, No.269, January 1925

Zervos, Christian, 'Choix des œuvres les plus expressives de la décoration contemporaine', *Les Arts de la Maison*, Paris, Winter 1924

Catalogues

Catalogue des ouvrages de peintures, sculpture, dessin, gravure, architecture et art décoratif exposés au Grand Palais des Champs-Élysées, 1 November – 17 December 1922, No.1077-1081, Société du Salon d'automne, Paris, Société français Editions, 1922

Catalogue du 14e Salon du 3 mai au 1er juillet 1923. Paris, Grand Palais des Champs-Élysées. Société des artistes décorateurs, Paris, Société des artistes décorateurs, 1923, No.308, No.309 and No.310

Catalogue du 15e Salon du 8 mai au 8 juillet 1923. Paris, Grand Palais des Champs-Élysées. Société des artistes décorateurs, Paris, Société des artistes décorateurs, 1924

Exposition Internationale des Arts Décoratifs et Industriels Modernes, 1925, General report, Vol. VI, Rapport de la Classe 13 – Tissu et Papier, Paris, 1928

Ancienne Collection Jacques Doucet: mobilier Art Déco provenant du Studio St James à Neuilly, sales catalogue, Audap, Godeau, Solanet, Paris Hôtel Drouot, 8 November 1972

Eileen Gray, Pioneer of Design, Exhibition Catalogue, London, Heinz Gallery, RIBA/Westerham Press, 1973

RIAI Catalogue, *Eileen Gray – Pioneer of Design*, Dublin, Royal Institute of the Architects of Ireland, 1973

Eileen Gray Carpets, Donegal Carpets, Donegal, 1974

Rééditions, Ecart, Paris, 2000

Camard, *20-21*, Paris, 6 April 2009

Christie's, *An Important Private Collection*, New York, 9-12 December 1994

Christie's, *Les Arts Décoratifs*, Paris, 20 May 2003

Christie's, *An Important Private Collection of Mid-20th Century Design*, New York, 26 September 2007

Christie's, *Collection Yves Saint Laurent et Pierre Bergé*, Paris, 23-25 February 2009

Christie's, *De Lorenzo – 30 years*, New York, 14 December 2010

Christie's, *Les Collections du Château de Gourdon*, Paris, 29-31 March 2011

Christie's, *The Steven A. Greenberg Collection, Masterpieces of French Art Deco*, New York, 12-13 December 2012

Sotheby's, *Collection Eileen Gray, Mobilier, Objets et Projets de sa Création*, Monaco, 25 May 1980

Sotheby's, *Mobilier Moderniste Provenant du Palais du Maharaja d'Indore*, 25 May 1980

Sotheby's, *Arts Décoratifs Styles 1900 et 1925*. Monaco, 25 June 1981

Sotheby's, *Important Twentieth Century Furniture*, New York, 6 May 1989

Sotheby's, *Arts Décoratifs du XXe Siècle*, Monaco, 13 October 1991

Sotheby's, *Arts Décoratifs du XXe Siècle et Design Contemporain*, Paris, 22 November 2011

Films

Bailey, Derek, 'Lacquer Lust: Eileen Gray', *Aquarius*, London Thames Television Productions, November 1975

Publications

Abel, Richard, *The Ciné Goes to Town: French cinema, 1896-1914,* Los Angeles, University of California Press, 1994

Adam, Marcelle, *Les Caricatures de Puvis de Chavannes,* Paris, Librairie Charles Delagrave, 1906.

Adam, Peter, *Eileen Gray: Architect/Designer: A Biography,* London, Thames and Hudson, 1987

Adam, Peter, *The Adjustable Table E.1027 by Eileen Gray,* Francfort-sur-le-Main, Verlag Form, 1998

Adam, Peter, *Eileen Gray: Architect/Designer: A Biography,* London, Thames and Hudson, 2000

Adam, Peter, *Eileen Gray, Her Life and Work,* London, Thames and Hudson, 2009

Adam, Peter, *Eileen Gray, sa vie, son œuvre,* Paris, Éditions de la Différence, 2012

Anscombe, Isabelle, *Arts and Crafts in Britain and America,* Van Nostrand Reinhold, 1983

Anscombe, Isabelle, *A Woman's Touch. Women in Design from 1860 to the Present Day,* London, Virago Press Ltd., 1984

Anscombe, Isabelle, *Arts and Crafts Style,* Phaidon, 1996

Antliff, Mark, *Inventing Bergson: Cultural Politics and the Parisian Avant-Garde,* Princeton, Princeton University Press, 1993

Apollinaire, Guillaume, *Les Peintres Cubistes*, Paris, Editions Eugène Figuière et Cie, 1913

Archieri, Jean-Francois, 'Jean Badovici: Une historie Confisquée', in Pitiot, Cloé, *Eileen Gray,* Paris, Éditions du Centre Pompidou, 2013

Arnold, Bruce, *Mainie Jellett and the Modern Movement in Ireland*, New Haven & London, Yale University Press, 1991

Arwas, Victor, *Art Deco,* London, Academy Editions, New York, Harry N. Abrams Editions Inc., 1980

Arwas, Victor, *the Art of Glass Art Nouveau to Art Deco,* Berkshire, Papadakis Publisher, 1997

Arwas, Victor, *From Mackintosh to Liberty – the Birth of a Style,* Berkshire, Papadakis Publisher, 2000

Arwas, Victor, *Art Nouveau- the French Aesthetic,* Berkshire, Papadakis Publisher, 2002

Atwood, John, *Edexcel A Level Design and Technology for Product Design: Resistant Materials,* Heinemann, 2009

Auslander, Leora, *Taste and Power, Furnishing Modern France,* Berkeley, Los Angeles and London, University of California Press, 1996

Badovici, Jean, *Maisons de Rapport de Charles Plumet,* Paris, Éditions Albert Morancé, 1923

Badovici, Jean, *Harmonies Intérieurs de Ruhlmann,* Paris Éditions Albert Morancé 1924

Badovici, Jean, *Intérieurs de Süe et Mare,* Paris Éditions Albert Morancé 1924

Badovici, Jean, *La Maison d'Aujourd'hui,* Paris Éditions Albert Morancé, 1925

Badovici, Jean, *Grandes Constructions, Béton Armé, Acier, Verre,* Paris, Éditions Albert Morancé, 1927

Badovici, Jean, *Deux Études de Paul Nelson,* Special edition of *L'Architecture Vivante*, Paris, Editions Albert Morancé, 1936

Badovici, Jean, *La Maison Suspendue. Recherche de Paul Nelson,* with text by Nelson, Paul, special edition of *L'Architecture Vivante*, Paris, Éditions Albert Morancé, 1939

Bailey, Stephen and Conran, Terence, *Design: Intelligence Made Visible,* Conran Octopus, 2007

Banham, Reyner, *Theory and Design in the First Machine Age,* London Architectural Press, 1960

Barney, Natalie, *Poem & Poèmes et autres alliances,* Paris, Editions Émile-Paul Frères, 1929

Bashkirtseff, Marie, *Journal de Marie Bashkirtseff,* Paris, Editions Mazarine, 1980

Battersby Martin, *The Decorative Twenties,* London, Studio Vista, 1969

Battersby, Martin, *The Decorative Thirties,* London, Herbert Press Ltd, 1988

Battersby, Martin, *Art Deco Fashion: French Designers, 1908-1925,* London, St Martin's Press, 1984

Baudot, Francois, *Eileen Gray,* Paris, London, Thames & Hudson, 1998

Bence-Jones, Mark, *A Guide to Irish Country Houses,* London, Constable and Company Ltd, 1988

Bennington, Jonathan, *Roderic O'Conor,* Dublin, Irish Academic Press, 1992

Benton, Tim, Benton, Charlotte, and Scharf, Aaron, *Design 1920s, Modernism in the Decorative Arts: Paris*

1910-1930, Milton Keynes, The Open University Press, 1975

Benton, Tim, *The Villas of Le Corbusier, 1920-1930, With photographs in the Lucien Hervé Collection,* New Haven/ London, Yale University Press, 1987

Benton, Tim, *LC FOTO Le Corbusier Secret Photographer,* Switzerland, Lar Müller Publishers, 2013

Bingham, Neil, *Wright to Gehry, Drawings from the Collection of Barbara Pine,* London, Sir John Soane's Museum, 2005

Boesiger, Willy. Le Corbusier: *Œuvre Complète* 1938-1946, Zurich Editions, 1946

Boesiger, Willy. Le Corbusier: *Œuvre Complète* 1946-1952, Zurich Editions, 1953

Boesiger, W. & Girsberger, H. *Le Corbusier, 1910-65,* Zurich Editions, 1967

Bonnevier, Katarina, 'A Queer analysis of Eileen Gray's E.1027', *Negotiating Domesticity – spatial productions of gender in modern architecture,* Routledge, London, 2005

Bordon, Ian, *Gender Space Architecture; an Interdisciplinary Introduction,* London, Routledge Press, 1999

Bourne, Jonathan, *Lacquer, An International History and Collector's Guide,* London, The Crowood Press, 1984

Bousquet Henri, *Catalogue Pathé des années 1896 à 1914,* Bassac, 1993-1996

Brande, Dorothea, *Wake Up and Live,* New York, Simon and Schuster, 1936

Brooks, H. Allen, *Le Corbusier's Formative Years,* Chicago and London, University of Chicago Press, 1997

Bruce, Kathleen, *Self Portrait of an Artist,* London, John Murray, 1949

Brunhammer, Yvonne, *Les Années 25: Collections du Musée des Arts Décoratifs,* Paris, Musée des Arts Décoratifs, 1966

Brunhammer, Yvonne, *The Nineteen Twenties Style,* London, Hamlyn, 1969

Brunhammer, Yvonne, *Le Style 1925*, Paris, Baschet Editions 1975

Brunhammer, Yvonne, *Art Nouveau Belgium and France,* Menil Collection, 1976

Brunhammer, Yvonne, *Art Deco Style,* London, St Martin's Press, 1984

Brunhammer, Yvonne, and Tise, Suzanne, *The Decorative Arts in France. La Société des artistes décorateurs 1900-1942,* New York, Rizzoli, 1989

Burke, Carolyn, *Becoming Modern, the Life of Mina Loy,* New York, Farrar, Straus and Giroux, 1996

Burke, Mary Alice, *Elizabeth Nourse, 1859-1938: A Salon Career,* Washington, Smithsonian, 1983

Butcher, Samuel Henry, and Lang, Andrew, (translation by), *The Odyssey of Homer,* New York Editions McMillan and Co., 1903.

Byers, Mel, *The Design Encyclopaedia*, London, Laurence King Publications, 1994

Campbell, Joan, *The German Werkbund, Politics of Reform and Applied Arts,* Princeton University Press, Princeton, New Jersey, 1978

Chapon, François, *Mystère et Splendeurs de Jacques Doucet 1853-1929,* Paris, J.C. Lattès, 1984

Chareau, Pierre, *Meubles,* Paris, Charles Moreau, 1929

Chavance, René, *Une Ambassade Française organisé par la Société des Artistes Décorateurs: Exposition Internationale des Arts Décoratifs et Industriels Modernes,* Paris: Charles Moreau, 1925

Chesterton, Gilbert K, *Heretics,* London, William Clowes and Sons Limited Editions, 1905

Chilvers, Ian, 'Roger Fry', *The Concise Oxford English Dictionary of Art and Artists,* London, 2003

Clapp, Susannah, *With Chatwin: Portrait of a Writer*, New York, Alfred A. Knopf, 1997

Coates, Michael, *The Visual Dictionary of Interior Architecture and Design,* Ava publishing, 2008

Cocteau, Jean, *Dessins,* Paris, Delamain, Boutelleau et Cie, 1923

Colomina, Beatriz, ed., *Sexuality and Space,* New York, Princeton Architectural Press, 1992

Colomina, Beatriz, *Privacy and Publicity – Modern Architecture as Mass Media,* MIT Press, 1994

Colomina, Beatriz, 'Battle Lines: E.1027', *The Sex of Architecture,* New York, Harry Abrams, 1996

Constant, Caroline, 'Eileen Gray: architecture and the politics of leisure', in *Form: Modernism and History, Festschrift in honour of Eduard F. Sekler*, edited by Alexander Von Hoffman, Cambridge: Graduate School of Design, 1996

Constant, Caroline, *Eileen Gray*, London, Phaidon, 2000

Copley, Antony, *Sexual Moralities in France, 1780-1980: New ideas on the family, divorce and homosexuality,*

London and New York, Routledge, 1989

Cranz, Galen, *The Chair rethinking culture, body and design,* New York, W. W. Norton & Co., 2000

Cronin, Vincent, *Paris City of Light: 1919-1939,* New York, Harper Collins, 1994

Crowley, Aleister*, The Mother's Tragedy,* London, Privately Printed, 1901

Crowley, Aleister, *Berashith, An Essay in Ontology with some remarks on Ceremonial Magic,* Paris, Clarke and Bishop Printers, 1902

Crowley, Aleister, *Tannhäuser, a Story of All Time,* London, Kegan Paul, Trench, Trübner & Co. Ltd, 1902

Crowley, Aleister, *The Star and the Garter,* London, Watts & Co, 1903

Crowley, Aleister, *The Confessions of Aleister Crowley,* London, Bantam Press, 1971

Cunard, Nancy, *Nous Gens d'Espagne*, Paris, Labau Press, December 1949

Curtis, William, *Le Corbusier Ideas and Forms*, London, Phaidon, 1986

Curtis, William, *Modern Architecture since 1900,* London, Phaidon, Third Edition, 1997

Czerwinski, Michael, *Fifty Chairs that changed the world,* Conran Octopus, 2009

Davies, Colin, *Key Houses of the Twentieth Century,* London, Lawrence King 2006

Day, Susan, *Art Deco and Modernist Carpets,* London, Thames and Hudson, 2002

Debrett's Peerage, Baronetage, Knightage and Companionage, London, Dean and Son Limited, 1906

Delarue Mardrus, Lucie, *Le Pain Blanc*, Paris, J Frenczi et Fils, 1923

Delarue Mardrus, Lucie, *L'Ange et les Pervers,* Paris, 1930

Delorme, Jean Claude and Clair, Philippe, *L'École de Paris : 10 architectes et leurs immeubles 1905-1937,* Paris, Editions du moniteur, 1981

Derouet, Christian, *Fernand Léger une correspondance d'affaires,* Éditions du Centre Pompidou, 1996

Derouet, Christian, *Fernand Léger une correspondance poste restante,* Éditions du Centre Pompidou, 1997

Derouet, Christian, Labrusse, Rémi, and Rochlitz, Rainer, *Cahiers D'Art Musée Zervos à Vézelay*, Éditions Musée Zervos, 2005

Derouet, Christian, *Zervos – Cahiers d'art,* Éditions du Centre Pompidou, 2011

Dottin, Georges, *L'Épopée Irlandaise,* Paris, La Renaissance du Livre, 1928

Duchamp, Marcel, *Le Surréalisme en 1947,* Paris, Galerie Maeght, 1947

Duncan, Alastair, *Art Deco Furniture. The French Designers,* London, Thames & Hudson, 1984

Fabre, Gladys 'Femme-Architecte et Modernité en Mouvement', *Charlotte Perriand,* Paris, Editions Centre Pompidou, 2006

Fesser, Andrea and Daly, Maureen, *The Materiality of Colour,* Farnham, Ashgate, 2012

Flammarion, Camille, *Death and Its Mystery*, Three Volumes, London, T. Fisher Unwin, 1921

Forestier, J.C.N., *Gardens : A Notebook of Plans and Sketches,* translated by Helen Morgenthau Fox, New York, Scribner's, 1924. Originally published as *Jardins: Carnet de plans et de dessins,* Paris, Émile-Paul Frères, 1920

Frampton, Kenneth, 'Oscar Nitzchke and the School of Paris', *Oscar Nitzchke Architect,* Gus Dudley (ed.), New York, Cooper Union, 1985

Frampton, Kenneth, 'Paul Nelson and the School of Paris', *The Filter of Reason: Work of Paul Nelson,* Terence Riley (ed.) and Joseph Abram, New York, Rizzoli, 1980

Franclieu, Françoise de, *Le Corbusier sketchbooks, 1957-1964,* Vol. 4, No.778, Cambridge (Mass), Architectural History Foundation, MIT Press, 1982

Franclieu, Françoise de (introduction*), Le Corbusier/ Savina, Dessins et sculptures*, Preface by Jean Jenger, Paris, Fondation Le Corbusier/ Philippe Sers, 1984

Friedman, Alice T., *Women and the Making of the Modern House, A Social and Architectural History,* New York, Harry N. Abrams, 1998

Gans, Deborah, *The Le Corbusier Guide,* Princeton Architectural Press, 1987

Garner, Philippe, *Eileen Gray 1878-1976, Designer and Architect,* Cologne, Benedikt Taschen, 1993

Garnier, Bénédicte, *Rodin, Le rêve japonais*, Paris, Éditions du Musée Rodin/Flammarion, 2007

Georges-Michel, Michel and George, Waldemar, *Les Ballets Russes de Serge de Diaghilew, Décors et costumes,* Paris, Galerie Billiet, 1930

Gleizes, Albert, and Metzinger, Jean, *Du Cubisme,* Paris, Éditions la Cible, 1912

Green, Christopher, *Cubism and its Enemies: Modern Movements and Reaction in French Art, 1916-1928,* New Haven, Yale University Press, 1987

Green, Christopher, *Léger and the Avant-Garde,* New Haven and London, Yale University Press, 1976

Greenhalgh, Paul (ed), *Art Nouveau 1890-1914,* London, V&A publications, 2000

Griffin, Roger, Delidow, Margo, McGlinchey, Chris, 'Peeling Back the Layers: Eileen Gray's Brick Screen', Paper given at the Vienna Conservation Congress, September 2012, New York, Maney Publishing, 2012

Gropius, Walter, *Staatliches Bauhaus in Weimar 1919-1923,* Weimar and München, Bauhaus Verlag, 1923

Hamnett, Nina, *Laughing Torso, Reminiscences of Nina Hamnett,* New York, Roy Long and Richard Smith, 1932

Hankey, W.J, *One Hundred Years of Neo-Platonism in France: a Brief Philosophical History,* published with *Levinas and the Greek Heritage* by Jean-Marc Narbonne, Studies in Philosophical Theology, Leuven, Paris, Dudley, MA: Peeters, 2006.

Haweis, Stephen, *The Book about the Sea Gardens of Nassau, Bahamas,* New York, PF Collier & Son, 1917

Haweis, Stephen, *Anything about Dominica?,* Advocate Co. Ltd, 1929

Haweis, Stephen, *Orts and Ends, Dominican Lyrics,* Roseau, Bulletin Office Edition, August 1963

Haweis, Stephen, *Verses of a West Indian Summer,* handwritten edition, 1963

Hecker, Stefan, and Müller, Christian, *Eileen Gray. Works and Projects,* Barcelona, Editorial Gustavo Gili, 1993.

Heide, Robert, and Gilm, N. John, *Popular Art Deco: Depression Era Style and Design,* New York, Abbeville, 1991

Heinze-Greenberg, Ita, 'I often fear the envy of the gods', *Erich Mendelsohn Dynamics and Function,* Germany, Hatje Cantz Publishers, 1999

Heller, Geneviève, *Propre en Ordre,* France, Editions d'en Bas, 1979

Henderson, Linda Dalrymple, *The Fourth Dimension and Non- Euclidean Geometry in Modern Art,* Cambridge (Mass), The MIT Press, 2013

Henry, Paul, *An Irish Portrait,* London, Batsford, 1951

Herbst, René, *25 années UAM, Union des artistes modernes, 1930-1955. Les formes utiles : l'architecture, les arts plastiques, les arts graphiques, le mobilier, l'équipment ménagerm* Paris, Éditions du Salons des arts ménagers, 1956. *u.a.m. (UAM)*

Hiller, Bevis, *Art Déco,* Minneapolis Institute of Arts, Studio Vista Editions, 1971

Hiller, Bevis, *The Style of the Century, 1900-1980,* New York, Dutton, 1983

Hinton, C. Howard, *The Fourth Dimension,* New York and London, 1904

Hudson, Derek, *For the Love of Painting, The Life of Sir Gerald Kelly,* London, Chaucer Press, 1975

Imbert, Dorothée, *The Modernist Garden in France,* New Haven and London, Yale University Press, 1993

Janneau, Guillaume, *Technique du Décor Intérieur Moderne,* Paris, Editions Albert Morancé, 1927

Janneau, Guillaume, *L'Architecture mineure. Technique du décor intérieur moderne,* Paris, Editions Albert Morancé, 1928

Jenger, Jean and Beamis, Caroline, *Le Corbusier Architect of New Age,* London, Thames and Hudson, 1996

Johnson, John Stewart, *Eileen Gray Designer,* London, Debrett's Peerage, 1979.

Kennedy, S.B., *Paul Henry – Paintings, Drawings, Illustrations,* Dublin, Yale, 2000

Kerner, Charlotte, *Die Nonkonformistin: Die Lebensgeschichte der Designerin und Architektin Eileen Gray,* Weinheim, Beltz & Gelberg, 2002

Kirsch, Karin, *The Weissenhofsiedlung: Experimental Housing Built for the Deutscher Werkbund, Stuttgart, 1927,* New York, Rizzoli, 1989

Klumpe, A.E., *Memoirs of an Artist*, L. Whiting, Boston, 1940

Koering, Elise, 'Les Intérieurs de Madame Mathieu Lévy', in Pitiot, Cloé, *Eileen Gray,* Paris, Éditions du Centre Pompidou, 2013

Koestler, Arthur, *Le Yogi et le Commissaire,* Paris, Editions Charlot Press, 1944

Lachman, Gary, *In Search of P.D. Ouspensky,* Wheaton, Illinois, Quest Books, 2006

Lane, John, *The Early Work of Aubrey Beardsley*, London, The Bodley Head, 1899

Laurent, Jennifer, 'Salon et Expositions : Les Décennies qui Précèdent L'UAM', in Pitiot, Cloé, *Eileen Gray,* Éditions du Centre Pompidou, Paris, 2013

Leatherbarrow, David and Moshen Mostafavi, *Surface Architecture,* Cambridge, MIT Press, 2005

Le Corbusier, *L'Art Décoratif d'Aujourd'hui,* Paris, Georges Crès et Cie, 1925

Le Corbusier, *Towards a New Architecture*, translated from the French by Frederick Etchells, London, The Architectural Press, 1927

Le Corbusier, *La Villa Radieuse,* Paris, Vincent Fréal et Cie, 1933

Le Corbusier, *Œuvre Plastique. Peintures et Dessins. Architecture,* Paris, Éditions Albert Morancé, 1938

Le Corbusier, 'Eileen Gray. Centre de vacances et de loisirs', *Des Canons, des munitions ? Merci ! Des Logis...S.V.P,* exhibition catalogue, Pavillon des temps nouveaux à l'Exposition Art et Techniques, 1937, Boulogne, Édition de l'Architecture d'Aujourd'hui, 1938

Le Corbusier, *L'Architecture d'Aujourd'hui*, Special edition, Boulogne, Editions Albert Morancé, April 1948

Le Corbusier, *The Radiant City*, trans. Pamela Knight, Eleanor Levieux and Derek Coltman, New York, Orion Press, 1967

Le Corbusier, *Une Petite Maison*, Basel, Birkhäuser Architecture Editions, 1989

Louis, Michel, 'Mallet Stevens et le cinéma 1919-1929', *Robert Mallet Stevens architecte,* Brussels, Editions des Archives d'Architecture Moderne, 1980

Loye, Brigitte, *Eileen Gray, 1879-1976; architecture, design* preface de Michael Raynaud, Analeph/ J.P. Viguier, Paris, 1984

Mackrell, B., *Paul Poiret,* New York, Holmes and Mier, 1990

Madge, John, The *Rehousing of Britain,* London, Editions Pivotal Press, 1946

Marcilhac, Félix, *Jean Dunand: His Life and Works,* London, Thames and Hudson, 1991

Matet, Maurice, *Tapis Modernes,* Paris, H. Ernst Publications, 1929

Mathey, François, *Les Années '25'*: *Art Déco/Bauhaus/ Stijl/Esprit Nouveau,* Paris, Musée des Art Décoratifs, 1966

Maugham, William Somerset, *The Magician,* London, Vintage Books, 2000

Mendelsohn, Eric, *Neues Haus Neue Welt,* Berlin, Gebr. Mann Verlag, 1997

McConkey, Kenneth, *A Free Spirit Irish Art 1860-1960*, London, Pyms Gallery 1990

McNeill Whistler, James, *The Gentle Art of Making Enemies,* New York, Frederick Stokes and Brother, 1890

Méral, Paul, *Le Dit des Jeux du Monde*, Paris, Presse de l'Imprimerie Studium, 1918

Miller, John, *Ten Twentieth-Century Houses,* London, Arts Council of Great Britain, 1980

Modersohn-Becker, Paula, *Paula Modersohn-Becker: The Letters and Journals,* editions Gunter Busch and Liselotte von Reinken, New York, Taplinger, 1983

Mondrian, Piet, *Neo Plasticisme,* Paris, Editions de l'Effort Moderne Léonce Rosenberg, 1920

Murray, Peter and Linda, *Dictionary of Art and Artists,* London, Penguin, 1991

Nelson, Paul, *Architecture Hospitalière*, Paris, Éditions Albert Morancé, 1936

Niggl, Reto, *The Maharaja's Palace in Indore: Architecture and Interior,* Arnoldsche, 1996

Olsen, Donald J., *The City as a Work of Art London, Paris, Vienna*, London, Yale University Press, 1986

Ouspensky, Peter, *The Fourth Dimension*, St Petersburg, 1909

Ozenfant, Amédée, *The Foundations of Modern Art*, Translation John Rodker, New York, Dover Publications, 1952

Ozenfant, Amédée, 'Für Erich Mendelsohn', in *Neues Haus Neue Welt*, Berlin, Gebr. Mann Verlag, 1997

Pater, Walter, *The Renaissance: Studies in Art and Poetry,* London and New York, MacMillan and Co., 1888

Pennell, Joseph and Elizabeth, *The Life of James McNeill Whistler,* London, William Heinemann, 1911.

Pitiot, Cloé, *Eileen Gray,* Paris, Éditions du Centre Pompidou, 2013

Poiret, Paul, '*My First Fifty Years*', translated by Stephen Haden Guest, London, Victor Gollancz Ltd, 1931

Polo, Roberto, *Eileen Gray-Œuvres sur papier,* Paris, Galerie Historismus, 2007

Rault, Jasmine, *Eileen Gray and the Design of Sapphic Modernity*, Farnham, Ashgate, 2011

Reichlin, Bruno, 'Corseaux: My Father Lived One Year in This House. The Scenery Fascinated Him', in Louis- Cohen, Jean, *Le Corbusier and Atlas of Modern Landscapes,* New York, The Museum of Modern Art, 2013

Ridder, André de, *Zadkine,* Brussels, Palais des Beaux-Arts, H. Wellens, W. Godenne rue de Roumanie Editions, January 1933

Robinson, Cervin and Haag Bletter, Rosemarie, *Skyscraper Style,* New York, Oxford University Press, 1975

Rodriguez, Susan, *Wild Heart Natalie Clifford Barney and the Decadence of Literary Paris,* New York, Harper Collins, 2002

Rowland, Penelope, Bartolucci Marisa, Cabra Raul, *Eileen Gray,* San Francisco, Chronicle Books, 2002

Ruhrberg, Schneckenburger, Fricke, Honnef, et al, 'Between Revolt & Acceptance', *Art of the Twentieth Century,* Spain, Benedikt Taschen, Verlag, 2000

Samuel, Flora, *Le Corbusier Architect and Feminist,* Wiley Academy, 2004

Schlemmer, Oskar, 'Man' 1928-29, translated by Hans M. Wingler in *Bauhaus: Weimar, Dessau, Berlin, Chicago,* Cambridge, (Mass), MIT Press, 1978

Scott, Kathleen, *Self Portrait of an Artist,* London, John Murray Editions, 1949

Smithson, Alison, and Smithson, Peter, *The Heroic Period of Modern Architecture,* New York, Rizzoli, 1981

Spalding, Francis, *Prunella Clough Regions Unmapped,* London, Lund Humphries, 2012

Sparke, Penny, *A Century of Design, Design Pioneers of the Twentieth Century,* London, Mitchel Beazley, 1998

Sparke, Penny, *The Modern Interior,* London, Reaktion Books, 2008

Sparke, Penny, Massey, Anne, Keeble, Trevor, Martin, Brenda and Wealleans, Anne, *Designing the Modern Interior: From the Victorians to Today,* London, BERG, 2009

Sparke, Penny and McKellar, Susie, (editors), *Interior Design and Identity – Studies in Design Anthology,* Manchester University Press, 2011

Spencer, Charles, *Léon Bakst and the Ballets Russes,* London, Academy Editions, 1995

Stalker, John and Parker, George, *Treatise of Japanning and Varnishing,* Oxford, 1688

Sutin, Lawrence, *Do What Thou Wilt, A Life of Aleister Crowley,* New York, St Martin's Press, 2000

Taylor, Brian Brace, *Pierre Chareau Designer and Architect,* Köln, Benedikt Taschen, 1992

Taylor, J, *Paths to Contemporary French Literature,* Vol. 1, New Jersey, Transaction Publishers, 2011

The Arts Council of Great Britain, *Plans for an Art Centre,* London, Lund Humphries & Co., 1945

Tinniswood, Adrian, *The Art Deco House. Avant-garde houses of the 1920s-1930s,* London, Mitchell Beazley, 2002

Tise, Suzanne, 'Contested Modernisms', *Eileen Gray: An Architecture for all Senses,* edited by Marietta Andreas, Rosamund Diamond, Brooke Hodge, Tübingen, Wasmuth, Harvard University Press, 1996

Troy, Nancy, *Modernism and the Decorative Arts in France,* New Haven and London, Yale University Press, 1991

Valéry, Paul, *Eupalinos or the Architect,* translation by William McCausland Stewart, London, Oxford University Press, 1932

Vallois, *Eileen Gray, biennale 2000,* Vallois Mobilier 1922-1930 Sculptures XXe Siècle, Paris, 2000

Van de Beek, Johan, 'Adolf Loos – Patterns of Townhouses', *Raumplaun versus Plan Libre,* Delft, Delft University Press, 1991

Van Doesburg, Theo, *Classique, Baroque Moderne,* Paris, Editions De Sikkel, Anvers et Léonce Rosenberg, December 1918

Verhaeren, Emile, *James Ensor,* Brussels, Librairie Nationale d'Art et d'Histoire, G. Van Oest & Cie, 1908.

Walker, Lynne, 'Architecture and Reputation', *Women's Places: Architecture and Design 1860-1960,* London, Routledge, 2003

Wang, Wilfred and Constant, Caroline, *An Architecture for All Senses,* edited by Marietta Andreas, Rosamund Diamond, Brooke Hodge, Tübingen, Wasmuth, Harvard University Press, 1996

Warncke, Carsten-Peter, *De Stijl 1917-1919,* Cologne, Taschen, 1998

Whiting, Lilian, *Paris the Beautiful,* Boston, Little Brown and Co., 1908

Whiting, Sarah, 'Talking in the Gray Zones', *Eileen Gray: An Architecture for all Senses,* edited by Marietta Andreas, Rosamund Diamond, Brooke Hodge, Tübingen, Wasmuth, Harvard University Press, 1996

Wickes, George, *The Amazon of Letters: The Life and Loves of Natalie Barney,* New York, Putnam's, 1976

Wilding, Paul, *In Defence of the Welfare State,* Manchester, Manchester University Press, 1986

Wilk, Christopher, *Marcel Breuer: Furniture and Interiors*, New York, Museum of Modern Art, 1981

Wilk, Christopher, *Thonet: 150 Years of Furniture,* New York and London, Barron's, 1980

Woods, Alice, *Edges,* Indianapolis: Bowen-Merrill, 1902

Woods, Christopher, *The Dictionary of Victorian Painters, Dictionary of British Art*, London, Antique Collectors Club Ltd, Second Edition, 1991

Zervos, Christian, *Les Arts de la Maison,* Paris, Winter 1926

Thesis

Goff, Jennifer, *The Eileen Gray Collection at the National Museum of Ireland,* Phd doctoral thesis, University College Dublin, 2013

Koering, Elise *Eileen Gray et Charlotte Perriand dans les années 1920 et la question de l'intérieur corbuséen. Essai d'analyse et de mise en perspective,* Phd doctoral thesis, université de Versailles-Saint-Quentin-en-Yvelynes, 2010

Loye, Brigitte, *Eileen Gray. Un autre chemin pour la modernité...une idée chorégraphique,* thesis, École nationale supérieure des beaux-arts, Paris, 1980

Lynch, Elizabeth, *Eileen Gray, Her Life and Work,* thesis, London, Polytechnic of North London, 1976

Pearson, C. 'Integrations of Art and Architecture in the work of Le Corbusier. Theory and Practice from Ornamentation to the Synthesis of the Major Arts', unpublished PhD thesis, Stanford University, 1995

Rault, Jasmine, *Eileen Gray. New Angles on Gender and Sexuality,* Phd doctoral thesis, Montreal, McGill University, Department of Art History and Communication Studies, 2006

9. Folding terrace chair, 1930-33, metal frame with upholstery
© Private Collection

Index

510 Eileen Gray